PMT	Payment of an annuity
PPP	Purchasing power parity
PV	Present value
PVA_N	Present value of an annuity for N years
Q	Quantity produced or sold
Q_{BE}	Break-even quantity
r	(1) A percentage discount rate, or cost of capital; also referred to as I
	(2) Nominal risk-adjusted required rate of return
$\bar{r}$	"r bar," historic, or realized, rate of return
$\hat{r}$	"r hat," an expected rate of return
r^*	Real risk-free rate of return
r_d	Before-tax cost of debt
$r_d(1 - T)$	After-tax cost of debt
r_e	Cost of new common stock (external equity)
r_f	Interest rate in foreign country
r_h	Interest rate in home country
r_i	Required return for an individual firm or security
r_M	Return on "the market," or on an "average" stock
r_{NOM}	Nominal rate of interest; also referred to as I_{NOM}
r_p	(1) Cost of preferred stock
	(2) Portfolio's return
r_{RF}	Rate of return on a risk-free security, equal to $r^* + IP$
r_s	(1) Cost of retained earnings
	(2) Required return on common stock
ρ	Correlation coefficient; also denoted as R when using historical data
ROA	Return on assets
ROE	Return on equity
ROIC	Return on invested capital
RP	Risk premium
RP_M	Market risk premium
S	(1) Sales
	(2) Estimated standard deviation for sample data
SML	Security Market Line
Σ	Summation sign
σ	Standard deviation
t	Time period
T	Marginal income tax rate
TIE	Times interest earned
V	(1) Variable cost per unit
	(2) Current value of a call option
V_B	Bond value
V_p	Value of preferred stock
VC	Total variable costs
WACC	Weighted average cost of capital
w_c	Percentage of common stock in capital structure
w_d	Percentage of debt in capital structure
w_p	Percentage of preferred stock in capital structure
YTC	Yield to call
YTM	Yield to maturity

DON'T THROW THIS CARD AWAY!
THIS MAY BE REQUIRED FOR YOUR COURSE!

6 MONTHS ACCESS FREE WITH THIS TEXT!

THOMSON ONE | Business School Edition

 THOMSON REUTERS

Congratulations!

Your purchase of this NEW textbook includes complimentary access to Thomson ONE – Business School Edition for Finance. Thomson ONE – Business School Edition is a Web-based portal product that provides integrated access to Thomson Reuters Financial content for the purpose of financial analysis. This is an educational version of the same financial resources used by Wall Street analysts on a daily basis!

For hundreds of companies, this online resource provides seamless access to:

– **Current and Past Company Data:** Worldscope which includes company profiles, financials and accounting results, market per-share data, annual information, and monthly prices going back to 1980.

– **Financial Analyst Data and Forecasts:** I/B/E/S Consensus Estimates which provides consensus estimates, analyst-by-analyst earnings coverage, and analysts' forecasts.

– **SEC Disclosure Statements:** Disclosure SEC Database which includes company profiles, annual and quarterly company financials, pricing information, and earnings.

– **And More!**

 SOUTH-WESTERN
CENGAGE Learning

THOMSON ONE
Business School Edition

 THOMSON REUTERS

ACCESS CODE

PH1H916PPJC9KW

HOW TO REGISTER YOUR ACCESS CODE

1. Launch a web browser and go to **http://www.cengage.com/thomsonone**

2. Click the "Register" button to enter your access code.

3. Enter your access code **exactly** as it appears here and create a unique User ID, or enter an existing User ID if you have previously registered for a different South-Western product via an access code.

4. When prompted, create a password (or enter an existing password, if you have previously registered for a different product via an access code.) Submit the necessary information when prompted. **Record your User ID and password in a secure location.**

5. Once registered, return to the URL above and select the "Enter" button; have your User ID and password handy.

Note: The duration of your access to the product begins when registration is complete.

For technical support, contact **1-800-423-0563** or email **support@cengage.com**.

Fundamentals of Financial Management

Concise

Eugene F. Brigham | Dr. Joel F. Houston

CENGAGE
Learning

Australia • Brazil • Japan • Korea • Mexico • Singapore • Spain • United Kingdom • United States

Fundamentals of Financial Management: Concise

Senior Manager, Student Engagement:

Linda deStefano

Janey Moeller

Manager, Student Engagement:

Julie Dierig

Marketing Manager:

Rachael Kloos

Manager, Production Editorial:

Kim Fry

Manager, Intellectual Property Project Manager:

Brian Methe

Senior Manager, Production and Manufacturing:

Donna M. Brown

Manager, Production:

Terri Daley

Source:

Fundamentals of Financial Management, Concise Edition, 8th Edition includes Thomson ONE - Business School Edition 6-Month Printed Access Card
Eugene F. Brigham | Dr. Joel F. Houston
© 2015, 2012, 2009 Cengage Learning. All rights reserved.

For product information and technology assistance, contact us at
Cengage Learning Customer & Sales Support, 1-800-354-9706

For permission to use material from this text or product,
submit all requests online at **cengage.com/permissions**
Further permissions questions can be emailed to
permissionrequest@cengage.com

This book contains select works from existing Cengage Learning resources and was produced by Cengage Learning Custom Solutions for collegiate use. As such, those adopting and/or contributing to this work are responsible for editorial content accuracy, continuity and completeness.

Compilation © 2014 Cengage Learning

ISBN-13: 978-1-305-02767-1

ISBN-10: 1-305-02767-1

WCN: 01-100-101

Cengage Learning

5191 Natorp Boulevard
Mason, Ohio 45040
USA

Cengage Learning is a leading provider of customized learning solutions with office locations around the globe, including Singapore, the United Kingdom, Australia, Mexico, Brazil, and Japan. Locate your local office at:
international.cengage.com/region.

Cengage Learning products are represented in Canada by Nelson Education, Ltd.
For your lifelong learning solutions, visit **www.cengage.com/custom.**
Visit our corporate website at **www.cengage.com.**

Printed in the United States of America

BRIEF CONTENTS

CONTENTS

Chapter 14
Distributions to Shareholders: Dividends and Share Repurchases 487

When the first edition of *Fundamentals* was published 36 years ago, we wanted to provide an introductory text that students would find interesting and easy to understand. *Fundamentals* immediately became the leading undergraduate finance text, and it has maintained that position ever since. However, over the years as *Fundamentals* got larger and larger, we heard more and more often that it was difficult to cover the entire book in a single term. These concerns led us to create *Fundamentals of Financial Management Concise* 18 years ago. When designing *Concise,* we had in mind those instructors who wanted to retain *Fundamentals'* depth and level but eliminate some less essential topics. As is the case with *Fundamentals,* our continuing goal is to produce a book and ancillary package that sets a new standard for finance textbooks.

Finance is an exciting and continually changing field. Since the last edition, many important changes have occurred within the global financial environment. In the midst of this changing environment, it is certainly an interesting time to be a finance student. In this latest edition, we highlight and analyze the events leading to these changes from a financial perspective. While the financial environment is ever-changing, the tried-and-true principles that the book has emphasized over the past three decades are now more important than ever.

STRUCTURE OF THE BOOK

Our target audience is a student taking his or her first, and perhaps only, finance course. Some of these students will decide to major in finance and go on to take courses in investments, money and capital markets, and advanced corporate finance. Others will choose marketing, management, or some other nonfinance business major. Still others will major in areas other than business and take finance plus a few other business courses to gain information that will help them in law, real estate, or other fields.

Our challenge has been to provide a book that serves all of these audiences well. We concluded that we should focus on the core principles of finance, including the basic topics of time value of money, risk analysis, and valuation. Moreover, we concluded that we should address these topics from two points of view: (1) that of an investor who is seeking to make intelligent investment choices and (2) that of a business manager trying to maximize the value of his or her firm's stock. Both investors and managers need to understand the same set of principles, so the core topics are important to students regardless of what they choose to do after they finish the course.

In planning the book's structure, we first listed the core topics in finance that are important to virtually everyone. Included were an overview of financial markets, methods used to estimate the cash flows that determine asset values, the time value of money, the determinants of interest rates, the basics of risk analysis, and the basics of bond and stock valuation procedures. We cover these core topics in the first nine chapters. Next, because most students in the course will probably work for a business firm, we want to show them how the core ideas are implemented in practice. Therefore, we go on to discuss cost of capital, capital budgeting, capital structure, dividend policy, working capital management, financial forecasting, and international operations.

Nonfinance majors sometimes wonder why they need to learn finance. As we structured the book, it quickly becomes obvious to everyone why they need to understand time value, risk, markets, and valuation. Virtually all students enrolled in the basic course expect at some point to have money to invest, and they quickly realize that the knowledge gained from Chapters 1 through 9 will help them make better investment decisions. Moreover, students who plan to go into the business world soon realize that their own success requires that their firms be successful, and the topics covered in Chapters 10 through 17 will be helpful here. For example, good capital budgeting decisions require accurate forecasts from people in sales, marketing, production, and human resources, and non-financial people need to understand how their actions affect the firm's profits and future performance.

ORGANIZATION OF THE CHAPTERS: A VALUATION FOCUS

As we discuss in Chapter 1, in an enterprise system such as that of the United States, the primary goal of financial management is to maximize their firms' values. At the same time, we stress that managers should not do "whatever it takes" to increase the firm's stock price. Managers have a responsibility to behave ethically, and when striving to maximize value, they must abide by constraints such as not polluting the environment, not engaging in unfair labor practices, not breaking the antitrust laws, and the like. In Chapter 1, we discuss the concept of valuation, explain how it depends on future cash flows and risk, and show why value maximization is good for society in general. This valuation theme runs throughout the text.

Stock and bond values are determined in the financial markets, so an understanding of those markets is essential to anyone involved with finance. Therefore, Chapter 2 covers the major types of financial markets, the rates of return that investors have historically earned on different types of securities, and the risks inherent in these securities. This information is important for anyone working in finance, and it is also important for anyone who has or hopes to own any financial assets. In this chapter, we also highlight how this environment has changed in the aftermath of the financial crisis.

Asset values depend in a fundamental way on earnings and cash flows as reported in the accounting statements. Therefore, we review those statements in Chapter 3 and then, in Chapter 4, show how accounting data can be analyzed and used to measure how well a company has operated in the past and how well it is likely to perform in the future.

Chapter 5 covers the time value of money (TVM), perhaps the most fundamental concept in finance. The basic valuation model, which ties together cash flows, risk, and interest rates, is based on TVM concepts, and these concepts are used throughout the remainder of the book. Therefore, students should allocate plenty of time to studying Chapter 5.

Chapter 6 deals with interest rates, a key determinant of asset values. We discuss how interest rates are affected by risk, inflation, liquidity, the supply of and demand for capital in the economy, and the actions of the Federal Reserve. The discussion of interest rates leads directly to the topics of bonds in Chapter 7 and stocks in Chapters 8 and 9, where we show how these securities (and all other financial assets) are valued using the basic TVM model.

The background material provided in Chapters 1 through 9 is essential to both investors and corporate managers. These are "Finance" topics, not "Business" or "Corporate Finance" topics as those terms are commonly used. Thus, Chapters 1 through 9 concentrate on the concepts and models used to establish values, whereas Chapters 10 through 17 focus on specific actions managers can take to maximize their firms' values.

Because most business students don't plan to specialize in finance, they might think the "business finance" chapters are not particularly relevant to them. This is most decidedly not true, and in the later chapters we show that all really important business decisions involve every one of a firm's departments—marketing, accounting, production, and so on. Thus, while a topic such as capital budgeting can be thought of as a financial issue, marketing people provide inputs on likely unit sales and sales prices, manufacturing people provide inputs on costs, and so on. Moreover, capital budgeting decisions influence the size of the firm, its products, its profits, and its stock price, and those factors affect all of the firm's employees, from the CEO to the mail room staff.

INNOVATIONS FOR THE EIGHTH EDITION

A great deal has happened in the financial markets and corporate America since the 7th edition was published. In this 8th edition, we have made several important changes to reflect this dynamic environment. Below, we provide a brief summary of the more significant changes.

1. Today's students are tomorrow's business and government leaders, and it is essential that they understand the key principles of finance, the important role that financial markets have on our economy, and the need to behave in an ethical fashion. With those concerns in mind, we changed the organization of Chapter 1 to emphasize the firm's main goal of creating value for shareholders and expanded the discussion of agency conflicts. We also reiterate that maximizing shareholder value does not mean "increase the stock price at all cost," and we discuss some recent events where companies have had to pay the price for actions that harmed society.

2. Since the last edition, a number of important events have significantly influenced the financial markets and finance in general. Over the last few years, we have witnessed continued weakness in the economy following the global financial crisis of 2008 and 2009, the European debt crisis, the escalating increase in the U.S. government's debt, the resulting downgrading of U.S. debt, U.S. budget woes, and sequestration. At the same time, the Federal Reserve's aggressive policy of quantitative easing has pushed interest rates to the lowest levels in years, which is partially responsible for the dramatic run-up in the U.S. stock market between August 2011 and August 2013. Throughout the 8th edition, we discuss these events and their implications for financial markets and corporate managers, and we use these examples to illustrate the importance of the key concepts covered in *Concise* for investors, businesses, and even government officials.

3. Instructors and students continually impress upon us the importance of having interesting and relevant real-world examples. Throughout the 8th edition we have added several new examples where recent events help illustrate the key concepts covered in the text. We have also expanded and updated the many tables where we present real-world data, and we have updated the Thomson One examples. Finally, as is always the case, we have also made significant changes to many of the opening vignettes that precede each chapter.

4. Behavioral finance theory continues to have an important influence on the academic literature and it has in many ways reshaped the way that many of us think about financial markets and corporate finance. As a reflection of its growing importance, in Chapter 2 we moved the discussion of behavioral finance and its impact on the efficient markets hypothesis from a separate box into its own section. In addition, we continue to highlight the importance of securitization, the role of derivatives, and the increasing importance of hedge funds, mutual funds, and private equity firms.

5. We updated the tax discussion in Chapter 3 to reflect 2013 tax rates and tax law changes. Impacts of these changes are discussed throughout the text especially in the capital structure and dividend chapters.

6. In Chapter 3, we also added a box about how excess cash holdings affect the calculation of net operating working capital.

7. In Chapter 4, we revised the definition of the debt ratio. We calculate it as interest-bearing debt divided by the sum of interest-bearing debt and equity. This revision is more consistent with our discussions in the capital budgeting, capital structure, and forecasting chapters.

8. We have added more "Quick Questions" that are designed to keep students actively involved and focused as they read the text. Here, in a separate box, we pose a question and then show students how to answer it. These "Quick Questions" go through examples to make the finance concepts more concrete, and in that sense they mimic what effective instructors often do in a classroom setting. Additional "Quick Questions" have been included in Chapters 3, 4, 6, 8, 13, and 17.

9. In Chapter 13, we changed the Bigbee illustration (that works through the calculations to determine the optimal capital structure) to reflect lower interest rates.

When revising the text, we always rely heavily on a team of reviewers who offer suggestions for making the text more readable and relevant to students. We give special thanks to these reviewers later in the preface; their comments and recommendations certainly helped us improve this 8th edition.

DIGITAL SOLUTIONS FOR THE EIGHTH EDITION

Changing technology and new ideas have had an exciting and dramatic influence on the ways we teach finance. Innovative instructors are developing and utilizing different classroom strategies, and new technology has allowed us to present key material in a more interesting and interactive fashion. As textbook authors, we think these new developments are tremendously exciting, and we have worked closely with our publisher's top team of innovative content and media developers, who have created a whole new set of revolutionary products for the 8th edition including:

MINDTAP™

MindTap™, Cengage Learning's fully online, highly personalized learning experience combines readings, multimedia activities, and assessments into a singular Learning Path. MindTap™ guides students through their course with ease and engagement with a learning path that includes an Interactive Chapter Reading, Problem Demonstrations, Blueprint Problems, and the Online Homework Assignment. Instructors can personalize the Learning Path for their students by customizing the robust suite of the Concise Eighth Edition resources and adding their own content via apps that integrate into the MindTap™ framework seamlessly with Learning Management Systems.

NEW! BLUEPRINT PROBLEMS

Written by the authors and located within CengageNOW™, Aplia™, and MindTap™, Blueprints teach students the fundamental finance concepts and their associated building blocks—going beyond memorization. By going through the problem step-by-step, they reinforce foundational concepts and allow students to demonstrate their understanding of the problem-solving process and business impact of each topic. Blueprints include rich feedback and explanations, providing students with an excellent learning resource to solidify their understanding.

NEW! CONCEPTCLIPS

Embedded throughout the new interactive eReader, finance ConceptClips present fundamental key topics to students in an entertaining and memorable way via short animated video clips. Developed by Mike Brandl of The Ohio State University, these vocabulary animations provide students with a memorable auditory and visual representation of the important terminology for the course.

NEW! PROBLEM WALK-THROUGHS

More than 100 Problem Walk-Through videos are embedded in the new interactive MindTap eReader and online homework. Each video walks students through solving a problem from start to finish, and students can play and replay the tutorials as they work through homework assignments or prepare for quizzes and tests, almost as though they had an instructor by their side the whole time.

APLIA™

Engage, prepare and educate your students with this ideal online learning solution. Aplia™ Finance improves comprehension and outcomes by increasing student effort and engagement. Students stay on top of coursework with regularly scheduled homework assignments while automatic grading provides detailed, immediate feedback. Aplia™ assignments match the language, style, and structure of the text which allows your students to apply what they learn directly to homework. Some of the features of Aplia™ include:

- MindTap™ eReader
- Auto-Graded Problem Sets
- Grade It Now
- Preparing for Finance Tutorials
- Finance in Action Modules
- Access to End-of-Chapter Problems, Blueprint Problems, and Test Bank
- Course Management System
- My Practice Reviews

For more information on how Aplia™ could benefit you, **visit www.aplia.com/ finance** today!

CENGAGENOW™

Designed by instructors for instructors, CengageNOW™ mirrors your natural workflow and provides time-saving, performance-enhancing tools for you and your students—all in one program! CengageNOW™ takes the best of current technology tools including online homework management; fully customizable algorithmic end-of-chapter problems and test bank; and course support materials such as online quizzing, videos, and tutorials to support your goals. With CengageNOW™, you can:

- **Plan** student assignments with an easy online homework management component
- **Manage** your grade book with ease
- **Reinforce** student comprehension with Personalized Study
- **Grade** automatically for seamless, immediate results

COGNERO™ TESTING SOFTWARE

Cengage Learning Testing Powered by Cognero™ is a flexible, online system that allows you to: author, edit, and manage test bank content from multiple Cengage Learning solutions; create multiple test versions in an instant; deliver tests from your LMS, your classroom or wherever you want. Revised to reflect Concise Eighth Edition, the Cognero™ Test Bank is tagged according to Tier I (AACSB Business Program Interdisciplinary Learning Outcomes) and Tier II (Finance-specific) topic, Bloom's Taxonomy, and difficulty level.

In addition to these changes, we have also significantly updated and improved our more traditional ancillary package, which includes the Instructor's Manual, Test Bank, Study Guide, Excel Chapter Models, Excel Chapter Integrated Case Models, Excel Spreadsheet Problem Models, and PowerPoints for Chapter Integrated Cases.

ACKNOWLEDGMENTS

The book reflects the efforts of a great many people, both those who worked on *Concise* and our related books in the past and those who worked specifically on this 8th edition. First, we would like to thank Dana Aberwald Clark, who worked closely with us at every stage of the revision—her assistance was absolutely invaluable. Second, Susan Whitman provided great typing and logistical support.

Our colleagues John Banko, Roy Crum, Jim Keys, Andy Naranjo, M. Nimalendran, Jay Ritter, Mike Ryngaert, Craig Tapley, and Carolyn Takeda Brown have given us many useful suggestions over the years regarding the ancillaries and many parts of the book, including the integrated cases. We also benefited from the work of Mike Ehrhardt and Phillip Daves of the University of Tennessee, who worked with us on companion books.

We would also like to thank the following professors, whose reviews and comments on our earlier books contributed to this edition:

Rebecca Abraham	Les Barenbaum	Bob Boldin	Bob Carlson
Robert Abraham	Charles	Keith Boles	Severin Carlson
Joe Adamo	Barngrover	Michael Bond	David Cary
Robert Adams	Sam Basu	Elizabeth Booth	Steve Celec
Mike Adler	Deborah Bauer	Geof Booth	Mary Chaffin
Cyrus Aleseyed	Greg Bauer	Waldo Born	Rajesh Chakrabarti
Sharif Ahkam	Laura A. Beal	Brian Boscaljon	Charles Chan
Syed Ahmad	David Becher	Steven Bouchard	Don Chance
Ed Altman	Bill Beedles	Kenneth Boudreaux	Antony Chang
Bruce Anderson	Brian Belt	Rick Boulware	Susan Chaplinsky
Ron Anderson	Moshe Ben-Horim	Helen Bowers	K. C. Chen
Tom Anderson	Gary Benesh	Oswald Bowlin	Jay Choi
John Andrews	Bill Beranek	Don Boyd	S. K. Choudhary
Bob Angell	Tom Berry	G. Michael Boyd	Lal Chugh
Vince Apilado	Al Berryman	Pat Boyer	Peter Clarke
Harvey Arbalaez	Will Bertin	Joe Brandt	Maclyn Clouse
Kavous Ardalan	Scott Besley	Elizabeth Brannigan	Thomas S. Coe
Henry Arnold	Dan Best	Mary Broske	Bruce Collins
Tom Arnold	Mark S. Bettner	Christopher Brown	Mitch Conover
Bob Aubey	Roger Bey	David T. Brown	Margaret Considine
Gil Babcock	Gilbert W.	Kate Brown	Phil Cooley
Peter Bacon	Bickum	Larry Brown	Joe Copeland
Chung Baek	Dalton Bigbee	Todd A. Brown	David Cordell
Bruce Bagamery	John Bildersee	Bill Brueggeman	Marsha Cornett
Kent Baker	Kenneth G.	Paul Bursik	M. P. Corrigan
Robert Balik	Bishop	Alva Butcher	John Cotner
Tom Bankston	Laurence E. Blose	Bill Campsey	Charles Cox
Babu Baradwaj	Russ Boisjoly	W. Thomas Carls	David Crary

John Crockett, Jr.
Julie Dahlquist
Brent Dalrymple
Bill Damon
Morris Danielson
Joel Dauten
Steve Dawson
Sankar De
Fred Dellva
Jim DeMello
Chad Denson
James Desreumaux
Thomas Devaney
Bodie Dickerson
Bernard Dill
Gregg Dimkoff
Les Dlabay
Nathan Dong
Mark Dorfman
Tom Downs
Frank Draper
Anne M. Drougas
Gene Drzycimski
Dean Dudley
David Durst
Ed Dyl
Fred J. Ebeid
Daniel Ebels
Richard Edelman
Charles Edwards
Scott Ehrhorn
U. Elike
John Ellis
George Engler
Suzanne Erickson
Dave Ewert
John Ezzell
Olubunmi Faleye
L. Franklin Fant
John Farns
John Farris
David Feller
Richard J. Fendler
Michael Ferri
Jim Filkins
John Finnerty
Robert Fiore
Susan Fischer
Peggy Fletcher
Steven Flint
Russ Fogler
Jennifer Foo
Jennifer Frazier
Dan French
Harry Gallatin
Partha
    Gangopadhyay
Michael Garlington
David Garraty
Sharon H. Garrison
Jim Garven
Adam Gehr, Jr.
Jim Gentry

Sudip Ghosh
Wafica Ghoul
Erasmo Giambona
Armand Gilinsky, Jr.
Philip Glasgo
Rudyard Goode
Raymond Gorman
Walt Goulet
Bernie Grablowsky
Theoharry
    Grammatikos
Georg Grassmueck
Greg Gregoriou
Owen Gregory
Ed Grossnickle
John Groth
Alan Grunewald
Manak Gupta
Darryl Gurley
Sam Hadaway
Don Hakala
Gerald Hamsmith
Mahfuzul Haque
William Hardin
John Harris
Mary Hartman
Paul Hastings
Bob Haugen
Steve Hawke
Stevenson Hawkey
Del Hawley
Eric M. Haye
Robert Hehre
Brian Henderson
Kath Henebry
David Heskel
George Hettenhouse
Hans Heymann
Kendall Hill
Roger Hill
Tom Hindelang
Linda Hittle
Ralph Hocking
Robert P. Hoffman
J. Ronald Hoffmeister
Robert Hollinger
Jim Horrigan
John Houston
John Howe
Keith Howe
Stephen Huffman
Steve Isberg
Jim Jackson
Kevin T. Jacques
Keith Jakob
Vahan Janjigian
Narayanan
    Jayaraman
Benjamas
    Jirasakuldech
Zhenhn Jin
Kose John
Craig Johnson

Keith Johnson
Ramon Johnson
Steve Johnson
Ray Jones
Frank Jordan
Manuel Jose
Sally Joyner
Alfred Kahl
Gus Kalogeras
Rajiv Kalra
Ravi Kamath
John Kaminarides
Ashok Kapoor
Howard Keen
Michael Keenan
Bill Kennedy
Peppi M. Kenny
Carol Kiefer
Joe Kiernan
Richard Kish
Robert Kleiman
Erich Knehans
Don Knight
Ladd Kochman
Dorothy Koehl
Jaroslaw
    Komarynsky
Duncan Kretovich
Harold Krogh
Charles Kroncke
Don Kummer
Robert A. Kunkel
Reinhold Lamb
Christopher J.
    Lambert
Joan Lamm
Larry Lang
David Lange
P. Lange
Howard Lanser
Edward Lawrence
Martin Lawrence
Jerry M. Leabman
Rick LeCompte
Alice Lee
Wayne Lee
Jim LePage
Vance Lesseig
David E. LeTourneau
Denise Letterman
Jules Levine
John Lewis
Jason Lin
Chuck Linke
Yi Liu
Bill Lloyd
Susan Long
Nancy L. Lumpkin
Yulong Ma
Judy Maese
Bob Magee
Ileen Malitz
Bob Malko

Phil Malone
Abbas Mamoozadeh
Terry Maness
Chris Manning
Surendra
    Mansinghka
Timothy Manuel
Barry Marchman
Brian Maris
Terry Martell
David Martin
D. J. Masson
John Mathys
Ralph May
John McAlhany
Andy McCollough
Ambrose McCoy
Thomas McCue
Bill McDaniel
John McDowell
Charles McKinney
Robyn McLaughlin
James McNulty
Jeanette Medewitz-
    Diamond
Jamshid Mehran
Larry Merville
Rick Meyer
Jim Millar
Ed Miller
John Miller
Jill Misuraca
John Mitchell
Carol Moerdyk
Bob Moore
Scott B. Moore
Jose F. Moreno
Matthew Morey
Barry Morris
Gene Morris
Dianne R. Morrison
John K. Mullen
Chris Muscarella
David Nachman
Tim Nantell
Don Nast
Edward Nelling
Bill Nelson
Bob Nelson
Tom C. Nelson
William Nelson
Duong Nguyen
Bob Niendorf
Bruce Niendorf
Ben Nonnally, Jr.
Tom O'Brien
William O'Connell
Dennis O'Connor
John O'Donnell
Jim Olsen
Robert Olsen
Dean Olson
R. Daniel Pace

Darshana Palkar
Jim Pappas
Stephen Parrish
Helen Pawlowski
Barron Peake
Michael Pescow
Glenn Petry
Jim Pettijohn
Rich Pettit
Dick Pettway
Aaron Phillips
Hugo Phillips
Michael Phillips
H. R. Pickett
John Pinkerton
Gerald Pogue
Eugene Poindexter
R. Potter
Franklin Potts
R. Powell
Dianna Preece
Chris Prestopino
John Primus
Jerry Prock
Howard Puckett
Herbert Quigley
George Racette
Bob Radcliffe
David Rakowski
Narendar V. Rao
Allen Rappaport
Charles R. Rayhorn
Bill Rentz
Thomas Rhee
Ken Riener
Charles Rini
John Ritchie
Bill Rives
Pietra Rivoli
Antonio Rodriguez
James Rosenfeld
Stuart Rosenstein
E. N. Roussakis

Dexter Rowell
Saurav
 Roychoudhury
Arlyn R. Rubash
Marjorie Rubash
Bob Ryan
Jim Sachlis
Abdul Sadik
Travis Sapp
Salil Sarkar
Thomas Scampini
Kevin Scanlon
Frederick Schadeler
Patricia L. Schaeff
David Schalow
Mary Jane Scheuer
David Schirm
Harold Schleef
Tom Schmidt
Oliver Schnusenberg
Robert Schwebach
Carol Schweser
John Settle
Alan Severn
James Sfiridis
Sol Shalit
Frederic Shipley
Dilip Shome
Ron Shrieves
Neil Sicherman
J. B. Silvers
Sudhir Singh
Clay Singleton
Amit Sinha
Joe Sinkey
Stacy Sirmans
Jaye Smith
Patricia Smith
Patricia Matisz Smith
Dean S. Sommers
Don Sorensen
David Speairs
Michal Spivey

Ken Stanley
Kenneth Stanton
Ed Stendardi
Alan Stephens
Don Stevens
Glenn L. Stevens
Jerry Stevens
Lowell E. Stockstill
Glen Strasburg
David Suk
Katherine Sullivan
Kathie Sullivan
Timothy G. Sullivan
Philip Swensen
Bruce Swenson
Ernest Swift
Paul Swink
Eugene Swinnerton
Gary Tallman
Dular Talukdar
Dennis Tanner
T. Craig Tapley
Russ Taussig
John Teall
Richard Teweles
Ted Teweles
Madeline Thimmes
Samantha Thapa
Francis D. Thomas
Andrew Thompson
John Thompson
Thomas H.
 Thompson
Arlene Thurman
Dogan Tirtirogu
Janet Todd
Holland J. Toles
William Tozer
Emery Trahan
George Trivoli
Eric Tsai
George Tsetsekos
David Tufte

David Upton
Lloyd Valentine
Howard Van Auken
Pretorious Van den
 Dool
Pieter Vandenberg
Paul Vanderheiden
David O. Vang
JoAnn Vaughan
Jim Verbrugge
Patrick Vincent
Steve Vinson
Susan Visscher
John Wachowicz
John Walker
Joe Walker
Mike Walker
Elizabeth J. Wark
Sam Weaver
Marsha Weber
Al Webster
Shelton Weeks
Kuo-Chiang Wei
Bill Welch
Fred Weston
Richard Whiston
Jeffrey Whitworth
Norm Williams
Tony Wingler
Ed Wolfe
Criss Woodruff
Don Woods
Yangru Wu
Robert Wyatt
Steve Wyatt
Sheng Yang
Elizabeth Yobaccio
Michael Yonan
David Zalewski
John Zietlow
Dennis Zocco
Sijing Zong
Kent Zumwalt

Special thanks are due to Shirley Love, Idaho State University, who wrote some chapter boxes relating to small-business issues; to Emery Trahan and Paul Bolster, Northeastern University, for their contributions; to Dilip Shome, Virginia Polytechnic Institute, who helped greatly with the capital structure chapter; to Dave Brown and Mike Ryngaert, University of Florida, who helped us with the bankruptcy material; to Roy Crum, Andy Naranjo, and Subu Venkataraman, who worked with us on the international materials; to Scott Below, East Carolina University, who developed the website information and references; to Laurie and Stan Eakins of East Carolina, who developed the Excel tutorial materials on the website; to Larry Wolken, Texas A&M University, who offered his hard work and advice for the development of the *Lecture Presentation Software*; and to Christopher Buzzard who helped us develop the Excel models, the website, and the PowerPoint presentations. Finally, we also want to acknowledge the contributions of the late Chris Barry who wrote some of the chapter boxes in earlier editions.

Finally, the Cengage Learning staff, especially Mike Reynolds, Kendra Brown, Jana Lewis, Jessica Robbe, Scott Fidler, Adele Scholtz, and Heather Mooney helped greatly with all phases of the book's development and production.

ERRORS IN THE TEXTBOOK

At this point, most authors make a statement such as this: "We appreciate all the help we received from the people listed above; but any remaining errors are, of course, our own responsibility." And generally there are more than enough remaining errors! Having experienced difficulties with errors ourselves, both as students and instructors, we resolved to avoid this problem in *Concise*. As a result of our detection procedures, we are convinced that few errors remain, but primarily because we want to detect any errors that may have slipped by so that we can correct them in subsequent printings, we decided to offer a reward of $10 per error to the first person who reports it to us. For purpose of this reward, errors are defined as misspelled words, nonrounding numerical errors, incorrect statements, and any other error that inhibits comprehension. Typesetting problems such as irregular spacing and differences of opinion regarding grammatical or punctuation conventions do not qualify for this reward. Given the ever-changing nature of the World Wide Web, changes in web addresses also do not qualify as errors, although we would like to learn about them. Finally, any qualifying error that has follow-through effects is counted as two errors only. Please report any errors to Joel Houston through e-mail at **concise@joelhouston.com** or by regular mail at the address below.

CONCLUSION

Finance is, in a real sense, the cornerstone of the enterprise system—good financial management is vitally important to the economic health of all firms and hence to the nation and the world. Because of its importance, finance should be widely and thoroughly understood, but this is easier said than done. The field is complex, and it undergoes constant change due to shifts in economic conditions. All of this makes finance stimulating and exciting, but challenging and sometimes perplexing. We sincerely hope that this 8th Edition of *Concise* will meet its own challenge by contributing to a better understanding of our financial system.

EUGENE F. BRIGHAM
JOEL F. HOUSTON
4723 N.W. 53rd Ave., Suite A
Gainesville, Florida 32653

November 2013

EUGENE F. BRIGHAM *UNIVERSITY OF FLORIDA*

Dr. Eugene F. Brigham is Graduate Research Professor Emeritus at the University of Florida, where he has taught since 1971. Dr. Brigham received his M.B.A. and Ph.D. from the University of California-Berkeley and his undergraduate degree from the University of North Carolina. Prior to joining the University of Florida, Dr. Brigham held teaching positions at the University of Connecticut, the University of Wisconsin, and the University of California-Los Angeles. Dr. Brigham has served as president of the Financial Management Association and has written many journal articles on the cost of capital, capital structure, and other aspects of financial management. He has authored or co-authored ten textbooks on managerial finance and managerial economics that are used at more than 1,000 universities in the United States and have been translated into 11 languages worldwide. He has testified as an expert witness in numerous electric, gas, and telephone rate cases at both federal and state levels. He has served as a consultant to many corporations and government agencies, including the Federal Reserve Board, the Federal Home Loan Bank Board, the U.S. Office of Telecommunications Policy, and the RAND Corporation. Dr. Brigham continues to teach, consult, and complete research in addition to his academic writing. He spends his spare time on the golf course, enjoying time with his family and dogs, and tackling outdoor adventure activities, such as biking through Alaska.

JOEL F. HOUSTON *UNIVERSITY OF FLORIDA*

Joel F. Houston is the John B. Hall Professor of Finance at the University of Florida. He received his M.A. and Ph.D. from the Wharton School at the University of Pennsylvania, and his undergraduate degree from Franklin and Marshall College. Prior to his appointment at the University of Florida, Dr. Houston was an Economist at the Federal Reserve Bank of Philadelphia. Joel's research is primarily in the areas of corporate finance and financial institutions, and his work has been published in a number of top journals including the *Journal of Finance, Journal of Financial Economics, Journal of Business, Journal of Financial and Quantitative Analysis* and *Financial Management*. Professor Houston also currently serves as an associate editor for the *Journal of Money, Credit and Banking, The Journal of Financial Services Research* and *The Journal of Financial Economic Policy*. Since arriving at the University of Florida in 1987, Joel has received 19 teaching awards, and has been actively involved in both undergraduate and graduate education. In addition to co-authoring leading textbooks in financial management, Dr. Houston has participated in management education programs for the PURC/World Bank Program, Southern Company, Exelon Corporation and Volume Services America. Joel enjoys playing golf and tennis and spending time with his wife (Sherry) and two children (Chris and Meredith). He is an avid sports fan who follows the Florida Gators, and the Pittsburgh Steelers, Pirates and Penguins.

PART 1

INTRODUCTION TO FINANCIAL MANAGEMENT

CHAPTER

1 An Overview of Financial Management

2 Financial Markets and Institutions

daniel acker/bloomberg/Getty Images

An Overview of Financial Management

Striking the Right Balance

In 1776, Adam Smith described how an "invisible hand" guides companies as they strive for profits, and that hand leads them to decisions that benefit society. Smith's insights led him to conclude that profit maximization is the right goal for a business and that the free enterprise system is best for society. But the world has changed since 1776. Firms today are much larger, they operate globally, they have thousands of employees, and they are owned by millions of stockholders. This makes us wonder if the "invisible hand" still provides reliable guidance: Should companies still try to maximize profits, or should they take a broader view and more balanced actions designed to benefit customers, employees, suppliers, and society as a whole?

Many academics and finance professionals today subscribe to the following modified version of Adam Smith's theory:

- A firm's principal goal should be to maximize the wealth of its stockholders, which means maximizing the value of its stock.

- Free enterprise is still the best economic system for society as a whole. Under the free enterprise framework, companies develop products and services that people want and that benefit society.

- However, some constraints are needed—firms should not be allowed to pollute the air and water, to engage in unfair employment practices, or to create monopolies that exploit consumers.

These constraints take a number of different forms. The first set of constraints is the costs that are assessed on companies if they take actions that harm society. Another set of constraints arises through the political process, where society imposes a wide range of regulations that are designed to keep companies from engaging in practices that are harmful to society. Properly imposed, these costs fairly transfer value to suffering parties and help create incentives that help prevent similar events from occurring in the future.

The recent financial crisis dramatically illustrates these points. We witnessed many Wall Street firms engaging in extremely risky activities that pushed the financial system to the brink of collapse in 2007 and 2008. Saving the financial system required a bailout of the banks and other financial companies, and that bailout imposed huge costs on taxpayers and helped push the economy into a deep recession. Apart from the huge costs imposed on society, the financial firms also paid a heavy price—a number of leading financial institutions saw a huge drop in their stock price, some failed and went out of business, and many Wall Street executives lost their jobs.

Arguably, these costs are not enough to prevent another financial crisis from occurring. Many maintain that the events surrounding the financial crisis illustrate that markets don't always work the way they should, and that there is a need for stronger regulation of the financial sector. For example, in his recent books, Nobel Laureate Joseph Stiglitz makes a strong case for enhanced regulation. At the same time, others with a different political persuasion continue to express concerns about the costs of excessive regulation.

Beyond the financial crisis, there is a broader question of whether laws and regulations are enough to compel firms to act in society's interest. An increasing number of companies continue to recognize the need to maximize shareholder value, but they also see their mission as more than just making money for shareholders. Google's well-known corporate motto is "Don't Be Evil." Consistent with this mission, the company has its own in-house foundation that has made large investments in a wide range of philanthropic ventures worldwide.

Looking at another industry, Whole Foods Markets' CEO John Mackey is an ardent defender of capitalism, and the company clearly states on its website, "We are stewards of our shareholders' investments and we take that responsibility very seriously. We are committed to increasing long term shareholder value." At the same time, Mackey has created a business model for Whole Foods that he refers to as "conscious capitalism." This model incorporates a broad set of core values. These values include:

- Selling the highest quality natural and organic products available
- Satisfying and delighting our customers
- Supporting team member excellence and happiness
- Creating wealth through profits and growth
- Caring about our communities and our environment
- Creating ongoing win-win partnerships with our suppliers
- Promoting the health of our stakeholders through healthy eating education.

Mackey makes a strong case that these core values work together and that the company's shareholders benefit from efforts to improve the welfare of its customers, employees, and surrounding communities. Realistically, however, there will still be cases where companies face conflicts between their various constituencies—for example, a company may enhance shareholder value by laying off some workers, or a change in policy may improve the environment but reduce shareholder value. In these instances, managers have to balance these competing interests and different managers will clearly make different choices. At the end of the day, all companies struggle to find the right balance. Enlightened managers recognize that there is more to life than money, but it often takes money to do good things.

Sources: Marc Gunther, "Money and Morals at GE," *Fortune*, November 15, 2004, pp. 176–182; Kevin J. Delaney, "Google: From 'Don't Be Evil' to How to Do Good," *The Wall Street Journal*, January 18, 2008, pp. B1–B2; Joseph E. Stiglitz, *Freefall: America, Free Markets, and the Sinking of the World Economy* (New York: W.W. Norton & Company, 2010); Joseph E. Stiglitz, *The Price of Inequality* (New York: W.W. Norton & Company, 2012); and http://wholefoodsmarket.com/mission-values/core-values.

PUTTING THINGS IN PERSPECTIVE

This chapter will give you an idea of what financial management is all about. We begin the chapter by describing how finance is related to the overall business environment, by pointing out that finance prepares students for jobs in different fields of business, and by discussing the different forms of business organization. For corporations, management's goal should be to maximize shareholder wealth, which means maximizing the value of the stock. When we say "maximizing the value of the stock,"

we mean the "true, long-run value," which may be different from the current stock price. In the chapter we discuss how firms must provide the right incentives for managers to focus on long-run value maximization. Good managers understand the importance of ethics, and they recognize that maximizing long-run value is consistent with being socially responsible.

When you finish this chapter, you should be able to:

- Explain the role of finance and the different types of jobs in finance.
- Identify the advantages and disadvantages of different forms of business organization.
- Explain the links between stock price, intrinsic value, and executive compensation.
- Identify the potential conflicts that arise within the firm between stockholders and managers and between stockholders and bondholders, and discuss the techniques that firms can use to mitigate these potential conflicts.
- Discuss the importance of business ethics and the consequences of unethical behavior.

1-1 What Is Finance?

Finance is defined by *Webster's Dictionary* as "the system that includes the circulation of money, the granting of credit, the making of investments, and the provision of banking facilities." Finance has many facets, which makes it difficult to provide one concise definition. The discussion in this section will give you an idea of what finance professionals do and what you might do if you enter the finance field after you graduate.

1-1a Areas of Finance

Finance as taught in universities is generally divided into three areas: (1) financial management, (2) capital markets, and (3) investments.

Financial management, also called corporate finance, focuses on decisions relating to how much and what types of assets to acquire, how to raise the capital needed to purchase assets, and how to run the firm so as to maximize its value. The same principles apply to both for-profit and not-for-profit organizations; and as the title suggests, much of this book is concerned with financial management.

Capital markets relate to the markets where interest rates, along with stock and bond prices, are determined. Also studied here are the financial institutions that supply capital to businesses. Banks, investment banks, stockbrokers, mutual funds, insurance companies, and the like bring together "savers" who have money to invest and businesses, individuals, and other entities that need capital for various purposes. Governmental organizations such as the Federal Reserve System, which regulates banks and controls the supply of money, and the Securities and Exchange Commission (SEC), which regulates the trading of stocks and bonds in public markets, are also studied as part of capital markets.

Investments relate to decisions concerning stocks and bonds and include a number of activities: (1) *Security analysis* deals with finding the proper values of individual securities (i.e., stocks and bonds). (2) *Portfolio theory* deals with the best way to structure portfolios, or "baskets," of stocks and bonds. Rational investors want to hold diversified portfolios in order to limit risks, so choosing a properly balanced portfolio is an important issue for any investor. (3) *Market analysis* deals with the issue of whether stock and bond markets at any given time are "too high," "too low," or "about right." Included in market analysis is *behavioral finance,* where investor psychology is examined in an effort to determine if stock prices have been bid up to unreasonable heights in a speculative bubble or driven down to unreasonable lows in a fit of irrational pessimism.

Although we separate these three areas, they are closely interconnected. Banking is studied under capital markets, but a bank lending officer evaluating a business' loan request must understand corporate finance to make a sound decision. Similarly, a corporate treasurer negotiating with a banker must understand banking if the treasurer is to borrow on "reasonable" terms. Moreover, a security analyst trying to determine a stock's true value must understand corporate finance and capital markets to do his or her job. In addition, financial decisions of all types depend on the level of interest rates; so all people in corporate finance, investments, and banking must know something about interest rates and the way they are determined. Because of these interdependencies, we cover all three areas in this book.

1-1b Finance Within an Organization

Most businesses and not-for-profit organizations have an organization chart similar to the one shown in Figure 1.1. The board of directors is the top governing body, and the chairperson of the board is generally the highest-ranking individual. The CEO comes next, but note that the chairperson of the board often also serves as the CEO. Below the CEO comes the chief operating officer (COO), who is often also designated as a firm's president. The COO directs the firm's operations, which include marketing, manufacturing, sales, and other operating departments. The chief financial officer (CFO), who is generally a senior vice president and the third-ranking officer, is in charge of accounting, finance, credit policy, decisions regarding asset acquisitions, and investor relations, which involves communications with stockholders and the press.

*The duties of the CFO have broadened over the years. CFO magazine's online service, **cfo.com**, is an excellent source of timely finance articles intended to help the CFO manage those new responsibilities.*

If the firm is publicly owned, the CEO and the CFO must both certify to the SEC that reports released to stockholders, and especially the annual report, are accurate. If inaccuracies later emerge, the CEO and the CFO could be fined or even jailed. This requirement was instituted in 2002 as a part of the **Sarbanes–Oxley Act**. The Act was passed by Congress in the wake of a series of corporate scandals involving now-defunct companies such as Enron and WorldCom, where investors, workers, and suppliers lost billions of dollars due to false information released by those companies.

Sarbanes–Oxley Act
A law passed by Congress that requires the CEO and CFO to certify that their firm's financial statements are accurate.

| FIGURE 1.1 | Finance Within the Organization |

© Cengage Learning 2015

1-1c FINANCE VERSUS ECONOMICS AND ACCOUNTING

Finance, as we know it today, grew out of economics and accounting. Economists developed the notion that an asset's value is based on the future cash flows the asset will provide, and accountants provided information regarding the likely size of those cash flows. People who work in finance need knowledge of both economics and accounting. Figure 1.1 illustrates that in the modern corporation, the accounting department typically falls under the control of the CFO. This further illustrates the link among finance, economics, and accounting.

SELF TEST

What three areas of finance does this book cover? Are these areas independent of one another, or are they interrelated in the sense that someone working in one area should know something about each of the other areas? Explain.

Who is the CFO, where does this individual fit into the corporate hierarchy? What are some of his or her responsibilities?

Does it make sense for not-for-profit organizations such as hospitals and universities to have CFOs? Why or why not?

What is the relationship among economics, finance, and accounting?

1-2 JOBS IN FINANCE

To find information about different finance careers, go to **careers-in-finance.com**. This website provides information about different finance areas and recommends different books about jobs in finance.

Finance prepares students for jobs in banking, investments, insurance, corporations, and government. Accounting students need to know marketing, management, and human resources; they also need to understand finance, for it affects decisions in all those areas. For example, marketing people propose advertising programs, but those programs are examined by finance people to judge the effects of the advertising on the firm's profitability. So to be effective in marketing, one needs to have a basic knowledge of finance. The same holds for management—indeed, most important management decisions are evaluated in terms of their effects on the firm's value.

Fins.com/Finance provides finance career news and advice including information on who's hiring in finance and accounting fields.

It is also worth noting that finance is important to individuals regardless of their jobs. Some years ago most employees received pensions from their employers upon retirement, so managing one's personal investments was not critically important. That's no longer true. Most firms today provide "defined contribution" pension plans, where each year the company puts a specified amount of money into an account that belongs to the employee. The employee must decide how those funds are to be invested—how much should be divided among stocks, bonds, or money funds—and how much risk they're willing to take with their stock and bond investments. These decisions have a major effect on people's lives, and the concepts covered in this book can improve decision-making skills.

1-3 FORMS OF BUSINESS ORGANIZATION

The basics of financial management are the same for all businesses, large or small, regardless of how they are organized. Still, a firm's legal structure affects its operations and thus should be recognized. There are four main forms of business organizations: (1) proprietorships, (2) partnerships, (3) corporations, and (4) limited liability companies (LLCs) and limited liability partnerships (LLPs). In terms of numbers, most businesses are proprietorships. However, based on the dollar value of sales, more than 80% of all business is done by corporations.[1] Because corporations conduct the most business and because most successful businesses eventually convert to corporations, we focus on them in this book. Still, it is important to understand the legal differences between types of firms.

A **proprietorship** is an unincorporated business owned by one individual. Going into business as a sole proprietor is easy—a person begins business operations. Proprietorships have three important advantages: (1) They are easy and inexpensive to form, (2) they are subject to few government regulations, and (3) they are subject to lower income taxes than are corporations. However, proprietorships also have three important limitations: (1) Proprietors have unlimited personal liability for the business' debts, so they can lose more than the amount of money they invested in the company. You might invest $10,000 to start a business but be sued for $1 million if, during company time, one of your employees runs over someone with a car. (2) The life of the business is limited to the life of the individual who created it; and to bring in new equity, investors require a change in the structure of the business. (3) Because of the first two points, proprietorships have difficulty obtaining large sums of capital; hence, proprietorships are used primarily for small businesses. However, businesses are frequently started as proprietorships and then converted to corporations when their growth results in the disadvantages outweighing the advantages.

A **partnership** is a legal arrangement between two or more people who decide to do business together. Partnerships are similar to proprietorships in that they can be established relatively easily and inexpensively. Moreover, the firm's income is allocated on a pro rata basis to the partners and is taxed on an individual basis. This allows the firm to avoid the corporate income tax. However, all of the partners are generally subject to unlimited personal liability, which means that if a partnership goes bankrupt and any partner is unable to meet his or her pro rata share of the firm's liabilities, the remaining partners will be responsible for making good on the unsatisfied claims. Thus, the actions of a Texas partner can bring ruin to a millionaire New York partner who had nothing to do with the actions that led to the downfall of the company. Unlimited liability makes it difficult for partnerships to raise large amounts of capital.[2]

A **corporation** is a legal entity created by a state, and it is separate and distinct from its owners and managers. It is this separation that limits stockholders' losses to the amount they invested in the firm—the corporation can lose all of its money, but its owners can lose only the funds that they invested in the company. Corporations also have unlimited lives, and it is easier to transfer shares of stock in a corporation than one's interest in an unincorporated business. These factors make it much easier for corporations to raise the capital necessary to operate large businesses. Thus, companies such as Hewlett-Packard and Microsoft generally begin as proprietorships or partnerships, but at some point they find it advantageous to become a corporation.

Proprietorship
An unincorporated business owned by one individual.

Partnership
An unincorporated business owned by two or more persons.

Corporation
A legal entity created by a state, separate and distinct from its owners and managers, having unlimited life, easy transferability of ownership, and limited liability.

---

[1]Refer to U.S. Census Bureau, *Statistical Abstract of the United States: 2012* (www.census.gov/compendia/statab), Table 744: Number of Tax Returns, Receipts, and Net Income by Type of Business: 1990 to 2008, p. 491.

[2]Originally, there were just straightforward partnerships; but over the years, lawyers have created a number of variations. We leave the variations to courses on business law, but we note that the variations are generally designed to limit the liabilities of some of the partners. For example, a *limited partnership* has a general partner, who has unlimited liability, and one or more limited partners, whose liability is limited to the amount of their investment. This sounds great from the standpoint of limited liability; but the limited partners must cede sole control to the general partner, which means that they have almost no say in the way the firm is managed. With a corporation, the owners (stockholders) have limited liability, but they also have the right to vote and thus change management if they think that a change is in order. Note too that LLCs and LLPs, discussed later in this section, are increasingly used in lieu of partnerships.

S Corporations

A special designation that allows small businesses that meet qualifications to be taxed as if they were a proprietorship or a partnership rather than a corporation.

Limited Liability Company (LLC)

A popular type of organization that is a hybrid between a partnership and a corporation.

Limited Liability Partnership (LLP)

Similar to an LLC but used for professional firms in the fields of accounting, law, and architecture. It provides personal asset protection from business debts and liabilities but is taxed as a partnership.

A major drawback to corporations is taxes. Most corporations' earnings are subject to double taxation—the corporation's earnings are taxed; and then when its after-tax earnings are paid out as dividends, those earnings are taxed again as personal income to the stockholders. However, as an aid to small businesses, Congress created **S corporations**, which are taxed as if they were proprietorships or partnerships; thus, they are exempt from the corporate income tax. To qualify for S corporation status, a firm can have no more than 100 stockholders, which limits their use to relatively small, privately owned firms. Larger corporations are known as *C corporations*. The vast majority of small corporations elect S status and retain that status until they decide to sell stock to the public, at which time they become C corporations.

A **limited liability company (LLC)** is a popular type of organization that is a hybrid between a partnership and a corporation. A **limited liability partnership (LLP)** is similar to an LLC. LLPs are used for professional firms in the fields of accounting, law, and architecture, while LLCs are used by other businesses. Similar to corporations, LLCs and LLPs provide limited liability protection, but they are taxed as partnerships. Further, unlike limited partnerships, where the general partner has full control of the business, the investors in an LLC or LLP have votes in proportion to their ownership interest. LLCs and LLPs have been gaining in popularity in recent years, but large companies still find it advantageous to be C corporations because of the advantages in raising capital to support growth. LLCs/LLPs were dreamed up by lawyers, and they are often structured in very complicated ways and their legal protections often vary by state. So, it is necessary to hire a good lawyer when establishing one.

When deciding on its form of organization, a firm must trade off the advantages of incorporation against a possibly higher tax burden. However, for the following reasons, the value of any business other than a relatively small one will probably be maximized if it is organized as a corporation:

1. Limited liability reduces the risks borne by investors; and other things held constant, the lower the firm's risk, the higher its value.

2. A firm's value is dependent on its growth opportunities, which are dependent on its ability to attract capital. Because corporations can attract capital more easily than other types of businesses, they are better able to take advantage of growth opportunities.

3. The value of an asset also depends on its liquidity, which means the time and effort it takes to sell the asset for cash at a fair market value. Because the stock of a corporation is easier to transfer to a potential buyer than is an interest in a proprietorship or partnership, and because more investors are willing to invest in stocks than in partnerships (with their potential unlimited liability), a corporate investment is relatively liquid. This too enhances the value of a corporation.

SELF TEST

What are the key differences among proprietorships, partnerships, and corporations?

How are LLCs and LLPs related to the other forms of organization?

What is an S corporation, and what is its advantage over a C corporation? Why don't firms such as IBM, GE, and Microsoft choose S corporation status?

What are some reasons why the value of a business other than a small one is generally maximized when it is organized as a corporation?

Suppose you are relatively wealthy and are looking for a potential investment. You do not plan to be active in the business. Would you be more interested in investing in a partnership or in a corporation? Why?

1-4 THE MAIN FINANCIAL GOAL: CREATING VALUE FOR INVESTORS

In public corporations, managers and employees work on behalf of the share-holders who own the business, and therefore they have an obligation to pursue policies that promote stockholder value. While many companies focus on max-imizing a broad range of financial objectives such as growth, earnings per share, and market share, these goals should not take precedence over the main financial goal, which is to create value for investors. Keep in mind that a company's stockholders are not just an abstract group—they represent individuals and orga-nizations who have chosen to invest their hard-earned cash into the company, and who are looking for a return on their investment in order to meet their long-term financial goals which might be saving for retirement, a new home, or a child's education.

If a manager is to maximize stockholder wealth, he or she must know how that wealth is determined. Throughout this book, we shall see that the value of any asset is the present value of the stream of cash flows that the asset provides to its owners over time. We discuss stock valuation in depth in Chapter 9, where we see that stock prices are based on cash flows expected in future years, not just in the current year. Thus, stock price maximization requires us to take a long-run view of operations. At the same time, managerial actions that affect a company's value may not immediately be reflected in the company's stock price.

1-4A DETERMINANTS OF VALUE

Figure 1.2 illustrates the situation. The top box indicates that managerial actions, combined with the economy, taxes, and political conditions, influence the level and riskiness of the company's future cash flows which ultimately determine the company's stock price. As you might expect, investors like higher expected cash flows, but they dislike risk; so the larger the expected cash flows and the lower the perceived risk, the higher the stock's price.

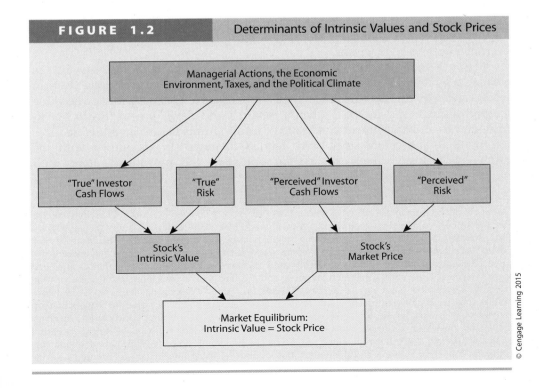

FIGURE 1.2 Determinants of Intrinsic Values and Stock Prices

© Cengage Learning 2015

The second row of boxes differentiates what we call "true" expected cash flows and "true" risk from "perceived" cash flows and "perceived" risk. By "true," we mean the cash flows and risk that investors would expect if they had all of the information that existed about a company. "Perceived" means what investors expect, given the limited information they have. To illustrate, in early 2001, investors had information that caused them to think Enron was highly profitable and would enjoy high and rising future profits. They also thought that actual results would be close to the expected levels and hence, that Enron's risk was low. However, true estimates of Enron's profits, which were known by its executives but not the investing public, were much lower; and Enron's true situation was extremely risky.

The third row of boxes shows that each stock has an **intrinsic value**, which is an estimate of the stock's "true" value as calculated by a competent analyst who has the best available data, and a **market price**, which is the actual market price based on perceived but possibly incorrect information as seen by the **marginal investor**.[3] Not all investors agree, so it is the "marginal" investor who determines the actual price.

When a stock's actual market price is equal to its intrinsic value, the stock is in **equilibrium**, which is shown in the bottom box in Figure 1.2. When equilibrium exists, there is no pressure for a change in the stock's price. Market prices can—and do—differ from intrinsic values; but eventually, as the future unfolds, the two values tend to converge.

1-4b Intrinsic Value

Actual stock prices are easy to determine—they can be found on the Internet and are published in newspapers every day. However, intrinsic values are estimates; and different analysts with different data and different views about the future form different estimates of a stock's intrinsic value. *Indeed, estimating intrinsic values is what security analysis is all about and is what distinguishes successful from unsuccessful investors.* Investing would be easy, profitable, and essentially riskless if we knew all stocks' intrinsic values; but, of course, we don't. We can estimate intrinsic values, but we can't be sure that we are right. A firm's managers have the best information about the firm's future prospects, so managers' estimates of intrinsic values are generally better than those of outside investors. However, even managers can be wrong.

Figure 1.3 graphs a hypothetical company's actual price and intrinsic value as estimated by its management over time.[4] The intrinsic value rises because the firm retains and reinvests earnings each year, which tends to increase profits. The value jumped dramatically in 2008, when a research and development (R&D) breakthrough raised management's estimate of future profits before investors had this information. The actual stock price tended to move up and down with the estimated intrinsic value; but investor optimism and pessimism, along with

Intrinsic Value
An estimate of a stock's "true" value based on accurate risk and return data. The intrinsic value can be estimated but not measured precisely.

Market Price
The stock value based on perceived but possibly incorrect information as seen by the marginal investor.

Marginal Investor
An investor whose views determine the actual stock price.

Equilibrium
The situation in which the actual market price equals the intrinsic value, so investors are indifferent between buying and selling a stock.

---

[3]Investors at the margin are the ones who actually set stock prices. Some stockholders think that a stock at its current price is a good deal, and they would buy more if they had more money. Others think that the stock is priced too high, so they would not buy it unless the price dropped sharply. Still others think that the current stock price is about where it should be; so they would buy more if the price fell slightly, sell it if the price rose slightly, and maintain their current holdings unless something were to change. These are the marginal investors, and it is their view that determines the current stock price. We discuss this point in more depth in Chapter 9, where we discuss the stock market in detail.
[4]We emphasize that the intrinsic value is an estimate and that different analysts have different estimates for a company at any given time. Managers should also estimate their firm's intrinsic value and then take actions to maximize that value. They should try to help outside security analysts improve their intrinsic value estimates by providing accurate information about the company's financial position and operations, but without releasing information that would help its competitors.

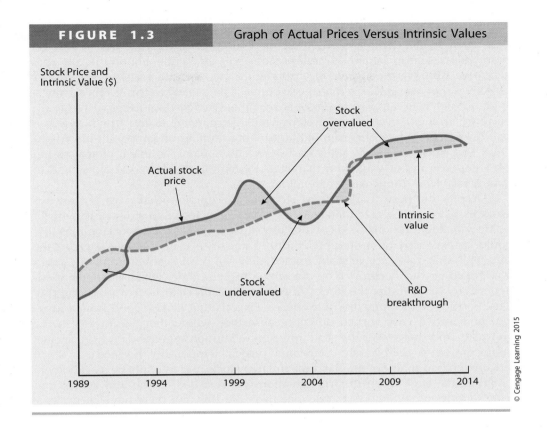

FIGURE 1.3 Graph of Actual Prices Versus Intrinsic Values

imperfect knowledge about the true intrinsic value, led to deviations between the actual prices and intrinsic values.

Intrinsic value is a long-run concept. *Management's goal should be to take actions designed to maximize the firm's intrinsic value, not its current market price.* Note, though, that maximizing the intrinsic value will maximize the *average* price over the long run, but not necessarily the current price at each point in time. For example, management might make an investment that lowers profits for the current year but raises expected future profits. If investors are not aware of the true situation, the stock price will be held down by the low current profit even though the intrinsic value was actually raised. Management should provide information that helps investors make better estimates of the firm's intrinsic value, which will keep the stock price closer to its equilibrium level. However, there are times when management cannot divulge the true situation because doing so would provide information that helps its competitors.[5]

1-4c CONSEQUENCES OF HAVING A SHORT-RUN FOCUS

Ideally, managers adhere to this long-run focus, but there are numerous examples in recent years where the focus for many companies shifted to the short run. Perhaps most notably, prior to the recent financial crisis, many Wall Street executives received huge bonuses for engaging in risky transactions that generated short-term profits. Subsequently, the value of these transactions collapsed causing many of these Wall Street firms to seek a massive government bailout.

[5]As we discuss in Chapter 2, many academics believe that stock prices embody all publicly available information—hence, that stock prices are typically reasonably close to their intrinsic values and thus at or close to equilibrium. However, almost no one doubts that managers have better information than the public at large, that at times stock prices and equilibrium values diverge, and thus that stocks can be temporarily undervalued or overvalued (as we suggest in Figure 1.3).

Apart from the recent problems on Wall Street, there have been other examples where managers have focused on short-run profits to the detriment of long-term value. Many academics and practitioners stress the important role that executive compensation plays in encouraging managers to focus on the proper objectives. For example, if a manager's bonus is tied solely to this year's earnings, it would not be a surprise to discover that the manager took steps to pump up current earnings—even if those steps were detrimental to the firm's long-run value. With these concerns in mind, a growing number of companies have used stock and stock options as a key part of executive pay. The intent of structuring compensation in this way is for managers to think more like stockholders and to continually work to increase shareholder value.

Despite the best of intentions, stock-based compensation does not always work as planned. To give managers an incentive to focus on stock prices, stockholders (acting through boards of directors) awarded executives stock options that could be exercised on a specified future date. An executive could exercise the option on that date, receive stock, immediately sell it, and earn a profit. The profit was based on the stock price on the option exercise date, which led some managers to try to maximize the stock price on that specific date, not over the long run. That, in turn, led to some horrible abuses. Projects that looked good from a long-run perspective were turned down because they would penalize profits in the short run and thus lower the stock price on the option exercise day. Even worse, some managers deliberately overstated profits, temporarily boosted the stock price, exercised their options, sold the inflated stock, and left outside stockholders "holding the bag" when the true situation was revealed. Enron and WorldCom are examples of companies whose managers did this, but there have been many others.

SELF TEST

What's the difference between a stock's current market price and its intrinsic value?

Do stocks have known and "provable" intrinsic values, or might different people reach different conclusions about intrinsic values? Explain.

Should managers estimate intrinsic values or leave that to outside security analysts? Explain.

If a firm could maximize either its current market price or its intrinsic value, what would stockholders (as a group) want managers to do? Explain.

Should a firm's managers help investors improve their estimates of the firm's intrinsic value? Explain.

1-5 STOCKHOLDER–MANAGER CONFLICTS[6]

It has long been recognized that managers' personal goals may compete with shareholder wealth maximization. In particular, managers might be more interested in maximizing their own wealth than their stockholders' wealth; therefore, managers might pay themselves excessive salaries.

---

[6]Conflicts between stockholders and managers, which are discussed in this section, and conflicts between stockholders and debtholders, which are discussed in the next section, are studied under the heading of "agency theory" in finance literature. The classic work on agency theory is Michael C. Jensen and William H. Meckling, "Theory of the Firm, Managerial Behavior, Agency Costs, and Ownership Structure," *Journal of Financial Economics*, vol. 3, no. 4 (October 1976), pp. 305–360.

Effective executive compensation plans motivate managers to act in their stockholders' best interests. Useful motivational tools include (1) reasonable compensation packages, (2) firing of managers who don't perform well, and (3) the threat of hostile takeovers.

1-5A COMPENSATION PACKAGES

Compensation packages should be sufficient to attract and retain able managers, but they should not go beyond what is needed. Compensation policies need to be consistent over time. Also, compensation should be structured so that managers are rewarded on the basis of the stock's performance over the long run, not the stock's price on an option exercise date. This means that options (or direct stock awards) should be phased in over a number of years so that managers have an incentive to keep the stock price high over time. When the intrinsic value can be measured in an objective and verifiable manner, performance pay can be based on changes in intrinsic value. However, because intrinsic value is not observable, compensation must be based on the stock's market price—but the price used should be an average over time rather than on a specific date.

1-5B DIRECT STOCKHOLDER INTERVENTION

Years ago most stock was owned by individuals. Today, however, the majority of stock is owned by institutional investors such as insurance companies, pension funds, hedge funds, and mutual funds; and private equity groups are ready and able to step in and take over underperforming firms. These institutional money managers have the clout to exercise considerable influence over firms' operations. First, they can speak with managers and make suggestions about how the business should be run. In effect, institutional investors such as Cal-PERS (California Public Employees' Retirement System, with $231 billion of assets) and TIAA-CREF (Teachers Insurance and Annuity Association-College Retirement Equity Fund, a retirement plan originally set up for professors at private colleges that now has more than $453 billion of assets) act as lobbyists for the body of stockholders. When such large stockholders speak, companies listen. Second, any shareholder who has owned $2,000 of a company's stock for one year can sponsor a proposal that may be voted on at the annual stockholders' meeting, even if management opposes the proposal.[7] Although shareholder-sponsored proposals are nonbinding, the results of such votes are heard by top management.

There has been an ongoing debate regarding how much influence shareholders should have through the proxy process. As a result of the passage of the Dodd–Frank Act, the SEC was given authority to make rules regarding shareholder access to company proxy materials. On August 25, 2010, the SEC adopted changes to federal proxy rules to give shareholders the right to nominate directors to a company's board. Rule 14a-11 under the 1934 SEC Act will require public companies to permit any shareholder owning at least 3% of a public company's voting stock for at least three years to include director nominations in the company's proxy materials.

Until recently, the probability of a large firm's management being ousted by its stockholders was so remote that it posed little threat. Most firms' shares were so widely distributed and the CEO had so much control over the voting mechanism that it was virtually impossible for dissident stockholders to get the votes

---

[7]Under current guidelines, shareholder proposals are restricted to governance issues and shareholders are not allowed to vote directly on items that are considered to be "operating issues." However, the SEC recently adopted rules (resulting from the passage of the Dodd–Frank Act) mandating an advisory vote on CEO compensation at least once every three years.

ARE CEOS OVERPAID?

In a 2012 survey of 300 large U.S. corporations, the Hay Group found that the median CEO received $10.1 million in total compensation (which includes salaries, bonuses, and long-term incentives such as stock options.). Compared to 2011, total CEO compensation increased 3.6%, while the average worker's pay raise was only 2.3%. The survey also found a somewhat stronger link between CEO pay and the firm's performance (as measured by profits and stock returns).

Over the past three years, total compensation has increased only slightly after accounting for inflation. Moreover, the structure of the average CEO compensation package has remained somewhat similar –the typical CEO has received a salary of $1.1 million, an annual bonus around $2 million, and stock options initially worth $7 million. Arguably, media scrutiny and investor concerns about excessive compensation have led some companies to limit the compensation paid to their top executives. A further concern are the recent "Say on Pay" provisions in the 2010 Dodd-Frank Act, which give shareholders an ability to vote on whether they approve of the CEO's compensation package. While these votes are nonbinding, they have put pressure on firms who want to avoid the negative publicity surrounding a shareholder vote to reject the pay plan.

While the increase in average CEO pay was fairly modest in 2012, many top CEOs still received extraordinarily high levels of total compensation. The top five highest paid CEOs were: Oracle's Larry Ellison ($94.6 million), CBS's Leslie Moonves ($58.8 million), Walt Disney Co.'s Robert Iger ($36.3 million), Nike's Mark Parker ($33.9 million), and Viacom's Philippe Dauman ($33.1 million). At the same time, many CEOs who have received stock options in previous years have seen the value of these options increase dramatically because of the recent run-up in the stock market.

The modest increase in CEO pay the past three years follows declines in median compensation in 2008 and 2009. Looking at a longer time frame, average compensation levels are significantly higher than they were a decade ago. (Average CEO compensation in 2002 was approximately $3.7 million.) The large shifts in CEO compensation over time can often be attributed to the increased importance of stock options. Relatedly, over the past few years, a small number of CEOs have attracted attention by announcing that they are only going to accept a $1 cash salary. A recent study finds that shareholders of these firms don't do particularly well, but the CEOs' total compensation doesn't suffer since they instead receive offsetting compensation in the form of stock and stock options. The study concludes that the primary reason that these managers announce their $1 salary is to "employ camouflage in compensation schemes to avoid public outrage over excessive private benefits."[8] On the plus side, stock options provide CEOs with a powerful incentive to raise their companies' stock prices. Indeed, most observers believe there is a strong causal relationship between CEO compensation procedures and stock price performance.

Other critics argue that although performance incentives are entirely appropriate as a method of compensation, the overall level of CEO compensation is just too high. The critics ask such questions as these: Would these CEOs have been unwilling to take their jobs if they had been offered only half as many stock options? Would they have put forth less effort, and would their firms' stock prices have not increased as much? It is hard to say. Other critics lament that the exercise of stock options has dramatically increased the compensation of not only truly excellent CEOs, but it has also dramatically increased the compensation of some pretty average CEOs, who were lucky enough to have had the job during a stock market boom that raised the stock prices of even poor-performing companies. In addition, huge CEO salaries are widening the gap between top executives and middle management salaries leading to employee discontent and declining employee morale and loyalty.

As the current survey indicates, the shift to better align CEO pay with corporate performance is modest and could reverse in the future. Stock returns and corporate financial results are only two factors impacting CEO pay. Other factors that influence CEO pay are the size of the firm (larger companies pay their CEOs more) and the type of industry (energy companies pay their CEOs more). Only time will tell if the modest results shown in the 2012 survey continue in future years.

Sources: Louis Lavelle, Frederick F. Jespersen, and Michael Arndt, "Executive Pay," *BusinessWeek*, April 15, 2002, pp. 80–86; Jason Zweig, "A Chance to Veto a CEO's Bonus," *The Wall Street Journal* (online.wsj.com), January 29, 2011; Jessica Dickler, "Employers To Hike Pay, But Only For A Select Few," *CNNMoney* (money.cnn.com), July 27, 2011; and Scott Thurm, "What's a CEO Worth? More Companies Answer $10 Million," *The Wall Street Journal*, May 16, 2013, p. B1.

needed to overthrow a management team. However, that situation has changed. In recent years, the top executives of Citigroup, AT&T, Coca-Cola, Merrill Lynch, Lehman Brothers, Fannie Mae, General Motors, Peugeot, IBM, and Xerox, to name a few, were forced out due to poor corporate performance.

---

[8]Gilberto R. Loureiro, Anil K. Makhija, and Dan Zhang, "Why Do Some CEOS Work for a One Dollar Salary?," Charles A. Dice Center Working Paper No. 2011-7 and Fisher College of Business Working Paper No. 2011-03-007, March 19, 2011. The paper is available at http://ssrn.com/abstract=1571823.

1-5c MANAGERS' RESPONSE

If a firm's stock is undervalued, **corporate raiders** will see it as a bargain and will attempt to capture the firm in a **hostile takeover**. If the raid is successful, the target's executives will almost certainly be fired. This situation gives managers a strong incentive to take actions to maximize their stock's price. In the words of one executive, "If you want to keep your job, never let your stock become a bargain."

Note that the price managers should be trying to maximize is not the price on a specific day. Rather, it is the average price over the long run, which will be maximized if management focuses on the stock's intrinsic value. However, managers must communicate effectively with stockholders (without divulging information that would aid their competitors) to keep the actual price close to the intrinsic value. It's bad for stockholders and managers when the intrinsic value is high but the actual price is low. In that situation, a raider may swoop in, buy the company at a bargain price, and fire the managers. To repeat our earlier message:

> *Managers should try to maximize their stock's intrinsic value and then communicate effectively with stockholders. That will cause the intrinsic value to be high and the actual stock price to remain close to the intrinsic value over time.*

Because the intrinsic value cannot be observed, it is impossible to know whether it is really being maximized. Still, as we will discuss in Chapter 9, there are procedures for estimating a stock's intrinsic value. Managers can use these valuation models to analyze alternative courses of action and thus see how these actions are likely to impact the firm's value. This type of value-based management is not precise, but it is the best way to run a business.

Corporate Raiders
Individuals who target corporations for takeover because they are undervalued.

Hostile Takeover
The acquisition of a company over the opposition of its management.

SELF TEST

What are three techniques stockholders can use to motivate managers to maximize their stock's long-run price?

Should managers focus directly on the stock's actual market price or its intrinsic value, or are both important? Explain.

1-6 STOCKHOLDER–DEBTHOLDER CONFLICTS

Conflicts can also arise between stockholders and debtholders. Debtholders, which include the company's bankers and its bondholders, generally receive fixed payments regardless of how well the company does, while stockholders do better when the company does better. This situation leads to conflicts between these two groups, to the extent that stockholders are typically more willing to take on risky projects.[9]

To illustrate this problem, consider the example in Table 1.1, where a company has raised $2,000 in capital, $1,000 from bondholders and $1,000 from stockholders. To keep things simple, we assume that the bonds have a one-year maturity and pay an 8% annual interest rate. The company's current plan is to invest its $2,000 in Project L, a relatively low-risk project that is expected to be worth $2,400 one year from now if the market is good and $2,000 if the market is bad. There is a 50% chance that the market will be good and a 50% chance the

---

[9]We are assuming here that managers make decisions on behalf of stockholders, so saying that there are conflicts between stockholders and debtholders is the same as saying there are conflicts between managers and debtholders.

TABLE 1.1 Stockholder–Debtholder Conflict Example

Project L:

	Money Invested Today	Martket Conditions One Year from Now		Expected Cash Flow	Expected Return
		GOOD	BAD		
Cash flow to firm		$2,400	$2,000	$2,200	
Bondholders' portion	$1,000	1,080	1,080	1,080	8.00%
Stockholders' portion	1,000	1,320	920	1,120	12.00

Project H:

	Money Invested Today	Martket Conditions One Year from Now		Expected Cash Flow	Expected Return
		GOOD	BAD		
Cash flow to firm		$4,400	$0	$2,200	
Bondholders' portion	$1,000	1,080	0	540	−46.00%
Stockholders' portion	1,000	3,320	0	1,660	66.00

market will be bad. In either case, there will be enough cash to pay the bondholders their money back plus the 8% annual interest rate that they were promised. The stockholders will receive whatever is left over after the bondholders have been paid. As expected, because they are paid last, the stockholders are bearing more risk (their payoff depends on the market), but they are also earning a higher expected return.

Now assume that the company discovers another project (Project H) that has considerably more risk. Project H has the same expected cash flow as Project L, but it will produce cash flows of $4,400 if the market is good but $0 if the market is bad. Clearly, the bondholders would not be interested in Project H, because they wouldn't receive any additional benefits if the market is good and they would lose everything if the market is bad. Notice, however, that Project H provides a higher rate of return for stockholders than Project L, because they capture all of the extra benefits if the market turns out to be good. While Project H is clearly riskier, in some circumstances managers acting on behalf of the stockholders may decide that the higher expected return is enough to justify the additional risk, and they would proceed with Project H, despite the strong objections of the bondholders.

Notice, however, that astute bondholders understand that managers and stockholders may have an incentive to shift to riskier projects. Recognizing this incentive, they will view the bonds as being riskier and will demand a higher rate of return, and in some cases the perceived risk may be so great that they will not invest in the company, unless the managers can credibly convince bondholders that the company will not pursue excessively risky projects.

Another type of stockholder–debtholder conflict arises over the use of additional debt. As we see later in this book, the more debt a firm uses to finance a given amount of assets, the riskier the firm becomes. For example, if a firm has $100 million of assets and finances them with $5 million of bonds and $95 million of common stock, things have to go terribly bad before the bondholders suffer a loss. On the other hand, if the firm uses $95 million of bonds and $5 million of stock, the bondholders suffer a loss even if the value of the assets declines only slightly.

Bondholders attempt to protect themselves by including covenants in the bond agreements that limit firms' use of additional debt and constrain managers' actions in other ways. We address these issues later in this book, but they are quite important and everyone should be aware of them.

SELF TEST

Why might conflicts arise between stockholders and debtholders?

How might astute bondholders react if stockholders take on risky projects?

How can bondholders protect themselves from managers' actions that negatively impact bondholders?

1-7 BALANCING SHAREHOLDER INTERESTS AND THE INTERESTS OF SOCIETY

Throughout this book, we focus primarily on publicly owned companies; hence, we operate on the assumption that management's primary goal is **shareholder wealth maximization**. At the same time, the managers know that this does not mean maximize shareholder value "at all costs." Managers have an obligation to behave ethically, and they must follow the laws and other society-imposed constraints that we discussed in the opening vignette to this chapter.

To understand how corporate managers balance the interests of society and shareholders, it is helpful to first look at those issues from the perspective of a sole proprietor. Consider Larry Jackson, the owner of a local sporting goods store. Jackson is in business to make money, but he likes to take time off to play golf on Fridays. He also has a few employees who are no longer very productive, but he keeps them on the payroll out of friendship and loyalty. Jackson is running the business in a way that is consistent with his own personal goals. He knows that he could make more money if he didn't play golf or if he replaced some of his employees. But he is comfortable with his choices; and because it is his business, he is free to make those choices.

By contrast, Linda Smith is CEO of a large corporation. Smith manages the company; however most of the stock is owned by shareholders who purchased it because they were looking for an investment that would help them retire, send their children to college, pay for a long-anticipated trip, and so forth. The shareholders elected a board of directors, which then selected Smith to run the company. Smith and the firm's other managers are working on behalf of the shareholders, and they were hired to pursue policies that enhance shareholder value.

Most managers understand that maximizing shareholder value does not mean that they are free to ignore the larger interests of society. Consider, for example, what would happen if Linda Smith narrowly focused on creating shareholder value, but in the process, her company was unresponsive to its employees and customers, hostile to its local community, and indifferent to the effects its actions had on the environment. In all likelihood, society would impose a wide range of costs on the company. It may find it hard to attract top-notch employees, its products may be boycotted, it may face additional lawsuits and regulations, and it may be confronted with negative publicity. These costs would ultimately lead to a reduction in shareholder value. So clearly when taking steps to maximize

Shareholder Wealth Maximization
The primary goal for managers of publicly owned companies implies that decisions should be made to maximize the long-run value of the firm's common stock.

INVESTING IN SOCIALLY RESPONSIBLE FUNDS

The same societal pressures that have encouraged consumers to buy products of companies that they believe to be socially responsible have also led some investors to search for ways to limit their investments to firms they deem to be socially responsible. Indeed, today there are a large number of mutual funds that only invest in companies that meet specified social goals. Each of these socially responsible funds applies different criteria, but typically they consider a company's environmental record, its commitment to social causes, and its employee relations. Many of these funds also avoid investments in companies that are involved with alcohol, tobacco, gambling, and nuclear power. Investment performance varies among funds from year to year. The accompanying chart compares the past performance of a representative socially responsible fund, the Domini Social Equity Fund, with that of the S&P 500 during the past 20+ years. While the general shape of each is similar, in the past decade the S&P 500 has outperformed this fund.

Recent Performance of Domini Social Equity Fund Versus S&P 500

Source: finance.yahoo.com, February 18, 2013.

shareholder value, enlightened managers need to also keep in mind these society-imposed constraints.[10]

From a broader perspective, firms have a number of different departments, including marketing, accounting, production, human resources, and finance. The finance department's principal task is to evaluate proposed decisions and judge how they will affect the stock price and thus shareholder wealth. For example, suppose the production manager wants to replace some old equipment with new automated machinery that will reduce labor costs. The finance staff will evaluate that proposal and determine whether the savings seem to be worth the cost. Similarly, if marketing wants to spend $10 million advertising during the Super Bowl, the financial staff will evaluate the proposal, look at the probable increase in sales, and reach a conclusion as to whether the money spent will lead to a higher stock price. Most significant decisions are evaluated in terms of their financial consequences, but astute managers recognize that they also need to take into account how these decisions affect society at large.

---

[10]A recent study highlights the various factors that motivate corporate managers to make socially responsible investments. Refer to Richard Borghesi, Joel F. Houston, and Andy Naranjo, "What Motivates Corporate Managers to Make Socially Responsible Investments?," November 4, 2012. The paper is available at http://ssrn.com/abstract=2171916.

1-8 BUSINESS ETHICS

As a result of the financial scandals occurring during the past decade, there has been a strong push to improve _business ethics._ This is occurring on many fronts—actions begun by former New York attorney general and former governor Elliot Spitzer and others who sued companies for improper acts; Congress' passing of the Sarbanes–Oxley bill to impose sanctions on executives who sign financial statements later found to be false; Congress' passing of the Dodd–Frank Act to implement an aggressive overhaul of the U.S. financial regulatory system aimed at preventing reckless actions that would cause another financial crisis; and business schools trying to inform students about proper versus improper business actions.

As noted earlier, companies benefit from having good reputations and are penalized by having bad ones; the same is true for individuals. Reputations reflect the extent to which firms and people are ethical. _Ethics_ is defined in _Webster's Dictionary_ as "standards of conduct or moral behavior." Business ethics can be thought of as a company's attitude and conduct toward its employees, customers, community, and stockholders. A firm's commitment to business ethics can be measured by the tendency of its employees, from the top down, to adhere to laws, regulations, and moral standards relating to product safety and quality, fair employment practices, fair marketing and selling practices, the use of confidential information for personal gain, community involvement, and the use of illegal payments to obtain business.

1-8A WHAT COMPANIES ARE DOING

Most firms today have strong written codes of ethical behavior; companies also conduct training programs to ensure that employees understand proper behavior in different situations. When conflicts arise involving profits and ethics, ethical considerations sometimes are so obviously important that they dominate. In other cases, however, the right choice is not clear. For example, suppose that Norfolk Southern's managers know that its coal trains are polluting the air; but the amount of pollution is within legal limits, and further reduction would be costly. Are the managers ethically bound to reduce pollution? Similarly, several years ago Merck's research indicated that its Vioxx pain medicine might be causing heart attacks. However, the evidence was not overly strong, and the product was clearly helping some patients. Over time, additional tests produced stronger evidence that Vioxx did pose a health risk. What should Merck have done, and when should Merck have done it? If the company released negative but perhaps incorrect information, this announcement would have hurt sales and possibly prevented some patients benefitting from the product. If the company delayed the release of this additional information, more patients might have suffered irreversible harm. At what point should Merck have made the potential problem known to the public? There are no obvious answers to questions such as these; but companies must deal with them, and a failure to handle them properly can lead to severe consequences.

1-8b CONSEQUENCES OF UNETHICAL BEHAVIOR

Over the past few years, ethical lapses have led to a number of bankruptcies. The collapses of Enron and WorldCom as well as the accounting firm Arthur Andersen dramatically illustrate how unethical behavior can lead to a firm's rapid decline. In all three cases, top executives came under fire because of misleading accounting practices that led to overstated profits. Enron and World-Com executives were busily selling their stock at the same time they were recommending the stock to employees and outside investors. These executives reaped millions before the stock declined, while lower-level employees and outside investors were left "holding the bag." Some of these executives are now in jail, and Enron's CEO had a fatal heart attack while awaiting sentencing after being found guilty of conspiracy and fraud. Moreover, Merrill Lynch and Citigroup, which were accused of facilitating these frauds, were fined hundreds of millions of dollars.

In other cases, companies avoid bankruptcy but face a damaging blow to their reputation. Safety concerns tarnished Toyota's once-sterling reputation for reliability. Ethical questions were raised regarding when the company's senior management became aware of the problems, and whether they were forthcoming in sharing these concerns with the public. In April 2010, the SEC brought forth a civil fraud suit against Goldman Sachs. The SEC contended that Goldman Sachs misled its investors when it created and marketed securities that were backed by subprime mortgages. In July 2010, Goldman Sachs ultimately reached a settlement where it agreed to pay $550 million. While just one example, many believe that too many Wall Street executives in recent years have been willing to compromise their ethics. In May 2011, Raj Rajararnam, the founder of the hedge fund Galleon Group LLC, was convicted of securities fraud and conspiracy in one of the government's largest insider trading cases. Mr. Rajararnam traded on information (worth approximately $63.8 million) from insiders at technology companies and others in the hedge fund industry. On October 13, 2011, he was sentenced to 11 years in prison. Even more recently, regulators have accused a number of high-profile institutions of actively manipulating the London Interbank Offer Rate (the LIBOR rate) to make additional profits on their trades. These accusations are particularly important because the LIBOR rate is used to set the terms in many financial contracts. These investigations are ongoing, but already regulators have fined Barclays Bank and UBS for their parts in this scandal.

The perception of widespread improper actions has caused many investors to lose faith in American business and to turn away from the stock market, which makes it difficult for firms to raise the capital they need to grow, create jobs, and stimulate the economy. So, unethical actions can have adverse consequences far beyond the companies that perpetrate them.

All this raises a question: Are *companies* unethical, or is it just a few of their employees? That was a central issue that came up in the case of Arthur Andersen, the accounting firm that audited Enron, WorldCom, and several other companies that committed accounting fraud. Evidence showed that relatively few of Andersen's accountants helped perpetrate the frauds. Its top managers argued that while a few rogue employees did bad things, most of the firm's 85,000 employees, and the firm itself, were innocent. The U.S. Justice Department disagreed, concluding that the firm was guilty because it fostered a climate where unethical behavior was permitted and that Andersen used an incentive system that made such behavior profitable to both the perpetrators and the firm. As a result, Andersen was put out of business, its partners lost millions of dollars, and its 85,000 employees lost their jobs. In most other cases, individuals rather than firms were tried; and while the firms survived, they suffered damage to their reputations, which greatly lowered their future profit potential and value.

1-8c HOW SHOULD EMPLOYEES DEAL WITH UNETHICAL BEHAVIOR?

Far too often the desire for stock options, bonuses, and promotions drives managers to take unethical actions such as fudging the books to make profits in the manager's division look good, holding back information about bad products that would depress sales, and failing to take costly but needed measures to protect the environment. Generally, these acts don't rise to the level of an Enron or a WorldCom, but they are still bad. If questionable things are going on, who should take action and what should that action be? Obviously, in situations such as Enron and WorldCom, where fraud was being perpetrated at or close to the top, senior managers knew about the illegal activities. In other cases, the problem is caused by a mid-level manager trying to boost his or her unit's profits and thus his or her bonus. In all cases, though, at least some lower-level employees are aware of what's happening; they may even be ordered to take fraudulent actions. Should the lower-level employees obey their boss's orders; refuse to obey those orders; or report the situation to a higher authority, such as the company's board of directors, the company's auditors, or a federal prosecutor?

In the WorldCom and Enron cases, it was clear to a number of employees that unethical and illegal acts were being committed; but in cases such as Merck's Vioxx product, the situation was less clear. Because early evidence that Vioxx led to heart attacks was weak and evidence of its pain reduction was strong, it was probably not appropriate to sound an alarm early on. However, as evidence accumulated, at some point the public needed to be given a strong warning or the product should have been taken off the market. But judgment comes into play when deciding on what action to take and when to take it. If a lower-level employee thinks that a product should be pulled but the boss disagrees, what should the employee do? If an employee decides to report the problem, trouble may ensue regardless of the merits of the case. If the alarm is false, the company will have been harmed and nothing will have been gained. In that case, the employee will probably be fired. Even if the employee is right, his or her career may still be ruined because many companies (or at least bosses) don't like "disloyal, troublemaking" employees.

Such situations arise fairly often ranging from accounting fraud to product liability and environmental cases. Employees jeopardize their jobs if they come forward over their bosses' objections. However, if they don't speak up, they may suffer emotional problems and contribute to the downfall of their companies and the accompanying loss of jobs and savings. Moreover, if employees obey orders regarding actions they know are illegal, they may end up going to jail. Indeed, in most of the scandals that have gone to trial, the lower-level people who physically entered the bad data received longer jail sentences than the bosses who presumably gave the directives. So employees can be "stuck between a rock and a hard place," that is, doing what they should do and possibly losing their jobs versus going along with the boss and possibly ending up in jail. This discussion shows why ethics is such an important consideration in business and in business schools—and why we are concerned with it in this book.

SELF TEST

How would you define "business ethics"?

Can a firm's executive compensation plan lead to unethical behavior? Explain.

Unethical acts are generally committed by unethical people. What are some things companies can do to help ensure that their employees act ethically?

TYING IT ALL TOGETHER

This chapter provides a broad overview of financial management. *Management's primary goal should be to maximize the long-run value of the stock, which means the intrinsic value as measured by the stock's price over time.* To maximize value, firms must develop products that consumers want, produce the products efficiently, sell them at competitive prices, and observe laws relating to corporate behavior. If firms are successful at maximizing the stock's value, they will also be contributing to social welfare and citizens' well-being.

Businesses can be organized as proprietorships, partnerships, corporations, limited liability companies (LLCs), or limited liability partnerships (LLPs). The vast majority of all business is done by corporations, and the most successful firms become corporations, which explains the focus on corporations in this book.

The primary tasks of the CFO are (1) to make sure the accounting system provides "good" numbers for internal decision making and for investors, (2) to ensure that the firm is financed in the proper manner, (3) to evaluate the operating units to make sure they are performing in an optimal manner, and (4) to evaluate all proposed capital expenditures to make sure they will increase the firm's value. In the remainder of this book, we discuss exactly how financial managers carry out these tasks.

SELF-TEST QUESTIONS AND PROBLEMS

(Solutions Appear in Appendix A)

ST-1 **KEY TERMS** Define each of the following terms:
a. Sarbanes–Oxley Act
b. Proprietorship; partnership; corporation
c. S corporation; limited liability company (LLC); limited liability partnership (LLP)
d. Intrinsic value; market price
e. Marginal investor; equilibrium
f. Corporate raider; hostile takeover
g. Stockholder wealth maximization
h. Business ethics

QUESTIONS

1-1 What is a firm's intrinsic value? Its current stock price? Is the stock's "true" long-run value more closely related to its intrinsic value or to its current price?

1-2 When is a stock said to be in equilibrium? Why might a stock at any point in time not be in equilibrium?

1-3 Suppose three honest individuals gave you their estimates of Stock X's intrinsic value. One person is your current roommate, the second person is a professional security analyst with an excellent reputation on Wall Street, and the third person is Company X's CFO. If the three estimates differed, in which one would you have the most confidence? Why?

1-4 Is it better for a firm's actual stock price in the market to be under, over, or equal to its intrinsic value? Would your answer be the same from the standpoints of stockholders in general and a CEO who is about to exercise a million dollars in options and then retire? Explain.

1-5 If a company's board of directors wants management to maximize shareholder wealth, should the CEO's compensation be set as a fixed dollar amount, or should the compensation depend on how well the firm performs? If it is to be based on performance, how should performance be measured? Would it be easier to measure performance by the growth rate in reported profits or the growth rate in the stock's intrinsic value? Which would be the better performance measure? Why?

1-6 What are the various forms of business organization? What are the advantages and disadvantages of each?

1-7 Should stockholder wealth maximization be thought of as a long-term or a short-term goal? For example, if one action increases a firm's stock price from a current level of $20 to $25 in 6 months and then to $30 in 5 years but another action keeps the stock at $20 for several years but then increases it to $40 in 5 years, which action would be better? Think of some specific corporate actions that have these general tendencies.

1-8 What are some actions that stockholders can take to ensure that management's and stockholders' interests are aligned?

1-9 The president of Southern Semiconductor Corporation (SSC) made this statement in the company's annual report: "SSC's primary goal is to increase the value of our common stockholders' equity." Later in the report, the following announcements were made:

a. The company contributed $1.5 million to the symphony orchestra in Birmingham, Alabama, its headquarters city.

b. The company is spending $500 million to open a new plant and expand operations in China. No profits will be produced by the Chinese operation for 4 years, so earnings will be depressed during this period versus what they would have been had the decision been made not to expand in China.

c. The company holds about half of its assets in the form of U.S. Treasury bonds, and it keeps these funds available for use in emergencies. In the future, though, SSC plans to shift its emergency funds from Treasury bonds to common stocks.

Discuss how SSC's stockholders might view each of these actions and how the actions might affect the stock price.

1-10 Investors generally can make one vote for each share of stock they hold. TIAA-CREF is the largest institutional shareholder in the United States; therefore, it holds many shares and has more votes than any other organization. Traditionally, this fund has acted as a passive investor, just going along with management. However, in 1993, it mailed a notice to all 1,500 companies whose stocks it held that henceforth, it planned to actively intervene if, in its opinion, management was not performing well. Its goal was to improve corporate performance to boost the prices of the stocks it held. It also wanted to encourage corporate boards to appoint a majority of independent (outside) directors; and it stated that it would vote against any directors of firms that "don't have an effective, independent board that can challenge the CEO."

In the past, TIAA-CREF responded to poor performance by "voting with its feet," which means selling stocks that were not doing well. However, by 1993, that position had become difficult to maintain for two reasons. First, the fund invested a large part of its assets in "index funds," which hold stocks in accordance with their percentage value in the broad stock market. Furthermore, TIAA-CREF owns such large blocks of stocks in many companies that if it tried to sell out, doing so would severely depress the prices of those stocks. Thus, TIAA-CREF is locked in to a large extent, which led to its decision to become a more active investor.

a. Is TIAA-CREF an ordinary shareholder? Explain.

b. Due to its asset size, TIAA-CREF owns many shares in a number of companies. The fund's management plans to vote those shares. However, TIAA-CREF is owned by many thousands of investors. Should the fund's managers vote its shares; or should it pass those votes, on a pro rata basis, back to its own shareholders? Explain.

1-11 Edmund Enterprises recently made a large investment to upgrade its technology. While these improvements won't have much effect on performance in the short run, they are expected to reduce future costs significantly. What effect will this investment have on Edmund Enterprises' earnings per share this year? What effect might this investment have on the company's intrinsic value and stock price?

1-12 Suppose you were a member of Company X's board of directors and chairperson of the company's compensation committee. What factors should your committee consider when setting the CEO's compensation? Should the compensation consist of a dollar salary, stock options that depend on the firm's performance, or a mix of the two? If "performance" is to be considered, how should it be measured? Think of both theoretical and practical (that is, measurement) considerations. If you were also a vice president of Company X, might your actions be different than if you were the CEO of some other company?

1-13 Suppose you are a director of an energy company that has three divisions—natural gas, oil, and retail (gas stations). These divisions operate independently from one another, but all division managers report to the firm's CEO. If you were on the compensation committee as discussed in Question 1-12 and your committee was asked to set the compensation for the three division managers, would you use the same criteria as that used for the firm's CEO? Explain your reasoning.

1-14 Bedrock Company has $70 million in debt and $30 million in equity. The debt matures in one year and has a 10% interest rate, so the company is promising to pay back $77 million to its debtholders one year from now.

The company is considering two possible investments, each of which will require an upfront cost of $100 million. Each investment will last for one year and the payoff from each investment depends on the strength of the overall economy. There is a 50% chance that the economy will be weak and a 50% chance it will be strong.

Here are the expected payoffs (all dollars are in millions) from the two investments:

	Payoff in One Year If the Economy Is Weak	Payoff in One Year If the Economy Is Strong	Expected Payoff
Investment L	$90.00	$130.00	$110.00
Investment H	50.00	170.00	110.00

Note that the two projects have the same expected payoff, but Project H has higher risk. The debtholders always get paid first and the stockholders receive any money that is available after the debtholders have been paid.

Assume that if the company doesn't have enough funds to pay off its debtholders one year from now, then Bedrock will declare bankruptcy. If bankruptcy is declared, the debtholders will receive all available funds and the stockholders will receive nothing.

a. Assume that the company selects Investment L. What is the expected payoff to the firm's debtholders? What is the expected payoff to the firm's stockholders?

b. Assume that the company selects Investment H. What is the expected payoff to the firm's debtholders? What is the expected payoff to the firm's stockholders?

c. Would the debtholders prefer that the company's managers select Project L or Project H? Briefly explain your reason.

d. Explain why the company's managers acting on behalf of the stockholders might select Project H even though it has greater risk.

e. What actions can debtholders take to protect their interests?

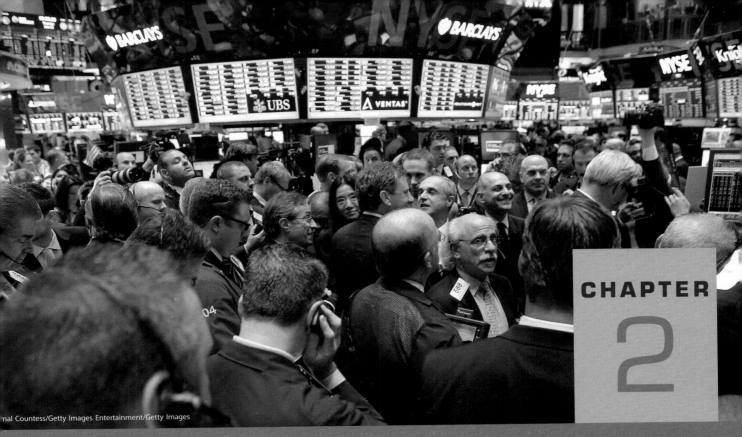

CHAPTER

2

Financial Markets and Institutions

Rebuilding the Financial System after the Crisis

History shows that a strong financial system is a necessary ingredient for a growing and prosperous economy. Companies raising capital to finance capital expenditures and investors saving to accumulate funds for future use require well-functioning financial markets and institutions.

Over the past few decades, changing technology and improving communications have increased cross-border transactions and expanded the scope and efficiency of the global financial system. Companies routinely raise funds throughout the world to finance projects all around the globe. Likewise, with the click of a mouse an individual investor in Pittsburgh can deposit funds in a European bank or purchase a mutual fund that invests in Chinese securities.

These innovations helped spur global economic growth by providing capital to an increasing number of individuals throughout the world. Along the way, the financial industry attracted a lot of talented people who created,

marketed, and traded a large number of new financial products. However, despite their benefits many of these same factors led to excesses which culminated in the recent financial crisis. While the early stage of the crisis occurred in 2007, it became front and center in 2008. Losses from its investments in securities backed by subprime mortgages led to the collapse of Bear Stearns in March 2008. A continued free fall in the housing market destroyed the value of many leading financial institutions and created a panic among many other firms that were connected to these institutions. By the end of 2008, a number of leading financial institutions including Lehman Brothers, AIG, Merrill Lynch, Washington Mutual, Wachovia, Fannie Mae, and Freddie Mac either failed, reorganized, or were forced to sell to other institutions at fire sale prices (often with government assistance).

At the height of the crisis, many were worried that the entire financial system could collapse, and in response regulators took emergency steps. Most notably through its Troubled Asset Relief Program (TARP), the U.S. government allocated a staggering $700 billion to purchase or insure the troubled assets of many of the surviving institutions. During this time period, the once well-functioning financial system suddenly became "frozen" as investors and financial institutions were unwilling or unable to provide funds to individual and corporate borrowers—even those with the highest credit rating. Waiting for the panic to subside, many of these investors put all of their money in cash and Treasury securities.

In the aftermath of the crisis, the financial sector is slowly recovering, but its effects continue. In many ways, the financial crisis dramatically illustrates that financial managers and investors don't operate in a vacuum—they make decisions within a large and complex financial environment. This environment includes financial markets and institutions, tax and regulatory policies, and the state of the economy. The environment both determines the available financial alternatives and affects the outcome of various decisions. Thus, it is crucial that investors and financial managers have a good understanding of the environment in which they operate.

PUTTING THINGS IN PERSPECTIVE

In Chapter 1, we saw that a firm's primary goal is to maximize its stock price. Stock prices are determined in the financial markets; so if financial managers are to make good decisions, they must understand how these markets operate. In addition, individuals make personal investment decisions; so they too need to know something about financial markets and the institutions that operate in those markets. Therefore, in this chapter, we describe the markets where capital is raised, securities are traded, and stock prices are established and the institutions that operate in these markets. We will also discuss the concept of market efficiency, and demonstrate how efficient markets help promote the effective allocation of capital.

In recent years, the dramatic price swings in the financial markets that have become increasingly common have led many to question whether markets are always efficient. In response, there has been increased interest in behavioral finance theory. This theory focuses on how psychological factors influence individual decisions (sometimes in perverse ways), and the resulting impact these decisions have on financial markets.

When you finish this chapter, you should be able to:

*For additional information regarding the financial crisis, students can refer to **timeline .stlouisfed.org.** Another good source can be found at **fcic .law.stanford.edu**, which focuses on the Financial Crisis Inquiry Commission.*

- Identify the different types of financial markets and financial institutions, and explain how these markets and institutions enhance capital allocation.
- Explain how the stock market operates, and list the distinctions between the different types of stock markets.
- Explain how the stock market has performed in recent years.
- Discuss the importance of market efficiency, and explain why some markets are more efficient than others.
- Develop a simple understanding of behavioral finance.

2-1 THE CAPITAL ALLOCATION PROCESS

Businesses, individuals, and governments often need to raise capital. For example, Carolina Power & Light Energy (CP&L) forecasts an increase in the demand for electricity in North and South Carolina, so it will build a new power plant to meet those needs. Because CP&L's bank account does not contain the $1 billion necessary to pay for the plant, the company must raise this capital in the financial markets. Similarly, the proprietor of a San Francisco hardware store, wants to expand into appliances. Where will he get the money to buy the initial inventory of TV sets, washers, and freezers? Or suppose the Johnson family wants to buy a home that costs $200,000, but they have only $50,000 in savings. Where will they obtain the additional $150,000? The city of New York needs $200 million to build a new sewer plant. Where can it obtain this money? Finally, the federal government needs more money than it receives from taxes. Where will the extra money come from?

On the other hand, some individuals and firms have incomes that exceed their current expenditures, in which case they have funds available to invest. For example, Carol Hawk has an income of $36,000, but her expenses are only $30,000. That leaves her with $6,000 to invest. Similarly, Microsoft has accumulated roughly $68.3 billion of cash and marketable securities. What can Microsoft do with this money until it is needed in the business?

People and organizations with surplus funds are saving today in order to accumulate funds for some future use. Members of a household might save to pay for their children's education and the parents' retirement, while a business might save to fund future investments. Those with surplus funds expect to earn a return on their investments, while people and organizations that need capital understand that they must pay interest to those who provide that capital.

In a well-functioning economy, capital flows efficiently from those with surplus capital to those who need it. This transfer can take place in the three ways described in Figure 2.1.

1. *Direct transfers* of money and securities, as shown in the top section, occur when a business sells its stocks or bonds directly to savers, without going through any type of financial institution. The business delivers its securities to savers, who, in turn, give the firm the money it needs. This procedure is used mainly by small firms, and relatively little capital is raised by direct transfers.

2. As shown in the middle section, transfers may also go through an investment bank (iBank) such as Morgan Stanley, which *underwrites* the issue. An underwriter facilitates the issuance of securities. The company sells its stocks

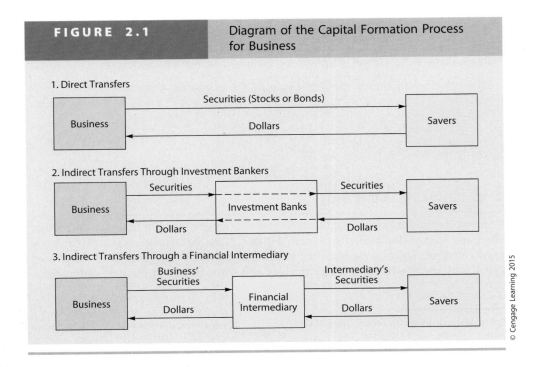

| FIGURE 2.1 | Diagram of the Capital Formation Process for Business |

1. Direct Transfers

Business → Securities (Stocks or Bonds) → Savers
Savers → Dollars → Business

2. Indirect Transfers Through Investment Bankers

Business → Securities → Investment Banks → Securities → Savers
Savers → Dollars → Investment Banks → Dollars → Business

3. Indirect Transfers Through a Financial Intermediary

Business → Business' Securities → Financial Intermediary → Intermediary's Securities → Savers
Savers → Dollars → Financial Intermediary → Dollars → Business

or bonds to the investment bank, which then sells these same securities to savers. The businesses' securities and the savers' money merely "pass through" the investment bank. However, because the investment bank buys and holds the securities for a period of time, it is taking a risk—it may not be able to resell the securities to savers for as much as it paid. Because new securities are involved and the corporation receives the sale proceeds, this transaction is called a *primary market transaction*.

3.   Transfers can also be made through a *financial intermediary* such as a bank, an insurance company, or a mutual fund. Here the intermediary obtains funds from savers in exchange for its securities. The intermediary uses this money to buy and hold businesses' securities, while the savers hold the intermediary's securities. For example, a saver deposits dollars in a bank, receiving a certificate of deposit; then the bank lends the money to a business in the form of a mortgage loan. Thus, intermediaries literally create new forms of capital—in this case, certificates of deposit, which are safer and more liquid than mortgages and thus better for most savers to hold. The existence of intermediaries greatly increases the efficiency of money and capital markets.

Often the entity needing capital is a business (and specifically a corporation); but it is easy to visualize the demander of capital being a home purchaser, a small business, or a government unit. For example, if your uncle lends you money to fund a new business, a direct transfer of funds will occur. Alternatively, if you borrow money to purchase a home, you will probably raise the funds through a financial intermediary such as your local commercial bank or mortgage banker. That banker could sell your mortgage to an investment bank, which then might use it as collateral for a bond that is purchased by a pension fund.

In a global context, economic development is highly correlated with the level and efficiency of financial markets and institutions.[1] It is difficult, if not impossible, for an economy to reach its full potential if it doesn't have access to a well-functioning financial system. In a well-developed economy like that of the United States, an extensive set of markets and institutions has evolved over time to facilitate the efficient allocation of capital. To raise capital efficiently, managers must understand how these markets and institutions work; and individuals need to know how the markets and institutions work to earn high rates of returns on their savings.

SELF TEST

Name three ways capital is transferred between savers and borrowers.

Why are efficient capital markets necessary for economic growth?

2-2 FINANCIAL MARKETS

People and organizations wanting to borrow money are brought together with those who have surplus funds in the *financial markets*. Note that *markets* is plural; there are many different financial markets in a developed economy such as that of the United States. We describe some of these markets and some trends in their development.

---

[1]For a detailed review of the evidence linking financial development to economic growth, see Ross Levine, "Finance and Growth: Theory and Evidence," Chapter 12 in *Handbook of Economic Growth*, edited by Philippe Aghion and Steven Durlauf (Amsterdam: Elsevier Science, 2005).

2-2A TYPES OF MARKETS

Different financial markets serve different types of customers or different parts of the country. Financial markets also vary depending on the maturity of the securities being traded and the types of assets used to back the securities. For these reasons, it is useful to classify markets along the following dimensions:

1. *Physical asset markets versus financial asset markets. Physical asset markets* (also called "tangible" or "real" asset markets) are for products such as wheat, autos, real estate, computers, and machinery. *Financial asset markets,* on the other hand, deal with stocks, bonds, notes, and mortgages. Financial markets also deal with *derivative securities* whose values are *derived* from changes in the prices of other assets. A share of Ford stock is a "pure financial asset," while an option to buy Ford shares is a derivative security whose value depends on the price of Ford stock.

2. *Spot markets versus futures markets.* **Spot markets** are markets in which assets are bought or sold for "on-the-spot" delivery (literally, within a few days). **Futures markets** are markets in which participants agree today to buy or sell an asset at some future date. For example, a farmer may enter into a futures contract in which he agrees today to sell 5,000 bushels of soybeans 6 months from now at a price of $13.75 a bushel. To continue that example, a food processor that needs soybeans in the future may enter into a futures contract in which it agrees to buy soybeans 6 months from now. Such a transaction can reduce, or *hedge,* the risks faced by both the farmer and the food processor.

3. *Money markets versus capital markets.* **Money markets** are the markets for short-term, highly liquid debt securities. The New York, London, and Tokyo money markets are among the world's largest. **Capital markets** are the markets for intermediate- or long-term debt and corporate stocks. The New York Stock Exchange, where the stocks of the largest U.S. corporations are traded, is a prime example of a capital market. There is no hard-and-fast rule, but in a description of debt markets, *short-term* generally means less than 1 year, *intermediate-term* means 1 to 10 years, and *long-term* means more than 10 years.

4. *Primary markets versus secondary markets.* **Primary markets** are the markets in which corporations raise new capital. If GE were to sell a new issue of common stock to raise capital, a primary market transaction would take place. The corporation selling the newly created stock, GE, receives the proceeds from the sale in a primary market transaction. **Secondary markets** are markets in which existing, already outstanding securities are traded among investors. Thus, if Jane Doe decided to buy 1,000 shares of GE stock, the purchase would occur in the secondary market. The New York Stock Exchange is a secondary market because it deals in outstanding, as opposed to newly issued, stocks and bonds. Secondary markets also exist for mortgages, other types of loans, and other financial assets. The corporation whose securities are being traded is not involved in a secondary market transaction and thus does not receive funds from such a sale.

5. *Private markets versus public markets.* **Private markets**, where transactions are negotiated directly between two parties, are differentiated from **public markets**, where standardized contracts are traded on organized exchanges. Bank loans and private debt placements with insurance companies are examples of private market transactions. Because these transactions are private, they may be structured in any manner to which the two parties agree. By contrast, securities that are traded in public markets (for example, common stock and corporate bonds) are held by a large number of individuals. These securities must have fairly standardized contractual

Spot Markets
The markets in which assets are bought or sold for "on-the-spot" delivery.

Futures Markets
The markets in which participants agree today to buy or sell an asset at some future date.

Money Markets
The financial markets in which funds are borrowed or loaned for short periods (less than one year).

Capital Markets
The financial markets for stocks and for intermediate- or long-term debt (one year or longer).

Primary Markets
Markets in which corporations raise capital by issuing new securities.

Secondary Markets
Markets in which securities and other financial assets are traded among investors after they have been issued by corporations.

Private Markets
Markets in which transactions are worked out directly between two parties.

Public Markets
Markets in which standardized contracts are traded on organized exchanges.

features because public investors do not generally have the time and expertise to negotiate unique, nonstandardized contracts. Broad ownership and standardization result in publicly traded securities being more liquid than tailor-made, uniquely negotiated securities.

Other classifications could be made, but this breakdown shows that there are many types of financial markets. Also note that the distinctions among markets are often blurred and unimportant except as a general point of reference. For example, it makes little difference if a firm borrows for 11, 12, or 13 months, that is, whether the transaction is a "money" or "capital" market transaction. You should be aware of the important differences among types of markets, but don't be overly concerned about trying to distinguish them at the boundaries.

A healthy economy is dependent on efficient funds transfers from people who are net savers to firms and individuals who need capital. Without efficient transfers, the economy could not function: Carolina Power & Light Energy could not raise capital, so Raleigh's citizens would have no electricity; the Johnson family would not have adequate housing; Carol Hawk would have no place to invest her savings; and so forth. Obviously, the level of employment and productivity (i.e., the standard of living) would be much lower. Therefore, it is essential that financial markets function efficiently—not only quickly, but also inexpensively.

Table 2.1 is a listing of the most important instruments traded in the various financial markets. The instruments are arranged in ascending order of typical length of maturity. As we go through this book, we will look in more detail at many of the instruments listed in Table 2.1. For example, we will see that there are many varieties of corporate bonds, ranging from "plain vanilla" bonds to bonds that can be converted to common stocks to bonds whose interest payments vary depending on the inflation rate. Still, the table provides an overview of the characteristics and costs of the instruments traded in the major financial markets.

2-2b RECENT TRENDS

Financial markets have experienced many changes in recent years. Technological advances in computers and telecommunications, along with the globalization of banking and commerce, have led to deregulation, which has increased competition throughout the world. As a result, there are more efficient, internationally linked markets, which are far more complex than what existed a few years ago. While these developments have been largely positive, they have also created problems for policy makers. With these concerns in mind, Congress and regulators have moved to reregulate parts of the financial sector following the recent financial crisis.

Globalization has exposed the need for greater cooperation among regulators at the international level, but the task is not easy. Factors that complicate coordination include (1) the different structures in nations' banking and securities industries; (2) the trend toward financial services conglomerates, which obscures developments in various market segments; and (3) the reluctance of individual countries to give up control over their national monetary policies. Still, regulators are unanimous about the need to close the gaps in the supervision of worldwide markets.

Derivative

Any financial asset whose value is derived from the value of some other "underlying" asset.

Another important trend in recent years has been the increased use of **derivatives**. A derivative is any security whose value is *derived* from the price of some other "underlying" asset. An option to buy IBM stock is a derivative, as is a contract to buy Japanese yen 6 months from now. The value of the IBM option depends on the price of IBM's stock and the value of the Japanese yen "future" depends on the exchange rate between yen and dollars. The market for derivatives has grown faster than any other market in recent years, providing investors with new opportunities, but also exposing them to new risks.

TABLE 2.1 Summary of Major Market Instruments, Market Participants, and Security Characteristics

Instrument (1)	Market (2)	Major Participants (3)	Security Characteristics		
			Riskiness (4)	Original Maturity (5)	Interest Rate on 2/19/13[a] (6)
U.S. Treasury bills	Money	Sold by U.S. Treasury to finance federal expenditures	Default-free, close to riskless	91 days to 1 year	0.104%
Bankers' acceptances	Money	A firm's note, but one guaranteed by a bank	Low degree of risk if guaranteed by a strong bank	Up to 180 days	0.28%
Commercial paper	Money	Issued by financially secure firms to large investors	Low default risk	Up to 270 days	0.08%
Negotiable certificates of deposit (CDs)	Money	Issued by major money-center commercial banks to large investors	Default risk depends on the strength of the issuing bank	Up to 1 year	0.22%
Money market mutual funds	Money	Invest in Treasury bills, CDs, and commercial paper; held by individuals and businesses	Low degree of risk	No specific maturity (instant liquidity)	0.50%
Eurodollar market time deposits	Money	Issued by banks outside the United States	Default risk depends on the strength of the issuing bank	Up to 1 year	0.20%
Consumer credit, including credit card debt	Money	Issued by banks, credit unions, and finance companies to individuals	Risk is variable	Variable	Variable, but average APR is 10.91%–16.36%
U.S. Treasury notes and bonds	Capital	Issued by U.S. government	No default risk, but price will decline if interest rates rise; hence, there is some risk	2 to 30 years	0.286% on 2-year to 3.173% on 30-year bonds
Mortgages	Capital	Loans to individuals and businesses secured by real estate; bought by banks and other institutions	Risk is variable; risk is high in the case of subprime loans	Up to 30 years	3.06% adjustable 5-year rate, 3.84% 30-year fixed rate
State and local government bonds	Capital	Issued by state and local governments; held by individuals and institutional investors	Riskier than U.S. government securities but exempt from most taxes	Up to 30 years	3.72% 20-year bonds, mixed quality debt

(Continued)

TABLE 2.1 Summary of Major Market Instruments, Market Participants, and Security Characteristics

Instrument (1)	Market (2)	Major Participants (3)	Riskiness (4)	Security Characteristics	
				Original Maturity (5)	Interest Rate on 2/19/13[a] (6)
Corporate bonds	Capital	Issued by corporations; held by individuals and institutional investors	Riskier than U.S. government securities but less risky than preferred and common stocks; varying degree of risk within bonds depends on strength of issuer	Up to 40 years[b]	3.90% on AAA bonds, 4.85% on BBB bonds
Leases	Capital	Similar to debt in that firms can lease assets rather than borrow and then buy the assets	Risk similar to corporate bonds	Generally 3 to 20 years	Similar to bond yields
Preferred stocks	Capital	Issued by corporations to individuals and institutional investors	Generally riskier than corporate bonds but less risky than common stock	Unlimited	5.5% to 9%
Common stocks[c]	Capital	Issued by corporations to individuals and institutional investors	Riskier than bonds and preferred stock; risk varies from company to company	Unlimited	NA

Notes:

[a] The yields reported are from *The Wall Street Journal* (online.wsj.com), February 19, 2013, and Board of Governors of the Federal Reserve System, "Selected Interest Rates (Daily)," www.federalreserve. gov/releases/H15/data/htm. Money market rates assume a 3-month maturity.

[b] A few corporations have issued 100-year bonds; however, the majority has issued bonds with maturities that are less than 40 years.

[c] While common stocks do not pay interest, they are expected to provide a "return" in the form of dividends and capital gains. Historically, stock returns have averaged between 9% and 12% a year, but they can be much higher or lower in a given year. Of course, if you purchase a stock, your actual return may be considerably higher or lower than these historical averages.

To illustrate the growing importance of derivatives, consider the case of *credit default swaps.*[2] Credit default swaps are contracts that offer protection against the default of a particular security. Suppose a bank wants to protect itself against the default of one of its borrowers. The bank could enter into a credit default swap where it agrees to make regular payments to another financial institution. In return, that financial institution agrees to insure the bank against losses that would occur if the borrower defaulted.

Derivatives can be used to reduce risks or to speculate. Suppose a wheat processor's costs rise and its net income falls when the price of wheat rises. The processor could reduce its risk by purchasing derivatives—wheat futures—whose value increases when the price of wheat rises. This is a *hedging operation,* and its purpose is to reduce risk exposure. Speculation, on the other hand, is done in the hope of high returns; but it raises risk exposure. For example, several years ago Procter & Gamble disclosed that it lost $150 million on derivative investments. More recently, losses on mortgage-related derivatives helped contribute to the credit collapse in 2008.

If a bank or any other company reports that it invests in derivatives, how can one tell if the derivatives are held as a hedge against something like an increase in the price of wheat or as a speculative bet that wheat prices will rise? The answer is that it is very difficult to tell how derivatives are affecting the firm's risk profile. In the case of financial institutions, things are even more complicated—the derivatives are generally based on changes in interest rates, foreign exchange rates, or stock prices; and a large international bank might have tens of thousands of separate derivative contracts. The size and complexity of these transactions concern regulators, academics, and members of Congress. Former Fed Chairperson Alan Greenspan noted that in theory, derivatives should allow companies to better manage risk, but that it is not clear whether recent innovations have "increased or decreased the inherent stability of the financial system."

2-3 Financial Institutions

Direct funds transfers are common among individuals and small businesses and in economies where financial markets and institutions are less developed. But large businesses in developed economies generally find it more efficient to enlist the services of a financial institution when it comes time to raise capital.

SELF TEST

Distinguish between physical asset markets and financial asset markets.

What's the difference between spot markets and futures markets?

Distinguish between money markets and capital markets.

What's the difference between primary markets and secondary markets?

Differentiate between private and public markets.

Why are financial markets essential for a healthy economy and economic growth?

---

[2]A 2010 article in *The New York Times* reported that this market had grown from $900 billion in 2000 to more than $30 trillion in 2008. The article also describes how credit default swaps helped contribute to the recent financial crises in the United States and Europe. Refer to "Times Topics: Credit Default Swaps," *The New York Times* (topics.nytimes.com), March 10, 2010.

In the United States and other developed nations, a set of highly efficient financial intermediaries has evolved. Their original roles were generally quite specific, and regulation prevented them from diversifying. However, in recent years regulations against diversification have been largely removed; and today the differences between institutions have become blurred. Still, there remains a degree of institutional identity. Therefore, it is useful to understand the major categories of financial institutions. Keep in mind, though, that one company can own a number of subsidiaries that engage in the different functions described next.

Investment Bank

An organization that underwrites and distributes new investment securities and helps businesses obtain financing.

1. **Investment banks** traditionally help companies raise capital. They (1) help corporations design securities with features that are currently attractive to investors, (2) buy these securities from the corporation, and (3) resell them to savers. Because the investment bank generally guarantees that the firm will raise the needed capital, the investment bankers are also called *underwriters.* The recent credit crisis has had a dramatic effect on the investment banking industry. Bear Stearns collapsed and was later acquired by J.P. Morgan, Lehman Brothers went bankrupt, and Merrill Lynch was forced to sell out to Bank of America. The two "surviving" major investment banks (Morgan Stanley and Goldman Sachs) received Federal Reserve approval to become commercial bank holding companies.

Commercial Bank

The traditional department store of finance serving a variety of savers and borrowers.

2. **Commercial banks,** such as Bank of America, Citibank, Wells Fargo, and JPMorgan Chase, are the traditional "department stores of finance" because they serve a variety of savers and borrowers. Historically, commercial banks were the major institutions that handled checking accounts and through which the Federal Reserve System expanded or contracted the money supply. Today, however, several other institutions also provide checking services and significantly influence the money supply. Note, too, that the larger banks are generally part of financial services corporations as described next.[3]

Financial Services Corporations

A firm that offers a wide range of financial services, including investment banking, brokerage operations, insurance, and commercial banking.

3. **Financial services corporations** are large conglomerates that combine many different financial institutions within a single corporation. Most financial services corporations started in one area but have now diversified to cover most of the financial spectrum. For example, Citigroup owns Citibank (a commercial bank), an investment bank, a securities brokerage organization, insurance companies, and leasing companies.

4. *Credit unions* are cooperative associations whose members are supposed to have a common bond, such as being employees of the same firm. Members' savings are loaned only to other members, generally for auto purchases, home improvement loans, and home mortgages. Credit unions are often the cheapest source of funds available to individual borrowers.

5. *Pension funds* are retirement plans funded by corporations or government agencies for their workers and administered primarily by the trust departments of commercial banks or by life insurance companies. Pension funds invest primarily in bonds, stocks, mortgages, and real estate.

6. *Life insurance companies* take savings in the form of annual premiums; invest these funds in stocks, bonds, real estate, and mortgages; and make payments

---

[3]Two other institutions that were important a few years ago were *savings and loan associations* and *mutual savings banks.* Most of these organizations have now been merged into commercial banks.

to the beneficiaries of the insured parties. In recent years, life insurance companies have also offered a variety of tax-deferred savings plans designed to provide benefits to participants when they retire.

7. **Mutual funds** are corporations that accept money from savers and then use these funds to buy stocks, long-term bonds, or short-term debt instruments issued by businesses or government units. These organizations pool funds and thus reduce risks by diversification. They also achieve economies of scale in analyzing securities, managing portfolios, and buying and selling securities. Different funds are designed to meet the objectives of different types of savers. Hence, there are bond funds for those who prefer safety, stock funds for savers who are willing to accept significant risks in the hope of higher returns, and **money market funds** that are used as interest-bearing checking accounts.

Another important distinction exists between actively managed funds and indexed funds. *Actively managed funds* try to outperform the overall markets, whereas *indexed funds* are designed to simply replicate the performance of a specific market index. For example, the portfolio manager of an actively managed stock fund uses his or her expertise to select what he or she thinks will be the best-performing stocks over a given time period. By contrast, an index fund that tracks the S&P 500 index will simply hold the basket of stocks that comprise the S&P 500. Both types of funds provide investors with valuable diversification, but actively managed funds typically have much higher fees— in large part, because of the extra costs involved in trying to select stocks that will (hopefully) outperform the market. In any given year, the very best actively managed funds will outperform the market index, but many will do worse than the overall market—even before taking into account their higher fees. Furthermore, it is extremely difficult to predict which actively managed funds will beat the market in a particular year. For this reason, many academics and practitioners have encouraged investors to rely more heavily on indexed funds.[4]

There are literally thousands of different mutual funds with dozens of different goals and purposes. Excellent information on the objectives and past performances of the various funds are provided in publications such as *Value Line Investment Survey* and *Morningstar Mutual Funds*, which are available in most libraries and on the Internet.

8. *Exchange Traded Funds* (ETFs) are similar to regular mutual funds and are often operated by mutual fund companies. ETFs buy a portfolio of stocks of a certain type—for example, the S&P 500 or media companies or Chinese companies—and then sell their own shares to the public. ETF shares are generally traded in the public markets, so an investor who wants to invest in the Chinese market, for example, can buy shares in an ETF that holds stocks in that particular market.

9. *Hedge funds* are also similar to mutual funds because they accept money from savers and use the funds to buy various securities, but there are some important differences. While mutual funds (and ETFs) are registered and regulated by the Securities and Exchange Commission (SEC), hedge funds are largely unregulated. This difference in regulation stems from the fact that mutual funds typically target small investors, whereas hedge funds typically have large minimum investments (often exceeding $1 million) and are marketed primarily to institutions and individuals with high net worths. Hedge funds received their name because they traditionally were used when an individual was trying to hedge risks. For example, a hedge fund manager

Mutual Funds
Organizations that pool investor funds to purchase financial instruments and thus reduce risks through diversification.

Money Market Funds
Mutual funds that invest in short-term, low-risk securities and allow investors to write checks against their accounts.

---

[4]Refer to Mark Hulbert, "The Index Funds Win Again," *The New York Times* (www.nytimes.com), February 21, 2009; and Rick Ferri, "Index Fund Portfolios Reign Superior," *Forbes* (www.forbes.com), August 20, 2012.

who believes that interest rate differentials between corporate and Treasury bonds are too large might simultaneously buy a portfolio of corporate bonds and sell a portfolio of Treasury bonds. In this case, the portfolio would be "hedged" against overall movements in interest rates, but it would perform especially well if the spread between these securities became smaller.

However, some hedge funds take on risks that are considerably higher than that of an average individual stock or mutual fund. For example, in 1998, Long-Term Capital Management (LTCM), a high-profile hedge fund (whose managers included several well-respected practitioners as well as two Nobel Prize–winning professors who were experts in investment theory), made some incorrect assumptions and "blew up."[5] LTCM had many billions of dollars under management, and it owed large amounts of money to a number of banks. To avert a worldwide crisis, the Federal Reserve orchestrated a buyout of the firm with a group of New York banks.

Table 2.2 lists the 10 largest hedge funds as of January 2, 2013. As evidence of their growing importance, each of these funds controls more than $20 billion in assets. As hedge funds have become more popular, many of them have begun to lower their minimum investment requirements. Perhaps not surprisingly, their rapid growth and shift toward smaller investors have also led to a call for more regulation.

10. *Private equity companies* are organizations that operate much like hedge funds; but rather than purchasing some of the stock of a firm, private equity players buy and then manage entire firms. Most of the money used to buy the target companies is borrowed. While private equity activity slowed around the financial crisis, over the past decade a number of high-profile companies (including Harrah's Entertainment, Albertson's, Neiman Marcus, and Clear Channel) have been acquired by private equity firms. More recently in 2013, two major deals were announced. Berkshire Hathaway (and its chairman Warren Buffett) partnered with the private equity firm 3G Capital to acquire H.J. Heinz Co. on June 7, 2013 for $28 billion. Around the same time, Dell Computer announced plans to go private with the assistance of the private equity firm, Silver Lake Partners. Some have criticized this deal for not offering enough payment to the existing shareholders, and there is a possibility that another private equity firm or outside investor will make a competing offer.[6] Other leading private equity firms include The Carlyle Group, Kohlberg Kravis Roberts, and The Blackstone Group.

With the exception of hedge funds and private equity companies, financial institutions are regulated to ensure the safety of these institutions and to protect investors. Historically, many of these regulations—which have included a prohibition on nationwide branch banking, restrictions on the types of assets the institutions could purchase, ceilings on the interest rates they could pay, and limitations on the types of services they could provide—tended to impede the free flow of capital and thus hurt the efficiency of the capital markets. Recognizing this fact, policy makers took several steps during the 1980s and 1990s to deregulate financial services companies. For example, the restriction barring nationwide branching by banks was eliminated in 1999.

---

[5]See Franklin Edwards, "Hedge Funds and the Collapse of Long-Term Capital Management," *Journal of Economic Perspectives*, vol. 13, no. 2 (Spring 1999), pp. 189–210, for a thoughtful review of the implications of the collapse of Long-Term Capital Management.

[6]In March 2013, the Blackstone Group and Carl Icahn (a well known activist investor) announced separate plans to acquire Dell. Blackstone has since dropped out, and Michael Dell and Silver Lake have offered shareholders a total deal worth $24.75 billion. The shareholder vote is scheduled for September 12, 2013. For additional information, refer to David Benoit, Kirsten Grind, and Sharon Terlep, "Dell Reaches New Deal With Founder," *The Wall Street Journal* (online.wsj.com), August 2, 2013.

| | Ten Largest Hedge Funds as of January 2, 2013 | **TABLE 2.2** |

Fund	Assets under Management ($ in billions)
Bridgewater Associates	83.30
J.P. Morgan Asset Management	54.80
Brevan Howard Asset Management	40.00
BlueCrest Capital Management	35.30
Och-Ziff Capital Management Group	31.90
Man Group	29.60
Baupost Group	26.70
BlackRock	26.63
Winton Capital Management	25.70
D.E. Shaw & Co.	23.40

Source: "The 2013 Hedge Fund 100," *Institutional Investor* (www.institutionalinvestor.com), May 28, 2013.

Many believed that excessive deregulation and insufficient supervision of the financial sector was partially responsible for the recent financial crisis. With these concerns in mind, Congress passed the Dodd–Frank Act. The legislation's main goals are to create a new agency for consumer protection, work to increase the transparency of derivative transactions, and force financial institutions to take steps to limit excessive risk-taking and to hold more capital.

Panel A of Table 2.3 lists the 10 largest U.S. bank holding companies, while Panel B shows the leading world banking companies. Among the world's 10 largest, none are based in the United States. While U.S. banks have grown dramatically as a result of recent mergers, they are still small by global standards. Panel C of the table lists the 10 leading underwriters in terms of dollar volume of new debt and equity issues. Eight of the top underwriters are also listed as major commercial banks or are part of bank holding companies shown in Panels A and B, which confirms the continued blurring of distinctions between different types of financial institutions.

| | | Largest Banks and Underwriters | **TABLE 2.3** |

Panel A U.S. Bank Holding Companies[a]	Panel B World Banking Companies[b]	Panel C Leading Global Underwriters[c]
JPMorgan Chase & Co.	Deutsche Bank AG (Frankfurt)	JPMorgan
Bank of America Corp.	BNP Paribas SA (Paris)	Deutsche Bank
Citigroup Inc.	Industrial & Commercial Bank of China Ltd. (Beijing)	Citi
Wells Fargo & Co.	Barclays Bank PLC (London)	Barclays Capital
Goldman Sachs Group Inc.	Japan Post Bank Co. Ltd. (Tokyo)	BofA-Merrill Lynch
Metlife Inc.	Credit Agricole SA (Paris)	Morgan Stanley
Morgan Stanley	Royal Bank of Scotland PLC (Edinburgh)	Goldman Sachs
U.S. Bancorp	China Construction Bank Corp. (Beijing)	Credit Suisse
Bank of New York Mellon Corporation	Bank of Tokyo-Mitsubishi UFJ Ltd. (Tokyo)	UBS
HSBC North America Holdings Inc.	Bank of China Ltd. (Beijing)	HSBC

Notes:
[a] Ranked by total assets as of December 31, 2012.
  Source: National Information Center, www.ffiec.gov/nicpubweb/nicweb/Top50Form.aspx.
[b] Ranked by total assets from balance sheet information available on February 18, 2013.
  Source: Bankersalmanac.com.
[c] Ranked by dollar amount raised through new issues (stocks and bonds) in 2012. For this ranking, the lead underwriter (manager) is given credit for the entire issue.
  Source: Adapted from *The Wall Street Journal*, January 2, 2013, p. R18.

SECURITIZATION HAS DRAMATICALLY TRANSFORMED THE BANKING INDUSTRY

At one time, commercial banking was a simpler business than it is today. A typical bank received money from its depositors and used it to make loans. In the vast majority of cases, the banker held the loan on its books until it matured. Because they originated the loan and continued to hold it on their books, the banks generally knew the risks involved. However, because banks often had limited funding, there was a cap on the number of loans they could hold on their books. And because most of the loans were made to individuals and businesses in their local market, banks were less able to spread their risk.

To address these concerns, financial engineers came up with the idea of securitizing loans. This is a process whereby an agent (such as an investment bank) creates an entity that buys a large number of loans from a wide range of banks and then issues securities that are backed by the loan payments. Securitization began in the 1970s when government-backed entities purchased pools of home mortgages and then issued securities backed by the cash flows from the diversified portfolio of mortgages. In many respects, securitization was a tremendous innovation. Banks no longer had to hold their mortgages, so they could quickly convert the originated loan to cash, enabling them to redeploy their capital to make other loans. At the same time, the newly created securities gave investors an opportunity to invest in a diversified portfolio of home mortgages. In addition, these securities traded on the open market so that investors were able to easily buy and sell them as their circumstances and views of the mortgage markets changed over time.

Over the last few decades, this process has accelerated. Bankers have securitized different types of loans into all types of different securities. One notable example is *collateralized debt obligations (CDOs),* where an entity issues several classes of securities backed by a portfolio of loans. For example, an investment bank purchases $100 million of mortgage loans from banks and mortgage brokers throughout the country. The investment bank uses the collateral to create $100 million in new securities, which are divided into three classes (often referred to as *tranches*). The Class A bonds have the first claim on the cash flows from the mortgages. Because they have the first claim, they are the least risky and are rated AAA by the rating agencies. The Class B bonds get paid after the Class A bonds are paid, but they too will generally have a high rating. Finally, the Class C bonds get paid. Because they are last in line, they will have the highest risk, but they will also sell for the lowest price. If the underlying mortgages perform well, the C bonds will realize the highest returns, but they will suffer the most if the underlying mortgages don't perform well.

CDOs backed by pools of higher risk (subprime) mortgages played a major role in the recent financial crisis. During the housing boom, financial institutions and mortgage brokers originated a large number of new mortgages, and investment bankers hungry for fees were more than happy to create new CDOs backed by these subprime mortgages. The securities created through these CDOs were sold primarily to other commercial and investment banks and to other financial institutions, such as hedge funds, mutual funds, and pension funds. Buoyed by the mistaken belief that housing prices would never fall, many viewed these securities as solid investments, and they received additional comfort from the fact that they were highly rated.

When the housing market collapsed, the value of these securities plummeted, destroying the balance sheets of many financial institutions. Making matters worse, it became very hard to value these securities because they were backed by such a large, diverse pool of mortgages. Not sure what they had on their books, many institutions tried to sell these securities at the same time, and the "rush to the exit" further depressed prices causing the cycle to deepen.

Following the crisis, many have looked to reform the securitization business, and others have criticized the rating agencies for routinely assigning high credit ratings to what in hindsight were extremely risky securities. At the same time, an article in *Barron's* highlights the important role that securitization plays in the capital markets and raises concerns that the economy won't thrive again until the securitization business recovers.

© Cengage Learning 2015

Source: David Adler, "A Flat Dow for 10 Years? Why It Could Happen," *Barron's* (online.barrons.com), December 28, 2009.

SELF TEST

What's the difference between a commercial bank and an investment bank?

List the major types of financial institutions and briefly describe the primary function of each.

What are some important differences between mutual funds, Exchange Traded Funds, and hedge funds? How are they similar?

2-4 THE STOCK MARKET

As noted earlier, outstanding, previously issued securities are traded in the secondary markets. By far, the most active secondary market—and the most important one to financial managers—is the *stock market,* where the prices of firms' stocks are established. Because the primary goal of financial managers is to maximize their firms' stock prices, knowledge of the stock market is important to anyone involved in managing a business.

There are a number of different stock markets. The two leaders are NYSE Euronext and NASDAQ. NYSE Euronext was formed through the 2007 merger of the New York Stock Exchange (NYSE) and Euronext, which at the time was the largest European exchange. Stocks are traded using a variety of market procedures, but there are two basic types: (1) *physical location exchanges,* which include the NYSE and several regional stock exchanges, and (2) *electronic dealer-based markets,* which include the NASDAQ, the less formal over-the-counter market, and the recently developed electronic communications networks (ECNs).

(See the box entitled, "The NYSE and NASDAQ Go Global.") Because the physical location exchanges are easier to describe and understand, we discuss them first.

2-4A PHYSICAL LOCATION STOCK EXCHANGES

Physical location exchanges are tangible entities. Each of the larger exchanges occupies its own building, allows a limited number of people to trade on its floor, and has an elected governing body—its board of governors. Members of the NYSE formerly had "seats" on the exchange, although everybody stood. Today the seats have been exchanged for trading licenses, which are auctioned to member organizations and cost about $50,000 per year. Most of the larger investment banks operate *brokerage departments.* They purchase seats on the exchanges and

Physical Location Exchanges
Formal organizations having tangible physical locations that conduct auction markets in designated ("listed") securities.

GLOBAL PERSPECTIVES

The NYSE and NASDAQ Go Global

Advances in computers and telecommunications that spurred consolidation in the financial services industry have also promoted online trading systems that bypass the traditional exchanges. These systems, which are known as *electronic communications networks (ECNs),* use electronic technology to bring buyers and sellers together. The rise of ECNs accelerated the move toward 24-hour trading. U.S. investors who wanted to trade after the U.S. markets closed could utilize an ECN, thus bypassing the NYSE and NASDAQ.

Recognizing the new threat, the NYSE and NASDAQ took action. First, both exchanges went public, which enabled them to use their stock as "currency" that could be used to buy ECNs and other exchanges across the globe. For example, NASDAQ acquired the Philadelphia Stock Exchange, several ECNs, and 25% of the London Stock Exchange; and it is actively seeking to merge with other exchanges around the world. The NYSE took similar actions, including a merger with the largest European exchange, Euronext, to form NYSE

Euronext and then acquiring the American Stock Exchange (AMEX).

Interestingly enough, on December 20, 2012, Intercontinental Exchange (ICE) announced plans to purchase NYSE Euronext for approximately $8.2 billion. In addition, it appears that Euronext may be spun off if the deal is completed. Of course, the sale will need to be approved by regulators. However, if it does go through, it will merge ICE's futures, over-the-counter, and derivatives trading with the NYSE's stock trading.

These actions illustrate the growing importance of global trading, especially electronic trading. Indeed, many pundits have concluded that the floor traders who buy and sell stocks on the NYSE and other physical exchanges will soon become a thing of the past. That may or may not be true, but it is clear that stock trading will continue to undergo dramatic changes in the upcoming years. To find a wealth of up-to-date information on the NYSE and NASDAQ, go to Google (or another search engine) and do NYSE history and NASDAQ history searches.

designate one or more of their officers as members. The exchanges are open on all normal working days, with the members meeting in a large room equipped with telephones and other electronic equipment that enable each member to communicate with his or her firm's offices throughout the country.

Like other markets, security exchanges facilitate communication between buyers and sellers. For example, Goldman Sachs (the seventh-largest brokerage firm) might receive an order from a customer who wants to buy shares of GE stock. Simultaneously, Morgan Stanley (the sixth-largest brokerage firm) might receive an order from a customer wanting to sell shares of GE. Each broker communicates electronically with the firm's representative on the NYSE. Other brokers throughout the country are also communicating with their own exchange members. The exchange members with *sell orders* offer the shares for sale, and they are bid for by the members with *buy orders*. Thus, the exchanges operate as *auction markets*.[7]

2-4B OVER-THE-COUNTER (OTC) AND THE NASDAQ STOCK MARKETS

Over-the-Counter (OTC) Market
A large collection of brokers and dealers, connected electronically by telephones and computers, that provides for trading in unlisted securities.

While the stocks of most large companies trade on the NYSE, a larger number of stocks trade off the exchange in what was traditionally referred to as the **over-the-counter (OTC) market**. An explanation of the term *over-the-counter* will help clarify how this term arose. As noted earlier, the exchanges operate as auction markets—buy and sell orders come in more or less simultaneously, and exchange members match these orders. When a stock is traded infrequently, perhaps because the firm is new or small, few buy and sell orders come in and matching them within a reasonable amount of time is difficult. To avoid this problem, some brokerage firms maintain an inventory of such stocks and stand prepared to make a market for them. These "dealers" buy when individual investors want to sell, and they sell part of their inventory when investors want to buy. At one time, the inventory of securities was kept in a safe; and the stocks, when bought and sold, were literally passed over the counter.

Dealer Markets
Includes all facilities that are needed to conduct security transactions not conducted on the physical location exchanges.

Today these markets are often referred to as **dealer markets**. A dealer market includes all facilities that are needed to conduct security transactions, but the transactions are not made on the physical location exchanges. The dealer market system consists of (1) the relatively few *dealers* who hold inventories of these securities and who are said to "make a market" in these securities; (2) the thousands of brokers who act as *agents* in bringing the dealers together with investors; and (3) the computers, terminals, and electronic networks that provide a communication link between dealers and brokers. The dealers who make a market in a

---

[7]The NYSE is actually a modified auction market wherein people (through their brokers) bid for stocks. Originally—in 1792—brokers would literally shout, "I have 100 shares of Erie for sale; how much am I offered?" and then sell to the highest bidder. If a broker had a buy order, he or she would shout, "I want to buy 100 shares of Erie; who'll sell at the best price?" The same general situation still exists, although the exchanges now have members known as *specialists* who facilitate the trading process by keeping an inventory of shares of the stocks in which they specialize. If a buy order comes in at a time when no sell order arrives, the specialist will sell some inventory. Similarly, if a sell order comes in, the specialist will buy and add to inventory. The specialist sets a *bid price* (the price the specialist will pay for the stock) and an *ask price* (the price at which shares will be sold out of inventory). The bid and ask prices are set at levels designed to keep the inventory in balance. If many buy orders start coming in because of favorable developments or many sell orders come in because of unfavorable events, the specialist will raise or lower prices to keep supply and demand in balance. Bid prices are somewhat lower than ask prices, with the difference, or *spread*, representing the specialist's profit margin.

Special facilities are available to help institutional investors such as mutual or pension funds sell large blocks of stock without depressing their prices. In essence, brokerage houses that cater to institutional clients will purchase blocks (defined as 10,000 or more shares) and then resell the stock to other institutions or individuals. Also, when a firm has a major announcement that is likely to cause its stock price to change sharply, it will ask the exchange to halt trading in its stock until the announcement has been made and the resulting information has been digested by investors.

particular stock quote the price at which they will pay for the stock (the *bid price)* and the price at which they will sell shares (the *ask price*). Each dealer's prices, which are adjusted as supply and demand conditions change, can be seen on computer screens across the world. The *bid–ask spread,* which is the difference between bid and ask prices, represents the dealer's markup, or profit. The dealer's risk increases when the stock is more volatile or when the stock trades infrequently. Generally, we would expect volatile, infrequently traded stocks to have wider spreads in order to compensate the dealers for assuming the risk of holding them in inventory.

Brokers and dealers who participate in the OTC market are members of a self-regulatory body known as the *Financial Industry Regulatory Authority* (FINRA), which licenses brokers and oversees trading practices. The computerized network used by FINRA is known as NASDAQ, which originally stood for "National Association of Securities Dealers Automated Quotations."

NASDAQ started as a quotation system, but it has grown to become an organized securities market with its own listing requirements. Over the past decade, the competition between the NYSE and NASDAQ has become increasingly fierce. As noted earlier, the NASDAQ has invested in the London Stock Exchange and other market makers, while the NYSE merged with Euronext and, pending regulatory approval, it may soon be purchased by Intercontinental Exchange—further adding to the competition. Because most of the larger companies trade on the NYSE, the market capitalization of NYSE-traded stocks is much higher than for stocks traded on NASDAQ.

Interestingly, many high-tech companies such as Microsoft, Google, and Intel have remained on NASDAQ even though they meet the listing requirements of the NYSE. At the same time, however, other high-tech companies have left NASDAQ for the NYSE. Despite these defections, NASDAQ's growth over the past decade has been impressive. In the years ahead, competition between NASDAQ and NYSE Euronext will no doubt remain fierce.

SELF TEST

What are the differences between the physical location exchanges and the NASDAQ stock market?

What is the bid–ask spread?

2-5 THE MARKET FOR COMMON STOCK

Some companies are so small that their common stocks are not actively traded; they are owned by relatively few people, usually the companies' managers. These firms are said to be *privately owned,* or **closely held, corporations;** and their stock is called *closely held stock.* In contrast, the stocks of most large companies are owned by thousands of investors, most of whom are not active in management. These companies are called **publicly owned corporations**, and their stock is called *publicly held stock.*

2-5A TYPES OF STOCK MARKET TRANSACTIONS

We can classify stock market transactions into three distinct categories:

1. *Outstanding shares of established publicly owned companies that are traded: the secondary market.* Allied Food Products, the company we study in Chapters 3

Closely Held Corporation
A corporation that is owned by a few individuals who are typically associated with the firm's management.

Publicly Owned Corporation
A corporation that is owned by a relatively large number of individuals who are not actively involved in the firm's management.

and 4, has 50 million shares of stock outstanding. If the owner of 100 shares sells his or her stock, the trade is said to have occurred in the *secondary market.* Thus, the market for outstanding shares, or *used shares,* is the secondary market. The company receives no new money when sales occur in this market.

2. *Additional shares sold by established publicly owned companies: the primary market.* If Allied Food decides to sell (or issue) an additional 1 million shares to raise new equity capital, this transaction is said to occur in the *primary market.*[8]

3. *Initial public offerings made by privately held firms: the IPO market.* Whenever stock in a closely held corporation is offered to the public for the first time, the company is said to be **going public.** The market for stock that is just being offered to the public is called the **initial public offering (IPO) market.**[9] In the summer of 2004, Google sold shares to the public for the first time at $85 per share. By mid-February, 2013, the stock was selling for more than $800. In 2006, McDonald's owned Chipotle Mexican Grill. McDonald's then sold its shares to the public for about $47.50 to raise capital to support its core business; and by mid-February 2013, Chipotle's stock price was more than $300. In some more recent examples, General Motors (GM) went public as part of its reorganization following its government bailout, and in May 2011, the professional-networking site LinkedIn Corp. created excitement when shares of its IPO more than doubled during its first day of trading.

The number of new IPOs rises and falls with the stock market. When the market is strong, many companies go public to bring in new capital and to give their founders an opportunity to cash out some of their shares. Table 2.4 lists the largest, the best performing, and the worst performing IPOs of 2012 and shows how they performed from their offering dates through year-end 2012. As the table shows, not all IPOs are as well received as Google, Chipotle, and LinkedIn. The most striking example is Facebook, which had the largest and highest-profile IPO of 2012. Amid much fanfare, the company went public on May 18, 2012 at a price of $38 per share. In the two weeks after the IPO, the stock had fallen to below $28, and just a few months later in September, the price reached a low of $17.55. By year-end 2012, the stock rebounded to $26.62, which was still 30% below the initial offering price. So, while Facebook raised a lot of money through its IPO, its initial investors did not quickly realize the big return that many were looking to capture.

Moreover, even if you are able to identify a "hot" issue, it is often difficult to purchase shares in the initial offering. These deals are often *oversubscribed,* which means that the demand for shares at the offering price exceeds the number of shares issued. In such instances, investment bankers favor large institutional investors (who are their best customers); and small investors find it hard, if not impossible, to get in on the ground floor. They can buy the stock in the after-market; but evidence suggests that when an investor does not get in on the ground floor, over the long run IPOs often underperform the overall market.[10]

Google's highly publicized IPO attracted attention because of its size (Google raised $1.67 billion in stock) and because of the way the sale was conducted. Rather than having the offer price set by its investment bankers, Google

Going Public
The act of selling stock to the public at large by a closely held corporation or its principal stockholders.

Initial Public Offering (IPO) Market
The market for stocks of companies that are in the process of going public.

For information on IPOs refer to Professor Jay Ritter's (University of Florida) web page bear.warrington.ufl .edu/ritter/ipodata.htm.

---

[8]Allied has 60 million shares authorized but only 50 million outstanding; thus, it has 10 million authorized but unissued shares. If it had no authorized but unissued shares, management could increase the authorized shares by obtaining stockholders' approval, which would generally be granted without any arguments.

[9]A number of years ago Coors, the beer company, offered some of its shares to the public. These shares were designated Class B, and they were nonvoting. The Coors family retained the founders' shares, called Class A stock, which carried full voting privileges. This illustrates how the managers of a company can use different classes of shares to maintain control.

[10]See Jay R. Ritter, "The Long-Run Performance of Initial Public Offerings," *Journal of Finance,* vol. 46, no. 1 (March 1991), pp. 3–27.

The Biggest IPOs

			Percent Change from Offer	
Issuer	**Issue Date**	**U.S. Proceeds (Millions)**	**First Day Trading**	**Through 12/31/12**
Facebook (U.S.)	05/17/12	$16,006.9	+0.6	−30.0%
Japan Airlines (Japan)	09/10/12	8,477.7	+1.1	−2.4
Grupo Financiero Santander Mexico SAB de CV (Mexico)	09/25/12	4,111.0	+6.9	−48.2
Telefonica Deutschland Holding AG (Germany)	10/29/12	1,874.6	+3.6	+3.1
MegaFon OAO (Russian Federation)	11/28/12	1,829.6	−2.0	+19.0
Banco BTG Pactual SA (Brazil)	04/24/12	1,726.4	+0.6	−0.8
Direct Line Insurance Group (U.K.)	10/11/12	1,449.4	+7.4	+23.4
LinnCo (U.S.)	10/11/12	1,269.7	+4.8	−1.0
Realogy Holding (U.S.)	10/10/12	1,242.0	+26.7	+55.3
Ziggo (Netherlands)	03/20/12	1,219.6	+14.9	+33.8

The Best Performers

				Percent Change from Offer	
Issuer	**Issue Date**	**Offer Price**	**U.S. Proceeds (Millions)**	**First Day Trading**	**Through 12/31/12**
Vipshop Holdings (China)	03/22/12	US$6.50	$ 71.5	−15.4%	+174.6%
Proto Labs (U.S.)	02/23/12	US$16.00	79.1	+81.3	+145.0
HomeStreet (U.S.)	02/10/12	US$44.00	96.0	+9.1	+133.3
Guidewire Software (U.S.)	01/24/12	US$13.00	132.3	+31.7	+128.3
Intercept Pharmaceuticals (U.S.)	10/10/12	US$15.00	86.3	+29.3	+127.1
Nationstar Mortgage Holdings (U.S.)	03/07/12	US$14.00	268.3	+1.4	+120.5
Eloqua (U.S.)	08/01/12	US$11.50	105.8	+12.1	+105.2
WageWorks (U.S.)	05/09/12	US$ 9.00	67.3	+40.0	+96.4
Changsha Sinocare (China)	03/05/12	RMB29.00	101.3	+18.5	+95.2
Workday (U.S.)	10/11/12	US$28.00	732.6	+73.9	+94.6

The Worst Performers

				Percent Change from Offer	
Issuer	**Issue Date**	**Offer Price**	**U.S. Proceeds (Millions)**	**First Day Trading**	**Through 12/31/12**
Envivio (U.S.)	04/24/12	US$9.00	$ 69.8	−5.7%	−81.1%
Ningbo Cixing (China)	03/19/12	RMB35.00	337.6	−13.7	−74.3
CafePress (U.S.)	03/28/12	US$19.00	85.5	+0.2	−69.6
XiAn Longi Silicon Materials (China)	03/29/12	RMB21.00	249.3	−6.0	−67.6
Hangzhou Everfine Photo-E-Info (China)	03/20/12	RMB45.00	106.7	−9.7	−67.1
Inside Secure SA (France)	02/17/12	EUR8.30	103.5	+10.8	−66.3
Ceres (U.S.)	02/21/12	US$13.00	74.8	+13.9	−64.9
Shenzhen ChangFang Light Emitting Diode Lighting (China)	03/09/12	RMB20.00	85.5	+6.6	−58.0
Beijing WKW Automotive Parts (China)	02/28/12	RMB20.00	238.2	+6.9	−57.8
Solar Company SA (Poland)	04/03/12	PZL13.00	50.3	+6.5	−56.9

Source: Telis Demos, "For IPOs, an Up-and-Down Year," *The Wall Street Journal*, January 2, 2013, p. R19.

conducted a Dutch auction, where individual investors placed bids for shares directly. In a *Dutch auction,* the actual transaction price is set at the highest price (the clearing price) that causes all of the offered shares to be sold. Investors who set their bids at or above the clearing price received all of the shares they subscribed to at the offer price, which turned out to be $85. While Google's IPO was in many ways precedent setting, few companies going public since then have been willing or able to use the Dutch auction method to allocate their IPO shares.

It is important to recognize that firms can go public without raising any additional capital. For example, the Ford Motor Company was once owned exclusively by the Ford family. When Henry Ford died, he left a substantial part of his stock to the Ford Foundation. When the Foundation later sold some of the stock to the general public, the Ford Motor Company went public, even though the company itself raised no capital in the transaction.

SELF TEST

Differentiate between closely held and publicly owned corporations.

Differentiate between primary and secondary markets.

What is an IPO?

What is a Dutch auction, and what company used this procedure for its IPO?

2-6 STOCK MARKETS AND RETURNS

Anyone who has invested in the stock market knows that there can be (and generally are) large differences between *expected* and *realized* prices and returns. Figure 2.2 shows how total realized portfolio returns have varied from year to year. As logic would suggest (and as is demonstrated in Chapter 9), a stock's

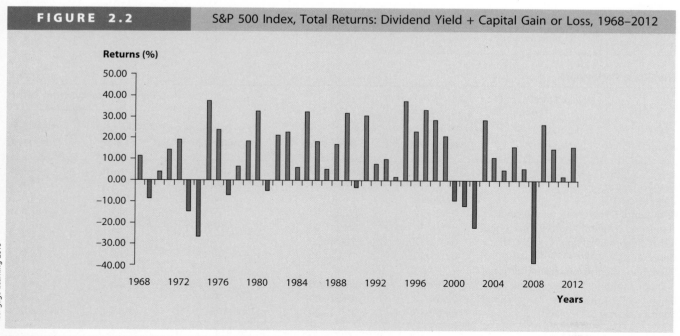

FIGURE 2.2 S&P 500 Index, Total Returns: Dividend Yield + Capital Gain or Loss, 1968–2012

Source: Data taken from various issues of *The Wall Street Journal* "Investment Scoreboard" section.

expected return as estimated by investors at the margin is always positive; otherwise, investors would not buy the stock. However, as Figure 2.2 shows, in some years, actual returns are negative.

2-6A STOCK MARKET REPORTING

Up until a few years ago, the best source of stock quotations was the business section of daily newspapers such as *The Wall Street Journal*. One problem with newspapers, however, is that they report yesterday's prices. Now it is possible to obtain quotes throughout the day from a wide variety of Internet sources. One of the best is Yahoo!'s finance.yahoo.com; Figure 2.3 shows a detailed quote for Facebook, Inc. (FB) stock for February 19, 2013. As the heading shows, Facebook is traded on the NASDAQGS (GS stands for Global Select Market) under the symbol FB. The information right below the company name and ticker symbol shows the real-time quote at 3:03 p.m. EST of $29.03, which is up $0.71 (or 2.51%) from the previous day's close. Facebook stock closed on Friday, February 15, 2013, at $28.32 per share and it opened for trading on Tuesday, February 19, 2013, at $28.19 per share.[11] So far during the day on February 19, 2013, Facebook's stock had traded from a low of $28.12 to a high of $29.08 and the price range during the past 52 weeks was between $17.55 and $45.00. Recall from our earlier discussion that Facebook went public on Friday, May 18, 2012, at a price of $38 per share, so the stock had not yet traded for a full year.

The next three lines give the bid (buy) and ask (sell) price range for the stock— the difference between the two represents the dealer's spread or profit. (In this example, a buyer had offered to purchase 4,000 shares at a bid price of $29.03, and a seller was offering to sell 4,500 shares at an ask price of $29.04.) The 1-year target estimate represents the median 1-year target price as forecasted by analysts covering the stock. On February 18, 33,729,430 shares of stock had traded hands. FB's average daily trading volume (based on the past 3 months) was 68,521,900

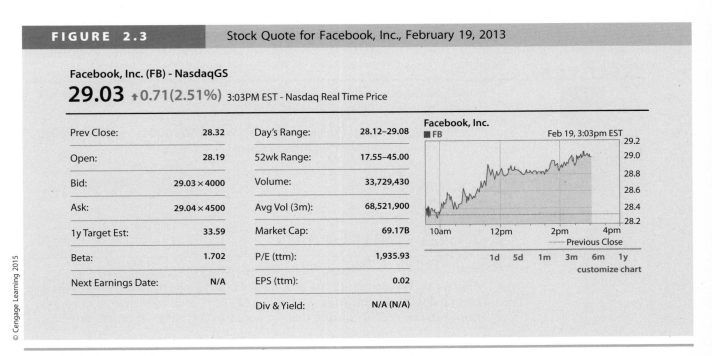

| **FIGURE 2.3** | Stock Quote for Facebook, Inc., February 19, 2013 |

Facebook, Inc. (FB) - NasdaqGS

29.03 ↑0.71(2.51%) 3:03PM EST - Nasdaq Real Time Price

Prev Close:	28.32	Day's Range:	28.12–29.08	
Open:	28.19	52wk Range:	17.55–45.00	
Bid:	29.03 × 4000	Volume:	33,729,430	
Ask:	29.04 × 4500	Avg Vol (3m):	68,521,900	
1y Target Est:	33.59	Market Cap:	69.17B	
Beta:	1.702	P/E (ttm):	1,935.93	
Next Earnings Date:	N/A	EPS (ttm):	0.02	
		Div & Yield:	N/A (N/A)	

Source: Facebook, Inc. (FB), finance.yahoo.com.

---

[11]The markets were closed on Monday, February 18, 2013, for President's Day.

shares, so trading on this day was about half the average daily trading volume. The total value of all of FB's stock, called its market cap, was $69.17 billion.

The last three lines report other market information for FB. The beta for the company is shown as 1.702. The firm's next earnings announcement is not given. FB's P/E ratio (price per share divided by the most recent 12 months' earnings) is 1,935.93, and its earnings per share for the most recent 12 months was $0.02. (The high P/E ratio is a direct result of the firm's low earnings per share number.) Facebook doesn't pay a dividend so the dividend and yield information is shown as NA (not applicable).

In Figure 2.3, the chart to the right plots the stock price during the day; however, the links below the chart allow you to pick different time intervals for plotting data. As you can see, Yahoo! provides a great deal of information in its detailed quote; and even more detail is available on the screen page below the basic quote information.

2-6B STOCK MARKET RETURNS

In Chapters 8 and 9, we discuss in detail how a stock's rate of return is calculated, what the connection is between risk and returns, and what techniques analysts use to value stocks. However, it is useful at this point to give you an idea of how stocks have performed in recent years. Figure 2.2 shows how the returns on large U.S. stocks have varied over the past years, and the box titled "Measuring the Market" provides information on the major U.S. stock market indices and their performances since the mid-1990s.

The market trend has been strongly up since 1968, but by no means does it go up every year. Indeed, as we can see from Figure 2.2, the overall market was down in 10 of the last 45 years, including the three consecutive years of 2000–2002. The stock prices of individual companies have likewise gone up and down.[12] Of course, even in bad years, some individual companies do well; so "the name of the game" in security analysis is to pick the winners. Financial managers attempt to do this, but they don't always succeed. In subsequent chapters, we will examine the decisions managers make to increase the odds that their firms will perform well in the marketplace.

SELF TEST

Would you expect a portfolio that consisted of the NYSE stocks to be more or less risky than a portfolio of NASDAQ stocks?

If we constructed a chart like Figure 2.2 for a typical S&P 500 stock, do you think it would show more or less volatility? Explain.

2-7 STOCK MARKET EFFICIENCY

To begin this section, consider the following definitions:

- *Market price:* The current price of a stock. For example, the Internet showed that on one day, Facebook's stock traded at $29.03. The market price had varied from $28.12 to $29.08 during that same day as buy and sell orders came in.

---

[12]If we constructed a graph like Figure 2.2 for individual stocks rather than for the index, far greater variability would be shown. Also, if we constructed a graph like Figure 2.2 for bonds, it would have similar ups and downs, but the bars would be far smaller, indicating that gains and losses on bonds are generally much smaller than those on stocks. Above-average bond returns occur in years when interest rates decline, losses occur when interest rates rise sharply, but interest payments tend to stabilize bonds' total returns. We discuss bonds in detail in Chapter 7.

MEASURING THE MARKET

Stock market indexes are designed to show the performance of the stock market. However, there are many stock indexes, and it is difficult to determine which index best reflects market actions. Some are designed to represent the entire stock market, some track the returns of certain industry sectors, and others track the returns of small-cap, mid-cap, or large-cap stocks. In addition, there are indexes for different countries. We discuss here the three leading U.S. indexes. These indexes are used as a benchmark for comparing individual stocks with the overall market, for measuring the trend in stock prices over time, and for determining how various economic factors affect the market.

Dow Jones Industrial Average

Unveiled in 1896 by Charles H. Dow, the Dow Jones Industrial Average (DJIA) began with just 10 stocks, was expanded in 1916 to 20 stocks, and then was increased to 30 stocks in 1928, when the editors of *The Wall Street Journal* began adjusting the index for stock splits and making periodic substitutions. Today the DJIA still includes 30 companies. They represent about a fifth of the market value of all U.S. stocks, and all are leading companies in their industries and widely held by individual and institutional investors. Visit djaverages.com to get more information about the DJIA. You can find out how it is calculated, the companies that make up the DJIA, and more history about the DJIA. In addition, a DJIA time line shows various historical events.

S&P 500 Index

Created in 1926, the S&P 500 Index is widely regarded as the standard for measuring large-cap U.S. stock market performance. The stocks in the S&P 500 are selected by the Standard & Poor's Index Committee, and they are the leading companies in the leading industries. It is weighted by each stock's market value, so the largest companies have the greatest influence. The S&P 500 is one of the most commonly used benchmarks for the U.S. stock market, and

approximately $376 billion is held in index funds designed to mirror the same performance of the index.

NASDAQ Composite Index

The NASDAQ Composite Index measures the performance of all stocks listed on the NASDAQ. Currently, it includes approximately 2,800 companies; and because many companies in the technology sector are traded on the computer-based NASDAQ exchange, this index is generally regarded as an economic indicator of the high-tech industry. Microsoft, Apple, Google, Cisco Systems, and Oracle are the five largest NASDAQ companies, and they make up a high percentage of the index's value-weighted market capitalization. For this reason, substantial movements in the same direction by these five companies can move the entire index.

Recent Performance

The accompanying figure plots the value that an investor would now have if he or she had invested $1 in each of the three indexes on January 1, 1995, through January 1, 2013. The returns on the three indexes are compared with an investment strategy that invests only in 1-year Treasury bills (T-bills). Each of these indexes performed quite well through 1999. However, for a couple of years, each index stumbled before beginning to rebound again in 2003 through mid-2008. Each index fell from mid-2008 until early 2009, when they began to rebound again. During the last 18 years, the average annualized returns of these indexes ranged from 6.7% for the S&P 500 to 8.2% for the NASDAQ. (The Dow's annualized return during this same period was 7.2%.) NASDAQ experienced a huge bubble in 1999, reflecting overly optimistic valuations of technology companies. However, in 2000, the bubble burst and technology stock valuations spiraled downward, causing the NASDAQ Index to revert back to a level comparable to the S&P 500 and Dow Jones Industrial Average Index. Since that time, the three indexes have closely tracked one another (see the line graph, below).

Growth of a $1 Investment Made On January 1, 1995, Through January 1, 2013

- *Intrinsic value:* The price at which the stock would sell if all investors had all knowable information about a stock. This concept was discussed in Chapter 1, where we saw that a stock's intrinsic value is based on its expected future cash flows and its risk. Moreover, the market price tends to fluctuate around the intrinsic value; and the intrinsic value changes over time as the company succeeds or fails with new projects, competitors enter or exit the market, and so forth. We can guess (or estimate) Facebook's intrinsic value, but different analysts will reach somewhat different conclusions.

- *Equilibrium price:* The price that balances buy and sell orders at any given time. When a stock is in equilibrium, the price remains relatively stable until new information becomes available and causes the price to change.

- *Efficient market:* A market in which prices are close to intrinsic values and stocks seem to be in equilibrium.

When markets are efficient, investors can buy and sell stocks and be confident that they are getting good prices. When markets are inefficient, investors may be afraid to invest and may put their money "under the pillow," which will lead to a poor allocation of capital and economic stagnation. From an economic standpoint, market efficiency is good.

Academics and financial professionals have studied the issue of market efficiency extensively.[13] As generally happens, some people think that markets are highly efficient, some think that markets are highly inefficient, and others think that the issue is too complex for a simple answer.

Those who believe that markets are efficient note that there are 100,000 or so full-time, highly trained professional analysts and traders operating in the market. Many have PhDs in physics, chemistry, and other technical fields in addition to advanced degrees in finance. Moreover, there are fewer than 3,000 major stocks; so if each analyst followed 30 stocks (which is about right, as analysts tend to focus on a specific industry), on average, 1,000 analysts would be following each stock. Further, these analysts work for organizations such as Goldman Sachs, JPMorgan Chase, and Deutsche Bank or for Warren Buffett and other billionaire investors who have billions of dollars available to take advantage of bargains. Also, the SEC has disclosure rules which, combined with electronic information networks, means that new information about a stock is received by all analysts at about the same time, causing almost instantaneous revaluations. All of these factors help markets to be efficient and cause stock prices to move toward their intrinsic values.

However, other people point to data that suggest that markets are not very efficient. For example, on May 6, 2010, the Dow Jones Index fell nearly 1,000 points only to rebound rapidly by the end of the day.[14] In 2000, Internet stocks rose to phenomenally high prices, and then fell to zero or close to it the following year. No truly important news was announced that could have caused either of these changes; and if the market was efficient, it's hard to see how such drastic changes could have occurred. Another situation that causes people to question market efficiency is the apparent ability of some analysts to consistently outperform the market over long periods. Warren Buffett comes to mind, but there are others. If markets are truly efficient, then each stock's price should be close to its intrinsic value. That would make it hard for any analyst to consistently pick stocks that outperform the market.

---

[13]The general name for these studies is the *efficient markets hypothesis,* or *EMH.* It was, and still is, a hypothesis that needs to be proved or disproved empirically. In the literature, researchers identified three levels of efficiency: *weak form,* which contends that information on past stock price movements cannot be used to predict future stock prices; *semi-strong form,* which contends that all publicly available information is immediately incorporated into stock prices (i.e., that one cannot analyze published reports and then beat the market); and *strong form,* which contends that even company insiders, with inside information, cannot earn abnormally high returns.

[14]Regulators are investigating the causes of this dramatic decline, and are particularly focusing on the role played by computerized trading. Refer to Tom Lauricella, Scott Patterson, and Carolyn Cui, "Computer Trading Is Eyed," *The Wall Street Journal* (online.wsj.com), May 8, 2010.

The diagram below sums up where most observers seem to be today. There is an "efficiency continuum," with the market for some companies' stocks being highly efficient and the market for other stocks being highly inefficient. The key factor is the size of the company—the larger the firm, the more analysts tend to follow it and thus the faster new information is likely to be reflected in the stock's price. Also, different companies communicate better with analysts and investors; and the better the communications, the more efficient the market for the stock.

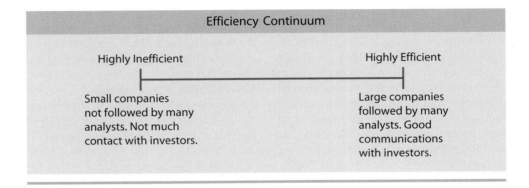

As an investor, would you prefer to purchase a stock whose price was determined in an efficient or an inefficient market? If you thought you knew something that others didn't know, you might prefer inefficient markets. But if you thought that those physics PhDs with unlimited buying power and access to company CEOs might know more than you, you would probably prefer efficient markets, where the price you paid was likely to be the "right" price. From an economic standpoint, it is good to have efficient markets in which everyone is willing to participate. So the SEC and other regulatory agencies should do everything they can to encourage market efficiency.

Thus far we have been discussing the market for individual stocks. But the notion of efficiency applies to the pricing of all assets. For example, the dramatic rise and subsequent collapse of housing prices in many U.S. markets, suggests that there was a lot of inefficiency in these markets. It is also important to realize that the level of market efficiency also varies over time. In one respect, we might expect that lower transactions costs and the increasing number of analysts would cause markets to become increasingly efficient over time. However, the recent housing bubble and the previous bubble for Internet stocks provides some contrary evidence. Indeed, these recent events have caused many experts to look for alternative reasons for this apparent irrational behavior. A lot of their research looks for psychologically based explanations, which we discuss in the next section.

2-7A BEHAVIORAL FINANCE THEORY

The *efficient markets hypothesis* (*EMH*) remains one of the cornerstones of modern finance theory. It implies that, on average, asset prices are about equal to their intrinsic values. The logic behind the EMH is straightforward. If a stock's price is "too low," rational traders will quickly take advantage of this opportunity and buy the stock, pushing prices up to the proper level. Likewise, if prices are "too high," rational traders will sell the stock, pushing the price down to its equilibrium level. Proponents of the EMH argue that these forces keep prices from being systematically wrong.

While the logic behind the EMH is compelling, many events in the real world seem inconsistent with the hypothesis, which has spurred a growing field called *behavioral finance*. Rather than assuming that investors are rational, behavioral finance theorists borrow insights from psychology to better understand how irrational behavior can be sustained over time. Pioneers in this field include psychologists Daniel Kahneman, Amos Tversky, and Richard Thaler. Their work has encouraged a growing number of scholars to work in this promising area of research.[15]

Professor Thaler and his colleague Nicholas Barberis argue that behavioral finance's criticism of the EMH rests on two key points. First, it is often difficult or risky for traders to take advantage of mispriced assets. For example, even if you know that a stock's price is too low because investors have overreacted to recent bad news, a trader with limited capital may be reluctant to purchase the stock for fear that the same forces that pushed the price down may work to keep it artificially low for a long time. Similarly, during the recent stock market bubble, many traders who believed (correctly) that stock prices were too high lost a great deal of money selling stocks short in the early stages of the bubble, because prices went even higher before they eventually collapsed. Thus, mispricings may persist.

The second point deals with why mispricings can occur in the first place. Here insights from psychology come into play. For example, Kahneman and Tversky suggested that individuals view potential losses and gains differently. If you ask average individuals whether they would rather have $500 with certainty or flip a fair coin and receive $1,000 if a head comes up and nothing if a tail comes up, most would prefer the certain $500, which suggests an aversion to risk. However, if you ask people whether they would rather pay $500 with certainty or flip a coin and pay $1,000 if it's a head and nothing if it's a tail, most would indicate that they prefer to flip the coin. Other studies suggest that people's willingness to take a gamble depends on recent performance. Gamblers who are ahead tend to take on more risk, whereas those who are behind tend to become more conservative.

These experiments suggest that investors and managers behave differently in down markets than they do in up markets, which might explain why those who made money early in the stock market bubble continued to invest their money in the market even as prices went ever higher. Other evidence suggests that individuals tend to overestimate their true abilities. For example, a large majority of people (upward of 90% in some studies) believe that they have above-average driving ability and above-average ability to get along with others. Barberis and Thaler point out that:

> *Overconfidence may in part stem from two other biases, self-attribution bias and hindsight bias. Self-attribution bias refers to people's tendency to ascribe any success they have in some activity to their own talents, while blaming failure on bad luck rather than on their ineptitude. Doing this repeatedly will lead people to the pleasing, but erroneous, conclusion that they are very talented. For example, investors might become overconfident after several quarters of investing success [Gervais and Odean (2001)]. Hindsight bias is the tendency of people to believe, after an event has occurred, that they predicted it before it happened. If people think they predicted the past better than they actually did, they may also believe that they can predict the future better than they actually can.[16]*

---

[15]Five noteworthy sources for students interested in behavioral finance are George Akerlof and Robert Shiller, *Animal Spirits: How Human Psychology Drives the Economy, and Why It Matters for Global Capitalism* (Princeton, NJ: Princeton University Press, 2009); Richard Thaler and Cass Sunstein, *Nudge: Improving Decisions about Health, Wealth, and Happiness* (New Haven, CT: Yale University Press, 2008); Richard H. Thaler, Editor, *Advances in Behavioral Finance* (New York: Russell Sage Foundation, 1993); Hersh Shefrin, "Behavioral Corporate Finance," *Journal of Applied Corporate Finance*, vol. 14, no. 3 (Fall 2001), pp. 113–125; and Nicholas Barberis and Richard Thaler, "A Survey of Behavioral Finance," Chapter 18 in *Handbook of the Economics of Finance*, edited by George Constantinides, Milt Harris, and René Stulz (New York: Elsevier/North-Holland, 2003). Students interested in learning more about the efficient markets hypothesis should consult Burton G. Malkiel, *A Random Walk Down Wall Street: The Time-Tested Strategy for Successful Investing*, 9th edition (New York: W.W. Norton & Company, 2007).

[16]Nicholas Barberis and Richard Thaler, "A Survey of Behavioral Finance," Chapter 18 in *Handbook of the Economics of Finance*, edited by George Constantinides, Milt Harris, and René Stulz (New York: Elsevier/North-Holland, 2003).

Behavioral finance has been studied in both the corporate finance and investments areas. Ulrike Malmendier of Stanford and Geoffrey Tate of Wharton found that overconfidence leads managers to overestimate their ability and thus the profitability of their projects.[17] This may explain why so many corporate projects fail to live up to their stated expectations.

2-7b Conclusions About Market Efficiency

As noted previously, if the stock market is efficient, it is a waste of time for most people to seek bargains by analyzing published data on stocks. That follows because if stock prices already reflect all publicly available information, they will be fairly priced; and a person can beat the market only with luck or inside information. So rather than spending time and money trying to find undervalued stocks, it would be better to buy an index fund designed to match the overall market as reflected in an index such as the S&P 500. However, if we worked for an institution with billions of dollars, we would try to find undervalued stocks or companies because even a small undervaluation would amount to a great deal of money when investing millions rather than thousands. Also, markets are more efficient for individual stocks than for entire companies; so for investors with enough capital, it does make sense to seek out badly managed companies that can be acquired and improved. Note, though, that a number of private equity players are doing exactly that; so the market for entire companies may soon be as efficient as that for individual stocks.

However, even if markets are efficient and all stocks and companies are fairly priced, an investor should still be careful when selecting stocks for his or her portfolio. Most importantly, the portfolio should be diversified, with a mix of stocks from various industries along with some bonds and other fixed-income securities. We will discuss diversification in greater detail in Chapter 8, but it is an important consideration for most individual investors.

SELF TEST

What does it mean for a market to be "efficient"?

Is the market for all stocks equally efficient? Explain.

Why is it good for the economy that markets be efficient?

Is it possible that the market for individual stocks could be highly efficient but the market for whole companies could be less efficient? Explain.

What is behavioral finance? What are the implications of behavioral finance for market efficiency?

TYING IT ALL TOGETHER

In this chapter, we provided a brief overview of how capital is allocated and discussed the financial markets, instruments, and institutions used in the allocation process. We discussed physical location exchanges and electronic markets for common stocks, stock market reporting, and stock indexes. We demonstrated that security prices are

---

[17]Ulrike Malmendier and Geoffrey Tate, "CEO Overconfidence and Corporate Investment," Stanford Graduate School of Business Research Paper #1799, June 2004.

volatile—investors expect to make money, which they generally do over time; but losses can be large in any given year. Finally, we discussed the efficiency of the stock market and developments in behavioral finance. After reading this chapter, you should have a general understanding of the financial environment in which businesses and individuals operate, realize that actual returns are often different from expected returns, and be able to read stock market quotations from business newspapers or various Internet sites. You should also recognize that the theory of financial markets is a "work in progress," and much work remains to be done.

SELF-TEST QUESTIONS AND PROBLEMS

(Solutions Appear in Appendix A)

ST-1 **KEY TERMS** Define each of the following terms:

a. Spot markets; futures markets

b. Money markets; capital markets

c. Primary markets; secondary markets

d. Private markets; public markets

e. Derivatives

f. Investment banks (iBanks); commercial banks; financial services corporations

g. Mutual funds; money market funds

h. Physical location exchanges; over-the-counter (OTC) market; dealer market

i. Closely held corporation; publicly owned corporation

j. Going public; initial public offering (IPO) market

k. Efficient markets hypothesis (EMH)

l. Behavioral finance

QUESTIONS

2-1 How does a cost-efficient capital market help reduce the prices of goods and services?

2-2 Describe the different ways in which capital can be transferred from suppliers of capital to those who are demanding capital.

2-3 Is an initial public offering an example of a primary or a secondary market transaction? Explain.

2-4 Indicate whether the following instruments are examples of money market or capital market securities.

a. U.S. Treasury bills

b. Long-term corporate bonds

c. Common stocks

d. Preferred stocks

e. Dealer commercial paper

2-5 What would happen to the U.S. standard of living if people lost faith in the safety of the financial institutions? Explain.

2-6 What types of changes have financial markets experienced during the last two decades? Have they been perceived as positive or negative changes? Explain.

2-7   Differentiate between dealer markets and stock markets that have a physical location.

2-8   Identify and briefly compare the two leading stock exchanges in the United States today.

2-9   Briefly explain what is meant by the term *efficiency continuum*.

2-10   Explain whether the following statements are true or false.

    a.   Derivative transactions are designed to increase risk and are used almost exclusively by speculators who are looking to capture high returns.

    b.   Hedge funds typically have large minimum investments and are marketed to institutions and individuals with high net worths.

    c.   Hedge funds have traditionally been highly regulated.

    d.   The New York Stock Exchange is an example of a stock exchange that has a physical location.

    e.   A larger bid–ask spread means that the dealer will realize a lower profit.

INTEGRATED CASE

SMYTH BARRY & COMPANY

2-1   **Financial Markets and Institutions** Assume that you recently graduated with a degree in finance and have just reported to work as an investment adviser at the brokerage firm of Smyth Barry & Co. Your first assignment is to explain the nature of the U.S. financial markets to Michelle Varga, a professional tennis player who recently came to the United States from Mexico. Varga is a highly ranked tennis player who expects to invest substantial amounts of money through Smyth Barry. She is very bright; therefore, she would like to understand in general terms what will happen to her money. Your boss has developed the following questions that you must use to explain the U.S. financial system to Varga.

    a.   What are the three primary ways in which capital is transferred between savers and borrowers? Describe each one.

    b.   What is a market? Differentiate between the following types of markets: physical asset markets versus financial asset markets, spot markets versus futures markets, money markets versus capital markets, primary markets versus secondary markets, and public markets versus private markets.

    c.   Why are financial markets essential for a healthy economy and economic growth?

    d.   What are derivatives? How can derivatives be used to reduce risk? Can derivatives be used to increase risk? Explain.

    e.   Briefly describe each of the following financial institutions: investment banks, commercial banks, financial services corporations, pension funds, mutual funds, exchange traded funds, hedge funds, and private equity companies.

    f.   What are the two leading stock markets? Describe the two basic types of stock markets.

    g.   If Apple Computer decided to issue additional common stock and Varga purchased 100 shares of this stock from Smyth Barry, the underwriter, would this transaction be a primary or a secondary market transaction? Would it make a difference if Varga purchased previously outstanding Apple stock in the dealer market? Explain.

    h.   What is an initial public offering (IPO)?

    i.   What does it mean for a market to be efficient? Explain why some stock prices may be more efficient than others.

    j.   After your consultation with Michelle, she wants to discuss these two possible stock purchases:

       1. While in the waiting room of your office, she overheard an analyst on a financial TV network say that a particular medical research company just received FDA approval for one of its products. On the basis of this "hot" information, Michelle wants to buy many shares of that company's stock. Assuming the stock market is highly efficient, what advice would you give her?

       2. She has read a number of newspaper articles about a huge IPO being carried out by a leading technology company. She wants to purchase as many shares in the IPO as possible and would even be willing to buy the shares in the open market immediately after the issue. What advice do you have for her?

    k.   How does behavioral finance explain the real world inconsistencies of the efficient markets hypothesis (EMH)?

PART 2

FUNDAMENTAL CONCEPTS IN FINANCIAL MANAGEMENT

CHAPTER

3 Financial Statements, Cash Flow, and Taxes

4 Analysis of Financial Statements

5 Time Value of Money

CHAPTER

3

Financial Statements, Cash Flow, and Taxes

Unlocking the Valuable Information in Financial Statements

In Chapter 1, we said that managers should make decisions that enhance long-term shareholder value, and they should be less concerned about short-term accounting measures such as earnings per share. With that important point in mind, you might reasonably wonder why are we now going to talk about accounting and financial statements. The simple answer is financial statements convey a lot of useful information that helps corporate managers assess the company's strengths and weaknesses and gauge the expected impact of various proposals. Good managers must have a solid understanding of the key financial statements. Outsiders also rely heavily on financial statements when deciding whether they want to buy the company's stock, lend money to the company, or enter into a long-term business relationship with the company.

At first glance, financial statements can be overwhelming—but if we know what we are looking for, we can quickly learn a great deal about a company after a quick review of its financial statements. Looking at the balance sheet we can see how large a company is, the types of assets it holds, and how it finances those assets. Looking at the income statement, we can see if the company's sales increased or declined and whether the company made a profit. Glancing at the statement of cash flows, we can see if the company made any new investments, if it raised funds through financing, repurchased debt or equity, or paid dividends.

For example, in early 2013, Starbucks released its first quarter financial statements. The news was good. The company earned $432.2 million in the first quarter of its fiscal year—a year earlier it had earned $382.1 million, and three years earlier it had earned only $64.3 million. Starbucks also announced a strong increase in same-store sales, and its income statement showed that operating costs grew less than revenues. Reviewing the company's annual report for 2012, at the end of its fiscal year (September 30, 2012), Starbucks showed total assets of $8.2 billion and total liabilities of $3.1 billion on its balance sheet. Finally, looking at the statement of cash flows, we see that the company used most of the cash generated from its operations to make new investments, to pay dividends, and to repurchase common stock. The net effect was that Starbucks' cash position increased only modestly from $1.15 billion to $1.19 billion during the year.

While we can learn a lot from a quick tour of the financial statements, a good financial analyst does not just accept these numbers at face value. The analyst digs deeper to see what's really driving the numbers and uses his or her intuition and knowledge of the industry to help assess the company's future direction. Keep in mind that just because a company reports great numbers doesn't mean that you should buy the stock. In the case of Starbucks, its stock price did rise after it announced its better-than-expected financial numbers for the first quarter. However, as is always the case, analysts have mixed feelings about the stock's future direction. It's these types of disagreements that make finance interesting, and as always, time will tell whether the optimists (the bulls) or the pessimists (the bears) are correct.

PUTTING THINGS IN PERSPECTIVE

A manager's primary goal is to maximize the value of his or her firm's stock, and value is based on the firm's future cash flows. But how do managers decide which actions are most likely to increase those flows, and how do investors estimate future cash flows? The answers to both questions lie in a study of financial statements that publicly traded firms must provide to investors. Here *investors* include both institutions (banks, insurance companies, pension funds, and the like) and individuals like you.

Much of the material in this chapter deals with concepts you covered in a basic accounting course. However, the information is important enough to warrant a review. Also, in accounting, you probably focused on how accounting statements are made; the focus here is on how investors and managers *interpret* and *use* them. Accounting is the basic language of business, so everyone engaged in business needs a good working knowledge of it. It is used to "keep score"; and if investors and managers do not know the score, they won't know whether their actions are appropriate. If you took midterm exams but were not told your scores, you would have a difficult time knowing whether you needed to improve. The same idea holds in business. If a firm's managers—whether they work in marketing, human resources, production, or finance—do not understand financial statements, they will not be able to judge the effects of their actions, which will make it hard for the firm to survive, much less to have a maximum value.

When you finish this chapter you should be able to:

- List each of the key financial statements and identify the kinds of information they provide to corporate managers and investors.
- Estimate a firm's free cash flow and explain why free cash flow has such an important effect on firm value.
- Discuss the major features of the federal income tax system.

3-1 FINANCIAL STATEMENTS AND REPORTS

Annual Report

A report issued annually by a corporation to its stockholders. It contains basic financial statements as well as management's analysis of the firm's past operations and future prospects.

The **annual report** is the most important report that corporations issue to stockholders, and it contains two types of information.[1] First, there is a verbal section, often presented as a letter from the chairperson, which describes the firm's operating results during the past year and discusses new developments that will affect future operations. Second, the report provides these four basic financial statements:

1. The *balance sheet,* which shows what assets the company owns and who has claims on those assets as of a given date—for example, December 31, 2014.

2. The *income statement,* which shows the firm's sales and costs (and thus profits) during some past period—for example, 2014.

3. The *statement of cash flows,* which shows how much cash the firm began the year with, how much cash it ended up with, and what it did to increase or decrease its cash.

4. The *statement of stockholders' equity,* which shows the amount of equity the stockholders had at the start of the year, the items that increased or decreased equity, and the equity at the end of the year.

These statements are related to one another; and taken together, they provide an accounting picture of the firm's operations and financial position.

The quantitative and verbal materials are equally important. The firm's financial statements report *what has actually happened* to its assets, earnings, and dividends over the past few years, whereas management's verbal statements attempt to explain why things turned out the way they did and what might happen in the future.

For discussion purposes, we use data for Allied Food Products, a processor and distributor of a wide variety of food products, to illustrate the basic financial statements. Allied was formed in 1983, when several regional firms merged; it has grown steadily while earning a reputation as one of the best firms in its industry. Allied's earnings dropped from $121.8 million in 2013 to $117.5 million in 2014. Management reported that the drop resulted from losses associated with a drought as well as increased costs due to a three-month strike. However, management then went on to describe a more optimistic picture for the future, stating that full operations had been resumed, that several unprofitable businesses had been eliminated, and that 2015 profits were expected to rise sharply. Of course, an increase in profitability may not occur; and analysts should compare management's past statements with subsequent results. In any event, *the information contained in the annual report can be used to help forecast future earnings and dividends.* Therefore, investors are very interested in this report.

We should note that Allied's financial statements are relatively simple and straightforward; we also omitted some details often shown in the statements. Allied finances with only debt and common stock—it has no preferred stock, convertibles, or complex derivative securities. Also, the firm has made no acquisitions that resulted in goodwill that must be carried on the balance sheet. Finally, all of its assets are used in its basic business operations; hence, no non-operating assets must be pulled out when we evaluate its operating performance. We deliberately chose such a company because this is an introductory text; as such,

---

[1]Firms also provide quarterly reports, but these are much less comprehensive than the annual report. In addition, larger firms file even more detailed statements with the Securities and Exchange Commission (SEC), giving breakdowns for each major division or subsidiary. These reports, called *10-K reports,* are made available to stockholders upon request to a company's corporate secretary. In this chapter, we focus on annual data—balance sheets at the ends of years and income statements for entire years rather than for shorter time periods.

GLOBAL PERSPECTIVES

Global Accounting Standards: Will It Ever Happen?

For the past decade, global accounting standards seemed all but certain. In 2005, the EU required the adoption of International Financial Reporting Standards (IFRS), and in 2007, the SEC eliminated the requirement for companies reporting under IFRS to reconcile their financial statements to U.S. Generally Accepted Accounting Principles (GAAP). To date, 100 countries have adopted IFRS. The most recent countries to adopt IFRS are Russia and Canada—even China is considering adopting IFRS. However, on July 13, 2012, the SEC staff issued a report that failed to recommend IFRS for U.S. adoption. Even though the ultimate decision will be up to the SEC commission, this report will play an important role in its decision.

The effort to internationalize accounting standards began in 1973 with the formation of the International Accounting Standards Committee. However, in 1998, it became apparent that a full-time rule-making body with global representation was necessary; so the International Accounting Standards Board (IASB) was established. The IASB was charged with the responsibility for creating a set of IFRS. The "convergence" process began in earnest in September 2002 with the "Norwalk Agreement," in which the Financial Accounting Standards Board (FASB) and IASB undertook a short-term project to remove individual differences between the FASB's U.S. GAAP and IFRS and agreed to coordinate their activities. The process was meant to narrow gaps between the two standards with the intention of making the transition for companies simpler and less expensive.

Obviously, the globalization of accounting standards is a huge endeavor—one that involves compromises between the IASB and FASB. However, in recent years the momentum behind this goal has diminished. Despite the best of intentions, progress towards consolidation was slowed by the 2007–2008 financial crisis and the resulting global recession. In addition, the leasing and financial instruments impairment projects progressed slowly and the chairs of both the FASB and IASB left their positions. It has become apparent that the cost to companies both large and small for switching from GAAP to IFRS will be significant. Finally, the SEC has been given the task of implementing the Dodd–Frank financial reform law—limiting its ability to focus on adopting global accounting standards.

The United States is an important economy, and without its participation it will be difficult to truly have global accounting standards. While this report is a setback, many CFOs and accounting professionals still expect the SEC to come out with an American version of IFRS to coexist with GAAP. However, it appears that any decision by the SEC will come after the November 2012 U.S. presidential election and even after January 1, 2013—maybe later. Global accounting standards are probably inevitable—it's just a question of time.

Sources: Lee Berton, "All Accountants Soon May Speak the Same Language," *The Wall Street Journal*, August 29, 1995, p. A15; James Turley (CEO, Ernst & Young), "Mind the GAAP," *The Wall Street Journal*, November 9, 2007, p. A18; David M. Katz, "The Path to Global Standards?," *CFO.com*, January 28, 2011; "Global Accounting Standards: Closing the GAAP," *The Economist* (economist.com), vol. 404, July 21, 2012; Joe Adler, "Is Effort to Unify Accounting Regimes Falling Apart?," *American Banker*, vol. 177, no. 145, July 30, 2012; Kathleen Hoffelder, "SEC Report Backs Away from Convergence," *CFO Magazine* (cfo.com/magazine), September 1, 2012; Ken Tysiac, "Still in Flux: Future of IFRS in U.S. Remains Unclear after SEC Report," *Journal of Accountancy* (journalofaccountancy.com), September 2012; and Tammy Whitehouse, "Ten Years on, Convergence Movement Starting to Wane," *Compliance Week* (complianceweek.com), October 2, 2012.

we want to explain the basics of financial analysis, not wander into arcane accounting matters that are best left to accounting and security analysis courses. We do point out some of the pitfalls that can be encountered when trying to interpret accounting statements, but we leave it to advanced courses to cover the intricacies of accounting.

SELF TEST

What is the annual report, and what two types of information does it provide?

What four financial statements are typically included in the annual report?

Why is the annual report of great interest to investors?

3-2 THE BALANCE SHEET

Balance Sheet

A statement of a firm's financial position at a specific point in time.

The balance sheet is a "snapshot" of a firm's position at a specific point in time. Figure 3.1 shows the layout of a typical **balance sheet**. The left side of the statement shows the assets that the company owns, while the right side shows the firm's liabilities and *stockholders' equity*, which are claims against the firm's assets. As Figure 3.1 shows, assets are divided into two major categories: current assets and fixed, or long-term, assets. Current assets consist of assets that should be converted to cash within one year; and they include cash and cash equivalents, accounts receivable, and inventory.[2] Long-term assets are assets expected to be used for more than one year; they include plant and equipment in addition to intellectual property such as patents and copyrights. Plant and equipment is generally reported net of accumulated depreciation. Allied's long-term assets consist entirely of net plant and equipment, and we often refer to them as "net fixed assets."

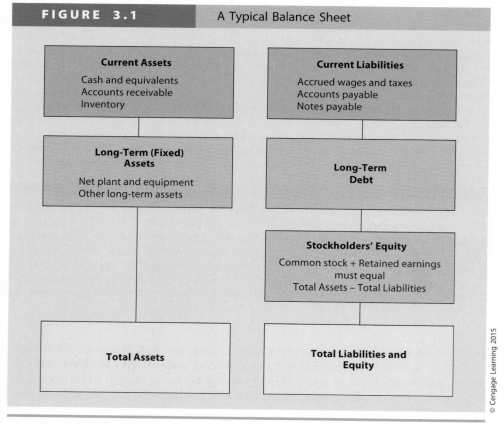

FIGURE 3.1 A Typical Balance Sheet

Note: This is the typical layout of a balance sheet for one year. When balance sheets for two or more years are shown, assets are listed in the top section; liabilities and equity, in the bottom section. See Table 3.1 for an illustration.

---

[2]Allied and most other companies hold some currency in addition to a bank checking account. They may also hold short-term interest-bearing securities that can be sold and thus converted to cash immediately with a simple telephone call. These securities are called "cash equivalents," and they are generally included with checking account balances for financial reporting purposes. If a company owns stocks or other marketable securities that it regards as short-term investments, these items will be shown separately on the balance sheet. Allied does not hold any marketable securities other than cash equivalents.

The claims against assets are of two basic types—liabilities (or money the company owes to others) and stockholders' equity. Current liabilities consist of claims that must be paid off within one year, including accounts payable, accruals (total of accrued wages and accrued taxes), and notes payable to banks and other short-term lenders that are due within one year. Long-term debt includes bonds that mature in more than a year.

Stockholders' equity can be thought of in two ways. First, it is the amount that stockholders paid to the company when they bought shares the company sold to raise capital, in addition to all of the earnings the company has retained over the years:[3]

$$\text{Stockholders' equity} = \text{Paid-in capital} + \text{Retained earnings}$$

The **retained earnings** are not just the earnings retained in the latest year—they are the cumulative total of all of the earnings the company has earned during its life.

Stockholders' equity can also be thought of as a residual:

$$\text{Stockholders' equity} = \text{Total assets} - \text{Total liabilities}$$

Stockholders' Equity
It represents the amount that stockholders paid the company when shares were purchased and the amount of earnings the company has retained since its origination.

Retained Earnings
They represent the cumulative total of all earnings kept by the company during its life.

If Allied had invested surplus funds in bonds backed by subprime mortgages and the bonds' value fell below their purchase price, the true value of the firm's assets would have declined. The amount of its liabilities would not have changed—the firm would still owe the amount it had promised to pay its creditors. Therefore, the reported value of the common equity must decline. The accountants would make a series of entries, and the result would be a reduction in retained earnings—and thus in common equity. In the end, assets would equal liabilities and equity and the balance sheet would balance. This example shows why common stock is more risky than bonds—any mistake that management makes has a big impact on the stockholders. Of course, gains from good decisions also go to the stockholders; so with risk come possible rewards.

Assets on the balance sheet are listed by the length of time before they will be converted to cash (inventories and accounts receivable) or used by the firm (fixed assets). Similarly, claims are listed in the order in which they must be paid: Accounts payable must generally be paid within a few days, accruals must also be paid promptly, notes payable to banks must be paid within one year, and so forth, down to the stockholders' equity accounts, which represent ownership and need never be "paid off."

3-2A ALLIED'S BALANCE SHEET

Table 3.1 shows Allied's year-end balance sheets for 2014 and 2013. From the 2014 statement, we see that Allied had $2 billion of assets—half current and half long term. These assets were financed with $310 million of current liabilities, $750 million of long-term debt, and $940 million of common equity. Comparing the balance sheets for 2014 and 2013, we see that Allied's assets grew by $320 million and its liabilities and equity necessarily grew by that same amount. Assets must, of course, equal liabilities and equity; otherwise, the balance sheet does not balance.

Several additional points about the balance sheet should be noted:

1. *Cash versus other assets.* Although assets are reported in dollar terms, only the cash and equivalents account represents actual spendable money. Accounts receivable represent credit sales that have not yet been collected. Inventories show the cost of raw materials, work in process, and finished goods. Net fixed

---

[3]On Allied's balance sheet, we simply show a common stock line representing the "paid-in" capital of stockholders when they purchased common shares of stock.

TABLE 3.1 Allied Food Products: December 31 Balance Sheets (Millions of Dollars)

	2014	2013
Assets		
Current assets:		
Cash and equivalents	$ 10	$ 80
Accounts receivable	375	315
Inventories	615	415
Total current assets	$1,000	$ 810
Net fixed assets:		
Net plant and equipment (cost minus depreciation)	1,000	870
Other assets expected to last more than a year	0	0
Total assets	$2,000	$1,680
Liabilities and Equity		
Current liabilities:		
Accounts payable	$ 60	$ 30
Accruals	140	130
Notes payable	110	60
Total current liabilities	$ 310	$ 220
Long-term bonds	750	580
Total liabilities	$1,060	$ 800
Common equity:		
Common stock (50,000,000 shares)	$ 130	$ 130
Retained earnings	810	750
Total common equity	$ 940	$ 880
Total liabilities and equity	$2,000	$1,680

© Cengage Learning 2015

Notes:

1. Inventories can be valued by several different methods, and the method chosen can affect both the balance sheet value and the cost of goods sold, and thus net income, as reported on the income statement. Similarly, companies can use different depreciation methods. The methods used must be reported in the notes to the financial statements, and security analysts can make adjustments when they compare companies if they think the differences are material.
2. Book value per share: Total common equity/Shares outstanding = $940/50 = $18.80.
3. A relatively few firms use preferred stock, which we discuss in Chapter 9. Preferred stock can take several different forms, but it is generally like debt because it pays a fixed amount each year. However, it is like common stock because a failure to pay the preferred dividend does not expose the firm to bankruptcy. If a firm does use preferred stock, it is shown on the balance sheet between total debt and common stock. There is no set rule on how preferred stock should be treated when financial ratios are calculated—it could be considered as debt or as equity. Bondholders often think of it as equity, while stockholders think of it as debt because it is a fixed charge. In truth, preferred stock is a hybrid, somewhere between debt and common equity.

assets represent the cost of the buildings and equipment used in operations minus the depreciation that has been taken on these assets. At the end of 2014, Allied has $10 million of cash; hence, it could write checks totaling that amount. The noncash assets should generate cash over time, but they do not represent cash in hand. And the cash they would bring in if they were sold today could be higher or lower than the values reported on the balance sheet.

Working Capital
Current assets.

2. *Working capital.* Current assets are often called **working capital** because these assets "turn over"; that is, they are used and then replaced throughout the year. When Allied buys inventory items on credit, its suppliers, in effect, lend it the money used to finance the inventory items. Allied could have borrowed

from its bank or sold stock to obtain the money, but it received the funds from its suppliers. These loans are shown as accounts payable, and they typically are "free" in the sense that they do not bear interest. Similarly, Allied pays its workers every two weeks and pays taxes quarterly; so Allied's labor force and tax authorities provide it with loans equal to its accrued wages and taxes. In addition to these "free" sources of short-term credit, Allied borrows from its bank on a short-term basis. These bank loans are shown as notes payable. While accounts payable and accruals do not bear interest, Allied pays interest on funds obtained from the bank. The total of accounts payable, accruals, and notes payable represent current liabilities on its balance sheet. If we subtract current liabilities from current assets, the difference is called **net working capital**.

Net Working Capital
Current assets minus current liabilities.

$$\text{Net working capital} = \text{Current assets} - \text{Current liabilities}$$
$$= \$1,000 - \$310 = \$690 \text{ million}$$

Current liabilities include accounts payable, accruals, and notes payable to the bank. Financial analysts often make an important distinction between the "free" liabilities (accruals and accounts payable) and interest-bearing notes payable (which incur interest expense that is included as a financing cost on the firm's income statement). With this distinction in mind, analysts often focus on **net operating working capital (NOWC)** which differs from net working capital because interest-bearing notes payable are subtracted from current liabilities.

Net Operating Working Capital (NOWC)
Current assets minus non-interest-bearing current liabilities.

$$\begin{array}{c}\text{Net operating}\\\text{work capital (NOWC)}\end{array} = \begin{array}{c}\text{Current}\\\text{assets}\end{array} - \left(\begin{array}{c}\text{Current}\\\text{liabilities}\end{array} - \begin{array}{c}\text{Notes}\\\text{payable}\end{array}\right) \qquad 3.1$$
$$= \$1,000 - (\$310 - \$110) = \$800 \text{ million}$$

Note that Allied's "free," or noninterest-bearing, current liabilities in 2014 total \$200 million (\$310 million in current liabilities less the \$110 million in interest-bearing notes payable).

 QUICK QUESTION

QUESTION:
Refer to Allied's balance sheets shown in Table 3.1 to answer the following questions:
a. What was Allied's net working capital on December 31, 2013?
b. What was Allied's net operating working capital on December 31, 2013?

ANSWER:
a. Net working capital$_{2013}$ = Current assets$_{2013}$ − Current liabilities$_{2013}$

   Net working capital$_{2013}$ = \$810 − \$220 = **\$590 million**

b. $\begin{array}{c}\text{Net operating}\\\text{working capital}_{2013}\end{array} = \begin{array}{c}\text{Current}\\\text{assets}_{2013}\end{array} - \left(\begin{array}{c}\text{Current}\\\text{liabilities}_{2013}\end{array} - \begin{array}{c}\text{Notes}\\\text{payable}_{2013}\end{array}\right)$

   $\begin{array}{c}\text{Net operating}\\\text{working capital}_{2013}\end{array} = \$810 - (\$220 - \$60)$

   $\begin{array}{c}\text{Net operating}\\\text{working capital}_{2013}\end{array} = \$810 - \$160 = \textbf{\$650 million}$

---

3. *Total debt versus total liabilities.* A company's total debt includes both its short-term and long-term interest-bearing liabilities. Total liabilities equal total debt

plus the company's "free" (non-interest bearing) liabilities. Allied's short-term debt is shown as notes payable on its balance sheet.[4]

$$\textbf{Total debt} = \textbf{Short-term debt} + \textbf{Long-term debt}$$
$$= \$110 + \$750 = \$860 \text{ million}$$

$$\textbf{Total liabilities} = \textbf{Total debt} + (\textbf{Accounts payable} + \textbf{Accruals})$$
$$= \$860 + (\$60 + \$140) = \$1{,}060 \text{ million} = \$1.06 \text{ billion}$$

 QUICK QUESTION

QUESTION:
Refer to Allied's balance sheets shown in Table 3.1. What was Allied's total debt on December 31, 2013?

ANSWER:
Total debt$_{2013}$ = Short-term debt$_{2013}$ + Long-term debt$_{2013}$
Total debt$_{2013}$ = $60 + $580 = **$640 million**

4. *Other sources of funds.* Most companies (including Allied) finance their assets with a combination of short-term debt, long-term debt, and common equity. Some companies also use "hybrid" securities such as preferred stock, convertible bonds, and long-term leases. Preferred stock is a hybrid between common stock and debt, while convertible bonds are debt securities that give the bondholder an option to exchange their bonds for shares of common stock. In the event of bankruptcy, debt is paid off first, and then preferred stock. Common stock is last, receiving a payment only when something remains after the debt and preferred stock are paid off.[5]

5. *Depreciation.* Most companies prepare two sets of financial statements—one is based on Internal Revenue Service (IRS) rules and is used to calculate taxes; the other is based on GAAP and is used for reporting to investors. Firms often use accelerated depreciation for tax purposes but straight-line depreciation for stockholder reporting. Allied uses accelerated depreciation for both.[6]

6. *Market values versus book values.* Companies generally use GAAP to determine the values reported on their balance sheets. In most cases, these accounting numbers (or "book values") are different from what the assets would sell for if they were offered for sale (or "market values"). For example, Allied purchased its headquarters in Chicago in 1990. Under GAAP, the company must report

---

[4]Companies also include the portion of their long-term bonds that is currently due as part of short-term debt.

[5]Other forms of financing are discussed in Chapter 20, "Hybrid Financing: Preferred Stock, Warrants, and Convertibles," of Brigham and Daves, *Intermediate Financial Management*, 11th edition, (Mason, OH: South-Western/Cengage Learning, 2013).

[6]Depreciation over an asset's life is equal to the asset's cost, but accelerated depreciation results in higher initial depreciation charges—and thus lower taxable income—than straight line. Due to the time value of money, it is better to delay taxes; so most companies use accelerated depreciation for tax purposes. Either accelerated or straight line can be used for stockholder reporting. Allied is a relatively conservative company; hence, it uses accelerated depreciation for stockholder reporting. Had Allied elected to use straight line for stockholder reporting, its 2014 depreciation expense would have been $25 million lower, the $1 billion shown for "net plant" on its balance sheet would have been $25 million higher, and its reported income would also have been higher.

Depreciation is also important in capital budgeting, where we make decisions regarding new investments in fixed assets. We will have more to say about depreciation in Chapter 12, when we discuss capital budgeting.

the value of this asset at its historical cost (what it originally paid for the building in 1990) less accumulated depreciation. Given that Chicago real estate prices have increased over the last 23 years (even considering the impact of the recent recession on real estate values), the market value of the building is higher than its book value. Other assets' market values also differ from their book values.

We can also see from Table 3.1 that the book value of Allied's common equity at the end of 2014 was $940 million. Because 50 million shares were outstanding, the book value per share was $940/50 = $18.80. However, the market value of the common stock was $23.06. As is true for most companies in 2014, shareholders are willing to pay more than book value for Allied's stock. This occurs in part because the values of assets have increased due to inflation and in part because shareholders expect earnings to grow. Allied, like most other companies, has learned how to make investments that will increase future profits.

> *Apple provides an example of the effect of growth on the stock price. When Apple first introduced new products such as the iPod, iPhone, and iPad, its balance sheet didn't budge; but investors recognized that these were great products that would lead to higher future profits. So Apple's stock quickly rose above its book value—at its peak in September 2012, the company's stock price was $705.07 versus a $125.86 book value. More recently, the assessments of the company's future prospects have dimmed somewhat, and we have seen the ratio of its market-to-book ratio narrow. On February 20, 2013, Apple's stock price closed at $448.85, while its book value for the most recent quarter was $135.62.*

If a company has problems, its stock price can fall below its book value. For example, SkyWest, a regional airline struggling during the slow economy and hurt by rising fuel costs, saw its stock price fall to around $11 at a time when its book value per share exceeded $26.

7. *Time dimension.* The balance sheet is a snapshot of the firm's financial position *at a point in time*—for example, on December 31, 2014. Thus, we see that on December 31, 2013, Allied had $80 million of cash; but that balance fell to $10 million by year-end 2014. The balance sheet changes every day as inventories rise and fall, as bank loans are increased or decreased, and so forth. A company such as Allied, whose business is seasonal, experiences especially

CASH HOLDINGS AND NET OPERATING WORKING CAPITAL: A CLOSER LOOK

To help keep things simple, our definition of net operating working capital (NOWC) assumes that all of the firm's current assets (including cash) are used for normal operating purposes. While this assumption may be reasonable, there are clear instances where firms hold more cash than they need to run their day-to-day operations. For example, at December 31, 2012, Microsoft had more than $68 billion in cash and short-term investments!

In practice, if a financial analyst believes that some of the firm's cash is being held for nonoperating purposes, he or she would subtract these excess cash holdings from the firm's current assets when calculating net operating working capital, as follows:

NOWC = (**Current assets − "Excess" cash**)
 − (**Current liabilities − Notes payable**)

To illustrate, if we make the extreme assumption that all of Allied's $10 million in cash is held for nonoperating purposes, then this $10 million in excess cash would be subtracted from its current assets, and its NOWC would be calculated as $790 million instead of the $800 million calculated earlier. While the difference for Allied is fairly small, assumptions about the level of excess cash become much more important when analyzing companies with very large cash holdings. However, unless otherwise noted, throughout this text we will assume that a firm's cash balance is used solely for operating purposes.

THE BALANCE SHEET OF AN "AVERAGE" AMERICAN HOUSEHOLD

Balance sheets are not unique to corporations. Every entity—including state and local governments, nonprofit agencies, and individual households—has a balance sheet.

We can learn a lot about a household's financial well-being by looking at its balance sheet. While obviously every household is different, economists can use available data to estimate the balance sheet of an average American household.

For example, in 2009, James Kwak posted his calculations of the average household balance sheet on his popular website *The Baseline Scenario* (baselinescenario.com), which provides interesting commentary on a variety of current economic and financial issues. The underlying data for his calculations came from the Federal Reserve Board's *Survey of Consumer Finances*.

Here is a summary of Kwak's calculations for 2004, 2007, and 2009:

	2004	**2007**	**2009**
Income	$ 47,500	$ 47,300	$ 47,300
Assets			
Bank accounts	3,300	2,700	2,700
Retirement savings	19,000	23,900	17,900
Vehicles	14,400	14,600	14,600
Primary residence	148,300	150,000	125,400
Total assets	$185,000	$191,200	$ 160,600
Liabilities			
Mortgage on			
primary residence	$ 84,800	$ 88,700	$ 88,700
Installment loans	11,800	12,800	12,800
Credit cards	2,400	2,400	2,400
Total liabilities	$ 99,000	$103,900	$ 103,900
Net worth	$ 86,000	$ 87,300	$ 56,700

Note: See Kwak's posting on *The Baseline Scenario* for more details about the methods that he used in his calculations.

While his calculations were only meant to give a broad picture of recent trends, they produce some interesting findings:

- The largest asset of the average household is its primary residence.
- The average American household does not have a large amount of savings in place for retirement.
- Perhaps somewhat surprisingly, average household debt levels have not increased dramatically in recent years.
- Average household net worth increased slightly from 2004 to 2007, but declined sharply from 2007 to 2009. The decline in net worth was due to two reasons: The

sharp decline in the housing market reduced the value of the average home and the sharp decline in the stock market reduced the value of the average amount of retirement savings.

While not broken down on a per-household level, updated information on aggregate household finances is on the Federal Reserve website. For example, numbers released in December 2012 indicate that aggregate household balance sheets have strengthened somewhat since 2009. These improvements reflect that many households have made progress in reducing their debt level. Household levels of net worth have also improved because of the large run-up in the stock market during this time period.[7]

Source: James Kwak, "Tracking the Household Balance Sheet," *The Baseline Scenario* (baselinescenario.com), February 15, 2009.

© Cengage Learning 2015

large balance sheet changes during the year. Its inventories are low just before the harvest season but high just after the fall crops have been harvested and processed. Similarly, most retailers have large inventories just before

---

[7]Refer to www.federalreserve.gov/releases/z1/current/z1r-5.pdf, Table B.100 "Balance Sheet of Households and Nonprofit Organizations (1)," December 6, 2012.

Christmas but low inventories (and high accounts receivable) just after Christmas. We will examine the effects of these changes in Chapter 4, when we compare companies' financial statements and evaluate their performance.

SELF TEST

What is the balance sheet, and what information does it provide?

How is the order in which items are shown on the balance sheet determined?

Explain in words the difference between net working capital and net operating working capital.

Explain in words the difference between total debt and total liabilities.

What items on Allied's December 31 balance sheet would probably be different from its June 30 values? Would these differences be as large if Allied were a grocery chain rather than a food processor? Explain.

3-3 THE INCOME STATEMENT

Income Statements
A report summarizing a firm's revenues, expenses, and profits during a reporting period, generally a quarter or a year.

Table 3.2 shows Allied's 2013 and 2014 **income statements**. Net sales are shown at the top of the statement; then operating costs, interest, and taxes are subtracted to obtain the net income available to common shareholders. We also show earnings and dividends per share, in addition to some other data, at the bottom of Table 3.2. Earnings per share (EPS) is often called "the bottom line," denoting that of all items on the income statement, EPS is the one that is most important to stockholders. Allied earned $2.35 per share in 2014, down from $2.44 in 2013. In spite of the decline in earnings, the firm still increased the dividend from $1.06 to $1.15.

Operating Income
Earnings from operations before interest and taxes (i.e., EBIT).

A typical stockholder focuses on the reported EPS, but professional security analysts and managers differentiate between *operating* and *non-operating* income. **Operating income** is derived from the firm's regular core business—in Allied's case, from producing and selling food products. Moreover, it is calculated before deducting interest expenses and taxes, which are considered to be non-operating costs. Operating income is also called EBIT, or earnings before interest and taxes. Here is its equation:

$$\text{Operating income (or EBIT)} = \text{Sales revenues} - \text{Operating costs}$$
$$= \$3,000.0 - \$2,716.2$$
$$= \$283.8 \text{ million}$$

3.2

This figure must, of course, match the one reported on the income statement.

Different firms have different amounts of debt, different tax carry-backs and carry-forwards, and different amounts of non-operating assets such as marketable securities. These differences can cause two companies with identical operations to report significantly different net incomes. For example, suppose two companies have identical sales, operating costs, and assets. However, one company uses some debt and the other uses only common equity. Despite their identical operating performances, the company with no debt (and therefore no interest expense) would report a higher net income because no interest was deducted from its

TABLE 3.2 Allied Food Products: Income Statements for Years Ending December 31 (Millions of Dollars, Except for Per-Share Data)

	2014	2013
Net sales	$3,000.0	$2,850.0
Operating costs except depreciation and amortization	2,616.2	2,497.0
Depreciation and amortization	100.0	90.0
Total operating costs	$2,716.2	$2,587.0
Operating income, or earnings before interest and taxes (EBIT)	$ 283.8	$ 263.0
Less interest	88.0	60.0
Earnings before taxes (EBT)	$ 195.8	$ 203.0
Taxes (40%)	78.3	81.2
Net income	$ 117.5	$ 121.8
Here are some related items:		
Total dividends	$ 57.5	$ 53.0
Addition to retained earnings = Net income − Total dividends	$ 60.0	$ 68.8
Per-share data:		
Common stock price	$ 23.06	$ 26.00
Earnings per share (EPS)[a]	$ 2.35	$ 2.44
Dividends per share (DPS)[a]	$ 1.15	$ 1.06
Book value per share (BVPS)[a]	$ 18.80	$ 17.60

© Cengage Learning 2015

Notes:

[a]Allied has 50 million shares of common stock outstanding. Note that EPS is based on net income available to common stockholders. Calculations of EPS, DPS, and BVPS for 2014 are as follows:

$$\text{Earnings per share} = \text{EPS} = \frac{\text{Net income}}{\text{Common shares outstanding}} = \frac{\$117,500,000}{50,000,000} = \$2.35$$

$$\text{Dividends per share} = \text{DPS} = \frac{\text{Dividends paid to common stockholders}}{\text{Common shares outstanding}} = \frac{\$57,500,000}{50,000,000} = \$1.15$$

$$\text{Book value per share} = \text{BVPS} = \frac{\text{Total common equity}}{\text{Common shares outstanding}} = \frac{\$940,000,000}{50,000,000} = \$18.80$$

When a firm has options or convertibles outstanding or it recently issued new common stock, a more comprehensive EPS, "diluted EPS," is calculated. Its calculation is a bit more complicated, but you may refer to any financial accounting text for a discussion.

operating income. Consequently, if you want to compare two companies' operating performances, it is best to focus on their operating income.[8]

From Allied's income statement, we see that its operating income increased from $263.0 million in 2013 to $283.8 million in 2014, or by $20.8 million. However, its 2014 net income declined. This decline occurred because it increased its debt in 2014, and the $28 million increase in interest lowered its net income.

Taking a closer look at the income statement, we see that depreciation and amortization are important components of operating costs. Recall from accounting

---

[8]Operating income is important for several reasons. Managers are generally compensated based on the performance of the units they manage. A division manager can control his or her division's performance but not the firm's capital structure policy or other corporate decisions. Second, if one firm is considering acquiring another, it will be interested in the value of the target firm's operations; that value is determined by the target firm's operating income. Third, operating income is normally more stable than total income, as total income can be heavily influenced by write-offs of bonds backed by subprime mortgages and the like. Therefore, analysts focus on operating income when they estimate firms' long-run stock values.

that **depreciation** is an annual charge against income that reflects the estimated dollar cost of the capital equipment and other tangible assets that were depleted in the production process. **Amortization** amounts to the same thing except that it represents the decline in value of intangible assets such as patents, copyrights, trademarks, and goodwill. Because depreciation and amortization are so similar, they are generally lumped together for purposes of financial analysis on the income statement and for other purposes. They both write off, or allocate, the costs of assets over their useful lives.

Even though depreciation and amortization are reported as costs on the income statements, they are not cash expenses—cash was spent in the past, when the assets being written off were acquired, but no cash is paid out to cover depreciation and amortization. Therefore, managers, security analysts, and bank loan officers who are concerned with the amount of cash a company is generating often calculate **EBITDA**, an acronym for earnings before interest, taxes, depreciation, and amortization. Allied has no amortization charges, so Allied's depreciation and amortization expense consists entirely of depreciation. In 2014, Allied's EBITDA was $383.8 million.

While the balance sheet represents a snapshot in time, the income statement reports on operations *over a period of time.* For example, during 2014, Allied had sales of $3 billion and its net income was $117.5 million. Income statements are prepared monthly, quarterly, and annually. The quarterly and annual statements are reported to investors, while the monthly statements are used internally by managers for planning and control purposes.

Finally, note that the income statement is tied to the balance sheet through the retained earnings account on the balance sheet. Net income as reported on the income statement less dividends paid is the retained earnings for the year (e.g., 2014). Those retained earnings are added to the cumulative retained earnings from prior years to obtain the year-end 2014 balance for retained earnings. The retained earnings for the year are also reported in the statement of stockholders' equity. All four of the statements provided in the annual report are interrelated.

Depreciation
The charge to reflect the cost of assets depleted in the production process. Depreciation is not a cash outlay.

Amortization
A noncash charge similar to depreciation except that it represents a decline in value of intangible assets.

EBITDA
Earnings before interest, taxes, depreciation, and amortization.

SELF TEST

Why is earnings per share called "the bottom line"? What is EBIT, or operating income?

What is EBITDA?

Which is more like a snapshot of the firm's operations—the balance sheet or the income statement? Explain your answer.

3-4 STATEMENT OF CASH FLOWS

Net income as reported on the income statement is not cash; and in finance, "cash is king." Management's goal is to maximize the price of the firm's stock; and the value of any asset, including a share of stock, is based on the cash flows the asset is expected to produce. Therefore, managers strive to maximize the cash flows available to investors. The **statement of cash flows** as shown in Table 3.3 is the accounting report that shows how much cash the firm is generating. The statement is divided into four sections, and we explain it on a line-by-line basis.[9]

Statement of Cash Flows
A report that shows how items that affect the balance sheet and income statement affect the firm's cash flows.

---

[9]Allied's statement of cash flows is relatively simple because it is a relatively uncomplicated company. Many cash flow statements are more complex; but if you understand Table 3.3, you should be able to follow more complex statements.

TABLE 3.3 Allied Food Products: Statement of Cash Flows for 2014 (Millions of Dollars)

		2014
a.	**I. Operating Activities**	
b.	Net income	$117.5
c.	Depreciation and amortization	100.0
d.	Increase in inventories	(200.0)
e.	Increase in accounts receivable	(60.0)
f.	Increase in accounts payable	30.0
g.	Increase in accrued wages and taxes	10.0
h.	Net cash provided by (used in) operating activities	($ 2.5)
i.	**II. Long-Term Investing Activities**	
j.	Additions to property, plant, and equipment	($230.0)
k.	Net cash used in investing activities	($230.0)
l.	**III. Financing Activities**	
m.	Increase in notes payable	$ 50.0
n.	Increase in bonds	170.0
o.	Payment of dividends to stockholders	(57.5)
p.	Net cash provided by financing activities	$162.5
q.	**IV. Summary**	
r.	Net decrease in cash (Net sum of 1, II, and III)	($ 70.0)
s.	Cash and equivalents at the beginning of the year	80.0
t.	Cash and equivalents at the end of the year	$ 10.0

© Cengage Learning 2015

Note: Here and throughout the book parentheses are sometimes used to denote negative numbers.

Here is a line-by-line explanation of the statement shown in Table 3.3:

a. *Operating activities.* This section deals with items that occur as part of normal ongoing operations.

b. *Net income.* The first operating activity is net income, which is the first source of cash. If all sales were for cash, if all costs required immediate cash payments, and if the firm were in a static situation, net income would equal cash from operations. However, these conditions don't hold, so net income is not equal to cash from operations. Adjustments shown in the remainder of the statement must be made.

c. *Depreciation and amortization.* The first adjustment relates to depreciation and amortization. Allied's accountants subtracted depreciation (it has no amortization expense), which is a noncash charge, when they calculated net income. Therefore, depreciation must be added back to net income when cash flow is determined.

d. *Increase in inventories.* To make or buy inventory items, the firm must use cash. It may receive some of this cash as loans from its suppliers and workers (payables and accruals); but ultimately, any increase in inventories requires cash. Allied increased its inventories by $200 million in 2014. That amount is shown in parentheses on Line d because it is negative (i.e., a use of cash). If Allied had reduced its inventories, it would have generated positive cash.

e. *Increase in accounts receivable.* If Allied chooses to sell on credit when it makes a sale, it will not immediately get the cash that it would have received had it not extended credit. To stay in business, it must replace the inventory that it sold on credit; but it won't yet have received cash from the credit sale. So if the firm's accounts receivable increase, this will amount to a use of cash. Allied's receivables rose by $60 million in 2014, and that use of cash is shown as a negative number on Line e. If Allied had reduced its receivables, this would be shown as a positive cash flow. (Once cash is received for the sale, the accompanying accounts receivable will be eliminated.)

f. *Increase in accounts payable.* Accounts payable represent a loan from suppliers. Allied bought goods on credit, and its payables increased by $30 million this year. That is treated as a $30 million increase in cash on Line f. If Allied had reduced its payables, that would have required, or used, cash. Note that as Allied grows, it will purchase more inventories. That will give rise to additional payables, which will reduce the amount of new outside funds required to finance inventory growth.

g. *Increase in accrued wages and taxes.* The same logic applies to accruals as to accounts payable. Allied's accruals increased by $10 million this year, which means that in 2014, it borrowed an additional $10 million from its workers and tax authorities. So this represents a $10 million cash inflow.

h. *Net cash provided by operating activities.* All of the previous items are part of normal operations—they arise as a result of doing business. When we sum them, we obtain the net cash flow from operations. Allied had positive flows from net income, depreciation, and increases in payables and accruals; but it used cash to increase inventories and to carry receivables. The net result was that operations led to a $2.5 million net cash outflow.

i. *Long-term investing activities.* All activities involving long-term assets are covered in this section. Allied had only one long-term investment activity—the acquisition of some fixed assets, as shown on Line j. If Allied had sold some fixed assets, its accountants would have reported it in this section as a positive amount (i.e., as a cash inflow).

j. *Additions to property, plant, and equipment.* Allied spent $230 million on fixed assets during the current year. This is an outflow; therefore, it is shown in parentheses. If Allied had sold some of its fixed assets, this would have been a cash inflow.[10]

k. *Net cash used in investing activities.* Because Allied had only one investment activity, the total on this line is the same as that on the previous line.

l. *Financing activities.* Allied's financing activities are shown in this section.

m. *Increase in notes payable.* Allied borrowed an additional $50 million from its bank this year, which was a cash inflow. When Allied repays the loan, this will be an outflow.

n. *Increase in bonds (long-term debt).* Allied borrowed an additional $170 million from long-term investors this year, issuing bonds in exchange for cash. This is shown as an inflow. When the bonds are repaid by the firm some years hence, this will be an outflow.

o. *Payment of dividends to stockholders.* Dividends are paid in cash, and the $57.5 million that Allied paid to stockholders is shown as a negative amount.

p. *Net cash provided by financing activities.* The sum of the three financing entries, which is a positive $162.5 million, is shown here. These funds were used to help pay for the $230 million of new plant and equipment and to help cover the deficit resulting from operations.

---

[10]The number on Line j is "gross" investment, or total expenditures. It is also equal to the change in net plant and equipment (from the balance sheet) plus depreciation as shown on Line c: Gross investment = Net investment + Depreciation = $130 + $100 = $230.

MASSAGING THE CASH FLOW STATEMENT

Profits as reported on the income statement can be "massaged" by changes in depreciation methods, inventory valuation procedures, and so on, but "cash is cash," so management can't mess with the cash flow statement, right? Nope—wrong. A 2005 article in *The Wall Street Journal* ("Little Campus Lab Shakes Big Firms") described how Ford, General Motors, and several other companies overstated their operating cash flows, the most important section of the cash flow statement. Indeed, GM reported more than twice as much cash from operations as it really generated, $7.6 billion versus a true $3.5 billion. When GM sold cars to a dealer on credit, it created an account receivable, which should be shown in the "Operating Activities" section as a use of cash. However, GM classified these receivables as loans to dealers and reported them as a financing activity. That decision more than doubled its reported cash flow from operations. It didn't affect the end-of-year cash balance, but it made operations look stronger than they really were.

If Allied Foods, in Table 3.3, had done this, the $60 million increase in receivables, which is correctly shown as a use of cash, would have been shifted to the "Financing Activities" section, causing Allied's cash provided by operations to rise from −$2.5 million to +$57.5 million. That would have made Allied look better to investors and credit analysts, but it would have been just smoke and mirrors.

GM's treatment was first reported by Charles Mulford, a professor at Georgia Tech. The SEC then sent GM a letter requiring it to change its procedures. The company issued a statement saying it thought that it was acting in accordance with GAAP but that it would reclassify its accounts in the future. GM's action was not in the league of WorldCom's or Enron's fraudulent accounting practices, but it does show that companies sometimes do things to make their statements look better than they really are.

Source: Diya Gullapalli, "Little Campus Lab Shakes Big Firms," *The Wall Street Journal*, March 1, 2005, p. C3.

q. *Summary.* This section summarizes the change in cash and cash equivalents over the year.

r. *Net decrease in cash.* The net sum of the operating activities, investing activities, and financing activities is shown here. These activities resulted in a $70 million net decrease in cash during 2014, mainly due to expenditures on new fixed assets.

s. *Cash and equivalents at the beginning of the year.* Allied began the year with $80 million of cash, which is shown here.

t. *Cash and equivalents at the end of the year.* Allied ended the year with $10 million of cash, the $80 million it started with minus the $70 million net decrease that occurred during the year. Clearly, Allied's cash position is weaker than it was at the beginning of the year.

Allied's statement of cash flows should be of concern to its managers and investors. The company was able to cover the small operating deficit and the large investment in fixed assets by borrowing and reducing its beginning balances of cash and equivalents. However, the firm can't continue to do this indefinitely. In the long run, Section I needs to show positive operating cash flows. In addition, we would expect Section II to show expenditures on fixed assets that are about equal to (1) its depreciation charges (to replace worn out fixed assets) along with (2) some additional expenditures to provide for growth. Section III would normally show some net borrowing in addition to a "reasonable" amount of dividends.[11] Finally, Section IV should show a reasonably stable year-to-year cash balance. These conditions don't hold for Allied, so some actions should be taken to correct the situation. We will consider corrective actions in Chapter 4, when we analyze the firm's financial statements.

---

[11]The average company pays out about one third of its earnings as dividends, but there is a great deal of variation between companies depending on each company's needs for retained earnings to support growth. We cover dividends in detail in Chapter 14.

What is the statement of cash flows, and what are some questions it answers?

Identify and briefly explain the four sections shown in the statement of cash flows.

If during the year a company has high cash flows from its operations, does this mean that cash on its balance sheet will be higher at the end of the year than it was at the beginning of the year? Explain.

3-5 STATEMENT OF STOCKHOLDERS' EQUITY

Changes in stockholders' equity during the accounting period are reported in the **statement of stockholders' equity**. Table 3.4 shows that Allied earned $117.5 million during 2014, paid out $57.5 million in common dividends, and plowed $60 million back into the business. Thus, the balance sheet item "Retained earnings" increased from $750 million at year-end 2013 to $810 million at year-end 2014.[12]

Note that "retained earnings" represents a *claim against assets,* not assets per se. Stockholders allow management to retain earnings and reinvest them in the business, use retained earnings for additions to plant and equipment, add to inventories, and the like. Companies *do not* just pile up cash in a bank account. *Thus, retained earnings as reported on the balance sheet do not represent cash and are not "available" for dividends or anything else.*[13]

Statement of Stockholders' Equity
A statement that shows by how much a firm's equity changed during the year and why this change occurred.

Allied Food Products: Statement of Stockholders' Equity, December 31, 2014 (Millions of Dollars)				**TABLE 3.4**
	COMMON STOCK			
	Shares (000)	**Amount**	**Retained Earnings**	**Total Stockholders' Equity**
Balances, December 31, 2013	50,000	$130.0	$750.0	$880.0
2014 Net income			117.5	
Cash dividends			(57.5)	
Addition to retained earnings				60.0
Balances, December 31, 2014	50,000	$130.0	$810.0	$940.0

© Cengage Learning 2015

[12]If they had been applicable, columns would have been used to show Additional Paid-in Capital and Treasury Stock. Also, additional rows would have contained information on such things as new issues of stock, treasury stock acquired or reissued, stock options exercised, and unrealized foreign exchange gains or losses.
[13]Cash (as of the balance sheet date) is found in the cash account, an asset account. A positive number in the retained earnings account indicates only that the firm has in the past earned income and has not paid it all out as dividends. Even though a company reports record earnings and shows an increase in retained earnings, it still may be short of cash if it is using its available cash to purchase current and fixed assets to support growth. The same situation holds for individuals. You might own a new BMW (no loan), many clothes, and an expensive stereo (hence, have a high net worth); but if you had only $0.23 in your pocket plus $5.00 in your checking account, you would still be short of cash.

What information does the statement of stockholders' equity provide?

Why do changes in retained earnings occur?

Explain why the following statement is true: The retained earnings account reported on the balance sheet does not represent cash and is not "available" for dividend payments or anything else.

3-6 USES AND LIMITATIONS OF FINANCIAL STATEMENTS

As we mentioned in the opening vignette to this chapter, financial statements provide a great deal of useful information. You can inspect the statements and answer a number of important questions such as these: How large is the company? Is it growing? Is it making or losing money? Is it generating cash through its operations or are operations actually losing cash?

At the same time, investors need to be cautious when they review financial statements. While companies are required to follow GAAP, managers still have a lot of discretion in deciding how and when to report certain transactions. (For an example, see the box in Section 3-4, "Massaging the Cash Flow Statement," on GM's treatment of receivables.)

Consequently, two firms in exactly the same situation may report financial statements that convey different impressions about their financial strength. Some variations may stem from legitimate differences of opinion about the correct way to record transactions. In other cases, managers may choose to report numbers in a manner that helps them present either higher or more stable earnings over time. As long as they follow GAAP, such actions are legal, but these differences make it difficult for investors to compare companies and gauge their true performances. In particular, watch out if senior managers receive bonuses or other compensation based on earnings in the short run—they may try to boost short-term reported income to boost their bonuses.

Unfortunately, there have also been cases where managers disregarded GAAP and reported fraudulent statements. One blatant example of cheating involved WorldCom, which reported asset values that exceeded their true value by about $11 billion. This led to an understatement of costs and a corresponding overstatement of profits. Enron is another high-profile example. It overstated the value of certain assets, reported those artificial value increases as profits, and transferred the assets to subsidiary companies to hide the true facts. Enron's and WorldCom's investors eventually learned what was happening, the companies were forced into bankruptcy, many of their top executives went to jail, the accounting firm that audited their books was forced out of business, and investors lost billions of dollars.

After the Enron and WorldCom fiascos, Congress in 2002 passed the Sarbanes–Oxley Act (SOX), which required companies to improve their internal auditing standards and required the CEO and CFO to certify that the financial statements were properly prepared. The SOX bill also created a new watchdog organization to help make sure that the outside accounting firms were doing their jobs.

More recently, a serious debate has arisen regarding the appropriate accounting for complicated investments held by financial institutions. In the recent financial crisis, many of these investments (particularly those related to subprime mortgages) turned out to be worth a lot less than their stated book value.

Currently, regulators and other policy makers are struggling to come up with the best way to account for and regulate many of these "toxic assets."[14]

Finally, keep in mind that even if investors receive accurate accounting data, it is cash flows, not accounting income, that matters most. Similarly, as we shall see in Chapters 11 and 12, when managers make capital budgeting decisions on which projects to accept, their focus should be on cash flow.

SELF TEST

Can investors be confident that if the financial statements of different companies are accurate and are prepared in accordance with GAAP, that the data reported by one company will be comparable to the data provided by another?

Why might different companies account for similar transactions in different ways?

3-7 FREE CASH FLOW

Thus far, we have focused on financial statements as they are prepared by accountants. However, accounting statements are designed primarily for use by creditors and tax collectors, not for managers and stock analysts. Therefore, corporate decision makers and security analysts often modify accounting data to meet their needs. The most important modification is the concept of **free cash flow (FCF)**, defined as "the amount of cash that could be withdrawn without harming a firm's ability to operate and to produce future cash flows." Here is the equation used to calculate free cash flow:

$$\text{FCF} = \left[\text{EBIT}(1 - \text{T}) + \begin{matrix} \text{Depreciation} \\ \text{and amortization} \end{matrix} \right] - \left[\begin{matrix} \text{Capital} \\ \text{expenditures} \end{matrix} + \begin{matrix} \Delta \text{Net operating} \\ \text{working capital} \end{matrix} \right] \qquad \textbf{3.3}$$

Free Cash Flow (FCF)
The amount of cash that could be withdrawn without harming a firm's ability to operate and to produce future cash flows.

The first term represents the amount of cash that the firm generates from its current operations. EBIT (1 − T) is often referred to as **NOPAT, or net operating profit after taxes**. Depreciation and amortization are added back because these are noncash expenses that reduce EBIT but do not reduce the amount of cash the company has available to pay its investors. The second bracketed term indicates the amount of cash that the company is investing in its fixed assets (capital expenditures) and operating working capital in order to sustain ongoing operations. A positive level of FCF indicates that the firm is generating more than enough cash to finance current investments in fixed assets and working capital. By contrast, negative free cash flow means that the company does not have sufficient internal funds to finance investments in fixed assets and working capital, and that it will have to raise new money in the capital markets in order to pay for these investments.

Net Operating Profit After Taxes (NOPAT)
The profit a company would generate if it had no debt and held only operating assets.

Consider the case of Home Depot. The first bracketed term in Equation 3.3 represents the amount of cash that Home Depot is generating from its existing stores. The second bracketed term represents the amount of cash that the company is spending this period to construct new stores. When Home Depot opens a new store it needs cash to purchase the land and construct the building—these are capital expenditures and they lead to a

---

[14]On May 12, 2011, the FASB and IASB jointly issued new guidance regarding how fair value measurement should be applied where its use is already required. It does not extend the use of fair value accounting.

corresponding increase in the firm's fixed assets on the balance sheet. However, when it opens a new store the company also needs to increase its net operating working capital. In particular, the company needs to stock the store with new inventory. Part of this inventory may be financed through accounts payable—for example, a supplier might ship Home Depot some flashlights today and allow Home Depot to pay for them later. In this case, there would be no increase in net operating working capital because the increase in current assets exactly equals the increase in current liabilities. Other portions of their inventory may not have an offsetting accounts payable, so there will be an increase in net operating working capital, and the company must come up with the cash today in order to pay for this increase. Putting everything together, the company as a whole is generating positive free cash flow if the money generated from operating existing stores exceeds the money required to build new stores.

Looking at Allied's key financial statements, we can collect the pieces that we need to calculate its free cash flow. First, we can obtain Allied's EBIT and depreciation and amortization expense from the income statement. Looking at Table 3.2, we see that Allied's 2014 operating income (EBIT) was $283.8 million. Because Allied's tax rate is 40%, it follows that its $NOPAT = EBIT(1 - T) = \$283.8(1 - 0.4) = \$170.3$ million. We also see that Allied's depreciation and amortization expense in 2014 was $100 million.

Allied's capital expenditures (the cash used to purchase new fixed assets) can be found under the investment activities on the Statement of Cash Flows. Looking at Table 3.3, we see that Allied's capital expenditures in 2014 totaled $230 million.[15] Finally, we need to calculate the change in net operating working capital (ΔNOWC). Recall that NOWC is current assets minus non-interest-bearing current liabilities (where non-interest-bearing current liabilities are calculated as current liabilities minus notes payable). We showed earlier that Allied's NOWC for 2014 was:

$$NOWC_{2014} = \$1,000 - (\$310 - \$110) = \$800 \text{ million}$$

Likewise, its NOWC for 2013 can be calculated as:

$$NOWC_{2013} = \$810 - (\$220 - \$60) = \$650 \text{ million}$$

Thus, Allied's change in net operating working capital (ΔNOWC) = $150 million ($800 million − $650 million). Putting everything together, we can now calculate Allied's 2014 free cash flow:

$$FCF = \left[EBIT(1 - T) + \begin{array}{c} \text{Depreciation} \\ \text{and amortization} \end{array} \right] - \left[\begin{array}{c} \text{Capital} \\ \text{expenditures} \end{array} + \begin{array}{c} \Delta\text{Net operating} \\ \text{working capital} \end{array} \right]$$

$$FCF_{2014} = [\$170.3 + \$100] - [\$230 + \$150]$$
$$= -\$109.7 \text{ million}$$

Allied's FCF is negative, which is not good. Note, though, that the negative FCF is largely attributable to the $230 million expenditure for a new processing plant. This plant is large enough to meet production for several years, so another new plant will not be needed until 2018. Therefore, Allied's FCF for 2015 and the next few years should increase, which means that Allied's financial situation is not as bad as the negative FCF might suggest.

Most rapidly growing companies have negative FCFs—the fixed assets and working capital needed to support a firm's rapid growth generally exceed cash

---

[15]Alternatively, we can calculate Allied's capital expenditures by looking at changes in net fixed assets on the balance sheet between 2013 and 2014 and then adding back depreciation and amortization for 2014. In this example, Allied's net fixed assets increased $130 million (from $870 million in 2013 to $1 billion in 2014), and its depreciation and amortization totaled $100 million in 2014. Consequently, gross capital expenditures were $130 million + $100 million = $230 million.

flows from its existing operations. This is not bad, provided a firm's new investments are eventually profitable and contribute to its FCF.

QUICK QUESTION

QUESTION:
A company has EBIT of $30 million, depreciation of $5 million, and a 40% tax rate. It needs to spend $10 million on new fixed assets and $15 million to increase its current assets. It expects its accounts payable to increase by $2 million, its accruals to increase by $3 million, and its notes payable to increase by $8 million. The firm's current liabilities consist of only accounts payable, accruals, and notes payable. What is its free cash flow?

ANSWER:
First, you need to determine the ΔNet operating working capital(ΔNOWC):

ΔNOWC = ΔCurrent assets – (ΔCurrent liabilities – ΔNotes payable)
ΔNOWC = $15 – ($13 – $8)
ΔNOWC = $15 – $5 = $10 million.

FCF = [EBIT(1 − T) + Depreciation and amortization] − [Capital expenditures + ΔNOWC]
FCF = [$30(1 − 0.4) + $5] − [$10 + $10]
FCF = [$18 + $5] − $20
FCF = **$3 million**

FREE CASH FLOW IS IMPORTANT FOR BUSINESSES BOTH SMALL AND LARGE

Free cash flow is important to large companies like Allied Foods. Security analysts use FCF to help estimate the value of the stock, and Allied's managers use it to assess the value of proposed capital budgeting projects and potential merger candidates. Note, though, that the concept is also relevant for small businesses.

Assume that your aunt and uncle own a small pizza shop and that their accountant prepares their financial statements. The income statement shows their accounting profit for each year. While they are certainly interested in this number, what they probably care more about is how much money they can take out of the business each year to maintain their standard of living. Let's assume that the shop's net income for 2014 was $75,000. However, your aunt and uncle had to spend $50,000 to refurbish the kitchen and restrooms.

So while the business is generating a great deal of "profit," your aunt and uncle can't take much money out because they have to put money back into the pizza shop. Stated another way, their free cash flow is much less than their net income. The required investments could be so large that they even exceed the money made from selling pizza. In this case, your aunt and uncle's free cash flow would be negative. If so, this means they must find funds from other sources just to maintain their pizza business.

As astute business owners, your aunt and uncle recognize that their restaurant investments, such as updating the kitchen and restrooms, are nonrecurring; and if nothing else happens unexpectedly, your aunt and uncle should be able to take more cash out of the business in future years, when their free cash flow increases. But some businesses never seem to produce cash for their owners—they consistently generate positive net income, but this net income is swamped by the amount of cash that has to be plowed back into the business. Thus, when it comes to valuing the pizza shop (or any business small or large), what really matters is the amount of free cash flow that the business generates over time.

Looking ahead, your aunt and uncle face competition from national chains that are moving into the area. To meet the competition, your aunt and uncle will have to modernize the dining room. This will again drain cash from the business and reduce its free cash flow, although the hope is that it will enable them to increase sales and free cash flow in the years ahead. As we will see in Chapters 11 and 12 which cover capital budgeting, evaluating projects require us to estimate whether the future increases in free cash flow are sufficient to more than offset the initial project cost. Therefore, the free cash flow calculation is critical to a firm's capital budgeting analysis.

© Cengage Learning 2015

Many analysts regard FCF as being the single most important number that can be developed from accounting statements, even more important than net income. After all, FCF shows how much cash the firm can distribute to its investors. We will discuss FCF again in Chapter 9, which covers stock valuation, and in Chapters 11 and 12, which cover capital budgeting.

SELF TEST

What is free cash flow (FCF)?

Why is FCF an important determinant of a firm's value?

3-8 MVA AND EVA

Items reported on the financial statements reflect historical, in-the-past, values, not current market values, and there are often substantial differences between the two. Changes in interest rates and inflation affect the market value of the company's assets and liabilities but often have no effect on the corresponding book values shown in the financial statements. Perhaps, more importantly, the market's assessment of value takes into account its ongoing assessment of current operations as well as future opportunities. For example, it cost Microsoft very little to develop its first operating system, but that system turned out to be worth many billions that were not shown on its balance sheet. For a given level of debt, these increases in asset value also lead to a corresponding increase in the market value of equity.

To illustrate, consider the following situation. A firm was started with $1 million of assets at book value (historical cost), $500,000 of which was provided by bondholders, and $500,000 by stockholders (50,000 shares purchased at $10 per share). However, this firm became very successful; the market value of the firm's equity is now worth $19.5 million, and its current stock price is $19,500,000/50,000 = $390 per share. Clearly the firm's managers have done a marvelous job for the stockholders.

The accounting statements do not reflect market values, so they are not sufficient for purposes of evaluating managers' performance. To help fill this void, financial analysts have developed two additional performance measures, the first of which is **MVA**, or **Market Value Added**.[16] MVA is simply the difference between the market value of a firm's equity and the book value as shown on the balance sheet, with market value found by multiplying the stock price by the number of shares outstanding. For our hypothetical firm, MVA is $19.5 million − $0.5 million = $19 million.

Market Value Added (MVA)
The excess of the market value of equity over its book value.

For Allied, which has 50 million shares outstanding and a stock price of $23.06, the market value of the equity is $1,153 million versus a book value as shown on the balance sheet in Table 3.1 of $940 million. Therefore, Allied's MVA is $1,153 − $940 = $213 million. This $213 million represents the difference between the money Allied's stockholders have invested in the corporation since

---

[16]The concepts of EVA and MVA were developed by Joel Stern and Bennett Stewart, co-founders of the consulting firm Stern Stewart & Company. Stern Stewart copyrighted the terms "MVA" and "EVA," so other consulting firms have given other names to these values. Still, MVA and EVA are the terms most commonly used in practice. For more on MVA and EVA, see G. Bennett Stewart, *The Quest for Value* (New York: HarperCollins, 1991, 1999).

its founding—including retained earnings—versus the cash they could receive if they sold the business. The higher its MVA, the better the job management is doing for the firm's shareholders. Boards of directors often look at MVA when deciding on the compensation a firm's managers deserve. Note though, that just as all ships rise in a rising tide, most firms' stock prices rise in a rising stock market, so a positive MVA may not be entirely attributable to management performance.

A related concept, **Economic Value Added (EVA)**, sometimes called "economic profit," is closely related to MVA and is found as follows:[17]

Economic Value Added (EVA)
Excess of NOPAT over capital costs.

$$EVA = \begin{array}{c} \text{Net operating profit} \\ \text{after taxes} \\ \text{(NOPAT)} \end{array} - \begin{array}{c} \text{Annual dollar} \\ \text{cost of} \\ \text{capital} \end{array}$$

3.4

$$= \quad EBIT(1-T) \quad - \left(\begin{array}{c} \text{Total} \\ \text{invested} \\ \text{capital} \end{array} \times \begin{array}{c} \text{After-tax} \\ \text{percentage} \\ \text{cost of capital} \end{array} \right)$$

Companies create value (and realize positive EVA) if the benefits of their investments exceed the cost of raising the necessary capital. Total invested capital represents the amount of money that the company has raised from debt, equity, and any other sources of capital (such as preferred stock). The annual dollar cost of capital is total invested capital multiplied by the after-tax percentage cost of this capital. So, for example, if the company has raised $1 million in capital, and the current cost of capital is 10%, the annual dollar cost of capital would be $100,000. The funds raised from this capital are invested in a variety of net fixed assets and net operating working capital. In any given year, NOPAT is the amount of money that these investments have generated for the company's investors after paying for operating costs and taxes—in this regard it represents the benefits of capital investments.

EVA is an estimate of a business' true economic profit for a given year, and it often differs sharply from accounting net income. The main reason for this difference is that while accounting income takes into account the cost of debt (the company's interest expense), it does not deduct for the cost of equity capital. By contrast, EVA takes into account the total dollar cost of all capital which includes both the cost of debt and equity capital.

If EVA is positive, then after-tax operating income exceeds the cost of the capital needed to produce that income, and management's actions are adding value for stockholders. Positive EVA on an annual basis will help ensure that MVA is also positive. Note that whereas MVA applies to the entire firm, EVA can be determined for divisions as well as for the company as a whole, so it is useful as a guide to "reasonable" compensation for divisional as well as top corporate managers.

SELF TEST

Define the terms Market Value Added (MVA) and Economic Value Added (EVA).

How does EVA differ from accounting net income?

---

[17]Another top consulting company, McKinsey & Company, uses the term "economic profit." Their definition of economic profit is:

(Total invested capital) × (Return on invested capital − Cost of capital)

Because the return on invested capital is [EBIT(1 − T)]/Total invested capital, you can show with a little bit of algebra that EVA and economic profit are identical.

The IRS website is **www .irs.gov**. Here you can find current filing information and current credits and deductions information, and order needed forms and publications.

3-9 INCOME TAXES

Individuals and corporations pay out a significant portion of their income as taxes, so taxes are important in both personal and corporate decisions. We summarize the key aspects of the U.S. tax system for individuals in this section and for corporations in the next section, using 2013 data. The details of our tax laws change fairly often—annually for items that are indexed for inflation—but the basic nature of the tax system is likely to remain intact.

3-9A INDIVIDUAL TAXES

Individuals pay taxes on wages and salaries, on investment income (dividends, interest, and profits from the sale of securities), and on the profits of proprietorships and partnerships. The tax rates are **progressive**—that is, the higher one's income, the larger the percentage paid in taxes. Table 3.5 provides the 2013 tax rates that taxpayers will pay for tax returns due April 15, 2014.

Progressive

A tax system where the tax rate is higher on higher incomes. The personal income tax in the United States, which ranges from 0% on the lowest incomes to 39.6% on the highest incomes, is progressive.

Taxable income is defined as "gross income less a set of exemptions and deductions." When filing a tax return in 2014 for the tax year 2013, taxpayers received an exemption of $3,900 for each dependent, including the taxpayer, which reduces taxable income. However, this exemption is indexed to rise with inflation, and the exemption is phased out (taken away) for high-income taxpayers. Also, certain expenses, including mortgage interest paid, state and local income taxes paid, and charitable contributions, can be deducted and thus be used to reduce taxable income; but again, high-income taxpayers lose most of these deductions.

Marginal Tax Rate

The tax rate applicable to the last unit of a person's income.

The **marginal tax rate** is defined as "the tax rate on the last dollar of income." Marginal rates begin at 10% and rise to 39.6%. Note, though, that when consideration is given to the phase-out of exemptions and deductions, to Social Security and Medicare taxes, and to state taxes, the marginal tax rate may actually exceed 50%. Average tax rates can be calculated from the data in Table 3.5. For example, if a single individual had taxable income of $37,000, his or her tax bill would be $4,991.25 + ($37,000 − $36,250)(0.25) = $4,991.25 + $187.50 = $5,178.75. Her **average tax rate** would be $5,178.75/$37,000 = 14% versus a marginal rate of 25%. If she received a raise of $1,000, bringing her income to $38,000, she would have to pay $250 of it as taxes; so her after-tax raise would be $750.

Average Tax Rate

Taxes paid divided by taxable income.

Note too that *interest income* received by individuals from corporate securities is added to other income and thus is taxed at federal rates going up to 39.6%, plus state taxes.[18] *Capital gains and losses*, on the other hand, are treated differently. Assets such as stocks, bonds, and real estate are defined as *capital assets*. When you buy a capital asset and later sell it for more than you paid, you earn a profit that is called a **capital gain**; when you suffer a loss, it is called a **capital loss**. If you held the asset for a year or less, you will have a *short-term gain or loss*, while if you held it for more than a year, you will have a *long-term gain or loss*. Thus, if you buy 100 shares of Disney stock for $51 per share and sell them for $61 per share, you have a capital gain of 100 × $10, or $1,000. However, if you sell the stock for $41 per share, you will have a $1,000 capital loss. Depending on how long you hold the stock, you will have a short-term or long-term gain or loss.[19] If you sell the stock for exactly $51 per share, you make neither a gain nor a loss; so no tax is due.

Capital Gain or Loss

The profit (loss) from the sale of a capital asset for more (less) than its purchase price.

---

[18]Under U.S. tax laws, interest on most state and local government bonds, called municipals or "munis," is not subject to federal income taxes. This has a significant effect on the values of munis and on their rates of return. We discuss rates and returns in Chapter 8.

[19]If you have a *net* capital loss (your capital losses exceed your capital gains) for the year, you can deduct up to $3,000 of this loss against your other income (for example, salary, interest, and dividends).

Single Individuals

If Your Taxable Income Is	You Pay This Amount on the Base of the Bracket	Plus This Percentage on the Excess over the Base (Marginal Rate)	Average Tax Rate at Top of Bracket
Up to $8,925	$ 0	10.0%	10.0%
$8,925–$36,250	892.50	15.0	13.8
$36,250–$87,850	4,991.25	25.0	20.4
$87,850–$183,250	17,891.25	28.0	24.3
$183,250–$398,350	44,603.25	33.0	29.0
$398,350–$400,000	115,586.25	35.0	29.0
Over $400,000	116,163.75	39.6	39.6

Married Couples Filing Joint Returns

If Your Taxable Income Is	You Pay This Amount on the Base of the Bracket	Plus This Percentage on the Excess over the Base (Marginal Rate)	Average Tax Rate at Top of Bracket
Up to $17,850	$ 0	10.0%	10.0%
$17,850–$72,500	1,785.00	15.0	13.8
$72,500–$146,400	9,982.50	25.0	19.4
$146,400–$223,050	28,457.50	28.0	22.4
$223,050–$398,350	49,919.50	33.0	27.1
$398,350–$450,000	107,768.50	35.0	28.0
Over $450,000	125,846.00	39.6	39.6

© Cengage Learning 2015

Notes:
1. These are the 2013 tax rates that will be paid on tax returns due April 15, 2014. The income ranges at which each tax rate takes effect are indexed with inflation, so they change each year.
2. The average tax rates are always below the marginal rates, but in 2013 the average at the top of the brackets approaches 39.6% as taxable income rises without limit.
3. In 2013, a *personal exemption* of $3,900 per person or dependent could be deducted from gross income to determine taxable income. Thus, a husband and wife with two children would have a 2013 exemption of 4 × $3,900 = $15,600. The exemption increases with inflation, but if gross income exceeds certain limits, the exemption is phased out, and this has the effect of raising the effective tax rate on incomes over the specified limit. In addition, taxpayers can claim *itemized deductions* for charitable contributions and certain other items, but these deductions are also phased out for high-income taxpayers. In addition, there are Social Security and Medicare taxes. These additional situations and payroll taxes push the 2013 effective tax rate up well above 39.6%.

A short-term capital gain is taxed at the same rate as ordinary income. However, long-term capital gains are taxed differently. For most taxpayers, the rate on long-term capital gains is only 15%. Thus, if in 2013, you were in the 35% tax bracket, any short-term capital gains you earned would be taxed just like ordinary income; but your long-term capital gains would only be taxed at 15%. However, beginning in 2013, the maximum tax rate on long-term capital gains was increased to 20% for single taxpayers with incomes over $400,000 and married taxpayers with incomes over $450,000. But even for individuals at these top tax brackets, the tax rate on long-term capital gains still remains considerably lower than the tax rate on ordinary income.

Beginning in 2013, the maximum tax rate on *qualified dividends* increased to 20% for single taxpayers with incomes over $400,000 and married taxpayers with incomes over \$450,000.[20] However, for most taxpayers the top tax rate on qualified dividends is 15%. Because corporations pay dividends out of earnings that have already been taxed, there is *double taxation of corporate income*—income is first taxed at the corporate rate; and when what is left is paid out as dividends, it is taxed again. This double taxation motivated Congress to tax dividends at a lower rate than the rate on ordinary income.

Tax rates on dividends and capital gains have varied over time, but they have generally been lower than rates on ordinary income. Congress wants the economy to grow. For growth, we need investment in productive assets; and low capital gains and dividend tax rates encourage investment. Individuals with money to invest understand the tax advantages associated with making equity investments in newly formed companies versus buying bonds, so new ventures have an easier time attracting capital under the tax system. All in all, lower capital gains and dividend tax rates stimulate capital formation and investment.

One other tax feature should be addressed—the **Alternative Minimum Tax (AMT)**. The AMT was created in 1969 because Congress learned that 155 millionaires with high incomes paid no taxes because they had so many tax shelters from items such as depreciation on real estate and municipal bond interest. Under the AMT law, people must calculate their tax under the "regular" system and then under the AMT system, where many deductions are added back to income and then taxed at a special AMT rate. For many years, the AMT was not indexed for inflation; and literally millions of taxpayers found themselves subject to this very complex tax.[21]

The new tax legislation also increased health care taxes for single taxpayers earning more than \$200,000 and married taxpayers earning more than \$250,000. These taxpayers will incur an additional 0.9% Medicare tax and a 3.8% investment income tax on certain types of investment income.

Alternative Minimum Tax (AMT)

Created by Congress to make it more difficult for wealthy individuals to avoid paying taxes through the use of various deductions.

3-9B CORPORATE TAXES

The corporate tax structure, shown in Table 3.6, is relatively simple. To illustrate, if a firm had \$65,000 of taxable income, its tax bill would be \$11,250.

$$\text{Taxes} = \$7,500 + 0.25(\$15,000)$$
$$= \$7,500 + \$3,750 = \$11,250$$

Its average tax rate would be \$11,250/\$65,000 = 17.3%. Note that corporate income above \$18,333,333 has an average and marginal tax rate of 35%.

Interest and Dividends Received by a Corporation

Corporations earn most of their income from operations, but they may also own securities—bonds and stocks—and receive interest and dividend income. Interest income received by a corporation is taxed as ordinary income at regular corporate tax rates. *However, dividends are taxed more favorably: 70% of dividends received is excluded from taxable income, while the remaining 30% is taxed at the ordinary tax rate.*[22]

---

[20]For a dividend to be "qualified," the investor must have owned the stock for more than 60 days during a 121-day period that begins 60 days prior to the ex-dividend date. We discuss dividends in Chapter 14; however, for now understand that the ex-dividend date is the date when the right to the current dividend leaves the stock.

[21]Beginning in 2013, the AMT exemption amounts are indexed to inflation. In 2013, the AMT exemption amounts are \$51,900 for single taxpayers, \$80,800 for those married and filing jointly, and \$40,400 for those married and filing separately. The corporate AMT exemption is \$40,000 and is phased out with alternative minimum taxable income between \$150,000 and \$310,000.

[22]The exclusion depends on the percentage of the paying company's stock the receiving company owns. If it owns 100% (hence, the payer is a subsidiary), all of the dividend will be excluded. If it owns less than 20%, which is the case if the stock held is just an investment, 70% will be excluded. Also, state tax rules vary; but in our example, we assume that Allied also has a state tax exclusion.

If a Corporation's Taxable Income Is	It Pays This Amount on the Base of the Bracket	Plus This Percentage on the Excess over the Base (Marginal Rate)	Average Tax Rate at Top of Bracket
Up to $50,000	$ 0	15%	15.0%
$50,000–$75,000	7,500	25	18.3
$75,000–$100,000	13,750	34	22.3
$100,000–$335,000	22,250	39	34.0
$335,000–$10,000,000	113,900	34	34.0
$10,000,000–$15,000,000	3,400,000	35	34.3
$15,000,000–$18,333,333	5,150,000	38	35.0
Over $18,333,333	6,416,667	35	35.0

2013 Corporate Tax Rates **TABLE 3.6**

© Cengage Learning 2015

Thus, a corporation earning more than $18,333,333 and paying a 40% marginal federal plus state tax rate would normally pay only $(0.30)(0.4) = 0.12 = 12\%$ of its dividend income as taxes. If this firm had $10,000 in pretax (B-T) dividend income, its after-tax (A-T) dividend income would be $8,800.

$$\text{A-T income} = \text{B-T income}(1 - T) = \$10,000(1 - 0.12) = \$8,800$$

The rationale behind this exclusion is that when a corporation receives dividends and then pays out its own after-tax income as dividends to its stockholders, the dividends received are subjected to triple taxation: (1) The original corporation is taxed, (2) the second corporation is taxed on the dividends it receives, and (3) the individuals who receive the final dividends are taxed again. This explains the 70% intercorporate dividend exclusion.

Suppose a firm has excess cash that it does not need for operations, and it plans to invest this cash in marketable securities. The tax factor favors stocks, which pay dividends, rather than bonds, which pay interest. For example, suppose Allied had $100,000 to invest, and it could buy bonds that paid 8% interest, or $8,000 per year, or stock that paid 7% in dividends, or $7,000. Allied is in the 40% federal-plus-state tax bracket. Therefore, if Allied bought bonds and received interest, its tax on the $8,000 of interest would be $0.4(\$8,000) = \$3,200$ and its after-tax income would be $4,800. If it bought stock, its tax would be $\$7,000(0.12) = \$840$ and its after-tax income would be $6,160. *Other factors might lead Allied to invest in bonds, but when the investor is a corporation the tax factor favors stock investments.*

Interest and Dividends Paid by a Corporation

A firm like Allied can finance its operations with either debt or stock. If a firm uses debt, it must pay interest, whereas if it uses stock, it is expected to pay dividends. *Interest paid can be deducted from operating income to obtain taxable income, but dividends paid cannot be deducted.* Therefore, Allied would need $1 of pretax income to pay $1 of interest; but because it is in the 40% federal-plus-state tax bracket, it must earn $1.67 of pretax income to pay $1 of dividends:

$$\frac{\text{Pretax income needed}}{\text{to pay \$1 of dividends}} = \frac{\$1}{1 - \text{Tax rate}} = \frac{\$1}{0.60} = \$1.67$$

Working backward, if Allied has $1.67 in pretax income, it must pay $0.67 in taxes $[(0.4)(\$1.67) = \$0.67]$. This leaves it with after-tax income of $1.00.

TABLE 3.7 Returns to Investors under Bond and Stock Financing

	Use Bonds (1)	Use Stocks (2)
Sales	$5,000,000	$5,000,000
Operating costs	3,500,000	3,500,000
Earnings before interest and taxes (EBIT)	$1,500,000	$1,500,000
Interest	1,500,000	0
Taxable income	$　　0	$1,500,000
Federal-plus-state taxes (40%)	0	600,000
After-tax income	$　　0	$ 900,000
Income to investors	$1,500,000	$ 900,000
Rate of return on $10 million of assets	15.0%	9.0%

© Cengage Learning 2015

Table 3.7 shows the situation for a firm with $10 million of assets, sales of $5 million, and $1.5 million of earnings before interest and taxes (EBIT). As shown in Column 1, if the firm were financed entirely by bonds and if it made interest payments of $1.5 million, its taxable income would be zero, taxes would be zero, and its investors would receive the entire $1.5 million. (The term *investors* includes both stockholders and bondholders.) However, as shown in Column 2, if the firm had no debt and was therefore financed entirely by stock, all of the $1.5 million of EBIT would be taxable income to the corporation, the tax would be $1,500,000(0.40) = $600,000, and investors would receive only $0.9 million versus $1.5 million under debt financing. Therefore, the rate of return to investors on their $10 million investment is much higher when debt is used.

Of course, it is generally not possible to finance exclusively with debt; and the risk of doing so would offset the benefits of the higher expected income. *Still, the fact that interest is a deductible expense has a profound effect on the way businesses are financed—the corporate tax system favors debt financing over equity financing.* This point is discussed in more detail in Chapters 10 and 13.[23]

Corporate Capital Gains

Before 1987, corporate long-term capital gains were taxed at lower rates than corporate ordinary income; so the situation was similar for corporations and individuals. Currently, though, corporations' capital gains are taxed at the same rates as their operating income.

Corporate Loss Carry-Back and Carry-Forward

Ordinary corporate operating losses can be carried back **(carry-back)** to each of the preceding 2 years and carried forward **(carry-forward)** for the next 20 years and used to offset taxable income in those years. For example, an operating loss in 2014 could be carried back and used to reduce taxable income in 2012 and 2013; it also could be carried forward, if necessary, and used in 2015, 2016, up until 2034. The loss is applied to the earliest year first, then to the next earliest year, and so forth, until losses have been used up or the 20-year carry-forward limit has been reached.

Tax Loss Carry-Back or Carry-Forward

Ordinary corporate operating losses can be carried backward for 2 years and carried forward for 20 years to offset taxable income in a given year.

---

[23]A company could, in theory, refrain from paying dividends to help prevent its stockholders from having to pay taxes on dividends received. The IRS has a rule against the *improper accumulation of retained earnings.* However, in our experience, it is easy for firms to justify retaining earnings; and we have never seen a firm have a problem with the improper accumulation rule.

	TABLE 3.8
Calculation of Loss Carry-Back and Carry-Forward for 2012–2013 Using a $12 Million 2014 Loss	

	2012	2013
Original taxable income	$ 2,000,000	$2,000,000
Carry-back credit	−2,000,000	−2,000,000
Adjusted profit	$ 0	$ 0
Taxes previously paid (40%)	800,000	800,000
Difference = Tax refund	$ 800,000	$ 800,000

Total refund check received in 2015: $800,000 + $800,000 = $1,600,000.

Amount of loss carry-forward available for use in 2015–2034:

2014 loss	$12,000,000
Carry-back losses used	4,000,000
Carry-forward losses still available	$ 8,000,000

© Cengage Learning 2015

To illustrate, suppose Company X had $2 million of pretax profits (taxable income) in 2012 and 2013 and then in 2014, it lost $12 million. Its federal-plus-state tax rate is 40%. As shown in Table 3.8, Company X would use the carry-back feature to recompute its taxes for 2012, using $2 million of the 2014 operating losses to reduce the 2012 pretax profit to zero. This would permit it to recover the taxes paid in 2012. Therefore, in 2014, it would receive a refund of its 2012 taxes because of the loss experienced in 2014. Because $10 million of the unrecovered losses would still be available, X would repeat this procedure for 2013. Thus, in 2014, the company would pay zero taxes for 2014 and would receive a refund for taxes paid in 2012 and 2013. It would still have $8 million of unrecovered losses to carry forward, subject to the 20-year limit. This $8 million could be used until the entire $12 million loss had been used to offset taxable income. The purpose of permitting this loss treatment is to avoid penalizing corporations whose incomes fluctuate substantially from year to year.

Consolidated Corporate Tax Returns

If a corporation owns 80% or more of another corporation's stock, it can aggregate income and file one consolidated tax return. This allows the losses of one company to be used to offset the profits of another. (Similarly, one division's losses can be used to offset another division's profits.) No business wants to incur losses; but tax offsets make it more feasible for large, multidivisional corporations to undertake risky new ventures or ventures that will suffer losses during a developmental period.

Taxation of Small Businesses: S Corporations

As we noted in Chapter 1, the Tax Code allows small businesses that meet certain conditions to be set up as corporations and thus receive the benefits of the corporate form of organization—especially limited liability—yet still be taxed as proprietorships or partnerships rather than as corporations. These corporations are called **S corporations**. (Regular corporations are called C corporations.) If a corporation elects to set up as an S corporation, all of its income is reported as personal income by its stockholders, on a pro rata basis, and thus is taxed at the stockholders' individual rates. Because the income is taxed only once, this is an important benefit to the owners of small corporations in which all or most of the

S Corporation
A small corporation that, under Subchapter S of the Internal Revenue Code, elects to be taxed as a proprietorship or a partnership yet retains limited liability and other benefits of the corporate form of organization.

income earned each year will be distributed as dividends. The situation is similar for LLCs.

Depreciation

Depreciation plays an important role in income tax calculations—the larger the depreciation, the lower the taxable income, the lower the tax bill, and thus the higher the operating cash flow. Congress specifies the life over which assets can be depreciated for tax purposes and the depreciation methods that can be used. We will discuss in detail how depreciation is calculated and how it affects income and cash flows when we study capital budgeting.

SELF TEST

Explain this statement: Our tax rates are progressive.

What's the difference between marginal and average tax rates?

What's the AMT, and what is its purpose?

What's a muni bond, and how are these bonds taxed?

What are long-term capital gains? Are they taxed like other income? Explain.

How does our tax system influence the use of debt financing by corporations?

What is the logic behind allowing tax loss carry-backs/carry-forwards?

Differentiate between S and C corporations.

TYING IT ALL TOGETHER

The primary purposes of this chapter were to describe the basic financial statements, to present background information on cash flows, to differentiate between cash flow and accounting income, and to provide an overview of the federal income tax system. In the next chapter, we build on this information to analyze a firm's financial statements and to determine its financial health.

SELF-TEST QUESTIONS AND PROBLEMS

(Solutions Appear in Appendix A)

ST-1 **KEY TERMS** Define each of the following terms:
  a. Annual report; balance sheet; income statement; statement of cash flows; statement of stockholders' equity
  b. Stockholders' equity; retained earnings; working capital; net working capital; net operating working capital (NOWC); total debt
  c. Depreciation; amortization; operating income; EBITDA; free cash flow (FCF)
  d. Net operating profit after taxes (NOPAT)

    e.   Market value added (MVA); economic value added (EVA)

    f.   Progressive tax; marginal tax rate; average tax rate

    g.   Tax loss carry-back; carry-forward; alternative minimum tax (AMT)

    h.   Capital gain (loss)

    i.   S corporation

ST-2   **NET INCOME AND CASH FLOW**   Last year Rattner Robotics had $5 million in operating income (EBIT). Its depreciation expense was $1 million, its interest expense was $1 million, and its corporate tax rate was 40%. At year-end, it had $14 million in current assets, $3 million in accounts payable, $1 million in accruals, $2 million in notes payable, and $15 million in net plant and equipment. Rattner uses only debt and common equity to fund its operations. (In other words, Rattner has no preferred stock on its balance sheet.) Rattner had no other current liabilities. Assume that Rattner's only noncash item was depreciation.

    a.   What was the company's net income?

    b.   What was its net operating working capital (NOWC)?

    c.   What was its net working capital (NWC)?

    d.   Rattner had $12 million in net plant and equipment the prior year. Its net operating working capital has remained constant over time. What is the company's free cash flow (FCF) for the year that just ended?

    e.   Rattner has 500,000 common shares outstanding and the common stock amount on the balance sheet is $5 million. The company has not issued or repurchased common stock during the year. Last year's balance in retained earnings was $11.2 million and the firm paid out dividends of $1.2 million during the year. Develop Rattner's end-of-year statement of stockholders' equity.

    f.   If the firm's stock price at year-end is $52, what is the firm's market value added (MVA)?

    g.   If the firm's after-tax percentage cost of capital is 9%, what is the firm's EVA at year-end?

QUESTIONS

3-1   What four financial statements are contained in most annual reports?

3-2   Who are some of the basic users of financial statements, and how do they use them?

3-3   If a "typical" firm reports $20 million of retained earnings on its balance sheet, could its directors declare a $20 million cash dividend without having any qualms about what they were doing? Explain your answer.

3-4   Explain the following statement: While the balance sheet can be thought of as a snapshot of a firm's financial position *at a point in time*, the income statement reports on operations *over a period of time*.

3-5   Financial statements are based on generally accepted accounting principles (GAAP) and are audited by CPA firms. Do investors need to worry about the validity of those statements? Explain your answer.

3-6   Refer to the box titled, "The Balance Sheet of an 'Average' American Household" when answering Parts a and b.

    a.   Based on this evidence, has the financial position of the average household improved during this period of time? Explain your answer.

    b.   What do you think the average household balance sheet looks like today? Explain your answer.

3-7   What is free cash flow? If you were an investor, why might you be more interested in free cash flow than net income?

3-8   Would it be possible for a company to report negative free cash flow and still be highly valued by investors; that is, could a negative free cash flow ever be viewed optimistically by investors? Explain your answer.

3-9   How are management's actions incorporated in EVA and MVA? How are EVA and MVA interconnected?

3-10   Explain the following statement: Our tax rates are progressive.

3-11   What does *double taxation of corporate income* mean? Could income ever be subject to *triple* taxation? Explain your answer.

3-12   How does the deductibility of interest and dividends by the paying corporation affect the choice of financing (that is, the use of debt versus equity)?

PROBLEMS

Easy Problems 1–7

3-1   **BALANCE SHEET**   The assets of Dallas & Associates consist entirely of current assets and net plant and equipment. The firm has total assets of $2.5 million and net plant and equipment equals $2 million. It has notes payable of $150,000, long-term debt of $750,000, and total common equity of $1.5 million. The firm does have accounts payable and accruals on its balance sheet. The firm only finances with debt and common equity, so it has no preferred stock on its balance sheet.

   a.   What is the company's total debt?
   b.   What is the amount of total liabilities and equity that appears on the firm's balance sheet?
   c.   What is the balance of current assets on the firm's balance sheet?
   d.   What is the balance of current liabilities on the firm's balance sheet?
   e.   What is the amount of accounts payable and accruals on its balance sheet? [Hint: Consider this as a single line item on the firm's balance sheet.]
   f.   What is the firm's net working capital?
   g.   What is the firm's net operating working capital?
   h.   What is the explanation for the difference in your answers to parts f and g?

3-2   **INCOME STATEMENT**   Little Books Inc. recently reported $3 million of net income. Its EBIT was $6 million, and its tax rate was 40%. What was its interest expense? [Hint: Write out the headings for an income statement and fill in the known values. Then divide $3 million of net income by $(1 − T) = 0.6$ to find the pretax income. The difference between EBIT and taxable income must be interest expense. Use this same procedure to complete similar problems.]

3-3   **INCOME STATEMENT**   Pearson Brothers recently reported an EBITDA of $7.5 million and net income of $1.8 million. It had $2.0 million of interest expense, and its corporate tax rate was 40%. What was its charge for depreciation and amortization?

3-4   **STATEMENT OF STOCKHOLDERS' EQUITY**   In its most recent financial statements, Newhouse Inc. reported $50 million of net income and $810 million of retained earnings. The previous retained earnings were $780 million. How much in dividends were paid to shareholders during the year? Assume that all dividends declared were actually paid.

3-5   **MVA**   Henderson Industries has $500 million of common equity on its balance sheet; its stock price is $60 per share; and its Market Value Added (MVA) is $130 million. How many common shares are currently outstanding?

3-6   **MVA**   Over the years, McLaughlin Corporation's stockholders have provided $35,000,000 of capital, when they purchased new issues of stock and allowed management to retain some of the firm's earnings. The firm now has 2,000,000 shares of common stock outstanding, and the shares sell at a price of $30 per share. How much value has McLaughlin's management added to stockholder wealth over the years, i.e., what is McLaughlin's MVA?

3-7   **EVA**   Britton Industries has operating income for the year of $3,000,000 and a 40% tax rate. Its total invested capital is $20,000,000 and its after-tax percentage cost of capital is 8%. What is the firm's EVA?

Intermediate Problems 8–13

3-8   **BALANCE SHEET**   Which of the following actions are most likely to directly increase cash as shown on a firm's balance sheet? Explain and state the assumptions that underlie your answer.

   a.   It issues $2 million of new common stock.
   b.   It buys new plant and equipment at a cost of $3 million.
   c.   It reports a large loss for the year.
   d.   It increases the dividends paid on its common stock.

3-9 **STATEMENT OF STOCKHOLDERS' EQUITY**   Computer World Inc. paid out $22.5 million in total common dividends and reported $278.9 million of retained earnings at year-end. The prior year's retained earnings were $212.3 million. What was the net income? Assume that all dividends declared were actually paid.

3-10 **EVA**   For 2014, Everyday Electronics reported $22.5 million of sales and $18 million of operating costs (including depreciation). The company has $15 million of total invested capital. Its after-tax cost of capital is 9% and its federal-plus-state income tax rate was 35%. What was the firm's Economic Value Added (EVA), that is, how much value did management add to stockholders' wealth during 2014?

3-11 **STATEMENT OF CASH FLOWS**   W.C. Cycling had $55,000 in cash at year-end 2013 and $25,000 in cash at year-end 2014. The firm invested in property, plant, and equipment totaling $250,000. Cash flow from financing activities totaled +$170,000.

   a.   What was the cash flow from operating activities?

   b.   If accruals increased by $25,000, receivables and inventories increased by $100,000, and depreciation and amortization totaled $10,000, what was the firm's net income?

3-12 **STATEMENT OF CASH FLOWS**   You have just been hired as a financial analyst for Basel Industries. Unfortunately, company headquarters (where all of the firm's records are kept) has been destroyed by fire. So, your first job will be to recreate the firm's cash flow statement for the year just ended. The firm had $100,000 in the bank at the end of the prior year and its working capital accounts except cash remained constant during the year. It earned $5 million in net income during the year but paid $750,000 in dividends to common shareholders. Throughout the year, the firm purchased $5.5 million of machinery that was needed for a new project. You have just spoken to the firm's accountants and learned that annual depreciation expense for the year is $450,000; however, the purchase price for the machinery represents additions to property, plant, and equipment before depreciation. Finally, you have determined that the only financing done by the firm was to issue long-term debt of $1 million at a 6% interest rate. What was the firm's end-of-year cash balance? Recreate the firm's cash flow statement to arrive at your answer.

3-13 **FREE CASH FLOW**   Bailey Corporation's financial statements (dollars and shares are in millions) are provided here.

Balance Sheets as of December 31

	2014	2013
Assets		
Cash and equivalents	$ 14,000	$ 13,000
Accounts receivable	30,000	25,000
Inventories	28,125	21,000
Total current assets	$ 72,125	$ 59,000
Net plant and equipment	50,000	47,000
Total assets	$122,125	$106,000
Liabilities and Equity		
Accounts payable	$ 10,800	$ 9,000
Accruals	7,600	6,000
Notes payable	6,700	5,150
Total current liabilities	$ 25,100	$ 20,150
Long-term bonds	15,000	15,000
Total liabilities	$ 40,100	$ 35,150
Common stock (5,000 shares)	50,000	50,000
Retained earnings	32,025	20,850
Common equity	$ 82,025	$ 70,850
Total liabilities and equity	$122,125	$106,000

Income Statement for Year Ending December 31, 2014

Sales	$214,000
Operating costs excluding depreciation and amortization	170,000
EBITDA	$ 44,000
Depreciation & amortization	5,000
EBIT	$ 39,000
Interest	1,750
EBT	$ 37,250
Taxes (40%)	14,900
Net income	$ 22,350
Dividends paid	$ 11,175

a.   What was net operating working capital for 2013 and 2014?

b.   What was Bailey's 2014 free cash flow?

c.   Construct Bailey's 2014 statement of stockholders' equity.

d.   What was Bailey's 2014 EVA? Assume that its after-tax cost of capital is 10%.

e.   What was Bailey's MVA at year-end 2014? Assume that its stock price at December 31, 2014 was $20.

Challenging Problems 14–16

3-14   INCOME STATEMENT   Hermann Industries is forecasting the following income statement:

Sales	$8,000,000
Operating costs excluding depreciation & amortization	4,400,000
EBITDA	$3,600,000
Depreciation and amortization	800,000
EBIT	$2,800,000
Interest	600,000
EBT	$2,200,000
Taxes (40%)	880,000
Net income	$1,320,000

The CEO would like to see higher sales and a forecasted net income of $2,500,000. Assume that operating costs (excluding depreciation and amortization) are 55% of sales and that depreciation and amortization and interest expenses will increase by 10%. The tax rate, which is 40%, will remain the same. (Note that while the tax rate remains constant, the taxes paid will change.) What level of sales would generate $2,500,000 in net income?

3-15   FINANCIAL STATEMENTS   The Davidson Corporation's balance sheet and income statement are provided here.

Davidson Corporation: Balance Sheet as of December 31, 2014
(Millions of Dollars)

Assets		Liabilities and Equity	
Cash and equivalents	$ 15	Accounts payable	$ 120
Accounts receivable	515	Accruals	280
Inventories	880	Notes payable	220
Total current assets	$1,410	Total current liabilities	$ 620
Net plant and equipment	2,590	Long-term bonds	1,520
		Total liabilities	$2,140
		Common stock (100 million shares)	260
		Retained earnings	1,600
		Common equity	$1,860
Total assets	$4,000	Total liabilities and equity	$4,000

Davidson Corporation: Income Statement for Year Ending December 31, 2014
(Millions of Dollars)

Sales	$6,250
Operating costs excluding depreciation and amortization	5,230
EBITDA	$1,020
Depreciation & amortization	220
EBIT	$ 800
Interest	180
EBT	$ 620
Taxes (40%)	248
Net income	$ 372
Common dividends paid	$ 146
Earnings per share	$ 3.72

a.   Construct the statement of stockholders' equity for December 31, 2014. No common stock was issued during 2014.
b.   How much money has been reinvested in the firm over the years?
c.   At the present time, how large a check could be written without it bouncing?
d.   How much money must be paid to current creditors within the next year?

3-16   FREE CASH FLOW   Financial information for Powell Panther Corporation is shown here.

Powell Panther Corporation: Income Statements for Year Ending December 31
(Millions of Dollars)

	2014	2013
Sales	$1,200.0	$1,000.0
Operating costs excluding depreciation and amortization	1,020.0	850.0
EBITDA	$ 180.0	$ 150.0
Depreciation & amortization	30.0	25.0
Earnings before interest and taxes (EBIT)	$ 150.0	$ 125.0
Interest	21.7	20.2
Earnings before taxes (EBT)	$ 128.3	$ 104.8
Taxes (40%)	51.3	41.9
Net income	$ 77.0	$ 62.9
Common dividends	$ 60.5	$ 46.4

Powell Panther Corporation: Balance Sheets as of December 31
(Millions of Dollars)

	2014	2013
Assets		
Cash and equivalents	$ 12.0	$ 10.0
Accounts receivable	180.0	150.0
Inventories	180.0	200.0
Total current assets	$372.0	$360.0
Net plant and equipment	300.0	250.0
Total assets	$672.0	$610.0

Powell Panther Corporation: Balance Sheets as of December 31
(Millions of Dollars)

	2014	2013
Liabilities and Equity		
Accounts payable	$108.0	$ 90.0
Accruals	72.0	60.0
Notes payable	67.0	51.5
Total current liabilities	$247.0	$201.5
Long-term bonds	150.0	150.0
Total liabilities	$397.0	$351.5
Common stock (50 million shares)	50.0	50.0
Retained earnings	225.0	208.5
Common equity	$275.0	$258.5
Total liabilities and equity	$672.0	$610.0

a. What was net operating working capital for 2013 and 2014?
b. What was the 2014 free cash flow?
c. How would you explain the large increase in 2014 dividends?

COMPREHENSIVE/SPREADSHEET PROBLEM

3-17 **FINANCIAL STATEMENTS, CASH FLOW, AND TAXES** Laiho Industries' 2013 and 2014 balance sheets (in thousands of dollars) are shown.

	2014	2013
Cash	$102,850	$ 89,725
Accounts receivable	103,365	85,527
Inventories	38,444	34,982
Total current assets	$244,659	$210,234
Net fixed assets	67,165	42,436
Total assets	$311,824	$252,670
Accounts payable	$ 30,761	$ 23,109
Accruals	30,477	22,656
Notes payable	16,717	14,217
Total current liabilities	$ 77,955	$ 59,982
Long-term debt	76,264	63,914
Total liabilities	$154,219	$123,896
Common stock	100,000	90,000
Retained earnings	57,605	38,774
Total common equity	$157,605	$128,774
Total liabilities and equity	$311,824	$252,670

a. Sales for 2014 were $455,150,000, and EBITDA was 15% of sales. Furthermore, depreciation and amortization were 11% of net fixed assets, interest was $8,575,000, the corporate tax rate was 40%, and Laiho pays 40% of its net income as dividends. Given this information, construct the firm's 2014 income statement.

b. Construct the statement of stockholders' equity for the year ending December 31, 2014, and the 2014 statement of cash flows.

c. Calculate 2013 and 2014 net operating working capital (NOWC) and 2014 free cash flow (FCF).

d. If Laiho increased its dividend payout ratio, what effect would this have on corporate taxes paid? What effect would this have on taxes paid by the company's shareholders?

e. Assume that the firm's after-tax cost of capital is 10.5%. What is the firm's 2014 EVA?

f. Assume that the firm's stock price is $22 per share and that at year-end 2014 the firm has 10 million shares outstanding. What is the firm's MVA at year-end 2014?

INTEGRATED CASE

D'LEON INC., PART I

3-18   **Financial Statements and Taxes**   Donna Jamison, a 2009 graduate of the University of Florida with 4 years of banking experience, was recently brought in as assistant to the chairperson of the board of D'Leon Inc., a small food producer that operates in north Florida and whose specialty is high-quality pecan and other nut products sold in the snack foods market. D'Leon's president, Al Watkins, decided in 2013 to undertake a major expansion and to "go national" in competition with Frito-Lay, Eagle, and other major snack foods companies. Watkins believed that D'Leon's products were of higher quality than the competition's; that this quality differential would enable it to charge a premium price; and that the end result would be greatly increased sales, profits, and stock price.

The company doubled its plant capacity, opened new sales offices outside its home territory, and launched an expensive advertising campaign. D'Leon's results were not satisfactory, to put it mildly. Its board of directors, which consisted of its president, vice president, and major stockholders (all of whom were local businesspeople), was most upset when directors learned how the expansion was going. Unhappy suppliers were being paid late; and the bank was complaining about the deteriorating situation, threatening to cut off credit. As a result, Watkins was informed that changes would have to be made—and quickly; otherwise, he would be fired. Also, at the board's insistence, Donna Jamison was brought in and given the job of assistant to Fred Campo, a retired banker who was D'Leon's chairperson and largest stockholder. Campo agreed to give up a few of his golfing days and help nurse the company back to health, with Jamison's help.

Jamison began by gathering the financial statements and other data given in Tables IC 3.1, IC 3.2, IC 3.3, and IC 3.4. Assume that you are Jamison's assistant. You must help her answer the following questions for Campo. (Note: We will continue with this case in Chapter 4, and you will feel more comfortable with the analysis there. But answering these questions will help prepare you for Chapter 4. Provide clear explanations.)

a.   What effect did the expansion have on sales, after-tax operating income, net operating working capital (NOWC), and net income?

b.   What effect did the company's expansion have on its free cash flow?

c.   D'Leon purchases materials on 30-day terms, meaning that it is supposed to pay for purchases within 30 days of receipt. Judging from its 2014 balance sheet, do you think that D'Leon pays suppliers on time? Explain, including what problems might occur if suppliers are not paid in a timely manner.

d.   D'Leon spends money for labor, materials, and fixed assets (depreciation) to make products—and spends still more money to sell those products. Then the firm makes sales that result in receivables, which eventually result in cash inflows. Does it appear that D'Leon's sales price exceeds its costs per unit sold? How does this affect the cash balance?

e.   Suppose D'Leon's sales manager told the sales staff to start offering 60-day credit terms rather than the 30-day terms now being offered. D'Leon's competitors react by offering similar terms, so sales remain constant. What effect would this have on the cash account? How would the cash account be affected if sales doubled as a result of the credit policy change?

f.   Can you imagine a situation in which the sales price exceeds the cost of producing and selling a unit of output, yet a dramatic increase in sales volume causes the cash balance to decline? Explain.

g.   Did D'Leon finance its expansion program with internally generated funds (additions to retained earnings plus depreciation) or with external capital? How does the choice of financing affect the company's financial strength?

h.   Refer to Tables IC 3.2 and IC 3.4. Suppose D'Leon broke even in 2014 in the sense that sales revenues equaled total operating costs plus interest charges. Would the asset expansion have caused the company to experience a cash shortage that required it to raise external capital? Explain.

i.   If D'Leon starts depreciating fixed assets over 7 years rather than 10 years, would that affect (1) the physical stock of assets, (2) the balance sheet account for fixed assets, (3) the company's reported net income, and (4) the company's cash position? Assume that the same depreciation method is used for stockholder reporting and for tax calculations and that the accounting change has no effect on assets' physical lives.

j.   Explain how earnings per share, dividends per share, and book value per share are calculated and what they mean. Why does the market price per share not equal the book value per share?

k.   Explain briefly the tax treatment of (1) interest and dividends paid, (2) interest earned and dividends received, (3) capital gains, and (4) tax loss carry-backs and carry-forwards. How might each of these items affect D'Leon's taxes?

TABLE IC 3.1   Balance Sheets

	2014	2013
Assets		
Cash	$ 7,282	$ 57,600
Accounts receivable	632,160	351,200
Inventories	1,287,360	715,200
Total current assets	$1,926,802	$1,124,000
Gross fixed assets	1,202,950	491,000
Less accumulated depreciation	263,160	146,200
Net fixed assets	$ 939,790	$ 344,800
Total assets	$2,866,592	$1,468,800
Liabilities and Equity		
Accounts payable	$ 524,160	$ 145,600
Accruals	489,600	136,000
Notes payable	636,808	200,000
Total current liabilities	$1,650,568	$ 481,600
Long-term debt	723,432	323,432
Common stock (100,000 shares)	460,000	460,000
Retained earnings	32,592	203,768
Total equity	$ 492,592	$ 663,768
Total liabilities and equity	$2,866,592	$1,468,800

© Cengage Learning 2015

TABLE IC 3.2   Income Statements

	2014	2013
Sales	$6,034,000	$3,432,000
Cost of goods sold	5,528,000	2,864,000
Other expenses	519,988	358,672
Total operating costs excluding depreciation and amortization	$6,047,988	$3,222,672
Depreciation and amortization	116,960	18,900
EBIT	($ 130,948)	$ 190,428
Interest expense	136,012	43,828
EBT	($ 266,960)	$ 146,600
Taxes (40%)	(106,784)[a]	58,640
Net income	($ 160,176)	$ 87,960
EPS	($ 1.602)	$ 0.880
DPS	$ 0.110	$ 0.220
Book value per share	$ 4.926	$ 6.638
Stock price	$ 2.25	$ 8.50
Shares outstanding	100,000	100,000
Tax rate	40.00%	40.00%
Lease payments	$ 40,000	$ 40,000
Sinking fund payments	0	0

© Cengage Learning 2015

[a]The firm had sufficient taxable income in 2012 and 2013 to obtain its full tax refund in 2014.

Statement of Stockholders' Equity, 2014				**TABLE IC 3.3**
	Common Stock			
	Shares	**Amount**	**Retained Earnings**	**Total Stockholders' Equity**
Balances, December 31, 2013	100,000	$460,000	$203,768	$663,768
2014 Net Income			(160,176)	
Cash Dividends			(11,000)	
Addition (Subtraction) to Retained Earnings				(171,176)
Balances, December 31, 2014	100,000	$460,000	$ 32,592	$ 492,592

© Cengage Learning 2015

Statement of Cash Flows, 2014	**TABLE IC 3.4**

Operating Activities

Net income	($160,176)
Depreciation and amortization	116,960
Increase in accounts payable	378,560
Increase in accruals	353,600
Increase in accounts receivable	(280,960)
Increase in inventories	(572,160)
Net cash provided by operating activities	($ 164,176)

Long-Term Investing Activities

Additions to property, plant, and equipment	($ 711,950)
Net cash used in investing activities	($ 711,950)

Financing Activities

Increase in notes payable	$ 436,808
Increase in long-term debt	400,000
Payment of cash dividends	(11,000)
Net cash provided by financing activities	$ 825,808

Summary

Net decrease in cash	($ 50,318)
Cash at beginning of year	57,600
Cash at end of year	$ 7,282

© Cengage Learning 2015

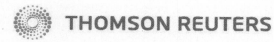
THOMSON REUTERS

Use the Thomson ONE—Business School Edition online database to answer this chapter's questions.

Exploring Starbucks' Financial Statements

Over the past decade, Starbucks coffee shops have become an increasingly familiar part of the urban landscape. In 2013, the company operated more than 17,600 coffee shops in all 50 states, in the District of Columbia, and in international markets, and it had approximately 160,000 employees.

Thomson ONE can access a wealth of financial information for companies such as Starbucks. To find some background information, begin by entering the company's ticker symbol, SBUX, and then selecting "GO." On the opening screen, you will see a great deal of useful information, including a summary of what Starbucks does, a chart of its recent stock price, EPS estimates, recent news stories, and a list of key financial data and ratios.

In researching a company's operating performance, a good place to start is the recent stock price performance. At the top of the Stock Price Chart, click on the section labeled "Interactive Chart." From this point, you can obtain a chart of the company's stock price performance relative to the overall market (as measured by the S&P 500) between 2003 and 2013. To obtain a 10-year chart, go to "Time Frame," under "Period:" click on the down arrow, and select "10 years." Then click on "Draw"; a 10-year price chart should appear. As you can see, Starbucks has had its ups and downs. But the company's overall performance has been quite strong, and it has beaten the overall market handily.

You can also find Starbucks' recent financial statements. Click on "Financials" to find the company's annual balance sheets for the past 5 years. Selecting Thomson Financials provides balance sheets, income statements, and statements of cash flows for various time periods. Clicking on the Microsoft Excel icon downloads these statements directly to a spreadsheet.

Discussion Questions

1. Looking at the most recent year available, what is the amount of total assets on Starbucks' balance sheet? What percentage is fixed assets, such as plant and equipment? What percentage is current assets? How much has the company grown over the years that are shown?
2. Does Starbucks have very much long-term debt? What are the chief ways in which Starbucks has financed assets?
3. Looking at the statement of cash flows, what factors can explain the change in the company's cash position over the last couple of years?
4. Looking at the income statement, what are the company's most recent sales and net income? Over the past several years, what has been the sales growth rate? What has been the growth rate in net income?
5. Over the past few years, has there been a strong correlation between stock price performance and reported earnings? Explain. [Hint: Change the Stock Price Chart so that it corresponds to a 5-year period—just as the financial statements show 5 years of data.]

ZUMA Press, Inc./Alamy

4

Analysis of Financial Statements

Can You Make Money Analyzing Stocks?

For many years, a debate has raged over this question. Some argue that the stock market is highly efficient and that all available information regarding a stock is already reflected in its price. The "efficient market advocates" point out that there are thousands of smart, well-trained analysts working for institutions with billions of dollars. These analysts have access to the latest information, and they spring into action—buying or selling—as soon as a firm releases any information that has a bearing on its future profits. The "efficient markets advocates" also point out that few mutual funds, which hire good people and pay them well, actually beat the averages. If these experts earn only average returns, how can the rest of us expect to beat the market?

Others disagree, arguing that analysis can pay off. They point out that some fund managers perform better than average year after year. Also, they note that some "activist" inves-

tors analyze firms carefully, identify those with weaknesses that appear to be correctable, and then persuade their managers to take actions to improve the firms' performances.

Arguably, the world's best-known investor is Warren Buffett. Through his company Berkshire Hathaway, Buffett has made significant investments in a number of well-known companies including Coca-Cola, American Express, IBM, and Wells Fargo. Buffett is well known for taking a long-run view of things. His value-investing approach, which borrows heavily from the ideas espoused decades ago by Benjamin Graham, looks for stocks trading at prices that are significantly lower than their estimated intrinsic value. Value investors rely heavily on the type of analysis described in this chapter to assess a company's strengths and weaknesses and to derive the key inputs for their estimates of intrinsic value.

Always looking for new opportunities, in June 2013 Berkshire Hathaway partnered with private equity firm 3G Capital and acquired H.J. Heinz Company for $28 billion. Heinz is the type of company that Buffett likes. It is an established business with well-known brands that has generated solid margins and steady earnings growth. On the other hand, the deal didn't come cheap. In the year before the announced deal, Heinz' stock had already been doing quite well—it had risen nearly 18% from a price of $51.70 per share in February 2012 to roughly $61 per share before the deal was first announced in February 2013. On top of that strong price, Berkshire Hathaway and 3G Capital offered

Heinz' shareholders an additional 20% premium for their shares. All of this suggests that, in his analysis, Buffett saw even greater room for improvement.

So, while many people regard financial statements as "just accounting," they really are much more. As you will see in this chapter, these statements provide a wealth of information that can be used for a wide variety of purposes by managers, investors, lenders, customers, suppliers, and regulators. An analysis of its statements can highlight a company's strengths and shortcomings, and this information can be used by management to improve the company's performance and by others to predict future results.

PUTTING THINGS IN PERSPECTIVE

The primary goal of financial management is to maximize shareholders' wealth, not accounting measures such as net income or earnings per share (EPS). However, accounting data influence stock prices, and this data can be used to see why a company is performing the way it is and where it is heading. Chapter 3 described the key financial statements and showed how they change as a firm's operations change. Now, in Chapter 4, we show how the statements are used by managers to improve the firm's stock price; by lenders to evaluate the likelihood that borrowers will be able to pay off loans; and by security analysts to forecast earnings, dividends, and stock prices.

If management is to maximize a firm's value, it must take advantage of the firm's strengths and correct its weaknesses. Financial analysis involves (1) comparing the firm's performance to that of other firms in the same industry and (2) evaluating trends in the firm's financial position over time. These studies help managers identify deficiencies and take corrective actions. In this chapter, we focus on how managers and investors evaluate a firm's financial position. Then, in later chapters, we examine the types of actions managers can take to improve future performance and thus increase the firm's stock price.

When you finish this chapter, you should be able to:

- Explain what ratio analysis is.
- List the five groups of ratios and identify, calculate, and interpret the key ratios in each group.
- Discuss each ratio's relationship to the balance sheet and income statement.
- Discuss why ROE is the key ratio under management's control and how the other ratios impact ROE, and explain how to use the DuPont equation for improving ROE.
- Compare a firm's ratios with those of other firms (benchmarking) and analyze a given firm's ratios over time (trend analysis).
- Discuss the tendency of ratios to fluctuate over time (which may or may not be problematic), explain how they can be influenced by accounting practices as well as other factors, and explain why they must be used with care.

4-1 RATIO ANALYSIS

Ratios help us evaluate financial statements. For example, at the end of 2014, Allied Food Products had $860 million of interest-bearing debt and interest charges of $88 million while Midwest Products had $52 million of interest-bearing debt and interest charges of $4 million. Which company is stronger? The burden of these debts and the companies' ability to repay them can best be evaluated by comparing each firm's total debt to its total capital and comparing interest expense to the income and cash available to pay that interest. Ratios are used to make such comparisons. We calculate Allied's ratios for 2014 using data from the balance sheets and income statements given in Tables 3.1 and 3.2. We also evaluate the ratios relative to food industry averages, using data in millions of dollars.[1] As you will see, we can calculate many different ratios, with different ones used to examine different aspects of the firm's operations. You will get to know some ratios by name, but it's better to understand what they are designed to do than to memorize names and equations.

We divide the ratios into five categories:

1. *Liquidity ratios,* which give an idea of the firm's ability to pay off debts that are maturing within a year.

2. *Asset management ratios,* which give an idea of how efficiently the firm is using its assets.

3. *Debt management ratios,* which give an idea of how the firm has financed its assets as well as the firm's ability to repay its long-term debt.

4. *Profitability ratios,* which give an idea of how profitably the firm is operating and utilizing its assets.

5. *Market value ratios,* which give an idea of what investors think about the firm and its future prospects.

Satisfactory liquidity ratios are necessary if the firm is to continue operating. Good asset management ratios are necessary for the firm to keep its costs low and thus its net income high. Debt management ratios indicate how risky the firm is and how much of its operating income must be paid to bondholders rather than stockholders. Profitability ratios combine the asset and debt management categories and show their effects on ROE. Finally, market value ratios tell us what investors think about the company and its prospects.

All of the ratios are important, but different ones are more important for some companies than for others. For example, if a firm borrowed too much in the past and its debt now threatens to drive it into bankruptcy, the debt ratios are key. Similarly, if a firm expanded too rapidly and now finds itself with excess inventory and manufacturing capacity, the asset management ratios take center stage. The ROE is always important; but a high ROE depends on maintaining liquidity, on efficient asset management, and on the proper use of debt. Managers are, of course, vitally concerned with the stock price; but managers have little direct

---

[1]Financial statement data for most publicly traded firms can be obtained from the Internet. Free sites that provide this information include Google Finance (google.com/finance) and Yahoo! Finance (finance.yahoo.com). These sites provide financial statements, which can be copied to an Excel file and used to create your own ratios; but the websites also provide calculated ratios.

In addition to the ratios discussed in this chapter, financial analysts often employ a tool known as *common size analysis.* To form a *common size balance sheet,* simply divide each asset, liability, and equity item by total assets and then express the results as percentages. To develop a *common size income statement,* divide each income statement item by sales. The resultant percentage statements can be compared with statements of larger or smaller firms or with those of the same firm over time. One would normally obtain the basic statements from a source such as Google Finance and copy them to Excel, so constructing common size statements is quite easy. Note too that industry average data are generally given as percentages, which make them easy to compare with a firm's own common size statements. We provide Allied Food Products' common size statements in Web Appendix 4A.

control over the stock market's performance while they do have control over their firm's ROE. So ROE tends to be the main focal point.

4-2 LIQUIDITY RATIOS

The liquidity ratios help answer this question: Will the firm be able to pay off its debts as they come due and thus remain a viable organization? If the answer is no, liquidity must be addressed.

A **liquid asset** is one that trades in an active market and thus can be quickly converted to cash at the going market price. As shown in Table 3.1 in Chapter 3, Allied has $310 million of current liabilities that must be paid off within the coming year. Will it have trouble meeting that obligation? A full liquidity analysis requires the use of a cash budget, which we discuss in Chapter 15; however, by relating cash and other current assets to current liabilities, ratio analysis provides a quick and easy-to-use measure of liquidity. Two of the most commonly used **liquidity ratios** are discussed below.

4-2A CURRENT RATIO

The primary liquidity ratio is the **current ratio**, which is calculated by dividing current assets by current liabilities:

$$\text{Current ratio} = \frac{\text{Current assets}}{\text{Current liabilities}}$$
$$= \frac{\$1,000}{\$310} = 3.2\times$$
$$\text{Industry average} = 4.2\times$$

Current assets include cash, marketable securities, accounts receivable, and inventories. Allied's current liabilities consist of accounts payable, accrued wages and taxes, and short-term notes payable to its bank, all of which are due within one year.

If a company is having financial difficulty, it typically begins to pay its accounts payable more slowly and to borrow more from its bank, both of which increase current liabilities. If current liabilities are rising faster than current assets, the current ratio will fall; and this is a sign of possible trouble. Allied's current ratio is 3.2, which is well below the industry average of 4.2. Therefore, its liquidity position is somewhat weak but by no means desperate.[2]

Although industry average figures are discussed later in some detail, note that an industry average is not a magic number that all firms should strive to maintain; in fact, some very well-managed firms may be above the average while other good firms are below it. However, if a firm's ratios are far removed from the averages for its industry, an analyst should be concerned about why this variance occurs. Thus, a deviation from the industry average should signal the analyst (or management) to check further. Note too that a high current ratio generally indicates a very strong, safe liquidity position; it might also indicate that the firm has too much old inventory that will have to be written off and too many old accounts receivable that may turn into bad debts. Or the high current ratio might indicate that the firm has too much cash, receivables, and inventory relative to its sales, in which case these assets are not being managed efficiently. So it is always necessary to thoroughly examine the full set of ratios before forming a judgment as to how well the firm is performing.

Liquid Asset

An asset that can be converted to cash quickly without having to reduce the asset's price very much.

Liquidity Ratios

Ratios that show the relationship of a firm's cash and other current assets to its current liabilities.

Current Ratio

This ratio is calculated by dividing current assets by current liabilities. It indicates the extent to which current liabilities are covered by those assets expected to be converted to cash in the near future.

---

[2]Because current assets should be convertible to cash within a year, it is likely that they could be liquidated at close to their stated value. With a current ratio of 3.2, Allied could liquidate current assets at only 31% of book value and still pay off current creditors in full: $1/3.2 = 0.31$, or 31%. Note also that $0.31(\$1,000) = \$310$, the current liabilities balance.

FINANCIAL ANALYSIS ON THE INTERNET

A wide range of valuable financial information is available on the Internet. With just a couple of clicks, an investor can find the key financial statements for most publicly traded companies.

Suppose you are thinking of buying some Disney stock, and you want to analyze its recent performance. Here's a partial (but by no means complete) list of sites you can access to get started:

- One source is Yahoo! Finance (finance.yahoo.com). Here you will find updated market information along with links to a variety of research sites. Enter a stock's ticker symbol, click "Get Quotes," and you will see the stock's current price along with recent news about the company. Click "Key Statistics" to find a report on the company's key financial ratios. Links to the company's financials (income statement, balance sheet, and statement of cash flows) can also be found. Yahoo! Finance also has a list of insider transactions that tell you whether a company's CEO and other key insiders are buying or selling the company's stock. In addition, the site has a message board where investors share opinions about the company and a link is provided to the company's filings with the Securities and Exchange Commission (SEC). Note also that, in most cases, a more complete listing of SEC filings can be found at the SEC website (sec.gov).

- Two other websites with similar information are Google Finance (google.com/finance) and MSN Money (money.msn.com). After entering a stock's ticker symbol, you will see the current stock price and a list of recent news stories. At either of these sites, you will find links to a company's financial statements and key ratios, as well as other information including analyst ratings, historical charts, earnings estimates, and a summary of insider transactions. Google Finance, MSN Money, and Yahoo! Finance allow you to export the financial statements and historical prices to an Excel spreadsheet.

- Other sources for up-to-date market information are CNNMoney.com (money.cnn.com), Zacks Investment Research (zacks.com), and MarketWatch (marketwatch.com), part of *The Wall Street Journal* Digital Network. On these sites, you also can obtain stock quotes, financial statements, links to Wall Street research and SEC filings, company profiles, and charts of a firm's stock price over time.

- If you're looking for data on bond yields, key money rates, and currency rates, Bloomberg (bloomberg.com) is an excellent source for this type of information.

- Another good place to look is Reuters (reuters.com). Here you can find links to analysts' research reports along with the key financial statements.

- A valuable subscriber website from *Value Line Investment Survey* (valueline.com) provides industry-specific and detailed company income statement data, capital structure data, returns data, EPS, book value per share, cash flow per share, and other investment data.

- If you're interested in obtaining baseline values on individual stocks, you will find ValuePro (valuepro.net) helpful. It identifies key financial numbers used to obtain a stock's value and allows the user to make changes and see their impact on the stock's value.

- After accumulating all of this information, you may want to look at a site that provides opinions regarding the direction of the overall market and a particular stock. Two popular sites are The Motley Fool (fool.com) and The Street (thestreet.com).

- A popular source is *The Wall Street Journal* website (online.wsj.com). It is a great resource, but you have to subscribe to access the full range of materials.

When analyzing ratios using different sources, it is important that you understand how each source calculates a particular ratio. Differences among sources could be attributable to timing differences (using an average number versus a trailing 12-month number) or to different definitions. It is quite possible that, if you were to examine the same ratio for a particular company, you might see different values for the same ratio depending on the source chosen. For example, Yahoo! Finance defines the inventory turnover ratio as the ratio of annual sales to average inventory, while MSN Money defines it as the cost of sales over the latest 12 months divided by the average inventory from the same period. You can often click on "Help" within the particular website and search for the site's specific finance glossary to determine how ratios are defined. Keep this in mind when conducting ratio analysis.

This list is just a small subset of the information available online. Sites come and go and change their content over time. In addition, new and interesting sites are constantly being added to the Internet.

4-2b QUICK, OR ACID TEST, RATIO

Quick (Acid Test) Ratio

This ratio is calculated by deducting inventories from current assets and then dividing the remainder by current liabilities.

The second liquidity ratio is the **quick**, or **acid test, ratio**, which is calculated by deducting inventories from current assets and then dividing the remainder by current liabilities:

$$\text{Quick, or acid test, ratio} = \frac{\text{Current assets} - \text{Inventories}}{\text{Current liabilities}}$$
$$= \frac{\$385}{\$310} = 1.2\times$$
$$\text{Industry average} = 2.2\times$$

Inventories are typically the least liquid of a firm's current assets; and if sales slow down, they might not be converted to cash as quickly as expected.[3] Also, inventories are the assets on which losses are most likely to occur in the event of liquidation. Therefore, the quick ratio, which measures the firm's ability to pay off short-term obligations without relying on the sale of inventories, is important.

The industry average quick ratio is 2.2, so Allied's 1.2 ratio is relatively low. Still, if the accounts receivable can be collected, the company can pay off its current liabilities even if it has trouble disposing of its inventories.

SELF TEST

What are the characteristics of a liquid asset? Give examples of some liquid assets.

What question are the two liquidity ratios designed to answer?

Which is the least liquid of the firm's current assets?

A company has current liabilities of $500 million, and its current ratio is 2.0. What is the total of its current assets? **($1,000 million)** If this firm's quick ratio is 1.6, how much inventory does it have? **($200 million)** (Hint: To answer this problem and some of the other problems in this chapter, write out the equation for the ratio in the question, insert the given data, and solve for the missing value.) Examples:
Current ratio = 2.0 = CA/CL = CA/$500, so CA = 2($500) = $1,000.
Quick ratio = 1.6 = (CA − Inventories)/CL = ($1,000 − Inventories)/$500, so $1,000 − Inventories = 1.6($500) and Inventories = $1,000 − $800 = $200.

4-3 ASSET MANAGEMENT RATIOS

Asset Management Ratios

A set of ratios that measure how effectively a firm is managing its assets.

The second group of ratios, the **asset management ratios**, measure how effectively the firm is managing its assets. These ratios answer this question: Does the amount of each type of asset seem reasonable, too high, or too low in view of current and projected sales? These ratios are important because when Allied and other companies acquire assets, they must obtain capital from banks or other sources and capital is expensive. Therefore, if Allied has too many assets, its cost of capital will be too high, which will depress its profits. On the other hand, if its assets are too low,

---

[3]Some companies also report "Other current assets" on their balance sheet. Our definition of the quick ratio would implicitly assume that these other current assets could be easily converted to cash. As an alternative measure, some analysts define the quick ratio as:

(Cash and equivalents + Accounts receivable)/Current liabilities

This alternative measure assumes that the other current assets cannot be easily converted to cash. In the case of Allied, since it has no other current assets, the two measures would yield the same number.

profitable sales will be lost. So Allied must strike a balance between too many and too few assets, and the asset management ratios will help it strike this proper balance.

4-3A INVENTORY TURNOVER RATIO

"Turnover ratios" divide sales by some asset: Sales/Various assets. As the name implies, these ratios show how many times the particular asset is "turned over" during the year. Here is the **inventory turnover ratio**:

Inventory Turnover Ratio
This ratio is calculated by dividing sales by inventories.

$$\text{Inventory turnover ratio} = \frac{\text{Sales}}{\text{Inventories}}$$
$$= \frac{\$3,000}{\$615} = 4.9\times$$
$$\text{Industry average} = 10.9\times$$

As a rough approximation, each item of Allied's inventory is sold and restocked, or "turned over," 4.9 times per year. *Turnover* is a term that originated many years ago with the old Yankee peddler who would load up his wagon with pots and pans, and then go off on his route to peddle his wares. The merchandise was called working capital because it was what he actually sold, or "turned over," to produce his profits, whereas his "turnover" was the number of trips he took each year. Annual sales divided by inventory equaled turnover, or trips per year. If he made 10 trips per year, stocked 100 pots and pans, and made a gross profit of $5 per item, his annual gross profit was (100)($5)(10) = $5,000. If he went faster and made 20 trips per year, his gross profit doubled, other things held constant. So his turnover directly affected his profits.

Allied's inventory turnover of 4.9 is much lower than the industry average of 10.9. This suggests that it is holding too much inventory. Excess inventory is, of course, unproductive and represents an investment with a low or zero rate of return. Allied's low inventory turnover ratio also makes us question its current ratio. With such a low turnover, the firm may be holding obsolete goods that are not worth their stated value.[4]

Note that sales occur over the entire year, whereas the inventory figure is for one point in time. For this reason, it might be better to use an average inventory measure.[5] If the business is highly seasonal or if there has been a strong upward or downward sales trend during the year, it is especially useful to make an adjustment. Allied's sales are not growing especially fast though; and to maintain comparability with industry averages, we used year-end rather than average inventories.

4-3B DAYS SALES OUTSTANDING

Accounts receivable are evaluated by the **days sales outstanding (DSO) ratio**, also called the average collection period (ACP).[6] It is calculated by dividing accounts receivable by the average daily sales to find how many days' sales are tied up in receivables. Thus, the DSO represents the average length of time the

Days Sales Outstanding (DSO) Ratio
This ratio is calculated by dividing accounts receivable by average sales per day. It indicates the average length of time the firm must wait after making a sale before it receives cash.

---

[4]Our measure of inventory turnover is frequently used by established compilers of financial ratio statistics such as Value Line (valueline.com) and Dun & Bradstreet (dnb.com). However, you should recognize that other sources calculate inventory using cost of goods sold in place of sales in the formula's numerator. The rationale for this alternative measure is that sales are stated at market prices; so if inventories are carried at cost, as they generally are, the calculated turnover overstates the true turnover ratio. Therefore, it might be more appropriate to use cost of goods sold in place of sales in the formula's numerator. When evaluating and comparing financial ratios from various sources, it is important to understand how those sources are specifically calculating financial ratios.

[5]Preferably, the average inventory value should be calculated by summing the monthly figures during the year and dividing by 12. If monthly data are not available, the beginning and ending figures can be added and then divided by 2. Both methods adjust for growth but not for seasonal effects.

[6]We could use the receivables turnover to evaluate receivables. Allied's receivables turnover is $3,000/$375 = 8×. However, the DSO ratio is easier to interpret and judge.

firm must wait after making a sale before receiving cash. Allied has 46 days' sales outstanding, well above the 36-day industry average:

$$\text{DSO} = \begin{array}{c} \text{Days} \\ \text{sales} \\ \text{outstanding} \end{array} = \frac{\text{Receivables}}{\text{Average sales per day}} = \frac{\text{Receivables}}{\text{Annual sales}/365}$$

$$= \frac{\$375}{\$3{,}000/365} = \frac{\$375}{\$8.2192} = 45.625 \text{ days} \approx 46 \text{ days}$$

Industry average = 36 days

The DSO can be compared with the industry average, but it is also evaluated by comparing it with Allied's credit terms. Allied's credit policy calls for payment within 30 days. So the fact that 46 days' sales are outstanding, not 30 days', indicates that Allied's customers, on average, are not paying their bills on time. This deprives the company of funds that could be used to reduce bank loans or some other type of costly capital. Moreover, the high average DSO indicates that if some customers are paying on time, quite a few must be paying very late. Late-paying customers often default, so their receivables may end up as bad debts that can never be collected.[7] Note too that the trend in the DSO over the past few years has been rising, but the credit policy has not been changed. This reinforces our belief that Allied's credit manager should take steps to collect receivables faster.

4-3c FIXED ASSETS TURNOVER RATIO

Fixed Assets Turnover Ratio
The ratio of sales to net fixed assets.

The **fixed assets turnover ratio**, which is the ratio of sales to net fixed assets, measures how effectively the firm uses its plant and equipment:

$$\text{Fixed assets turnover ratio} = \frac{\text{Sales}}{\text{Net fixed assets}}$$

$$= \frac{\$3{,}000}{\$1{,}000} = 3.0\times$$

Industry average = 2.8×

Allied's ratio of 3.0 times is slightly above the 2.8 industry average, indicating that it is using its fixed assets at least as intensively as other firms in the industry. Therefore, Allied seems to have about the right amount of fixed assets relative to its sales.

Potential problems may arise when interpreting the fixed assets turnover ratio. Recall that fixed assets are shown on the balance sheet at their historical costs less depreciation. Inflation has caused the value of many assets that were purchased in the past to be seriously understated. Therefore, if we compare an old firm whose fixed assets have been depreciated with a new company with similar operations that acquired its fixed assets only recently, the old firm will probably have the higher fixed assets turnover ratio. However, this would be more reflective of the age of the assets than of inefficiency on the part of the new firm. The accounting profession is trying to develop procedures for making financial statements reflect current values rather than historical values, which would help us make better comparisons. However, at the moment, the problem still exists; so financial analysts must recognize this problem and deal with it judgmentally. In Allied's case, the issue is not serious because all firms in the industry have been expanding at about the same rate; hence, the balance sheets of the comparison firms are reasonably comparable.[8]

---

[7]For example, if further analysis along the lines suggested in Part 6 of this text (Working Capital Management) indicates that 85% of the customers pay in 30 days, for the DSO to average 46 days, the remaining 15% must be paying, on average, in 136.67 days. Paying that late suggests financial difficulties. A DSO of 46 days would alert a good analyst of the need to dig deeper.

[8]Refer to FASB Accounting Standards Codification Topic 255, Changing Prices, for a discussion of the effects of inflation on financial statements. ASC 255 references FAS 89, Financial Reporting and Changing Prices, issued in December 1986.

4-3D TOTAL ASSETS TURNOVER RATIO

The final asset management ratio, the **total assets turnover ratio**, measures the turnover of all of the firm's assets; and it is calculated by dividing sales by total assets:

$$\text{Total assets turnover ratio} = \frac{\text{Sales}}{\text{Total assets}}$$
$$= \frac{\$3,000}{\$2,000} = 1.5\times$$
$$\text{Industry average} = 1.8\times$$

Total Assets Turnover Ratio
This ratio is calculated by dividing sales by total assets.

Allied's ratio is somewhat below the industry average, indicating that it is not generating enough sales given its total assets. We just saw that Allied's fixed assets turnover is in line with the industry average; so the problem is with its current assets, inventories and accounts receivable, whose ratios were below the industry standards. Inventories should be reduced and receivables collected faster, which would improve operations.

SELF TEST

Write the equations for four ratios that are used to measure how effectively a firm manages its assets.

If one firm is growing rapidly and another is not, how might this distort a comparison of their inventory turnover ratios?

If you wanted to evaluate a firm's DSO, with what could you compare it?

How might different ages distort comparisons of different firms' fixed assets turnover ratios?

A firm has annual sales of $100 million, $20 million of inventory, and $30 million of accounts receivable. What is its inventory turnover ratio? **(5×)** What is its DSO? **(109.5 days)**

4-4 DEBT MANAGEMENT RATIOS

The use of debt will increase, or "leverage up," a firm's ROE if the firm earns more on its assets than the interest rate it pays on debt. However, debt exposes the firm to more risk than if it financed only with equity. In this section we discuss **debt management ratios**.

Table 4.1 illustrates the potential benefits and risks associated with debt.[9] Here we analyze two companies that are identical except for how they are financed. Firm U (for *Unleveraged*) has no debt; thus, it uses 100% common equity. Firm L (for *Leveraged*) obtained 50% of its capital as debt at an interest rate of 10%. Both firms have $100 of assets, and their sales are expected to range from a high of $150 down to $75 depending on business conditions. Some of their operating costs (e.g., rent and the president's salary) are fixed and will be the same regardless of

Debt Management Ratios
A set of ratios that measure how effectively a firm manages its debt.

---

[9]We discuss ROE in more depth later in this chapter, and we examine the effects of leverage in detail in Chapter 13. The relationship between various debt management ratios and bond ratings is discussed in Chapter 7 and illustrated in Table 7.4.

TABLE 4.1 The Effects of Financial Leverage

Firm U—Unleveraged (No Debt)

Current assets	$ 50	Debt	$ 0
Fixed assets	50	Common equity	100
Total assets	$100	Total liabilities and equity	$100

		State of the Economy		
		Good	**Expected**	**Bad**
Sales revenues		$150.0	$100.0	$75.0
Operating costs	Fixed	45.0	45.0	45.0
	Variable	60.0	40.0	30.0
Total operating costs		105.5	85.0	75.0
Operating income (EBIT)		$ 45.0	$ 15.0	$ 0.0
Interest (Rate = 10%)		0.0	0.0	0.0
Earnings before taxes (EBT)		$ 45.0	$ 15.0	$ 0.0
Taxes (Rate = 40%)		18.0	6.0	0.0
Net income (NI)		$ 27.0	$ 9.0	$ 0.0
ROE_U		27.0%	9.0%	0.0%

Firm L—Leveraged (Some Debt)

Current assets	$ 50	Debt	$ 50
Fixed assets	50	Common equity	50
Total assets	$100	Total liabilities and equity	$100

		State of the Economy		
		Good	**Expected**	**Bad**
Sales revenues		$150.0	$100.0	$ 75.0
Operating costs	Fixed	45.0	45.0	45.0
	Variable	60.0	40.0	30.0
Total operating costs		105.0	85.0	75.0
Operating income (EBIT)		$ 45.0	$ 15.0	$ 0.0
Interest (Rate = 10%)		5.0	5.0	5.0
Earnings before taxes (EBT)		$ 40.0	$ 10.0	−$ 5.0
Taxes (Rate = 40%)		16.0	4.0	0.0
Net income (NI)		$ 24.0	$ 6.0	−$ 5.0
ROE_L		48.0%	12.0%	−10.0%

© Cengage Learning 2015

the level of sales, while other costs (e.g., manufacturing labor and materials costs) vary with sales.[10]

Notice that everything is the same in the table for the leveraged and unleveraged firms down through operating income—thus, their EBITs are the same in

---

[10]The financial statements do not show the breakdown between fixed and variable operating costs, but companies can and do make this breakdown for internal purposes. Of course, the distinction is not always clear because a fixed cost in the very short run can become a variable cost over a longer time horizon. It's interesting to note that companies are moving toward making more of their costs variable, using such techniques as increasing bonuses rather than base salaries, switching to profit-sharing plans rather than fixed pension plans, and outsourcing various operations.

each state of the economy. However, things differ below operating income. Firm U has no debt, it pays no interest, its taxable income is the same as its operating income, it pays a 40% state and federal tax rate, and its net income ranges from $27 under good conditions down to $0 under bad conditions. When U's net income is divided by its common equity, its ROEs range from 27% to 0% depending on the state of the economy.

Firm L has the same EBIT as U under each state of the economy, but L uses $50 of debt with a 10% interest rate; so it has $5 of interest charges regardless of the economy. This $5 is deducted from EBIT to arrive at taxable income; taxes are taken out; and the result is net income, which ranges from $24 to –$5 depending on conditions.[11] At first, it looks as though Firm U is better off under all conditions, but this is not correct—we need to consider how much the two firms' stockholders have invested. Firm L's stockholders have put up only $50; so when that investment is divided into net income, we see that their ROE under good conditions is a whopping 48% (versus 27% for U) and is 12% (versus 9% for U) under expected conditions. However, L's ROE falls to –10% under bad conditions, which means that Firm L would go bankrupt if those conditions persisted for several years.

Thus, firms with relatively high debt ratios typically have higher expected returns when the economy is normal but lower returns and possibly bankruptcy if the economy goes into a recession. Therefore, decisions about the use of debt require firms to balance higher expected returns against increased risk. Determining the optimal amount of debt is a complicated process, and we defer a discussion of that subject until Chapter 13. For now, we simply look at two procedures that analysts use to examine the firm's debt: (1) They check the balance sheet to determine the proportion of total funds represented by debt; and (2) they review the income statement to see the extent to which interest is covered by operating profits.

4-4A TOTAL DEBT TO TOTAL CAPITAL

The ratio of **total debt to total capital** measures the percentage of the firm's capital provided by debtholders:

$$\frac{\text{Total debt}}{\text{Total capital}} = \frac{\text{Total debt}}{\text{Total debt} + \text{Equity}}$$
$$= \frac{\$110 + \$750}{\$1,800} = \frac{\$860}{\$1,800} = 47.8\%$$

Industry average = 36.4%

Total Debt to Total Capital
The ratio of total debt to total capital.

Recall from Chapter 3 that total debt includes all short-term and long-term interest-bearing debt, but it does not include operating items such as accounts payable and accruals. Allied has total debt of $860 million, which consists of $110 million in short-term notes payable and $750 million in long-term bonds. Its total capital is $1.80 billion: $860 million of debt plus $940 million in total equity. To keep things simple, unless we say otherwise, we will generally refer to the total debt to total capital ratio as the company's *debt ratio*.[12] Creditors prefer low debt ratios because the lower the ratio, the greater the cushion against creditors' losses in the event of

---

[11]As we discussed in the last chapter, firms can carry losses back or forward for several years. Therefore, if firm L had profits and thus paid taxes in 2013, it could carry back the 2014 loss under bad conditions and receive a credit (a check from the government). In Table 4.1, we disregard the carry-back/carry-forward provision.

[12]Two other debt ratios are often used in financial analysis:
1. Some analysts like to look at a broader debt ratio which includes all total liabilities (including accounts payables and accruals) divided by total assets. For Allied, the total liabilities-to-assets ratio is 53% ($1,060 million divided by $2,000 million), while the industry average is 40%.
2. Another measure, the debt-to-equity ratio equals total debt divided by total equity. Allied's debt-to-equity ratio is 860 million/940 million = 91.5%.

liquidation. Stockholders, on the other hand, may want more leverage because it can magnify expected earnings, as we saw in Table 4.1.

Allied's debt ratio is 47.8%, which means that its creditors have supplied roughly half of its total funds. As we will discuss in Chapter 13, a number of factors affect a company's optimal debt ratio. Nevertheless, the fact that Allied's debt ratio exceeds the industry average by a large amount raises a red flag, and this will make it relatively costly for Allied to borrow additional funds without first raising more equity. Creditors will be reluctant to lend the firm more money, and management would probably be subjecting the firm to too high a risk of bankruptcy if it sought to borrow a substantial amount of additional funds.

4-4b TIMES-INTEREST-EARNED RATIO

Times-Interest-Earned (TIE) Ratio

The ratio of earnings before interest and taxes (EBIT) to interest charges; a measure of the firm's ability to meet its annual interest payments.

The **times-interest-earned (TIE) ratio** is determined by dividing earnings before interest and taxes (EBIT in Table 3.2) by the interest charges:

$$\text{Times-interest-earned (TIE) ratio} = \frac{\text{EBIT}}{\text{interest charges}}$$
$$= \frac{\$283.8}{\$88} = 3.2\times$$
$$\text{Industry average} = 6.0\times$$

The TIE ratio measures the extent to which operating income can decline before the firm is unable to meet its annual interest costs. Failure to pay interest will bring legal action by the firm's creditors and probably result in bankruptcy. Note that earnings before interest and taxes, rather than net income, are used in the numerator. Because interest is paid with pretax dollars, the firm's ability to pay current interest is not affected by taxes.

Allied's interest is covered 3.2 times. The industry average is 6 times, so Allied is covering its interest charges by a much lower margin of safety than the average firm in the industry. Thus, the TIE ratio reinforces our conclusion from the debt ratio, namely, that Allied would face difficulties if it attempted to borrow additional money.[13]

SELF TEST

How does the use of financial leverage affect stockholders' control position?

How does the U.S. tax structure influence a firm's willingness to finance with debt?

How does the decision to use debt involve a risk-versus-return trade-off?

Explain the following statement: Analysts look at both balance sheet and income statement ratios when appraising a firm's financial condition.

Name two ratios that are used to measure financial leverage and write their equations.

---

[13]Another commonly used debt management ratio, using earnings before interest, taxes, depreciation, and amortization (EBITDA), is the EBITDA coverage ratio calculated as:

$$\text{EBITDA coverage ratio} = \frac{\text{EBITDA} + \text{Lease payments}}{\text{Interest} + \text{Principal payments} + \text{Lease payments}}$$

This ratio is more complete than the TIE ratio because it recognizes that depreciation and amortization expenses are not cash expenses, and thus are available to service debt, and that lease payments and principal repayments on debt are fixed charges. For more on this ratio, see E. F. Brigham and P. R. Daves, *Intermediate Financial Management*, 11th edition (Mason, OH: South-Western/Cengage Learning, 2013), Chapter 8.

4-5 PROFITABILITY RATIOS

Accounting statements reflect events that happened in the past, but they also provide clues about what's really important—that is, what's likely to happen in the future. The liquidity, asset management, and debt ratios covered thus far tell us something about the firm's policies and operations. Now we turn to the **profitability ratios**, which reflect the net result of all of the firm's financing policies and operating decisions.

Profitability Ratios
A group of ratios that show the combined effects of liquidity, asset management, and debt on operating results.

4-5A OPERATING MARGIN

The **operating margin**, calculated by dividing operating income (EBIT) by sales, gives the operating profit per dollar of sales:

$$\text{Operating margin} = \frac{\text{EBIT}}{\text{Sales}}$$
$$= \frac{\$283.8}{\$3,000} = 9.5\%$$
$$\text{Industry average} = 10.0\%$$

Allied's 9.5% operating margin is below the industry average of 10.0%. This subpar result indicates that Allied's operating costs are too high. This is consistent with the low inventory turnover and high days' sales outstanding ratios that we calculated earlier.

Operating Margin
This ratio measures operating income, or EBIT, per dollar of sales; it is calculated by dividing operating income by sales.

4-5B PROFIT MARGIN

The **profit margin**, also sometimes called the *net profit margin*, is calculated by dividing net income by sales:

$$\text{Profit margin} = \frac{\text{Net income}}{\text{Sales}}$$
$$= \frac{\$117.5}{\$3,000} = 3.9\%$$
$$\text{Industry average} = 5.0\%$$

Profit Margin
This ratio measures net income per dollar of sales and is calculated by dividing net income by sales.

Allied's 3.9% profit margin is below the industry average of 5.0%, and this subpar result occurred for two reasons. First, Allied's operating margin was below the industry average because of the firm's high operating costs. Second, the profit margin is negatively impacted by Allied's heavy use of debt. To see this second point, recognize that net income is *after interest*. Suppose two firms have identical operations in the sense that their sales, operating costs, and operating income are identical. However, one firm uses more debt; hence, it has higher interest charges. Those interest charges pull down its net income; and because sales are identical, the result is a relatively low profit margin for the firm with more debt. We see then that Allied's operating inefficiency and its high debt ratio combine to lower its profit margin below the food processing industry average. It also follows that when two companies have the same operating margin but different debt ratios, we can expect the company with a higher debt ratio to have a lower profit margin.

Note too that while a high return on sales is good, we must also be concerned with turnover. If a firm sets a very high price on its products, it may earn a high return on each sale but fail to make many sales. It might generate a high profit margin, but realize low sales, and hence experience a low net income. We will see shortly how, through the use of the DuPont equation, profit margins, the use of debt, and turnover ratios interact to affect overall stockholder returns.

4-5c RETURN ON TOTAL ASSETS

Return on Total Assets (ROA)

The ratio of net income to total assets.

Net income divided by total assets gives us the **return on total assets (ROA)**:

$$\text{Return on total assets (ROA)} = \frac{\text{Net income}}{\text{Total assets}}$$
$$= \frac{\$117.5}{\$2,000} = 5.9\%$$
$$\text{Industry average} = 9.0\%$$

Allied's 5.9% return is well below the 9.0% industry average. This is not good—it is obviously better to have a higher than a lower return on assets. Note, though, that a low ROA can result from a conscious decision to use a great deal of debt, in which case high interest expenses will cause net income to be relatively low. That is part of the reason for Allied's low ROA. Never forget—you must look at a number of ratios, see what each suggests, and then look at the overall situation before you judge the performance of a company and consider what actions it should undertake to improve.

4-5d RETURN ON COMMON EQUITY

Return on Common Equity (ROE)

The ratio of net income to common equity; measures the rate of return on common stockholders' investment.

Another important accounting ratio is the **return on common equity (ROE)**, which is found as follows:

$$\text{Return on common equity (ROE)} = \frac{\text{Net income}}{\text{Common equity}}$$
$$= \frac{\$117.5}{\$940} = 12.5\%$$
$$\text{Industry average} = 15.0\%$$

Stockholders expect to earn a return on their money, and this ratio tells how well they are doing in an accounting sense. Allied's 12.5% return is below the 15.0% industry average, but not as far below as the return on total assets. This somewhat better ROE results from the company's greater use of debt, a point discussed earlier in the chapter.

4-5e RETURN ON INVESTED CAPITAL

Return on Invested Capital (ROIC)

The ratio of after-tax operating income to total invested capital; it measures the total return that the company has provided for its investors.

The **return on invested capital (ROIC)** measures the total return that the company has provided for its investors.

$$\text{Return on invested capital (ROIC)} = \frac{\text{EBIT}(1-T)}{\text{Total invested capital}}$$
$$= \frac{\text{EBIT}(1-T)}{\text{Debt} + \text{Equity}} = \frac{\$170.3}{\$1,800} = 9.5\%$$
$$\text{Industry average} = 10.8\%$$

ROIC differs from ROA in two ways. First its return is based on total invested capital rather than total assets. Second, in the numerator it uses after-tax operating income (NOPAT) rather than net income. The key difference is that net income subtracts the company's after-tax interest expense and therefore represents the total amount of income available to shareholders, while NOPAT is the amount of funds available to pay both stockholders and debtholders.

QUICK QUESTION

QUESTION:

A company has $20 billion of sales and $1 billion of net income. Its total assets are $10 billion. The company's total assets equal total invested capital, and its capital consists of half debt and half common equity. The firm's interest rate is 5% and its tax rate is 40%.

a. What is its profit margin?
b. What is its ROA?
c. What is its ROE?
d. What is its ROIC?
e. Would this firm's ROA increase if it used less leverage? (The size of the firm does not change.)

ANSWER:

a. Profit margin $= \dfrac{\text{Net income}}{\text{Sales}} = \dfrac{\$1 \text{ billion}}{\$20 \text{ billion}} = 5\%$.

b. ROA $= \dfrac{\text{Net income}}{\text{Total assets}} = \dfrac{\$1 \text{ billion}}{\$10 \text{ billion}} = 10\%$.

c. ROE $= \dfrac{\text{Net income}}{\text{Common equity}} = \dfrac{\$1 \text{ billion}}{\$5 \text{ billion}} = 20\%$.

d. First, we need to calculate the firm's EBIT by working up the firm's income statement:

EBIT	$1,916,666,667	EBT + Interest
Interest	250,000,000	0.05 × 0.5 × $10,000,000,000
EBT	$1,666,666,667	$1,000,000,000/(1 − 0.4)
Taxes (40%)	666,666,667	EBT × 0.4
Net income	$1,000,000,000	

$$\text{ROIC} = \frac{\text{EBIT}(1-T)}{\text{Total invested capital}} = \frac{\$1,916,666,667(0.6)}{\$10,000,000,000} = 11.5\%.$$

e. If the company used less debt, it would increase net income because interest expense would be reduced. Because assets would not change and net income increases, ROA will increase.

4-5F BASIC EARNING POWER (BEP) RATIO

The **basic earning power (BEP) ratio** is calculated by dividing operating income (EBIT) by total assets:

$$\text{Basic earning power (BEP)} = \frac{\text{EBIT}}{\text{Total assets}}$$
$$= \frac{\$283.8}{\$2,000} = 14.2\%$$

Industry average $= 18.0\%$

Basic Earning Power (BEP) Ratio
This ratio indicates the ability of the firm's assets to generate operating income; it is calculated by dividing EBIT by total assets.

This ratio shows the raw earning power of the firm's assets before the influence of taxes and debt, and it is useful when comparing firms with different debt and tax situations. Because of its low turnover ratios and poor profit margin on sales, Allied has a lower BEP ratio than the average food processing company.

Identify six profitability ratios and write their equations.

Why does the use of debt lower the profit margin and the ROA?

Using more debt lowers profits and thus the ROA. Why doesn't debt have the same negative effect on the ROE?

A company has a 10% ROA. Assume that a company's total assets equals total invested capital, and that the company has no debt, so its total invested capital equals total equity. What is the company's ROE and ROIC? **(10%, 10%)**

4-6 MARKET VALUE RATIOS

ROE reflects the effects of all of the other ratios, and it is the single best accounting measure of performance. Investors like a high ROE, and high ROEs are correlated with high stock prices. However, other things come into play. For example, financial leverage generally increases the ROE but also increases the firm's risk; so if a high ROE is achieved by using a great deal of debt, the stock price might end up lower than if the firm had been using less debt and had a lower ROE. We use the final set of ratios—the **market value ratios**, which relate the stock price to earnings and book value price—to help address this situation. If the liquidity, asset management, debt management, and profitability ratios all look good and if investors think these ratios will continue to look good in the future, the market value ratios will be high, the stock price will be as high as can be expected, and management will be judged as having done a good job.

Market Value Ratios
Ratios that relate the firm's stock price to its earnings and book value per share.

The market value ratios are used in three primary ways: (1) by investors when they are deciding to buy or sell a stock, (2) by investment bankers when they are setting the share price for a new stock issue (an IPO), and (3) by firms when they are deciding how much to offer for another firm in a potential merger.

4-6A PRICE/EARNINGS RATIO

Price/Earnings (P/E) Ratio
The ratio of the price per share to earnings per share; shows the dollar amount investors will pay for $1 of current earnings.

The **price/earnings (P/E) ratio** shows how much investors are willing to pay per dollar of reported profits. Allied's stock sells for $23.06; so with an EPS of $2.35, its P/E ratio is 9.8×:

$$\text{Price/Earnings (P/E) ratio} = \frac{\text{Price per share}}{\text{Earnings per share}}$$

$$= \frac{\$23.06}{\$2.35} = 9.8\times$$

$$\text{Industry average} = 11.3\times$$

As we will see in Chapter 9, P/E ratios are relatively high for firms with strong growth prospects and little risk but low for slowly growing and risky firms. Allied's P/E ratio is below its industry average; so this suggests that the company is regarded as being relatively risky, as having poor growth prospects, or both.[14]

P/E ratios vary considerably over time and across firms.[15] In February 2013, the S&P 500's P/E ratio was 27.4×. At this same point in time, US Airways Group had a

---

[14]Security analysts also look at the Price-to-Free-Cash-Flow ratio. In addition, analysts consider the PEG, or P/E to growth, ratio where the P/E is divided by the firm's forecasted growth rate. Allied's growth rate as forecasted by a number of security analysts for the next 5 years is 7.0%, so its PEG = 9.8/7.0 = 1.4×. The lower the ratio, the better; and most firms have ratios in the range of 1.0× to 2.0×. We note, though, that P/E ratios jump around from year to year because earnings and forecasted growth rates fluctuate. Like other ratios, PEG ratios are interesting, but must be interpreted with care and judgment.

[15]On his website (www.econ.yale.edu/~shiller/data.htm), Professor Robert Shiller reports the annual P/E ratio of the overall stock market dating back to 1871. His calculations show that the historical average P/E ratio for the market has been 16.4×, and it has ranged from 4.8× to 44.2×.

P/E of 4.3×, while Under Armour, Inc., a rapidly growing apparel company, had a P/E of 39.2×. Moreover, once high-flying growth stocks such as Intel and Exxon Mobil (both of which a decade ago had P/E ratios above 20), have seen their P/Es fall to around 9× as they become larger, more stable companies with fewer growth opportunities.

4-6B MARKET/BOOK RATIO

The ratio of a stock's market price to its book value gives another indication of how investors regard the company. Companies that are well regarded by investors—which means low risk and high growth—have high M/B ratios. For Allied, we first find its book value per share:

$$\text{Book value per share} = \frac{\text{Common equity}}{\text{Shares outstanding}}$$
$$= \frac{\$940}{50} = \$18.80$$

We then divide the market price per share by the book value per share to get the **market/book (M/B) ratio**, which for Allied is 1.2×:

$$\text{Market/Book (M/B) ratio} = \frac{\text{Market price per share}}{\text{Book value per share}}$$
$$= \frac{\$23.06}{\$18.80} = 1.2\times$$
$$\text{Industry average} = 1.7\times$$

Market/Book (M/B) Ratio
The ratio of a stock's market price to its book value.

Investors are willing to pay less for a dollar of Allied's book value than for one of an average food processing company. This is consistent with our other findings. M/B ratios typically exceed 1.0, which means that investors are willing to pay more for stocks than the accounting book values of the stocks. This situation occurs primarily because asset values, as reported by accountants on corporate balance sheets, do not reflect either inflation or goodwill. Assets purchased years ago at pre-inflation prices are carried at their original costs even though inflation might have caused their actual values to rise substantially; and successful companies' values rise above their historical costs, whereas unsuccessful ones have low M/B ratios.[16] This point is demonstrated by Google and Bank of America: In February 2013, Google's M/B ratio was 3.68× while Bank of America's was only 0.57×. Google's stockholders now have $3.68 in market value per $1.00 of equity, whereas Bank of America's stockholders have only $0.57 for each dollar they invested.

SELF TEST

Describe two ratios that relate a firm's stock price to its earnings and book value per share and write their equations.

In what sense do these market value ratios reflect investors' opinions about a stock's risk and expected future growth?

What does the price/earnings (P/E) ratio show? If one firm's P/E ratio is lower than that of another firm, what factors might explain the difference?

How is book value per share calculated? Explain how inflation and R&D programs might cause book values to deviate from market values.

---

[16]The second point is known as *survivor bias*. Successful companies survive and are reflected in the averages, whereas unsuccessful companies vanish and their low numbers are not reflected in the averages.

4-7 TYING THE RATIOS TOGETHER: THE DUPONT EQUATION

DuPont Equation

A formula that shows that the rate of return on equity can be found as the product of profit margin, total assets turnover, and the equity multiplier. It shows the relationships among asset management, debt management, and profitability ratios.

We have discussed many ratios, so it would be useful to see how they work together to determine the ROE. For this, we use the **DuPont equation**, a formula developed by the chemical giant's financial staff in the 1920s. It is shown here for Allied and the food processing industry.

$$ROE = ROA \times \text{Equity multiplier}$$
$$= \text{Profit margin} \times \text{Total assets turnover} \times \text{Equity multiplier}$$
$$= \frac{\text{Net income}}{\text{Sales}} \times \frac{\text{Sales}}{\text{Total assets}} \times \frac{\text{Total assets}}{\text{Total common equity}}$$
$$= \frac{\$117.5}{\$3,000} \times \frac{\$3,000}{\$2,000} \times \frac{\$2,000}{\$940}$$
$$= 3.92\% \times 1.5 \text{ times} \times 2.13 \text{ times} = 12.5\%$$

4.1

$$\text{Industry} = 5.0\% \times 1.8 \text{ times} \times 1.67 \text{ times} = 15.0\%$$

- The first term, the profit margin, tells us how much the firm earns on its sales. This ratio depends primarily on costs and sales prices—if a firm can command a premium price and hold down its costs, its profit margin will be high, which will help its ROE.

- The second term is the total assets turnover. It is a "multiplier" that tells us how many times the profit margin is earned each year—Allied earned 3.92% on each dollar of sales, and its assets were turned over 1.5 times each year; so its return on assets was $3.92\% \times 1.5 = 5.9\%$. Note, though, that this entire 5.9% belongs to the common stockholders—the bondholders earned a return in the form of interest, and that interest was deducted before we calculated net income to stockholders. So the whole 5.9% return on assets belongs to the stockholders. Therefore, the return on assets must be adjusted upward to obtain the return on equity.

- That brings us to the third term, the equity multiplier, which is the adjustment factor. Allied's assets are 2.13 times its equity, so we must multiply the 5.9% return on assets by the 2.13× equity multiplier to arrive at its ROE of 12.5%.[17]

Note that ROE as calculated using the DuPont equation is identical to Allied's ROE, 12.5%, which we calculated earlier. What's the point of going through all of the steps required to implement the DuPont equation to find ROE? The answer is that the DuPont equation helps us see *why* Allied's ROE is only 12.5% versus 15.0% for the industry. First, its profit margin is below average, which indicates that its costs are not being controlled as well as they should be and that it cannot charge premium prices. In addition, because it uses more debt than most companies, its high interest charges also reduce its profit margin. Second, its total assets turnover is below the industry average, which indicates that it has more assets than it needs. Finally, because its equity multiplier is relatively high, its heavy use of debt offsets to some extent its low profit margin and turnover. However, the high debt ratio exposes Allied to above-average bankruptcy risk; so it might want

---

[17]The equity multiplier relates to the firm's use of debt. The industry equity multiplier can be obtained by using the industry ROE and ROA. The equity multiplier = Total assets divided by common equity. ROE = Net income/Common equity and ROA = Net income/Total assets. So, ROE ÷ ROA = Equity multiplier as shown below:

$$\frac{ROE}{ROA} = \frac{NI}{Equity} \div \frac{NI}{Assets} = \frac{NI}{Equity} \times \frac{Assets}{NI} = \frac{Assets}{Equity} = \text{Equity multiplier}$$

MICROSOFT EXCEL: A TRULY ESSENTIAL TOOL

Microsoft Excel is an essential tool for anyone dealing with business issues—not just finance and accounting professionals but also lawyers, marketers, auto sales managers, government employees, and many others. Indeed, anyone who works with numbers will be more efficient and productive if they know the basics of Excel, so it's a necessity for anyone who hopes to hold a managerial position.

As you go through this book, you will see that Excel is used in four main ways:

1. *As a financial calculator.* Excel can add, subtract, multiply, and divide, and it can retain results from one operation for use in subsequent operations. For example, we created the financial statements in Chapter 3 with Excel, and we use it to analyze those statements in the current chapter. We could have done this with a calculator or pencil and paper, but it was a lot easier with Excel. As we will see throughout the text, Excel also has a large number of built-in financial functions that can be used to simply calculate the answers to a wide range of financial problems. For example, using Excel, it is straightforward to calculate the return on an investment, the price of a bond, or the value of a project.

2. *To modify the work when things change.* Suppose your boss asked you to create the statements in Chapter 3, but when you finished she said, "Thanks, but the accounting department just informed us that inventories in 2014 were overstated by $100 million, which means that total assets were also overstated. To make the balance sheet balance, we must reduce retained earnings, common equity, and total claims against assets. Please make those adjustments and give me a revised set of statements before the board meeting tomorrow morning."

    If you were working with a calculator, you'd be looking at an all-nighter, but with Excel you could make just one change—reduce 2014 inventories by $100 million—

and Excel would instantly revise the statements. If your company had two people working on problems like this, who would get promoted and who would get a pink slip?

3. *Sensitivity analysis.* We use ratios to analyze financial statements and assess how well a company is managed, and if weaknesses are detected management can make changes to improve the situation. For example, Allied's return on equity (ROE), a key determinant of its stock price, is below the industry average. ROE depends on a number of factors, including the level of inventories, and using Excel one can see how ROE would change if inventories were increased or decreased. Then, management can investigate alternative inventory policies to see how they would impact profits and the ROE. In theory, one could do this analysis with a calculator, but this would be inefficient, and in a competitive world efficiency is essential to survival.

4. *Risk assessments.* Sensitivity analysis can be used to assess the risk inherent in different policies. For example, *forecasted* returns on equity are generally higher if a firm increases its debt, but the more debt the firm carries, the worse the effects of an economic downturn. We can use Excel to quantify the effects of changing economic conditions with different amounts of debt, and thus the probability that the firm will go bankrupt in a recession. Many firms learned about this during the 2008–2009 recession, so the survivors are now more interested than ever in risk models.

This listing gives you an idea of what Excel can do and why it is important in business today. We illustrate it throughout the book, and you should make an effort to understand how to use it. The Excel chapter models can be found on the text's website, www.cengagebrain.com. You will find an understanding of Excel very helpful when you begin interviewing for a job.[18]

to cut back on its financial leverage. But if it reduced its debt to the same level as the average firm in its industry without any other changes, its ROE would decline significantly, to $3.92\% \times 1.5 \times 1.67 = 9.8\%$.[19]

Allied's management can use the DuPont equation to help identify ways to improve its performance. Focusing on the profit margin, its marketing people can

---

[18]It is often impractical for professors to test students on their ability to integrate Excel into financial management, so some students conclude that knowing more about Excel won't help them on tests and thus they ignore it. That's unfortunate, and we can only say that there's more to school than grades alone, and in the long run knowing something about Excel is one of the most valuable tools you can learn in school.

[19]The ROE reduction would actually be somewhat less because if debt were lowered, interest payments would also decline, which would raise Allied's profit margin. Allied's analysts determined that the net effect of a reduction in debt would still be a significant reduction in ROE.

study the effects of raising sales prices or of introducing new products with higher margins. Its cost accountants can study various expense items and, working with engineers, purchasing agents, and other operating personnel, seek ways to cut costs. The credit manager can investigate ways to speed up collections, which would reduce accounts receivable and therefore improve the quality of the total assets turnover ratio. And the financial staff can analyze the effects of alternative debt policies, showing how changes in leverage would affect both the expected ROE and the risk of bankruptcy.

As a result of this analysis, Ellen Jackson, Allied's chief executive officer (CEO), undertook a series of moves that are expected to cut operating costs by more than 20%. Jackson and Allied's other executives have a strong incentive to improve the firm's financial performance—their compensation depends on how well the company operates.

SELF TEST

Write the equation for the DuPont equation.

What is the equity multiplier, and why is it used?

How can management use the DuPont equation to analyze ways of improving the firm's performance?

4-8 POTENTIAL MISUSES OF ROE

While ROE is an important measure of performance, we know that managers should strive to maximize shareholder wealth. If a firm takes steps that improve its ROE, does that mean that shareholder wealth will also be increased? The answer is, "not necessarily." Indeed, three problems are likely to arise if a firm relies too heavily on ROE to measure performance.

First, ROE does not consider risk. Shareholders care about ROE, but they also care about risk. To illustrate, consider two divisions within the same firm. Division S has stable cash flows and a predictable 15% ROE. Division R has a 16% expected ROE, but its cash flows are quite risky; so the expected ROE may not materialize. If managers were compensated solely on the basis of ROE and if the expected ROEs were actually achieved during the coming year, Division R's manager would receive a higher bonus than S's even though S might actually be creating more value for shareholders as a result of its lower risk. Similarly, financial leverage can increase expected ROE, but more leverage means higher risk; so raising ROE through the use of leverage may not be good.

Second, ROE does not consider the amount of invested capital. To illustrate, consider a company that is choosing between two mutually exclusive projects. Project A calls for investing $50,000 at an expected ROE of 50%, while Project B calls for investing $1,000,000 at a 45% ROE. The projects are equally risky, and the company's cost of capital is 10%. Project A has the higher ROE, but it is much smaller. Project B should be chosen because it would add more to shareholder wealth.

Third, a focus on ROE can cause managers to turn down profitable projects. For example, suppose you manage a division of a large firm and the firm determines bonuses solely on the basis of ROE. You project that your division's ROE for the year will be an impressive 45%. Now you have an opportunity to invest in a large, low-risk project with an estimated ROE of 35%, which is well above the firm's 10% cost of capital. Even though this project is extremely profitable, you might still be reluctant to undertake it because it would reduce your division's average ROE and therefore your year-end bonus.

ECONOMIC VALUE ADDED (EVA) VERSUS NET INCOME

As we mentioned in Chapter 3, Economic Value Added (EVA) is a measure of how much management has added to shareholders' wealth during the year. To better understand the idea behind EVA, let's look at Allied's 2014 numbers (in millions). Allied's total invested capital consists of $110 of notes payable, $750 of long-term debt, and $940 of common equity, totaling $1,800. Debt represents 47.78% of this total, and common equity is 52.22% of this total. Later in the text we will discuss how to calculate the cost of Allied's capital; but for now, to simplify things, we estimate its capital cost at 10%. Thus, the firm's total dollar cost of capital (which includes both debt and common equity) per year is 0.10($1,800) = $180.

Now let's look at Allied's income statement. Its operating income, EBIT, is $283.8; and its interest expense is $88.0. Therefore, its taxable income is $283.8 − $88.0 = $195.8. Taxes equal 40% of taxable income, or 0.4($195.8) = $78.3; so the firm's net income is $117.5. Its return on equity, ROE, is $117.5/$940 = 12.5%.

Given this data, we can now calculate Allied's EVA. The basic formula for EVA (as discussed in Chapter 3) is as follows:

$$\text{EVA} = \text{EBIT}(1-T) - \left(\begin{array}{c}\text{Total}\\\text{invested capital}\end{array}\right) \times \left(\begin{array}{c}\text{After-tax}\\\text{cost of capital}\end{array}\right)$$

$$= \$283.8(1-0.40) - (\$1,800)(0.10)$$

$$= \$170.3 - \$180$$

$$= -\$9.7$$

This negative EVA indicates that Allied's shareholders actually earned $9.7 million less than they could have earned elsewhere by investing in other stocks with the same risk as Allied. To see where this −$9.7 comes from, let's trace what happened to the money:

- The firm generated $283.8 of operating income.
- $78.3 went to the government to pay taxes, leaving $205.5 available for investors—stockholders and bondholders.

- $88.0 went to the bondholders in the form of interest payments, thus leaving $117.5 for the stockholders.
- However, Allied's shareholders must also earn a return on the equity capital they have invested in the firm because they could have invested in other companies of comparable risk. We call this the cost of Allied's equity.
- Once Allied's shareholders are "paid" their return, the firm comes up $9.7 million short—that's the economic value management added, and it is negative. In a sense, Allied's management created *negative* wealth because it provided shareholders with a lower return than they could have earned on alternative investments with the same risk as Allied's stock.
- In practice, it is often necessary to make several adjustments to arrive at a "better" measure of EVA. The adjustments deal with nonoperating assets, leased assets, depreciation, and other accounting details that we leave for discussion in advanced finance courses.

The Connection between ROE and EVA

EVA is different from traditional accounting profit *because EVA reflects the cost of equity as well as the cost of debt*. Indeed, using the previous example, we could also express EVA as net income minus the dollar cost of equity:

$$\text{EVA} = \text{Net income} - (\text{Equity} \times \text{Cost of equity})$$

This expression above could be rewritten as follows:

$$\text{EVA} = (\text{Equity})(\text{Net income}/\text{Equity} - \text{Cost of equity})$$

which can be rewritten as:

$$\text{EVA} = \text{Equity}(\text{ROE} - \text{Cost of equity})$$

This last expression implies that EVA depends on three factors: rate of return, as reflected in ROE; risk, which affects the cost of equity; and size, which is measured by the equity employed. Recall that earlier in this chapter, we said that shareholder value depends on risk, return, and capital invested. This final equation illustrates that point.

These three examples suggest that a project's ROE must be combined with its size and risk to determine its effect on shareholder value as we illustrate in the diagram below:

We will discuss this in more depth when we consider capital budgeting, where we look in detail at how projects are selected so as to maximize stock prices, and consequently, shareholder value.

4-9 Using Financial Ratios to Assess Performance

While financial ratios help us evaluate financial statements, it is often hard to evaluate a company by just looking at the ratios. For example, if you see that a company has a current ratio of 1.2, it is hard to know if that is good or bad, unless you put the ratio in its proper perspective. Allied's management could look at industry averages, it could compare itself to specific companies or "benchmarks," and it can analyze the trends in each ratio. We look at all three approaches in this section.

4-9A Comparison to Industry Average

As we have done for Allied, one way to assess performance, is to compare the company's key ratios to the industry averages. Table 4.2 provides a summary of the ratios we have discussed in this chapter. This table is useful as a quick reference, and the calculated ratios and accompanying comments give a good sense of Allied's strengths and weaknesses relative to the average food processing company. To give you a further sense of some "real-world" ratios, Table 4.3 provides a list of ratios for a number of different industries in February 2013.

4-9B Benchmarking

Benchmarking

The process of comparing a particular company with a subset of top competitors in their industry.

Ratio analysis involves comparisons with industry average figures, but Allied and many other firms also compare themselves with a subset of top competitors in their industry. This is called **benchmarking**, and the companies used for the comparison are called benchmark companies. Allied's management benchmarks against Campbell Soup, a leading manufacturer of canned soups; Dean Foods, a processor of canned and frozen vegetables; Fresh Del Monte Produce, a processor of fruits and vegetables; Flowers Foods, a producer of bakery and snack-food goods; Hershey Foods, a producer of chocolates and nonchocolate confectionary products; and Kellogg Company, a manufacturer of ready-to-eat cereals and convenience foods. Ratios are calculated for each company, then listed in descending order as shown below for the profit margin (the firms' latest 12 months' results reported by MSN Money (money.msn.com) as of February 25, 2013):

Company	Profit Margin
Flowers Foods	31.62%
Hershey Foods	9.95
Campbell Soup	9.01
Kellogg	6.51
Fresh Del Monte Produce	4.16
Allied Food Products	**3.90**
Dean Foods	1.34

	Allied Food Products: Summary of Financial Ratios (Millions of Dollars)				**TABLE 4.2**

Ratio	Formula	Calculation	Ratio	Industry Average	Comment
Liquidity					
Current	$\dfrac{\text{Current assets}}{\text{Current liabilities}}$	$\dfrac{\$1,000}{\$310}$	= 3.2×	4.2×	Poor
Quick	$\dfrac{\text{Current assets} - \text{Inventories}}{\text{Current liabilities}}$	$\dfrac{\$385}{\$310}$	= 1.2×	2.2×	Poor
Asset Management					
Inventory turnover	$\dfrac{\text{Sales}}{\text{Inventories}}$	$\dfrac{\$3,000}{\$615}$	= 4.9×	10.9×	Poor
Days sales outstanding (DSO)	$\dfrac{\text{Receivables}}{\text{Annual sales}/365}$	$\dfrac{\$375}{\$8.2192}$	= 46 days	36 days	Poor
Fixed assets turnover	$\dfrac{\text{Sales}}{\text{Net fixed assets}}$	$\dfrac{\$3,000}{\$1,000}$	= 3.0×	2.8×	OK
Total assets turnover	$\dfrac{\text{Sales}}{\text{Total assets}}$	$\dfrac{\$3,000}{\$2,000}$	= 1.5×	1.8×	Somewhat low
Debt Management					
Total debt to total capital	$\dfrac{\text{Total debt}}{\text{Total capital}}$	$\dfrac{\$860}{\$1,800}$	= 47.8%	36.4%	High (risky)
Times-interest-earned (TIE)	$\dfrac{\text{Earnings before interest and taxes (EBIT)}}{\text{Interest charges}}$	$\dfrac{\$283.8}{\$88}$	= 3.2×	6.0×	Low (risky)
Profitability					
Operating margin	$\dfrac{\text{Operating income (EBIT)}}{\text{Sales}}$	$\dfrac{\$283.8}{\$3,000}$	= 9.5%	10.0%	Low
Profit margin	$\dfrac{\text{Net income}}{\text{Sales}}$	$\dfrac{\$117.5}{\$3,000}$	= 3.9%	5.0%	Poor
Return on total assets (ROA)	$\dfrac{\text{Net income}}{\text{Total assets}}$	$\dfrac{\$117.5}{\$2,000}$	= 5.9%	9.0%	Poor
Return on common equity (ROE)	$\dfrac{\text{Net income}}{\text{Common equity}}$	$\dfrac{\$117.5}{\$940}$	= 12.5%	15.0%	Poor
Return on invested capital (ROIC)	$\dfrac{\text{EBIT}(1-T)}{\text{Total invested capital}}$	$\dfrac{\$170.3}{\$1,800}$	= 9.5%	10.8%	Poor
Basic earning power (BEP)	$\dfrac{\text{Earnings before interest and taxes (EBIT)}}{\text{Total assets}}$	$\dfrac{\$283.8}{\$2,000}$	= 14.2%	18.0%	Poor
Market Value					
Price/Earnings (P/E)	$\dfrac{\text{Price per share}}{\text{Earnings per share}}$	$\dfrac{\$23.06}{\$2.35}$	= 9.8×	11.3×	Low
Market/Book (M/B)	$\dfrac{\text{Market price per share}}{\text{Book value per share}}$	$\dfrac{\$23.06}{\$18.80}$	= 1.2×	1.7×	Low

The benchmarking setup makes it easy for Allied's management to see exactly where it stands relative to the competition. As the data show, Allied is near the bottom of its benchmark group relative to its profit margin, so it has lots of room for improvement. Other ratios are analyzed similarly.

Comparative ratios are available from a number of sources, including both Yahoo! Finance and MSN Money. Useful ratios are also compiled by Value Line, Dun and Bradstreet (D&B), and the Risk Management Association, which is the national association of bank loan officers. Also, financial statement data for thousands of publicly owned corporations are available on other Internet sites, and as brokerage houses, banks, and other financial institutions have access to these data, security analysts can and do generate comparative ratios tailored to their specific needs.

TABLE 4.3 Key Financial Ratios for Selected Industries[a]

Industry Name	Current Ratio	Inventory Turnover[b]	Total Assets Turnover	LT Debt/ LT Capital[c]	Days Sales Outstanding[d]	Net Profit Margin	Return on Assets	Return on Equity
Aerospace/defense	1.6	5.9	0.9	94.8%	42.44	6.7%	5.6%	87.0%
Apparel stores	2.3	4.2	1.8	21.3	4.64	6.5	11.9	3359.0
Auto manufacturing—major	1.0	9.0	0.7	62.0	32.30	4.7	3.6	15.6
Beverage (soft drink)	1.2	7.5	0.8	51.0	36.87	14.1	8.2	27.1
Electronics—diversified	3.9	5.1	0.7	19.4	24.50	8.8	4.7	6.7
Food wholesalers	1.7	13.5	3.0	43.2	25.35	2.3	6.9	17.6
Grocery stores	1.1	17.2	2.3	84.9	6.90	2.9	5.8	14.7
Health services—specialized	1.8	21.9	0.8	55.8	64.04	9.5	6.9	21.4
Lodging	1.1	165.1	0.7	50.7	13.93	9.6	5.8	18.3
Newspapers	0.5	7.4	0.2	6.5	214.71	7.0	1.0	2.3
Paper and paper products	2.1	6.6	0.7	51.5	52.14	0.7	1.2	4.6
Railroad	1.1	15.0	0.5	41.2	33.80	15.9	7.3	18.7
Restaurant	0.7	25.9	0.8	61.5	9.58	13.7	6.4	21.3
Retail (department stores)	1.5	5.8	1.9	29.6	2.80	5.1	10.6	22.9
Scientific and technical instruments	2.9	8.6	0.7	37.5	41.01	8.3	6.2	14.3
Sporting goods	2.3	3.4	2.0	36.7	27.24	1.3	4.9	15.4
Steel and iron	2.0	3.9	0.9	42.2	40.11	5.1	4.0	8.0
Tobacco (cigarettes)	1.1	2.7	1.3	57.3	14.43	16.1	18.2	35.8

Notes:

[a]The ratios presented are averages for each industry. Ratios for the individual companies are also available.

[b]The inventory turnover ratio in this table is calculated as the company's latest 12 months of cost of sales divided by the average of its inventory for the last quarter and the comparable year earlier quarter.

[c]LT debt/LT capital is calculated as LT debt/(LT debt + Equity) by using MSN's Debt/Equity ratio as follows:

$$\frac{D/E}{(1 + D/E)}$$

[d]The days sales outstanding ratio in this table was calculated as 365/Receivable turnover. The receivable turnover is calculated as the company's latest 12 months of sales divided by the average of its receivables for the last quarter and the comparable year earlier quarter.

Source: Data obtained from MSN Money, Key Ratios (money.msn.com), February 25, 2013.

Each of the data-supplying organizations uses a somewhat different set of ratios designed for its own purposes. For example, D&B deals mainly with small firms, many of which are proprietorships, and it sells its services primarily to banks and other lenders. Therefore, D&B is concerned largely with the creditor's viewpoint, and its ratios emphasize current assets and liabilities, not market value ratios. So, when you select a comparative data source, you should be sure that your emphasis is similar to that of the agency whose ratios you plan to use. Additionally, there are often definitional differences in the ratios presented by different sources, so before using a source, be sure to verify the exact definitions of the ratios to ensure consistency with your own work.

Trend Analysis

An analysis of a firm's financial ratios over time; used to estimate the likelihood of improvement or deterioration in its financial condition.

4-9C TREND ANALYSIS

As a final comparison, Allied compares its ratios to its own past levels. It is important to analyze trends in ratios as well as their absolute levels, for trends give clues as to whether a firm's financial condition is likely to improve or to deteriorate. To do a **trend analysis**, simply plot a ratio over time, as shown in Figure 4.1. This graph shows that Allied's ROE has been declining since 2011 even

FIGURE 4.1   Rate of Return on Common Equity, 2010–2014

though the industry average has been relatively stable. All the other ratios could be analyzed similarly, and such an analysis can be quite useful in gaining insights as to why the ROE behaved as it did.

SELF TEST

Why might railroads have such low total assets turnovers and food wholesalers and grocery stores such high turnovers?

If competition causes all companies to have similar ROEs in the long run, would companies with high turnovers tend to have high or low profit margins? Explain your answer.

Why are comparative ratio analyses useful?

How does one do a trend analysis?

What important information does a trend analysis provide?

4-10 USES AND LIMITATIONS OF RATIOS

As noted earlier, ratio analysis is used by three main groups: (1) *managers,* who use ratios to help analyze, control, and thus improve their firms' operations; (2) *credit analysts,* including bank loan officers and bond rating analysts, who analyze ratios to help judge a company's ability to repay its debts; and (3) *stock analysts,* who are interested in a company's efficiency, risk, and growth prospects. In later chapters, we will look more closely at the basic factors that underlie each ratio. Note, though, that while ratio analysis can provide useful information concerning a company's operations and financial condition, it does have limitations. Some potential problems are listed here:

To find information about a company quickly, link to **reuters.com**. *Here you can find company profiles and snapshots, stock price quotes and share information, key ratios, and comparative ratios.*

1. Many firms have divisions that operate in different industries; and for such companies, it is difficult to develop a meaningful set of industry averages. Therefore, ratio analysis is more useful for narrowly focused firms than for multidivisional ones.

2. Most firms want to be better than average, so merely attaining average performance is not necessarily good. As a target for high-level performance, it is best to focus on the industry leaders' ratios. Benchmarking helps in this regard.

3. Inflation has distorted many firms' balance sheets—book values are often different from market values. Market values would be more appropriate for most purposes, but we cannot generally get market value figures because assets such as used machinery are not traded in the marketplace. Further, inflation affects asset values, depreciation charges, inventory costs, and thus profits. Therefore, a ratio analysis for one firm over time or a comparative analysis of firms of different ages must be interpreted with care and judgment.

4. Seasonal factors can also distort a ratio analysis. For example, the inventory turnover ratio for a food processor will be radically different if the balance sheet figure used for inventory is the one just before versus just after the close of the canning season. This problem can be mitigated by using monthly averages for inventory (and receivables) when calculating turnover ratios.

"Window Dressing" Techniques

Techniques employed by firms to make their financial statements look better than they really are.

5. Firms can employ **"window dressing" techniques** to improve their financial statements. To illustrate, people tend to think that larger hedge funds got large because their high returns attracted many investors. However, we learned in 2007 that some funds simply borrowed and invested money to increase their apparent size. One fund, Wharton Asset Management, reported $2 billion "under management," but it had actually attracted less than $100 million of investors' capital.

6. Different accounting practices can distort comparisons. As noted earlier, inventory valuation and depreciation methods can affect financial statements and thus distort comparisons among firms. Also, if one firm leases much of its productive equipment, its fixed assets turnover may be artificially high because leased assets often do not appear on the balance sheet. At the same time, the liability associated with the lease may not appear as debt, keeping the debt ratio low even though failure to make lease payments can bankrupt the firm. Therefore, leasing can artificially improve both turnover and the debt ratios. The accounting profession has taken steps to reduce this problem, but it still can cause distortions.

7. It is difficult to generalize about whether a particular ratio is "good" or "bad." For example, a high current ratio may indicate a strong liquidity position, which is good, but it can also indicate excessive cash, which is bad because excess cash in the bank is a nonearning asset. Similarly, a high fixed assets turnover ratio may indicate that the firm uses its assets efficiently, but it could also indicate that the firm is short of cash and cannot afford to make needed fixed asset investments.

8. Firms often have some ratios that look "good" and others that look "bad," making it difficult to tell whether the company is, on balance, strong or weak. To deal with this problem, banks and other lending organizations often use statistical procedures to analyze the *net effects* of a set of ratios and to classify firms according to their probability of getting into financial trouble.[20]

We see then that ratio analysis is useful, but analysts should be aware of the problems just listed and make adjustments as necessary. Ratio analysis conducted

---

[20]The technique used is discriminant analysis. The seminal work on this subject was undertaken by Edward I Altman, "Financial Ratios, Discriminant Analysis, and the Prediction of Corporate Bankruptcy," *Journal of Finance*, vol. 23, no. 4 (September 1968), pp. 589–609.

LOOKING FOR WARNING SIGNS WITHIN THE FINANCIAL STATEMENTS

Financial scandals have spurred a renewed interest in financial accounting, and analysts now scour companies' financial statements to see if trouble is lurking. This renewed interest has led to a list of red flags to consider when reviewing a company's financial statements. For example, after conferring with New York University Accounting Professor Baruch Lev, *Fortune* magazine's Shawn Tully identified the following warning signs:

- Year after year a company reports restructuring charges and/or write-downs. This practice raises concerns because companies can use write-downs to mask operating expenses, which results in overstated earnings.

- A company's earnings have been propped up through a series of acquisitions. Acquisitions can increase earnings if the acquiring company has a higher P/E ratio than the acquired firm, but such "growth" cannot be sustained over the long run.

- A company depreciates its assets more slowly than the industry average. Lower depreciation boosts current earnings, but again this cannot be sustained because eventually depreciation must be recognized.

- A company routinely has high earnings but low cash flow. As Tully points out, this warning sign would have exposed Enron's problems. In the second quarter of 2001

(a few months before its problems began to unfold), Enron reported earnings of $423 million versus a cash flow of minus $527 million.

Along similar lines, after consulting with various professionals, Ellen Simon of the *Newark Star Ledger* came up with her list of red flags:

- You wouldn't buy the stock at today's price.
- You don't really understand the company's financial statements.
- The company is in a business that lends itself to "creative accounting."
- The company keeps taking nonrecurring charges.
- Accounts receivable and inventory are increasing faster than sales revenues.
- The company's insiders are selling their stock.
- The company is making aggressive acquisitions, especially in unrelated fields.

There is some overlap between these two lists. Also, none of these items automatically means there is something wrong with the company—instead, the items should be viewed as warning signs that cause you to take a closer look at the company's performance before making an investment.

in a mechanical, unthinking manner is dangerous; but used intelligently and with good judgment, it can provide useful insights into firms' operations. Your judgment in interpreting ratios is bound to be weak at this point, but it will improve as you go through the remainder of the book.

SELF TEST

List three types of users of ratio analysis. Would the different users emphasize the same or different types of ratios? Explain.

List several potential difficulties with ratio analysis.

4-11 LOOKING BEYOND THE NUMBERS

Working through this chapter should increase your ability to understand and interpret financial statements. This is critically important for anyone making business decisions or forecasting stock prices. However, sound financial analysis involves more than just numbers—good analysis requires that certain qualitative

*Students might want to refer to AAII's educational website at **aaii.com**. The site provides information on investing basics, financial planning, and portfolio management, so that individuals can manage their own assets more effectively.*

factors also be considered. These factors, as summarized by the American Association of Individual Investors (AAII), include the following:

1. Are the company's revenues tied to one key customer? If so, the company's performance may decline dramatically if that customer goes elsewhere. On the other hand, if the customer has no alternative to the company's products, this might actually stabilize sales.

2. To what extent are the company's revenues tied to one key product? Firms that focus on a single product are often efficient, but a lack of diversification also increases risk because having revenues from several products stabilizes profits and cash flows in a volatile world.

3. To what extent does the company rely on a single supplier? Depending on a single supplier may lead to an unanticipated shortage and a hit to sales and profits.

4. What percentage of the company's business is generated overseas? Companies with a large percentage of overseas business are often able to realize higher growth and larger profit margins. However, overseas operations may expose the firm to political risks and exchange rate problems.

5. How much competition does the firm face? Increases in competition tend to lower prices and profit margins; so when forecasting future performance, it is important to assess the likely actions of current competitors and the entry of new ones.

6. Is it necessary for the company to continually invest in research and development? If so, its future prospects will depend critically on the success of new products in the pipeline. For example, investors in a pharmaceutical company want to know whether the company has a strong pipeline of potential blockbuster drugs and whether those products are doing well in the required tests.

7. Are changes in laws and regulations likely to have important implications for the firm? For example, when the future of electric utilities is forecasted, it is crucial to factor in the effects of proposed regulations affecting the use of coal, nuclear, and gas-fired plants.

As a good illustration of the need to look beyond the numbers, consider the recent rise of Netflix. While Netflix's financial statements have improved over time, the rapid improvement in the company's stock price is more due to the market's expectations regarding its future prospects. Many investors believe that households will increasingly access movies directly through streaming video, and that Netflix is well positioned to take advantage of this changing technology. At the same time, the above factors suggest that Netflix's success is far from guaranteed. Indeed, many suggest that confronted with this technology the company will face a new set of digital/on-demand competitors from cable companies and from other sources, such as Apple's iTunes. It will be interesting for both consumers and Netflix's shareholders to see how this plays out in the years ahead.

SELF TEST

What are some qualitative factors that analysts should consider when evaluating a company's likely future financial performance?

TYING IT ALL TOGETHER

In the last chapter, we discussed the key financial statements; and in this one, we described how ratios are used to analyze the statements to identify weaknesses that need to be strengthened to maximize the stock price. Ratios are grouped into five categories:

- Liquidity
- Asset management
- Debt management
- Profitability
- Market value

The firm's ratios are compared with averages for its industry and with the leading firms in the industry (benchmarking), and these comparisons are used to help formulate policies that will lead to improved future performance. Similarly, the firm's own ratios can be analyzed over time to see if its financial situation is getting better or worse (trend analysis).

The single most important ratio over which management has control is the ROE—the other ratios are also important, but mainly because they affect the ROE. One tool used to show how ROE is determined is the DuPont equation: ROE = Profit margin × Total assets turnover × Equity multiplier. If the firm's ROE is below the industry average and that of the benchmark companies, a DuPont analysis can help identify problem areas that should be strengthened. In later chapters, we consider specific actions that can be taken to improve ROE and thus a firm's stock price. One closing note: Although ratio analysis is useful, it must be applied with care and good judgment. Actions taken to improve one ratio can have negative effects on other ratios. For example, it might be possible to improve the ROE by using more debt, but the risk of the additional debt may lead to a decrease in the P/E ratio and thus in the firm's stock price. Quantitative analysis such as ratio analysis can be useful, but thinking through the results is even more important.

SELF-TEST QUESTIONS AND PROBLEMS

(Solutions Appear in Appendix A)

ST-1 **KEY TERMS**   Define each of the following terms:

a. Liquid asset

b. Liquidity ratios: current ratio; quick (acid test) ratio

c. Asset management ratios: inventory turnover ratio; days sales outstanding (DSO); fixed assets turnover ratio; total assets turnover ratio

d. Debt management ratios: total debt to total capital; times-interest-earned (TIE) ratio

e. Profitability ratios: operating margin; profit margin; return on total assets (ROA); return on common equity (ROE); return on invested capital (ROIC); basic earning power (BEP) ratio

f. Market value ratios: price/earnings (P/E) ratio; market/book (M/B) ratio

g. DuPont equation; benchmarking; trend analysis

h. "Window dressing" techniques

ST-2   **TOTAL DEBT TO TOTAL CAPITAL**   Last year K. Billingsworth & Co. had earnings per share of $4 and dividends per share of $2. Total retained earnings increased by $12 million during the year, while book value per share at year-end was $40. Billingsworth has no preferred stock, and no new common stock was issued during the year. If its year-end total debt was $120 million, what was the company's year-end total debt to total capital ratio?

ST-3   **RATIO ANALYSIS**   The following data apply to A.L. Kaiser & Company (millions of dollars):

Cash and equivalents	$ 100.00
Fixed assets	283.50
Sales	1,000.00
Net income	50.00
Current liabilities	105.50
Notes payable to bank	20.00
Current ratio	3.00×
DSO[a]	40.55 days
ROE	12.00%

[a]This calculation is based on a 365-day year.

Kaiser has no preferred stock—only common equity, current liabilities, and long-term debt.

a.   Find Kaiser's (1) accounts receivable, (2) current assets, (3) total assets, (4) ROA, (5) common equity, (6) quick ratio, and (7) long-term debt.

b.   In Part a, you should have found that Kaiser's accounts receivable (A/R) = $111.1 million. If Kaiser could reduce its DSO from 40.55 days to 30.4 days while holding other things constant, how much cash would it generate? If this cash were used to buy back common stock (at book value), thus reducing common equity, how would this affect (1) the ROE, (2) the ROA, and (3) the total debt/total capital ratio?

QUESTIONS

4-1   Financial ratio analysis is conducted by three main groups of analysts: credit analysts, stock analysts, and managers. What is the primary emphasis of each group, and how would that emphasis affect the ratios on which they focus?

4-2   Why would the inventory turnover ratio be more important for someone analyzing a grocery store chain than an insurance company?

4-3   Over the past year, M.D. Ryngaert & Co. had an increase in its current ratio and a decline in its total assets turnover ratio. However, the company's sales, cash and equivalents, DSO, and fixed assets turnover ratio remained constant. What balance sheet accounts must have changed to produce the indicated changes?

4-4   Profit margins and turnover ratios vary from one industry to another. What differences would you expect to find between the turnover ratios, profit margins, and DuPont equations for a grocery chain and a steel company?

4-5   How does inflation distort ratio analysis comparisons for one company over time (trend analysis) and for different companies that are being compared? Are only balance sheet items or both balance sheet and income statement items affected?

4-6   If a firm's ROE is low and management wants to improve it, explain how using more debt might help.

4-7   Give some examples that illustrate how (a) seasonal factors and (b) different growth rates might distort a comparative ratio analysis. How might these problems be alleviated?

4-8   Why is it sometimes misleading to compare a company's financial ratios with those of other firms that operate in the same industry?

4-9 Suppose you were comparing a discount merchandiser with a high-end merchandiser. Suppose further that both companies had identical ROEs. If you applied the DuPont equation to both firms, would you expect the three components to be the same for each company? If not, explain what balance sheet and income statement items might lead to the component differences.

4-10 Refer to an online finance source such as Yahoo! Finance or Google Finance to look up the P/E ratios for Verizon Communications and Walmart. Which company has the higher P/E ratio? What factors could explain this?

4-11 Differentiate between ROE and ROIC.

4-12 Indicate the effects of the transactions listed in the following table on total current assets, current ratio, and net income. Use (+) to indicate an increase, (–) to indicate a decrease, and (0) to indicate either no effect or an indeterminate effect. Be prepared to state any necessary assumptions and assume an initial current ratio of more than 1.0. (Note: A good accounting background is necessary to answer some of these questions; if yours is not strong, answer the questions you can.)

		Total Current Assets	Current Ratio	Effect on Net Income
a.	Cash is acquired through issuance of additional common stock.	_____	_____	_____
b.	Merchandise is sold for cash.	_____	_____	_____
c.	Federal income tax due for the previous year is paid.	_____	_____	_____
d.	A fixed asset is sold for less than book value.	_____	_____	_____
e.	A fixed asset is sold for more than book value.	_____	_____	_____
f.	Merchandise is sold on credit.	_____	_____	_____
g.	Payment is made to trade creditors for previous purchases.	_____	_____	_____
h.	A cash dividend is declared and paid.	_____	_____	_____
i.	Cash is obtained through short-term bank loans.	_____	_____	_____
j.	Short-term notes receivable are sold at a discount.	_____	_____	_____
k.	Marketable securities are sold below cost.	_____	_____	_____
l.	Advances are made to employees.	_____	_____	_____
m.	Current operating expenses are paid.	_____	_____	_____
n.	Short-term promissory notes are issued to trade creditors in exchange for past due accounts payable.	_____	_____	_____
o.	10-year notes are issued to pay off accounts payable.	_____	_____	_____
p.	A fully depreciated asset is retired.	_____	_____	_____
q.	Accounts receivable are collected.	_____	_____	_____
r.	Equipment is purchased with short-term notes.	_____	_____	_____
s.	Merchandise is purchased on credit.	_____	_____	_____
t.	The estimated taxes payable are increased.	_____	_____	_____

PROBLEMS

Easy Problems 1–6

4-1 **DAYS SALES OUTSTANDING** Baker Brothers has a DSO of 40 days, and its annual sales are $7,300,000. What is its accounts receivable balance? Assume that it uses a 365-day year.

4-2 **DEBT TO CAPITAL RATIO** Bartley Barstools has a market/book ratio equal to 1. Its stock price is $14 per share and it has 5 million shares outstanding. The firm's total capital is $125 million and it finances with only debt and common equity. What is its debt-to-capital ratio?

4-3 **DuPONT ANALYSIS** Doublewide Dealers has an ROA of 10%, a 2% profit margin, and an ROE of 15%. What is its total assets turnover? What is its equity multiplier?

4-4 **MARKET/BOOK RATIO** Jaster Jets has $10 billion in total assets. Its balance sheet shows $1 billion in current liabilities, $3 billion in long-term debt, and $6 billion in common equity. It has 800 million shares of common stock outstanding, and its stock price is $32 per share. What is Jaster's market/book ratio?

4-5 **PRICE/EARNINGS RATIO** A company has an EPS of $2.00, a book value per share of $20, and a market/book ratio of 1.2×. What is its P/E ratio?

4-6 **DuPONT AND ROE** A firm has a profit margin of 2% and an equity multiplier of 2.0. Its sales are $100 million, and it has total assets of $50 million. What is its ROE?

Intermediate
Problems
7–19

4-7 **ROE AND ROIC** Hilyard Industries' net income is $25,000, its interest expense is $5,000, and its tax rate is 40%. Its notes payable equals $25,000, long-term debt equals $75,000, and common equity equals $250,000. The firm finances with only debt and common equity, so it has no preferred stock. What are the firm's ROE and ROIC?

4-8 **DuPONT AND NET INCOME** Ebersoll Mining has $6 million in sales, its ROE is 12%, and its total assets turnover is 3.2×. Common equity on the firm's balance sheet is 50% of its total assets. What is its net income?

4-9 **BEP, ROE, AND ROIC** Duval Manufacturing recently reported the following information:

Net income	$ 600,000
ROA	8%
Interest expense	$ 225,000
Accounts payable and accruals	$1,000,000

Duval's tax rate is 35%. Duval finances with only debt and common equity, so it has no preferred stock. 40% of its total invested capital is debt, while 60% of its total invested capital is common equity. Calculate its basic earning power (BEP), its return on equity (ROE), and its return on invested capital (ROIC).

4-10 **M/B AND SHARE PRICE** You are given the following information: Stockholders' equity as reported on the firm's balance sheet = $3.75 billion, price/earnings ratio = 3.5, common shares outstanding = 50 million, and market/book ratio = 1.9. Calculate the price of a share of the company's common stock.

4-11 **RATIO CALCULATIONS** Assume the following relationships for the Brauer Corp.:

Sales/Total assets	1.5×
Return on assets (ROA)	3.0%
Return on equity (ROE)	5.0%

Calculate Brauer's profit margin and debt-to-capital ratio assuming the firm uses only debt and common equity, so total assets equal total invested capital.

4-12 **RATIO CALCULATIONS** Graser Trucking has $12 billion in assets, and its tax rate is 40%. Its basic earning power (BEP) ratio is 15%, and its return on assets (ROA) is 5%. What is its times-interest-earned (TIE) ratio?

4-13 **TIE AND ROIC RATIOS** The H.R. Pickett Corp. has $500,000 of interest-bearing debt outstanding, and it pays an annual interest rate of 10%. In addition, it has $700,000 of common stock on its balance sheet. It finances with only debt and common equity, so it has no preferred stock. Its annual sales are $2 million, its average tax rate is 30%, and its profit margin is 5%. What are its TIE ratio and its return on invested capital (ROIC)?

4-14 **RETURN ON EQUITY** Midwest Packaging's ROE last year was only 3%; but its management has developed a new operating plan that calls for a debt-to-capital ratio of 60%, which will result in annual interest charges of $300,000. The firm has no plans to use preferred stock and total assets equal total invested capital. Management projects an EBIT of $1,000,000 on sales of $10,000,000, and it expects to have a total assets turnover ratio of 2.0. Under these conditions, the tax rate will be 34%. If the changes are made, what will be the company's return on equity?

4-15 **RETURN ON EQUITY AND QUICK RATIO** Lloyd Inc. has sales of $200,000, a net income of $15,000, and the following balance sheet:

Cash	$ 10,000	Accounts payable	$ 30,000
Receivables	50,000	Notes payable to bank	20,000
Inventories	150,000	Total current liabilities	$ 50,000
Total current assets	$210,000	Long-term debt	50,000
Net fixed assets	90,000	Common equity	200,000
Total assets	$300,000	Total liabilities and equity	$300,000

The new owner thinks that inventories are excessive and can be lowered to the point where the current ratio is equal to the industry average, 2.5×, without affecting sales or net income. If inventories are sold and not replaced (thus reducing the current ratio to 2.5×), if the funds generated are used to reduce common equity (stock can be repurchased at book value), and if no other changes occur, by how much will the ROE change? What will be the firm's new quick ratio?

4-16 **RETURN ON EQUITY** Central City Construction (CCC) needs $1 million of assets to get started, and it expects to have a basic earning power ratio of 20%. CCC will own no securities, so all of its income will be operating income. If it so chooses, CCC can finance up to 50% of its assets with debt, which will have an 8% interest rate. If it chooses to use debt, the firm will finance using only debt and common equity, so no preferred stock will be used. Assuming a 40% tax rate on all taxable income, what is the *difference* between CCC's expected ROE if it finances these assets with 50% debt versus its expected ROE if it finances these assets entirely with common stock?

4-17 **CONCEPTUAL: RETURN ON EQUITY** Which of the following statements is most correct? (Hint: Work Problem 4-16 before answering 4-17 and consider the solution setup for 4-16 as you think about 4-17.)

  a. If a firm's expected basic earning power (BEP) is constant for all of its assets and exceeds the interest rate on its debt, adding assets and financing them with debt will raise the firm's expected return on common equity (ROE).
  b. The higher a firm's tax rate, the lower its BEP ratio, other things held constant.
  c. The higher the interest rate on a firm's debt, the lower its BEP ratio, other things held constant.
  d. The higher a firm's debt ratio, the lower its BEP ratio, other things held constant.
  e. Statement a is false; but statements b, c, and d are true.

4-18 **TIE RATIO** AEI Incorporated has $5 billion in assets, and its tax rate is 40%. Its basic earning power (BEP) ratio is 10%, and its return on assets (ROA) is 5%. What is AEI's times-interest-earned (TIE) ratio?

4-19 **CURRENT RATIO** The Petry Company has $1,312,500 in current assets and $525,000 in current liabilities. Its initial inventory level is $375,000, and it will raise funds as additional notes payable and use them to increase inventory. How much can its short-term debt (notes payable) increase without pushing its current ratio below 2.0?

Challenging Problems 20–24

4-20 **DSO AND ACCOUNTS RECEIVABLE** Harrelson Inc. currently has $750,000 in accounts receivable, and its days sales outstanding (DSO) is 55 days. It wants to reduce its DSO to 35 days by pressuring more of its customers to pay their bills on time. If this policy is adopted, the company's average sales will fall by 15%. What will be the level of accounts receivable following the change? Assume a 365-day year.

4-21 **P/E AND STOCK PRICE** Fontaine Inc. recently reported net income of $2 million. It has 500,000 shares of common stock, which currently trades at $40 a share. Fontaine continues to expand and anticipates that 1 year from now, its net income will be $3.25 million. Over the next year, it also anticipates issuing an additional 150,000 shares of stock so that 1 year from now it will have 650,000 shares of common stock. Assuming Fontaine's price/earnings ratio remains at its current level, what will be its stock price 1 year from now?

4-22 **BALANCE SHEET ANALYSIS** Complete the balance sheet and sales information using the following financial data:

Total assets turnover: 1.5×

Days sales outstanding: 36.5 days[a]

Inventory turnover ratio: 5×

Fixed assets turnover: 3.0×

Current ratio: 2.0×

Gross profit margin on sales: (Sales − Cost of goods sold)/Sales = 25%

[a]Calculation is based on a 365-day year.

Balance Sheet

Cash	_____		Current liabilities	_____
Accounts receivable	_____		Long-term debt	60,000
Inventories	_____		Common stock	
Fixed assets	_____		Retained earnings	97,500
Total assets	$300,000		Total liabilities and equity	_____
Sales	_____		Cost of goods sold	_____

4-23 **RATIO ANALYSIS** Data for Barry Computer Co. and its industry averages follow.

a. Calculate the indicated ratios for Barry.

b. Construct the DuPont equation for both Barry and the industry.

c. Outline Barry's strengths and weaknesses as revealed by your analysis.

d. Suppose Barry had doubled its sales as well as its inventories, accounts receivable, and common equity during 2014. How would that information affect the validity of your ratio analysis? (Hint: Think about averages and the effects of rapid growth on ratios if averages are not used. No calculations are needed.)

Barry Computer Company:
Balance Sheet as of December 31, 2014 (in Thousands)

Cash	$ 77,500		Accounts payable	$129,000
Receivables	336,000		Other current liabilities	117,000
Inventories	241,500		Notes payable to bank	84,000
Total current assets	$655,000		Total current liabilities	$330,000
			Long-term debt	256,500
Net fixed assets	292,500		Common equity	361,000
Total assets	$947,500		Total liabilities and equity	$947,500

Barry Computer Company: Income Statement for Year Ended
December 31, 2014 (in Thousands)

Sales		$1,607,500
Cost of goods sold		
Materials	$717,000	
Labor	453,000	
Heat, light, and power	68,000	
Indirect labor	113,000	
Depreciation	41,500	1,392,500
Gross profit		$ 215,000
Selling expenses		115,000
General and administrative expenses		30,000
Earnings before interest and taxes (EBIT)		$ 70,000
Interest expense		24,500
Earnings before taxes (EBT)		$ 45,500
Federal and state income taxes (40%)		18,200
Net income		$ 27,300

Ratio	Barry	Industry Average
Current	_____	2.0×
Quick	_____	1.3×
Days sales outstanding[a]	_____	35 days
Inventory turnover	_____	6.7×
Total assets turnover	_____	3.0×
Profit margin	_____	1.2%

[a]Calculation is based on a 365-day year.

Ratio	Barry	Industry Average
ROA	_____	3.6%
ROE	_____	9.0%
ROIC	_____	7.5%
TIE	_____	3.0×
Debt/Total capital	_____	47.0%

4-24 **DUPONT ANALYSIS** A firm has been experiencing low profitability in recent years. Perform an analysis of the firm's financial position using the DuPont equation. The firm has no lease payments but has a $2 million sinking fund payment on its debt. The most recent industry average ratios and the firm's financial statements are as follows:

Industry Average Ratios

Current ratio	3×	Fixed assets turnover	6×
Debt-to-capital ratio	20%	Total assets turnover	3×
Times interest earned	7×	Profit margin	3%
EBITDA coverage	9×	Return on total assets	9%
Inventory turnover	10×	Return on common equity	12.86%
Days sales outstanding[a]	24 days	Return on invested capital	11.50%

[a]Calculation is based on a 365-day year.

Balance Sheet as of December 31, 2014 (Millions of Dollars)

Cash and equivalents	$ 78	Accounts payable	$ 45
Accounts receivable	66	Other current liabilities	11
Inventories	159	Notes payable	29
Total current assets	$303	Total current liabilities	$ 85
		Long-term debt	50
		Total liabilities	$135
Gross fixed assets	225	Common stock	114
Less depreciation	78	Retained earnings	201
Net fixed assets	$147	Total stockholders' equity	$315
Total assets	$450	Total liabilities and equity	$450

Income Statement for Year Ended December 31, 2014 (Millions of Dollars)

Net sales	$795.0
Cost of goods sold	660.0
Gross profit	$135.0
Selling expenses	73.5
EBITDA	$ 61.5
Depreciation expense	12.0
Earnings before interest and taxes (EBIT)	$ 49.5
Interest expense	4.5
Earnings before taxes (EBT)	$ 45.0
Taxes (40%)	18.0
Net income	$ 27.0

a. Calculate the ratios you think would be useful in this analysis.
b. Construct a DuPont equation and compare the company's ratios to the industry average ratios.
c. Do the balance sheet accounts or the income statement figures seem to be primarily responsible for the low profits?
d. Which specific accounts seem to be most out of line relative to other firms in the industry?
e. If the firm had a pronounced seasonal sales pattern or if it grew rapidly during the year, how might that affect the validity of your ratio analysis? How might you correct for such potential problems?

COMPREHENSIVE/SPREADSHEET PROBLEM

4-25   RATIO ANALYSIS   The Corrigan Corporation's 2013 and 2014 financial statements follow, along with some industry average ratios.

a. Assess Corrigan's liquidity position and determine how it compares with peers and how the liquidity position has changed over time.

b. Assess Corrigan's asset management position and determine how it compares with peers and how its asset management efficiency has changed over time.

c. Assess Corrigan's debt management position and determine how it compares with peers and how its debt management has changed over time.

d. Assess Corrigan's profitability ratios and determine how they compare with peers and how its profitability position has changed over time.

e. Assess Corrigan's market value ratios and determine how its valuation compares with peers and how it has changed over time.

f. Calculate Corrigan's ROE as well as the industry average ROE using the DuPont equation. From this analysis, how does Corrigan's financial position compare with the industry average numbers?

g. What do you think would happen to its ratios if the company initiated cost-cutting measures that allowed it to hold lower levels of inventory and substantially decreased the cost of goods sold? No calculations are necessary. Think about which ratios would be affected by changes in these two accounts.

Corrigan Corporation: Balance Sheets as of December 31

	2014	2013
Cash	$ 72,000	$ 65,000
Accounts receivable	439,000	328,000
Inventories	894,000	813,000
Total current assets	$1,405,000	$1,206,000
Land and building	238,000	271,000
Machinery	132,000	133,000
Other fixed assets	61,000	57,000
Total assets	$1,836,000	$1,667,000
Accounts payable	$ 80,000	$ 72,708
Accrued liabilities	45,010	40,880
Notes payable	476,990	457,912
Total current liabilities	$ 602,000	$ 571,500
Long-term debt	404,290	258,898
Common stock	575,000	575,000
Retained earnings	254,710	261,602
Total liabilities and equity	$1,836,000	$1,667,000

Corrigan Corporation: Income Statements for Years Ending December 31

	2014	2013
Sales	$4,240,000	$3,635,000
Cost of goods sold	3,680,000	2,980,000
Gross operating profit	$ 560,000	$ 655,000
General administrative and selling expenses	303,320	297,550
Depreciation	159,000	154,500
EBIT	$ 97,680	$ 202,950

Corrigan Corporation: Income Statements for Years Ending December 31

	2014	2013
Interest	67,000	43,000
Earnings before taxes (EBT)	$ 30,680	$ 159,950
Taxes (40%)	12,272	63,980
Net income	$ 18,408	$ 95,970

Per-Share Data

	2014	2013
EPS	$ 0.80	$ 4.17
Cash dividends	$ 1.10	$ 0.95
Market price (average)	$12.34	$23.57
P/E ratio	15.42×	5.65×
Number of shares outstanding	23,000	23,000

Industry Financial Ratios[a]

	2014
Current ratio	2.7×
Inventory turnover[b]	7.0×
Days sales outstanding[c]	32.0 days
Fixed assets turnover[b]	13.0×
Total assets turnover[b]	2.6×
Return on assets	9.1%
Return on equity	18.2%
Return on invested capital	14.5%
Profit margin	3.5%
Debt-to-capital ratio	50.0%
P/E ratio	6.0×

[a]Industry average ratios have been constant for the past 4 years.
[b]Based on year-end balance sheet figures.
[c]Calculation is based on a 365-day year.

INTEGRATED CASE

D'LEON INC., PART II

4-26 **FINANCIAL STATEMENTS AND TAXES**   Part I of this case, presented in Chapter 3, discussed the situation of D'Leon Inc., a regional snack foods producer, after an expansion program. D'Leon had increased plant capacity and undertaken a major marketing campaign in an attempt to "go national." Thus far, sales have not been up to the forecasted level, costs have been higher than were projected, and a large loss occurred in 2014 rather than the expected profit. As a result, its managers, directors, and investors are concerned about the firm's survival.

Donna Jamison was brought in as assistant to Fred Campo, D'Leon's chairman, who had the task of getting the company back into a sound financial position. D'Leon's 2013 and 2014 balance sheets and income statements, together with projections for 2015, are given in Tables IC 4.1 and IC 4.2. In addition, Table IC 4.3 gives the company's 2013 and 2014 financial ratios, together with industry average data. The 2015 projected financial statement data represent Jamison's and Campo's best guess for 2015 results, assuming that some new financing is arranged to get the company "over the hump."

Jamison examined monthly data for 2014 (not given in the case), and she detected an improving pattern during the year. Monthly sales were rising, costs were falling, and large losses in the early months had turned to a small profit by December. Thus, the annual data look somewhat worse than final monthly data. Also, it appears to be taking longer for the advertising program to get the message out, for the new sales offices to generate sales, and for the new manufacturing facilities to operate efficiently. In other words, the lags between spending money and deriving benefits were longer than D'Leon's managers had anticipated. For these reasons, Jamison and Campo see hope for the company—provided it can survive in the short run.

Jamison must prepare an analysis of where the company is now, what it must do to regain its financial health, and what actions should be taken. Your assignment is to help her answer the following questions. Provide clear explanations, not yes or no answers.

a. Why are ratios useful? What are the five major categories of ratios?

b. Calculate D'Leon's 2015 current and quick ratios based on the projected balance sheet and income statement data. What can you say about the company's liquidity positions in 2013, in 2014, and as projected for 2015? We often think of ratios as being useful (1) to managers to help run the business, (2) to bankers for credit analysis, and (3) to stockholders for stock valuation. Would these different types of analysts have an equal interest in the company's liquidity ratios? Explain your answer.

c. Calculate the 2015 inventory turnover, days sales outstanding (DSO), fixed assets turnover, and total assets turnover. How does D'Leon's utilization of assets stack up against other firms in the industry?

d. Calculate the 2015 debt-to-capital and times-interest-earned ratios. How does D'Leon compare with the industry with respect to financial leverage? What can you conclude from these ratios?

e. Calculate the 2015 operating margin, profit margin, basic earning power (BEP), return on assets (ROA), return on equity (ROE), and return on invested capital (ROIC). What can you say about these ratios?

f. Calculate the 2015 price/earnings ratio and market/book ratio. Do these ratios indicate that investors are expected to have a high or low opinion of the company?

g. Use the DuPont equation to provide a summary and overview of D'Leon's financial condition as projected for 2015. What are the firm's major strengths and weaknesses?

h. Use the following simplified 2015 balance sheet to show, in general terms, how an improvement in the DSO would tend to affect the stock price. For example, if the company could improve its collection procedures and thereby lower its DSO from 45.6 days to the 32-day industry average without affecting sales, how would that change "ripple through" the financial statements (shown in thousands below) and influence the stock price?

Accounts receivable	$ 878	Current liabilities	$ 845
Other current assets	1,802	Debt	700
Net fixed assets	817	Equity	1,952
Total assets	$3,497	Liabilities plus equity	$3,497

i. Does it appear that inventories could be adjusted? If so, how should that adjustment affect D'Leon's profitability and stock price?

j. In 2014, the company paid its suppliers much later than the due dates; also, it was not maintaining financial ratios at levels called for in its bank loan agreements. Therefore, suppliers could cut the company off, and its bank could refuse to renew the loan when it comes due in 90 days. On the basis of data provided, would you, as a credit manager, continue to sell to D'Leon on credit? (You could demand cash on delivery—that is, sell on terms of COD—but that might cause D'Leon to stop buying from your company.) Similarly, if you were the bank loan officer, would you recommend renewing the loan or demanding its repayment? Would your actions be influenced if, in early 2015, D'Leon showed you its 2015 projections along with proof that it was going to raise more than $1.2 million of new equity?

k. In hindsight, what should D'Leon have done in 2013?

l. What are some potential problems and limitations of financial ratio analysis?

m. What are some qualitative factors that analysts should consider when evaluating a company's likely future financial performance?

Balance Sheets			TABLE IC 4.1
	2015E	**2014**	**2013**
Assets			
Cash	$ 85,632	$ 7,282	$ 57,600
Accounts receivable	878,000	632,160	351,200
Inventories	1,716,480	1,287,360	715,200
Total current assets	$2,680,112	$1,926,802	$1,124,000
Gross fixed assets	1,197,160	1,202,950	491,000
Less accumulated depreciation	380,120	263,160	146,200
Net fixed assets	$ 817,040	$ 939,790	$ 344,800
Total assets	$3,497,152	$2,866,592	$1,468,800
Liabilities and Equity			
Accounts payable	$ 436,800	$ 524,160	$ 145,600
Accruals	408,000	489,600	136,000
Notes payable	300,000	636,808	200,000
Total current liabilities	$1,144,800	$1,650,568	$ 481,600
Long-term debt	400,000	723,432	323,432
Common stock	1,721,176	460,000	460,000
Retained earnings	231,176	32,592	203,768
Total equity	$1,952,352	$ 492,592	$ 663,768
Total liabilities and equity	$3,497,152	$2,866,592	$1,468,800

Note: E indicates estimated. The 2015 data are forecasts.

Income Statements			TABLE IC 4.2
	2015E	**2014**	**2013**
Sales	$7,035,600	$6,034,000	$3,432,000
Cost of goods sold	5,875,992	5,528,000	2,864,000
Other expenses	550,000	519,988	358,672
Total operating costs excluding depreciation and amortization	$6,425,992	$ 6,047,988	$3,222,672
EBITDA	$ 609,608	($ 13,988)	$ 209,328
Depreciation & amortization	116,960	116,960	18,900
EBIT	$ 492,648	($ 130,948)	$ 190,428
Interest expense	70,008	136,012	43,828
EBT	$ 422,640	($ 266,960)	$ 146,600
Taxes (40%)	169,056	(106,784)[a]	58,640
Net income	$ 253,584	($ 160,176)	$ 87,960
EPS	$ 1.014	($ 1.602)	$ 0.880
DPS	$ 0.220	$ 0.110	$ 0.220
Book value per share	$ 7.809	$ 4.926	$ 6.638
Stock price	$ 12.17	$ 2.25	$ 8.50
Shares outstanding	250,000	100,000	100,000
Tax rate	40.00%	40.00%	40.00%
Lease payments	$40,000	$40,000	$40,000
Sinking fund payments	0	0	0

Note: E indicates estimated. The 2015 data are forecasts.
[a]The firm had sufficient taxable income in 2012 and 2013 to obtain its full tax refund in 2014.

TABLE IC 4.3   Ratio Analysis

	2015E	2014	2013	Industry Average
Current		1.2×	2.3×	2.7×
Quick		0.4×	0.8×	1.0×
Inventory turnover		4.7×	4.8×	6.1×
Days sales outstanding (DSO)[a]		38.2	37.4	32.0
Fixed assets turnover		6.4×	10.0×	7.0×
Total assets turnover		2.1×	2.3×	2.6×
Debt-to-capital ratio		73.4%	44.1%	40.0%
TIE		−1.0×	4.3×	6.2×
Operating margin		−2.2%	5.5%	7.3%
Profit margin		−2.7%	2.6%	3.5%
Basic earning power		−4.6%	13.0%	19.1%
ROA		−5.6%	6.0%	9.1%
ROE		−32.5%	13.3%	18.2%
ROIC		−4.2%	9.6%	14.5%
Price/earnings		−1.4×	9.7×	14.2×
Market/book		0.5×	1.3×	2.4×
Book value per share		$4.93	$6.64	n.a.

© Cengage Learning 2015

Note: E indicates estimated. The 2015 data are forecasts.
[a]Calculation is based on a 365-day year.

  THOMSON REUTERS

Use the Thomson ONE—Business School Edition online database to answer this chapter's questions.

CONDUCTING A FINANCIAL RATIO ANALYSIS ON HEWLETT PACKARD CO.

In Chapter 3, we looked at Starbucks' financial statements. Now we use Thomson ONE to analyze Hewlett Packard Co. Enter Hewlett Packard's ticker symbol (HPQ) and select "GO." Select "Financials" and "Thomson Financials" to find Hewlett Packard's key financial statements for the past several years. Click on "Worldscope" under "Financial Ratios." From here you can select annual ratios, annual average ratios, annual balance sheet ratios, annual income statement ratios, or annual cash flow ratios.

   Under annual ratios, there is an in-depth summary of Hewlett Packard's various ratios over the past 5 years. This information enables you to evaluate Hewlett Packard's performance over time for each of the ratio categories mentioned in the text (liquidity, asset management, debt management, profitability, and market-based ratios).

   The text mentions that financial statement analysis has two major components: a trend analysis, where we evaluate changes in the key ratios over time, and a peer analysis, where we compare financial ratios with firms that are in the same industry and/or line of business. We have already used Thomson ONE to conduct a trend analysis—next, we use this tool to conduct a peer analysis. Click on "Comparables" to find some summary financial information for Hewlett Packard and a few of its peers. By clicking on the Peer

Sets, you can modify the list of peer firms. The default setup is "Peers set by SIC Code." To obtain a comparison of many of the key ratios presented in the text, click on "Key Financial Ratios."

Discussion Questions

1. What has happened to Hewlett Packard's liquidity position over the past 5 years? How does Hewlett Packard's liquidity compare with that of its peers? (Hint: You may use both the peer key financial ratios and liquidity comparison to answer this question.)
2. Take a look at Hewlett Packard's inventory turnover ratio. How does this ratio compare with that of its peers? Have there been any interesting changes over time in this measure? Do you consider Hewlett Packard's inventory management to be a strength or a weakness? Explain.
3. Construct a DuPont analysis for Hewlett Packard and its peers. What are Hewlett Packard's strengths and weaknesses compared to those of its competitors?

CHAPTER
5

Time Value of Money

Will You Be Able to Retire?

For an interesting website that looks at global savings rates, refer to **http://www.gfmag .com/tools/global-database/ economic-data/12065- household-savings-rates .html#axzz20fpvnu2g.**

Your reaction to that question is probably, "First things first! I'm worried about getting a job, not about retiring!" However, understanding the retirement situation can help you land a job because (1) this is an important issue today, (2) employers like to hire people who know what's happening in the real world, and (3) professors often test on the time value of money with problems related to saving for future purposes (including retirement).

A recent study by the Employee Benefit Research Institute suggests that many U.S. workers are not doing enough to prepare for retirement. The survey found that 57% of workers had less than $25,000 in savings and investments (not including the value of their homes). Equally concerning, 28% of those surveyed said they had "no confidence" that they would be able to retire

comfortably. This is the highest percentage recorded since the survey was established 23 years ago.[1] Unfortunately, there is no easy solution. In order to reach their retirement goals, many current workers will need to work longer, spend less and save more, and hopefully earn higher returns on their current savings.

Historically, many Americans have relied on Social Security as an important source of their retirement income. However, given current demographics, it is likely that this important program will need to be restructured down the road in order to maintain its viability. While the average personal savings rate in the United States had edged up in recent years, it still stands at a fairly low level of 4%.[2] In addition, the ratio of U.S. workers to retirees has steadily declined over the

---

[1]Refer to Kelly Greene and Vipal Monga, "Workers Saving Too Little to Retire," *The Wall Street Journal*, March 19, 2013, pp. A1, A6.

[2]Refer to the U.S. Department of Commerce: Bureau of Economic Analysis, *Personal Saving Rate: January 1, 1959–December 1, 2012,* (http://research.stlouisfed.org/fred2/data/PSAVERT.txt).

past half century. In 1955, there were 8.6 workers supporting each retiree, but by 1975, that number had declined to 3.2 workers for every one retiree. From 1975 through 2009, the ratio remained between 3.0 and 3.4 workers for every retiree. Current projections show this ratio significantly declining in the years ahead—the forecast is for 2.0 workers per retiree in 2035 and 1.9 workers per retiree in 2085.[3] With so few people paying into the Social Security system and so many drawing funds out, Social Security is going to be in serious trouble. In fact, for the first time since its inception, in 2010 (and 7 years ahead of schedule), Social Security was in the red—paying out

more in benefits than it received in tax revenues. Considering these facts, many people may have trouble maintaining a reasonable standard of living after they retire, and many of today's college students will have to support their parents.

This is an important issue for millions of Americans, but many don't know how to deal with it. Most Americans have been ignoring what is most certainly going to be a huge personal and social problem. However, if you study this chapter carefully, you can use the tools and techniques presented here to avoid the trap that has caught, and is likely to catch, so many people.

PUTTING THINGS IN PERSPECTIVE

*Excellent retirement calculators are available at **money.msn.com/ retirement**, **ssa.gov**, and **choosetosave.org/ calculators**. These calculators allow you to input hypothetical retirement savings information; the program then shows if current retirement savings will be sufficient to meet retirement needs.*

Time value analysis has many applications, including planning for retirement, valuing stocks and bonds, setting up loan payment schedules, and making corporate decisions regarding investing in new plants and equipment. *In fact, of all financial concepts, time value of money is the single most important concept. Indeed, time value analysis is used throughout the book; so it is vital that you understand this chapter before continuing.*

You need to understand basic time value concepts, but conceptual knowledge will do you little good if you can't do the required calculations. Therefore, this chapter is heavy on calculations. Most students studying finance have a financial or scientific calculator; some also own or have access to a computer. One of these tools is necessary to work many finance problems in a reasonable length of time. However, when students begin reading this chapter, many of them don't know how to use the time value functions on their calculator or computer. If you are in that situation, you will find yourself simultaneously studying concepts and trying to learn to use your calculator, and you will need more time to cover this chapter than you might expect.[4]

When you finish this chapter, you should be able to:

- **Explain how the time value of money works and discuss why it is such an important concept in finance.**
- **Calculate the present value and future value of lump sums.**
- **Identify the different types of annuities, calculate the present value and future value of both an ordinary annuity and an annuity due, and calculate the relevant annuity payments.**

[3]Refer to the U.S. Social Security Administration, *2012 Annual Report of the Board of Trustees of the Federal Old-Age and Survivors Insurance and Federal Disability Insurance Trust Funds,* Table IV.B2.
[4]Calculator manuals tend to be long and complicated, partly because they cover a number of topics that aren't required in the basic finance course. We provide tutorials for the most commonly used calculators on the textbook website and you can access these by going to www.cengagebrain.com and searching ISBN 9781285065137. The tutorials are keyed to this chapter, and they show exactly how to do the required calculations. If you don't know how to use your calculator, go to the textbook's website, find the relevant tutorial, and work through it as you study the chapter.

- Calculate the present value and future value of an uneven cash flow stream. You will use this knowledge in later chapters that show how to value common stocks and corporate projects.
- Explain the difference between nominal, periodic, and effective interest rates. An understanding of these concepts is necessary when comparing rates of returns on alternative investments.
- Discuss the basics of loan amortization and develop a loan amortization schedule that you might use when considering an auto loan or home mortgage loan.

5-1 TIME LINES

Time Line

An important tool used in time value analysis; it is a graphical representation used to show the timing of cash flows

The first step in time value analysis is to set up a **time line**, which will help you visualize what's happening in a particular problem. As an illustration, consider the following diagram, where PV represents $100 that is on hand today and FV is the value that will be in the account on a future date:

The intervals from 0 to 1, 1 to 2, and 2 to 3 are time periods such as years or months. Time 0 is today, and it is the beginning of Period 1; Time 1 is one period from today, and it is both the end of Period 1 and the beginning of Period 2; and so forth. Although the periods are often years, periods can also be quarters or months or even days. Note that each tick mark corresponds to both the *end* of one period and the *beginning* of the next one. Thus, if the periods are years, the tick mark at Time 2 represents the *end* of Year 2 and the *beginning* of Year 3.

Cash flows are shown directly below the tick marks, and the relevant interest rate is shown just above the time line. Unknown cash flows, which you are trying to find, are indicated by question marks. Here the interest rate is 5%; a single cash outflow, $100, is invested at Time 0; and the Time 3 value is an unknown inflow. In this example, cash flows occur only at Times 0 and 3, with no flows at Times 1 or 2. Note that in our example, the interest rate is constant for all 3 years. That condition is generally true; but if it were not, we would show different interest rates for the different periods.

Time lines are essential when you are first learning time value concepts, but even experts use them to analyze complex finance problems; and we use them throughout the book. We begin each problem by setting up a time line to illustrate the situation, after which we provide an equation that must be solved to find the answer. Then we explain how to use a regular calculator, a financial calculator, and a spreadsheet to find the answer.

SELF TEST

Do time lines deal only with years, or can other time periods be used?

Set up a time line to illustrate the following situation: You currently have $2,000 in a 3-year certificate of deposit (CD) that pays a guaranteed 4% annually.

5-2 FUTURE VALUES

A dollar in hand today is worth more than a dollar to be received in the future because if you had it now, you could invest it, earn interest, and own more than a dollar in the future. The process of going to **future value (FV)** from **present value (PV)** is called **compounding**. For an illustration, refer back to our 3-year time line and assume that you plan to deposit $100 in a bank that pays a guaranteed 5% interest each year. How much would you have at the end of Year 3? We first define some terms, and then we set up a time line to show how the future value is calculated.

Future Value (FV)
The amount to which a cash flow or series of cash flows will grow over a given period of time when compounded at a given interest rate.

Present Value (PV)
The value today of a future cash flow or series of cash flows.

Compounding
The arithmetic process of determining the final value of a cash flow or series of cash flows when compound interest is applied.

PV = Present value, or beginning amount. In our example, PV = $100.

FV_N = Future value, or ending amount, of your account after N periods. Whereas PV is the value now, or the *present value*, FV_N is the value N periods into the *future*, after the interest earned has been added to the account.

CF_t = Cash flow. Cash flows can be positive or negative. The cash flow for a particular period is often given as a subscript, CF_t, where t is the period. Thus, CF_0 = PV = the cash flow at Time 0, whereas CF_3 is the cash flow at the end of Period 3.

I = Interest rate earned per year. Sometimes a lowercase i is used. Interest earned is based on the balance at the beginning of each year, and we assume that it is paid at the end of the year. Here I = 5% or, expressed as a decimal, 0.05. Throughout this chapter, we designate the interest rate as I because that symbol (or I/YR, for interest rate per year) is used on most financial calculators. Note, though, that in later chapters, we use the symbol r to denote rates because r (for rate of return) is used more often in the finance literature. Note, too, that in this chapter we generally assume that interest payments are guaranteed by the U.S. government; hence, they are certain. In later chapters, we will consider risky investments, where the interest rate earned might differ from its expected level.

INT = Dollars of interest earned during the year = Beginning amount × I. In our example, INT = $100(0.05) = $5.

N = Number of periods involved in the analysis. In our example, N = 3. Sometimes the number of periods is designated with a lowercase n, so both N and n indicate the number of periods involved.

We can use four different procedures to solve time value problems.[5] These methods are described in the following sections.

5-2A STEP-BY-STEP APPROACH

The time line used to find the FV of $100 compounded for 3 years at 5%, along with some calculations, is shown. Multiply the initial amount and each succeeding amount by $(1 + I) = (1.05)$:

---

[5]A fifth procedure, using tables that show "interest factors," was used before financial calculators and computers became available. Now, though, calculators and spreadsheet applications such as Microsoft Excel are programmed to calculate the specific factor needed for a given problem and then to use it to find the FV. This is more efficient than using the tables. Moreover, calculators and spreadsheets can handle fractional periods and fractional interest rates, such as the FV of $100 after 3.75 years when the interest rate is 5.375%, whereas tables provide numbers only for whole periods and rates. For these reasons, tables are not used in business today; hence, we do not discuss them in the text.

Time

	0		1	2	3
		5%			

Amount at beginning of period $100.00 ----► $105.00 ----► $110.25 ----► $115.76

You start with $100 in the account—this is shown at t = 0:

- You earn $100(0.05) = $5 of interest during the first year, so the amount at the end of Year 1 (or t = 1) is $100 + $5 = $105.

- You begin the second year with $105, earn 0.05($105) = $5.25 on the now larger beginning-of-period amount, and end the year with $110.25. Interest during Year 2 is $5.25; and it is higher than the first year's interest, $5.00, because you earned $5(0.05) = $0.25 interest on the first year's interest. This is called compounding, and interest earned on interest is called compound interest.

- This process continues; and because the beginning balance is higher each successive year, the interest earned each year increases.

- The total interest earned, $15.76, is reflected in the final balance, $115.76.

The step-by-step approach is useful because it shows exactly what is happening. However, this approach is time-consuming, especially when a number of years are involved; so streamlined procedures have been developed.

5-2B FORMULA APPROACH

In the step-by-step approach, we multiply the amount at the beginning of each period by $(1 + I) = (1.05)$. If N = 3, we multiply by $(1 + I)$ three different times, which is the same as multiplying the beginning amount by $(1 + I)^3$. This concept can be extended, and the result is this key equation:

Compound Interest

Occurs when interest is earned on prior periods' interest.

$$FV_N = PV(1 + I)^N$$

5.1

Simple Interest

Occurs when interest is not earned on interest.

We can apply Equation 5.1 to find the FV in our example:

$$FV_3 = \$100(1.05)^3 = \$115.76$$

Equation 5.1 can be used with any calculator that has an exponential function, making it easy to find FVs no matter how many years are involved.

SIMPLE VERSUS COMPOUND INTEREST

Interest earned on the interest earned in prior periods, as was true in our example and is always true when we apply Equation 5.1, is called **compound interest**. If interest is not earned on interest, we have **simple interest**. The formula for FV with simple interest is FV = PV + PV(I)(N); so in our example, FV would have been $100 + $100(0.05)(3) = $100 + $15 = $115 based on simple interest. Most financial contracts are based on compound interest; but in legal proceedings, the law often specifies that simple interest must be used. For example, Maris Distributing, a company founded by home-run king Roger Maris, won a lawsuit against Anheuser-Busch (A-B) because A-B had breached a contract and taken away Maris's franchise to sell Budweiser

beer. The judge awarded Maris $50 million plus interest at 10% from 1997 (when A-B breached the contract) until the payment was actually made. The interest award was based on simple interest, which as of 2005 (when a settlement was reached between A-B and the Maris family) had raised the total from $50 million to $50 million + 0.10($50 million) (8 years) = $90 million. (No doubt the sheer size of this award and the impact of the interest, even simple interest, influenced A-B to settle.) If the law had allowed compound interest, the award would have totaled ($50 million)(1.10)^8 = $107.18 million, or $17.18 million more. This legal procedure dates back to the days before calculators and computers. The law moves slowly!

5-2c FINANCIAL CALCULATORS

Financial calculators are extremely helpful in working time value problems. Their manuals explain calculators in detail; and on the textbook's website, we provide summaries of the features needed to work the problems in this book for several popular calculators. Also see the box entitled "Hints on Using Financial Calculators," on page 145, for suggestions that will help you avoid common mistakes. If you are not yet familiar with your calculator, we recommend that you work through the tutorial as you study this chapter.

First, note that financial calculators have five keys that correspond to the five variables in the basic time value equations. We show the inputs for our text example above the respective keys and the output, the FV, below its key. Because there are no periodic payments, we enter 0 for PMT. We describe the keys in more detail after this calculation.

3	5	−100	0	FV
N	I/YR	PV	PMT	115.76

Where:

   N = Number of periods. Some calculators use n rather than N.

I/YR = Interest rate per period. Some calculators use i or I rather than I/YR.

  PV = Present value. In our example, we begin by making a deposit, which is an outflow (the cash leaves our wallet and is deposited at one of many financial institutions); so the PV should be entered with a negative sign. On most calculators, you must enter the 100, then press the +/− key to switch from +100 to −100. If you enter −100 directly, 100 will be subtracted from the last number in the calculator, giving you an incorrect answer.

 PMT = Payment. This key is used when we have a series of equal, or constant, payments. Because there are no such payments in our illustrative problem, we enter PMT = 0. We will use the PMT key when we discuss annuities later in this chapter.

  FV = Future value. In this example, the FV is positive because we entered the PV as a negative number. If we had entered the 100 as a positive number, the FV would have been negative.

As noted in our example, you enter the known values (N, I/YR, PV, and PMT) and then press the FV key to get the answer, 115.76. Again, note that if you enter the PV as 100 without a minus sign, the FV will be shown on the calculator display as a negative number. The calculator *assumes* that either the PV or the FV is negative. This should not be confusing if you think about what you are doing. When PMT is zero, it doesn't matter what sign you enter for PV as your calculator will automatically assign the opposite sign to FV. We will discuss this point in greater detail later in the chapter when we cover annuities.

5-2d SPREADSHEETS[6]

Students generally use calculators for homework and exam problems; but in business, people generally use spreadsheets for problems that involve the time value of money (TVM). Spreadsheets show in detail what is happening, and they

---

[6]If you have never worked with spreadsheets, you may choose to skip this section. However, you might want to read through it and refer to this chapter's Excel model to get an idea of how spreadsheets work.

help reduce both conceptual and data-entry errors. The spreadsheet discussion can be skipped without loss of continuity; but if you understand the basics of Excel and have access to a computer, we recommend that you read through this section. Even if you aren't familiar with spreadsheets, the discussion will still give you an idea of how they operate.

We used Excel to create Table 5.1, which is part of the spreadsheet model that corresponds to this chapter. Table 5.1 summarizes the four methods of finding the FV and shows the spreadsheet formulas toward the bottom. Note that spreadsheets can be used to do calculations; but they can also be used like a word processor to create exhibits like Table 5.1, which includes text, drawings, and calculations. The letters across the top designate columns, the numbers to the left designate rows, and the rows and columns jointly designate cells. Thus, C14 is the cell in which we specify the −$100 investment, C15 shows the interest rate, and C16 shows the number of periods. We then created a time line on Rows 17 to 19; and on Row 21, we have Excel go through the step-by-step calculations, multiplying the beginning-of-year values by $(1 + I)$ to find the compounded value at the end of each period. Cell G21 shows the final result. Then on Row 23, we illustrate the formula approach, using Excel to solve Equation 5.1, and find the FV, $115.76. Next, on Rows 25 to 27, we show a picture of the calculator solution. Finally, on Rows 30 and 31, we use Excel's built-in FV function to find the answers given in Cells G30 and G31. The G30 answer is based on fixed inputs, while the G31 answer is based on cell references, which makes it easy to change inputs and see the effects on the output.

For example, if you wanted to quickly see how the future value changes if the interest rate was 7% instead of 5%, all you need to do is change Cell C15 to 7%. Looking at Cell G30, you will immediately see that the future value is now $122.50.

Students can download the Excel chapter models from the student companion site on the text's website. Once downloaded onto your computer, retrieve the Excel chapter model and follow along as you read this chapter.

Summary of Future Value Calculations **TABLE 5.1**

	A	B	C	D	E	F	G
14	Investment	= CF$_0$ = PV =	-$100.00				
15	Interest rate	= I =	5.00%				
16	No. of periods =	N =	3				
17			Periods:	0	1	2	3
18							
19			Cash Flow Time Line:	-$100			FV = ?
20							
21	Step-by-Step Approach:			$100	$105.00	$110.25	$115.76
22							
23	Formula Approach: FV$_N$ = PV(1 + I)^N			FV$_N$ =	$100(1.05)^3	=	$115.76
24							
25			3	5	-$100.00	$0	
26	Calculator Approach:		N	I/YR	PV	PMT	FV
27							$115.76
28							
29	Excel Approach:		FV function:	FV$_N$ =	=FV(rate,nper,pmt,pv,type)		
30			Fixed inputs:	FV$_N$ =	=FV(0.05,3,0,-100) =		$115.76
31			Cell references:	FV$_N$ =	=FV(C15,C16,0,C14) =		$115.76
32	In the Excel formula, the terms are entered in this sequence: interest, periods, 0 to indicate no intermediate cash flows, and then the PV. The data can be entered as fixed numbers or as cell references.						

© Cengage Learning 2015

HINTS ON USING FINANCIAL CALCULATORS

When using a financial calculator, make sure it is set up as indicated here. Refer to your calculator manual or to our calculator tutorial on the text's website for information on setting up your calculator.

- *One payment per period.* Many calculators "come out of the box" assuming that 12 payments are made per year; that is, monthly payments. However, in this book, we generally deal with problems in which only one payment is made each year. *Therefore, you should set your calculator at one payment per year and leave it there. See our tutorial or your calculator manual if you need assistance.*

- *End mode.* With most contracts, payments are made at the end of each period. However, some contracts call for payments at the beginning of each period. You can switch between "End Mode" and "Begin Mode" depending on the problem you are solving. *Because most of the problems in this book call for end-of-period payments, you should return your calculator to End Mode after you work a problem where payments are made at the beginning of periods.*

- *Negative sign for outflows.* Outflows must be entered as negative numbers. This generally means typing the outflow as a positive number and then pressing the +/− key to convert from + to − before hitting the enter key.

- *Decimal places.* With most calculators, you can specify from 0 to 11 decimal places. When working with dollars, we generally specify two decimal places. When dealing with interest rates, we generally specify two places after the decimal when the rate is expressed as a percentage (e.g., 5.25%), but we specify four decimal places when the rate is expressed as a decimal (e.g., 0.0525).

- *Interest rates.* For arithmetic operations with a nonfinancial calculator, 0.0525 must be used; but with a financial calculator and its TVM keys, you must enter 5.25, not 0.0525, because financial calculators assume that rates are stated as percentages.

If you are using Excel, there are a few things to keep in mind:

- When calculating time value of money problems in Excel, interest rates are entered as percentages or decimals (e.g., .05 or 5%). However, when using the time value of money function on most financial calculators you generally enter the interest rate as a whole number (e.g., 5).

- When calculating time value of money problems in Excel, the abbreviation for the number of periods is nper, whereas for most financial calculators the abbreviation is simply N. Throughout the text, we will use these terms interchangeably.

- When calculating time value of money problems in Excel, you will often be prompted to enter Type. Type refers to whether the payments come at the end of the year (in which case Type = 0, or you can just omit it), or at the beginning of the year (in which case Type = 1). Most financial calculators have a BEGIN/END mode function that you toggle on or off to indicate whether the payments come at the beginning or at the end of the period.

Table 5.1 demonstrates that all four methods get the same result, but they use different calculating procedures. It also shows that with Excel, all inputs are shown in one place, which makes checking data entries relatively easy. Finally, it shows that Excel can be used to create exhibits, which are quite important in the real world. In business, it's often as important to explain what you are doing as it is to "get the right answer" because if decision makers don't understand your analysis, they may reject your recommendations.

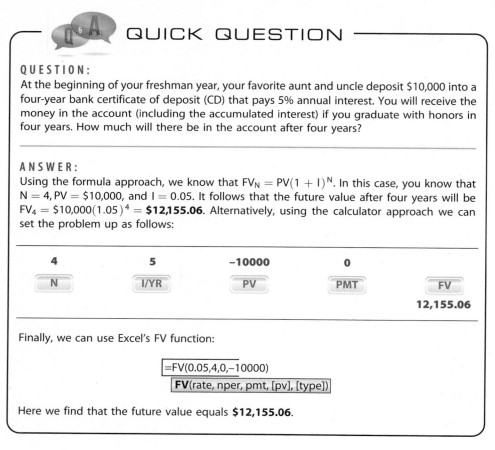

QUICK QUESTION

QUESTION:

At the beginning of your freshman year, your favorite aunt and uncle deposit $10,000 into a four-year bank certificate of deposit (CD) that pays 5% annual interest. You will receive the money in the account (including the accumulated interest) if you graduate with honors in four years. How much will there be in the account after four years?

ANSWER:

Using the formula approach, we know that $FV_N = PV(1 + I)^N$. In this case, you know that $N = 4, PV = \$10,000$, and $I = 0.05$. It follows that the future value after four years will be $FV_4 = \$10,000(1.05)^4 = \mathbf{\$12,155.06}$. Alternatively, using the calculator approach we can set the problem up as follows:

4	5	–10000	0	
N	I/YR	PV	PMT	FV
				12,155.06

Finally, we can use Excel's FV function:

=FV(0.05,4,0,–10000)
FV(rate, nper, pmt, [pv], [type])

Here we find that the future value equals **$12,155.06**.

5-2e Graphic View of the Compounding Process

Figure 5.1 shows how a $1 investment grows over time at different interest rates. We made the curves by solving Equation 5.1 with different values for N and I. The interest rate is a growth rate: If a sum is deposited and earns 5% interest per year,

FIGURE 5.1	Growth of $1 at Various Interest Rates and Time Periods

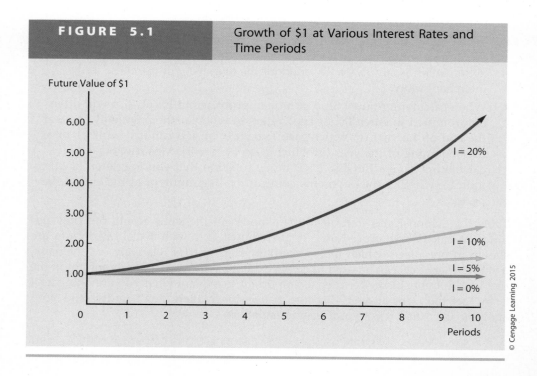

the funds on deposit will grow by 5% per year. Note also that time value concepts can be applied to anything that grows—sales, population, earnings per share, or future salary.

SELF TEST

Explain why this statement is true: A dollar in hand today is worth more than a dollar to be received next year.

What is compounding? What's the difference between simple interest and compound interest? What would the future value of $100 be after 5 years at 10% *compound* interest? At 10% *simple* interest? **($161.05; $150.00)**

Suppose you currently have $2,000 and plan to purchase a 3-year certificate of deposit (CD) that pays 4% interest compounded annually. How much will you have when the CD matures? How would your answer change if the interest rate were 5% or 6% or 20%? **($2,249.73; $2,315.25; $2,382.03; $3,456.00. Hint: With a calculator, enter N = 3, I/YR = 4, PV = −2000, and PMT = 0; then press FV to get 2,249.73. Enter I/YR = 5 to override the 4% and press FV again to get the second answer. In general, you can change one input at a time to see how the output changes.)**

A company's sales in 2014 were $100 million. If sales grow at 8%, what will they be 10 years later, in 2024? **($215.89 million)**

How much would $1, growing at 5% per year, be worth after 100 years? What would the FV be if the growth rate was 10%? **($131.50; $13,780.61)**

5-3 PRESENT VALUES

Finding a present value is the reverse of finding a future value. Indeed, we simply solve Equation 5.1, the formula for the future value, for the PV to produce the basic present value Equation, 5.2:

$$\text{Future value} = FV_N = PV(1 + I)^N$$

 5.1

$$\text{Present value} = PV = \frac{FV_N}{(1 + I)^N}$$

 5.2

We illustrate PVs with the following example. A broker offers to sell you a Treasury bond that will pay $115.76 three years from now. Banks are currently offering a guaranteed 5% interest on 3-year certificates of deposit (CDs); and if you don't buy the bond, you will buy a CD. The 5% rate paid on the CDs is defined as your **opportunity cost**, or the rate of return you could earn on an alternative investment of similar risk. Given these conditions, what's the most you should pay for the bond? We answer this question using the four methods discussed in the last section—step-by-step, formula, calculator, and spreadsheet. Table 5.2 summarizes the results.

First, recall from the future value example in the last section that if you invested $100 at 5%, it would grow to $115.76 in 3 years. You would also have $115.76 after 3 years if you bought the T-bond. Therefore, the most you should pay for the bond is $100—this is its "fair price." If you could buy the bond for *less than* $100, you should buy it rather than invest in the CD. Conversely, if its price was *more than* $100, you should buy the CD. If the bond's price was exactly $100, you should be indifferent between the T-bond and the CD.

Opportunity Cost
The rate of return you could earn on an alternative investment of similar risk.

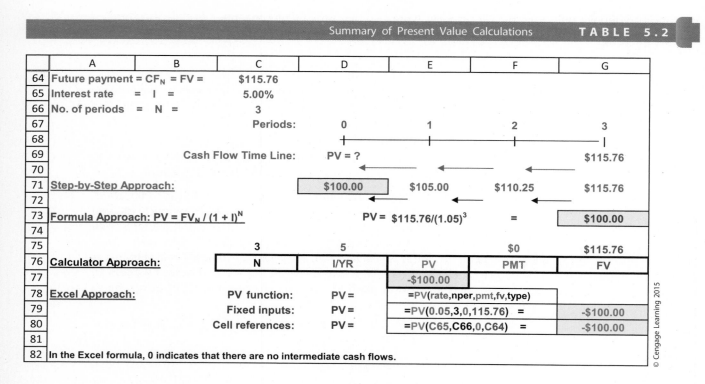

TABLE 5.2 Summary of Present Value Calculations

	A	B	C	D	E	F	G
64	Future payment = CF$_N$ = FV =		$115.76				
65	Interest rate = I =		5.00%				
66	No. of periods = N =		3				
67			Periods:	0	1	2	3
68							
69			Cash Flow Time Line:	PV = ?			$115.76
70							
71	Step-by-Step Approach:			$100.00	$105.00	$110.25	$115.76
72							
73	Formula Approach: PV = FV$_N$ / (1 + I)^N				PV = $115.76/(1.05)^3	=	$100.00
74							
75			3	5		$0	$115.76
76	Calculator Approach:		N	I/YR	PV	PMT	FV
77					-$100.00		
78	Excel Approach:		PV function:	PV =	=PV(rate,nper,pmt,fv,type)		
79			Fixed inputs:	PV =	=PV(0.05,3,0,115.76) =		-$100.00
80			Cell references:	PV =	=PV(C65,C66,0,C64) =		-$100.00
81							
82	In the Excel formula, 0 indicates that there are no intermediate cash flows.						

The $100 is defined as the present value, or PV, of $115.76 due in 3 years when the appropriate interest rate is 5%. In general, *the present value of a cash flow due N years in the future is the amount which, if it were on hand today, would grow to equal the given future amount.* Because $100 would grow to $115.76 in 3 years at a 5% interest rate, $100 is the present value of $115.76 due in 3 years at a 5% rate. Finding present values is called **discounting**; and as noted above, it is the reverse of compounding—if you know the PV, you can compound to find the FV, while if you know the FV, you can discount to find the PV.

Discounting

The process of finding the present value of a cash flow or a series of cash flows; discounting is the reverse of compounding.

The top section of Table 5.2 calculates the PV using the step-by-step approach. When we found the future value in the previous section, we worked from left to right, multiplying the initial amount and each subsequent amount by (1 + I). To find present values, we work backward, or from right to left, dividing the future value and each subsequent amount by (1 + I). This procedure shows exactly what's happening, which can be quite useful when you are working complex problems. However, it's inefficient, especially when you are dealing with a large number of years.

With the formula approach, we use Equation 5.2, simply dividing the future value by (1 + I)^N. This is more efficient than the step-by-step approach, and it gives the same result. Equation 5.2 is built into financial calculators; and as shown in Table 5.2, we can find the PV by entering values for N, I/YR, PMT, and FV and then pressing the PV key. Finally, Excel's PV function,

=PV(0.05,3,0,–115.76)

PV(rate, nper, pmt, [fv], [type])

can be used. It is essentially the same as the calculator and solves Equation 5.2.

The fundamental goal of financial management is to maximize the firm's value, and the value of a business (or any asset, including stocks and bonds) is the *present value* of its expected future cash flows. Because present value lies at the heart of the valuation process, we will have much more to say about it in the remainder of this chapter and throughout the book.

5-3A GRAPHIC VIEW OF THE DISCOUNTING PROCESS

Figure 5.2 shows that the present value of a sum to be received in the future decreases and approaches zero as the payment date is extended further into the future and that the present value falls faster at higher interest rates. At relatively high rates, funds due in the future are worth very little today; and even at relatively low rates, present values of sums due in the very distant future are quite small. For example, at a 20% discount rate, $1 million due in 100 years would be worth only $0.0121 today. This is because $0.0121 would grow to $1 million in 100 years when compounded at 20%.

| FIGURE 5.2 | Present Value of $1 at Various Interest Rates and Time Periods |

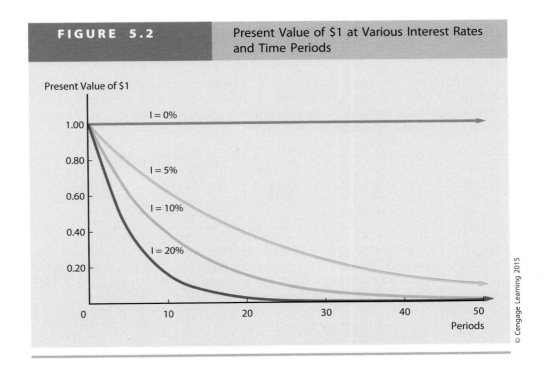

© Cengage Learning 2015

SELF TEST

What is discounting, and how is it related to compounding? How is the future value equation (5.1) related to the present value equation (5.2)?

How does the present value of a future payment change as the time to receipt is lengthened? As the interest rate increases?

Suppose a U.S. government bond promises to pay $2,249.73 three years from now. If the going interest rate on three-year government bonds is 4%, how much is the bond worth today? How would your answer change if the bond matured in 5 years rather than 3? What if the interest rate on the 5-year bond was 6% rather than 4%? **($2,000; $1,849.11; $1,681.13)**

How much would $1,000,000 due in 100 years be worth today if the discount rate was 5%? If the discount rate was 20%? **($7,604.49; $0.0121)**

5-4 FINDING THE INTEREST RATE, I

Thus far we have used Equations 5.1 and 5.2 to find future and present values. Those equations have four variables; and if we know three of the variables, we can solve for the fourth. Thus, if we know PV, I, and N, we can solve Equation 5.1 for FV, while if we know FV, I, and N, we can solve Equation 5.2 to find PV. That's what we did in the preceding two sections.

Now suppose we know PV, FV, and N and want to find I. For example, suppose we know that a given bond has a cost of $100 and that it will return $150 after 10 years. Thus, we know PV, FV, and N and we want to find the rate of return we will earn if we buy the bond. Here's the situation:

$$FV = PV(1 + I)^N$$
$$\$150 = \$100(1 + I)^{10}$$
$$\$150/\$100 = (1 + I)^{10}$$
$$1.5 = (1 + I)^{10}$$

Unfortunately, we can't factor I out to produce as simple a formula as we could for FV and PV. We can solve for I, but it requires a bit more algebra.[7] However, financial calculators and spreadsheets can find interest rates almost instantly. Here's the calculator setup:

10		−100	0	150
N	I/YR	PV	PMT	FV
	4.14			

Enter N = 10, PV = −100, PMT = 0 because there are no payments until the security matures, and FV = 150. Then when you press the I/YR key, the calculator gives the answer, 4.14%. You would get this same answer using the RATE function in Excel:

=RATE(10,0,−100,150)
RATE(nper, pmt, pv, [fv], [type], [guess])

Here we find that the interest rate is equal to 4.14%.[8]

SELF TEST

The U.S. Treasury offers to sell you a bond for $585.43. No payments will be made until the bond matures 10 years from now, at which time it will be redeemed for $1,000. What interest rate would you earn if you bought this bond for $585.43? What rate would you earn if you could buy the bond for $550? For $600? **(5.5%; 6.16%; 5.24%)**

Microsoft earned $0.94 per share in 2002. Ten years later in 2012 it earned $2.72. What was the growth rate in Microsoft's earnings per share (EPS) over the 10-year period? If EPS in 2012 had been $2.25 rather than $2.72, what would the growth rate have been? **(11.21%; 9.12%)**

---

[7]Raise the left side of the equation, the 1.5, to the power 1/N = 1/10 = 0.1, getting 1.0414. That number is 1 plus the interest rate, so the interest rate is 0.0414 = 4.14%.

[8]The RATE function prompts you to make a "guess." In many cases, you can leave this blank, but if Excel is unable to find a solution to the problem, you should enter a reasonable "guess," which will help the program converge to the correct solution.

5-5 FINDING THE NUMBER OF YEARS, N

We sometimes need to know how long it will take to accumulate a certain sum of money, given our beginning funds and the rate we will earn on those funds. For example, suppose we believe that we could retire comfortably if we had $1 million. We want to find how long it will take us to acquire $1 million, assuming we now have $500,000 invested at 4.5%. We cannot use a simple formula—the situation is like that with interest rates. We can set up a formula that uses logarithms, but calculators and spreadsheets find N very quickly. Here's the calculator setup:

	4.5	–500000	0	1000000
N	I/YR	PV	PMT	FV
15.7473				

Enter I/YR = 4.5, PV = –500000, PMT = 0, and FV = 1000000. Then when you press the N key, you get the answer, 15.7473 years. If you plug N = 15.7473 into the FV formula, you can prove that this is indeed the correct number of years:

$$FV = PV(1 + I)^N = \$500{,}000(1.045)^{15.7473} = \$1{,}000{,}000$$

You can also use Excel's NPER function:

=NPER(0.045,0,–500000,1000000)
NPER(rate, pmt, pv, [fv], [type])

Here we find that it will take 15.7473 years for $500,000 to double at a 4.5% interest rate.

SELF TEST

How long would it take $1,000 to double if it was invested in a bank that paid 6% per year? How long would it take if the rate was 10%? **(11.9 years; 7.27 years)**

Microsoft's 2012 earnings per share were $2.72, and its growth rate during the prior 10 years was 11.21% per year. If that growth rate was maintained, how long would it take for Microsoft's EPS to double? **(6.52 years)**

5-6 ANNUITIES

Thus far we have dealt with single payments, or "lump sums." However, many assets provide a series of cash inflows over time; and many obligations, such as auto, student, and mortgage loans, require a series of payments. When the payments are equal and are made at fixed intervals, the series is an **annuity**. For example, $100 paid at the end of each of the next 3 years is a 3-year annuity. If the payments occur at the *end* of each year, the annuity is an **ordinary (or deferred) annuity**. If the payments are made at the *beginning* of each year, the annuity is an **annuity due**. Ordinary annuities are more common in finance; so when we use the term *annuity* in this book, assume that the payments occur at the ends of the periods unless otherwise noted.

Annuity
A series of equal payments at fixed intervals for a specified number of periods.

Ordinary (Deferred) Annuity
An annuity whose payments occur at the end of each period.

Annuity Due
An annuity whose payments occur at the beginning of each period.

Here are the time lines for a $100, 3-year, 5% ordinary annuity and for the same annuity on an annuity due basis. With the annuity due, each payment is shifted to the left by one year. A $100 deposit will be made each year, so we show the payments with minus signs:

Ordinary Annuity:

Annuity Due:

As we demonstrate in the following sections, we can find an annuity's future and present values, the interest rate built into annuity contracts, and the length of time it takes to reach a financial goal using an annuity. Keep in mind that annuities must have *constant payments* and *a fixed number of periods.* If these conditions don't hold, then the payments do not constitute an annuity.

SELF TEST

What's the difference between an ordinary annuity and an annuity due?

Why would you prefer to receive an annuity due for $10,000 per year for 10 years than an otherwise similar ordinary annuity?

5-7 FUTURE VALUE OF AN ORDINARY ANNUITY

The future value of an annuity can be found using the step-by-step approach or using a formula, a financial calculator, or a spreadsheet. As an illustration, consider the ordinary annuity diagrammed earlier, where you deposit $100 at the end of each year for 3 years and earn 5% per year. How much will you have at the end of the third year? The answer, $315.25, is defined as the future value of the annuity, **FVA$_N$**; it is shown in Table 5.3.

FVA$_N$

The future value of an annuity over N periods.

As shown in the step-by-step section of the table, we compound each payment out to Time 3, then sum those compounded values to find the annuity's FV, FVA$_3$ = $315.25. The first payment earns interest for two periods, the second payment earns interest for one period, and the third payment earns no interest at all because it is made at the end of the annuity's life. This approach is straightforward; but if the annuity extends out for many years, the approach is cumbersome and time-consuming.

As you can see from the time line diagram, with the step-by-step approach, we apply the following equation, with N = 3 and I = 5%:

$$FVA_N = PMT(1 + I)^{N-1} + PMT(1 + I)^{N-2} + PMT(1 + I)^{N-3}$$
$$= \$100(1.05)^2 + \$100(1.05)^1 + \$100(1.05)^0$$
$$= \$315.25$$

| TABLE 5.3 | | Summary: Future Value of an Ordinary Annuity | | | | |

	A	B	C	D	E	F	G
131	Payment amount	= PMT =	$100.00				
132	Interest rate	= I =	5.00%				
133	Number of periods	= N =	3				
134							
135		Periods:	0	1	2	3	
136							
137		Cash Flow Time Line:		-$100	-$100	-$100	
138	**Step-by-Step Approach:**						
139	Multiply each payment by					-$100.00	
140	$(1+I)^{N-t}$ and sum these FVs to					-105.00	
141	find FVA_N:					-110.25	
142						-$315.25	
143							
144	**Formula Approach:**						
145							
146		FVA_N =	$PMT \times \left(\dfrac{(1+I)^N - 1}{I} \right)$		=	$315.25	
147							
148							
149			3	5	$0	-$100.00	
150	**Calculator Approach:**		N	I/YR	PV	PMT	FV
151							$315.25
152	**Excel Function Approach:**		FV function:	FVA_N =	=FV(rate,nper,pmt,pv,type)		
153			Fixed inputs:	FVA_N =	=FV(0.05,3,-100,0) =	$315.25	
154			Cell references:	FVA_N =	=FV(C132,C133,-C131,0) =	$315.25	
155		In the Excel formula, a 0 entered for type (or left blank) indicates that cash flows occur at the <u>end</u> of each period. A 1 would indicate beginning-of-period payments, i.e., an annuity due.					

© Cengage Learning 2015

We can generalize and streamline the equation as follows:

$$FVA_N = PMT(1+I)^{N-1} + PMT(1+I)^{N-2} + PMT(1+I)^{N-3} + \ldots + PMT(1+I)^0$$

$$= PMT \left[\frac{(1+I)^N - 1}{I} \right]$$

5.3

The first line shows the equation in its long form. It can be transformed to the second form on the last line, which can be used to solve annuity problems with a nonfinancial calculator.[9] This equation is also built into financial calculators and spreadsheets. With an annuity, we have recurring payments; hence, the PMT key is used. Here's the calculator setup for our illustrative annuity:

3	5	0	−100	End Mode
N	I/YR	PV	PMT	FV
				315.25

We enter PV = 0 because we start off with nothing, and we enter PMT = −100 because we plan to deposit this amount in the account at the end of each year. When we press the FV key, we get the answer, FVA_3 = 315.25.

---

[9] The long form of the equation is a geometric progression that can be reduced to the second form.

Because this is an ordinary annuity, with payments coming at the *end* of each year, we must set the calculator appropriately. As noted earlier, calculators "come out of the box" set to assume that payments occur at the end of each period, that is, to deal with ordinary annuities. However, there is a key that enables us to switch between ordinary annuities and annuities due. For ordinary annuities the designation is "End Mode" or something similar, while for annuities due the designation is "Begin" or "Begin Mode" or "Due" or something similar. If you make a mistake and set your calculator on Begin Mode when working with an ordinary annuity, each payment will earn interest for one extra year. That will cause the compounded amounts, and thus the FVA, to be too large.

The last approach in Table 5.3 shows the spreadsheet solution using Excel's built-in function. We can put in fixed values for N, I, PV, and PMT or set up an Input Section, where we assign values to those variables, and then input values into the function as cell references. Using cell references makes it easy to change the inputs to see the effects of changes on the output.

 QUICK QUESTION

QUESTION:

Your grandfather urged you to begin a habit of saving money early in your life. He suggested that you put $5 a day into an envelope. If you follow his advice, at the end of the year you will have $1,825 (365 × $5). Your grandfather further suggested that you take that money at the end of the year and invest it in an online brokerage mutual fund account that has an annual expected return of 8%.

You are 18 years old. If you start following your grandfather's advice today, and continue saving in this way the rest of your life, how much do you expect to have in the brokerage account when you are 65 years old?

ANSWER:

This problem is asking you to calculate the future value of an ordinary annuity. More specifically, you are making 47 payments of $1,825, where the annual interest rate is 8%.

To quickly find the answer, enter the following inputs into a financial calculator: N = 47; I/YR = 8; PV = 0; and PMT = −1825. Then solve for the FV of the ordinary annuity by pressing the FV key, FV = **$826,542.78**.

In addition, we can use Excel's FV function:

=FV(0.08,47,−1825,0)

FV(rate, nper, pmt, [pv], [type])

Here we find that the future value is **$826,542.78**.

You can see your grandfather is right—it definitely pays to start saving early!

SELF TEST

For an ordinary annuity with five annual payments of $100 and a 10% interest rate, how many years will the first payment earn interest? What will this payment's value be at the end? Answer this same question for the fifth payment. **(4 years, $146.41; 0 years, $100)**

Assume that you plan to buy a condo 5 years from now, and you estimate that you can save $2,500 per year. You plan to deposit the money in a bank that pays 4% interest, and you will make the first deposit at the end of the year. How much will you have after 5 years? How will your answer change if the interest rate is increased to 6% or lowered to 3%? **($13,540.81; $14,092.73; $13,272.84)**

5-8 FUTURE VALUE OF AN ANNUITY DUE

Because each payment occurs one period earlier with an annuity due, all of the payments earn interest for one additional period. Therefore, the FV of an annuity due will be greater than that of a similar ordinary annuity. If you went through the step-by-step procedure, you would see that our illustrative annuity due has an FV of $331.01 versus $315.25 for the ordinary annuity.

With the formula approach, we first use Equation 5.3; but because each payment occurs one period earlier, we multiply the Equation 5.3 result by $(1 + I)$:

$$\text{FVA}_{\text{due}} \; = \; \text{FVA}_{\text{ordinary}}(1 + I)$$

 5.4

Thus, for the annuity due, $\text{FVA}_{\text{due}} = \$315.25(1.05) = \$331.01$, which is the same result when the period-by-period approach is used. With a calculator, we input the variables just as we did with the ordinary annuity; but now we set the calculator to Begin Mode to get the answer, $331.01.

SELF TEST

Why does an annuity due always have a higher future value than an ordinary annuity?

If you calculated the value of an ordinary annuity, how could you find the value of the corresponding annuity due?

Assume that you plan to buy a condo 5 years from now and you need to save for a down payment. You plan to save $2,500 per year (with the first deposit made *immediately*), and you will deposit the funds in a bank account that pays 4% interest. How much will you have after 5 years? How much will you have if you make the deposits at the end of each year? **($14,082.44; $13,540.81)**

PVA$_N$

The present value of an annuity of N periods.

5-9 PRESENT VALUE OF AN ORDINARY ANNUITY

The present value of an annuity, **PVA$_N$**, can be found using the step-by-step, formula, calculator, or spreadsheet method. Look back at Table 5.3. To find the FV of the annuity, we compounded the deposits. To find the PV, we discount them, dividing each payment by $(1 + I)^t$. The step-by-step procedure is diagrammed as follows:

Periods	0		1	2	3
		5%			
Payments			−$100	−$100	−$100

$ 95.24
90.70
86.38
$272.32 = Present value of the annuity (PVA$_N$)

Equation 5.5 expresses the step-by-step procedure in a formula. The bracketed form of the equation can be used with a scientific calculator, and it is helpful if the annuity extends out for a number of years:

$$PVA_N = PMT/(1+I)^1 + PMT/(1+I)^2 + \ldots + PMT/(1+I)^N$$

$$= PMT \left[\frac{1 - \dfrac{1}{(1+I)^N}}{I} \right]$$

5.5

$$= \$100 \times [1 - 1/(1.05)^3]/0.05 = \$272.32$$

Calculators are programmed to solve Equation 5.5; so we merely input the variables and press the PV key, *making sure the calculator is set to End Mode.* The calculator setup follows for both an ordinary annuity and an annuity due. Note that the PV of the annuity due is larger because each payment is discounted back one less year. Note too that you can find the PV of the ordinary annuity and then multiply by $(1 + I) = 1.05$, calculating $\$272.32(1.05) = \$285.94$, the PV of the annuity due.

3	5		−100	0	End Mode
N	I/YR	PV	PMT	FV	(Ordinary Annuity)
		272.32			

3	5		−100	0	Begin Mode
N	I/YR	PV	PMT	FV	(Annuity Due)
		285.94			

QUICK QUESTION

QUESTION:

You just won the Florida lottery. To receive your winnings, you must select one of the two following choices:

1. You can receive $1,000,000 a year at the end of each of the next 30 years; OR
2. You can receive a one-time payment of $15,000,000 today.

Assume that the current interest rate is 6%. Which option is most valuable?

ANSWER:

The most valuable option is the one with the largest present value. You know that the second option has a present value of $15,000,000, so we need to determine whether the present value of the $1,000,000 30-year ordinary annuity exceeds $15,000,000.

Using the formula approach, we see that the present value of the annuity is:

$$PVA_N = PMT \left[\frac{1 - \dfrac{1}{(1 + I)^N}}{I} \right]$$

$$= \$1,000,000 \left[\frac{1 - \dfrac{1}{(1.06)^{30}}}{0.06} \right]$$

$$= \$13,764,831.15$$

Alternatively, using the calculator approach we can set up the problem as follows:

30	6		−1000000	0
N	I/YR	PV	PMT	FV
		13,764,831.15		

Finally, we can use Excel's PV function:

=PV(0.06,30,−1000000,0)

PV(rate, nper, pmt, [fv], [type])

Here we find that the present value is **$13,764,831.15**.

Because the present value of the 30-year annuity is less than $15,000,000, you should choose to receive your winnings as a one-time upfront payment.

SELF TEST

Why does an annuity due have a higher present value than a similar ordinary annuity?

If you know the present value of an ordinary annuity, how can you find the PV of the corresponding annuity due?

What is the PVA of an ordinary annuity with 10 payments of $100 if the appropriate interest rate is 10%? What would the PVA be if the interest rate was 4%? What if the interest rate was 0%? How would the PVA values differ if we were dealing with annuities due? **($614.46; $811.09; $1,000.00; $675.90; $843.53; $1,000.00)**

Assume that you are offered an annuity that pays $100 at the end of each year for 10 years. You could earn 8% on your money in other investments with equal risk. What is the most you should pay for the annuity? If the payments began immediately, how much would the annuity be worth? **($671.01; $724.69)**

5-10 Finding Annuity Payments, Periods, and Interest Rates

We can find payments, periods, and interest rates for annuities. Here five variables come into play: N, I, PMT, FV, and PV. If we know any four, we can find the fifth.

5-10a Finding Annuity Payments, PMT

Suppose we need to accumulate $10,000 and have it available 5 years from now. Suppose further that we can earn a return of 6% on our savings, which are currently zero. Thus, we know that FV = 10,000, PV = 0, N = 5, and I/YR = 6. We can enter these values in a financial calculator and press the PMT key to find how large our deposits must be. The answer will, of course, depend on whether we make deposits at the end of each year (ordinary annuity) or at the beginning (annuity due). Here are the results for each type of annuity:

Ordinary Annuity:

5	6	0		10000	End Mode
N	I/YR	PV	PMT	FV	(Ordinary Annuity)
			−1,773.96		

We can also use Excel's PMT function:

```
=PMT(0.06,5,0,10000
PMT(rate, nper, pv, [fv], [type])
```

Because the deposits are made at the end of the year, we can leave "type" blank. Here we find that an annual deposit of $1,773.96 is needed to reach your goal.

Annuity Due:

5	6	0		10000	Begin Mode
N	I/YR	PV	PMT	FV	(Annuity Due)
			−1,673.55		

Alternatively, Excel's PMT function can be used to calculate the annual deposit for the annuity due:

=PMT(0.06,5,0,10000,1)
PMT(rate, nper, pv, [fv], [type])

Because the deposits are now made at the beginning of the year, enter 1 for type. Here we find that an annual deposit of $1,673.55 is needed to reach your goal.

Thus, you must save $1,773.96 per year if you make deposits at the *end* of each year, but only $1,673.55 if the deposits begin *immediately*. Note that the required annual deposit for the annuity due is calculated as the ordinary annuity payment divided by $(1 + I)$: $1,773.96/1.06 = $1,673.55.

5-10B FINDING THE NUMBER OF PERIODS, N

Suppose you decide to make end-of-year deposits, but you can save only $1,200 per year. Again assuming that you would earn 6%, how long would it take to reach your $10,000 goal? Here is the calculator setup:

	6	0	−1200	10000	End Mode
N	I/YR	PV	PMT	FV	
6.96					

With these smaller deposits, it would take 6.96 years to reach your $10,000 goal. If you began the deposits immediately, you would have an annuity due and N would be a bit smaller, 6.63 years.

You can also use Excel's NPER function to arrive at both of these answers. If we assume end-of-year payments Excel's NPER function looks like this:

=NPER(0.06,−1200,0,10000)
NPER(rate, pmt, pv, [fv], [type])

Here we find that it will take 6.96 years to reach your goal.

If we assume beginning-of-year payments Excel's NPER function looks like this:

=NPER(0.06,−1200,0,10000,1)
NPER(rate, pmt, pv, [fv], [type])

Here we find that it will take only 6.63 years to reach your goal.

5-10C FINDING THE INTEREST RATE, I

Now suppose you can save only $1,200 annually, but you still need the $10,000 in 5 years. What rate of return would enable you to achieve your goal? Here is the calculator setup:

5		0	−1200	10000	End Mode
N	I/YR	PV	PMT	FV	
	25.78				

Excel's RATE function will arrive at the same answer:

$$\boxed{\text{=RATE(5,−1200,0,10000)}}$$
$$\boxed{\textbf{RATE}\text{(nper, pmt, pv, [fv], [type], [guess])}}$$

Here we find that the interest rate is 25.78%.

You must earn a whopping 25.78% to reach your goal. About the only way to earn such a high return would be to invest in speculative stocks or head to the casinos in Las Vegas. Of course, investing in speculative stocks and gambling aren't like making deposits in a bank with a guaranteed rate of return, so there's a good chance you'd end up with nothing. You might consider changing your plans—save more, lower your $10,000 target, or extend your time horizon. It might be appropriate to seek a somewhat higher return, but trying to earn 25.78% in a 6% market would require taking on more risk than would be prudent.

It's easy to find rates of return using a financial calculator or a spreadsheet. However, to find rates of return without one of these tools, you would have to go through a trial-and-error process, which would be very time-consuming if many years were involved.

SELF TEST

Suppose you inherited $100,000 and invested it at 7% per year. What is the most you could withdraw at the *end* of each of the next 10 years and have a zero balance at Year 10? How would your answer change if you made withdrawals at the *beginning* of each year? **($14,237.75; $13,306.31)**

If you had $100,000 that was invested at 7% and you wanted to withdraw $10,000 at the end of each year, how long would your funds last? How long would they last if you earned 0%? How long would they last if you earned the 7% but limited your withdrawals to $7,000 per year? **(17.8 years; 10 years; forever)**

Your uncle named you beneficiary of his life insurance policy. The insurance company gives you a choice of $100,000 today or a 12-year annuity of $12,000 at the end of each year. What rate of return is the insurance company offering? **(6.11%)**

Assume that you just inherited an annuity that will pay you $10,000 per year for 10 years, with the first payment being made today. A friend of your mother offers to give you $60,000 for the annuity. If you sell it, what rate of return would your mother's friend earn on his investment? If you think a "fair" return would be 6%, how much should you ask for the annuity? **(13.70%; $78,016.92)**

5-11 PERPETUITIES

Perpetuity
A stream of equal payments at fixed intervals expected to continue forever.

A **perpetuity** is simply an annuity with an extended life. Because the payments go on forever, you can't apply the step-by-step approach. However, it's easy to find the PV of a perpetuity with a formula found by solving Equation 5.5 with N set at infinity:[10]

---

[10]Equation 5.6 was found by letting N in Equation 5.5 approach infinity.

$$\text{PV of a perpetuity} = \frac{\text{PMT}}{\text{I}}$$

 5.6

Let's say, for example, that you buy preferred stock in a company that pays you a fixed dividend of $2.50 each year the company is in business. If we assume that the company will go on indefinitely, the preferred stock can be valued as a perpetuity. If the discount rate on the preferred stock is 10%, the present value of the perpetuity, the preferred stock, is $25:

$$\text{PV of a perpetuity} = \frac{\$2.50}{0.10} = \$25$$

SELF TEST

What's the present value of a perpetuity that pays $1,000 per year beginning one year from now if the appropriate interest rate is 5%? What would the value be if payments on the annuity began immediately? **($20,000, $21,000. Hint: Just add the $1,000 to be received immediately to the value of the annuity.)**

5-12 UNEVEN CASH FLOWS

The definition of an annuity includes the words *constant payment*—in other words, annuities involve payments that are equal in every period. Although many financial decisions involve constant payments, many others involve **uneven**, or **nonconstant, cash flows**. For example, the dividends on common stocks typically increase over time, and investments in capital equipment almost always generate uneven cash flows. Throughout the book, we reserve the term **payment (PMT)** for annuities with their equal payments in each period and use the term **cash flow (CF$_t$)** to denote uneven cash flows, where t designates the period in which the cash flow occurs.

There are two important classes of uneven cash flows: (1) a stream that consists of a series of annuity payments plus an additional final lump sum and (2) all other uneven streams. Bonds represent the best example of the first type, while stocks and capital investments illustrate the second type. Here are numerical examples of the two types of flows:

Uneven (Nonconstant) Cash Flows
A series of cash flows where the amount varies from one period to the next.

Payment (PMT)
This term designates equal cash flows coming at regular intervals.

Cash Flow (CF$_t$)
This term designates a cash flow that's not part of an annuity.

1. Annuity plus additional final payment:

Periods	0		1	2	3	4	5
		I = 12%					
Cash flows	$0		$100	$100	$100	$100	$ 100
							1,000
							$1,100

2. Irregular cash flows:

Periods	0		1	2	3	4	5
		I = 12%					
Cash flows	$0		$100	$300	$300	$300	$500

We can find the PV of either stream by using Equation 5.7 and following the step-by-step procedure, where we discount each cash flow and then sum them to find the PV of the stream:

$$PV = \frac{CF_1}{(1+I)^1} + \frac{CF_2}{(1+I)^2} + \ldots + \frac{CF_N}{(1+I)^N} = \sum_{t=1}^{N} \frac{CF_t}{(1+I)^t} \qquad \textbf{5.7}$$

If we did this, we would find the PV of Stream 1 to be $927.90 and the PV of Stream 2 to be $1,016.35.

The step-by-step procedure is straightforward; but if we have a large number of cash flows, it is time-consuming. However, financial calculators speed up the process considerably. First, consider Stream 1; notice that we have a 5-year, 12% ordinary annuity plus a final payment of $1,000. We could find the PV of the annuity, and then find the PV of the final payment and sum them to obtain the PV of the stream. Financial calculators do this in one simple step—use the five TVM keys, enter the data as shown below, and press the PV key to obtain the answer, $927.90.

5	12		100	1000
N	I/YR	PV	PMT	FV
		−927.90		

The solution procedure is different for the second uneven stream. Here we must use the step-by-step approach as shown in Figure 5.3. Even calculators and spreadsheets solve the problem using the step-by-step procedure, but they do it quickly and efficiently. First, you enter all of the cash flows and the interest rate; then the calculator or computer discounts each cash flow to find its present value and sums these PVs to produce the PV of the stream. You must enter the cash flows in the calculator's "cash flow register," enter the interest rate, and then press the NPV key to find the PV of the stream. NPV stands for "net present value." We cover the calculator mechanics in the calculator tutorial, and we discuss the process in more detail in Chapters 9 and 11, where we use the NPV calculation to analyze stocks and proposed capital budgeting projects. If you don't know how to do the calculation with your calculator, it would be worthwhile to review the tutorial or your calculator manual, learn the steps, and make sure you can do this calculation. Because you will have to learn to do it eventually, now is a good time to begin.

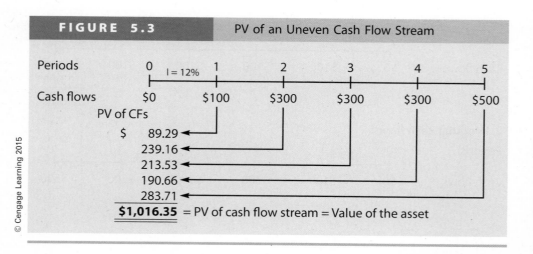

FIGURE 5.3 PV of an Uneven Cash Flow Stream

© Cengage Learning 2015

How could you use Equation 5.2 to find the PV of an uneven stream of cash flows?

What's the present value of a 5-year ordinary annuity of $100 plus an additional $500 at the end of Year 5 if the interest rate is 6%? What is the PV if the $100 payments occur in Years 1 through 10 and the $500 comes at the end of Year 10? **($794.87; $1,015.21)**

What's the present value of the following uneven cash flow stream: $0 at Time 0, $100 in Year 1 (or at Time 1), $200 in Year 2, $0 in Year 3, and $400 in Year 4 if the interest rate is 8%? **($558.07)**

Would a typical common stock provide cash flows more like an annuity or more like an uneven cash flow stream? Explain.

5-13 FUTURE VALUE OF AN UNEVEN CASH FLOW STREAM

We find the future value of uneven cash flow streams by compounding rather than discounting. Consider Cash Flow Stream 2 in the preceding section. We discounted those cash flows to find the PV, but we would compound them to find the FV. Figure 5.4 illustrates the procedure for finding the FV of the stream using the step-by-step approach.

The values of all financial assets—stocks, bonds, and business capital investments—are found as the present values of their expected future cash flows. Therefore, we need to calculate present values very often, far more often than future values. As a result, all financial calculators provide automated functions for finding PVs, but they generally do not provide automated FV functions. On the relatively few occasions when we need to find the FV of an uneven cash flow stream, we generally use the step-by-step procedure shown in Figure 5.4. That approach works for all cash flow streams, even those for which some cash flows are zero or negative.

| FIGURE 5.4 | FV of an Uneven Cash Flow Stream |

5-14 SOLVING FOR I WITH UNEVEN CASH FLOWS[11]

Before financial calculators and spreadsheets existed, it was *extremely difficult* to find I when the cash flows were uneven. With spreadsheets and financial calculators, however, it's relatively easy to find I. If you have an annuity plus a final lump sum, you can input values for N, PV, PMT, and FV into the calculator's TVM registers and then press the I/YR key. Here is the setup for Stream 1 from Section 5-12, assuming we must pay $927.90 to buy the asset. The rate of return on the $927.90 investment is 12%.

5		−927.90	100	1000
N	I/YR	PV	PMT	FV
	12.00			

Finding the interest rate for an uneven cash flow stream such as Stream 2 is a bit more complicated. First, note that there is no simple procedure—finding the rate requires a trial-and-error process, which means that a financial calculator or a spreadsheet is needed. With a calculator, we enter the CFs into the cash flow register and then press the IRR key to get the answer. IRR stands for "internal rate of return," and it is the rate of return the investment provides. The investment is the cash flow at Time 0, and it must be entered as a negative value. As an illustration, consider the cash flows given here, where $CF_0 = -\$1,000$ is the cost of the asset.

Periods	0	1	2	3	4	5
Cash flows	−$1,000	$100	$300	$300	$300	$500
IRR = I =	12.55%					

When we enter those cash flows into the calculator's cash flow register and press the IRR key, we get the rate of return on the $1,000 investment, 12.55%. You get the same answer using Excel's IRR function. This process is covered in the calculator tutorial; it is also discussed in Chapter 11, where we study capital budgeting.

---

[11]This section is relatively technical. It can be deferred at this point, but the calculations will be required in Chapter 11.

SELF TEST

An investment costs $465 and is expected to produce cash flows of $100 at the end of each of the next 4 years, then an extra lump sum payment of $200 at the end of the fourth year. What is the expected rate of return on this investment? **(9.05%)**

An investment costs $465 and is expected to produce cash flows of $100 at the end of Year 1, $200 at the end of Year 2, and $300 at the end of Year 3. What is the expected rate of return on this investment ? **(11.71%)**

5-15 SEMIANNUAL AND OTHER COMPOUNDING PERIODS

In all of our examples thus far, we assumed that interest was compounded once a year, or annually. This is called **annual compounding**. Suppose, however, that you deposit $100 in a bank that pays a 5% annual interest rate but credits interest each 6 months. So in the second 6-month period, you earn interest on your original $100 plus interest on the interest earned during the first 6 months. This is called **semiannual compounding**. Note that banks generally pay interest more than once a year; virtually all bonds pay interest semiannually; and most mortgages, student loans, and auto loans require monthly payments. Therefore, it is important to understand how to deal with nonannual compounding.

For an illustration of semiannual compounding, assume that we deposit $100 in an account that pays 5% and leave it there for 10 years. First, consider again what the future value would be under *annual* compounding:

$$FV_N = PV(1 + I)^N = \$100(1.05)^{10} = \$162.89$$

We would, of course, get the same answer using a financial calculator or a spreadsheet.

How would things change in this example if interest was paid semiannually rather than annually? First, whenever payments occur more than once a year, you must make two conversions: (1) Convert the stated interest rate into a "periodic rate" and (2) convert the number of years into "number of periods." The conversions are done as follows, where I is the stated annual rate, M is the number of compounding periods per year, and N is the number of years:

$$\text{Periodic rate } (I_{PER}) = \frac{\text{Stated annual rate}}{\text{Number of payments per year}} = I/M \qquad \textbf{5.8}$$

With a stated annual rate of 5%, compounded semiannually, the periodic rate is 2.5%:

$$\text{Periodic rate} = 5\%/2 = 2.5\%$$

The number of compounding periods is found with Equation 5.9:

$$\text{Number of periods} = (\text{Number of years})(\text{Periods per year}) = NM \qquad \textbf{5.9}$$

With 10 years and semiannual compounding, there are 20 periods:

$$\text{Number of periods} = 10(2) = 20 \text{ periods}$$

Annual Compounding
The arithmetic process of determining the final value of a cash flow or series of cash flows when interest is added once a year.

Semiannual Compounding
The arithmetic process of determining the final value of a cash flow or series of cash flows when interest is added twice a year.

Under semiannual compounding, our $100 investment will earn 2.5% every 6 months for 20 semiannual periods, not 5% per year for 10 years. The periodic rate and number of periods, not the annual rate and number of years, must be shown on time lines and entered into the calculator or spreadsheet whenever you are working with nonannual compounding.[12]

With this background, we can find the value of $100 after 10 years if it is held in an account that pays a stated annual rate of 5.0% but with semiannual compounding. Here's the time line and the future value:

Periods | 0 | I = 2.5% | 1 | 2 | ••• | 19 | 20

Cash flows −$100 ⟶ $PV (1 + I)^N = \$100(1.025)^{20} = FV_{20} = \$163.86$

With a financial calculator, we get the same result using the periodic rate and number of periods:

20	2.5	−100	0	
N	I/YR	PV	PMT	FV
				163.86

The future value under semiannual compounding, $163.86, exceeds the FV under annual compounding, $162.89, because interest starts accruing sooner; thus, you earn more interest on interest.

How would things change in our example if interest was compounded quarterly or monthly or daily? With quarterly compounding, there would be $NM = 10(4) = 40$ periods and the periodic rate would be $I/M = 5\%/4 = 1.25\%$ per quarter. Using those values, we would find FV = $164.36. If we used monthly compounding, we would have $10(12) = 120$ periods, the monthly rate would be $5\%/12 = 0.416667\%$, and the FV would rise to $164.70. If we went to daily compounding, we would have $10(365) = 3,650$ periods, the daily rate would be $5\%/365 = 0.0136986\%$ per day, and the FV would be $164.87 (based on a 365-day year).

The same logic applies when we find present values under semiannual compounding. Again, we use Equation 5.8 to convert the stated annual rate to the periodic (semiannual) rate and Equation 5.9 to find the number of semiannual periods. We then use the periodic rate and number of periods in the calculations. For example, we can find the PV of $100 due after 10 years when the stated annual rate is 5%, with semiannual compounding:

$$\text{Periodic rate} = 5\%/2 = 2.5\% \text{ per period}$$
$$\text{Number of periods} = 10(2) = 20 \text{ periods}$$
$$\text{PV of } \$100 = \$100/(1.025)^{20} = \$61.03$$

---

[12]With some financial calculators, you can enter the annual (nominal) rate and the number of compounding periods per year rather than make the conversions we recommend. We prefer the conversions because they must be used on time lines and because it is easy to forget to reset your calculator after you change its settings, which may lead to an error on your next problem.

We would get this same result with a financial calculator:

20	2.5		0	−100
N	I/YR	PV	PMT	FV
		61.03		

If we increased the number of compounding periods from 2 (semiannual) to 12 (monthly), the PV would decline to $60.72; and if we went to daily compounding, the PV would fall to $60.66.

SELF TEST

Would you rather invest in an account that pays 7% with annual compounding or 7% with monthly compounding? Would you rather borrow at 7% and make annual or monthly payments? Why?

What's the *future value* of $100 after 3 years if the appropriate interest rate is 8% compounded annually? Compounded monthly? **($125.97; $127.02)**

What's the *present value* of $100 due in three years if the appropriate interest rate is 8% compounded annually? Compounded monthly? **($79.38; $78.73)**

5-16 COMPARING INTEREST RATES

Different compounding periods are used for different types of investments. For example, bank accounts generally pay interest daily; most bonds pay interest semiannually; stocks pay dividends quarterly; and mortgages, auto loans, and other instruments require monthly payments.[13] If we are to compare investments or loans with different compounding periods properly, we need to put them on a common basis. Here are some terms you need to understand:

- The **nominal interest rate (I_{NOM})**, also called the **annual percentage rate (APR)** (or **quoted** or **stated rate**), is the rate that credit card companies, student loan officers, auto dealers, and other lenders tell you they are charging on loans. Note that if two banks offer loans with a stated rate of 8% but one requires monthly payments and the other quarterly payments, they are not charging the same "true" rate. The one that requires monthly payments is charging more than the one with quarterly payments because it will receive your money sooner. So to compare loans across lenders, or interest rates earned on different securities, you should calculate effective annual rates as described here.[14]

Nominal (Quoted, Or Stated) Interest Rate, I_{NOM}
The contracted interest rate.

Annual Percentage Rate (APR)
The periodic rate times the number of periods per year.

---

[13]Some banks even pay interest compounded continuously. Continuous compounding is discussed in Web Appendix 5A.

[14]Note, though, that if you are comparing two bonds that both pay interest semiannually, it's OK to compare their nominal rates. Similarly, you can compare the nominal rates on two money funds that pay interest daily. But don't compare the nominal rate on a semiannual bond with the nominal rate on a money fund that compounds daily because that will make the money fund look worse than it really is.

Effective (Equivalent) Annual Rate (EFF% or EAR)

The annual rate of interest actually being earned, as opposed to the quoted rate.

- The **effective annual rate**, abbreviated **EFF%**, is also called the **equivalent annual rate (EAR)**. This is the rate that would produce the same future value under annual compounding as would more frequent compounding at a given nominal rate.

- If a loan or an investment uses annual compounding, its nominal rate is also its effective rate. However, if compounding occurs more than once a year, the EFF% is higher than I_{NOM}.

- To illustrate, a nominal rate of 10% with semiannual compounding is equivalent to a rate of 10.25% with annual compounding because both rates will cause $100 to grow to the same amount after 1 year. The top line in the following diagram shows that $100 will grow to $110.25 at a nominal rate of 10.25%. The lower line shows the situation if the nominal rate is 10% but semiannual compounding is used.

```
0      Nom = EFF% = 10.25%                                        1
├──────────────────────────────────────────────────────────────┤
$100.00 - - - - - - - - - - - - - - - - - - - - - - - - - - - - -▶ $110.25


0      Nom = 10.00% semi; EFF% = 10.25%          1               2
├───────────────────────────────────────────────┼───────────────┤
$100.00 - - - - - - - - - - - - - - - -▶ $105 ───────────────────▶ $110.25
```

Given the nominal rate and the number of compounding periods per year, we can find the effective annual rate with this equation:

$$\text{Effective annual rate (EFF\%)} = \left[1 + \frac{I_{NOM}}{M}\right]^M - 1.0$$

 5.10

Here I_{NOM} is the nominal rate expressed as a decimal and M is the number of compounding periods per year. In our example, the nominal rate is 10%; but with semiannual compounding, $I_{NOM} = 10\% = 0.10$ and $M = 2$. This results in EFF% = 10.25%:

$$\text{Effective annual rate (EFF\%)} = \left[1 + \frac{0.10}{2}\right]^2 - 1 = 0.1025 = 10.25\%$$

We can also use the EFFECT function in Excel to solve for the effective rate:

```
=EFFECT (0.1,2)
EFFECT(nominal_rate, npery)
```

Here we find that the effective rate is 10.25%. NPERY refers to the number of payments per year. Likewise, if you know the effective rate and want to solve for the nominal rate, you can use the NOMINAL function in Excel.[15] Thus, if one investment promises to pay 10% with semiannual compounding and an equally risky investment promises 10.25% with annual compounding, we would be indifferent between the two.

---

[15]Most financial calculators are programmed to find the EFF% or, given the EFF%, to find the nominal rate. This is called *interest rate conversion*. You enter the nominal rate and the number of compounding periods per year and then press the EFF% key to find the effective annual rate. However, we generally use Equation 5.10 because it's as easy to use as the interest conversion feature and the equation reminds us of what we are really doing. If you use the interest rate conversion feature on your calculator, don't forget to reset your calculator settings. Interest rate conversion is discussed in the calculator tutorials.

QUICK QUESTION

QUESTION:

You just received your first credit card and decided to purchase a new Apple iPad. You charged the iPad's $500 purchase price on your new credit card. Assume that the nominal interest rate on the credit card is 18% and that interest is compounded monthly.

The minimum payment on the credit card is only $10 a month. If you pay the minimum and make no other charges, how long will it take you to fully pay off the credit card?

ANSWER:

Here we are given that the nominal interest rate is 18%. It follows that the monthly periodic rate is 1.5% (18%/12). Using a financial calculator, we can solve for the number of months that it takes to pay off the credit card.

	1.5	500	−10	0
N	I/YR	PV	PMT	FV
93.11				

We can also use Excel's NPER function:

=NPER(0.015,−10,500,0)

NPER(rate, pmt, pv, [fv], [type])

Here we find that it will take **93**.11 months to pay off the credit card.

Note that it would take you almost 8 years to pay off your iPad purchase. Now, you see why you can quickly get into financial trouble if you don't manage your credit cards wisely!

SELF TEST

Define the terms *annual percentage rate (APR)*, *effective annual rate (EFF%)*, and *nominal interest rate (I_{NOM})*.

A bank pays 5% with daily compounding on its savings accounts. Should it advertise the nominal or effective rate if it is seeking to attract new deposits?

By law, credit card issuers must print their annual percentage rate on their monthly statements. A common APR is 18% with interest paid monthly. What is the EFF% on such a loan? **[EFF% = $(1 + 0.18/12)^{12} − 1 = 0.1956 = 19.56\%$]**

Some years ago banks didn't have to reveal the rates they charged on credit cards. Then Congress passed the Truth in Lending Act that required banks to publish their APRs. Is the APR really the "most truthful" rate, or would the EFF% be "more truthful"? Explain.

5-17 FRACTIONAL TIME PERIODS

Thus far we have assumed that payments occur at the beginning or the end of periods but not *within* periods. However, we often encounter situations that require compounding or discounting over fractional periods. For example, suppose you deposited $100 in a bank that pays a nominal rate of 10% but adds interest daily, based on a 365-day year. How much would you have after 9 months? The answer is $107.79, found as follows:[16]

$$\text{Periodic rate} = I_{PER} = 0.10/365 = 0.000273973 \text{ per day}$$

$$\text{Number of days} = (9/12)(365) = 0.75(365) = 273.75 \text{ rounded to 274}$$

$$\text{Ending amount} = \$100(1.000273973)^{274} = \$107.79$$

Now suppose you borrow $100 from a bank whose nominal rate is 10% per year simple interest, which means that interest is not earned on interest. If the loan is outstanding for 274 days, how much interest would you have to pay? Here we would calculate a daily interest rate, I_{PER}, as just shown, but multiply it by 274 rather than use the 274 as an exponent:

$$\text{Interest owed} = \$100(0.000273973)(274) = \$7.51$$

You would owe the bank a total of $107.51 after 274 days. This is the procedure that most banks use to calculate interest on loans, except that they require borrowers to pay the interest on a monthly basis rather than after 274 days.

---

[16]Bank loan contracts specifically state whether they are based on a 360- or a 365-day year. If a 360-day year is used, the daily rate is higher, which means that the effective rate is also higher. Here we assumed a 365-day year. Also note that in real-world calculations, banks' computers have built-in calendars so they can calculate the exact number of days, taking account of 30-day, 31-day, and 28- or 29-day months.

5-18 AMORTIZED LOANS[17]

An important application of compound interest involves loans that are paid off in installments over time. Included are automobile loans, home mortgage loans, student loans, and many business loans. A loan that is to be repaid in equal amounts on a monthly, quarterly, or annual basis is called an **amortized loan.**[18]

Table 5.4 illustrates the amortization process. A homeowner borrows $100,000 on a mortgage loan, and the loan is to be repaid in five equal payments at the end of each of the next 5 years.[19] The lender charges 6% on the balance at the beginning of each year. Our first task is to determine the payment the homeowner must make each year. Here's a picture of the situation:

Amortized Loan
A loan that is repaid in equal payments over its life.

The payments must be such that the sum of their PVs equals $100,000:

$$\$100{,}000 = \frac{PMT}{(1.06)^1} + \frac{PMT}{(1.06)^2} + \frac{PMT}{(1.06)^3} + \frac{PMT}{(1.06)^4} + \frac{PMT}{(1.06)^5} = \sum_{t=1}^{5} \frac{PMT}{(1.06)^t}$$

We could insert values into a calculator as follows to get the required payments, $23,739.64:[20]

5	6	100000		0
N	I/YR	PV	PMT	FV
			−23,739.64	

Therefore, the borrower must pay the lender $23,739.64 per year for the next 5 years.

Each payment will consist of two parts—interest and repayment of principal. This breakdown is shown on an **amortization schedule** such as the one in Table 5.4. The interest component is relatively high in the first year, but it declines as the loan balance decreases. For tax purposes, the borrower would deduct the interest component while the lender would report the same amount as taxable income.

Amortization Schedule
A table showing precisely how a loan will be repaid. It gives the required payment on each payment date and a breakdown of the payment, showing how much is interest and how much is repayment of principal.

SELF TEST

Suppose you borrowed $30,000 on a student loan at a rate of 8% and must repay it in three equal installments at the end of each of the next 3 years. How large would your payments be, how much of the first payment would represent interest, how much would be principal, and what would your ending balance be after the first year? **(PMT = $11,641.01; Interest = $2,400; Principal = $9,241.01; Balance at end of Year 1 = $20,758.99)**

---

[17]Amortized loans are important, but this section can be omitted without loss of continuity.

[18]The word *amortized* comes from the Latin *mors*, meaning "death"; so an amortized loan is one that is "killed off" over time.

[19]Most mortgage loans call for monthly payments over 10 to 30 years, but we use a shorter period to reduce the calculations.

[20]You could also factor out the PMT term; find the value of the remaining summation term (4.212364); and divide it into the $100,000 to find the payment, $23,739.64.

TABLE 5.4   Loan Amortization Schedule, $100,000 at 6% for 5 Years

Amount borrowed: $100,000
Years: 5
Rate: 6%
PMT: −$23,739.64

Year	Beginning Amount (1)	Payment (2)	Interest[a] (3)	Repayment of Principal[b] (4)	Ending Balance (5)
1	$100,000.00	$23,739.64	$6,000.00	$17,739.64	$82,260.36
2	82,260.36	23,739.64	4,935.62	18,804.02	63,456.34
3	63,456.34	23,739.64	3,807.38	19,932.26	43,524.08
4	43,524.08	23,739.64	2,611.44	21,128.20	22,395.89
5	22,395.89	23,739.64	1,343.75	22,395.89	0.00

© Cengage Learning 2015

Notes:
[a]Interest in each period is calculated by multiplying the loan balance at the beginning of the year by the interest rate. Therefore, interest in Year 1 is $100,000.00(0.06) = $6,000; in Year 2, it is $4,935.62; and so forth.
[b]Repayment of principal is equal to the payment of $23,739.64 minus the interest charge for the year.

TYING IT ALL TOGETHER

In this chapter, we worked with single payments, ordinary annuities, annuities due, perpetuities, and uneven cash flow streams. One fundamental equation, Equation 5.1, is used to calculate the future value of a given amount. The equation can be transformed to Equation 5.2 and then used to find the present value of a given future amount. We used time lines to show when cash flows occur; and we saw that time value problems can be solved in a step-by-step manner when we work with individual cash flows, with formulas that streamline the approach, with financial calculators, and with spreadsheets.

As we noted at the outset, TVM is the single most important concept in finance and the procedures developed in Chapter 5 are used throughout this book. Time value analysis is used to find the values of stocks, bonds, and capital budgeting projects. It is also used to analyze personal finance problems, such as the retirement issue set forth in the opening vignette. You will become more familiar with time value analysis as you go through the book, but we *strongly recommend* that you get a good handle on Chapter 5 before you continue.

SELF-TEST QUESTIONS AND PROBLEMS

(Solutions Appear in Appendix A)

ST-1 **KEY TERMS** Define each of the following terms:

a. Time line

b. FV_N; PV; I; INT; N; FVA_N; PMT; PVA_N

c. Compounding; discounting

d. Simple interest; compound interest

e. Opportunity cost

f. Annuity; ordinary (deferred) annuity; annuity due; perpetuity

g. Uneven (nonconstant) cash flow; payment (PMT); cash flow (CF_t)

h. Annual compounding; semiannual compounding

i. Nominal (quoted) interest rate; annual percentage rate (APR); effective (equivalent) annual rate (EAR or EFF%)

j. Amortized loan; amortization schedule

ST-2 **FUTURE VALUE** It is now January 1, 2014. Today you will deposit $1,000 into a savings account that pays 8%.

a. If the bank compounds interest annually, how much will you have in your account on January 1, 2017?

b. What will your January 1, 2017, balance be if the bank uses quarterly compounding?

c. Suppose you deposit $1,000 in three payments of $333.333 each on January 1 of 2015, 2016, and 2017. How much will you have in your account on January 1, 2017, based on 8% annual compounding?

d. How much will be in your account if the three payments begin on January 1, 2014?

e. Suppose you deposit three equal payments into your account on January 1 of 2015, 2016, and 2017. Assuming an 8% interest rate, how large must your payments be to have the same ending balance as in Part a?

ST-3 **TIME VALUE OF MONEY** It is now January 1, 2014; and you will need $1,000 on January 1, 2018, in 4 years. Your bank compounds interest at an 8% annual rate.

a. How much must you deposit today to have a balance of $1,000 on January 1, 2018?

b. If you want to make four equal payments on each January 1 from 2015 through 2018 to accumulate the $1,000, how large must each payment be? (Note that the payments begin a year from today.)

c. If your father offers to make the payments calculated in Part b ($221.92) or to give you $750 on January 1, 2015 (a year from today), which would you choose? Explain.

d. If you have only $750 on January 1, 2015, what interest rate, compounded annually for 3 years, must you earn to have $1,000 on January 1, 2018?

e. Suppose you can deposit only $200 each January 1 from 2015 through 2018 (4 years). What interest rate, with annual compounding, must you earn to end up with $1,000 on January 1, 2018?

f. Your father offers to give you $400 on January 1, 2015. You will then make six additional equal payments each 6 months from July 2015 through January 2018. If your bank pays 8% compounded semiannually, how large must each payment be for you to end up with $1,000 on January 1, 2018?

g. What is the EAR, or EFF%, earned on the bank account in Part f? What is the APR earned on the account?

ST-4 **EFFECTIVE ANNUAL RATES** Bank A offers loans at an 8% nominal rate (its APR) but requires that interest be paid quarterly; that is, it uses quarterly compounding. Bank B wants to charge the same effective rate on its loans but it wants to collect interest on a monthly basis, that is, to use monthly compounding. What nominal rate must Bank B set?

QUESTIONS

5-1   What is an *opportunity cost?* How is this concept used in TVM analysis, and where is it shown on a time line? Is a single number used in all situations? Explain.

5-2   Explain whether the following statement is true or false: $100 a year for 10 years is an annuity; but $100 in Year 1, $200 in Year 2, and $400 in Years 3 through 10 does *not* constitute an annuity. However, the second series *contains* an annuity.

5-3   If a firm's earnings per share grew from $1 to $2 over a 10-year period, the *total growth* would be 100%, but the *annual growth rate* would be *less than* 10%. True or false? Explain. (Hint: If you aren't sure, plug in some numbers and check it out.)

5-4   Would you rather have a savings account that pays 5% interest compounded semiannually or one that pays 5% interest compounded daily? Explain.

5-5   To find the present value of an uneven series of cash flows, you must find the PVs of the individual cash flows and then sum them. Annuity procedures can never be of use, even when some of the cash flows constitute an annuity, because the entire series is not an annuity. True or false? Explain.

5-6   The present value of a perpetuity is equal to the payment on the annuity, PMT, divided by the interest rate, I : PV = PMT/I. What is the *future value* of a perpetuity of PMT dollars per year? (Hint: The answer is infinity, but explain why.)

5-7   Banks and other lenders are required to disclose a rate called the APR. What is this rate? Why did Congress require that it be disclosed? Is it the same as the effective annual rate? If you were comparing the costs of loans from different lenders, could you use their APRs to determine the loan with the lowest effective interest rate? Explain.

5-8   What is a loan amortization schedule, and what are some ways these schedules are used?

PROBLEMS

**Easy
Problems
1–8**

5-1   **FUTURE VALUE**   If you deposit $10,000 in a bank account that pays 10% interest annually, how much will be in your account after 5 years?

5-2   **PRESENT VALUE**   What is the present value of a security that will pay $5,000 in 20 years if securities of equal risk pay 7% annually?

5-3   **FINDING THE REQUIRED INTEREST RATE**   Your parents will retire in 18 years. They currently have $250,000 saved, and they think they will need $1,000,000 at retirement. What annual interest rate must they earn to reach their goal, assuming they don't save any additional funds?

5-4   **TIME FOR A LUMP SUM TO DOUBLE**   If you deposit money today in an account that pays 6.5% annual interest, how long will it take to double your money?

5-5   **TIME TO REACH A FINANCIAL GOAL**   You have $42,180.53 in a brokerage account, and you plan to deposit an additional $5,000 at the end of every future year until your account totals $250,000. You expect to earn 12% annually on the account. How many years will it take to reach your goal?

5-6   **FUTURE VALUE: ANNUITY VERSUS ANNUITY DUE**   What's the future value of a 7%, 5-year ordinary annuity that pays $300 each year? If this was an annuity due, what would its future value be?

5-7   **PRESENT AND FUTURE VALUES OF A CASH FLOW STREAM**   An investment will pay $100 at the end of each of the next 3 years, $200 at the end of Year 4, $300 at the end of Year 5, and $500 at the end of Year 6. If other investments of equal risk earn 8% annually, what is its present value? Its future value?

5-8   **LOAN AMORTIZATION AND EAR**   You want to buy a car, and a local bank will lend you $20,000. The loan will be fully amortized over 5 years (60 months), and the nominal interest rate will be 12% with interest paid monthly. What will be the monthly loan payment? What will be the loan's EAR?

Intermediate Problems 9–26

5-9   **PRESENT AND FUTURE VALUES FOR DIFFERENT PERIODS**   Find the following values *using the equations* and then a financial calculator. Compounding/discounting occurs annually.

a.   An initial $500 compounded for 1 year at 6%
b.   An initial $500 compounded for 2 years at 6%
c.   The present value of $500 due in 1 year at a discount rate of 6%
d.   The present value of $500 due in 2 years at a discount rate of 6%

5-10   **PRESENT AND FUTURE VALUES FOR DIFFERENT INTEREST RATES**   Find the following values. Compounding/discounting occurs annually.

a.   An initial $500 compounded for 10 years at 6%
b.   An initial $500 compounded for 10 years at 12%
c.   The present value of $500 due in 10 years at 6%
d.   The present value of $1,552.90 due in 10 years at 12% and at 6%
e.   Define *present value* and illustrate it using a time line with data from Part d. How are present values affected by interest rates?

5-11   **GROWTH RATES**   Shalit Corporation's 2013 sales were $12 million. Its 2008 sales were $6 million.

a.   At what rate have sales been growing?
b.   Suppose someone made this statement: "Sales doubled in 5 years. This represents a growth of 100% in 5 years; so dividing 100% by 5, we find the growth rate to be 20% per year." Is the statement correct?

5-12   **EFFECTIVE RATE OF INTEREST**   Find the interest rates earned on each of the following:

a.   You *borrow* $700 and promise to pay back $749 at the end of 1 year.
b.   You *lend* $700 and the borrower promises to pay you $749 at the end of 1 year.
c.   You *borrow* $85,000 and promise to pay back $201,229 at the end of 10 years.
d.   You *borrow* $9,000 and promise to make payments of $2,684.80 at the end of each year for 5 years.

5-13   **TIME FOR A LUMP SUM TO DOUBLE**   How long will it take $200 to double if it earns the following rates? Compounding occurs once a year.

a.   7%
b.   10%
c.   18%
d.   100%

5-14   **FUTURE VALUE OF AN ANNUITY**   Find *the future values* of these *ordinary annuities*. Compounding occurs once a year.

a. $400 per year for 10 years at 10%
b. $200 per year for 5 years at 5%
c. $400 per year for 5 years at 0%
d.   Rework Parts a, b, and c assuming they are *annuities due*.

5-15   **PRESENT VALUE OF AN ANNUITY**   Find the *present values* of these *ordinary annuities*. Discounting occurs once a year.

a. $400 per year for 10 years at 10%
b. $200 per year for 5 years at 5%
c. $400 per year for 5 years at 0%
d.   Rework Parts a, b, and c assuming they are *annuities due*.

5-16   **PRESENT VALUE OF A PERPETUITY**   What is the present value of a $100 perpetuity if the interest rate is 7%? If interest rates doubled to 14%, what would its present value be?

5-17   **EFFECTIVE INTEREST RATE**   You borrow $85,000; the annual loan payments are $8,273.59 for 30 years. What interest rate are you being charged?

5-18   **UNEVEN CASH FLOW STREAM**

a.   Find the present values of the following cash flow streams at an 8% discount rate.

	0	1	2	3	4	5
Stream A	$0	$100	$400	$400	$400	$300
Stream B	$0	$300	$400	$400	$400	$100

    b.   What are the PVs of the streams at a 0% discount rate?

5-19   **FUTURE VALUE OF AN ANNUITY**   Your client is 40 years old. She wants to begin saving for retirement with the first payment to come one year from now. She can save $5,000 per year, and you advise her to invest it in the stock market, which you expect to provide an average return of 9% in the future.

    a.   If she follows your advice, how much money will she have at 65?

    b.   How much will she have at 70?

    c.   She expects to live for 20 years if she retires at 65 and for 15 years if she retires at 70. If her investments continue to earn the same rate, how much will she be able to withdraw at the end of each year after retirement at each retirement age?

5-20   **PV OF A CASH FLOW STREAM**   A rookie quarterback is negotiating his first NFL contract. His opportunity cost is 10%. He has been offered three possible 4-year contracts. Payments are guaranteed, and they would be made at the end of each year. Terms of each contract are as follows:

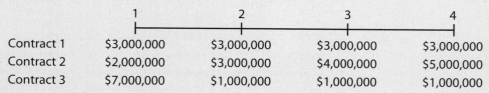

	1	2	3	4
Contract 1	$3,000,000	$3,000,000	$3,000,000	$3,000,000
Contract 2	$2,000,000	$3,000,000	$4,000,000	$5,000,000
Contract 3	$7,000,000	$1,000,000	$1,000,000	$1,000,000

As his adviser, which contract would you recommend that he accept?

5-21   **EVALUATING LUMP SUMS AND ANNUITIES**   Crissie just won the lottery, and she must choose among three award options. She can elect to receive a lump sum today of $61 million, to receive 10 end-of-year payments of $9.5 million, or to receive 30 end-of-year payments of $5.5 million.

    a.   If she thinks she can earn 7% annually, which should she choose?

    b.   If she expects to earn 8% annually, which is the best choice?

    c.   If she expects to earn 9% annually, which option would you recommend?

    d.   Explain how interest rates influence her choice.

5-22   **LOAN AMORTIZATION**   Jan sold her house on December 31 and took a $10,000 mortgage as part of the payment. The 10-year mortgage has a 10% nominal interest rate, but it calls for semiannual payments beginning next June 30. Next year Jan must report on Schedule B of her IRS Form 1040 the amount of interest that was included in the two payments she received during the year.

    a.   What is the dollar amount of each payment Jan receives?

    b.   How much interest was included in the first payment? How much repayment of principal was included? How do these values change for the second payment?

    c.   How much interest must Jan report on Schedule B for the first year? Will her interest income be the same next year?

    d.   If the payments are constant, why does the amount of interest income change over time?

5-23   **FUTURE VALUE FOR VARIOUS COMPOUNDING PERIODS**   Find the amount to which $500 will grow under each of these conditions:

    a.   12% compounded annually for 5 years

    b.   12% compounded semiannually for 5 years

    c.   12% compounded quarterly for 5 years

    d.   12% compounded monthly for 5 years

    e.   12% compounded daily for 5 years

    f.   Why does the observed pattern of FVs occur?

5-24   **PRESENT VALUE FOR VARIOUS DISCOUNTING PERIODS**   Find the present value of $500 due in the future under each of these conditions:

     a.   12% nominal rate, semiannual compounding, discounted back 5 years

     b.   12% nominal rate, quarterly compounding, discounted back 5 years

     c.   12% nominal rate, monthly compounding, discounted back 1 year

     d.   Why do the differences in the PVs occur?

5-25   **FUTURE VALUE OF AN ANNUITY**   Find the future values of the following ordinary annuities:

     a.   FV of $400 paid each 6 months for 5 years at a nominal rate of 12% compounded semiannually

     b.   FV of $200 paid each 3 months for 5 years at a nominal rate of 12% compounded quarterly

     c.   These annuities receive the same amount of cash during the 5-year period and earn interest at the same nominal rate, yet the annuity in Part b ends up larger than the one in Part a. Why does this occur?

5-26   **PV AND LOAN ELIGIBILITY**   You have saved $4,000 for a down payment on a new car. The largest monthly payment you can afford is $350. The loan will have a 12% APR based on end-of-month payments. What is the most expensive car you can afford if you finance it for 48 months? For 60 months?

Challenging Problems 27–40

5-27   **EFFECTIVE VERSUS NOMINAL INTEREST RATES**   Bank A pays 4% interest compounded annually on deposits, while Bank B pays 3.5% compounded daily.

     a.   Based on the EAR (or EFF%), which bank should you use?

     b.   Could your choice of banks be influenced by the fact that you might want to withdraw your funds during the year as opposed to at the end of the year? Assume that your funds must be left on deposit during an entire compounding period in order to receive any interest.

5-28   **NOMINAL INTEREST RATE AND EXTENDING CREDIT**   As a jewelry store manager, you want to offer credit, with interest on outstanding balances paid monthly. To carry receivables, you must borrow funds from your bank at a nominal 6%, monthly compounding. To offset your overhead, you want to charge your customers an EAR (or EFF%) that is 2% more than the bank is charging you. What APR rate should you charge your customers?

5-29   **BUILDING CREDIT COST INTO PRICES**   Your firm sells for cash only, but it is thinking of offering credit, allowing customers 90 days to pay. Customers understand the time value of money, so they would all wait and pay on the 90th day. To carry these receivables, you would have to borrow funds from your bank at a nominal 12%, daily compounding based on a 360-day year. You want to increase your base prices by exactly enough to offset your bank interest cost. To the closest whole percentage point, by how much should you raise your product prices?

5-30   **REACHING A FINANCIAL GOAL**   Erika and Kitty, who are twins, just received $30,000 each for their 25th birthday. They both have aspirations to become millionaires. Each plans to make a $5,000 annual contribution to her "early retirement fund" on her birthday, beginning a year from today. Erika opened an account with the Safety First Bond Fund, a mutual fund that invests in high-quality bonds whose investors have earned 6% per year in the past. Kitty invested in the New Issue Bio-Tech Fund, which invests in small, newly issued bio-tech stocks and whose investors have earned an average of 20% per year in the fund's relatively short history.

     a.   If the two women's funds earn the same returns in the future as in the past, how old will each be when she becomes a millionaire?

     b.   How large would Erika's annual contributions have to be for her to become a millionaire at the same age as Kitty, assuming their expected returns are realized?

     c.   Is it rational or irrational for Erika to invest in the bond fund rather than in stocks?

5-31   **REQUIRED LUMP SUM PAYMENT**   Starting next year, you will need $10,000 annually for 4 years to complete your education. (One year from today you will withdraw the first $10,000.) Your uncle deposits an amount *today* in a bank paying 5% annual interest, which will provide the needed $10,000 payments.

     a.   How large must the deposit be?

     b.   How much will be in the account immediately after you make the first withdrawal?

5-32   **REACHING A FINANCIAL GOAL**   Six years from today you need $10,000. You plan to deposit $1,500 annually, with the first payment to be made a year from today, in an account that pays an 8% effective annual rate. Your last deposit, which will occur at the end of Year 6, will be for less than $1,500 if less is needed to reach $10,000. How large will your last payment be?

5-33   **FV OF UNEVEN CASH FLOW**   You want to buy a house within 3 years, and you are currently saving for the down payment. You plan to save $5,000 at the end of the first year, and you anticipate that your annual savings will increase by 10% annually thereafter. Your expected annual return is 7%. How much will you have for a down payment at the end of Year 3?

5-34   **AMORTIZATION SCHEDULE**

a.   Set up an amortization schedule for a $25,000 loan to be repaid in equal installments at the end of each of the next 3 years. The interest rate is 10% compounded annually.

b.   What percentage of the payment represents interest and what percentage represents principal for each of the 3 years? Why do these percentages change over time?

5-35   **AMORTIZATION SCHEDULE WITH A BALLOON PAYMENT**   You want to buy a house that costs $100,000. You have $10,000 for a down payment, but your credit is such that mortgage companies will not lend you the required $90,000. However, the realtor persuades the seller to take a $90,000 mortgage (called a seller take-back mortgage) at a rate of 7%, provided the loan is paid off in full in 3 years. You expect to inherit $100,000 in 3 years; but right now all you have is $10,000, and you can afford to make payments of no more than $7,500 per year given your salary. (The loan would call for monthly payments, but assume end-of-year annual payments to simplify things.)

a.   If the loan was amortized over 3 years, how large would each annual payment be? Could you afford those payments?

b.   If the loan was amortized over 30 years, what would each payment be? Could you afford those payments?

c.   To satisfy the seller, the 30-year mortgage loan would be written as a balloon note, which means that at the end of the third year, you would have to make the regular payment plus the remaining balance on the loan. What would the loan balance be at the end of Year 3, and what would the balloon payment be?

5-36   **NONANNUAL COMPOUNDING**

a.   You plan to make five deposits of $1,000 each, one every 6 months, with the first payment being made in 6 months. You will then make no more deposits. If the bank pays 4% nominal interest, compounded semiannually, how much will be in your account after 3 years?

b.   One year from today you must make a payment of $10,000. To prepare for this payment, you plan to make two equal quarterly deposits (at the end of Quarters 1 and 2) in a bank that pays 4% nominal interest compounded quarterly. How large must each of the two payments be?

5-37   **PAYING OFF CREDIT CARDS**   Simon recently received a credit card with an 18% nominal interest rate. With the card, he purchased an Apple iPhone 5 for $372.71. The minimum payment on the card is only $10 per month.

a.   If Simon makes the minimum monthly payment and makes no other charges, how many months will it be before he pays off the card? Round to the nearest month.

b.   If Simon makes monthly payments of $35, how many months will it be before he pays off the debt? Round to the nearest month.

c.   How much more in total payments will Simon make under the $10-a-month plan than under the $35-a-month plan? Make sure you use three decimal places for N.

5-38   **PV AND A LAWSUIT SETTLEMENT**   It is now December 31, 2013 (t = 0), and a jury just found in favor of a woman who sued the city for injuries sustained in a January 2012 accident. She requested recovery of lost wages plus $100,000 for pain and suffering plus $20,000 for legal expenses. Her doctor testified that she has been unable to work since the accident and that she will not be able to work in the future. She is now 62, and the jury decided that she would have worked for another 3 years. She was scheduled to have earned $34,000 in 2012. (To simplify this problem, assume that the entire annual salary amount would have been received on December 31, 2012.) Her employer testified that she probably would have received raises of 3% per year. The actual payment for the jury award will be made on December 31, 2014. The judge stipulated that all dollar amounts are to be adjusted to a present value basis on December 31, 2014, using a 7% annual interest rate and using compound, not simple, interest. Furthermore, he stipulated that the pain and suffering and legal expenses should be based on a December 31, 2013, date. How large a check must the city write on December 31, 2014?

5-39   **REQUIRED ANNUITY PAYMENTS**   Your father is 50 years old and will retire in 10 years. He expects to live for 25 years after he retires, until he is 85. He wants a fixed retirement income value of his retirement income will decline annually after he retires.) His *retirement income will begin the day he retires,* 10 years from today, at which time he will receive 24 additional annual payments. Annual inflation is expected to be 5%. He currently has $100,000 saved, and he expects to earn 8% annually on his savings. How much must he save during each of the next 10 years (end-of-year deposits) to meet his retirement goal?

5-40 **REQUIRED ANNUITY PAYMENTS** A father is now planning a savings program to put his daughter through college. She is 13, plans to enroll at the university in 5 years, and should graduate 4 years later. Currently, the annual cost (for everything—food, clothing, tuition, books, transportation, and so forth) is $15,000, but these costs are expected to increase by 5% annually. The college requires total payment at the start of the year. She now has $7,500 in a college savings account that pays 6% annually. Her father will make six equal annual deposits into her account; the first deposit today and the sixth on the day she starts college. How large must each of the six payments be? [Hint: Calculate the cost (inflated at 5%) for each year of college and find the total present value of those costs, discounted at 6%, as of the day she enters college. Then find the compounded value of her initial $7,500 on that same day. The difference between the PV of costs and the amount that would be in the savings account must be made up by the father's deposits, so find the six equal payments that will compound to the required amount.]

COMPREHENSIVE/SPREADSHEET PROBLEM

5-41 **TIME VALUE OF MONEY** Answer the following questions:

a. Assuming a rate of 10% annually, find the FV of $1,000 after 5 years.

b. What is the investment's FV at rates of 0%, 5%, and 20% after 0, 1, 2, 3, 4, and 5 years?

c. Find the PV of $1,000 due in 5 years if the discount rate is 10%.

d. What is the rate of return on a security that costs $1,000 and returns $2,000 after 5 years?

e. Suppose California's population is 36.5 million people and its population is expected to grow by 2% annually. How long will it take for the population to double?

f. Find the PV of an ordinary annuity that pays $1,000 each of the next 5 years if the interest rate is 15%. What is the annuity's FV?

g. How will the PV and FV of the annuity in Part f change if it is an annuity due?

h. What will the FV and the PV be for $1,000 due in 5 years if the interest rate is 10%, semiannual compounding?

i. What will the annual payments be for an ordinary annuity for 10 years with a PV of $1,000 if the interest rate is 8%? What will the payments be if this is an annuity due?

j. Find the PV and the FV of an investment that pays 8% annually and makes the following end-of-year payments:

k. Five banks offer nominal rates of 6% on deposits; but A pays interest annually, B pays semiannually, C pays quarterly, D pays monthly, and E pays daily.

1. What effective annual rate does each bank pay? If you deposit $5,000 in each bank today, how much will you have in each bank at the end of 1 year? 2 years?

2. If all of the banks are insured by the government (the FDIC) and thus are equally risky, will they be equally able to attract funds? If not (and the TVM is the only consideration), what nominal rate will cause all of the banks to provide the same effective annual rate as Bank A?

3. Suppose you don't have the $5,000 but need it at the end of 1 year. You plan to make a series of deposits—annually for A, semiannually for B, quarterly for C, monthly for D, and daily for E—with payments beginning today. How large must the payments be to each bank?

4. Even if the five banks provided the same effective annual rate, would a rational investor be indifferent between the banks? Explain.

l. Suppose you borrow $15,000. The loan's annual interest rate is 8%, and it requires four equal end-of-year payments. Set up an amortization schedule that shows the annual payments, interest payments, principal repayments, and beginning and ending loan

INTEGRATED CASE

FIRST NATIONAL BANK

5-42   TIME VALUE OF MONEY ANALYSIS   You have applied for a job with a local bank. As part of its evaluation process, you must take an examination on time value of money analysis covering the following questions:

a. Draw time lines for (1) a $100 lump sum cash flow at the end of Year 2; (2) an ordinary annuity of $100 per year for 3 years; and (3) an uneven cash flow stream of −$50, $100, $75, and $50 at the end of Years 0 through 3.

b. 1. What's the future value of $100 after 3 years if it earns 4%, annual compounding?
    2. What's the present value of $100 to be received in 3 years if the interest rate is 4%, annual compounding?

c. What annual interest rate would cause $100 to grow to $119.10 in 3 years?

d. If a company's sales are growing at a rate of 10% annually, how long will it take sales to double?

e. What's the difference between an ordinary annuity and an annuity due? What type of annuity is shown here? How would you change it to the other type of annuity?

f. 1. What is the future value of a 3-year, $100 ordinary annuity if the annual interest rate is 4%?
    2. What is its present value?
    3. What would the future and present values be if it was an annuity due?

g. A 5-year $100 ordinary annuity has an annual interest rate of 4%.
    1. What is its present value?
    2. What would the present value be if it was a 10-year annuity?
    3. What would the present value be if it was a 25-year annuity?
    4. What would the present value be if this was a perpetuity?

h. A 20-year-old student wants to save $5 a day for her retirement. Every day she places $5 in a drawer. At the end of each year, she invests the accumulated savings ($1,825) in a brokerage account with an expected annual return of 8%.
    1. If she keeps saving in this manner, how much will she have accumulated at age 65?
    2. If a 40-year-old investor began saving in this manner, how much would he have at age 65?
    3. How much would the 40-year-old investor have to save each year to accumulate the same amount at 65 as the 20-year-old investor?

i. What is the present value of the following uneven cash flow stream? The annual interest rate is 4%.

j. 1. Will the future value be larger or smaller if we compound an initial amount more often than annually (e.g., semiannually, holding the stated (nominal) rate constant)? Why?
    2. Define (a) the stated (or quoted or nominal) rate, (b) the periodic rate, and (c) the effective annual rate (EAR or EFF%).
    3. What is the EAR corresponding to a nominal rate of 4% compounded semiannually? Compounded quarterly? Compounded daily?
    4. What is the future value of $100 after 3 years under 4% semiannual compounding? Quarterly compounding?

k.   When will the EAR equal the nominal (quoted) rate?

l.   1. What is the value at the end of Year 3 of the following cash flow stream if interest is 4% compounded semiannually? (Hint: You can use the EAR and treat the cash flows as an ordinary annuity or use the periodic rate and compound the cash flows individually.)

   2. What is the PV?
   3. What would be wrong with your answer to Parts 1(1) and 1(2) if you used the nominal rate, 4%, rather than the EAR or the periodic rate, $I_{NOM}/2 = 4\%/2 = 2\%$, to solve the problems?

m. 1. Construct an amortization schedule for a $1,000, 4% annual interest loan with three equal installments.
   2. What is the annual interest expense for the borrower and the annual interest income for the lender during Year 2?

PART 3

FINANCIAL ASSETS

CHAPTER

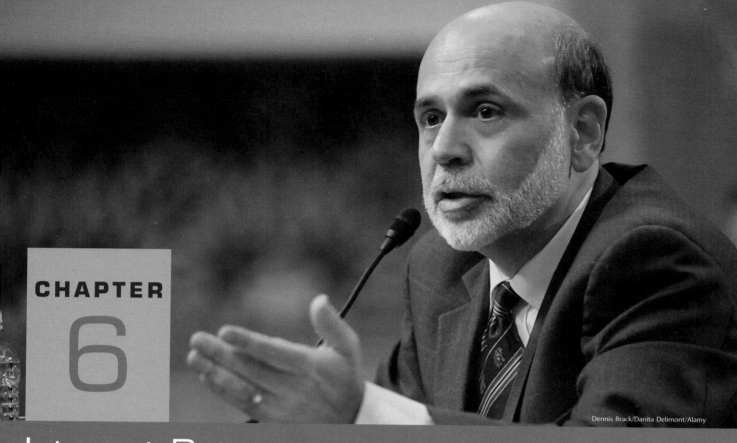

CHAPTER

6

Interest Rates

Interest Rates Remain Low as the Economy Recovers from Recession and Financial Crisis

The U.S. economy performed well from the early 1990s through 2007. Economic growth was positive, unemployment was fairly low, and inflation remained under control. One reason for the economy's good performance was the low level of interest rates over most of that period, with the rate on 10-year Treasury bonds generally at or below 5%, a level last seen in the 1960s, and rates on most other bonds correspondingly low. These low interest rates reduced the cost of capital for businesses, which encouraged corporate investment. They also stimulated consumer spending and helped produce a massive growth in the housing market. Indeed, some critics argue that by keeping interest rates too low for too long, the Federal Reserve and other policymakers contributed to an unsustainable boom in housing prices.

When the housing market collapsed, many homeowners struggled to pay their mortgages

and the financial institutions holding these mortgages suffered huge losses. In this environment financial institutions no longer felt comfortable lending to other financial institutions, turning a bad situation into a full-blown financial crisis. Struggling to survive, many banks stopped providing credit to individuals and businesses, and this helped push the economy into a deep recession. To keep the economy afloat, the Federal Reserve maintained extremely low interest rates. Five years after the crisis, it appears that policymakers have successfully kept the economy from completely collapsing, but the economy is still weak and unemployment remains stubbornly high.

In response to the economy's continued sluggishness, the Federal Reserve has re-doubled its efforts to strengthen the economy with its policy of "quantitative easing." Through this policy, the Fed has systematically purchased large amounts of longer-term financial assets from leading financial institutions. The Fed pays for these assets by injecting new funds into the economy, which helps put downward pressure on interest rates. In December 2012, the Federal Reserve announced that it would maintain this policy until the unemployment rate fell below 6.5% or the inflation rate rose above 2.5%. As a result of their actions, the 10-year Treasury rate was pushed below 2%, and shorter-term Treasury rates were close to zero.

Six months later, as the economy began to show signs of life, the Federal Reserve reaffirmed its policy. However, the Federal Reserve also suggested that in the months ahead it might "taper" its aggressive bond-buying program. In response, the 10-year Treasury rate rose above 2.5%.

While the Federal Reserve has a tremendous influence on interest rates, other factors have helped keep interest rates low. Most notably, inflation remains low, and foreign investors have maintained a strong willingness to purchase

U.S. securities. Looking ahead, there is a concern that some of these forces may start working in reverse. While the Federal Reserve has kept interest rates low for the time being, there are fears that we will pay the price later in the form of higher inflation. At the same time, a rapidly growing federal budget deficit is also pushing upward pressure on interest rates. To the extent that deficits and inflation fears combine with a weakening dollar, foreign investors may sell U.S. bonds, which would put even more upward pressure on rates.

Because corporations and individuals are greatly affected by interest rates, this chapter takes a closer look at the major factors that determine those rates. As we will see, there is no single interest rate—various factors determine the rate that each borrower pays—and in some cases, rates on different types of debt move in different directions. With these issues in mind, we will also consider the various factors influencing the spreads between long- and short-term interest rates and between Treasury and corporate bonds.

Source: Jeff Cox, "Fed to Keep Easing, Sets Target for Rates," www.cnbc.com, December 12, 2012.

PUTTING THINGS IN PERSPECTIVE

Companies raise capital in two main forms: debt and equity. In a free economy, capital, like other items, is allocated through a market system, where funds are transferred and prices are established. The interest rate is the price that lenders receive and borrowers pay for debt capital. Similarly, equity investors expect to receive dividends and capital gains, the sum of which represents the cost of equity. We take up the cost of equity in a later chapter, but our focus in this chapter is on the cost of debt. We begin by examining the factors that affect the supply of and demand for capital, which, in turn, affects the cost of money. We will see that there is no single interest rate—interest rates on different types of debt vary depending on the borrower's risk, the use of the funds borrowed, the type of collateral used to back the loan, and the length of time the money is needed. In this chapter, we concentrate mainly on how these various factors affect the cost of debt for individuals; but in later chapters, we delve into the cost of debt for a business and its role in investment decisions. As you will see in Chapters 7 and 9, the cost of debt is a key determinant of bond and stock prices; it is also an important component of the cost of corporate capital, which we cover in Chapter 10.

When you finish this chapter, you should be able to:

- List the various factors that influence the cost of money.
- Discuss how market interest rates are affected by borrowers' need for capital, expected inflation, different securities' risks, and securities' liquidity.
- Explain what the yield curve is, what determines its shape, and how you can use the yield curve to help forecast future interest rates.

6-1 The Cost of Money

The four most fundamental factors affecting the cost of money are (1) **production opportunities**, (2) **time preferences for consumption**, (3) **risk**, and (4) **inflation**. To see how these factors operate, visualize an isolated island community where people live on fish. They have a stock of fishing gear that permits them to survive reasonably well, but they would like to have more fish. Now suppose one of the island's inhabitants, Mr. Crusoe, had a bright idea for a new type of fishnet that would enable him to double his daily catch. However, it would take him a year to perfect the design, build the net, and learn to use it efficiently. Mr. Crusoe would probably starve before he could put his new net into operation. Therefore, he might suggest to Ms. Robinson, Mr. Friday, and several others that if they would give him one fish each day for a year, he would return two fish a day the next year. If someone accepted the offer, the fish that Ms. Robinson and the others gave to Mr. Crusoe would constitute *savings*, these savings would be *invested* in the fishnet, and the extra fish the net produced would constitute a *return on the investment*.

Obviously, the more productive Mr. Crusoe thought the new fishnet would be, the more he could afford to offer potential investors for their savings. In this example, we assume that Mr. Crusoe thought he would be able to pay (and thus he offered) a 100% rate of return—he offered to give back two fish for every one he received. He might have tried to attract savings for less—for example, he might have offered only 1.5 fish per day next year for every one he received this year, which would represent a 50% rate of return to Ms. Robinson and the other potential savers.

How attractive Mr. Crusoe's offer appeared to a potential saver would depend in large part on the saver's *time preference for consumption*. For example, Ms. Robinson might be thinking of retirement, and she might be willing to trade fish today for fish in the future on a one-for-one basis. On the other hand, Mr. Friday might have a wife and several young children and need his current fish; so he might be unwilling to "lend" a fish today for anything less than three fish next year. Mr. Friday would be said to have a high time preference for current consumption, and Ms. Robinson, a low time preference. Note also that if the entire population was living right at the subsistence level, time preferences for current consumption would necessarily be high, aggregate savings would be low, interest rates would be high, and capital formation would be difficult.

The *risk* inherent in the fishnet project (and thus in Mr. Crusoe's ability to repay the loan) also affects the return that investors require: The higher the perceived risk, the higher the required rate of return. Also, in a more complex society, there are many businesses like Mr. Crusoe's, many goods other than fish, and many savers like Ms. Robinson and Mr. Friday. Therefore, people use money as a medium of exchange rather than barter with fish. When money is used, its value in the future, which is affected by *inflation*, comes into play: The higher the expected rate of inflation, the larger the required dollar return. We discuss this point in detail later in the chapter.

Thus, we see that the interest rate paid to savers depends (1) on the rate of return that producers expect to earn on invested capital, (2) on savers' time preferences for current versus future consumption, (3) on the riskiness of the loan, and (4) on the expected future rate of inflation. Producers' expected returns on their business investments set an upper limit to how much they can pay for savings, while consumers' time preferences for consumption establish how much consumption they are willing to defer and, hence, how much they will save at different interest rates.[1] Higher risk and higher inflation also lead to higher interest rates.

---

[1] The term *producers* in this example is too narrow. A better word might be *borrowers*, which would include corporations, home purchasers, people borrowing to go to college, and even people borrowing to buy autos or to pay for vacations. Also, the wealth of a society and its demographics influence its people's ability to save and thus their time preferences for current versus future consumption.

What is the price paid to borrow debt capital called?

What are the two items whose sum is the cost of equity?

What four fundamental factors affect the cost of money?

Which factor sets an upper limit on how much can be paid for savings?

Which factor determines how much will be saved at different interest rates?

How do risk and inflation impact interest rates in the economy?

6-2 INTEREST RATE LEVELS

Borrowers bid for the available supply of debt capital using interest rates: The firms with the most profitable investment opportunities are willing and able to pay the most for capital, so they tend to attract it away from inefficient firms and firms whose products are not in demand. At the same time, government policy can also influence the allocation of capital and the level of interest rates. For example, the federal government has agencies that help designated individuals or groups obtain credit on favorable terms. Among those eligible for this kind of assistance are small businesses, certain minorities, and firms willing to build plants in areas with high unemployment. Still, most capital in the United States is allocated through the price system, where the interest rate is the price.

Figure 6.1 shows how supply and demand interact to determine interest rates in two capital markets. Markets L and H represent two of the many capital markets in existence. The supply curve in each market is upward-sloping, which indicates that investors are willing to supply more capital the higher the interest rate they receive on their capital. Likewise, the downward-sloping demand curve indicates that borrowers will borrow more if interest rates are lower. The interest rate in each market is the point where the supply and demand curves intersect. The going interest rate, designated as r, is initially 5% for the low-risk securities in Market L. Borrowers whose credit is strong enough to participate in this market can obtain funds at a cost of 5%, and investors who want to put their money to

FIGURE 6.1	Interest Rates as a Function of Supply and Demand for Funds

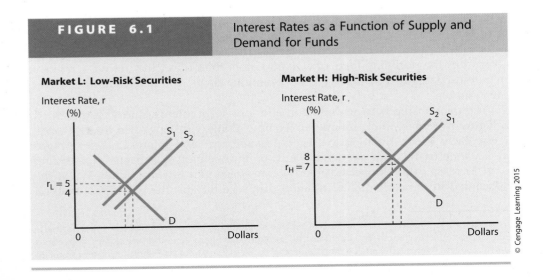

© Cengage Learning 2015

work without much risk can obtain a 5% return. Riskier borrowers must obtain higher-cost funds in Market H, where investors who are more willing to take risks expect to earn a 7% return but also realize that they might receive much less. In this scenario, investors are willing to accept the higher risk in Market H in exchange for a *risk premium* of 7% − 5% = 2%.

Now let's assume that because of changing market forces, investors perceive that Market H has become relatively more risky. This changing perception will induce many investors to shift toward safer investments—referred to as a "flight to quality." As investors move their money from Market H to Market L, the supply of funds is increased in Market L from S_1 to S_2; and the increased availability of capital will push down interest rates in this market from 5% to 4%. At the same time, as investors move their money out of Market H, there will be a decreased supply of funds in that market; and tighter credit in that market will force interest rates up from 7% to 8%. In this new environment, money is transferred from Market H to Market L and the risk premium rises from 2% to 8% − 4% = 4%.

There are many capital markets in the United States, and Figure 6.1 highlights the fact that they are interconnected. U.S. firms also invest and raise capital throughout the world, and foreigners both borrow and lend in the United States. There are markets for home loans; farm loans; business loans; federal, state, and local government loans; and consumer loans. Within each category, there are regional markets as well as different types of sub-markets. For example, in real estate, there are separate markets for first and second mortgages and for loans on single-family homes, apartments, office buildings, shopping centers, and vacant land. And, of course, there are separate markets for prime and subprime mortgage loans. Within the business sector, there are dozens of types of debt securities and there are several different markets for common stocks.

There is a price for each type of capital, and these prices change over time as supply and demand conditions change. Figure 6.2 shows how long- and short-term interest rates to business borrowers have varied since the early 1970s. Notice that short-term interest rates are especially volatile, rising rapidly during booms and falling equally rapidly during recessions. (The shaded areas of the chart indicate recessions.) In particular, note the dramatic drop in short-term interest rates during the recent recession. When the economy is expanding, firms need capital; and this demand pushes rates up. Inflationary pressures are strongest during business booms, also exerting upward pressure on rates. Conditions are reversed during recessions: Slack business reduces the demand for credit, inflation falls, and the Federal Reserve increases the supply of funds to help stimulate the economy. The result is a decline in interest rates.

These tendencies do not hold exactly, as demonstrated by the period after 1984. Oil prices fell dramatically in 1985 and 1986, reducing inflationary pressures on other prices and easing fears of serious long-term inflation. Earlier these fears had pushed interest rates to record levels. The economy from 1984 to 1987 was strong, but the declining fears of inflation more than offset the normal tendency for interest rates to rise during good economic times; the net result was lower interest rates.[2]

The relationship between inflation and long-term interest rates is highlighted in Figure 6.3, which plots inflation over time along with long-term interest rates. In the early 1960s, inflation averaged 1% per year and interest rates on high-quality long-term bonds averaged 4%. Then the Vietnam War heated up, leading to an increase in inflation; and interest rates began an upward climb. When the war ended in the early 1970s, inflation dipped a bit; but then the 1973 Arab oil

---

[2]Short-term rates are responsive to current economic conditions, whereas long-term rates primarily reflect long-run expectations for inflation. As a result, short-term rates are sometimes above and sometimes below long-term rates. The relationship between long-term and short-term rates is called the *term structure of interest rates,* and it is discussed later in this chapter.

FIGURE 6.2	Long- and Short-Term Interest Rates, 1972–2013

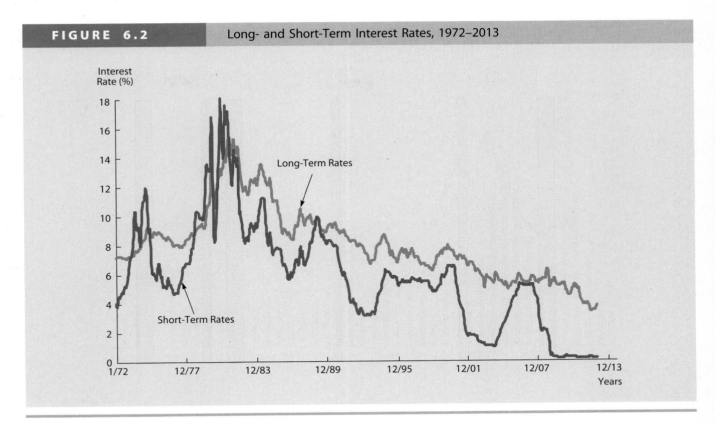

Notes:

1. The shaded areas designate business recessions.
2. Short-term rates are measured by 3- to 6-month loans to very large, strong corporations; long-term rates are measured by AAA corporate bonds.

Source: St. Louis Federal Reserve, FRED database, research.stlouisfed.org/fred2.

embargo led to rising oil prices, much higher inflation rates, and sharply higher interest rates.

Inflation peaked at about 13% in 1980. But interest rates continued to increase into 1981 and 1982, and they remained quite high until 1985 because people feared another increase in inflation. Thus, the "inflationary psychology" created during the 1970s persisted until the mid-1980s. People gradually realized that the Federal Reserve was serious about keeping inflation down, that global competition was keeping U.S. auto producers and other corporations from raising prices as they had in the past, and that constraints on corporate price increases were diminishing labor unions' ability to push through cost-increasing wage hikes. As these realizations set in, interest rates declined.

The current interest rate minus the current inflation rate (which is also the gap between the inflation bars and the interest rate curve in Figure 6.3) is defined as the "current real rate of interest." It is called a "real rate" because it shows how much investors really earned after the effects of inflation are removed. The real rate was extremely high during the mid-1980s, but it has generally been in the range of 1% to 4% since 1987.[3]

In recent years, inflation has been quite low, averaging about 2% a year, and it was even negative in 2009, as prices fell in the midst of the deep recession. However, long-term interest rates have been volatile because investors are not

---

[3]Refer to Carmen M. Reinhart and Kenneth S. Rogoff, *This Time Is Different: Eight Centuries of Financial Folly* (Princeton, New Jersey: Princeton University Press, 2009).

| FIGURE 6.3 | Relationship Between Annual Inflation Rates and Long-Term Interest Rates, 1972–2013 |

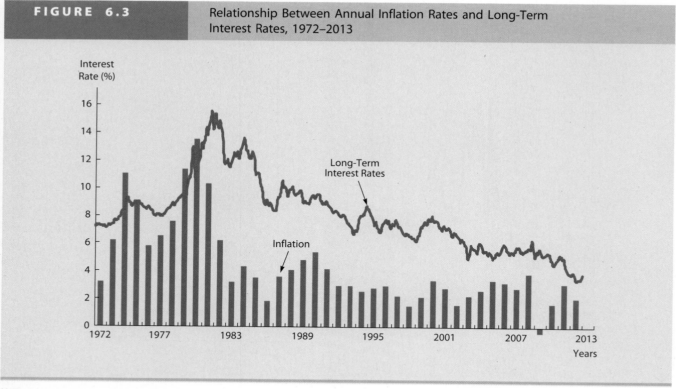

Notes:

1. Interest rates are rates on AAA long-term corporate bonds.
2. Inflation is measured as the annual rate of change in the consumer price index (CPI).

Source: St. Louis Federal Reserve, FRED database, research.stlouisfed.org/fred2.

sure if inflation is truly under control or is about to jump back to the higher levels of the 1980s. In the years ahead, we can be sure of two things: (1) Interest rates will vary, and (2) they will increase if inflation appears to be headed higher or decrease if inflation is expected to decline.

SELF TEST

What role do interest rates play in allocating capital to different potential borrowers?

What happens to market-clearing, or equilibrium, interest rates in a capital market when the supply of funds declines? What happens when expected inflation increases or decreases?

How does the price of capital tend to change during a boom? During a recession?

How does risk affect interest rates?

If inflation during the last 12 months was 2% and the interest rate during that period was 5%, what was the real rate of interest? If inflation is expected to average 4% during the next year and the real rate is 3%, what should the current interest rate be? **(3%; 7%)**

6-3 THE DETERMINANTS OF MARKET INTEREST RATES

In general, the quoted (or nominal) interest rate on a debt security, r, is composed of a real risk-free rate, r*, plus several premiums that reflect inflation, the security's risk, its liquidity (or marketability), and the years to its maturity. This relationship can be expressed as follows:

$$\text{Quoted interest rate} = r = r^* + IP + DRP + LP + MRP$$ **6.1**

Where:
   r = the quoted, or nominal, rate of interest on a given security.[4]
   r* = the real risk-free rate of interest, r* is pronounced "r-star," and it is the rate that would exist on a riskless security in a world where no inflation was expected.
   r_{RF} = r* + IP. It is the quoted rate on a risk-free security such as a U.S. Treasury bill, which is very liquid and is free of most types of risk. Note that the premium for expected inflation, IP, is included in r_{RF}.
   IP = inflation premium. IP is equal to the average expected rate of inflation over the life of the security. The expected future inflation rate is not necessarily equal to the current inflation rate, so IP is not necessarily equal to current inflation as shown in Figure 6.3.
   DRP = default risk premium. This premium reflects the possibility that the issuer will not pay the promised interest or principal at the stated time. DRP is zero for U.S. Treasury securities, but it rises as the riskiness of the issuer increases.
   LP = liquidity (or marketability) premium. This is a premium charged by lenders to reflect the fact that some securities cannot be converted to cash on short notice at a "reasonable" price. LP is very low for Treasury securities and for securities issued by large, strong firms; but it is relatively high on securities issued by small, privately held firms.
   MRP = maturity risk premium. As we will explain later, longer-term bonds, even Treasury bonds, are exposed to a significant risk of price declines due to increases in inflation and interest rates; and a maturity risk premium is charged by lenders to reflect this risk.

Because r_{RF} = r* + IP, we can rewrite Equation 6.1 as follows:

$$\text{Nominal, or quoted, rate} = r = r_{RF} + DRP + LP + MRP$$

We discuss the components whose sum makes up the quoted, or nominal, rate on a given security in the following sections.

6-3A THE REAL RISK-FREE RATE OF INTEREST, r*

The **real risk-free rate of interest, r***, is the interest rate that would exist on a riskless security if no inflation were expected. It may be thought of as the rate of interest on short-term U.S. Treasury securities in an inflation-free world. The real

Real Risk-Free Rate of interest, r*
The rate of interest that would exist on default-free U.S. Treasury securities if no inflation were expected.

---

[4]The term *nominal* as it is used here means the *stated* rate as opposed to the *real* rate, where the real rate is adjusted to remove inflation's effects. If you had bought a 30-year Treasury bond in February 2013, the quoted, or nominal, rate would have been about 3.2%; but if inflation averages 2.0% over the next 30 years, the real rate would turn out to be about 3.2% − 2.0% = 1.2%. Also note that in later chapters, when we discuss both debt and equity, we use the subscripts *d* and *s* to designate returns on debt and stock, that is, r_d and r_s.

risk-free rate is not static—it changes over time depending on economic conditions, especially on (1) the rate of return that corporations and other borrowers expect to earn on productive assets and (2) people's time preferences for current versus future consumption. Borrowers' expected returns on real assets set an upper limit on how much borrowers can afford to pay for funds, while savers' time preferences for consumption establish how much consumption savers will defer—hence, the amount of money they will lend at different interest rates. It is difficult to measure the real risk-free rate precisely, but most experts think that r^* has typically fluctuated in the range of 1% to 3% in recent years.[5] The best estimate of r^* is the rate of return on indexed Treasury bonds, which are discussed later in the chapter.

6-3B THE NOMINAL, OR QUOTED, RISK-FREE RATE OF INTEREST, $r_{RF} = r^* + IP$

Nominal, (Quoted) Risk-Free Rate, r_{RF}

The rate of interest on a security that is free of all risk; r_{RF} is proxied by the T-bill rate or the T-bond rate; r_{RF} includes an inflation premium.

The **nominal, or quoted, risk-free rate, r_{RF},** is the real risk-free rate plus a premium for expected inflation: $r_{RF} = r^* + IP$. To be strictly correct, the risk-free rate should be the interest rate on a totally risk-free security—one that has no default risk, no maturity risk, no liquidity risk, no risk of loss if inflation increases, and no risk of any other type. However, as the recent downgrade of U.S. Treasuries illustrates, there is no such security, hence, there is no observable truly risk-free rate. However, one security is free of most risks—a Treasury Inflation Protected Security (TIPS), whose value increases with inflation. Short-term TIPS are free of default, maturity, and liquidity risks and of risk due to changes in the general level of interest rates. However, they are not free of changes in the real rate.[6]

If the term *risk-free rate* is used without the modifiers *real* or *nominal*, people generally mean the quoted (or nominal) rate; and we follow that convention in this book. Therefore, when we use the term *risk-free rate, r_{RF}*, we mean the nominal risk-free rate, which includes an inflation premium equal to the average expected inflation rate over the remaining life of the security. In general, we use the T-bill rate to approximate the short-term risk-free rate and the T-bond rate to approximate the long-term risk-free rate. So whenever you see the term *risk-free rate*, assume that we are referring to the quoted U.S. T-bill rate or to the quoted T-bond rate. Our definition of the risk-free rate assumes that, despite the recent downgrade, Treasury securities have no meaningful default risk. And for convenience, we will assume in our subsequent problems and examples that Treasury securities have no default risk.

---

[5]The real rate of interest as discussed here is different from the *current* real rate as discussed in connection with Figure 6.3. The current real rate is the current interest rate minus the current (or latest past) inflation rate, while the real rate (without the word *current*) is the current interest rate minus the *expected future* inflation rate over the life of the security. For example, suppose the current quoted rate for a one-year Treasury bill is 2.0%, inflation during the latest year was 1.0%, and inflation expected for the coming year is 1.5%. The *current* real rate would be 2.0% − 1.0% = 1.0%, but the *expected* real rate would be 2.0% − 1.5% = 0.5%. The rate on a 10-year bond would be related to the average expected inflation rate over the next 10 years, and so on. In the press, the term *real rate* generally means the current real rate; but in economics and finance (hence, in this book unless otherwise noted), the real rate means the one based on *expected* inflation rates.

[6]Indexed Treasury securities are the closest thing we have to a riskless security, but even they are not totally riskless because r^* can change and cause a decline in the prices of these securities. For example, between its issue date in April 1998 and December 2000, the price of the TIPS that matures on April 15, 2028, declined because during this time period the real rate on long-term securities *increased*. Conversely, between December 2000 and February 2013, the real rate on this security has *decreased*. As a result, the bond's price during this time increased almost 48%.

6-3c INFLATION PREMIUM (IP)

Inflation has a major impact on interest rates because it erodes the real value of what you receive from the investment. To illustrate, suppose you have saved $10,000 to purchase a car. Rather than buying a car today, you could invest the money with the hope of buying a better car one year from now. If you decide to invest in a one-year Treasury bill that pays a 1% interest rate, you will have a little bit more money ($10,100—your original money plus $100 in interest) at the end of the year. Now suppose that the overall inflation rate increased by 3% that year. In this case, a similar version of the $10,000 car that you would have purchased at the beginning of the year would cost 3% more ($10,300) at the end of the year. Notice, in this case, the additional interest that you earn on the Treasury bill is not enough to compensate for the expected increase in the price of the car. In real terms you are worse off because the nominal interest rate is less than the expected inflation rate.

Investors are well aware of all this; so when they lend money, they build an **inflation premium (IP)** equal to the average expected inflation rate over the life of the security into the rate they charge. As discussed previously, the actual interest rate on a short-term default-free U.S. Treasury bill, $r_{T\text{-bill}}$, would be the real risk-free rate, r^*, plus the inflation premium (IP):

$$r_{T\text{-bill}} = r_{RF} = r^* + IP$$

Therefore, if the real risk-free rate was $r^* = 1.7\%$ and if inflation was expected to be 1.5% (and hence IP = 1.5%) during the next year, the quoted rate of interest on one-year T-bills would be 1.7% + 1.5% = 3.2%.

It is important to note that the inflation rate built into interest rates is the *inflation rate expected in the future,* not the rate experienced in the past. Thus, the latest reported figures might show an annual inflation rate of 3% over the past 12 months, but that is for the *past* year. If people, on average, expect a 4% inflation rate in the future, 4% would be built into the current interest rate. Note also that the inflation rate reflected in the quoted interest rate on any security is the *average inflation rate expected over the security's life.* Thus, the inflation rate built into a 1-year bond is the expected inflation rate for the next year, but the inflation rate built into a 30-year bond is the average inflation rate expected over the next 30 years.[7]

Expectations for future inflation are closely, but not perfectly, correlated with past inflation rates. Therefore, if the inflation rate reported for last month increased, people would tend to raise their expectations for future inflation; and this change in expectations would increase current rates. Also, consumer prices change with a lag following changes at the producer level. Thus, if the price of oil increases this month, gasoline prices are likely to increase in the coming months. This lagged situation between final product and producer goods prices exists throughout the economy.

Note that Japan and Switzerland have, over the past several years, had lower inflation rates than the United States; hence, their interest rates have generally been lower than those of the United States. The United Kingdom, Australia, and most South American countries have experienced higher inflation, so their rates have been higher than those of the United States. For example, in February 2013, Brazil's inflation rate was around 6%, while the Central Bank's benchmark interest

Inflation Premium (IP)
A premium equal to expected inflation that investors add to the real risk-free rate of return.

*Students should go to **Bloomberg.com/markets** to find current interest rates in the United States as well as in Australia, Brazil, Germany, Japan, and Great Britain.*

---

[7]To be theoretically precise, we should use a *geometric average.* Also, because millions of investors are active in the market, it is impossible to determine exactly the consensus-expected inflation rate. Survey data are available, however, that give us a reasonably good idea of what investors expect over the next few years. For example, in 1980, the University of Michigan's Survey Research Center reported that people expected inflation during the next year to be 11.9% and that the average rate of inflation expected over the next 5 to 10 years was 10.5%. Those expectations led to record-high interest rates. However, the economy cooled thereafter; and as Figure 6.3 showed, actual inflation dropped sharply. This led to a gradual reduction in the *expected future* inflation rate; and as inflationary expectations dropped, so did quoted market interest rates.

rate was above 7%. On the other hand, the U.S. inflation rate was much lower (around 2%) and the Fed's targeted interest rate was 0.25%.

Students should go to **tradingeconomics.com** *for information on a number of economic indicators such as interest rates, inflation, and GDP.*

Default Risk Premium (DRP)

The difference between the interest rate on a U.S. Treasury bond and a corporate bond of equal maturity and marketability.

Liquidity Premium (LP)

A premium added to the equilibrium interest rate on a security if that security cannot be converted to cash on short notice and at close to its "fair market value."

Interest Rate Risk

The risk of capital losses to which investors are exposed because of changing interest rates.

6-3d Default Risk Premium (DRP)

The risk that a borrower will *default*, which means the borrower will not make scheduled interest or principal payments, also affects the market interest rate on a bond: The greater the bond's risk of default, the higher the market rate. Once again, we are assuming that Treasury securities have no default risk; hence, they carry the lowest interest rates on taxable securities in the United States. For corporate bonds, bond ratings are often used to measure default risk. The higher the bond's rating, the lower its default risk and, consequently, the lower its interest rate.[8] The difference between the quoted interest rate on a T-bond and that on a corporate bond with similar maturity, liquidity, and other features is the **default risk premium (DRP)**. The average default risk premiums vary over time, and tend to get larger when the economy is weaker and borrowers are more likely to have a hard time paying off their debts.

6-3e Liquidity Premium (LP)

A "liquid" asset can be converted to cash quickly at a "fair market value." Real assets are generally less liquid than financial assets, but different financial assets vary in their liquidity. Because they prefer assets that are more liquid, investors include a **liquidity premium (LP)** in the rates charged on different debt securities. Although it is difficult to measure liquidity premiums accurately, we can get some sense of an asset's liquidity by looking at its trading volume. Assets with higher trading volume are generally easier to sell, and are therefore more liquid. The average liquidity premiums also vary over time. During the recent financial crisis, the liquidity premiums on many assets soared. The market for many assets that were once highly liquid suddenly dried up as everyone rushed to sell them at the same time. The liquidity of real assets also varies over time. For example, at the height of the housing boom, many homes in "hot" real estate markets were often sold the first day they were listed. After the bubble burst, homes in these same markets often sat unsold for months.

6-3f Interest Rate Risk and the Maturity Risk Premium (MRP)

Despite a few recent concerns about the Treasury's long-run ability to service its growing debt, we generally assume that U.S. Treasury securities are free of default risk in the sense that one can be virtually certain that the federal government will pay interest on its bonds and pay them off when they mature. Therefore, we assume that the default risk premium on Treasury securities is zero. Further, active markets exist for Treasury securities, so we assume that their liquidity premium is also zero.[9] Thus, as a first approximation, the rate of interest on a Treasury security should be the risk-free rate, r_{RF}, which is the real risk-free rate plus an inflation premium, $r_{RF} = r^* + IP$. However, the prices of long-term bonds decline whenever interest rates rise; and because interest rates can and do occasionally rise, all long-term bonds, even Treasury bonds, have an element of risk called **interest rate risk**. As a general rule, the bonds of any organization

---

[8]Bond ratings and bonds' riskiness in general are discussed in detail in Chapter 7. For now, merely note that bonds rated AAA are judged to have less default risk than bonds rated AA, while AA bonds are less risky than A bonds, and so forth. Ratings are designated AAA or Aaa, AA or Aa, and so forth, depending on the rating agency. In this book, the designations are used interchangeably.

[9]While it is a reasonable approximation to assume that the liquidity premium is zero for Treasury securities, in reality some Treasury securities are more liquid than others. In particular, bonds tend to be less liquid if it has been a long time since the bonds were originally issued.

An Almost Riskless Treasury Bond

Investors who purchase bonds must constantly worry about inflation. If inflation turns out to be greater than expected, bonds will provide a lower-than-expected real return. To protect themselves against expected increases in inflation, investors build an inflation risk premium into their required rate of return. This raises borrowers' costs.

To provide investors with an inflation-protected bond and to reduce the cost of debt to the government, the U.S. Treasury issues Treasury Inflation Protected Securities (TIPS), which are bonds that are indexed to inflation. For example, in 2009, the Treasury issued 10-year TIPS with a $2\frac{1}{8}$% coupon. These bonds pay an interest rate of $2\frac{1}{8}$% plus an additional amount that is just sufficient to offset inflation. At the end of each 6-month period, the principal (originally set at par or $1,000) is adjusted by the inflation rate. To understand how TIPS work, consider that during the first 6-month interest period, inflation (as measured by the CPI) declined by 0.55% (1/15/09 CPI = 214.69971 and 7/15/09 CPI = 213.51819). The inflation-adjusted principal was then calculated as $1,000(1 − 0.0055) = $1,000 × 0.9945 = $994.50. So on July 15, 2009, each bond paid interest of (0.02125/2) × $994.50 = $10.57. Note that the interest rate is divided by 2 because interest on Treasury (and most other) bonds is paid twice a year. This same adjustment process will continue each year until the bonds mature on January 15, 2019, at which time they will pay the adjusted maturity value. On January 15, 2013, the change in the CPI from when the bonds were originally issued was 7.509%. The inflation-adjusted principal was calculated as $1,000 × 1.07509 = $1,075.09. So on January 15, 2013, each bond paid interest of (0.02125/2) × $1,075.09 = $11.42. Thus, the cash income

provided by the bonds rises and falls by exactly enough to cover inflation or a decline in inflation, producing a real inflation-adjusted rate of $2\frac{1}{8}$% for those who hold the bond from its original issue date until its maturity. Further, because the principal also rises and falls by the inflation rate or its decline, it too is protected from inflation.

Both the annual interest received and the increase in principal are taxed each year as interest income, even though cash from the appreciation will not be received until the bond matures. Therefore, these bonds are not good for accounts subject to current income taxes; but they are excellent for individual retirement accounts (IRAs) and 401(k) plans, which are not taxed until funds are withdrawn.

The Treasury regularly conducts auctions to issue indexed bonds. The $2\frac{1}{8}$% coupon rate was based on the relative supply and demand for the issue, and it will remain fixed over the life of the bond. However, after the bonds are issued, they continue to trade in the open market; and their price will vary as investors' perceptions of the real rate of interest changes. Indeed, as we can see in the following graph, the real rate of interest on this bond has varied quite a bit since it was issued; and as the real rate changes, so does the price of the bond. Real rates fell in early 2009, but rose from April to July of that same year. After July 2009, real rates fell again, then rose in the latter half of 2010 and early 2011, and fell again during 2012. However midway through 2013, real rates have begun to rise. Thus, despite their protection against inflation, indexed bonds are not completely riskless. The real rate can change; and if r* rises, the prices of indexed bonds will decline. This confirms again that there is no such thing as a free lunch or a riskless security.

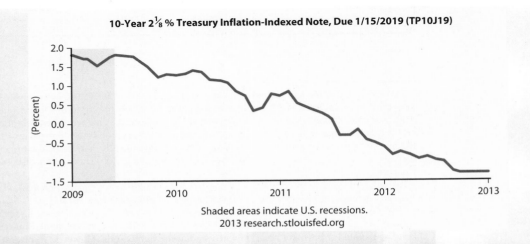

10-Year $2\frac{1}{8}$ % Treasury Inflation-Indexed Note, Due 1/15/2019 (TP10J19)

Shaded areas indicate U.S. recessions.
2013 research.stlouisfed.org

Source: Dow Jones & Company, Haver Analytics, and St. Louis Federal Reserve, FRED database, research.stlouisfed.org/fred2.

Maturity Risk Premium (MRP)

A premium that reflects interest rate risk.

Reinvestment Rate Risk

The risk that a decline in interest rates will lead to lower income when bonds mature and funds are reinvested.

have more interest rate risk the longer the maturity of the bond.[10] Therefore, a **maturity risk premium (MRP)**, which is higher the greater the years to maturity, is included in the required interest rate.

The effect of maturity risk premiums is to raise interest rates on long-term bonds relative to those on short-term bonds. This premium, like the others, is difficult to measure; but (1) it varies somewhat over time, rising when interest rates are more volatile and uncertain, and then falling when interest rates are more stable and (2) in recent years, the maturity risk premium on 20-year T-bonds has generally been in the range of one to two percentage points.[11]

We should also note that although long-term bonds are heavily exposed to interest rate risk, short-term bills are heavily exposed to **reinvestment rate risk**. When short-term bills mature and the principal must be reinvested, or "rolled over," a decline in interest rates would necessitate reinvestment at a lower rate, which would result in a decline in interest income. To illustrate, suppose you had $100,000 invested in T-bills and you lived on the income. In 1981, short-term Treasury rates were about 15%, so your income would have been about $15,000. However, your income would have declined to about $9,000 by 1983 and to just $70 by February 2013. Had you invested your money in long-term T-bonds, your income (but not the value of the principal) would have been stable.[12] Thus, although "investing short" preserves one's principal, the interest income provided by short-term T-bills is less stable than that on long-term bonds.

QUICK QUESTION

QUESTION:

An analyst evaluating securities has obtained the following information. The real rate of interest is 2% and is expected to remain constant for the next 3 years. Inflation is expected to be 3% next year, 3.5% the following year, and 4% the third year. The maturity risk premium is estimated to be $0.1 \times (t - 1)\%$, where t = number of years to maturity. The liquidity premium on relevant 3-year securities is 0.25% and the default risk premium on relevant 3-year securities is 0.6%.

a. What is the yield on a 1-year T-bill?
b. What is the yield on a 3-year T-bond?
c. What is the yield on a 3-year corporate bond?

---

[10]For example, if someone had bought a 20-year Treasury bond for $1,000 in October 1998, when the long-term interest rate was 5.3%, and sold it in May 2002, when long-term T-bond rates were about 5.8%, the value of the bond would have declined to about $942. That would represent a loss of 5.8%; and it demonstrates that long-term bonds, even U.S. Treasury bonds, are not riskless. However, had the investor purchased short-term T-bills in 1998 and subsequently reinvested the principal each time the bills matured, he or she would still have had the original $1,000. This point is discussed in detail in Chapter 7.

[11]The MRP for long-term bonds has averaged 1.5% over the last 87 years. See *Ibbotson Stocks, Bonds, Bills, and Inflation: 2013 Valuation Yearbook* (Chicago: Morningstar Inc., 2013).

[12]Most long-term bonds also have some reinvestment rate risk. If a person is saving and investing for some future purpose (say, to buy a house or to retire), to actually earn the quoted rate on a long-term bond, each interest payment must be reinvested at the quoted rate. However, if interest rates fall, the interest payments would be reinvested at a lower rate; so the realized return would be less than the quoted rate. Note, though, that reinvestment rate risk is lower on long-term bonds than on short-term bonds because only the interest payments (rather than interest plus principal) on a long-term bond are exposed to reinvestment rate risk. Noncallable zero coupon bonds, which are discussed in Chapter 7, are completely free of reinvestment rate risk during their lifetime.

ANSWER:

a. A Treasury security has no default risk premium or liquidity risk premium. Therefore,

$r_{T1} = r^* + IP_1 + MRP_1$

$r_{T1} = 2\% + 3\% + 0.1(1 - 1)\%$

$r_{T1} = 5\%.$

b. A Treasury security has no default risk premium or liquidity risk premium. Therefore,

$r_{T3} = r^* + IP_3 + MRP_3$

$r_{T3} = 2\% + [(3\% + 3.5\% + 4\%)/3] + 0.1(3 - 1)\%$

$r_{T3} = 2\% + 3.5\% + 0.2\%$

$r_{T3} = 5.7\%.$

c. Unlike Treasury securities, corporate bonds have both a default risk premium and a liquidity risk premium.

$r_{C3} = r^* + IP_3 + MRP_3 + DRP + LP.$

Realize that the first three terms in this equation are identical to the terms in the Part b equation. So we can rewrite this equation as follows:

$r_{C3} = r_{T3} + DRP + LP.$

Now, we can insert the known values for these variables.

$r_{C3} = 5.7\% + 0.6\% + 0.25\%$

$r_{C3} = 6.55\%.$

SELF TEST

Write an equation for the nominal interest rate on any security.

Distinguish between the *real* risk-free rate of interest, r*, and the *nominal,* or *quoted,* risk-free rate of interest, r_{RF}.

How do investors deal with inflation when they determine interest rates in the financial markets?

Does the interest rate on a T-bond include a default risk premium? Explain.

Distinguish between liquid and illiquid assets and list some assets that are liquid and some that are illiquid.

Briefly explain the following statement: Although long-term bonds are heavily exposed to interest rate risk, short-term T-bills are heavily exposed to reinvestment rate risk. The maturity risk premium reflects the net effects of those two opposing forces.

Assume that the real risk-free rate is r* = 2% and the average expected inflation rate is 3% for each future year. The DRP and LP for Bond X are each 1%, and the applicable MRP is 2%. What is Bond X's interest rate? Is Bond X (1) a Treasury bond or a corporate bond and (2) more likely to have a 3-month or a 20-year maturity? **(9%, corporate, 20-year)**

6-4 THE TERM STRUCTURE OF INTEREST RATES

The **term structure of interest rates** describes the relationship between long- and short-term rates. The term structure is important to corporate treasurers deciding whether to borrow by issuing long- or short-term debt and to investors who are deciding whether to buy long- or short-term bonds. Therefore, both borrowers and lenders should understand (1) how long- and short-term rates relate to each other and (2) what causes shifts in their relative levels.

Interest rates for bonds with different maturities can be found in a variety of publications, including *The Wall Street Journal* and the *Federal Reserve Bulletin,* and

Term Structure of Interest rates
The relationship between bond yields and maturities.

on a number of websites, including those of Bloomberg, Yahoo!, CNN Financial, and the Federal Reserve Board. Using interest rate data from these sources, we can determine the term structure at any given point in time. For example, the table section of Figure 6.4 presents interest rates for different maturities on three different dates. The set of data for a given date, when plotted on a graph such as Figure 6.4, is called the **yield curve** for that date.

Yield Curve

A graph showing the relationship between bond yields and maturities.

As the figure shows, the yield curve changes in position and in slope over time. In March 1980, all rates were quite high because high inflation was expected. However, the rate of inflation was expected to decline; so short-term rates were higher than long-term rates, and the yield curve was thus *downward sloping*. By February 2000, inflation had indeed declined; thus, all rates were lower, and the yield curve had become *humped*—intermediate-term rates were higher than either short- or long-term rates. By February 2013, all rates had fallen below the 2000 levels; and because short-term rates had dropped below long-term rates, the yield curve was *upward sloping*.

Figure 6.4 shows yield curves for U.S. Treasury securities; but we could have constructed curves for bonds issued by GE, IBM, Delta Air Lines, or any other company that borrows money over a range of maturities. Had we constructed such corporate yield curves and plotted them on Figure 6.4, they would have been above those for Treasury securities because corporate yields include default risk

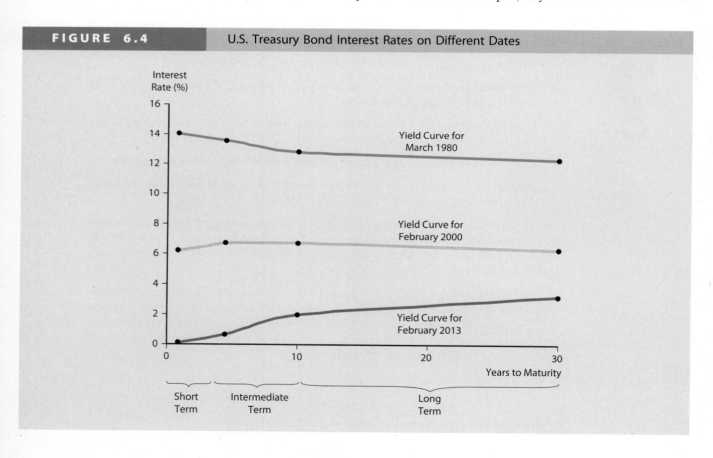

| **FIGURE 6.4** | U.S. Treasury Bond Interest Rates on Different Dates |

| | | **INTEREST RATE** | |
Term to Maturity	**March 1980**	**February 2000**	**February 2013**
1 year	14.0%	6.2%	0.1%
5 years	13.5	6.7	0.8
10 years	12.8	6.7	2.0
30 years	12.3	6.3	3.2

premiums and somewhat higher liquidity premiums. Even so, the corporate yield curves would have had the same general shape as the Treasury curves. Also, the riskier the corporation, the higher its yield curve. For example, in February 2013, Verizon Communications' bonds with a 10-year maturity were rated A by S&P and yielded 2.92%, while Royal Bank of Scotland had 10-year bonds outstanding that were rated BBB− and had a yield of 5.45%. At the same point in time, 10-year Treasury securities had an interest rate of 2.0%.

Historically, long-term rates are generally above short-term rates because of the maturity risk premium; so all yield curves usually slope upward. For this reason, people often call an upward-sloping yield curve a **"normal" yield curve** and a yield curve that slopes downward an **inverted** or **"abnormal" yield curve**. Thus, in Figure 6.4, the yield curve for March 1980 was inverted, while the one for February 2013 was normal. However, the February 2000 curve is humped—a **humped yield curve**—which means that interest rates on intermediate-term maturities were higher than rates on both short- and long-term maturities. We will explain in detail why an upward slope is the normal situation. Briefly, however, the reason is that short-term securities have less interest rate risk than longer-term securities; hence, they have smaller MRPs. So short-term rates are normally lower than long-term rates.

"Normal" Yield Curve
An upward-sloping yield curve.

Inverted ("Abnormal") Yield Curve
A downward-sloping yield curve.

Humped Yield Curve
A yield curve where interest rates on intermediate-term maturities are higher than rates on both short- and long-term maturities.

SELF TEST

What is a yield curve, and what information would you need to draw this curve?

Distinguish among the shapes of a "normal" yield curve, an "abnormal" curve, and a "humped" curve.

If the interest rates on 1-, 5-, 10-, and 30-year bonds are 4%, 5%, 6%, and 7%, respectively, how would you describe the yield curve? If the rates were reversed, how would you describe it?

6-5 WHAT DETERMINES THE SHAPE OF THE YIELD CURVE?

Because maturity risk premiums are positive, if other things were held constant, long-term bonds would always have higher interest rates than short-term bonds. However, market interest rates also depend on expected inflation, default risk, and liquidity, each of which can vary with maturity.

Expected inflation has an especially important effect on the yield curve's shape, especially the curve for U.S. Treasury securities. Treasuries have essentially no default or liquidity risk, so the yield on a Treasury bond that matures in t years can be expressed as follows:

$$\text{T-bond yield} = r_t^* + IP_t + MRP_t$$

 6.2

While the real risk-free rate, r^*, varies somewhat over time because of changes in the economy and demographics, these changes are random rather than predictable. Therefore, the best forecast for the future value of r^* is its current value. However, the inflation premium, IP, varies significantly over time and in a somewhat predictable manner. Recall that the inflation premium is the average level of expected inflation over the life of the bond. Thus, if the market expects inflation to increase in the future (say, from 3% to 4% to 5% over the next 3 years), the inflation premium will be higher on a 3-year bond than on a 1-year bond. On the other hand, if the market expects inflation to decline in the future, long-term bonds will have a smaller inflation premium than will short-term bonds. Finally, since investors consider long-term bonds to be riskier than short-term bonds

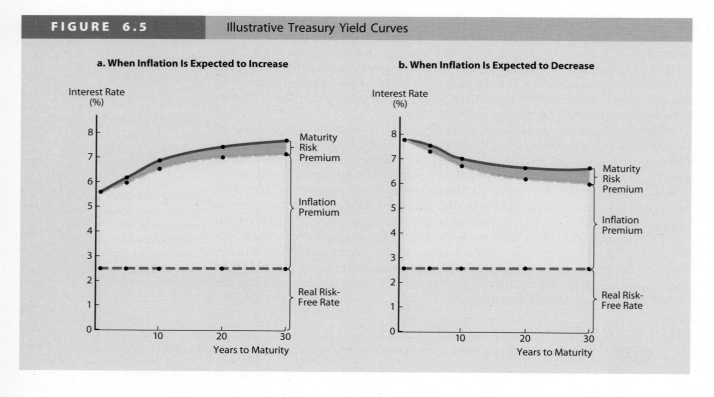

FIGURE 6.5   Illustrative Treasury Yield Curves

a. When Inflation Is Expected to Increase

b. When Inflation Is Expected to Decrease

	With Inflation Expected to Increase						With Inflation Expected to Decrease			
Maturity	r*	IP	MRP	Yield		Maturity	r*	IP	MRP	Yield
1 year	2.50%	3.00%	0.00%	5.50%		1 year	2.50%	5.00%	0.00%	7.50%
5 years	2.50	3.40	0.18	6.08		5 years	2.50	4.60	0.18	7.28
10 years	2.50	4.00	0.28	6.78		10 years	2.50	4.00	0.28	6.78
20 years	2.50	4.50	0.42	7.42		20 years	2.50	3.50	0.42	6.42
30 years	2.50	4.67	0.53	7.70		30 years	2.50	3.33	0.53	6.36

© Cengage Learning 2015

because of interest rate risk, the maturity risk premium always increases with maturity.

Figure 6.5 shows two illustrative yield curves—one where inflation is expected to increase over time and another where inflation is expected to decrease. Note that these hypothetical interest rates are similar to historical rates, but they are much higher than current interest rates. Panel a shows the Treasury yield curve when inflation is expected to increase. Here long-term bonds have higher yields for two reasons: (1) Inflation is expected to be higher in the future, and (2) there is a positive maturity risk premium. Panel b shows the yield curve when inflation is expected to decline. Such a downward-sloping yield curve often foreshadows an economic downturn because weaker economic conditions generally lead to declining inflation, which, in turn, results in lower long-term rates.[13]

Now let's consider the yield curve for corporate bonds. Recall that corporate bonds include a default risk premium (DRP) and a liquidity premium (LP).

---

[13]Note that yield curves tend to rise or fall relatively sharply over the first 5 to 10 years and then flatten out. One reason this occurs is that when forecasting future interest rates, people often predict relatively high or low inflation for the next few years, after which they assume an average long-run inflation rate. Consequently, the short end of the yield curve tends to have more curvature and the long end of the yield curve tends to be more stable.

Therefore, the yield on a corporate bond that matures in t years can be expressed as follows:

$$\text{Corporate bond yield} = r_t^* + IP_t + MRP_t + DRP_t + LP_t$$

6.3

Comparing the Treasury bond yield in Equation 6.2 and the corporate bond yield in Equation 6.3, we can calculate the corporate bond yield spread:

$$\begin{matrix}\text{Corporate bond} \\ \text{yield spread}\end{matrix} = \text{Corporate bond yield} - \text{Treasury bond yield} = DRP_t + LP_t$$

One recent study estimates that both the default risk premium and liquidity premium vary over time, and that the majority of the corporate bond yield spread

THE LINKS BETWEEN EXPECTED INFLATION AND INTEREST RATES: A CLOSER LOOK

Throughout the text, we use the following equation to describe the link between expected inflation and the nominal risk-free rate of interest, r_{RF}:

$$r_{RF} = r^* + IP$$

Recall that r^* is the real risk-free interest rate and IP is the corresponding inflation premium. This equation suggests that there is a simple link between expected inflation and nominal interest rates.

It turns out, however, that this link is a bit more complex. To fully understand this relationship, first recognize that individuals get utility through the consumption of real goods and services such as bread, water, haircuts, pizza, and textbooks. When we save money, we are giving up the opportunity to consume these goods today in return for being able to consume more of them in the future. Our gain from waiting is measured by the real rate of interest, r^*.

To illustrate this point, consider the following example. Assume that a loaf of bread costs $1 today. Also assume that the real rate of interest is 3% and that inflation is expected to be 5% over the next year. The 3% real rate indicates that the average consumer is willing to trade 100 loaves of bread today for 103 loaves next year. If a "bread bank" were available, consumers who wanted to defer consumption until next year could deposit 100 loaves today and withdraw 103 loaves next year. In practice, most of us do not directly trade real goods such as bread—instead, we purchase these goods with money because in a well-functioning economy, it is more efficient to exchange money than goods. However, when we lend money over time, we worry that borrowers might pay us back with dollars that aren't worth as much due to inflation. To compensate for this risk, lenders build in a premium for expected inflation.

With these concerns in mind, let's compare the dollar cost of 100 loaves of bread today to the cost of 103 loaves next year. Given the current price, 100 loaves of bread today would cost $100. Because expected inflation is 5%, this means that a loaf of bread is expected to cost $1.05 next year. Consequently, 103 loaves of bread are expected to cost $108.15 next year (103 × $1.05). So if consumers were to deposit $100 in a bank today, they would need to earn 8.15% to realize a real return of 3%.

Putting this all together, we see that the 1-year nominal interest rate can be calculated as follows:

$$r_{RF} = (1 + r^*)(1 + IP) - 1$$
$$= (1.03)(1.05) - 1 = 0.0815 = 8.15\%$$

Note that this expression can be rewritten as follows:

$$r_{RF} = r^* + IP + (r^* \times IP)$$

That equation is identical to our original expression for the nominal risk-free rate except that it includes a "cross-term," $r^* \times IP$. When real interest rates and expected inflation are relatively low, the cross-term turns out to be quite small and thus is often ignored. Because it is normally insignificant we disregard the cross-term in the text unless stated otherwise. (When working problems, we will tell you when to include the cross-term; otherwise, ignore this term when solving problems.)

One last point—you should recognize that while it may be reasonable to ignore the cross-term when interest rates are low (as they are in the United States today), it is a mistake to do so when investing in a market where interest rates and inflation are quite high, as is often the case in many emerging markets. In these markets, the cross-term can be significant and thus should not be disregarded.

can be attributed to default risk.[14] Corporate bonds' default and liquidity risks are affected by their maturities. For example, the default risk on Coca-Cola's short-term debt is very small because there is almost no chance that Coca-Cola will go bankrupt over the next few years. However, Coke has some bonds that have a maturity of almost 100 years; and while the odds of Coke defaulting on those bonds might not be very high, there is still a higher probability of default risk on Coke's long-term bonds than on its short-term bonds.

Longer-term corporate bonds also tend to be less liquid than shorter-term bonds. Because short-term debt has less default risk, someone can buy a short-term bond without doing as much credit checking as would be necessary for a long-term bond. Thus, people can move in and out of short-term corporate debt relatively rapidly. As a result, a corporation's short-term bonds are typically more liquid and thus have lower liquidity premiums than its long-term bonds.

Figure 6.6 shows yield curves for two hypothetical corporate bonds—an AA-rated bond with minimal default risk and a BBB-rated bond with more default risk—along with the yield curve for Treasury securities taken from Panel a of Figure 6.5. Here we assume that inflation is expected to increase, so the

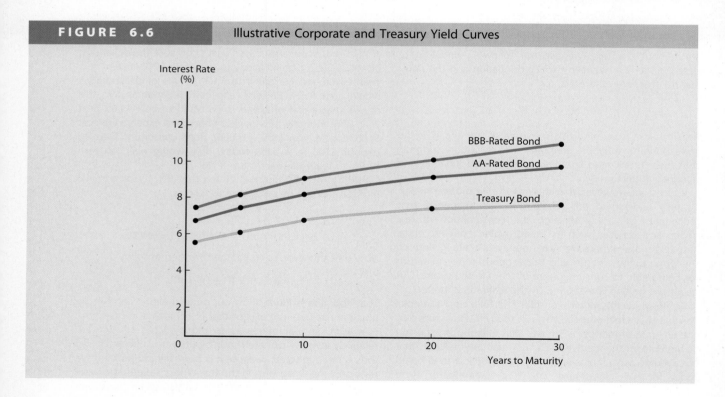

FIGURE 6.6 Illustrative Corporate and Treasury Yield Curves

	Interest Rate		
	Treasury Bond	**AA-Rated Bond**	**BBB-Rated Bond**
1 year	5.5%	6.7%	7.4%
5 years	6.1	7.4	8.1
10 years	6.8	8.2	9.1
20 years	7.4	9.2	10.2
30 years	7.7	9.8	11.1

[14]Refer to Francis A. Longstaff, Sanjay Mithal, and Eric Neis, "Corporate Yield Spreads: Default Risk or Liquidity? New Evidence from the Credit Default Swap Market," *Journal of Finance*, vol. 60, no. 5 (October 2005), pp. 2213–2253.

Treasury yield curve is upward-sloping. Because of their additional default and liquidity risk, corporate bonds yield more than Treasury bonds with the same maturity and BBB-rated bonds yield more than AA-rated bonds. Finally, note that the yield spread between corporate and Treasury bonds is larger the longer the maturity. This occurs because longer-term corporate bonds have more default and liquidity risk than shorter-term bonds, and both of these premiums are absent in Treasury bonds.

SELF TEST

How do maturity risk premiums affect the yield curve?

If the inflation rate is expected to increase, would this increase or decrease the slope of the yield curve?

If the inflation rate is expected to remain constant at the current level in the future, would the yield curve slope up, slope down, or be horizontal? Consider all factors that affect the yield curve, not just inflation.

Explain why corporate bonds' default and liquidity premiums are likely to increase with their maturity.

Explain why corporate bonds always yield more than Treasury bonds and why BBB-rated bonds always yield more than AA-rated bonds.

6-6 USING THE YIELD CURVE TO ESTIMATE FUTURE INTEREST RATES[15]

In the last section, we saw that the slope of the yield curve depends primarily on two factors: (1) expectations about future inflation and (2) effects of maturity on bonds' risk. We also saw how to calculate the yield curve, given inflation and maturity-related risks. Note, though, that people can reverse the process: They can look at the yield curve and use information embedded in it to estimate the market's expectations regarding future inflation, risk, and short-term interest rates. For example, suppose a company is in the midst of a 5-year expansion program and the treasurer knows that she will need to borrow short-term funds a year from now. She knows the current cost of 1-year money, read from the yield curve, but she wants to know the cost of 1-year money next year. That information can be "backed out" by analyzing the current yield curve, as will be discussed.

The estimation process is straightforward provided we (1) focus on Treasury bonds and (2) assume that Treasury bonds contain no maturity risk premiums.[16] This position has been called the **pure expectations theory** of the term structure of

Pure Expectations Theory
A theory that states that the shape of the yield curve depends on investors' expectations about future interest rates.

---

[15]This section is relatively technical, but instructors can omit it without loss of continuity.

[16]Although most evidence suggests that there is a positive maturity risk premium, some academics and practitioners contend that this second assumption is reasonable, at least as an approximation. They argue that the market is dominated by large bond traders who buy and sell securities of different maturities each day, that these traders focus only on short-term returns, and that they are not concerned with maturity risk. According to this view, a bond trader is just as willing to buy a 20-year bond to pick up a short-term profit as he or she is to buy a 3-month security. Proponents of this view argue that the shape of the Treasury yield curve is therefore determined only by market expectations about future interest rates. Later in this section we show what happens when we include the effects of maturity risk premiums.

interest rates, often simply referred to as the "expectations theory." The expectations theory assumes that bond traders establish bond prices and interest rates strictly on the basis of expectations for future interest rates and that they are indifferent to maturity because they do not view long-term bonds as being riskier than short-term bonds. If this were true, the maturity risk premium (MRP) would be zero and long-term interest rates would simply be a weighted average of current and expected future short-term interest rates.

To illustrate the pure expectations theory, assume that a 1-year Treasury bond currently yields 5.00% while a 2-year bond yields 5.50%. Investors who want to invest for a 2-year horizon have two primary options:

Option 1: *Buy a two-year security and hold it for 2 years.*
Option 2: *Buy a 1-year security; hold it for 1 year; and then at the end of the year, reinvest the proceeds in another 1-year security.*

If they select Option 1, for every dollar they invest today, they will have accumulated $1.113025 by the end of Year 2:

$$\text{Funds at end of Year 2} = \$1 \times (1.055)^2 = \$1.113025$$

If they select Option 2, they should end up with the same amount; but this equation is used to find the ending amount:

$$\text{Funds at end of Year 2} = \$1 \times (1.05) \times (1 + X)$$

Here X is the expected interest rate on a 1-year Treasury security 1 year from now.

If the expectations theory is correct, each option must provide the same amount of cash at the end of 2 years, which implies the following:

$$(1.05)(1 + X) = (1.055)^2$$

We can rearrange this equation and then solve for X:

$$1 + X = (1.055)^2/1.05$$
$$= (1.055)^2/1.05 - 1 = 0.0600238 = 6.00238\%$$

Therefore, X, the 1-year rate 1 year from today, must be 6.00238%; otherwise, one option will be better than the other and the market will not be in equilibrium. However, if the market is not in equilibrium, buying and selling will quickly bring about equilibrium. For example, suppose investors expect the 1-year Treasury rate to be 6.00238% a year from now but a 2-year bond now yields 5.25%, not the 5.50% rate required for equilibrium. Bond traders could earn a profit by adopting the following strategy:

1. Borrow money for 2 years at the 2-year rate, 5.25% per year.

2. Invest the money in a series of 1-year securities, expecting to earn 5.00% this year and 6.00238% next year, for an overall expected return over the 2 years of $[1.05 \times 1.0600238]^{1/2} - 1 = 5.50\%$.

Borrowing at 5.25% and investing to earn 5.50% is a good deal, so bond traders would rush to borrow money (demand funds) in the 2-year market and invest (or supply funds) in the 1-year market.

Recall from Figure 6.1 that a decline in the supply of funds raises interest rates, while an increase in the supply lowers rates. Likewise, an increase in the demand for funds raises rates, while a decline in demand lowers rates. Therefore, bond traders would push up the 2-year yield and simultaneously lower the yield on 1-year bonds. This buying and selling would cease when the 2-year rate becomes a weighted average of expected future 1-year rates.[17]

Let's suppose that the yield curve looks as follows:

1-year T-bond: 5.00%
2-year T-bond: 5.50%
4-year T-bond: 6.25%

An investor would like to purchase a 1-year T-bond today and then to invest in a 3-year T-bond one year from now. What yield would this investor expect to earn on the 3-year T-bond one year from now? You have enough information from the yield curve above to determine the expected yield on the 3-year T-bond one year from today. Here's the equation setup:

$$(1.0625)^4 = (1.05) \times (1 + X)^3$$
$$(1.0625)^4/1.05 = (1 + X)^3$$
$$1.213742 = (1 + X)^3$$
$$(1.213742)^{1/3} = 1 + X$$
$$1.0667 = 1 + X, \text{ so } X = 6.67\%.$$

To eliminate the exponent, each side of the equation is raised to the 1/3 power.

The investor would expect to earn one year from today a yield of 6.67% for three years on the 3-year T-bond. Note that the investor would expect to earn the same yield investing in a 4-year T-bond today as he would investing in a 1-year T-bond today and then investing in a 3-year T-bond one year from now.

The preceding analysis was based on the assumption that the maturity risk premium is zero. However, most evidence suggests that a positive maturity risk premium exists. For example, assume once again that 1- and 2-year maturities yield 5.00% and 5.50%, respectively; so we have a rising yield curve. However, now assume that the maturity risk premium on the 2-year bond is 0.20% versus zero for the 1-year bond. This premium means that in equilibrium, the expected annual return on a 2-year bond (5.50%) must be 0.20% higher than the expected return on a series of two 1-year bonds (5.00% and X%). Therefore, the expected return on the series must be 5.50% − 0.20% = 5.30%:

$$\text{Expected return on 2-year series} = \text{Rate on 2-year bond} - \text{MRP}$$
$$= 0.055 - 0.002 = 0.053 = 5.30\%$$

Now recall that the annual expected return from the series of two 1-year bonds can be expressed as follows, where X is the 1-year rate next year:

$$(1.05)(1 + X) = (1 + \text{Expected return on 2-year series})^2 = (1.053)^2$$
$$1.05X = (1.053)^2 - 1.05$$
$$X = \frac{0.0588090}{1.05} = 0.0560086 = 5.60086\%.$$

Under these conditions, equilibrium requires that market participants expect the 1-year rate next year to be 5.60086%.

Note that the rate read from the yield curve rises by 0.50% when the years to maturity increase from one to two: 5.50% − 5.00% = 0.50%. Of this 0.50% increase, 0.20% is attributable to the MRP and the remaining 0.30% is due to the increase in expected 1-year rates next year.

---

[17]In our calculations, we used the geometric average of the current and expected 1-year rates: [1.05 × 1.0600238]$^{1/2}$ − 1 = 0.055 or 5.50%. The arithmetic average of the two rates is (5% + 6.00238%)/2 = 5.50119%. The geometric average is theoretically correct, but the difference is only 0.00119%. With interest rates at the levels they have been in the United States and most other nations in recent years, the geometric and arithmetic averages are so close that many people use the arithmetic average, especially given the other assumptions that underlie the estimation of future 1-year rates.

Putting all of this together, we see that one can use the yield curve to estimate what the market expects the short-term rate to be next year. However, this requires an estimate of the maturity risk premium; and if our estimated MRP is incorrect, then so will our yield-curve-based interest rate forecast. Thus, while the yield curve can be used to obtain insights into what the market thinks future interest rates will be, the calculations above (although they appear to be precise) will only approximate these expectations unless the pure expectations theory holds or we know with certainty the exact maturity risk premium. Because neither of these conditions holds, it is difficult to know for sure what the market is forecasting.

Note too that even if we could determine the market's consensus forecast for future rates, the market is not always right. So a forecast of next year's rate based on the yield curve could be wrong. Therefore, obtaining an accurate forecast of rates for next year—or even for next month—is extremely difficult.

SELF TEST

What key assumption underlies the pure expectations theory?

Assuming that the pure expectations theory is correct, how are expected short-term rates used to calculate expected long-term rates?

According to the pure expectations theory, what would happen if long-term rates were not an average of expected short-term rates?

Most evidence suggests that a positive maturity risk premium exists. How would this affect your calculations when determining interest rates?

Assume that the interest rate on a 1-year T-bond is currently 7% and the rate on a 2-year bond is 9%. If the maturity risk premium is zero, what is a reasonable forecast of the rate on a 1-year bond next year? What would the forecast be if the maturity risk premium on the 2-year bond was 0.5% versus zero for the 1-year bond? **(11.04%; 10.02%)**

6-7 MACROECONOMIC FACTORS THAT INFLUENCE INTEREST RATE LEVELS

The home page for the Board of Governors of the Federal Reserve System can be found at **federalreserve.gov**. You can access general information about the Federal Reserve, including press releases, speeches, and monetary policy.

We described how key components such as expected inflation, default risk, maturity risk, and liquidity concerns influence the level of interest rates over time and across different markets. On a day-to-day basis, a variety of macro-economic factors may influence one or more of these components; hence, macroeconomic factors have an important effect on both the general level of interest rates and the shape of the yield curve. The primary factors are (1) Federal Reserve policy; (2) the federal budget deficit or surplus; (3) international factors, including the foreign trade balance and interest rates in other countries; and (4) the level of business activity.

6-7A FEDERAL RESERVE POLICY

As you probably learned in your economics courses, (1) the money supply has a significant effect on the level of economic activity, inflation, and interest rates, and (2) in the United States, the Federal Reserve Board controls the money supply. If the Fed wants to stimulate the economy, it increases the money supply. The Fed buys and sells short-term securities, so the initial effect of a monetary easing would be to cause short-term rates to decline. However, a larger money supply might lead to an increase in expected future inflation, which would cause long-term rates to rise even as short-term rates fell. The reverse holds if the Fed tightens the money supply. The Fed's job is to promote economic growth while keeping inflation at bay. This is a delicate balancing act.

As you can see from Figure 6.2, interest rates in recent years have been relatively low, with short-term rates especially low during the last 4 years shown (January 2009 through February 2013). Economists anticipate that rates will remain low for the foreseeable future; however, some worry that the Fed might be increasing the risk of inflation down the road.

During the last several years, the Fed has been trying to increase business investment to generate growth in our economy. In addition to lower interest rates, the Fed through its program of "Quantitative Easing" has pumped trillions of dollars into the economy by purchasing mortgage-backed securities and long-term Treasury securities and through special lending programs. As we write this, the Fed is still purchasing mortgage-backed securities. The Fed's third quantitative easing program was announced in September 2012—and it is open ended. The Fed has stated that it will purchase $40 billion dollars of mortgage-backed securities per month until there is substantial improvement in the labor market. 2012 was the best year for the housing industry since the 2008 financial crisis due to record lows in mortgage rates. Job growth has been steady, although the unemployment rate is at 7.9%. However, there is concern that once the Fed stops purchasing mortgage-backed securities mortgage rates will rise. If the Fed anticipates inflation returning, it could be forced to raise rates or to reduce the money supply.

Actions that lower short-term rates won't necessarily lower long-term rates. Lower rates could cause foreigners to sell their holdings of U.S. bonds. These investors would be paid with dollars, which they would then sell to buy their own currencies. The sale of dollars and the purchase of other currencies would lower the value of the dollar relative to other currencies, which would make U.S. goods less expensive, which would help manufacturers and thus lower the trade deficit. Note also that during periods when the Fed is actively intervening in the markets, the yield curve may be temporarily distorted. Short-term rates may be driven below the long-run equilibrium level if the Fed is easing credit and above the equilibrium rate if the Fed is tightening credit. Long-term rates are not affected as much by Fed intervention.

6-7B FEDERAL BUDGET DEFICITS OR SURPLUSES

If the federal government spends more than it takes in as taxes, it runs a deficit; and that deficit must be covered by additional borrowing (selling more Treasury bonds) or by printing money. If the government borrows, this increases the demand for funds and thus pushes up interest rates. If the government prints money, investors recognize that with "more money chasing a given amount of goods," the result will be increased inflation, which will also increase interest rates. So the larger the federal deficit, other things held constant, the higher the level of interest rates.

Over the past several decades, the federal government has generally run large budget deficits. There were some surpluses in the late 1990s; but the September 11, 2001, terrorist attacks, the subsequent recession, and the Iraq war all boosted government spending and caused the deficits to return.

6-7C INTERNATIONAL FACTORS

Businesses and individuals in the United States buy from and sell to people and firms all around the globe. If they buy more than they sell (that is, if there are more imports than exports), they are said to be running a **foreign trade deficit**. When trade deficits occur, they must be financed, and this generally means borrowing from nations with export surpluses. Thus, if the United States imported $200 billion of goods but exported only $100 billion, it would run a trade deficit of $100 billion while other countries would have a $100 billion trade surplus.

Foreign Trade Deficit
The situation that exists when a country imports more than it exports.

The United States would probably borrow the $100 billion from the surplus nations.[18] At any rate, the larger the trade deficit, the higher the tendency to borrow. Note that foreigners will hold U.S. debt if and only if the rates on U.S. securities are competitive with rates in other countries. This causes U.S. interest rates to be highly dependent on rates in other parts of the world.

All this interdependency limits the ability of the Federal Reserve to use monetary policy to control economic activity in the United States. For example, if the Fed attempts to lower U.S. interest rates and this causes rates to fall below rates abroad, foreigners will begin selling U.S. bonds. Those sales will depress bond prices, which will push up rates in the United States. Thus, the large U.S. trade deficit (and foreigners' holdings of U.S. debt that resulted from many years of deficits) hinders the Fed's ability to combat a recession by lowering interest rates.

For about 25 years following World War II, the United States ran large trade surpluses and the rest of the world owed it many billions of dollars. However, the situation changed, and the United States has been running trade deficits since the mid-1970s. (The U.S. annual 2012 international trade deficit for goods and services was $540.4 billion.) The cumulative effect of these deficits has been to change the United States from being the largest creditor nation to being the largest debtor nation of all time. As a result, interest rates are very much influenced by interest rates in other countries—higher or lower rates abroad lead to higher or lower U.S. rates. Because of all of this, U.S. corporate treasurers and everyone else who is affected by interest rates should keep up with developments in the world economy.

6-7D BUSINESS ACTIVITY

You can examine Figure 6.2 to see how business conditions influence interest rates. Here are the key points revealed by the graph:

1. Because inflation increased from 1972 to 1981, the general tendency during that period was toward higher interest rates. However, since the 1981 peak, the trend has generally been downward.

2. The shaded areas in the graph represent recessions, during which (a) the demand for money and the rate of inflation tended to fall and (b) the Federal Reserve tended to increase the money supply in an effort to stimulate the economy. As a result, there is a tendency for interest rates to decline during recessions. For example, the economy began to slow down in 2000, and the country entered a mild recession in 2001. In response, the Federal Reserve cut interest rates. In 2004, the economy began to rebound; so the Fed began to raise rates. However, the subprime debacle hit in 2007; so the Fed began lowering rates in September 2007. By February 2008, the Fed's target rate had fallen from 5.25% to 3.00%. In February 2013, the Federal Reserve target rate ranged from 0% to 0.25%.

3. During recessions, short-term rates decline more sharply than long-term rates. This occurs for two reasons: (a) The Fed operates mainly in the short-term sector, so its intervention has the strongest effect there, (b) Long-term rates reflect the average expected inflation rate over the next 20 to 30 years; and this expectation generally does not change much, even when the current inflation rate is low because of a recession or high because of a boom. So short-term rates are more volatile than long-term rates. Taking another look at Figure 6.2, we see that short-term rates did decline recently by much more than long-term rates.

---

[18]The deficit could also be financed by selling assets, including gold, corporate stocks, entire companies, and real estate. The United States has financed its massive trade deficits by all of these means in recent years. Although the primary method has been by borrowing from foreigners, in recent years, there has been a sharp increase in foreign purchases of U.S. assets, especially oil exporters' purchases of U.S. businesses.

SELF TEST

Identify some macroeconomic factors that influence interest rates and explain the effects of each.

How does the Fed stimulate the economy? How does the Fed affect interest rates?

Does the Fed have complete control over U.S. interest rates? That is, can it set rates at any level it chooses? Why or why not?

6-8 INTEREST RATES AND BUSINESS DECISIONS

As you might expect, companies look carefully at the level of interest rates and the shape of the yield curve when making important business decisions. For example, assume that Leading Edge Co. is considering building a new plant with a 30-year life that will cost $1 million and it plans to raise the $1 million by borrowing rather than by issuing new stock. At the time of its decision in April 2013, the company faces an upward sloping yield curve. If it borrows on a short-term basis from a bank—say for 1 year—its annual interest cost would be only 1.0%, or $10,000. On the other hand, if it issued long-term bonds, then its annual cost would be 4.0%, or $40,000. Therefore, at first glance, it would seem that Leading Edge should use short-term debt.

However, this could prove to be a horrible mistake. If it used short-term debt, it will have to renew its loan every year; and the rate charged on each new loan will reflect the then-current short-term rate. Interest rates could dramatically increase in which case the company's interest payments would soar over time. Those high interest payments would cut into and perhaps eliminate its profits. Even more concerning, if at some point in time, the company's lenders refused to renew the loan and demanded its repayment, as they would have every right to do, Leading Edge might have to sell assets at a loss, which could result in bankruptcy. On the other hand, if the company used long-term financing in 2013, its interest costs would remain constant at $40,000 per year; so it would not be directly hurt if interest rates in the economy increased over time.

Does all of this suggest that firms should avoid short-term debt? Not at all. If inflation falls over the next few years, so will interest rates. If Leading Edge had borrowed on a long-term basis in April 2013, it would be at a disadvantage if it was locked into 4.0% debt while its competitors (who used short-term debt in 2013) had a borrowing cost of only 1.0%.

Financing decisions would be easy if we could make accurate forecasts of future interest rates. Unfortunately, predicting interest rates with consistent accuracy is nearly impossible. However, although it is difficult to predict future interest rate *levels*, it is easy to predict that interest rates will *fluctuate*—they always have, and they always will. That being the case, sound financial policy calls for using a mix of long- and short-term debt as well as equity to position the firm so that it can survive in any interest rate environment. Further, the optimal financial policy depends in an important way on the nature of the firm's assets—the easier it is to sell assets to generate cash, the more feasible it is to use more short-term debt. This makes it logical for a firm to finance current assets such as inventories and receivables with short-term debt and to finance fixed assets such as buildings and equipment with long-term debt. We will return to this issue later in the book when we discuss capital structure and financing policy.

Changes in interest rates also have implications for savers. For example, if you had a 401(k) plan—and someday most of you will—you would probably want to invest some of your money in a bond mutual fund. You could choose a fund that had an average maturity of 25 years, 20 years, or on down to only a few months (a money market fund). How would your choice affect your investment results and hence your retirement income? First, your decision would affect your annual interest income. For example, if the yield curve was upward-sloping, as it normally is, you would earn more interest if you chose a fund that held long-term bonds. Note, though, that if you chose a long-term fund and interest rates then rose, the market value of your fund would decline. For example, as we will see in Chapter 7, if you had $100,000 in a fund whose average bond had a maturity of 25 years and a coupon rate of 6% and if interest rates then rose from 6% to 10%, the market value of your fund would decline from $100,000 to about $63,500. On the other hand, if rates declined, your fund would increase in value. If you invested in a short-term fund, its value would be more stable, but it would probably provide less interest per year. In any event, your choice of maturity would have a major effect on your investment performance and, therefore, on your future income.

SELF TEST

If short-term interest rates are lower than long-term rates, why might a borrower still choose to finance with long-term debt?

Explain the following statement: The optimal financial policy depends in an important way on the nature of the firm's assets.

TYING IT ALL TOGETHER

In this chapter, we discussed the way interest rates are determined, the term structure of interest rates, and some of the ways interest rates affect business decisions. We saw that the interest rate on a given bond, r, is based on this equation:

$$r = r^* + IP + DRP + LP + MRP$$

Here r^* is the real risk-free rate, IP is the premium for expected inflation, DRP is the premium for potential default risk, LP is the premium for lack of liquidity, and MRP is the premium to compensate for the risk inherent in bonds with long maturities. Both r^* and the various premiums can and do change over time depending on economic conditions, Federal Reserve actions, and the like. Because changes in these factors are difficult to predict, it is hard to forecast the future direction of interest rates.

The yield curve, which relates bonds' interest rates to their maturities, usually has an upward slope; but it can slope up or down, and both its slope and level change over time. The main determinants of the slope of the curve are expectations for future inflation and the MRP. We can analyze yield curve data to estimate what market participants think future interest rates are likely to be. We will use the insights gained from this chapter in later chapters when we analyze the values of bonds and stocks and when we examine various corporate investment and financing decisions.

SELF-TEST QUESTIONS AND PROBLEMS

(Solutions Appear in Appendix A)

ST-1 **KEY TERMS** Define each of the following terms:

a. Production opportunities; time preferences for consumption; risk; inflation

b. Real risk-free rate of interest, r*; nominal (quoted) risk-free rate of interest, r_{RF}

c. Inflation premium (IP)

d. Default risk premium (DRP)

e. Liquidity premium (LP); maturity risk premium (MRP)

f. Interest rate risk; reinvestment rate risk

g. Term structure of interest rates; yield curve

h. "Normal" yield curve; inverted ("abnormal") yield curve; humped yield curve

i. Pure expectations theory

j. Foreign trade deficit

ST-2 **INFLATION AND INTEREST RATES** The real risk-free rate of interest, r*, is 3%; and it is expected to remain constant over time. Inflation is expected to be 2% per year for the next 3 years and 4% per year for the next 5 years. The maturity risk premium is equal to $0.1 \times (t-1)\%$, where t = the bond's maturity. The default risk premium for a BBB-rated bond is 1.3%.

a. What is the average expected inflation rate over the next 4 years?

b. What is the yield on a 4-year Treasury bond?

c. What is the yield on a 4-year BBB-rated corporate bond with a liquidity premium of 0.5%?

d. What is the yield on an 8-year Treasury bond?

e. What is the yield on an 8-year BBB-rated corporate bond with a liquidity premium of 0.5%?

f. If the yield on a 9-year Treasury bond is 7.3%, what does that imply about expected inflation in 9 years?

ST-3 **PURE EXPECTATIONS THEORY** The yield on 1-year Treasury securities is 6%, 2-year securities yield 6.2%, 3-year securities yield 6.3%, and 4-year securities yield 6.5%. There is no maturity risk premium. Using expectations theory and geometric averages, forecast the yields on the following securities:

a. A 1-year security, 1 year from now

b. A 1-year security, 2 years from now

c. A 2-year security, 1 year from now

d. A 3-year security, 1 year from now

QUESTIONS

6-1 Suppose interest rates on residential mortgages of equal risk are 5.5% in California and 7.0% in New York. Could this differential persist? What forces might tend to equalize rates? Would differentials in borrowing costs for businesses of equal risk located in California and New York be more or less likely to exist than differentials in residential mortgage rates? Would differentials in the cost of money for New York and California firms be more likely to exist if the firms being compared were very large or if they were very small? What are the implications of all of this with respect to nationwide branching?

6-2 Which fluctuate more—long-term or short-term interest rates? Why?

6-3 Suppose you believe that the economy is just entering a recession. Your firm must raise capital immediately, and debt will be used. Should you borrow on a long-term or a short-term basis? Why?

6-4   Suppose the population of Area Y is relatively young and the population of Area O is relatively old, but everything else about the two areas is the same.

a.   Would interest rates likely be the same or different in the two areas? Explain.

b.   Would a trend toward nationwide branching by banks and the development of nationwide diversified financial corporations affect your answer to Part a? Explain.

6-5   Suppose a new process was developed that could be used to make oil out of seawater. The equipment required is quite expensive; but it would, in time, lead to low prices for gasoline, electricity, and other types of energy. What effect would this have on interest rates?

6-6   Suppose a new and more liberal Congress and administration are elected. Their first order of business is to take away the independence of the Federal Reserve System and to force the Fed to greatly expand the money supply. What effect will this have:

a.   On the level and slope of the yield curve immediately after the announcement?

b.   On the level and slope of the yield curve that would exist two or three years in the future?

6-7   It is a fact that the federal government (1) encouraged the development of the savings and loan industry, (2) virtually forced the industry to make long-term fixed-interest-rate mortgages, and (3) forced the savings and loans to obtain most of their capital as deposits that were withdrawable on demand.

a.   Would the savings and loans have higher profits in a world with a "normal" or an inverted yield curve? Explain your answer.

b.   Would the savings and loan industry be better off if the individual institutions sold their mortgages to federal agencies and then collected servicing fees or if the institutions held the mortgages that they originated?

6-8   Suppose interest rates on Treasury bonds rose from 5% to 9% as a result of higher interest rates in Europe. What effect would this have on the price of an average company's common stock?

6-9   What does it mean when it is said that the United States is running a trade deficit? What impact will a trade deficit have on interest rates?

6-10   Suppose you have noticed that the slope of the corporate yield curve has become steeper over the past few months. What factors might explain the change in the slope?

PROBLEMS

Easy Problems 1–7

6-1   **YIELD CURVES**   Yields on U.S. Treasury securities were as follows:

Term	Rate
6 months	5.1%
1 year	5.5
2 years	5.6
3 years	5.7
4 years	5.8
5 years	6.0
10 years	6.1
20 years	6.5
30 years	6.3

a.   Plot a yield curve based on these data.

b.   What type of yield curve is shown?

c.   What information does this graph tell you?

d.   Based on this yield curve, if you needed to borrow money for longer than 1 year, would it make sense for you to borrow short term and renew the loan or borrow long term? Explain.

6-2 **REAL RISK-FREE RATE** You read in *The Wall Street Journal* that 30-day T-bills are currently yielding 5.5%. Your brother-in-law, a broker at Safe and Sound Securities, has given you the following estimates of current interest rate premiums:

- Inflation premium= 3.25%
- Liquidity premium = 0.6%
- Maturity risk premium = 1.8%
- Default risk premium = 2.15%

On the basis of these data, what is the real risk-free rate of return?

6-3 **EXPECTED INTEREST RATE** The real risk-free rate is 3%. Inflation is expected to be 2% this year and 4% during the next 2 years. Assume that the maturity risk premium is zero. What is the yield on 2-year Treasury securities? What is the yield on 3-year Treasury securities?

6-4 **DEFAULT RISK PREMIUM** A Treasury bond that matures in 10 years has a yield of 6%. A 10-year corporate bond has a yield of 8%. Assume that the liquidity premium on the corporate bond is 0.5%. What is the default risk premium on the corporate bond?

6-5 **MATURITY RISK PREMIUM** The real risk-free rate is 3%, and inflation is expected to be 3% for the next 2 years. A 2-year Treasury security yields 6.2%. What is the maturity risk premium for the 2-year security?

6-6 **INFLATION CROSS-PRODUCT** An analyst is evaluating securities in a developing nation where the inflation rate is very high. As a result, the analyst has been warned not to ignore the cross-product between the real rate and inflation. If the real risk-free rate is 5% and inflation is expected to be 16% each of the next 4 years, what is the yield on a 4-year security with no maturity, default, or liquidity risk? (Hint: Refer to "The Links between Expected Inflation and Interest Rates: A Closer Look" on page 201.)

6-7 **EXPECTATIONS THEORY** One-year Treasury securities yield 5%. The market anticipates that 1 year from now, 1-year Treasury securities will yield 6%. If the pure expectations theory is correct, what is the yield today for 2-year Treasury securities? Calculate the yield using a geometric average.

Intermediate Problems 8–16

6-8 **EXPECTATIONS THEORY** Interest rates on 4-year Treasury securities are currently 7%, while 6-year Treasury securities yield 7.5%. If the pure expectations theory is correct, what does the market believe that 2-year securities will be yielding 4 years from now? Calculate the yield using a geometric average.

6-9 **EXPECTED INTEREST RATE** The real risk-free rate is 3%. Inflation is expected to be 3% this year, 4% next year, and 3.5% thereafter. The maturity risk premium is estimated to be $0.05 \times (t - 1)\%$, where t = number of years to maturity. What is the yield on a 7-year Treasury note?

6-10 **INFLATION** Due to a recession, expected inflation this year is only 3%. However, the inflation rate in Year 2 and thereafter is expected to be constant at some level above 3%. Assume that the expectations theory holds and the real risk-free rate (r*) is 2%. If the yield on 3-year Treasury bonds equals the 1-year yield plus 2%, what inflation rate is expected after Year 1?

6-11 **DEFAULT RISK PREMIUM** A company's 5-year bonds are yielding 7.75% per year. Treasury bonds with the same maturity are yielding 5.2% per year, and the real risk-free rate (r*) is 2.3%. The average inflation premium is 2.5%; and the maturity risk premium is estimated to be $0.1 \times (t - 1)\%$, where t = number of years to maturity. If the liquidity premium is 1%, what is the default risk premium on the corporate bonds?

6-12 **MATURITY RISK PREMIUM** An investor in Treasury securities expects inflation to be 2.5% in Year 1, 3.2% in Year 2, and 3.6% each year thereafter. Assume that the real risk-free rate is 2.75% and that this rate will remain constant. Three-year Treasury securities yield 6.25%, while 5-year Treasury securities yield 6.80%. What is the difference in the maturity risk premiums (MRPs) on the two securities; that is, what is $MRP_5 - MRP_3$?

6-13 **DEFAULT RISK PREMIUM** The real risk-free rate, r*, is 2.5%. Inflation is expected to average 2.8% a year for the next 4 years, after which time inflation is expected to average 3.75% a year. Assume that there is no maturity risk premium. An 8-year corporate bond has a yield of 8.3%, which includes a liquidity premium of 0.75%. What is its default risk premium?

6-14 **EXPECTATIONS THEORY AND INFLATION** Suppose 2-year Treasury bonds yield 4.5%, while 1-year bonds yield 3%. r* is 1%, and the maturity risk premium is zero.

a. Using the expectations theory, what is the yield on a 1-year bond 1 year from now? Calculate the yield using a geometric average.

b. What is the expected inflation rate in Year 1? Year 2?

6-15 **EXPECTATIONS THEORY** Assume that the real risk-free rate is 2% and that the maturity risk premium is zero. If a 1-year Treasury bond yield is 5% and a 2-year Treasury bond yields 7%, what is the 1-year interest rate that is expected for Year 2? Calculate this yield using a geometric average. What inflation rate is expected during Year 2? Comment on why the average interest rate during the 2-year period differs from the 1-year interest rate expected for Year 2.

6-16 **INFLATION CROSS-PRODUCT** An analyst is evaluating securities in a developing nation where the inflation rate is very high. As a result, the analyst has been warned not to ignore the cross-product between the real rate and inflation. A 6-year security with no maturity, default, or liquidity risk has a yield of 20.84%. If the real risk-free rate is 6%, what average rate of inflation is expected in this country over the next 6 years? (Hint: Refer to "The Links between Expected Inflation and Interest Rates: A Closer Look" on page 201.)

Challenging Problems 17–19

6-17 **INTEREST RATE PREMIUMS** A 5-year Treasury bond has a 5.2% yield. A 10-year Treasury bond yields 6.4%, and a 10-year corporate bond yields 8.4%. The market expects that inflation will average 2.5% over the next 10 years ($IP_{10} = 2.5\%$). Assume that there is no maturity risk premium (MRP = 0) and that the annual real risk-free rate, r*, will remain constant over the next 10 years. (Hint: Remember that the default risk premium and the liquidity premium are zero for Treasury securities: DRP = LP = 0.) A 5-year corporate bond has the same default risk premium and liquidity premium as the 10-year corporate bond described. What is the yield on this 5-year corporate bond?

6-18 **YIELD CURVES** Suppose the inflation rate is expected to be 7% next year, 5% the following year, and 3% thereafter. Assume that the real risk-free rate, r*, will remain at 2% and that maturity risk premiums on Treasury securities rise from zero on very short-term bonds (those that mature in a few days) to 0.2% for 1-year securities. Furthermore, maturity risk premiums increase 0.2% for each year to maturity, up to a limit of 1.0% on 5-year or longer-term T-bonds.

a. Calculate the interest rate on 1-, 2-, 3-, 4-, 5-, 10-, and 20-year Treasury securities and plot the yield curve.

b. Suppose a AAA-rated company (which is the highest bond rating a firm can have) had bonds with the same maturities as the Treasury bonds. Estimate and plot what you believe a AAA-rated company's yield curve would look like on the same graph with the Treasury bond yield curve. (Hint: Think about the default risk premium on its long-term versus its short-term bonds.)

c. On the same graph, plot the approximate yield curve of a much riskier lower-rated company with a much higher risk of defaulting on its bonds.

6-19 **INFLATION AND INTEREST RATES** In late 1980, the U.S. Commerce Department released new data showing inflation was 15%. At the time, the prime rate of interest was 21%, a record high. However, many investors expected the new Reagan administration to be more effective in controlling inflation than the Carter administration had been. Moreover, many observers believed that the extremely high interest rates and generally tight credit, which resulted from the Federal Reserve System's attempts to curb the inflation rate, would lead to a recession, which, in turn, would lead to a decline in inflation and interest rates. Assume that, at the beginning of 1981, the expected inflation rate for 1981 was 13%; for 1982, 9%; for 1983, 7%; and for 1984 and thereafter, 6%.

a. What was the average expected inflation rate over the 5-year period 1981–1985? (Use the arithmetic average.)

b. Over the 5-year period, what average *nominal* interest rate would be expected to produce a 2% real risk-free return on 5-year Treasury securities? Assume MRP = 0.

c. Assuming a real risk-free rate of 2% and a maturity risk premium that equals $0.1 \times (t)\%$, where t is the number of years to maturity, estimate the interest rate in January 1981 on bonds that mature in 1, 2, 5, 10, and 20 years. Draw a yield curve based on these data.

d. Describe the general economic conditions that could lead to an upward-sloping yield curve.

e. If investors in early 1981 expected the inflation rate for every future year to be 10% (that is, $I_t = I_{t+1} = 10\%$ for t = 1 to ∞), what would the yield curve have looked like? Consider all the factors that are likely to affect the curve. Does your answer here make you question the yield curve you drew in Part c?

COMPREHENSIVE/SPREADSHEET PROBLEM

6-20 **INTEREST RATE DETERMINATION AND YIELD CURVES**

a. What effect would each of the following events likely have on the level of nominal interest rates?

   1. Households dramatically increase their savings rate.
   2. Corporations increase their demand for funds following an increase in investment opportunities.
   3. The government runs a larger-than-expected budget deficit.
   4. There is an increase in expected inflation.

b. Suppose you are considering two possible investment opportunities: a 12-year Treasury bond and a 7-year, A-rated corporate bond. The current real risk-free rate is 4%; and inflation is expected to be 2% for the next 2 years, 3% for the following 4 years, and 4% thereafter. The maturity risk premium is estimated by this formula: $MRP = 0.02(t - 1)\%$. The liquidity premium (LP) for the corporate bond is estimated to be 0.3%. You may determine the default risk premium (DRP), given the company's bond rating, from the table below. Remember to subtract the bond's LP from the corporate spread given in the table to arrive at the bond's DRP. What yield would you predict for each of these two investments?

	Rate	Corporate Bond Yield Spread = DRP + LP
U.S. Treasury	0.83%	——
AAA corporate	0.93	0.10%
AA corporate	1.29	0.46
A corporate	1.67	0.84

c. Given the following Treasury bond yield information, construct a graph of the yield curve.

Maturity	Yield
1 year	5.37%
2 years	5.47
3 years	5.65
4 years	5.71
5 years	5.64
10 years	5.75
20 years	6.33
30 years	5.94

d. Based on the information about the corporate bond provided in Part b, calculate yields and then construct a new yield curve graph that shows both the Treasury and the corporate bonds.

e. Which part of the yield curve (the left side or right side) is likely to be most volatile over time?

f. Using the Treasury yield information in Part c, calculate the following rates using geometric averages:

   1. The 1-year rate 1 year from now
   2. The 5-year rate 5 years from now
   3. The 10-year rate 10 years from now
   4. The 10-year rate 20 years from now

INTEGRATED CASE

MORTON HANDLEY & COMPANY

6-21   INTEREST RATE DETERMINATION Maria Juarez is a professional tennis player, and your firm manages her money. She has asked you to give her information about what determines the level of various interest rates. Your boss has prepared some questions for you to consider.

a. What are the four most fundamental factors that affect the cost of money, or the general level of interest rates, in the economy?

b. What is the real risk-free rate of interest (r*) and the nominal risk-free rate (r_{RF})? How are these two rates measured?

c. Define the terms *inflation premium (IP)*, *default risk premium (DRP)*, *liquidity premium (LP)*, and *maturity risk premium (MRP)*. Which of these premiums is included in determining the interest rate on (1) short-term U.S. Treasury securities, (2) long-term U.S. Treasury securities, (3) short-term corporate securities, and (4) long-term corporate securities? Explain how the premiums would vary over time and among the different securities listed.

d. What is the term structure of interest rates? What is a yield curve?

e. Suppose most investors expect the inflation rate to be 5% next year, 6% the following year, and 8% thereafter. The real risk-free rate is 3%. The maturity risk premium is zero for bonds that mature in 1 year or less and 0.1% for 2-year bonds; then the MRP increases by 0.1% per year thereafter for 20 years, after which it is stable. What is the interest rate on 1-, 10-, and 20-year Treasury bonds? Draw a yield curve with these data. What factors can explain why this constructed yield curve is upward-sloping?

f. At any given time, how would the yield curve facing a AAA-rated company compare with the yield curve for U.S. Treasury securities? At any given time, how would the yield curve facing a BB-rated company compare with the yield curve for U.S. Treasury securities? Draw a graph to illustrate your answer.

g. What is the pure expectations theory? What does the pure expectations theory imply about the term structure of interest rates?

h. Suppose you observe the following term structure for Treasury securities:

Maturity	Yield
1 year	6.0%
2 years	6.2
3 years	6.4
4 years	6.5
5 years	6.5

Assume that the pure expectations theory of the term structure is correct. (This implies that you can use the yield curve provided to "back out" the market's expectations about future interest rates.) What does the market expect will be the interest rate on 1-year securities 1 year from now? What does the market expect will be the interest rate on 3-year securities 2 years from now? Calculate these yields using geometric averages.

i. Describe how macroeconomic factors affect the level of interest rates. How do these factors explain why interest rates have been lower in recent years?

© John Clark/Shutterstock.com

Bonds and Their Valuation

Sizing Up Risk in the Bond Market

Many people view Treasury securities as a lackluster but ultrasafe investment. From a default standpoint, Treasuries are indeed our safest investments; but their prices can still decline in any given year if interest rates increase. This is especially true for long-term Treasury bonds, which lost nearly 15% in 2009. However, bonds can also perform well—Treasury bonds earned a return of nearly 26% in 2008, and they out-gained stocks in 7 of the 13 years between 2000 and 2012.

Not all bonds are alike, and they don't always move in the same direction. For example, corporate bonds are often callable and issuers can default on them, whereas Treasury bonds are not exposed to these risks. To compensate investors for these additional risks, corporate bonds typically have higher yields. When the economy is strong, corporate bonds generally produce higher returns than Treasuries because their promised returns are higher, and most make their promised payments because few go into default. However, when the economy weakens, concerns about defaults rise, which leads to declines in corporate bond prices. Furthermore, at any point in time, there are widespread differences among corporate bonds. For example, in February 2013, bonds issued by American Home Products Corporation with an AA credit rating maturing in 2023 were trading at a yield to maturity of 3.01%. At the same point in time, bonds issued by Brunswick Corporation with a BB– credit rating maturing in 2023 were trading at a yield to maturity of 6.47%.

A 2009 article in *The Wall Street Journal* highlighted the concerns that bond investors face in today's environment. The article offers what it refers to as "five key pointers":

1. *Watch Out for Defaults.* Investors should be wary of low-rated corporate bonds on the edge of default. The article cautions investors about increased default risk in the municipal market as state and local governments struggle to balance their budgets.

2. *Limit Your Rate Risk.* Rates are likely to increase over time as the economy hopefully continues to recover. As we see in this chapter, increasing interest rates reduce the value of bonds, and this effect is particularly important for investors of long-term bonds. For this reason, *The Wall Street Journal* writer suggests that some bond investors may want to gradually shift away from longer-maturity bonds.

3. *Consider a Passive Strategy.* This advice is directed specifically to investors in bond mutual funds. Rather than investing in actively managed funds where the portfolio manager is constantly moving in and out of different bonds, the author suggests that investors invest in index funds or exchange-traded funds (ETFs) that track a broad index of bonds.

4. *Have an Inflation Hedge.* Many analysts worry that down the road, higher government spending and a relaxed monetary policy will ultimately lead to higher levels of inflation. As we will see in this chapter, one way to hedge against rising inflation is to invest in Treasury securities that are indexed to inflation.

5. *Don't Try to Time the Market.* As we have seen in recent years, bond prices can move quickly and dramatically, which makes it difficult to effectively bet on where the market is heading next. Rather than trying to time the next move in the market, the article urges investors to adopt a more steady long-term strategy when it comes to bonds.

While these pointers are relevant in today's market, in many ways the advice is timeless. In the face of similar risks in 2001, a *BusinessWeek Online* article gave investors the following similar advice, which is still applicable today:

Take the same diversified approach to bonds as you do with stocks. Blend in U.S. government, corporate—both high-quality and high-yield—and perhaps even some foreign government debt. If you're investing taxable dollars, consider tax-exempt municipal bonds. And it doesn't hurt to layer in some inflation-indexed bonds.

Sources: Michael A. Pollack, "The New Bond Equation," *The Wall Street Journal* (online.wsj.com), August 3, 2009; "Ahead of the Tape: Junk Yields Flashing Back to '01 Slump," *The Wall Street Journal*, January 30, 2008, p. C1; *Ibbotson Stocks, Bonds, Bills, and Inflation: 2013 Valuation Yearbook* (Chicago: Morningstar, Inc., 2013); and Susan Scherreik, "Getting the Most Bang Out of Your Bonds," *BusinessWeek Online* (businessweek.com), November 12, 2001.

PUTTING THINGS IN PERSPECTIVE

In previous chapters, we noted that companies raise capital in two main forms: debt and equity. In this chapter, we examine the characteristics of bonds and discuss the various factors that influence bond prices. In Chapter 9, we will turn our attention to stocks and their valuation.

If you skim through *The Wall Street Journal,* you will see references to a wide variety of bonds. This variety may seem confusing; but in actuality, only a few characteristics distinguish the various types of bonds.

When you finish this chapter, you should be able to:

- Identify the different features of corporate and government bonds.
- Discuss how bond prices are determined in the market, what the relationship is between interest rates and bond prices, and how a bond's price changes over time as it approaches maturity.
- Calculate a bond's yield to maturity and yield to call if it is callable, and determine the "true" yield.
- Explain the different types of risk that bond investors and issuers face, and discuss how a bond's terms and collateral can be changed to affect its interest rate.

7-1 WHO ISSUES BONDS?

A **bond** is a long-term contract under which a borrower agrees to make payments of interest and principal on specific dates to the holders of the bond. Bonds are issued by corporations and government agencies that are looking for long-term debt capital. For example, on January 3, 2014, Allied Food Products borrowed $170 million by issuing $170 million of bonds. For convenience, we assume that Allied sold 170,000 individual bonds for $1,000 each. Actually, it could have sold one $170 million bond, 17 bonds each with a $10 million face value, or any other combination that totaled $170 million. In any event, Allied received the $170 million; and in exchange, it promised to make annual interest payments and to repay the $170 million on a specified maturity date.

Until the 1970s, most bonds were beautifully engraved pieces of paper and their key terms, including their face values, were spelled out on the bonds. Today, though, virtually all bonds are represented by electronic data stored in secure computers, much like the "money" in a bank checking account.

Bonds are grouped in several ways. One grouping is based on the issuer: the U.S. Treasury, corporations, state and local governments, and foreigners. Each bond differs with respect to risk and consequently its expected return.

Treasury bonds, generally called Treasuries and sometimes referred to as government bonds, are issued by the federal government.[1] It is reasonable to assume that the U.S. government will make good on its promised payments, so Treasuries have no default risk. However, these bonds' prices do decline when interest rates rise; so they are not completely riskless.

Corporate bonds are issued by business firms. Unlike Treasuries, corporates are exposed to default risk—if the issuing company gets into trouble, it may be unable to make the promised interest and principal payments and bondholders may suffer losses. Corporate bonds have different levels of default risk depending on the issuing company's characteristics and the terms of the specific bond. Default risk is often referred to as "credit risk"; and as we saw in Chapter 6, the larger this risk, the higher the interest rate investors demand.

Municipal bonds, or munis, is the term given to bonds issued by state and local governments. Like corporates, munis are exposed to some default risk; but they have one major advantage over all other bonds: As we discussed in Chapter 3, the interest earned on most munis is exempt from federal taxes and from state taxes if the holder is a resident of the issuing state. Consequently, the market interest rate on a muni is considerably lower than on a corporate bond of equivalent risk.

Foreign bonds are issued by a foreign government or a foreign corporation. All foreign corporate bonds are exposed to default risk, as are some foreign government bonds. Indeed in recent months, concerns have risen about possible defaults in many countries including Greece, Ireland, Portugal, and Spain. An additional risk exists when the bonds are denominated in a currency other than that of the investor's home currency. Consider, for example, a U.S. investor who purchases a corporate bond denominated in Japanese yen. At some point, the investor will want to close out his investment and convert the yen back to U.S. dollars. If the Japanese yen unexpectedly falls relative to the dollar, the investor will have fewer dollars than he originally expected to receive. Consequently, the investor could still lose money even if the bond does not default.

Bond
A long-term debt instrument.

Treasury Bonds
Bonds issued by the federal government, sometimes referred to as government bonds.

Corporate Bonds
Bonds issued by corporations.

Municipal Bonds
Bonds issued by state and local governments.

Foreign Bonds
Bonds issued by foreign governments or by foreign corporations.

---

[1]The U.S. Treasury actually calls its debt "bills," "notes," or "bonds." T-bills generally have maturities of 1 year or less at the time of issue, notes generally have original maturities of 2 to 7 years, and bonds originally mature in 8 to 30 years. There are technical differences between bills, notes, and bonds; but they are not important for our purposes. So we generally call all Treasury securities "bonds." Note too that a 30-year T-bond at the time of issue becomes a 29-year bond the next year, and it is a 1-year bond after 29 years.

SELF TEST

What is a bond?

What are the four main issuers of bonds?

Why are U.S. Treasury bonds not completely riskless?

In addition to default risk, what key risk do investors in foreign bonds face? Explain.

An excellent website on bonds is **finance.yahoo.com/bonds**. Yahoo's Bonds Center provides educational information as well as current information on treasury, municipal, and corporate bonds. In addition, it provides a bond screener that allows you to search for bonds with specified criteria.

7-2 KEY CHARACTERISTICS OF BONDS

Although all bonds have some common characteristics, different types of bonds can have different contractual features. For example, most corporate bonds have provisions that allow the issuer to pay them off early ("call" features), but the specific call provisions vary widely among different bonds. Similarly, some bonds are backed by specific assets that must be turned over to the bondholders if the issuer defaults, while other bonds have no such collateral backup. Differences in contractual provisions (and in the fundamental underlying financial strength of the companies backing the bonds) lead to differences in bonds' risks, prices, and expected returns. To understand bonds, it is essential that you understand the following terms.

7-2A PAR VALUE

Par Value
The face value of a bond.

The **par value** is the stated face value of the bond; for illustrative purposes, we generally assume a par value of $1,000, although any multiple of $1,000 (e.g., $10,000 or $10 million) can be used. The par value generally represents the amount of money the firm borrows and promises to repay on the maturity date.

7-2B COUPON INTEREST RATE

Coupon Payment
The specified number of dollars of interest paid each year.

Allied Food Products' bonds require the company to pay a fixed number of dollars of interest each year. This payment, generally referred to as the **coupon payment**, is set at the time the bond is issued and remains in force during the bond's life.[2] Typically, at the time a bond is issued, its coupon payment is set at a level that will induce investors to buy the bond at or near its par value. Most of the examples and problems throughout this text will focus on bonds with fixed coupon rates.

Coupon Interest Rate
The stated annual interest rate on a bond.

When this annual coupon payment is divided by the par value, the result is the **coupon interest rate**. For example, Allied's bonds have a $1,000 par value, and they pay $100 in interest each year. The bond's coupon payment is $100, so its coupon interest rate is $100/$1,000 = 10%. In this regard, the $100 is the annual income that an investor receives when he or she invests in the bond.

---

[2]Back when bonds were engraved pieces of paper rather than electronic information stored on a computer, each bond had a number of small (1/2- by 2-inch) dated coupons attached to them. On each interest payment date, the owner would "clip the coupon" for that date, send it to the company's paying agent, and receive a check for the interest. A 30-year semiannual bond would start with 60 coupons, whereas a 5-year annual payment bond would start with only 5 coupons. Today no physical coupons are involved, and interest checks are mailed or deposited automatically to the bonds' registered owners on the payment date. Even so, people continue to use the terms *coupon* and *coupon interest rate* when discussing bonds. You can think of the coupon interest rate as the *promised rate*.

Allied's bonds are **fixed-rate bonds** because the coupon rate is fixed for the life of the bond. In some cases, however, a bond's coupon payment is allowed to vary over time. These **floating-rate bonds** work as follows: The coupon rate is set for an initial period, often 6 months, after which it is adjusted every 6 months based on some open market rate. For example, the bond's rate may be adjusted so as to equal the 10-year Treasury bond rate plus a "spread" of 1.5 percentage points. Other provisions can be included in corporate bonds. For example, some can be converted at the holders' option into fixed-rate debt, and some floaters have upper limits (caps) and lower limits (floors) on how high or low the rate can go.

Some bonds pay no coupons at all but are offered at a discount below their par values and hence provide capital appreciation rather than interest income. These securities are called **zero coupon bonds** *(zeros)*. Other bonds pay some coupon interest, but not enough to induce investors to buy them at par. In general, any bond originally offered at a price significantly below its par value is called an **original issue discount (OID) bond**. Some of the details associated with issuing or investing in zero coupon bonds are discussed more fully in Web Appendix 7A.

7-2c MATURITY DATE

Bonds generally have a specified **maturity date** on which the par value must be repaid. Allied's bonds, which were issued on January 3, 2014, will mature on January 2, 2029; thus, they had a 15-year maturity at the time they were issued. Most bonds have **original maturities** (the maturity at the time the bond is issued) ranging from 10 to 40 years, but any maturity is legally permissible.[3] Of course, the effective maturity of a bond declines each year after it has been issued. Thus, Allied's bonds had a 15-year original maturity. But in 2015, a year later, they will have a 14-year maturity; a year after that, they will have a 13-year maturity; and so on.

7-2d CALL PROVISIONS

Many corporate and municipal bonds contain a **call provision** that gives the issuer the right to call the bonds for redemption. The call provision generally states that the issuer must pay the bondholders an amount greater than the par value if they are called. The additional sum, which is termed a *call premium,* is often equal to one year's interest. For example, the call premium on a 10-year bond with a 10% annual coupon and a par value of $1,000 might be $100, which means that the issuer would have to pay investors $1,100 (the par value plus the call premium) if it wanted to call the bonds. In most cases, the provisions in the bond contract are set so that the call premium declines over time as the bonds approach maturity. Also, while some bonds are immediately callable, in most cases, bonds are often not callable until several years after issue, generally 5 to 10 years. This is known as a *deferred call,* and such bonds are said to have *call protection.*

Companies are not likely to call bonds unless interest rates have declined significantly since the bonds were issued. Suppose a company sold bonds when interest rates were relatively high. Provided the issue is callable, the company could sell a new issue of low-yielding securities if and when interest rates drop, use the proceeds of the new issue to retire the high-rate issue, and thus reduce its interest expense. This process is called a *refunding operation.* Thus, the call

Fixed-Rate Bonds
Bonds whose interest rate is fixed for their entire life.

Floating-Rate Bonds
Bonds whose interest rate fluctuates with shifts in the general level of interest rates.

Zero Coupon Bonds
Bonds that pay no annual interest but are sold at a discount below par, thus compensating investors in the form of capital appreciation.

Original Issue Discount (OID) Bond
Any bond originally offered at a price below its par value.

Maturity Date
A specified date on which the par value of a bond must be repaid.

Original Maturity
The number of years to maturity at the time a bond is issued.

Call Provision
A provision in a bond contract that gives the issuer the right to redeem the bonds under specified terms prior to the normal maturity date.

---

[3]In July 1993, The Walt Disney Company, attempting to lock in a low interest rate, stretched the meaning of "long-term bond" by issuing the first 100-year bonds sold by any borrower in modern times. Soon after, Coca-Cola became the second company to sell 100-year bonds. Other companies that have issued 100-year bonds include Columbia/HCA Healthcare Corporation, BellSouth Telecommunications, Wisconsin Electric Power Company, and IBM.

privilege is valuable to the firm but detrimental to long-term investors, who will need to reinvest the funds they receive at the new and lower rates. Accordingly, the interest rate on a new issue of callable bonds will exceed that on the company's new noncallable bonds. For example, on February 28, 2014, Pacific Timber Company sold a bond issue yielding 6% that was callable immediately. On the same day, Northwest Milling Company sold an issue with similar risk and maturity that yielded only 5.5%; but its bonds were noncallable for 10 years. Investors were willing to accept a 0.5% lower coupon interest rate on Northwest's bonds for the assurance that the 5.5% interest rate would be earned for at least 10 years. Pacific, on the other hand, had to incur a 0.5% higher annual interest rate for the option of calling the bonds in the event of a decline in rates.

Note that the refunding operation is similar to a homeowner refinancing his or her home mortgage after a decline in interest rates. Consider, for example, a homeowner with an outstanding mortgage at 7%. If mortgage rates fall to 4%, the homeowner will probably find it beneficial to refinance the mortgage. There may be some fees involved in the refinancing, but the lower rate may be more than enough to offset those fees. The analysis required is essentially the same for homeowners and corporations.

7-2e SINKING FUNDS

Sinking Fund Provision
A provision in a bond contract that requires the issuer to retire a portion of the bond issue each year.

Some bonds include a **sinking fund provision** that facilitates the orderly retirement of the bond issue. Years ago firms were required to deposit money with a trustee, which invested the funds and then used the accumulated sum to retire the bonds when they matured. Today, though, sinking fund provisions require the issuer to buy back a specified percentage of the issue each year. A failure to meet the sinking fund requirement constitutes a default, which may throw the company into bankruptcy. Therefore, a sinking fund is a mandatory payment.

Suppose a company issued $100 million of 20-year bonds and it is required to call 5% of the issue, or $5 million of bonds, each year. In most cases, the issuer can handle the sinking fund requirement in either of two ways:

1. It can call in for redemption, at par value, the required $5 million of bonds. The bonds are numbered serially, and those called for redemption would be determined by a lottery administered by the trustee.

2. The company can buy the required number of bonds on the open market.

The firm will choose the least-cost method. If interest rates have fallen since the bond was issued, the bond will sell for more than its par value. In this case, the firm will use the call option. However, if interest rates have risen, the bonds will sell at a price below par; so the firm can and will buy $5 million par value of bonds in the open market for less than $5 million. Note that a call for sinking fund purposes is generally different from a refunding call because most sinking fund calls require no call premium. However, only a small percentage of the issue is normally callable in a given year.

Although sinking funds are designed to protect investors by ensuring that the bonds are retired in an orderly fashion, these funds work to the detriment of bondholders if the bond's coupon rate is higher than the current market rate. For example, suppose the bond has a 10% coupon but similar bonds now yield only 7.5%. A sinking fund call at par would require a long-term investor to give up a bond that pays $100 of interest and then to reinvest in a bond that pays only $75 per year. This is an obvious disadvantage to those bondholders whose bonds are called. On balance, however, bonds that have a sinking fund are regarded as being safer than those without such a provision; so at the time they are issued, sinking fund bonds have lower coupon rates than otherwise similar bonds without sinking funds.

7-2f OTHER FEATURES

Several other types of bonds are used sufficiently often to warrant mention.[4] First, **convertible bonds** are bonds that are exchangeable into shares of common stock at a fixed price at the option of the bondholder. Convertibles offer investors the chance for capital gains if the stock price increases, but that feature enables the issuing company to set a lower coupon rate than on nonconvertible debt with similar credit risk. Bonds issued with **warrants** are similar to convertibles; but instead of giving the investor an option to exchange the bonds for stock, warrants give the holder an option to buy stock for a stated price, thereby providing a capital gain if the stock's price rises. Because of this factor, bonds issued with warrants, like convertibles, carry lower coupon rates than otherwise similar non-convertible bonds.

Whereas callable bonds give the *issuer* the right to retire the debt prior to maturity, **putable bonds** allow *investors* to require the company to pay in advance. If interest rates rise, investors will put the bonds back to the company and reinvest in higher coupon bonds. Yet another type of bond is the **income bond**, which pays interest only if the issuer has earned enough money to pay the interest. Thus, income bonds cannot bankrupt a company; but from an investor's standpoint, they are riskier than "regular" bonds. Yet another bond is the **indexed,** or **purchasing power, bond**. The interest rate is based on an inflation index such as the consumer price index (CPI); so the interest paid rises automatically when the inflation rate rises, thus protecting bondholders against inflation. As we mentioned in Chapter 6, the U.S. Treasury is the main issuer of indexed bonds. Recall that these Treasury Inflation Protected Securities (TIPS) generally pay a real return varying from 1% to 3%, plus the rate of inflation during the past year.

Convertible Bonds
Bonds that are exchangeable at the option of the holder for the issuing firm's common stock.

Warrants
Long-term options to buy a stated number of shares of common stock at a specified price.

Putable Bonds
Bonds with a provision that allows investors to sell them back to the company prior to maturity at a prearranged price.

Income Bond
A bond that pays interest only if it is earned.

Indexed (Purchasing Power) Bond
A bond that has interest payments based on an inflation index so as to protect the holder from inflation.

SELF TEST

Define floating-rate bonds, zero coupon bonds, callable bonds, putable bonds, income bonds, convertible bonds, and inflation-indexed bonds (TIPS).

Which is riskier to an investor, other things held constant—a callable bond or a putable bond? Explain.

In general, how is the rate on a floating-rate bond determined?

What are the two ways sinking funds can be handled? Which alternative will be used if interest rates have risen? If interest rates have fallen?

---

[4]An article by John D. Finnerty and Douglas R. Emery reviews new types of debt (and other) securities that have been created in recent years. See "Corporate Securities Innovations: An Update," *Journal of Applied Finance: Theory, Practice, Education*, vol. 12, no. 1 (Spring–Summer 2002), pp. 21–47.

7-3 BOND VALUATION

The value of any financial asset—a stock, a bond, a lease, or even a physical asset such as an apartment building or a piece of machinery—is the present value of the cash flows the asset is expected to produce. The cash flows for a standard coupon-bearing bond, like those of Allied Foods, consist of interest payments during the bond's 15-year life plus the amount borrowed (generally the par value) when the bond matures. In the case of a floating-rate bond, the interest payments vary over time. For zero coupon bonds, there are no interest payments, so the only cash flow is the face amount when the bond matures. For a "regular" bond with a fixed coupon, like Allied's, here is the situation:

Where:
r_d = the market rate of interest on the bond, 10%. This is the discount rate used to calculate the present value of the cash flows, which is also the bond's price. In Chapter 6, we discussed in detail the various factors that determine market interest rates. Note that r_d is *not* the coupon interest rate. However, r_d is equal to the coupon rate at times, especially the day the bond is issued; and when the two rates are equal, as in this case, the bond sells at par.

N = the number of years before the bond matures = 15. N declines over time after the bond has been issued; so a bond that had a maturity of 15 years when it was issued (original maturity = 15) will have N = 14 after 1 year, N = 13 after 2 years, and so forth. At this point, we assume that the bond pays interest once a year, or annually; so N is measured in years. Later on we will analyze semiannual payment bonds, which pay interest every 6 months.

INT = dollars of interest paid each year = Coupon rate × Par value = 0.10($1,000) = $100. In calculator terminology, INT = PMT = 100. If the bond had been a semiannual payment bond, the payment would have been $50 every 6 months. The payment would have been zero if Allied had issued zero coupon bonds, and it would have varied over time if the bond had been a "floater."

M = the par, or maturity, value of the bond = $1,000. This amount must be paid at maturity. Back in the 1970s and before, when paper bonds with paper coupons were used, most bonds had a $1,000 value. Now with computer-entry bonds, the par amount purchased can vary; but in the text we use $1,000 for simplicity.

We can now redraw the time line to show the numerical values for all variables except the bond's value (and price, assuming an equilibrium exists), V_B:

The following general equation can be solved to find the value of any bond:

$$\text{Bond's value} = V_B = \frac{INT}{(1+r_d)^1} + \frac{INT}{(1+r_d)^2} + \cdots + \frac{INT}{(1+r_d)^N} + \frac{M}{(1+r_d)^N}$$

$$= \sum_{t=1}^{N} \frac{INT}{(1+r_d)^t} + \frac{M}{(1+r_d)^N}$$

7.1

Inserting values for the Allied bond, we have

$$V_B = \sum_{t=1}^{15} \frac{\$100}{(1.10)^t} + \frac{\$1,000}{(1.10)^{15}}$$

The cash flows consist of an annuity of N years plus a lump sum payment at the end of Year N, and this fact is reflected in Equation 7.1.

We could simply discount each cash flow back to the present and sum those PVs to find the bond's value; see Figure 7.1 for an example. However, this procedure is not very efficient, especially when the bond has many years to maturity. Therefore, we use a financial calculator to solve the problem. Here is the setup:

15	10		100	1000
N	I/YR	PV	PMT	FV
		= −1,000		

Simply input $N = 15, r_d = I/YR = 10, INT = PMT = 100$, and $M = FV = 1000$; then press the PV key to find the bond's value, $1,000.[5] Because the PV is an outflow to the investor, it is shown with a negative sign. The calculator is programmed to solve Equation 7.1. It finds the PV of an annuity of $100 per year for 15 years discounted at 10%; then it finds the PV of the $1,000 maturity payment; then it adds those two PVs to find the bond's value. In this Allied example, the bond is selling at a price equal to its par value.

Whenever the bond's market, or going, rate, r_d, is equal to its coupon rate, a *fixed-rate* bond will sell at its par value. Normally, the coupon rate is set at the going rate in the market the day a bond is issued, causing it to sell at par initially.

The coupon rate remains fixed after the bond is issued, but interest rates in the market move up and down. Looking at Equation 7.1, we see that an *increase* in the market interest rate (r_d) causes the price of an outstanding bond to *fall*, whereas a *decrease* in the rate causes the bond's price to *rise*. For example, if the market interest rate on Allied's bond increased to 15% immediately after it was issued, we would recalculate the price with the new market interest rate as follows:

15	15		100	1000
N	I/YR	PV	PMT	FV
		= −707.63		

---

[5]Spreadsheets can also be used to solve for the bond's value. The PV of this bond can be calculated using Excel's PV function:

= PV(0.1,15,100,1000)

PV(rate, nper, pmt, [fv], [type])

This gives the bond's value as $1,000. Note that type is left blank because cash flows occur at year-end.

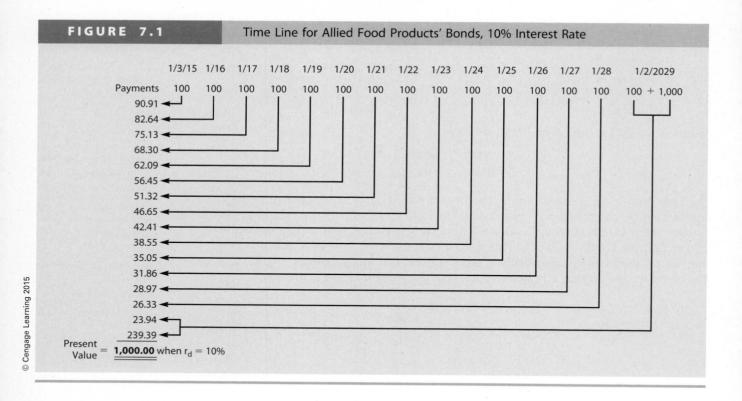

FIGURE 7.1   Time Line for Allied Food Products' Bonds, 10% Interest Rate

The bond's price would fall to $707.63, well below par, as a result of the increase in interest rates. Whenever the going rate of interest *rises above* the coupon rate, a fixed-rate bond's price will fall *below* its par value; this type of bond is called a **discount bond**.

On the other hand, bond prices rise when market interest rates fall. For example, if the market interest rate on Allied's bond decreased to 5% immediately after it was issued, we would once again recalculate its price as follows:

Discount Bond

A bond that sells below its par value; occurs whenever the going rate of interest is above the coupon rate.

= −1,518.98

In this case, the price rises to $1,518.98. In general, whenever the going interest rate *falls below* the coupon rate, a fixed-rate bond's price will rise *above* its par value; this type of bond is called a **premium bond**.

To summarize, here is the situation:

Premium Bond

A bond that sells above its par value; occurs whenever the going rate of interest is below the coupon rate.

r_d = coupon rate, fixed-rate bond sells at par; hence, it is a *par bond*.
r_d > coupon rate, fixed-rate bond sells below par; hence, it is a *discount bond*.
r_d < coupon rate, fixed-rate bond sells above par; hence, it is a *premium bond*.

QUICK QUESTION

QUESTION:

A friend of yours just invested in an outstanding bond with a 5% annual coupon and a remaining maturity of 10 years. The bond has a par value of $1,000 and the market interest rate is currently 7%. How much did your friend pay for the bond? Is it a par, premium, or discount bond?

ANSWER:

Using a financial calculator, we can determine that your friend paid **$859.53** for the bond.

10	7		50	1000
N	I/YR	PV	PMT	FV
		= −859.53		

Using Excel's PV function we solve for the bond's value as follows:

$$= PV(0.07,10,50,1000)$$

PV(rate, nper, pmt, [fv], [type])

Here we find that the bond's value is equal to **$859.53**.

Because the bond's coupon rate (5%) is less than the current market interest rate (7%), the bond is a discount bond—reflecting that interest rates have increased since this bond was originally issued.

SELF TEST

A bond that matures in 8 years has a par value of $1,000 and an annual coupon payment of $70; its market interest rate is 9%. What is its price? **($889.30)**

A bond that matures in 12 years has a par value of $1,000 and an annual coupon rate of 10%; the market interest rate is 8%. What is its price? **($1,150.72)**

Which of those two bonds is a discount bond, and which is a premium bond? Explain.

7-4 BOND YIELDS

If you examine the bond market table of *The Wall Street Journal* or a price sheet put out by a bond dealer, you will typically see information regarding each bond's maturity date, price, and coupon interest rate. You will also see a reported yield. Unlike the coupon interest rate, which is fixed, the bond's yield varies from day to day depending on current market conditions.

To be most useful, the bond's yield should give us an estimate of the rate of return we would earn if we purchased the bond today and held it over its remaining life. If the bond is not callable, its remaining life is its years to maturity. If it is callable, its remaining life is the years to maturity if it is not called or the years to the call if it is called. In the following sections, we explain how to calculate those two possible yields and which one is likely to be earned by an investor.

7-4A YIELD TO MATURITY

Yield to Maturity (YTM)
The rate of return earned on a bond if it is held to maturity.

Suppose you were offered a 14-year, 10% annual coupon, $1,000 par value bond at a price of $1,494.93. What rate of interest would you earn on your investment if you bought the bond, held it to maturity, and received the promised interest and maturity payments? This rate is called the bond's **yield to maturity (YTM)**, and it is the interest rate generally discussed by investors when they talk about rates of return and the rate reported by *The Wall Street Journal* and other publications. To find the YTM, all you need to do is solve Equation 7.1 for r_d as follows:

$$V_B = \frac{INT}{(1+r_d)^1} + \frac{INT}{(1+r_d)^2} + \cdots + \frac{INT}{(1+r_d)^N} + \frac{M}{(1+r_d)^N}$$

$$\$1,494.93 = \frac{\$100}{(1+r_d)^1} + \cdots + \frac{\$100}{(1+r_d)^{14}} + \frac{\$1,000}{(1+r_d)^{14}}$$

You can substitute values for r_d until you find a value that "works" and force the sum of the PVs in the equation to equal $1,494.93. However, finding r_d = YTM by trial and error would be a tedious, time-consuming process. However, as you might guess, the calculation is easy with a financial calculator.[6] Here is the setup:

Simply enter N = 14, PV = −1494.93, PMT = 100, and FV = 1000; then press the I/YR key. The answer, 5%, will appear.

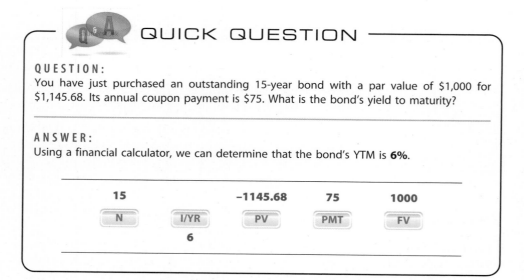

QUICK QUESTION

QUESTION:
You have just purchased an outstanding 15-year bond with a par value of $1,000 for $1,145.68. Its annual coupon payment is $75. What is the bond's yield to maturity?

ANSWER:
Using a financial calculator, we can determine that the bond's YTM is **6%**.

---

[6]You can also find the YTM with a spreadsheet. In Excel, you use the RATE function:

= RATE(14,100,−1494.93,1000)

RATE(nper, pmt, pv, [fv], [type], [guess])

This gives the YTM as 5%. Note that we didn't need to specify a value for type (because the cash flows occur at the end of the year) or guess.

Using Excel's RATE function we solve for the bond's YTM as follows:

$$= \text{RATE}(15,75,-1145.68,1000)$$

RATE(nper, pmt, pv, [fv], [type], [guess])

Here we find the bond's YTM is equal to **6%**.

Because the bond's coupon rate ($75/$1,000 = 7.5%) is greater than its YTM (6%), the bond is a premium bond—indicating that interest rates have declined since the bond was originally issued.

The yield to maturity can also be viewed as the bond's *promised rate of return,* which is the return that investors will receive if all of the promised payments are made. However, the yield to maturity equals the *expected rate of return* only when (1) the probability of default is zero and (2) the bond cannot be called. If there is some default risk or the bond may be called, there is some chance that the promised payments to maturity will not be received, in which case the calculated yield to maturity will exceed the expected return.

Note also that a bond's calculated yield to maturity changes whenever interest rates in the economy change, which is almost daily. An investor who purchases a bond and holds it until it matures will receive the YTM that existed on the purchase date, but the bond's calculated YTM will change frequently between the purchase date and the maturity date.

7-4b YIELD TO CALL

If you purchase a bond that is callable and the company calls it, you do not have the option of holding it to maturity. Therefore, the yield to maturity would not be earned. For example, if Allied's 10% coupon bonds were callable and if interest rates fell from 10% to 5%, the company could call in the 10% bonds, replace them with 5% bonds, and save $100 − $50 = $50 interest per bond per year. This would be beneficial to the company but not to its bondholders.

If current interest rates are well below an outstanding bond's coupon rate, a callable bond is likely to be called; and investors will estimate its most likely rate of return as the **yield to call (YTC)** rather than the yield to maturity. To calculate the YTC, we modify Equation 7.1, using years to call as N and the call price rather than the maturity value as the ending payment. Here's the modified equation:

Yield to Call (YTC)
The rate of return earned on a bond when it is called before its maturity date.

$$\text{Price of bond} = \sum_{t=1}^{N} \frac{\text{INT}}{(1+r_d)^t} + \frac{\text{Call price}}{(1+r_d)^N} \qquad \textbf{7.2}$$

Here N is the number of years until the company can call the bond; call price is the price the company must pay in order to call the bond (it is often set equal to the par value plus one year's interest); and r_d is the YTC.

To illustrate, suppose Allied's bonds had a deferred call provision that permitted the company, if it desired, to call them 10 years after their issue date at a price of $1,100. Suppose further that interest rates had fallen and that 1 year after issuance, the going interest rate had declined, causing their price to rise to $1,494.93. Here is the time line and the setup for finding the bonds' YTC with a financial calculator:

0		1		2		8		9
YTC = ?					•••			
−1,494.93		100		100		100		100
								1,100

9		−1494.93	100	1100
N	I/YR	PV	PMT	FV
	4.21			

The YTC is 4.21%—this is the return you would earn if you bought an Allied bond at a price of $1,494.93 and it was called 9 years from today. (It could not be called until 10 years after issuance. One year has gone by, so there are 9 years left until the first call date.)

 QUICK QUESTION

QUESTION:
You have just purchased an outstanding 15-year bond with a par value of $1,000 for $1,145.68. Its annual coupon payment is $75. We calculated the YTM of this bond (6%) in the Quick Question box on page 228. Now, assume that this bond is callable in 7 years at a price of $1,075. What is the bond's YTC? If the yield curve remains flat at its current level during this time period, would you expect to earn the YTM or YTC?

ANSWER:
Using a financial calculator, we can determine that the bond's YTC is **5.81%**.

7		−1145.68	75	1075
N	I/YR	PV	PMT	FV
	5.81			

Using Excel's RATE function we solve for the bond's YTC as follows:

= RATE(7,75,−1145.68,1075)

RATE(nper, pmt, pv, [fv], [type], [guess])

Here we find the bond's YTC is equal to **5.81%**.

This bond sells at a premium so interest rates have declined since the bond was originally issued. If the yield curve remained flat at this current level during the next 7 years, you would expect the firm to call the bond and issue bonds at the lower 6% interest rate, assuming the cost of doing so was lower than the $75 − $60 = $15 savings per bond.

A company is more likely to call its bonds if they are able to replace their current high-coupon debt with cheaper financing. Broadly speaking, a bond is more likely to be called if its price is above par—because a price above par means that the going market interest rate (the yield to maturity) is less than the coupon rate. So, do you think Allied *will* call its 10% bonds when they become callable? Allied's action will depend on what the going interest rate is when they become callable. If the going rate remains at $r_d = 5\%$, Allied could save 10% − 5% = 5%, or $50 per bond per year; so it would call the 10% bonds and replace them with a new 5% issue. There would be some cost to the company to refund the bonds; but because the interest savings would most likely be worth the cost, Allied would probably refund them. Therefore, you should expect to earn the YTC = 4.21% rather than the YTM = 5% if you purchased the bond under the indicated conditions.

In the balance of this chapter, we assume that bonds are not callable unless otherwise noted. However, some of the end-of-chapter problems deal with yield to call.[7]

Explain the difference between yield to maturity (YTM) and yield to call (YTC).

Halley Enterprises' bonds currently sell for $975. They have a 7-year maturity, an annual coupon of $90, and a par value of $1,000. What is their yield to maturity? **(9.51%)**

The Henderson Company's bonds currently sell for $1,275. They pay a $120 annual coupon, have a 20-year maturity, and a par value of $1,000, but they can be called in 5 years at $1,120. What are their YTM and their YTC, and if the yield curve remained flat which rate would investors expect to earn? **(8.99%; 7.31%; YTC)**

7-5 CHANGES IN BOND VALUES OVER TIME

When a coupon bond is issued, the coupon is generally set at a level that causes the bond's market price to equal its par value. If a lower coupon were set, investors would not be willing to pay $1,000 for the bond; but if a higher coupon were set, investors would clamor for it and bid its price up over $1,000. Investment bankers can judge quite precisely the coupon rate that will cause a bond to sell at its $1,000 par value.

A bond that has just been issued is known as a *new issue*. Once it has been issued, it is an *outstanding bond*, also called a *seasoned issue*. Newly issued bonds generally sell at prices very close to par, but the prices of outstanding bonds can vary widely from par. Except for floating-rate bonds, coupon payments are constant; so when economic conditions change, a bond with a $100 coupon that sold at its $1,000 par value when it was issued will sell for more or less than $1,000 thereafter.

Among its outstanding bonds, Allied currently has three equally risky issues that will mature in 15 years:

- Allied's just-issued 15-year bonds have a 10% annual coupon. They were issued at par, which means that the market interest rate on their issue date was also 10%. Because the coupon rate equals the market interest rate, these bonds are trading at par, or $1,000.

- Five years ago Allied issued 20-year bonds with a 7% annual coupon. These bonds currently have 15 years remaining until maturity. They were originally issued at par, which means that 5 years ago the market interest rate was 7%. Currently, this bond's coupon rate is less than the 10% market rate, so they sell

---

[7]Brokerage houses occasionally report a bond's *current yield,* defined as the annual interest payment divided by the current price. For example, if Allied's 10% coupon bonds were selling for $985, the current yield would be $100/$985 = 10.15%. Unlike the YTM or YTC, the current yield *does not* represent the actual return that investors should expect because it does not account for the capital gain or loss that will be realized if the bond is held until it matures or is called. The current yield was popular before calculators and computers came along because it was easy to calculate. However, it can be misleading, and now it's easy enough to calculate the YTM and YTC.

at a discount. Using a financial calculator or spreadsheet, we can quickly find that they have a price of $771.82. (Set N = 15, I/YR = 10, PMT = 70, and FV = 1000 and solve for the PV to calculate the price.)

- Ten years ago Allied issued 25-year bonds with a 13% annual coupon. These bonds currently have 15 years remaining until maturity. They were originally issued at par, which means that 10 years ago the market interest rate must have been 13%. Because their coupon rate is greater than the current market rate, they sell at a premium. Using a financial calculator or spreadsheet, we can find that their price is $1,228.18. (Set N = 15, I/YR = 10, PMT = 130, and FV = 1000 and solve for the PV to determine the price.)

Each of these three bonds has a 15-year maturity; each has the same credit risk; and thus each has the same market interest rate, 10%. However, the bonds have different prices because of their different coupon rates.

Now let's consider what would happen to the prices of these three bonds over the 15 years until they mature, assuming that market interest rates remain constant at 10% and Allied does not default on its payments. Table 7.1 demonstrates how the prices of each of these bonds will change over time if market interest rates remain at 10%. One year from now each bond will have a maturity of 14 years—that is, N = 14. With a financial calculator, override N = 15 with N = 14 and press the PV key; that gives you the value of each bond 1 year from now. Continuing, set N = 13, N = 12, and so forth, to see how the prices change over time.

Table 7.1 also shows the current yield (which is the coupon interest divided by the bond's price), the capital gains yield, and the total return over time. For any given year, the *capital gains yield* is calculated as the bond's annual change in price divided by the beginning-of-year price. For example, if a bond was selling for $1,000 at the beginning of the year and $1,035 at the end of the year, its capital gains yield for the year would be $35/$1,000 = 3.5%. (If the bond was selling at a premium, its price would decline over time. Then the capital gains yield would be negative, but it would be offset by a high current yield.) A bond's total return is equal to the current yield plus the capital gains yield. In the absence of default risk and assuming market equilibrium, the total return is also equal to YTM and the market interest rate, which in our example is 10%.

Figure 7.2 plots the three bonds' predicted prices as calculated in Table 7.1. Notice that the bonds have very different price paths over time but that at maturity, all three will sell at their par value of $1,000. Here are some points about the prices of the bonds over time:

- The price of the 10% coupon bond trading at par will remain at $1,000 if the market interest rate remains at 10%. Therefore, its current yield will remain at 10% and its capital gains yield will be zero each year.

- The 7% bond trades at a discount; but at maturity, it must sell at par because that is the amount the company will pay its bondholders. Therefore, its price must rise over time.

- The 13% coupon bond trades at a premium. However, its price must be equal to its par value at maturity; so the price must decline over time.

While the prices of the 7% and 13% coupon bonds move in opposite directions over time, each bond provides investors with the same total return, 10%, which is also the total return on the 10% coupon par value bond. The discount bond has a low coupon rate (and therefore a low current yield), but it provides a capital gain

TABLE 7.1 Calculation of Current Yields, Capital Gains Yields, and Total Returns for 7%, 10%, and 13% Coupon Bonds When the Market Rate Remains Constant at 10%

Number of Years until Maturity	7% Coupon Bond				10% Coupon Bond				13% Coupon Bond			
	Price[a]	Expected Current Yield[b]	Expected Capital Gains Yield[c]	Expected Total Return[d]	Price[a]	Expected Current Yield[b]	Expected Capital Gains Yield[c]	Expected Total Return[d]	Price[a]	Expected Current Yield[b]	Expected Capital Gains Yield[c]	Expected Total Return[d]
15	$771.82	9.1%	0.9%	10.0%	$1,000.00	10.0%	0.0%	10.0%	$1,228.18	10.6%	−0.6%	10.0%
14	779.00	9.0	1.0	10.0	1,000.00	10.0	0.0	10.0	1,221.00	10.6	−0.6	10.0
13	786.90	8.9	1.1	10.0	1,000.00	10.0	0.0	10.0	1,213.10	10.7	−0.7	10.0
12	795.59	8.8	1.2	10.0	1,000.00	10.0	0.0	10.0	1,204.41	10.8	−0.8	10.0
11	805.15	8.7	1.3	10.0	1,000.00	10.0	0.0	10.0	1,194.85	10.9	−0.9	10.0
10	815.66	8.6	1.4	10.0	1,000.00	10.0	0.0	10.0	1,184.34	11.0	−1.0	10.0
9	827.23	8.5	1.5	10.0	1,000.00	10.0	0.0	10.0	1,172.77	11.1	−1.1	10.0
8	839.95	8.3	1.7	10.0	1,000.00	10.0	0.0	10.0	1,160.05	11.2	−1.2	10.0
7	853.95	8.2	1.8	10.0	1,000.00	10.0	0.0	10.0	1,146.05	11.3	−1.3	10.0
6	869.34	8.1	1.9	10.0	1,000.00	10.0	0.0	10.0	1,130.66	11.5	−1.5	10.0
5	886.28	7.9	2.1	10.0	1,000.00	10.0	0.0	10.0	1,113.72	11.7	−1.7	10.0
4	904.90	7.7	2.3	10.0	1,000.00	10.0	0.0	10.0	1,095.10	11.9	−1.9	10.0
3	925.39	7.6	2.4	10.0	1,000.00	10.0	0.0	10.0	1,074.61	12.1	−2.1	10.0
2	947.93	7.4	2.6	10.0	1,000.00	10.0	0.0	10.0	1,052.07	12.4	−2.4	10.0
1	972.73	7.2	2.8	10.0	1,000.00	10.0	0.0	10.0	1,027.27	12.7	−2.7	10.0
0	1,000.00				1,000.00				1,000.00			

Notes:
[a] Using a financial calculator, the price of each bond is calculated by entering the data for N, I/YR, PMT, and FV, then solving for PV = the bond's value.
[b] The expected current yield is calculated as the annual interest divided by the price of the bond.
[c] The expected capital gains yield is calculated as the difference between the end-of-year bond price and the beginning-of-year bond price divided by the beginning-of-year bond price.
[d] The expected total return is the sum of the expected current yield and the expected capital gains yield.

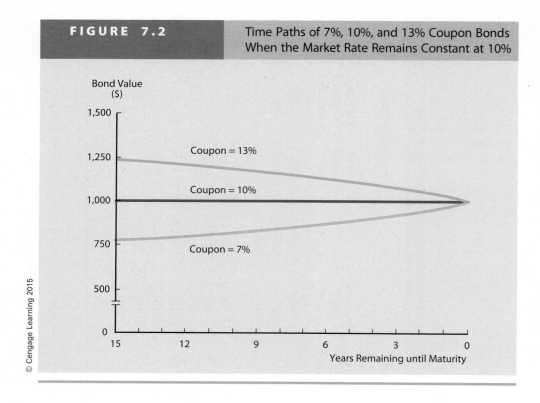

FIGURE 7.2 Time Paths of 7%, 10%, and 13% Coupon Bonds When the Market Rate Remains Constant at 10%

© Cengage Learning 2015

each year. In contrast, the premium bond has a high current yield, but it has an expected capital loss each year.[8]

SELF TEST

What is meant by the terms *new issue* and *seasoned issue?*

Last year a firm issued 20-year, 8% annual coupon bonds at a par value of $1,000.

a. Suppose that one year later the going market interest rate drops to 6%. What is the new price of the bonds assuming they now have 19 years to maturity? **($1,223.16)**

b. Suppose that one year after issue, the going market interest rate is 10% (rather than 6%). What would the price have been? **($832.70)**

Why do the prices of fixed-rate bonds fall if expectations for inflation rise?

7-6 BONDS WITH SEMIANNUAL COUPONS

Although some bonds pay interest annually, the vast majority actually make payments semiannually. To evaluate semiannual bonds, we must modify the valuation model (Equation 7.1) as follows:

---

[8]In this example (and throughout the text), we ignore the tax effects associated with purchasing different types of bonds. For coupon bonds, under the current Tax Code (June 2013), coupon payments are taxed as ordinary income, whereas long-term capital gains are taxed at the long-term capital gains tax rate. As we mentioned in Chapter 3, for most investors, the long-term capital gains tax rate is lower than the personal tax rate. Moreover, while coupon payments are taxed each year, capital gains taxes are deferred until the bond is sold or matures. Consequently, all else equal, investors end up paying lower taxes on discount bonds because a greater percentage of their total return comes in the form of capital gains. For details on the tax treatment of zero coupon bonds, see Web Appendix 7A.

1. Divide the annual coupon interest payment by 2 to determine the dollars of interest paid each six months.
2. Multiply the years to maturity, N, by 2 to determine the number of semiannual periods.
3. Divide the nominal (quoted) interest rate, r_d, by 2 to determine the periodic (semiannual) interest rate.

On a time line, there would be twice as many payments, but each would be half as large as with an annual payment bond. Making the indicated changes results in the following equation for finding a semiannual bond's value:

$$V_B = \sum_{t=1}^{2N} \frac{INT/2}{(1 + r_d/2)^t} + \frac{M}{(1 + r_d/2)^{2N}}$$

 7.1a

To illustrate, assume that Allied Food's 15-year bonds as discussed in Section 7-3 pay $50 of interest each 6 months rather than $100 at the end of each year. Thus, each interest payment is only half as large but there are twice as many of them. We would describe the coupon rate as "10% with semiannual payments."[9]

When the going (nominal) rate is $r_d = 5\%$ with semiannual compounding, the value of a 15-year, 10% semiannual coupon bond that pays $50 interest every 6 months is found as follows:

30	2.5		50	1000
N	I/YR	PV	PMT	FV
		= −1,523.26		

Enter N = 30, r_d = I/YR = 2.5, PMT = 50, and FV = 1000; then press the PV key to obtain the bond's value, $1,523.26. The value with semiannual interest payments is slightly larger than $1,518.98, the value when interest is paid annually as we calculated in Section 7-3. This higher value occurs because each interest payment is received somewhat faster under semiannual compounding.

Alternatively, when we know the price of a semiannual bond, we can easily back out the bond's nominal yield to maturity. In the previous example, if you were told that a 15-year bond with a 10% semiannual coupon was selling for $1,523.26, you could solve for the bond's periodic interest rate as follows:

30		−1523.26	50	1000
N	I/YR	PV	PMT	FV
	2.5			

---

[9]In this situation, the coupon rate of "10% paid semiannually" is the rate that bond dealers, corporate treasurers, and investors generally discuss. Of course, if this bond were issued at par, its *effective annual rate* would be higher than 10%.

$$EAR = EFF\% = \left(1 + \frac{r_{NOM}}{M}\right)^M - 1 = \left(1 + \frac{0.10}{2}\right)^2 - 1 = (1.05)^2 - 1 = 10.25\%$$

Because 10% with annual payments is quite different from 10% with semiannual payments, we have assumed a change in effective rates in this section from the situation in Section 7-3, where we assumed 10% with annual payments.

In this case, enter N = 30, PV = −1523.26, PMT = 50, and FV = 1000; then press the I/YR key to obtain the interest rate per semiannual period, 2.5%. Multiplying by 2, we calculate the bond's nominal yield to maturity to be 5%.[10]

QUICK QUESTION

QUESTION:

You have just purchased an outstanding noncallable, 15-year bond with a par value of $1,000. Assume that this bond pays interest of 7.5%, with semiannual compounding. If the going (nominal) annual rate is 6%, what price did you pay for this bond? How does the price compare to the price of the annual coupon bond?

ANSWER:

Using a financial calculator, we can determine that the bond's price is **$1,147.00**.

30	3		37.50	1000
N	I/YR	PV	PMT	FV

$$= −1,147.00$$

Using Excel's PV function we solve for the semiannual bond's price as follows:

= PV(0.03,30,37.5,1000)

PV(rate, nper, pmt, [fv], [type])

Here we find that the bond's value is equal to **$1,147.00**.

In the Quick Question box on page 228 we calculated the YTM on this annual bond whose price was $1,145.68. Notice that the semiannual bond's price is $1,147.00 − $1,145.68 = $1.32 greater due to the interest payments being received semiannually rather than on an annual basis.

SELF TEST

Describe how the annual payment bond valuation formula is changed to evaluate semiannual coupon bonds and write the revised formula.

Hartwell Corporation's bonds have a 20-year maturity, an 8% semiannual coupon, and a face value of $1,000. The going nominal annual interest rate (r_d) is 7%. What is the bond's price? **($1,106.78)**

7-7 ASSESSING A BOND'S RISKINESS

In this section, we identify and explain the two key factors that impact a bond's riskiness. Once those factors are identified, we differentiate between them and discuss how you can minimize these risks.

---

[10]We can use a similar process to calculate the nominal yield to call for a semiannual bond. The only difference would be that N should represent the number of semiannual periods until the bond is callable and FV should be the bond's call price rather than its par value.

7-7A PRICE RISK

As we saw in Chapter 6, interest rates fluctuate over time and when they rise, the value of outstanding bonds decline. This risk of a decline in bond values due to an increase in interest rates is called **price risk (or interest rate risk)**. To illustrate, refer back to Allied's bonds; assume once more that they have a 10% annual coupon; and assume that you bought one of these bonds at its par value, $1,000. Shortly after your purchase, the going interest rate rises from 10% to 15%.[11] As we saw in Section 7-3, this interest rate increase would cause the bond's price to fall from $1,000 to $707.63, so you would have a loss of $292.37 on the bond.[12] Because interest rates can and do rise, rising rates cause losses to bondholders; people or firms who invest in bonds are exposed to risk from increasing interest rates.

Price (Interest Rate) Risk
The risk of a decline in a bond's price due to an increase in interest rates.

Price risk is higher on bonds that have long maturities than on bonds that will mature in the near future.[13] This follows because the longer the maturity, the longer before the bond will be paid off and the bondholder can replace it with another bond with a higher coupon. This point can be demonstrated by showing how the value of a 1-year bond with a 10% annual coupon fluctuates with changes in r_d and then comparing those changes with changes on a 15-year bond. The 1-year bond's values at different interest rates are shown below.

Value of a 1-year bond at:

$r_d = 5\%$:	1	5		100	1000
	N	I/YR	PV	PMT	FV
			= −1,047.62		

$r_d = 10\%$:	1	10		100	1000
	N	I/YR	PV	PMT	FV
			= −1,000.00		

$r_d = 15\%$:	1	15		100	1000
	N	I/YR	PV	PMT	FV
			= −956.52		

---

[11]An immediate increase in rates from 10% to 15% would be quite unusual, and it would occur only if something quite bad were revealed about the company or happened in the economy. Smaller but still significant rate increases that adversely affect bondholders do occur fairly often.
[12]You would have an accounting (and tax) loss only if you sold the bond; if you held it to maturity, you would not have such a loss. However, even if you did not sell, you would still have suffered a real economic loss in an opportunity cost sense because you would have lost the opportunity to invest at 15% and would be stuck with a 10% bond in a 15% market. In an economic sense, "paper losses" are just as bad as realized accounting losses.
[13]Actually, a bond's maturity and coupon rate both affect price risk. Low coupons mean that most of the bond's return will come from repayment of principal, whereas on a high-coupon bond with the same maturity, more of the cash flows will come in during the early years due to the relatively large coupon payments.

You would obtain the first value with a financial calculator by entering N = 1, I/YR = 5, PMT = 100, and FV = 1000 and then pressing PV to get $1,047.62. With all the data still in your calculator, enter I/YR = 10 to override the old I/YR = 5 and press PV to find the bond's value at a 10% rate; it drops to $1,000. Then enter I/YR = 15 and press the PV key to find the last bond value, $956.52.

The effects of increasing rates on the 15-year bond value as found earlier in Section 7-3 can be compared with the just-calculated effects for the 1-year bond. This comparison is shown in Figure 7.3, where we show bond prices at several rates and then plot those prices on the graph. Compared to the 1-year bond, the 15-year bond is far more sensitive to changes in rates. At a 10% interest rate, both the 15-year and 1-year bonds are valued at $1,000. When rates rise to 15%, the 15-year bond falls to $707.63, but the 1-year bond falls only to $956.52. The price decline for the 1-year bond is only 4.35%, while that for the 15-year bond is 29.24%.

For bonds with similar coupons, this differential interest rate sensitivity always holds true—the longer a bond's maturity, the more its price changes in response to a given change in interest rates. Thus, even if the risk of default on two bonds is exactly the same, the one with the longer maturity is typically exposed to more risk from a rise in interest rates.[14]

The logical explanation for this difference in price risk is simple. Suppose you bought a 15-year bond that yielded 10%, or $100 a year. Now suppose interest rates on comparable-risk bonds rose to 15%. You would be stuck receiving only $100 of interest for the next 15 years. On the other hand, had you bought a 1-year bond, you would have earned a low return for only 1 year. At the end of the year, you would have received your $1,000 back; then you could have reinvested it and earned 15%, or $150 per year, for the next 14 years.

7-7b REINVESTMENT RISK

As we saw in the preceding section, an *increase* in interest rates hurts bondholders because it leads to a decline in the current value of a bond portfolio. But can a *decrease* in interest rates also hurt bondholders? The answer is yes because if interest rates fall, long-term investors will suffer a reduction in income. For example, consider a retiree who has a bond portfolio and lives off the income it produces. The bonds in the portfolio, on average, have coupon rates of 10%. Now suppose interest rates decline to 5%. Many of the bonds will mature or be called; as this occurs, the bondholder will have to replace 10% bonds with 5% bonds. Thus, the retiree will suffer a reduction of income.[15]

Reinvestment Risk
The risk that a decline in interest rates will lead to a decline in income from a bond portfolio.

The risk of an income decline due to a drop in interest rates is called **reinvestment risk**, and its importance has been demonstrated to all bondholders in recent years as a result of the sharp drop in rates since the mid-1980s. Reinvestment risk is obviously high on callable bonds. It is also high on short-term bonds because the shorter the bond's maturity, the fewer the years before the relatively high old-coupon bonds will be replaced with the new low-coupon issues. Thus, retirees whose primary holdings are short-term bonds or other debt securities will be hurt badly by a decline in rates, but holders of noncallable long-term bonds will continue to enjoy the old high rates.

---

[14]If a 10-year bond were plotted on the graph in Figure 7.3, its curve would lie between those of the 15-year and the 1-year bonds. The curve of a 1-month bond would be almost horizontal, indicating that its price would change very little in response to an interest rate change; but a 100-year bond would have a very steep slope, and the slope of a perpetuity would be even steeper. Also, a zero coupon bond's price is quite sensitive to interest rate changes; and the longer its maturity, the greater its price sensitivity. Therefore, a 30-year zero coupon bond would have a huge amount of price risk.

[15]Charles Schwab makes this point in a recent opinion piece in *The Wall Street Journal*, where he argues that continued low interest rates have had a devastating effect on many senior citizens who live off of the interest generated from their investments. For additional information, refer to Charles Schwab, "Low Interest Rates Are Squeezing Seniors," *The Wall Street Journal* (online.wsj.com), March 30, 2010.

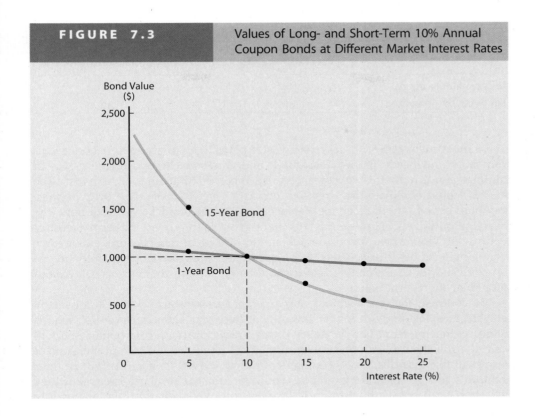

FIGURE 7.3	Values of Long- and Short-Term 10% Annual Coupon Bonds at Different Market Interest Rates

Current Market Interest Rate, r_d	Value of	
	1-Year Bond	**15-Year Bond**
5%	$1,047.62	$1,518.98
10	1,000.00	1,000.00
15	956.52	707.63
20	916.67	532.45
25	880.00	421.11

Note: Bond values were calculated using a financial calculator assuming annual, or once-a-year, compounding.

7-7c COMPARING PRICE RISK AND REINVESTMENT RISK

Note that price risk relates to the *current market value* of the bond portfolio, while reinvestment risk relates to the *income* the portfolio produces. If you hold long-term bonds, you will face significant price risk because the value of your portfolio will decline if interest rates rise, but you will not face much reinvestment risk because your income will be stable. On the other hand, if you hold short-term bonds, you will not be exposed to much price risk, but you will be exposed to significant reinvestment risk. Table 7.2 summarizes how a bond's maturity and coupon rate affect its price risk and reinvestment risk. For example, a long-term zero coupon bond will have a very high level of price risk and relatively little reinvestment risk. In contrast, a short-term bond with a high coupon rate will have low price risk, but considerable reinvestment risk.

Which type of risk is "more relevant" to a given investor depends on how long the investor plans to hold the bonds—this is often referred to as his or her **investment horizon**. To illustrate, consider an investor who has a relatively short

Investment Horizon
The period of time an investor plans to hold a particular investment.

TABLE 7.2   Comparing Price Risk and Reinvestment Risk

Bond	Level of Price Risk	Level of Reinvestment Risk
Longer maturity bonds	High	Low
Higher coupon bonds	Low	High

1-year investment horizon—say, the investor plans to go to graduate school a year from now and needs money for tuition and expenses. Reinvestment risk is of minimal concern to this investor because there is little time to reinvest. The investor could eliminate price risk by buying a 1-year Treasury security because he would be assured of receiving the face value of the bond 1 year from now (the investment horizon). However, if this investor were to buy a long-term Treasury security, he would bear a considerable amount of price risk because, as we have seen, long-term bond prices decline when interest rates rise. Consequently, investors with shorter investment horizons should view long-term bonds as being more risky than short-term bonds.

By contrast, the reinvestment risk inherent in short-term bonds is especially relevant to investors with longer investment horizons. Consider a retiree who is living on income from her portfolio. If this investor buys 1-year bonds, she will have to "roll them over" every year; and if rates fall, her income in subsequent years will likewise decline. A younger couple saving for their retirement or their children's college costs, for example, would be affected similarly because if they buy short-term bonds, they too will have to roll over their portfolio at possibly much lower rates. Because of the uncertainty today about the rates that will be earned on these reinvested cash flows, long-term investors should be especially concerned about the reinvestment risk inherent in short-term bonds.

Duration

The weighted average of the time it takes to receive each of the bond's cash flows.

To account for the effects related to both a bond's maturity and coupon, many analysts focus on a measure called **duration**. A bond's duration is the weighted average of the time it takes to receive each of the bond's cash flows. It follows that a zero coupon bond whose only cash flow is paid at maturity has a duration equal to its maturity. On the other hand, a coupon bond will have a duration that is less than its maturity. You can use Excel's DURATION function to calculate a bond's duration. We discuss duration in greater detail in Web Appendix 7B.

One way to manage both price and reinvestment risk is to buy a zero coupon Treasury bond with a duration equal to the investor's investment horizon. A very simple way to do this is to buy a zero coupon bond with a maturity that matches the investment horizon. For example, assume your investment horizon is 10 years. If you buy a 10-year zero, you will receive a guaranteed payment in 10 years equal to the bond's face value.[16] Moreover, as there are no coupons to reinvest, there is no reinvestment risk. This explains why investors with specific goals often invest in zero coupon bonds.[17]

---

[16]Note that in this example, the 10-year zero technically has a considerable amount of price risk because its *current* price is highly sensitive to changes in interest rates. However, the year-to-year movements in price should not be of great concern to an investor with a 10-year investment horizon because the investor knows that, regardless of what happens to interest rates, the bond's price will still be $1,000 when it matures.

[17]Two words of caution about zeros are in order. First, as we show in Web Appendix 7A, investors in zeros must pay taxes each year on their accrued gain in value even though the bonds don't pay any cash until they mature. Second, buying a zero coupon bond with a maturity equal to your investment horizon enables you to lock in a nominal cash payoff, but the *real* value of that payment still depends on what happens to inflation during your investment horizon.

Recall from Chapter 6 that maturity risk premiums are generally positive.[18] Moreover, a positive maturity risk premium implies that investors, on average, regard longer-term bonds as being riskier than shorter-term bonds. That, in turn, suggests that the average investor is more concerned with price risk. Still, it is appropriate for each investor to consider his or her own situation, to recognize the risks inherent in bonds with different maturities, and to construct a portfolio that deals best with the investor's most relevant risk.

SELF TEST

Differentiate between price risk and reinvestment risk.

To which type of risk are holders of long-term bonds more exposed? Short-term bondholders?

What type of security can be used to minimize both price risk and reinvestment risk for an investor with a fixed investment horizon? Does this security protect the real payoff? Explain.

7-8 DEFAULT RISK

Potential default is another important risk that bondholders face. If the issuer defaults, investors will receive less than the promised return. Recall from Chapter 6 that the quoted interest rate includes a default risk premium—the higher the probability of default, the higher the premium and thus the yield to maturity. Default risk on Treasuries is zero, but this risk is substantial for lower-grade corporate and municipal bonds.

To illustrate, suppose two bonds have the same promised cash flows—their coupon rates, maturities, liquidity, and inflation exposures are identical; but one has more default risk than the other. Investors will naturally pay more for the one with less chance of default. As a result, bonds with higher default risk have higher market rates: $r_d = r^* + IP + DRP + LP + MRP$. If a bond's default risk changes, r_d and thus the price will be affected. Thus, if the default risk on Allied's bonds increases, their price will fall and the yield to maturity (YTM = r_d) will increase.

7-8A VARIOUS TYPES OF CORPORATE BONDS

Default risk is influenced by the financial strength of the issuer and the terms of the bond contract, including whether collateral has been pledged to secure the bond. The characteristics of some key types of bonds are described in this section.

Mortgage Bonds

Under a **mortgage bond**, the corporation pledges specific assets as security for the bond. To illustrate, in 2014, Billingham Corporation needed $10 million to build a regional distribution center. Bonds in the amount of $4 million, secured by *a first mortgage* on the property, were issued. (The remaining $6 million was financed with equity capital.) If Billingham defaults on the bonds, the bondholders can foreclose on the property and sell it to satisfy their claims.

Mortgage Bond
A bond backed by fixed assets. First mortgage bonds are senior in priority to claims of second mortgage bonds.

---

[18]The fact that maturity risk premiums are positive suggests that most investors have relatively short investment horizons, or at least worry about short-term changes in their net worth. See *Ibbotson Stocks, Bonds, Bills, and Inflation: 2013 Valuation Yearbook* (Chicago: Morningstar, Inc., 2013), which finds that the maturity risk premium for long-term bonds has averaged 1.5% over the past 87 years.

If Billingham had chosen to, it could have issued *second mortgage bonds* secured by the same $10 million of assets. In the event of liquidation, the holders of the second mortgage bonds would have a claim against the property, but only after the first mortgage bondholders had been paid in full. Thus, second mortgages are sometimes called *junior mortgages* because they are junior in priority to the claims of *senior mortgages,* or *first mortgage bonds.*

All mortgage bonds are subject to an **indenture**, which is a legal document that spells out in detail the rights of the bondholders and the corporation. The indentures of many major corporations were written 20, 30, 40, or more years ago. These indentures are generally "open-ended," meaning that new bonds can be issued from time to time under the same indenture. However, the amount of new bonds that can be issued is usually limited to a specified percentage of the firm's total "bondable property," which generally includes all land, plant, and equipment. And, of course, the coupon interest rate on newly issued bonds changes over time, along with the market rate on the older bonds.

Indenture

A formal agreement between the issuer and the bondholders.

Debentures

A **debenture** is an unsecured bond; and as such, it provides no specific collateral as security for the obligation. Therefore, debenture holders are general creditors whose claims are protected by property not otherwise pledged. In practice, the use of debentures depends on the nature of the firm's assets and on its general credit strength. Extremely strong companies such as General Electric and Exxon Mobil can use debentures because they do not need to put up property as security for their debt. Debentures are also issued by weak companies that have already pledged most of their assets as collateral for mortgage loans. In this case, the debentures are quite risky and that risk will be reflected in their interest rates.

Debenture

A long-term bond that is not secured by a mortgage on specific property.

Subordinated Debentures

The term *subordinate* means "below" or "inferior to"; and in the event of bankruptcy, subordinated debt has a claim on assets only after senior debt has been paid in full. **Subordinated debentures** may be subordinated to designated notes payable (usually bank loans) or to all other debt. In the event of liquidation or reorganization, holders of subordinated debentures receive nothing until all senior debt, as named in the debentures' indenture, has been paid. Precisely how subordination works and how it strengthens the position of senior debtholders are explained in detail in Web Appendix 7C.

Subordinated Debentures

Bonds having a claim on assets only after the senior debt has been paid in full in the event of liquidation.

7-8b Bond Ratings

Since the early 1900s, bonds have been assigned quality ratings that reflect their probability of going into default. The three major rating agencies are Moody's Investors Service (Moody's), Standard & Poor's Corporation (S&P), and Fitch Investors Service. Moody's and S&P's rating designations are shown in Table 7.3.[19] The triple- and double-A bonds are extremely safe. Single-A and triple-B bonds are also strong enough to be called **investment-grade bonds**, and they are the lowest-rated bonds that many banks and other institutional investors are permitted by law to hold. Double-B and lower bonds are speculative, or **junk, bonds**; and they have a significant probability of going into default.

Investment-Grade Bonds

Bonds rated triple-B or higher; many banks and other institutional investors are permitted by law to hold only investment-grade bonds.

Junk Bonds

High-risk, high-yield bonds.

Bond Rating Criteria

The framework used by rating agencies examines both qualitative and quantitative factors. Quantitative factors relate to financial risk—examining a firm's financial ratios such as those discussed in Chapter 4. Published ratios are, of course,

---

[19]In the discussion to follow, reference to the S&P rating is intended to imply the Moody's and Fitch's ratings as well. Thus, triple-B bonds mean both BBB and Baa bonds; double-B bonds mean both BB and Ba bonds; and so forth.

	Investment Grade				Junk			
Moody's	Aaa	Aa	A	Baa	Ba	B	Caa	C
S&P	AAA	AA	A	BBB	BB	B	CCC	C

Moody's and S&P Bond Ratings — **TABLE 7.3**

Note: Both Moody's and S&P use "modifiers" for bonds rated below triple A. S&P uses a plus and minus system. Thus, A+ designates the strongest A-rated bonds; A–, the weakest. Moody's uses a 1, 2, or 3 designation, with 1 denoting the strongest and 3 denoting the weakest; thus, within the double-A category, Aa1 is the best, Aa2 is average, and Aa3 is the weakest.

historical—they show the firm's condition in the past, whereas bond investors are more interested in the firm's condition in the future. Qualitative factors considered include an analysis of a firm's business risk, such as its competitiveness within its industry and the quality of its management. Determinants of bond ratings include the following:

1. *Financial Ratios.* All of the ratios are potentially important, but those related to financial risk are key. The rating agencies' analysts perform a financial analysis along the lines discussed in Chapter 4 and forecast future ratios along the lines described in Chapter 16.

2. *Qualitative Factors: Bond Contract Terms.* Every bond is covered by a contract, often called an indenture, between the issuer and the bondholders. The indenture spells out all the terms related to the bond. Included in the indenture are the maturity, the coupon interest rate, a statement of whether the bond is secured by a mortgage on specific assets, any sinking fund provisions, and a statement of whether the bond is guaranteed by some other party with a high credit ranking. Other provisions might include *restrictive covenants* such as requirements that the firm not let its debt ratio exceed a stated level and that it keep its times-interest-earned ratio at or above a given level. Some bond indentures are hundreds of pages long, while others are quite short and cover just the terms of the loan.

3. *Miscellaneous Qualitative Factors.* Included here are issues like the sensitivity of the firm's earnings to the strength of the economy, the way it is affected by inflation, a statement of whether it is having or likely to have labor problems, the extent of its international operations (including the stability of the countries in which it operates), potential environmental problems, and potential antitrust problems. Today the most important factor is exposure to subprime loans, including the difficulty to determine the extent of this exposure as a result of the complexity of the assets backed by such loans.

We see that bond ratings are determined by a great many factors, some quantitative and some qualitative (or subjective). Also, the rating process is dynamic—at times, one factor is of primary importance; at other times, some other factor is key. Table 7.4 provides some of the criteria a rating agency examines when rating a company's bonds. Not surprisingly, companies with lower business risk, lower debt ratios, higher cash flow to debt, and lower debt to EBITDA typically have higher bond ratings.

Importance of Bond Ratings

Bond ratings are important to both firms and investors. First, because a bond's rating is an indicator of its default risk, the rating has a direct, measurable influence on the bond's interest rate and the firm's cost of debt. Second, most bonds are purchased by institutional investors rather than individuals and many

TABLE 7.4   Bond Rating Criteria: Business Risk/Financial Risk

	Financial Risk Profile				
Business Risk Profile	**Minimal**	**Modest**	**Intermediate**	**Aggressive**	**Highly Leveraged**
Excellent	AAA	AA	A	BBB	BB
Strong	AA	A	A−	BBB−	BB−
Satisfactory	A	BBB+	BBB	BB+	B+
Weak	BBB	BBB−	BB+	BB−	B
Vulnerable	BB	B+	B+	B	B−
Financial Risk Indicative Ratios[a]	**Minimal**	**Modest**	**Intermediate**	**Aggressive**	**Highly Leveraged**
Cash flow (Funds from operations/Debt)	>60%	45%–60%	30%–45%	15%–30%	<15%
Debt leverage (Total debt/Capital)	<25%	25%–35%	35%–45%	45%–55%	>55%
Debt/EBITDA	<1.4×	1.4×–2.0×	2.0×–3.0×	3.0×–4.5×	>4.5×

Note:
[a] Fully adjusted, historically demonstrated, and expected to continue consistently.

Source: *Standard & Poor's 2008 Corporate Ratings Criteria* (New York: McGraw-Hill, 2008), p. 21.

institutions are restricted to investment-grade securities. Thus, if a firm's bonds fall below BBB, it will have a difficult time selling new bonds because many potential purchasers will not be allowed to buy them.

As a result of their higher risk and more restricted market, lower-grade bonds have higher required rates of return, r_d, than high-grade bonds. Figure 7.4 illustrates this point. In each of the years shown on the graph, U.S. government bonds have had the lowest yields, AAA bonds have been next, and BBB bonds have had the highest yields. The figure also shows that the gaps between yields on the three types of bonds vary over time, indicating that the cost differentials, or yield spreads, fluctuate from year to year. Most recently there was a dramatic increase in the yield spreads between corporate and Treasury securities in the aftermath of the recent financial crisis. In the years since the crisis, these spreads have narrowed as investors have slowly become once again more willing to hold riskier securities. This point is highlighted in Figure 7.5, which gives the yields on the three types of bonds and the yield spreads for AAA and BBB bonds over Treasuries in January 2009 and January 2013.[20] Note first from Figure 7.5 that the risk-free rate, or vertical axis intercept, was lower in January 2013 than it was in January 2009, primarily reflecting the decline in both rates and expected inflation over the past

---

[20]A yield spread is related to but not identical to risk premiums on corporate bonds. The true *risk premium* reflects only the difference in expected (and required) returns between two securities that results from differences in their risk. However, yield spreads reflect (1) a true risk premium; (2) a liquidity premium, which reflects the fact that U.S. Treasury bonds are more readily marketable than most corporate bonds; (3) a call premium because most Treasury bonds are not callable whereas corporate bonds are; and (4) an expected loss differential, which reflects the probability of loss on the corporate bonds. As an example of the last point, suppose the yield to maturity on a BBB bond was 6.0% versus 4.8% on government bonds but there was a 5% probability of total default loss on the corporate bond. In this case, the *expected* return on the BBB bond would be 0.95(6.0%) + 0.05(0%) = 5.7% and the yield spread would be 0.9%, not the full 1.2 percentage points difference in "promised" yields to maturity.

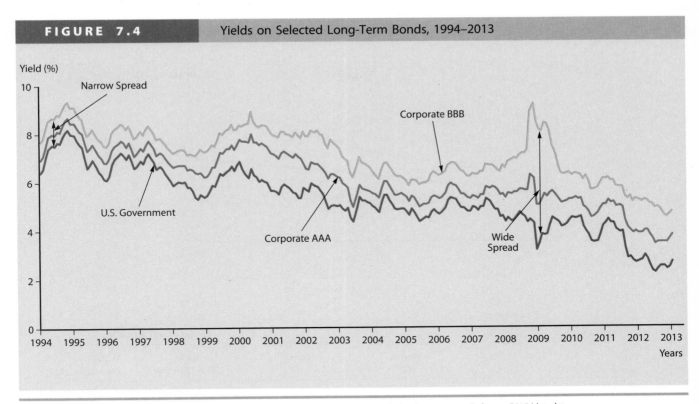

FIGURE 7.4   Yields on Selected Long-Term Bonds, 1994–2013

Source: *Federal Reserve Statistical Release*, Selected Interest Rates (Historical Data), federalreserve.gov/releases/H15/data.htm.

few years. Second, the slope of the line has decreased. In the crisis period of 2009, investors were both pessimistic and risk-averse; so spreads were quite high. As noted above, these spreads have subsequently fallen as economic conditions have slowly improved.

Changes in Ratings

Changes in a firm's bond rating affect its ability to borrow funds and its cost of that capital. Rating agencies review outstanding bonds on a periodic basis, occasionally upgrading or downgrading a bond as a result of its issuer's changed circumstances. For example, on January 17, 2013, S&P raised the corporate credit rating from BB+ to BBB– of Fidelity National Information Services Inc., a global banking and payment technologies provider. S&P's decision to upgrade the firm's credit rating was due to the company's consistent strong operating results and its reduced debt levels. On February 28, 2013, S&P lowered the corporate credit rating from B– to CCC+ of J.C. Penney, a clothing and household goods retailer. S&P's decision to downgrade the firm's credit rating was due to the company's weak fourth-quarter results, poor operating margins, and a weak liquidity position. The company has shifted its marketing strategy from steady promotions to everyday low pricing; however, this strategy hurt sales.

Over the long run, rating agencies have done a reasonably good job of measuring the average credit risk of bonds and of changing ratings whenever there is a significant change in credit quality. However, it is important to understand that ratings do not adjust immediately to changes in credit quality; and in some cases, there can be a considerable lag between a change in credit quality and a change in rating. For example, Enron's bonds still carried an investment-grade rating on a Friday in December 2001, but the company declared bankruptcy 2 days later, on Sunday. More recently, the rating agencies have come under considerable fire for significantly underestimating the risks of many of the securities

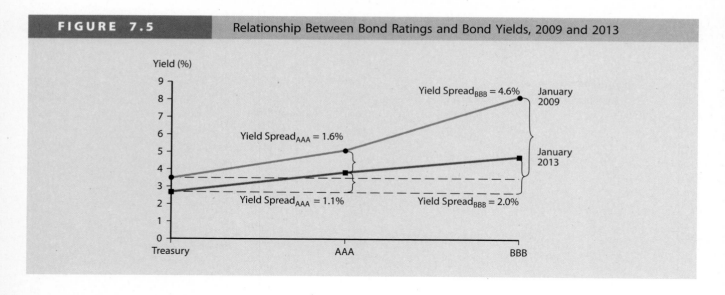

FIGURE 7.5   Relationship Between Bond Ratings and Bond Yields, 2009 and 2013

	Long-Term Government Bonds (Default-Free) (1)	AAA Corporate Bonds (2)	BBB Corporate Bonds (3)	Yield Spreads	
				AAA (4) = (2) − (1)	BBB (5) = (3) − (1)
January 2009	3.5%	5.1%	8.1%	1.6%	4.6%
January 2013	2.7	3.8	4.7	1.1	2.0

Source: *Federal Reserve Statistical Release*, Selected Interest Rates (Historical Data), federalreserve.gov/releases/H15/data.htm.

that were backed by subprime mortgages. Many worry that rating agencies don't have the proper incentives to measure risk because they are paid by the issuing firms. In response to these concerns, many have called for Congress and the SEC to reform the rating agencies.[21]

7-8c BANKRUPTCY AND REORGANIZATION

When a business becomes *insolvent*, it doesn't have enough cash to meet its interest and principal payments. A decision must then be made whether to dissolve the firm through *liquidation* or to permit it to *reorganize* and thus continue to operate. These issues are addressed in Chapter 7 and Chapter 11 of the federal bankruptcy statutes, and the final decision is made by a federal bankruptcy court judge.

The decision to force a firm to liquidate versus permitting it to reorganize depends on whether the value of the reorganized business is likely to be greater than the value of its assets if they were sold off piecemeal. In a reorganization, the firm's creditors negotiate with management on the terms of a potential reorganization. The reorganization plan may call for *restructuring* the debt, in which case the interest rate may be reduced, the term to maturity lengthened, or some of the debt may be exchanged for equity. The point of the restructuring is to reduce the financial charges to a level that is supportable by the firm's projected cash flows. Of course, the common stockholders also have to "take a haircut"—they generally see their position diluted as a result of additional

---

[21]See Aaron Lucchetti, Serena Ng, and Greg Hitt, "Rating Agencies Face Curbs," *The Wall Street Journal* (online.wsj.com), May 12, 2010.

shares being given to debtholders in exchange for accepting a reduced amount of debt principal and interest. A trustee may be appointed by the court to oversee the reorganization, but the existing management generally is allowed to retain control.

Liquidation occurs if the company is deemed to be worth more "dead" than "alive." If the bankruptcy court orders a liquidation, assets are auctioned off and the cash obtained is distributed as specified in Chapter 7 of the Bankruptcy Act. Web Appendix 7C provides an illustration of how a firm's assets are distributed after liquidation. For now, you should know that (1) the federal bankruptcy statutes govern reorganization and liquidation, (2) bankruptcies occur frequently, (3) a priority of the specified claims must be followed when the assets of a liquidated firm are distributed, (4) bondholders' treatment depends on the terms of the bond, and (5) stockholders generally receive little in reorganizations and nothing in liquidations because the assets are usually worth less than the amount of debt outstanding.

SELF TEST

Differentiate between mortgage bonds and debentures.

Name the major rating agencies and list some factors that affect bond ratings.

Why are bond ratings important to firms and investors?

Do bond ratings adjust immediately to changes in credit quality? Explain.

Differentiate between Chapter 7 liquidations and Chapter 11 reorganizations. In general, when should each be used?

7-9 BOND MARKETS

Corporate bonds are traded primarily in the over-the-counter market. Most bonds are owned by and traded among large financial institutions (for example, life insurance companies, mutual funds, hedge funds, and pension funds, all of which deal in very large blocks of securities), and it is relatively easy for over-the-counter bond dealers to arrange the transfer of large blocks of bonds among the relatively few holders of the bonds. It would be more difficult to conduct similar operations in the stock market among the literally millions of large and small stockholders, so a higher percentage of stock trades occur on the exchanges.

A number of leading business publications and websites routinely report key developments in the Treasury, corporate, and municipal bond markets. For example, *The Wall Street Journal* provides a list of bonds whose yield spreads (relative to Treasury securities) widened and narrowed the most in the previous day. Table 7.5 reprints a portion of this data for a given day in March 2013. The table also reports the company's previous day's stock performance, which enables an investor to easily see how recent news has affected both the company's stock price and the interest rate on its debt. As part of its reported data, *The Wall Street Journal* also includes interesting data regarding a number of bond indices and a snapshot of government bond rates in different countries. Other helpful sources include the bond sections of Yahoo Finance, Google Finance, and Morningstar.com.

Corporate Debt

Price moves by a company's debt in the credit markets sometimes mirror and sometimes anticipate moves in that same company's share price. Here's a look at both for two companies in the news.

Investment-Grade

Freeport-McMoRan 3.55% notes due Mar. 01, 2022,
Copper & Gold Inc.: yielding 3.620%

The mining giant sold the biggest bond deal of 2013 on Thursday.

High Yield (junk-rated)

J.C. Penney Co.:   5.65% notes due Jun. 01, 2020,
yielding 9.314%

The department store's losses widened in the fourth-quarter on weak sales and margins.

Investment-grade spreads that tightened the most ...

Issuer	Symbol	Coupon (%)	Maturity	SPREAD*, In basis points Current	one-day change	Last week	STOCK PERFORMANCE Close ($)	% chg
FirstEnergy Solutions	FE	6.050	Aug. 15, '21	155	–43	196	...	...
Hewlett-Packard	HPQ	5.500	March 1, '18	224	–20	250	20.14	1.87
Banro	BAA	10.000	March 1, '17	1401	–18	n.a.	2.28	–0.87
Juniper Networks	JNPR	3.100	March 15, '16	98	–16	n.a.	20.68	–0.19
General Electric Capital	GE	4.875	March 4, '15	41	–15	60	...	...
Comcast Cable Holdings	CMCSA	8.750	Aug. 1, '15	56	–14	68	...	...
Goldman Sachs Capital	GS	6.345	Feb. 15, '34	279	–12	270	...	...
Wynn Las Vegas	WYNN	5.375	March 15, '22	260	–11	257	...	...

... And spreads that widened the most

Issuer	Symbol	Coupon (%)	Maturity	Current	one-day change	Last week	Close ($)	% chg
SAIC	SAI	5.950	Dec. 1, '40	255	30	258	11.82	2.07
FirstEnergy	FE	7.375	Nov. 15, '31	260	19	219	39.48	0.08
France Telecom S.A.	FRTEL	8.500	March 1, '31	191	17	176	...	...
El Du Pont de Nemours	DD	2.800	Feb. 15, '23	75	15	76	47.90	0.82
Residential Capital	RESCAP	9.625	May 15, '15	487	14	490	...	...
UnitedHealth	UNH	2.875	March 15, '23	103	14	n.a.	53.45	–0.78
BP Capital Markets	BPLN	3.125	Oct. 1, '15	55	12	55	...	...
Petrohawk Energy	BHP	7.250	Aug. 15, '18	80	11	51	...	...

High-yield issues with the biggest price increases ...

Issuer	Symbol	Coupon (%)	Maturity	BOND PRICE as % of face value Current	one-day change	Last week	STOCK PERFORMANCE Close ($)	% chg
New Albertsons	SVU	7.450	Aug. 1, '29	73.000	2.50	71.000	...	...
Gymboree	GYMB	9.125	Dec. 1, '18	95.875	2.38	93.250	...	...
Tesoro	TSO	5.375	Oct. 1, '22	106.625	2.31	104.000	56.24	1.24
Overseas Shipholding	OSG	8.125	March 30, '18	42.000	2.00	39.500	...	...
Basic Energy Services	BAS	7.750	Feb. 15, '19	103.988	1.99	101.000	14.63	2.52
Regency Energy Partners	RGP	5.500	April 15, '23	106.000	1.38	n.a.	23.79	–0.25
Chesapeake Energy	CHK	6.775	March 15, '19	103.750	1.25	102.250	20.16	0.10
Continental Resources	CLR	5.000	Sept. 15, '22	108.313	1.25	106.030	88.00	4.80

... And with the biggest price decreases

Issuer	Symbol	Coupon (%)	Maturity	Current	one-day change	Last week	Close ($)	% chg
Ford Motor Credit	F	5.000	May 15, '18	100.344	–10.01	110.227	...	...
JC Penney	JCP	6.375	Oct. 15, '36	75.250	–1.75	77.875	17.57	–16.97
Cablevision Systems	CVC	5.875	Sept. 15, '22	97.125	–1.38	97.750	13.99	–9.57
CCO Holdings	CCMM	5.250	Sept. 30, '22	98.750	–1.19	99.625	...	...
Cincinnati Bell	CBB	8.375	Oct. 15, '20	105.500	–1.00	107.270	3.25	0.62
MGM Resorts International	MGM	7.500	June 1, '16	108.505	–1.00	109.750	12.49	0.08
Qwest Capital Funding	CTL	6.875	June 15, '28	98.080	–0.92	99.500	...	...
Clear Channel Communications	CCMO	9.000	March 1, '21	90.500	–0.88	92.250	...	...

*Estimated spread over 2-year, 3-year, 5-year, 10-year or 30-year hot-run Treasury; 100 basis points*one percentage pt.; change in spread shown is for Z-spread.
Note: Data are for the most active issue of bonds with maturities of two years or more

Sources: MarketAxess Corporate BondTicker; WSJ Market Data Group.

ACCRUED INTEREST AND THE PRICING OF COUPON BONDS

In this chapter, we have demonstrated the various factors that influence bond prices. But in practice, how much you are willing to pay for a bond also depends on when the next coupon payment is due. Clearly, all else equal, you would be willing to pay more for a bond the day before a coupon is paid, than you would the day after it has been paid. So, if you purchase a bond between coupon payments, you also have to pay what is called *accrued interest*. Accrued interest represents the amount of interest that has accumulated between coupon payments, and it can be calculated as follows:

$$\text{Accrued interest} = \text{Coupon payment} \times \frac{\text{Number of days since the last coupon payment}}{\text{Number of days in the coupon period}}$$

Let's consider, for example, a corporate bond that was issued on February 22, 2013. The bond has an 8% semiannual coupon and a par value of $1,000—which means six months later on August 22, 2013, the bond will pay its first $40 coupon, and on February 22, 2014, it will pay its second $40 coupon. If you buy the bond on May 11, 2013 (79 days since the bond's last coupon payment on February 22), you will have to pay the seller $17.56 in accrued interest:[22]

$$\text{Accrued interest} = \$40 \times (79/180) = \$17.56$$

In most cases, bonds are quoted net of accrued interest—in what is often referred to as a *clean price*. The actual invoice price you pay (often referred to as the *dirty price*) is the clean price plus accrued interest. In the case of the above bond, let's assume that the bond's nominal yield to maturity is the same as it was when the bond was issued (8%), which means that excluding accrued interest the bond continues to trade at par. It follows that:

$$\text{Clean price (quoted price)} = \$1,000$$
$$\text{Accrued interest} = \$17.56$$
$$\text{Dirty price (invoice price)} = \text{Clean price} + \text{Accrued interest}$$
$$= \$1,017.56$$

You can also use the Accrued Interest function in Excel (ACCRINT) to easily calculate a bond's accrued interest.[23] As a final point, in the examples we use in the text, when we refer to a bond's price we are referring to the bond's quoted or clean price. But you should keep in mind that if you buy or sell a bond, the actual price paid or received is the dirty price which includes accrued interest.

SELF TEST

Why do most bond trades occur in the over-the-counter market?

How is accrued interest calculated?

What is meant by the terms clean price and dirty price?

TYING IT ALL TOGETHER

This chapter described the different types of bonds governments and corporations issue, explained how bond prices are established, and discussed how investors estimate rates of return on bonds. It also discussed various types of risks that investors face when they purchase bonds.

---

[22]If you look up accrued interest in Yahoo! Finance's glossary you will see more details regarding the payment of accrued interest. Most notably, it points out that accrued interest is calculated slightly differently for corporate and Treasury bonds:

Interest on most bonds and fixed-income securities is paid twice a year. On corporate and municipal bonds, interest is calculated on 30-day months and a 360-day year. For government bonds, interest is calculated on actual days and a 365-day year.

[23]Refer to the Accrued Interest tab on the Chapter 7 Excel Model.

When an investor purchases a company's bonds, the investor is providing the company with capital. Moreover, when a firm issues bonds, *the return that investors require on the bonds represents the cost of debt capital to the firm.* This point is extended in Chapter 10, where the ideas developed in this chapter are used to help determine a company's overall cost of capital, which is a basic component of the capital budgeting process.

In recent years, many companies have used zero coupon bonds to raise billions of dollars, while bankruptcy is an important consideration for companies that issue debt and for investors. These two related issues are discussed in detail in Web Appendixes 7A and 7C. Duration, a measurement involving a weighted average of the bond's cash flows, is discussed in Web Appendix 7B. These appendixes can be accessed through the textbook's website.

SELF-TEST QUESTIONS AND PROBLEMS

(Solutions Appear in Appendix A)

ST-1 **KEY TERMS** Define each of the following terms:

a. Bond; treasury bond; corporate bond; municipal bond; foreign bond

b. Par value; maturity date; original maturity

c. Coupon payment; coupon interest rate

d. Fixed-rate bond; floating-rate bond; zero coupon bond; original issue discount (OID) bond

e. Call provision; sinking fund provision

f. Convertible bond; warrant; putable bond; income bond; indexed, or purchasing power, bond

g. Discount bond; premium bond

h. Yield to maturity (YTM); yield to call (YTC)

i. Current yield; capital gains yield; total return

j. Price risk; reinvestment risk; investment horizon; default risk; duration

k. Mortgage bond; indenture; debenture; subordinated debenture

l. Investment-grade bond; junk bond

ST-2 **BOND VALUATION** The Pennington Corporation issued a new series of bonds on January 1, 1990. The bonds were sold at par ($1,000); had a 12% coupon; and mature in 30 years, on December 31, 2019. Coupon payments are made semiannually (on June 30 and December 31).

a. What was the YTM on January 1, 1990?

b. What was the price of the bonds on January 1, 1995, 5 years later, assuming that interest rates had fallen to 10%?

c. Find the current yield, capital gains yield, and total return on January 1, 1995, given the price as determined in Part b.

d. On July 1, 2013, 6½ years before maturity, Pennington's bonds sold for $916.42. What were the YTM, the current yield, the capital gains yield, and the total return at that time?

e. Now assume that you plan to purchase an outstanding Pennington bond on March 1, 2013, when the going rate of interest given its risk was 15.5%. How large a check must you write to complete the transaction? (This is a difficult question.)

ST-3 **SINKING FUND** The Vancouver Development Company (VDC) is planning to sell a $100 million, 10-year, 12%, semiannual payment bond issue. Provisions for a sinking fund to retire the issue over its life will be included in the indenture. Sinking fund payments will be made at the end of each year, and each payment must be sufficient to retire 10% of the original amount of the issue. The last sinking fund payment will retire the last of the bonds. The bonds to be retired each period can be purchased on the open market or obtained by calling up to 5% of the original issue at par, at VDC's option.

a. How large must each sinking fund payment be if the company (1) uses the option to call bonds at par or (2) decides to buy bonds on the open market? For Part (2), you can only answer in words.

b. What will happen to debt service requirements per year associated with this issue over its 10-year life?

c. Now consider an alternative plan where VDC sets up its sinking fund so that *equal annual amounts* are paid into a sinking fund trust held by a bank, with the proceeds being used to buy government bonds that are expected to pay 7% annual interest. The payments, plus accumulated interest, must total $100 million at the end of 10 years, when the proceeds will be used to retire the issue. How large must the annual sinking fund payments be? Is this amount known with certainty, or might it be higher or lower?

d. What are the annual cash requirements for covering bond service costs under the trusteeship arrangement described in Part c? (Note: Interest must be paid on Vancouver's outstanding bonds but not on bonds that have been retired.) Assume level interest rates for purposes of answering this question.

e. What would have to happen to interest rates to cause the company to buy bonds on the open market rather than call them under the plan where some bonds are retired each year?

QUESTIONS

7-1 A sinking fund can be set up in one of two ways:

- The corporation makes annual payments to the trustee, who invests the proceeds in securities (frequently government bonds) and uses the accumulated total to retire the bond issue at maturity.

- The trustee uses the annual payments to retire a portion of the issue each year, calling a given percentage of the issue by a lottery and paying a specified price per bond or buying bonds on the open market, whichever is cheaper.

What are the advantages and disadvantages of each procedure from the viewpoint of the firm and the bondholders?

7-2 Can the following equation be used to find the value of a bond with N years to maturity that pays interest once a year? Assume that the bond was issued several years ago.

$$V_B = \sum_{t=1}^{N} \frac{\text{Annual interest}}{(1 + r_d)^t} + \frac{\text{Par value}}{(1 + r_d)^N}$$

7-3 The values of outstanding bonds change whenever the going rate of interest changes. In general, short-term interest rates are more volatile than long-term interest rates. Therefore, short-term bond prices are more sensitive to interest rate changes than are long-term bond prices. Is that statement true or false? Explain. (Hint: Make up a "reasonable" example based on a 1-year and a 20-year bond to help answer the question.)

7-4 If interest rates rise after a bond issue, what will happen to the bond's price and YTM? Does the time to maturity affect the extent to which interest rate changes affect the bond's price? (Again, an example might help you answer this question.)

7-5 Discuss the following statement: A bond's yield to maturity is the bond's promised rate of return, which equals its expected rate of return.

7-6 If you buy a *callable* bond and interest rates decline, will the value of your bond rise by as much as it would have risen if the bond had not been callable? Explain.

7-7   Assume that you have a short investment horizon (less than 1 year). You are considering two investments: a 1-year Treasury security and a 20-year Treasury security. Which of the two investments would you view as being riskier? Explain.

7-8   Indicate whether each of the following actions will increase or decrease a bond's yield to maturity:

a.   The bond's price increases.

b.   The bond is downgraded by the rating agencies.

c.   A change in the bankruptcy code makes it more difficult for bondholders to receive payments in the event the firm declares bankruptcy.

d.   The economy seems to be shifting from a boom to a recession. Discuss the effects of the firm's credit strength in your answer.

e.   Investors learn that the bonds are subordinated to another debt issue.

7-9   Why is a call provision advantageous to a bond issuer? When would the issuer be likely to initiate a refunding call?

7-10 Are securities that provide for a sinking fund more or less risky from the bondholder's perspective than those without this type of provision? Explain.

7-11 What's the difference between a call for sinking fund purposes and a refunding call?

7-12 Why are convertibles and bonds with warrants typically offered with lower coupons than similarly rated straight bonds?

7-13 Explain whether the following statement is true or false: Only weak companies issue debentures.

7-14 Would the yield spread on a corporate bond over a Treasury bond with the same maturity tend to become wider or narrower if the economy appeared to be heading toward a recession? Would the change in the spread for a given company be affected by the firm's credit strength? Explain.

7-15 A bond's expected return is sometimes estimated by its YTM and sometimes by its YTC. Under what conditions would the YTM provide a better estimate, and when would the YTC be better?

Problems

Easy
Problems
1–4

7-1   **BOND VALUATION**   Callaghan Motors' bonds have 10 years remaining to maturity. Interest is paid annually, they have a $1,000 par value, the coupon interest rate is 8%, and the yield to maturity is 9%. What is the bond's current market price?

7-2   **YIELD TO MATURITY AND FUTURE PRICE**   A bond has a $1,000 par value, 10 years to maturity, and a 7% annual coupon and sells for $985.

a.   What is its yield to maturity (YTM)?

b.   Assume that the yield to maturity remains constant for the next 3 years. What will the price be 3 years from today?

7-3   **BOND VALUATION**   Nungesser Corporation's outstanding bonds have a $1,000 par value, a 9% semiannual coupon, 8 years to maturity, and an 8.5% YTM. What is the bond's price?

7-4   **YIELD TO MATURITY**   A firm's bonds have a maturity of 10 years with a $1,000 face value, have an 8% semiannual coupon, are callable in 5 years at $1,050, and currently sell at a price of $1,100. What are their nominal yield to maturity and their nominal yield to call? What return should investors expect to earn on these bonds?

Intermediate
Problems
5–14

7-5   **BOND VALUATION**   An investor has two bonds in his portfolio that have a face value of $1,000 and pay a 10% annual coupon. Bond L matures in 15 years, while Bond S matures in 1 year.

a.   What will the value of each bond be if the going interest rate is 5%, 8%, and 12%? Assume that only one more interest payment is to be made on Bond S at its maturity and that 15 more payments are to be made on Bond L.

b.   Why does the longer-term bond's price vary more than the price of the shorter-term bond when interest rates change?

7-6 BOND VALUATION   An investor has two bonds in her portfolio, Bond C and Bond Z. Each bond matures in 4 years, has a face value of $1,000, and has a yield to maturity of 9.6%. Bond C pays a 10% annual coupon, while Bond Z is a zero coupon bond.

a. Assuming that the yield to maturity of each bond remains at 9.6% over the next 4 years, calculate the price of the bonds at each of the following years to maturity:

Years to Maturity	Price of Bond C	Price of Bond Z
4	_____	_____
3	_____	_____
2	_____	_____
1	_____	_____
0	_____	_____

b. Plot the time path of prices for each bond.

7-7 INTEREST RATE SENSITIVITY   An investor purchased the following 5 bonds. Each bond had a par value of $1,000 and an 8% yield to maturity on the purchase day. Immediately after the investor purchased them, interest rates fell and each then had a new YTM of 7%. What is the percentage change in price for each bond after the decline in interest rates? Fill in the following table:

	Price @ 8%	Price @ 7%	Percentage Change
10-year, 10% annual coupon	_____	_____	_____
10-year zero	_____	_____	_____
5-year zero	_____	_____	_____
30-year zero	_____	_____	_____
$100 perpetuity	_____	_____	_____

7-8 YIELD TO CALL   Six years ago the Singleton Company issued 20-year bonds with a 14% annual coupon rate at their $1,000 par value. The bonds had a 9% call premium, with 5 years of call protection. Today Singleton called the bonds. Compute the realized rate of return for an investor who purchased the bonds when they were issued and held them until they were called. Explain why the investor should or should not be happy that Singleton called them.

7-9 YIELD TO MATURITY   Heymann Company bonds have 4 years left to maturity. Interest is paid annually, and the bonds have a $1,000 par value and a coupon rate of 9%.

a. What is the yield to maturity at a current market price of (1) $829 and (2) $1,104?

b. Would you pay $829 for each bond if you thought that a "fair" market interest rate for such bonds was 12%—that is, if r_d = 12%? Explain your answer.

7-10 CURRENT YIELD, CAPITAL GAINS YIELD, AND YIELD TO MATURITY   Hooper Printing Inc. has bonds outstanding with 9 years left to maturity. The bonds have an 8% annual coupon rate and were issued 1 year ago at their par value of $1,000. However, due to changes in interest rates, the bond's market price has fallen to $901.40. The capital gains yield last year was −9.86%.

a. What is the yield to maturity?

b. For the coming year, what are the expected current and capital gains yields? (Hint: Refer to Footnote 7 for the definition of the current yield and to Table 7.1.)

c. Will the actual realized yields be equal to the expected yields if interest rates change? If not, how will they differ?

7-11 BOND YIELDS   Last year Clark Company issued a 10-year, 12% semiannual coupon bond at its par value of $1,000. Currently, the bond can be called in 4 years at a price of $1,060 and it sells for $1,100.

a. What are the bond's nominal yield to maturity and its nominal yield to call? Would an investor be more likely to earn the YTM or the YTC?

b. What is the current yield? Is this yield affected by whether the bond is likely to be called? (Hint: Refer to Footnote 7 for the definition of the current yield and to Table 7.1.)

c. What is the expected capital gains (or loss) yield for the coming year? Is this yield dependent on whether the bond is expected to be called? Explain your answer.

7-12   **YIELD TO CALL**   It is now January 1, 2014, and you are considering the purchase of an outstanding bond that was issued on January 1, 2012. It has a 9.5% annual coupon and had a 30-year original maturity. (It matures on December 31, 2041.) There is 5 years of call protection (until December 31, 2016), after which time it can be called at 109—that is, at 109% of par, or $1,090. Interest rates have declined since it was issued; and it is now selling at 116.575% of par, or $1,165.75.

a. What is the yield to maturity? What is the yield to call?

b. If you bought this bond, which return would you actually earn? Explain your reasoning.

c. Suppose the bond had been selling at a discount rather than a premium. Would the yield to maturity have been the most likely return, or would the yield to call have been most likely?

7-13   **PRICE AND YIELD**   An 8% semiannual coupon bond matures in 5 years. The bond has a face value of $1,000 and a current yield of 8.21%. What are the bond's price and YTM? (Hint: Refer to Footnote 7 for the definition of the current yield and to Table 7.1.)

7-14   **EXPECTED INTEREST RATE**   Lloyd Corporation's 14% coupon rate, semiannual payment, $1,000 par value bonds, which mature in 30 years, are callable 5 years from today at $1,050. They sell at a price of $1,353.54, and the yield curve is flat. Assume that interest rates are expected to remain at their current level.

a. What is the best estimate of these bonds' remaining life?

b. If Lloyd plans to raise additional capital and wants to use debt financing, what coupon rate would it have to set in order to issue new bonds at par?

Challenging Problems 15–18

7-15   **BOND VALUATION**   Bond X is noncallable and has 20 years to maturity, a 9% annual coupon, and a $1,000 par value. Your required return on Bond X is 10%; if you buy it, you plan to hold it for 5 years. You (and the market) have expectations that in 5 years, the yield to maturity on a 15-year bond with similar risk will be 8.5%. How much should you be willing to pay for Bond X today? (Hint: You will need to know how much the bond will be worth at the end of 5 years.)

7-16   **BOND VALUATION**   You are considering a 10-year, $1,000 par value bond. Its coupon rate is 9%, and interest is paid semiannually. If you require an "effective" annual interest rate (not a nominal rate) of 8.16%, how much should you be willing to pay for the bond?

7-17   **BOND RETURNS**   Last year Joan purchased a $1,000 face value corporate bond with an 11% annual coupon rate and a 10-year maturity. At the time of the purchase, it had an expected yield to maturity of 9.79%. If Joan sold the bond today for $1,060.49, what rate of return would she have earned for the past year?

7-18   **YIELD TO MATURITY AND YIELD TO CALL**   Kaufman Enterprises has bonds outstanding with a $1,000 face value and 10 years left until maturity. They have an 11% annual coupon payment, and their current price is $1,175. The bonds may be called in 5 years at 109% of face value (Call price = $1,090).

a. What is the yield to maturity?

b. What is the yield to call if they are called in 5 years?

c. Which yield might investors expect to earn on these bonds? Why?

d. The bond's indenture indicates that the call provision gives the firm the right to call the bonds at the end of each year beginning in Year 5. In Year 5, the bonds may be called at 109% of face value; but in each of the next 4 years, the call percentage will decline by 1%. Thus, in Year 6, they may be called at 108% of face value; in Year 7, they may be called at 107% of face value; and so forth. If the yield curve is horizontal and interest rates remain at their current level, when is the latest that investors might expect the firm to call the bonds?

COMPREHENSIVE/SPREADSHEET PROBLEM

7-19   **BOND VALUATION**   Clifford Clark is a recent retiree who is interested in investing some of his savings in corporate bonds. His financial planner has suggested the following bonds:

• Bond A has a 7% annual coupon, matures in 12 years, and has a $1,000 face value.

• Bond B has a 9% annual coupon, matures in 12 years, and has a $1,000 face value.

• Bond C has an 11% annual coupon, matures in 12 years, and has a $1,000 face value.

Each bond has a yield to maturity of 9%.

a. Before calculating the prices of the bonds, indicate whether each bond is trading at a premium, at a discount, or at par.

b. Calculate the price of each of the three bonds.

c. Calculate the current yield for each of the three bonds. (Hint: Refer to Footnote 7 for the definition of the current yield and to Table 7.1.)

d. If the yield to maturity for each bond remains at 9%, what will be the price of each bond 1 year from now? What is the expected capital gains yield for each bond? What is the expected total return for each bond?

e. Mr. Clark is considering another bond, Bond D. It has an 8% semiannual coupon and a $1,000 face value (i.e., it pays a $40 coupon every 6 months). Bond D is scheduled to mature in 9 years and has a price of $1,150. It is also callable in 5 years at a call price of $1,040.

   1. What is the bond's nominal yield to maturity?

   2. What is the bond's nominal yield to call?

   3. If Mr. Clark were to purchase this bond, would he be more likely to receive the yield to maturity or yield to call? Explain your answer.

f. Explain briefly the difference between price risk and reinvestment risk. Which of the following bonds has the most price risk? Which has the most reinvestment risk?

   - A 1-year bond with a 9% annual coupon
   - A 5-year bond with a 9% annual coupon
   - A 5-year bond with a zero coupon
   - A 10-year bond with a 9% annual coupon
   - A 10-year bond with a zero coupon

g. Only do this part if you are using a spreadsheet. Calculate the price of each bond (A, B, and C) at the end of each year until maturity, assuming interest rates remain constant. Create a graph showing the time path of each bond's value similar to Figure 7.2.

   1. What is the expected interest yield for each bond in each year?

   2. What is the expected capital gains yield for each bond in each year?

   3. What is the total return for each bond in each year?

INTEGRATED CASE

WESTERN MONEY MANAGEMENT INC.

7-20   **BOND VALUATION**   Robert Black and Carol Alvarez are vice presidents of Western Money Management and codirectors of the company's pension fund management division. A major new client, the California League of Cities, has requested that Western present an investment seminar to the mayors of the represented cities. Black and Alvarez, who will make the presentation, have asked you to help them by answering the following questions.

a. What are a bond's key features?

b. What are call provisions and sinking fund provisions? Do these provisions make bonds more or less risky?

c. How is the value of any asset whose value is based on expected future cash flows determined?

d. How is a bond's value determined? What is the value of a 10-year, $1,000 par value bond with a 10% annual coupon if its required return is 10%?

e. 1. What is the value of a 13% coupon bond that is otherwise identical to the bond described in Part d? Would we now have a discount or a premium bond?

   2. What is the value of a 7% coupon bond with these characteristics? Would we now have a discount or premium bond?

   3. What would happen to the values of the 7%, 10%, and 13% coupon bonds over time if the required return remained at 10%? [Hint: With a financial calculator, enter PMT, I/YR, FV, and N; then change (override) N to see what happens to the PV as it approaches maturity.]

f. 1. What is the yield to maturity on a 10-year, 9%, annual coupon, $1,000 par value bond that sells for $887.00? That sells for $1,134.20? What does the fact that it sells at a discount or at a premium tell you about the relationship between r_d and the coupon rate?

   2. What are the total return, the current yield, and the capital gains yield for the discount bond? Assume that it is held to maturity and the company does not default on it. (Hint: Refer to Footnote 7 for the definition of the current yield and to Table 7.1.)

g. What is *price risk?* Which has more price risk, an annual payment 1-year bond or a 10-year bond? Why?

h. What is *reinvestment risk?* Which has more reinvestment risk, a 1-year bond or a 10-year bond?

i. How does the equation for valuing a bond change if semiannual payments are made? Find the value of a 10-year, semiannual payment, 10% coupon bond if nominal $r_d = 13\%$.

j. Suppose for $1,000 you could buy a 10%, 10-year, annual payment bond or a 10%, 10-year, semiannual payment bond. They are equally risky. Which would you prefer? If $1,000 is the proper price for the semiannual bond, what is the equilibrium price for the annual payment bond?

k. Suppose a 10-year, 10%, semiannual coupon bond with a par value of $1,000 is currently selling for $1,135.90, producing a nominal yield to maturity of 8%. However, it can be called after 4 years for $1,050.

   1. What is the bond's *nominal yield to call* (YTC)?

   2. If you bought this bond, would you be more likely to earn the YTM or the YTC? Why?

l. Does the yield to maturity represent the promised or expected return on the bond? Explain.

m. These bonds were rated AA− by S&P. Would you consider them investment-grade or junk bonds?

n. What factors determine a company's bond rating?

o. If this firm were to default on the bonds, would the company be immediately liquidated? Would the bondholders be assured of receiving all of their promised payments? Explain.

© Blend Images/Alamy

Risk and Rates of Return

Managing Risk in Difficult Times

Over the past few decades, the U.S. stock market has seen more than its share of ups and downs. To give you a quick sense of the market's recent performance, consider that in April 1993, the S&P 500 index had a value around 440. In the following seven years, the market roared to a high of 1,516. Slightly more than two years later—following the 2001 terrorist attacks and the resulting recession—the index had lost nearly half of its value. Five bumpy years later, in September 2007, the market finally recovered back to where it was trading near its old highs above 1,500. But then the housing market collapsed and the financial crisis began, and by March 2009, the S&P 500 plunged to a level below 700. A little more than four years later, in March 2013, the market once again rebounded to a new all-time high.

In many cases, the returns on individual stocks have been even more volatile than the S&P 500 index. For example, in a recent three and a half year period, Apple Inc.'s stock rose more than 450%—from a price below $120 per share in March 2009 to more than $700 per share in September 2012. But following this incredible run-up, the stock's price subsequently plummeted to $420 per share six months later.

As we see in this chapter, one way to reduce the risk of investing is to hold a diversified portfolio of stocks. One approach is to invest in mutual funds or exchange traded funds (ETFs) that track the overall market. An even broader diversification strategy is to invest in a wide range of global assets including stocks, bonds, commodities, and real estate. While many U.S. investors are reluctant to invest in foreign stocks and bonds, many foreign markets have performed well, and their performance has not been perfectly correlated with U.S. markets. Therefore, global diversification offers U.S. investors an opportunity to increase returns and at the same time reduce risk. To be sure, however, these other investments can also be quite risky at times.

While many investors are trained to expect some risk, the huge and dramatic swings we have seen in recent years have been unnerving to many. Consequently, there has been increased interest in understanding these extreme price swings. In his bestselling book, *The Black Swan*, Professor Nassim Taleb defines a Black Swan event as:

> …a highly improbable event with three principal characteristics. It is unpredictable, it carries a massive impact, and after the fact, we concoct an explanation that makes it appear less random, and more predictable than it was.

Over the past decade, we have had a series of what could be characterized as Black Swan events—for example, the rise of Google, the terrorist attacks in 2001, the financial crisis, and the tsunami disaster in Japan. Arguably, these events have contributed largely to the high levels of volatility in the overall stock market.

While diversification is important, the events of the past decade show all too well that even fully diversified investors can suffer large losses in short periods of time. As a result, many have become more conservative with their money and are holding larger amounts of cash and other safe assets in their portfolio. Many are convinced that these investors won't return to the market unless they are reasonably assured that the expected returns are enough to justify the risks of stocks and other more speculative investments.

In this chapter, we explore these ideas in more detail, and specifically consider the different types of risk that investors face, the benefits of diversification, and the fundamental trade-off between risk and return. After studying the concepts in this chapter, you should be able to avoid some of the investing pitfalls that a number of investors have faced recently in their quest for wealth.

Source: Nassim Nicholas Taleb, *The Black Swan: The Impact of the Highly Improbable* (New York: Random House, 2007).

PUTTING THINGS IN PERSPECTIVE

We start this chapter from the basic premise that investors like returns and dislike risk; hence, they will invest in risky assets only if those assets offer higher expected returns. We define what risk means as it relates to investments, examine procedures that are used to measure risk, and discuss the relationship between risk and return. Investors should understand these concepts, as should corporate managers as they develop the plans that will shape their firms' futures.

Risk can be measured in different ways, and different conclusions about an asset's riskiness can be reached depending on the measure used. Risk analysis can be confusing, but it will help if you keep the following points in mind:

1. All business assets are expected to produce *cash flows,* and the riskiness of an asset is based on the riskiness of its cash flows. The riskier the cash flows, the riskier the asset.

2. Assets can be categorized as *financial assets,* especially stocks and bonds, and as *real assets,* such as trucks, machines, and whole businesses. In theory, risk analysis for all types of assets is similar, and the same fundamental concepts apply to all assets. However, in practice, differences in the types of available data lead to different procedures for stocks, bonds, and real assets. Our focus in this chapter is on financial assets, especially stocks. We considered bonds in Chapter 7; and we take up real assets in the capital budgeting chapters, especially Chapter 12.

3. A stock's risk can be considered in two ways: (a) on a *stand-alone, or single-stock, basis,* or (b) in a *portfolio context,* where a number of stocks are combined and their consolidated cash flows are analyzed.[1] There is an important difference between stand-alone and portfolio risk, and a stock that has a great deal of risk held by itself may be much less risky when held as part of a larger portfolio.

4. In a portfolio context, a stock's risk can be divided into two components: (a) *diversifiable risk,* which can be diversified away and is thus of little concern to diversified investors, and (b) *market risk,* which reflects the risk of a general stock market decline and cannot be eliminated by diversification (hence, does concern investors). Only market risk is *relevant* to rational investors because diversifiable risk can and will be eliminated.

5. A stock with high market risk must offer a relatively high expected rate of return to attract investors. Investors in general are *averse to risk,* so they will not buy risky assets unless they are compensated with high expected returns.

6. If investors, on average, think a stock's expected return is too low to compensate for its risk, they will start selling it, driving down its price and boosting its expected return. Conversely, if the expected return on a stock is more than enough to compensate for the risk, people will start buying it, raising its price and thus lowering its expected return. The stock will be in equilibrium, with neither buying nor selling pressure, when its expected return is exactly sufficient to compensate for its risk.

7. Stand-alone risk, the topic of Section 8-2, is important in stock analysis primarily as a lead-in to portfolio risk analysis. However, stand-alone risk is extremely important when analyzing real assets such as capital budgeting projects.

When you finish this chapter, you should be able to:

- Explain the difference between stand-alone risk and risk in a portfolio context.
- Describe how risk aversion affects a stock's required rate of return.
- Discuss the difference between diversifiable risk and market risk, and explain how each type of risk affects well-diversified investors.
- Describe what the CAPM is and illustrate how it can be used to estimate a stock's required rate of return.
- Discuss how changes in the general stock and bond markets could lead to changes in the required rate of return on a firm's stock.
- Discuss how changes in a firm's operations might lead to changes in the required rate of return on the firm's stock.

8-1 THE RISK-RETURN TRADE-OFF

As we mention above, we start from a very simple premise that investors like returns and they dislike risk. This premise suggests that there is a fundamental trade-off between risk and return: to entice investors to take on more risk, you have to provide them with higher expected returns. This trade-off is illustrated in Figure 8.1.

The slope of the risk-return line in Panel A of Figure 8.1 indicates how much additional return an individual investor requires in order to take on a higher level of risk. A steeper line suggests that an investor is very averse to taking on

---

[1]A *portfolio* is a collection of investment securities. If you owned stock in General Motors, Exxon Mobil, and IBM, you would be holding a three-stock portfolio. Because diversification lowers risk without sacrificing much, if any, expected return, most stocks are held in portfolios.

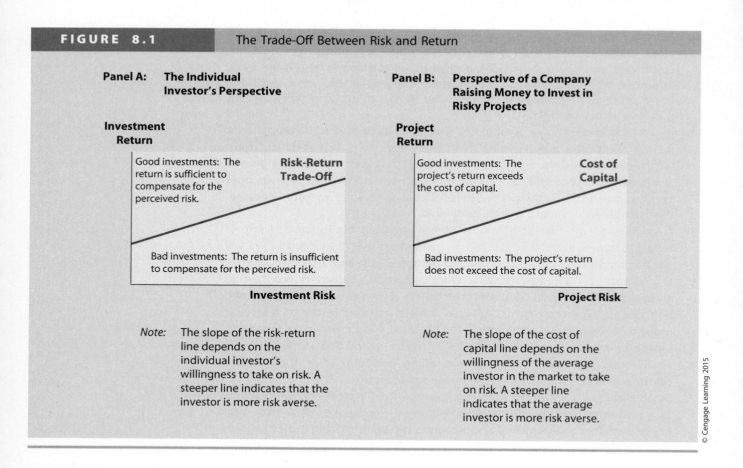

FIGURE 8.1   The Trade-Off Between Risk and Return

Panel A: The Individual Investor's Perspective

Investment Return

Good investments: The return is sufficient to compensate for the perceived risk.

Risk-Return Trade-Off

Bad investments: The return is insufficient to compensate for the perceived risk.

Investment Risk

Note: The slope of the risk-return line depends on the individual investor's willingness to take on risk. A steeper line indicates that the investor is more risk averse.

Panel B: Perspective of a Company Raising Money to Invest in Risky Projects

Project Return

Good investments: The project's return exceeds the cost of capital.

Cost of Capital

Bad investments: The project's return does not exceed the cost of capital.

Project Risk

Note: The slope of the cost of capital line depends on the willingness of the average investor in the market to take on risk. A steeper line indicates that the average investor is more risk averse.

risk, whereas a flatter line would suggest that the investor is more comfortable bearing risk. Not surprisingly, investors who are less comfortable bearing risk tend to gravitate toward lower-risk investments, while investors with a greater-risk appetite tend to put more of their money into higher-risk, higher-return investments. The average investor's willingness to take on risk also varies over time. For example, prior to the recent financial crisis, an increasing number of investors were putting their money into riskier investments that included high-growth stocks, junk bonds, and emerging market funds. In the aftermath of the crisis, there was a tremendous "flight to quality" where investors rapidly moved away from riskier investments and instead flocked toward safer investments such as Treasury securities and money market funds. At any point in time, an investor's goal should be to earn returns that are more than sufficient to compensate for the perceived risk of the investment—in other words, getting above the risk-return trade-off line illustrated in Panel A of Figure 8.1.

The trade-off between risk and return is also an important concept for companies trying to create value for their shareholders. Panel B of Figure 8.1 suggests that if a company is investing in riskier projects, it must offer its investors (both bondholders and stockholders) higher expected returns. As we showed in Chapter 7, higher-risk companies must pay higher yields on their bonds to compensate bondholders for the additional default risk. Likewise, as we will see in this chapter, riskier companies trying to increase their stock price must generate higher returns to compensate their stockholders for the additional risk. It is important to understand that the returns that companies have to pay their investors represent the companies' costs of obtaining capital. Thus from a company's perspective, the risk-return line in Panel B of Figure 8.1 represents its cost of obtaining capital, and the slope of the risk-return line reflects the average investor's current willingness to take on risk. As we will see in Chapters 10 through 12, companies create value by investing in projects where the returns on the investments exceed their costs of capital. Once again, this translates into operating above the risk-return trade-off line.

Throughout the rest of this chapter, we discuss these simple ideas in greater detail. We begin by discussing the concept of risk. Later we discuss returns, and we provide a model for estimating the trade-off between risk and return.

SELF TEST

Briefly explain the fundamental trade-off between risk and return.

What do the slopes of the risk-return lines illustrated in Figure 8.1 indicate?

Does the average investor's willingness to take on risk vary over time? Explain.

What do you think the average investor's risk perception is now? In what types of investments do you think the average investor is investing currently?

Should companies completely avoid high-risk projects? Explain.

8-2 STAND-ALONE RISK

Risk is defined by *Webster's Dictionary* as "a hazard; a peril; exposure to loss or injury." Thus, risk refers to the chance that some unfavorable event will occur. If you engage in skydiving, you are taking a chance with your life—skydiving is risky. If you bet on the horses, you are risking your money.

As we saw in previous chapters, individuals and firms invest funds today with the expectation of receiving additional funds in the future. Bonds offer relatively low returns, but with relatively little risk—at least if you stick to Treasury and high-grade corporate bonds. Stocks offer the chance of higher returns, but stocks are generally riskier than bonds. If you invest in speculative stocks (or, really, *any* stock), you are taking a significant risk in the hope of making an appreciable return.

An asset's risk can be analyzed in two ways: (1) on a stand-alone basis, where the asset is considered by itself, and (2) on a portfolio basis, where the asset is held as one of a number of assets in a portfolio. Thus, an asset's **stand-alone risk** is the risk an investor would face if he or she held only this one asset. Most financial assets, and stocks in particular, are held in portfolios; but it is necessary to understand stand-alone risk to understand risk in a portfolio context.

To illustrate stand-alone risk, suppose an investor buys $100,000 of short-term Treasury bills with an expected return of 5%. In this case, the investment's return, 5%, can be estimated quite precisely; and the investment is defined as being essentially *risk-free*. This same investor could also invest the $100,000 in the stock of a company just being organized to prospect for oil in the mid-Atlantic. Returns on the stock would be much harder to predict. In the worst case, the company would go bankrupt and the investor would lose all of his or her money, in which case the return would be −100%. In the best-case scenario, the company would discover huge amounts of oil and the investor would receive a 1,000% return. When evaluating this investment, the investor might analyze the situation and conclude that the *expected* rate of return, in a statistical sense, is 20%; but the *actual* rate of return could range from, say, +1,000% to −100%. Because there is a significant danger of earning much less than the expected return, such a stock would be relatively risky.

No investment should be undertaken unless the expected rate of return is high enough to compensate for the perceived risk. In our example, it is clear that few if any investors would be willing to buy the oil exploration stock if its expected return didn't exceed that of the T-bill. This is an extreme example. Generally, things are much less

Risk
The chance that some unfavorable event will occur.

Stand-Alone Risk
The risk an investor would face if he or she held only one asset.

obvious, and we need to measure risk in order to decide whether a potential investment should be undertaken. Therefore, we need to define risk more precisely.

As you will see, the risk of an asset is different when the asset is held by itself versus when it is held as a part of a group, or portfolio, of assets. We look at stand-alone risk in this section, and then at portfolio risk in later sections. It's necessary to know something about stand-alone risk in order to understand portfolio risk. Also, stand-alone risk is important to the owners of small businesses and in our examination of physical assets in the capital budgeting chapters. For stocks and most financial assets, though, it is portfolio risk that is most important. Still, you need to understand the key elements of both types of risk.

8-2A STATISTICAL MEASURES OF STAND-ALONE RISK

This is not a statistics book, and we won't spend a great deal of time on statistics. However, you do need an intuitive understanding of the relatively simple statistics presented in this section. All of the calculations can be done easily with a calculator or with Excel; and while we show pictures of the Excel setup, Excel is not needed for the calculations.

Here are the five key items that are covered:

- Probability distributions
- Expected rates of return, $\hat{r}$ ("r hat")
- Historical, or past realized, rates of return, $\bar{r}$ ("r bar")
- Standard deviation, σ (sigma)
- Coefficient of variation (CV)

Probability Distributions
Listings of possible outcomes or events with a probability (chance of occurrence) assigned to each outcome.

Table 8.1 gives the **probability distributions** for Martin Products, which makes engines for long-haul trucks (18-wheelers), and for U.S. Water, which supplies an essential product and thus has very stable sales and profits. Three possible states of the economy are shown in Column 1; and the probabilities of these outcomes, expressed as decimals rather than percentages, are given in Column 2 and then repeated in Column 5. There is a 30% chance of a strong economy and thus strong demand, a 40% probability of normal demand, and a 30% probability of weak demand.

Columns 3 and 6 show the returns for the two companies under each state of the economy. Returns are relatively high when demand is strong and low when demand is weak. Notice, though, that Martin's rate of return could vary far more widely than U.S. Water's. Indeed, there is a fairly high probability that Martin's stock will suffer a 60% loss, while at worst, U.S. Water should have a 5% return.[2]

TABLE 8.1 Probability Distributions and Expected Returns

	A	B	C	D	E	F	G	H
16			Martin Products				U.S. Water	
17			Rate of				Rate of	
18	Economy,	Probability	Return			Probability	Return	
19	Which	of This	if This			of This	if This	
20	Affects	Demand	Demand	Product		Demand	Demand	Product
21	Demand	Occurring	Occurs	(2) × (3)		Occurring	Occurs	(5) × (6)
22	(1)	(2)	(3)	(4)		(5)	(6)	(7)
23	Strong	0.30	80%	24%		0.30	15%	4.5%
24	Normal	0.40	10%	4%		0.40	10%	4.0%
25	Weak	0.30	−60%	−18%		0.30	5%	1.5%
26		1.00	Expected return =	10%		1.00	Expected return =	10.0%
27								

---

[2]While this example is illustrative, it is also somewhat unrealistic. In reality, most stocks have at least some chance of producing a negative return.

Columns 4 and 7 show the products of the probabilities times the returns under the different demand levels. When we sum these products, we obtain the **expected rate of return, r̂** ("r-hat"), for each stock. Both stocks have an expected return of 10%.[3]

We can graph the data in Table 8.1 as shown in Figure 8.2. The height of each bar indicates the probability that a given outcome will occur. The range of possible returns for Martin is from −60% to +80%, and the expected return is 10%. The expected return for U.S. Water is also 10%, but its possible range (and thus maximum loss) is much narrower.

In Figure 8.2, we assumed that only three economic states could occur: strong, normal, and weak. Actually, the economy can range from a deep depression to a fantastic boom; and there are an unlimited number of possibilities in between. Suppose we had the time and patience to assign a probability to each possible level of demand (with the sum of the probabilities still equaling 1.0) and to assign a rate of return to each stock for each level of demand. We would have a table similar to Table 8.1 except that it would have many more demand levels. This table could be used to calculate expected rates of return as shown previously, and

Expected Rate of Return, r̂
The rate of return expected to be realized from an investment; the weighted average of the probability distribution of possible results.

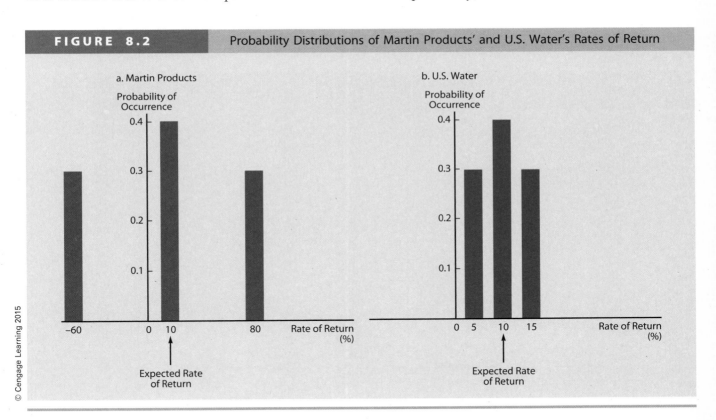

FIGURE 8.2   Probability Distributions of Martin Products' and U.S. Water's Rates of Return

[3]The expected return can also be calculated with an equation that does the same thing as the table:

$$\text{Expected rate of return} = \hat{r} = P_1r_1 + P_2r_2 + \ldots + P_Nr_N$$
$$= \sum_{i=1}^{N} P_ir_i$$

8.1

The second form of the equation is a shorthand expression in which sigma (Σ) means "sum up," or add, the values of N factors. If i = 1, then P_ir_i, = P_1r_1; if i = 2, then P_ir_i, = P_2r_2; and so forth; until i = N, the last possible outcome. The symbol $\sum_{i=1}^{N}$ simply says, "Go through the following process: First, let i = 1 and find the first product; then let i = 2 and find the second product; then continue until each individual product up to N has been found. Add these individual products to find the expected rate of return."

the probabilities and outcomes could be represented by continuous curves such as those shown in Figure 8.3. Here we changed the assumptions so that there is essentially no chance that Martin's return will be less than −60% or more than 80% or that U.S. Water's return will be less than 5% or more than 15%. However, virtually any return within these limits is possible.

The tighter (or more peaked) the probability distributions, the more likely the actual outcome will be close to the expected value and, consequently, the less likely the actual return will end up far below the expected return. *Thus, the tighter the probability distribution, the lower the risk.* As shown in Figure 8.3, because U.S. Water has a relatively tight distribution, its actual return is likely to be closer to its 10% expected return than is true for Martin; so U.S. Water is less risky.[4]

8-2B MEASURING STAND-ALONE RISK: THE STANDARD DEVIATION [5]

It is useful to measure risk for comparative purposes, but risk can be defined and measured in several ways. A common definition that is satisfactory for our purpose is based on probability distributions such as those shown in Figure 8.3: *The tighter the probability distribution of expected future returns, the smaller the risk of a*

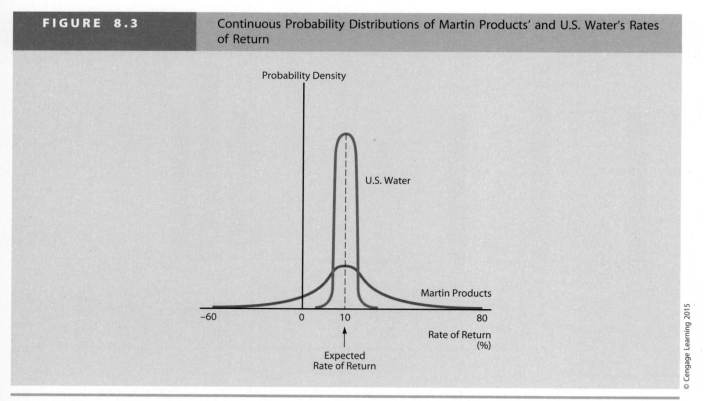

| FIGURE 8.3 | Continuous Probability Distributions of Martin Products' and U.S. Water's Rates of Return |

© Cengage Learning 2015

Note: The assumptions regarding the probabilities of various outcomes have been changed from those in Figure 8.2. There the probability of obtaining exactly 10% was 40%; here it is *much smaller* because there are many possible outcomes instead of just three. With continuous distributions, it is more appropriate to ask what the probability is of obtaining at least some specified rate of return than to ask what the probability is of obtaining exactly that rate. This topic is covered in detail in statistics courses.

---

[4]In this example, we implicitly assume that the state of the economy is the only factor that affects returns. In reality, many factors, including labor, materials, and development costs, influence returns. This is discussed at greater length in the chapters on capital budgeting.

[5]This section is relatively technical, but it can be omitted without loss of continuity.

given investment. According to this definition, U.S. Water is less risky than Martin Products because there is a smaller chance that the actual return of U.S. Water will end up far below its expected return.

We can use the standard deviation (σ, pronounced "sigma") to quantify the tightness of the probability distribution.[6] The smaller the standard deviation, the tighter the probability distribution and, accordingly, the lower the risk. We calculate Martin's σ in Table 8.2. We picked up Columns 1, 2, and 3 from Table 8.1. Then in Column 4, we find the deviation of the return in each demand state from the expected return: Actual return − Expected 10% return. The deviations are squared and shown in Column 5. Each squared deviation is then multiplied by the relevant probability and shown in Column 6. The sum of the products in Column 6 is the *variance* of the distribution. Finally, we find the square root of the variance—this is the *standard deviation,* and it is shown at the bottom of Column 6 both as a fraction and a percentage.[7]

The **standard deviation, σ,** is a measure of how far the actual return is likely to deviate from the expected return. Martin's standard deviation is 54.22%, so its actual return is likely to be quite different from the expected 10%.[8] U.S. Water's standard deviation is 3.87%, so its actual return should be much closer to the expected return of 10%. The average publicly traded firm's σ has been in the range of 20% to 30% in recent years; so Martin is more risky than most stocks, while U.S. Water is less risky.

Standard Deviation, σ
A statistical measure of the variability of a set of observations.

8-2C USING HISTORICAL DATA TO MEASURE RISK [9]

In the last section, we found the mean and standard deviation based on a subjective probability distribution. If we had actual historical data instead, the standard deviation of returns could be found as shown in

	A	B	C	D	E	F	G	H
			Rate of	Deviation:				
	Economy,	Probability	Return	Actual −				
	Which	of This	if This	10%			Squared	
	Affects	Demand	Demand	Expected		Deviation	Deviation	
	Demand	Occurring	Occurs	Return		Squared	× Prob.	
38	(1)	(2)	(3)	(4)		(5)	(6)	
39	Strong	0.30	80%	70%		0.4900	0.1470	
40	Normal	0.40	10%	0%		0.0000	0.0000	
41	Weak	0.30	−60%	−70%		0.4900	0.1470	
42		1.00				Σ = Variance:	0.2940	
43			Standard deviation = square root of variance: σ =				0.5422	
44			Standard deviation expressed as a percentage: σ =				54.22%	

TABLE 8.2 Calculating Martin Products' Standard Deviation

© Cengage Learning 2015

[6]There are actually two types of standard deviations, one for complete distributions and one for situations that involve only a sample. Different formulas and notations are used. Also, the standard deviation should be modified if the distribution is not normal, or bell-shaped. Because our purpose is simply to get the general idea across, we leave the refinements to advanced finance and statistics courses.

[7]This formula summarizes what we did in Table 8.2:

$$\text{Standard deviation} = \sigma = \sqrt{\sum_{i=1}^{N}(r_i - \hat{r})^2 P_i}$$

8.2

[8]With a normal (bell-shaped) distribution, the actual return should be within one σ about 68% of the time.
[9]Again, this section is relatively technical, but it can be omitted without loss of continuity.

TABLE 8.3   Finding σ Based on Historical Data

	A	B	C	D	E	F	G	H
73				Deviation				
74				from			Squared	
75	Year	Return		Average			Deviation	
76	(1)	(2)		(3)			(4)	
77	2011	30.0%		19.8%			0.0390	
78	2012	–10.0%		–20.3%			0.0410	
79	2013	–19.0%		–29.3%			0.0856	
80	2014	40.0%		29.8%			0.0885	
81	Average	10.3%		Sum of Squared Devs (SSDevs):			0.2541	
82				SSDevs/(N – 1) = SSDevs/3:			0.0847	
83			Standard deviation = Square root of SSDevs/3: σ =				29.10%	
84			Excel Function: STDEV(B77:B80) σ =				29.10%	

Table 8.3.[10] Because past results are often repeated in the future, the historical σ is often used as an estimate of future risk.[11] A key question that arises when historical data is used to forecast the future is how far back in time we should go. Unfortunately, there is no simple answer. Using a longer historical time series has the benefit of giving more information, but some of that information may be misleading if you believe that the level of risk in the future is likely to be very different from the level of risk in the past.

All financial calculators (and Excel) have easy-to-use functions for finding σ based on historical data.[12] Simply enter the rates of return and press the key marked S (or S_x) to obtain the standard deviation. However, neither calculators nor Excel have a built-in formula for finding σ where probabilistic data are involved. In those cases, you must go through the process outlined in Table 8.2.

8-2D MEASURING STAND-ALONE RISK: THE COEFFICIENT OF VARIATION

If a choice has to be made between two investments that have the same expected returns but different standard deviations, most people would choose the one with the lower standard deviation and, therefore, the lower risk. Similarly, given a choice between two investments with the same risk (standard deviation) but different expected returns, investors would generally prefer the investment with the higher expected return. To most people, this is common sense—return

---

[10]The 4 years of historical data are considered to be a "sample" of the full (but unknown) set of data, and the procedure used to find the standard deviation is different from the one used for probabilistic data. Here is the equation for sample data, and it is the basis for Table 8.3:

$$\text{Estimated } \sigma = \sqrt{\frac{\sum_{t=1}^{N} (\bar{r}_t - \bar{r}_{Avg})^2}{N-1}}$$

8.2a

Here $\bar{r}_t$ ("r bar t") denotes the past realized rate of return in Period t, and $\bar{r}_{Avg}$ is the average annual return earned over the last N years.

[11]The average return for the past period (10.3% in our example) may also be used as an estimate of future returns, but this is problematic because the average historical return varies widely depending on the period examined. In our example, if we went from 2011 to 2013, we would get a different average from the 10.3%. The average historical return stabilizes with more years of data, but that brings into question whether data from many years ago are still relevant today.

[12]See our tutorials on the text's website or your calculator manual for instructions on calculating historical standard deviations.

is "good" and risk is "bad"; consequently, investors want as much return and as little risk as possible. But how do we choose between two investments if one has the higher expected return but the other has the lower standard deviation? To help answer that question, we use another measure of risk, the **coefficient of variation (CV)**, which is the standard deviation divided by the expected return:

$$\text{Coefficient of variation} = CV = \frac{\sigma}{\hat{r}} \qquad \boxed{8.3}$$

Coefficient of Variation (CV)
The standardized measure of the risk per unit of return; calculated as the standard deviation divided by the expected return.

The coefficient of variation shows the risk per unit of return, and it provides a more meaningful risk measure when the expected returns on two alternatives are not the same. Because U.S. Water and Martin Products have the same expected return, the coefficient of variation is not necessary in this case. In this example, the firm with the larger standard deviation, Martin, must also have the larger coefficient of variation. In fact, the coefficient of variation for Martin is $54.22/10 = 5.42$ and the coefficient of variation for U.S. Water is $3.87/10 = 0.39$. Thus, Martin is about 14 times riskier than U.S. Water on the basis of this criterion.

8-2E RISK AVERSION AND REQUIRED RETURNS

Suppose you inherited \$1 million, which you plan to invest and then retire on the income. You can buy a 5% U.S. Treasury bill, and you will be sure of earning \$50,000 of interest. Alternatively, you can buy stock in R&D Enterprises. If R&D's research programs are successful, your stock will increase to \$2.1 million. However, if the research is a failure, the value of your stock will be zero and you will be penniless. You regard R&D's chances of success or failure as 50-50, so the expected value of the stock a year from now is $0.5(\$0) + 0.5(\$2,100,000) = \$1,050,000$. Subtracting the \$1 million cost leaves an expected \$50,000 profit and a 5% rate of return, the same as for the T-bill:

$$\begin{aligned}
\text{Expected rate of return} &= \frac{\text{Expected ending value} - \text{Cost}}{\text{Cost}} \\[6pt]
&= \frac{\$1,050,000 - \$1,000,000}{\$1,000,000} \\[6pt]
&= \frac{\$50,000}{\$1,000,000} = 5\%
\end{aligned}$$

Given the choice of the sure \$50,000 profit (and 5% rate of return) and the risky expected \$50,000 profit and 5% return, which one would you choose? *If you choose the less risky investment, you are risk-averse. Most investors are risk-averse, and certainly the average investor is with regard to his or her "serious money." Because this is a well-documented fact, we assume **risk aversion** in our discussions throughout the remainder of the book.*

What are the implications of risk aversion for security prices and rates of return? *The answer is that, other things held constant, the higher a security's risk, the higher its required return; and if this situation does not hold, prices will change to bring about the required condition.* To illustrate this point, look back at Figure 8.3 and consider again the U.S. Water and Martin Products stocks. Suppose each stock sells for \$100 per share and each has an expected rate of return of 10%. Investors are averse to risk; so under those conditions, there would be a general preference for U.S. Water. People with money to invest would bid for U.S. Water, and Martin's stockholders would want to sell and use the money to buy U.S. Water. Buying pressure would quickly drive U.S. Water's stock price up, and selling pressure would simultaneously cause Martin's price to fall.

Risk Aversion
Risk-averse investors dislike risk and require higher rates of return as an inducement to buy riskier securities.

These price changes, in turn, would change the expected returns of the two securities. Suppose, for example, that U.S. Water's stock price was bid up from \$100 to \$125 and Martin's stock price declined from \$100 to \$77. These price changes would cause U.S. Water's expected return to fall to 8% and Martin's

THE HISTORICAL TRADE-OFF BETWEEN RISK AND RETURN

The table accompanying this box summarizes the historical trade-off between risk and return for different classes of investments from 1926 through 2012. As the table shows, those assets that produced the highest average returns also had the highest standard deviations and the widest ranges of returns. For example, small-company stocks had the highest average annual return, 16.5%, but the standard deviation of their returns, 32.3%, was also the highest. By contrast, U.S. Treasury bills had the lowest standard deviation, 3.1%, but they also had the lowest average return, 3.6%. While there is no guarantee that history will repeat itself, the returns and standard deviations observed in the past are often used as a starting point for estimating future returns.

Selected Realized Returns, 1926–2012

	Average Return	Standard Deviation
Small-company stocks	16.5%	32.3%
Large-company stocks	11.8	20.2
Long-term corporate bonds	6.4	8.3
Long-term government bonds	6.1	9.7
U.S. Treasury bills	3.6	3.1

Source: Based on *Ibbotson Stocks, Bonds, Bills, and Inflation: 2013 Valuation Yearbook* (Chicago: Morningstar, Inc., 2013), p. 23.

Risk Premium (RP)

The difference between the expected rate of return on a given risky asset and that on a less risky asset.

return to rise to 13%.[13] The difference in returns, 13% − 8% = 5%, would be a **risk premium (RP),** which represents the additional compensation investors require for bearing Martin's higher risk.

This example demonstrates a very important principle: *In a market dominated by risk-averse investors, riskier securities compared to less risky securities must have higher expected returns as estimated by the marginal investor. If this situation does not exist, buying and selling will occur until it does exist.* Later in the chapter we will consider the question of how much higher the returns on risky securities must be, after we see how diversification affects the way risk should be measured.

SELF TEST

What does *investment risk* mean?

Set up an illustrative probability distribution table for an investment with probabilities for different conditions, returns under those conditions, and the expected return.

Which of the two stocks graphed in Figure 8.3 is less risky? Why?

Explain why you agree or disagree with this statement: Most investors are risk-averse.

How does risk aversion affect rates of return?

An investment has a 50% chance of producing a 20% return, a 25% chance of producing an 8% return, and a 25% chance of producing a −12% return. What is its expected return? **(9%)**

---

[13]We assume that each stock is expected to pay shareholders $10 a year in perpetuity. The price of this perpetuity can be found by dividing the annual cash flow by the stock's return. Thus, if the stock's expected return is 10%, the price must be $10/0.10 = $100. Likewise, an 8% expected return would be consistent with a $125 stock price ($10/0.08 = $125) and a 13% return with a $77 stock price ($10/0.13 = $77).

8-3 RISK IN A PORTFOLIO CONTEXT: THE CAPM

In this section, we discuss the risk of stocks when they are held in portfolios rather than as stand-alone assets. Our discussion is based on an extremely important theory, the **Capital Asset Pricing Model, or CAPM**, that was developed in the 1960s.[14] We do not attempt to cover the CAPM in detail—rather, we simply use its intuition to explain how risk should be considered in a world where stocks and other assets are held in portfolios. If you go on to take a course in investments, you will cover the CAPM in detail.

Capital Asset Pricing Model (CAPM)
A model based on the proposition that any stock's required rate of return is equal to the risk-free rate of return plus a risk premium that reflects only the risk remaining after diversification.

Thus far in the chapter we have considered the riskiness of assets when they are held in isolation. This is generally appropriate for small businesses, many real estate investments, and capital budgeting projects. However, the risk of a stock held in a portfolio is typically lower than the stock's risk when it is held alone. Because investors dislike risk and because risk can be reduced by holding portfolios, most stocks are held in portfolios. Banks, pension funds, insurance companies, mutual funds, and other financial institutions are required by law to hold diversified portfolios. Most individual investors—at least those whose security holdings constitute a significant part of their total wealth—also hold portfolios. Therefore, the fact that one particular stock's price increases or decreases is not important—*what is important is the return on the portfolio and the portfolio's risk. Logically, then, the risk and return of an individual stock should be analyzed in terms of how the security affects the risk and return of the portfolio in which it is held.*

To illustrate, Pay Up Inc. is a collection agency that operates nationwide through 37 offices. The company is not well known, its stock is not very liquid, and its earnings have experienced sharp fluctuations in the past. This suggests that Pay Up is risky and that its required rate of return, r, should be relatively high. However, Pay Up's required return in 2014 (and all other years) was quite low in comparison to most other companies. This indicates that investors think Pay Up is a low-risk company in spite of its uncertain profits. *This counterintuitive finding has to do with diversification and its effect on risk.* Pay Up's earnings rise during recessions, whereas most other companies' earnings decline when the economy slumps. Thus, Pay Up's stock is like insurance—it pays off when other investments go bad—so adding Pay Up to a portfolio of "regular" stocks stabilizes the portfolio's returns and makes it less risky.

8-3A EXPECTED PORTFOLIO RETURNS, $\hat{r}_p$

The **expected return on a portfolio, $\hat{r}_p$**, is the weighted average of the expected returns of the individual assets in the portfolio, with the weights being the percentage of the total portfolio invested in each asset:

Expected Return on a Portfolio, $\hat{r}_p$
The weighted average of the expected returns on the assets held in the portfolio.

$$\hat{r}_p = w_1\hat{r}_1 + w_2\hat{r}_2 + \ldots + w_N\hat{r}_N$$
$$= \sum_{i=1}^{N} w_i\hat{r}_i$$

8.4

Here $\hat{r}_i$ is the expected return on the ith stock; the w_i's are the stocks' weights, or the percentage of the total value of the portfolio invested in each stock; and N is the number of stocks in the portfolio.

Table 8.4 can be used to implement the equation. Here we assume that an analyst estimated returns on the four stocks shown in Column 1 for the coming year, as shown in Column 2. Suppose further that you had $100,000 and you planned to invest $25,000, or 25% of the total, in each stock. You could multiply

---

[14]The CAPM was originated by Professor William F. Sharpe in his article "Capital Asset Prices: A Theory of Market Equilibrium Under Conditions of Risk," *Journal of Finance*, vol. 19, no. 3 (1964), pp. 425–442. Literally thousands of articles exploring various aspects of the CAPM have been published subsequently, and it is very widely used in investment analysis.

TABLE 8.4   Expected Return on a Portfolio, $\hat{r}_p$

	A	B	C	D	E	F	G	H
101		Expected	Dollars	Percent of		Product:		
102	Stock	Return	Invested	Total (w_i)		(2) × (4)		
103	(1)	(2)	(3)	(4)		(5)		
104	Microsoft	7.70%	$25,000	25.0%		1.925%		
105	IBM	8.20%	$25,000	25.0%		2.050%		
106	GE	9.45%	$25,000	25.0%		2.363%		
107	Exxon Mobil	7.45%	$25,000	25.0%		1.863%		
108		8.20%	$100,000	100.0%		8.200%	= Expected r_p	
109								

© Cengage Learning 2015

each stock's percentage weight as shown in Column 4 by its expected return; obtain the product terms in Column 5; and then sum Column 5 to calculate the expected portfolio return, 8.20%.

If you added a fifth stock with a higher expected return, the portfolio's expected return would increase, and vice versa if you added a stock with a lower expected return. *The key point to remember is that the expected return on a portfolio is a weighted average of expected returns on the stocks in the portfolio.*

Several additional points should be made:

1. The expected returns in Column 2 would be based on a study of some type, but they would still be essentially subjective and judgmental because different analysts could look at the same data and reach different conclusions. Therefore, this type of analysis must be viewed with a critical eye. Nevertheless, it is useful, indeed necessary, if one is to make intelligent investment decisions.

2. If we added companies such as Delta Airlines and GM, which are generally considered to be relatively risky, their expected returns as estimated by the marginal investor would be relatively high; otherwise, investors would sell them, drive down their prices, and force the expected returns above the returns on safer stocks.

Realized Rates of Return, $\bar{r}$
Returns that were actually earned during some past period. Actual returns ($\bar{r}$) usually turn out to be different from expected returns ($\hat{r}$) except for riskless assets.

3. After the fact and a year later, the actual **realized rates of return**, $\bar{r}_i$, on the individual stocks—the $\bar{r}_i$, or "r-bar," values—would almost certainly be different from the initial expected values. That would cause the portfolio's actual return, $\bar{r}_p$, to differ from the expected return, $\hat{r}_p = 8.20\%$. For example, Microsoft's price might double and thus provide a return of +100%, whereas IBM might have a terrible year, fall sharply, and have a return of −75%. Note, though, that those two events would be offsetting; so the portfolio's return still might be close to its expected return even though the returns on the individual stocks were far from their expected values.

8-3B PORTFOLIO RISK

Although the expected return on a portfolio is simply the weighted average of the expected returns on its individual stocks, the portfolio's risk, σ_p, is *not* the weighted average of the individual stocks' standard deviations. The portfolio's risk is generally *smaller* than the average of the stocks' σs because diversification lowers the portfolio's risk.

To illustrate this point, consider the situation in Figure 8.4. The bottom section gives data on Stocks W and M individually and data on a portfolio with 50% in each stock. The left graph plots the data in a time series format, and it shows that the returns on the individual stocks vary widely from year to year. Therefore, the individual stocks are risky. However, the portfolio's returns are constant at 15%,

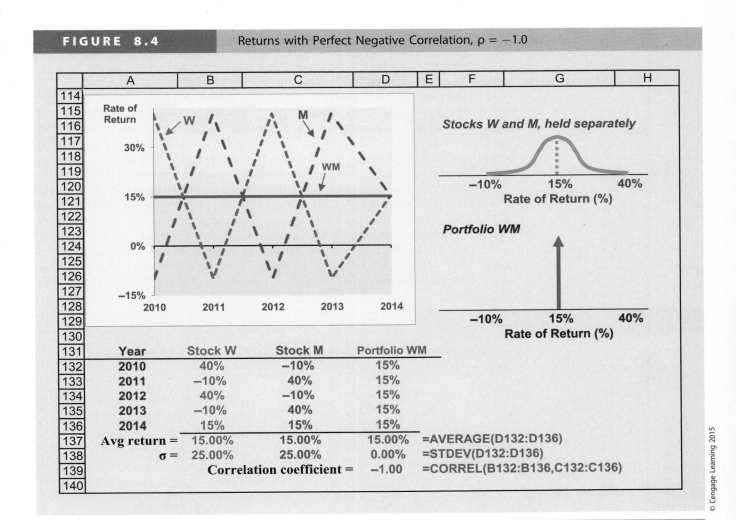

FIGURE 8.4 Returns with Perfect Negative Correlation, ρ = −1.0

Year	Stock W	Stock M	Portfolio WM	
2010	40%	−10%	15%	
2011	−10%	40%	15%	
2012	40%	−10%	15%	
2013	−10%	40%	15%	
2014	15%	15%	15%	
Avg return =	15.00%	15.00%	15.00%	=AVERAGE(D132:D136)
σ =	25.00%	25.00%	0.00%	=STDEV(D132:D136)
Correlation coefficient =			−1.00	=CORREL(B132:B136,C132:C136)

indicating that it is not risky at all. The probability distribution graphs to the right show the same thing—the two stocks would be quite risky if they were held in isolation; but when they are combined to form Portfolio WM, they have no risk whatsoever.

If you invested all of your money in Stock W, you would have an expected return of 15%, but you would face a great deal of risk. The same thing would hold if you invested entirely in Stock M. However, if you invested 50% in each stock, you would have the same expected return of 15%, but with no risk whatsoever. Being rational and averse to risk, you and all other rational investors would choose to hold the portfolio, not the stocks individually.

Stocks W and M can be combined to form a riskless portfolio because their returns move countercyclically to each other—when W's fall, M's rise, and vice versa. The tendency of two variables to move together is called **correlation**, and the **correlation coefficient, ρ** (pronounced "rho"), measures this tendency.[15]

Correlation
The tendency of two variables to move together.

Correlation Coefficient, ρ
A measure of the degree of relationship between two variables.

---

[15]The correlation coefficient, ρ, can range from +1.0, denoting that the two variables move up and down in perfect synchronization, to −1.0, denoting that the variables move in exactly opposite directions. A correlation coefficient of zero indicates that the two variables are not related to each other—that is, changes in one variable are independent of changes in the other. It is easy to calculate correlation coefficients with a financial calculator. Simply enter the returns on the two stocks and press a key labeled "r." For W and M, ρ = −1.0. See our tutorial on the text's website or your calculator manual for the exact steps. Also, note that the correlation coefficient is often denoted by the term r. We use ρ here to avoid confusion with r used to denote the rate of return.

In statistical terms, we say that the returns on Stocks W and M are *perfectly negatively correlated*, with $\rho = -1.0$. The opposite of perfect negative correlation is *perfect positive correlation*, with $\rho = +1.0$. If returns are not related to one another at all, they are said to be *independent* and $\rho = 0$.

The returns on two perfectly positively correlated stocks with the same expected return would move up and down together, and a portfolio consisting of these stocks would be exactly as risky as the individual stocks. If we drew a graph like Figure 8.4, we would see just one line because the two stocks and the portfolio would have the same return at each point in time. *Thus, diversification is completely useless for reducing risk if the stocks in the portfolio are perfectly positively correlated.*

We see then that when stocks are perfectly negatively correlated ($\rho = -1.0$), all risk can be diversified away; but when stocks are perfectly positively correlated ($\rho = +1.0$), diversification does no good. In reality, most stocks are positively correlated but not perfectly so. Past studies have estimated that on average, the correlation coefficient between the returns of two randomly selected stocks is about 0.30.[16] *Under this condition, combining stocks into portfolios reduces risk but does not completely eliminate it.*[17] Figure 8.5 illustrates this point using two stocks

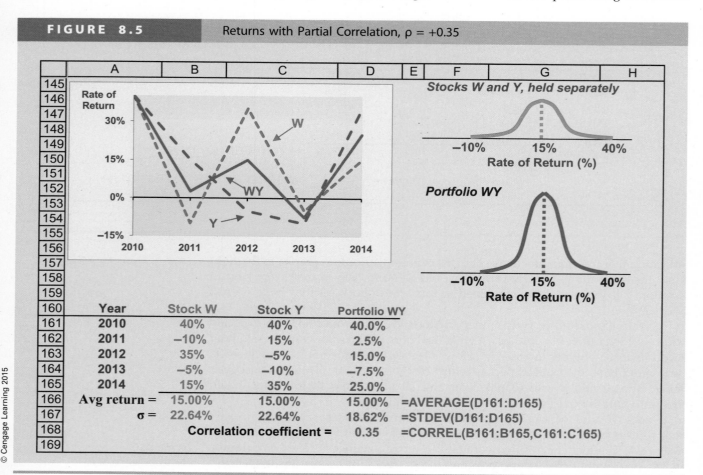

FIGURE 8.5	Returns with Partial Correlation, $\rho = +0.35$

Year	Stock W	Stock Y	Portfolio WY	
2010	40%	40%	40.0%	
2011	−10%	15%	2.5%	
2012	35%	−5%	15.0%	
2013	−5%	−10%	−7.5%	
2014	15%	35%	25.0%	
Avg return =	15.00%	15.00%	15.00%	=AVERAGE(D161:D165)
σ =	22.64%	22.64%	18.62%	=STDEV(D161:D165)
Correlation coefficient =		0.35	=CORREL(B161:B165,C161:C165)	

---

[16]A study by Chan, Karceski, and Lakonishok (1999) estimated that the average correlation coefficient between two randomly selected stocks was 0.28, while the average correlation coefficient between two large-company stocks was 0.33. The time period of their sample was 1968 to 1998. See Louis K. C. Chan, Jason Karceski, and Josef Lakonishok, "On Portfolio Optimization: Forecasting Covariance and Choosing the Risk Model," *The Review of Financial Studies*, vol. 12, no. 5 (Winter 1999), pp. 937–974.

[17]If we combined a large number of stocks with $\rho = 0$, we could form a riskless portfolio. However, there are not many stocks with $\rho = 0$. Stocks' returns tend to move together, not to be independent of one another.

whose correlation coefficient is ρ = +0.35. The portfolio's average return is 15%, which is the same as the average return for the two stocks; but its standard deviation is 18.62%, which is below the stocks' standard deviations and their average σ. Again, a rational, risk-averse investor would be better off holding the portfolio rather than just one of the individual stocks.

In our examples, we considered portfolios with only two stocks. What would happen if we increased the number of stocks in the portfolio? *As a rule, on average, portfolio risk declines as the number of stocks in a portfolio increases.*

If we added enough partially correlated stocks, could we completely eliminate risk? In general, the answer is no. For an illustration, see Figure 8.6 which shows that a portfolio's risk declines as stocks are added. Here are some points to keep in mind about the figure:

1. The portfolio's risk declines as stocks are added, but at a decreasing rate; and once 40 to 50 stocks are in the portfolio, additional stocks do little to reduce risk.

2. The portfolio's total risk can be divided into two parts, **diversifiable risk** and **market risk**. Diversifiable risk is the risk that is eliminated by adding stocks. Market risk is the risk that remains even if the portfolio holds every stock in the market.

Diversifiable Risk

That part of a security's risk associated with random events; it can be eliminated by proper diversification. This risk is also known as company-specific, or unsystematic, risk.

Market Risk

The risk that remains in a portfolio after diversification has eliminated all company-specific risk. This risk is also known as non-diversifiable or systematic or beta risk.

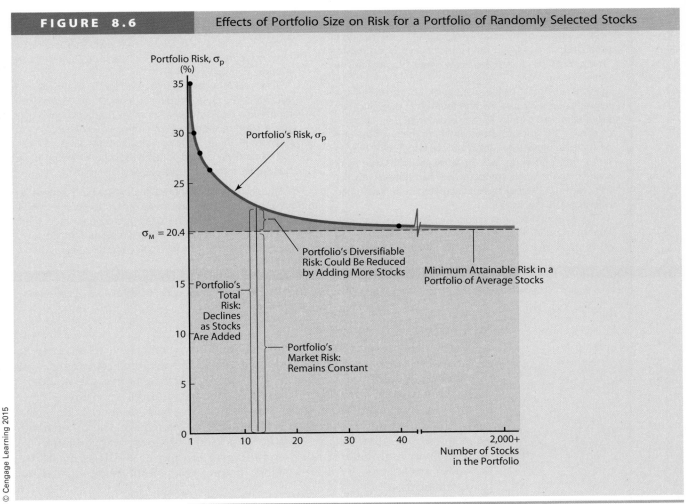

| FIGURE 8.6 | Effects of Portfolio Size on Risk for a Portfolio of Randomly Selected Stocks |

Note: This graph assumes that stocks in the portfolio are randomly selected from the universe of large, publicly traded stocks listed on the NYSE.

ADDING MORE STOCKS DOESN'T ALWAYS REDUCE THE RISK OF YOUR PORTFOLIO

While Figure 8.6 illustrates the importance of diversification, it is important to realize that in some cases adding more stocks to your portfolio does not always reduce risk. In fact, in some cases, it can even increase risk. To understand why this is so, assume that the first stock you randomly select for your portfolio is a very safe utility firm, but the second stock you randomly select for your portfolio is a very risky biotechnology firm. In this case, your two-stock portfolio is likely to have more risk, even though you are realizing some benefits from diversification.

A recent article in *The Wall Street Journal* sheds more light on this issue. The article discusses some recent research by Professor Don Chance of Louisiana State University. Professor Chance conducted a classroom study where he asked students to first select a stock for their portfolio, and then to keep adding stocks until they had a portfolio of 30 stocks. Here's a summary of his findings:

> Prof. Chance wanted to prove to his students that diversification works. On average, for the group as a whole, diversifying from one stock to 20 cut the riskiness of portfolios by roughly 40%, just as the research predicted. "It was like a magic trick," says Prof. Chance. "The classes produced the exact same graph that's in their textbook."
>
> But then Prof. Chance went back and analyzed the results student by student, and found that diversification failed remarkably often. As they broadened their holdings from a single stock to a basket of 30, many of the students raised their risk instead of lowering it. One in nine times, they ended up with 30-stock portfolios that were riskier than the single company they had started with. For 23%, the final 30-stock basket fluctuated more than it had with only five stocks in it.
>
> The lesson: For any given investor, the averages mightn't apply. "We send this message out that you don't need that many stocks to diversify," says Prof.

Chance, "but that's just not true." What accounts for these odd results?

> Leave it to a professor called Chance to show that even a random process produces seemingly unlikely outliers. Thirteen percent of the time, a 20-stock portfolio generated by computer will be riskier than a one-stock portfolio.

Also note that if instead of randomly adding stocks to your portfolio, you keep adding the same types of stocks (for example, all technology stocks or all financial stocks) to your portfolio then the benefits of diversification will be considerably less dramatic. Keep in mind, however, the larger point. On average, you will have a hard time reducing risk if you only hold a small number of stocks in your portfolio. With this point in mind, many analysts recommend that individual investors invest in index funds that provide extensive diversification with low transactions costs. Echoing this argument, *The Wall Street Journal* article concludes by offering the following observation and recommendation:

> According to the Federal Reserve's Survey of Consumer Finances, 84% of households that own shares directly have no more than nine stocks; 36% hold shares in only a single company.
>
> That's way too few. But 30 or 40 isn't enough either. If you want to pick stocks directly, put 90% to 95% of your money in a total stock-market index fund, which will give you a stake in thousands of companies at low cost. Put the rest in three to five stocks, at most, that you can follow closely and hold patiently. Beyond a handful, more companies may well leave you less diversified.

You should note that Figure 8.6 shows what happens *on average* if you *randomly* add more stocks to your portfolio. But while the picture shows what happens on average, there is certainly no guarantee that every time you add stocks to your portfolio that the portfolio's risk will decline.

3. Diversifiable risk is caused by such random, unsystematic events as lawsuits, strikes, successful and unsuccessful marketing and R&D programs, the winning or losing of a major contract, and other events that are unique to the particular firm. Because these events are random, their effects on a portfolio can be eliminated by diversification—bad events for one firm will be offset by good events for another. Market risk, on the other hand, stems from factors that systematically affect most firms: war, inflation, recessions, high interest rates, and other macro factors. Because most stocks are affected by macro factors, market risk cannot be eliminated by diversification.

4. If we carefully selected the stocks included in the portfolio rather than adding them randomly, the graph would change. In particular, if we chose

stocks with low correlations with one another and with low stand-alone risk, the portfolio's risk would decline faster than if random stocks were added. The reverse would hold if we added stocks with high correlations and high σs.

5. Most investors are rational in the sense that they dislike risk, other things held constant. That being the case, why would an investor ever hold one (or a few) stocks? Why not hold a **market portfolio** consisting of all stocks? There are several reasons. First, high administrative costs and commissions would more than offset the benefits for individual investors. Second, index funds can be used by investors for diversification, and many individuals can and do get broad diversification through these funds. Third, some people think they can pick stocks that will "beat the market"; so they buy them rather than the broad market. And fourth, some people can, through superior analysis, beat the market; so they find and buy undervalued stocks and sell overvalued ones and, in the process, cause most stocks to be properly valued, with their expected returns consistent with their risks.

Market Portfolio
A portfolio consisting of all stocks.

6. One key question remains: How should the risk of an individual stock be measured? The standard deviation of expected returns, σ, is not appropriate because it includes risk that can be eliminated by holding the stock in a portfolio. How then should we measure a stock's risk in a world where most people hold portfolios? That's the subject of the next section.

8-3c Risk in a Portfolio Context: The Beta Coefficient

When a stock is held by itself, its risk can be measured by the standard deviation of its expected returns. However, σ is not appropriate when the stock is held in a portfolio, as stocks generally are. So how do we measure a stock's **relevant risk** in a portfolio context?

First, note that all risk except that related to broad market movements can and will be diversified away by most investors—rational investors will hold enough stocks to move down the risk curve in Figure 8.6 to the point where only market risk remains in their portfolios.

Relevant Risk
The risk that remains once a stock is in a diversified portfolio is its contribution to the portfolio's market risk. It is measured by the extent to which the stock moves up or down with the market.

> *The risk that remains once a stock is in a diversified portfolio is its contribution to the portfolio's market risk, and that risk can be measured by the extent to which the stock moves up or down with the market.*

The tendency of a stock to move with the market is measured by its **beta coefficient, b**. Ideally, when estimating a stock's beta, we would like to have a crystal ball that tells us how the stock is going to move relative to the overall stock market in the future. But because we can't look into the future, we often use historical data and assume that the stock's historical beta will give us a reasonable estimate of how the stock will move relative to the market in the future.

Beta Coefficient, b
A metric that shows the extent to which a given stock's returns move up and down with the stock market. Beta measures market risk.

To illustrate the use of historical data, consider Figure 8.7, which shows the historical returns on three stocks and a market index. In Year 1, "the market," as defined by a portfolio containing all stocks, had a total return (dividend yield plus capital gains yield) of 10%, as did the three individual stocks. In Year 2, the market went up sharply and its return was 20%. Stocks H (for high) soared to 30%; A (for average) returned 20%, the same as the market; and L (for low) returned 15%. In Year 3, the market dropped sharply; its return was −10%. The three stocks' returns also fell—H's return was −30%, A's was −10%, and L broke even with a 0% return. In Years 4 and 5, the market returned 0% and 5%, respectively, and the three stocks' returns were as shown in the figure.

FIGURE 8.7	Betas: Relative Volatility of Stocks H, A, and L

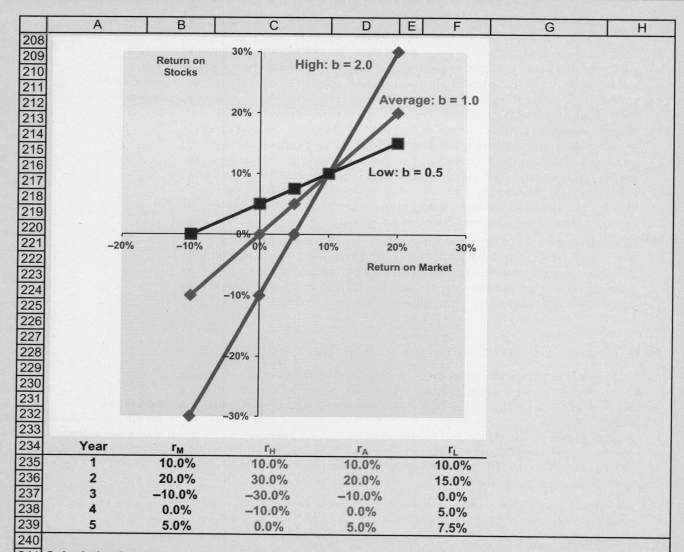

	A	B	C	D	E	F
234	**Year**	r_M	r_H	r_A		r_L
235	1	10.0%	10.0%	10.0%		10.0%
236	2	20.0%	30.0%	20.0%		15.0%
237	3	−10.0%	−30.0%	−10.0%		0.0%
238	4	0.0%	−10.0%	0.0%		5.0%
239	5	5.0%	0.0%	5.0%		7.5%

Calculating beta:

1. Rise-Over-Run. Divide the vertical axis change that results from a given change on the horizontal axis, i.e., the change in the stock's return divided by the change in the market return. For Stock H, when the Market rises from −10% to +20%, or by 30%, the stock's return goes from −30% to +30%, or by 60%. Thus, beta H by the rise-over-run method is 60/30 = 2.0. In the same way, we find beta A to be 1.0 and beta L to be 0.5. This procedure is easy in our example because all the points lie on a straight line, but if the points were scattered around the trend line, we could not calculate an exact beta in this manner.

2. Financial Calculator. Financial calculators have a built-in function that can be used to calculate beta. The procedure differs somewhat from calculator to calculator. See our tutorial on the text's website for instructions on several calculators.

3. Excel. Excel's Slope function can be used to calculate betas. Here are the functions for our three stocks:

Beta$_H$	2.0	=SLOPE(C235:C239,B235:B239)
Beta$_A$	1.0	=SLOPE(D235:D239,B235:B239)
Beta$_L$	0.5	=SLOPE(F235:F239,B235:B239)

A plot of the data shows that the three stocks moved up or down with the market but that H was twice as volatile as the market, A was exactly as volatile as the market, and L had only half the market's volatility. It is apparent that the steeper the line, the greater the stock's volatility and thus the larger its loss in a down market. *The slopes of the lines are the stocks' beta coefficients.* We see in the figure that the slope coefficient for H is 2.0; for A, it is 1.0; and for L, it is 0.5.[18] Thus, beta measures a given stock's volatility relative to the market, and an **average stock's beta, b_A = 1.0.**

Stock A is defined as an *average-risk stock* because it has a beta of b = 1.0 and thus moves up and down in step with the general market. Thus, an average stock will, in general, move up by 10% when the market moves up by 10% and fall by 10% when the market falls by 10%. A large portfolio of such b = 1.0 stocks would (1) have all of its diversifiable risk removed but (2) would still move up and down with the broad market averages and thus have a degree of risk.

Stock H, which has b = 2.0, is twice as volatile as an average stock, which means that it is twice as risky. The value of a portfolio consisting of b = 2.0 stocks could double—or halve—in a short time; and if you held such a portfolio, you could quickly go from being a millionaire to being a pauper. Stock L, on the other hand, with b = 0.5, is only half as volatile as the average stock, and a portfolio of such stocks would rise and fall only half as rapidly as the market. Thus, its risk would be half that of an average-risk portfolio with b = 1.0.

Betas for literally thousands of companies are calculated and published by Value Line, Yahoo!, Google, and numerous other organizations; and the beta coefficients of some well-known companies are shown in Table 8.5. Most stocks have betas in the range of 0.50 to 1.50; and the average beta for all stocks is 1.0, which indicates that the average stock moves in sync with the market.[19]

Average Stock's Beta, b_A
By definition, b_A = 1 because an average-risk stock is one that tends to move up and down in step with the general market.

Illustrative List of Beta Coefficients   TABLE 8.5

Stock	Beta
Bank of America	1.90
Daimler AG	1.55
Harley-Davidson	1.50
Dow Chemical	1.30
General Electric	1.20
NCR Corporation	1.20
eBay	1.10
Best Buy	1.10
Cracker Barrel	1.00
Chipotle Mexican Grill	0.95
Microsoft	0.85
Exxon Mobil	0.75
NextEra Energy	0.70
Coca-Cola	0.60
Procter & Gamble	0.60

© Cengage Learning 2005

Source: Adapted from *Value Line Investment Survey* (valueline.com), April 2013.

[18]For more on calculating betas, see Brigham and Daves, *Intermediate Financial Management*, 11th edition (South-Western/Mason, OH: South-Western/Cengage Learning, 2013), Chapters 2 and 3.
[19]While fairly uncommon, it is possible for a stock to have a negative beta. In that case, the stock's returns would tend to rise whenever the returns on other stocks fell.

If a stock whose beta is greater than 1.0 (say 1.5) is added to a $b_p = 1.0$ portfolio, the portfolio's beta and consequently its risk will increase. Conversely, if a stock whose beta is less than 1.0 is added to a $b_p = 1.0$ portfolio, the portfolio's beta and risk will decline. *Thus, because a stock's beta reflects its contribution to the riskiness of a portfolio, beta is the theoretically correct measure of the stock's riskiness.*

We can summarize our discussion up to this point as follows:

1. A stock's risk has two components, diversifiable risk and market risk.

2. Diversifiable risk can be eliminated; and most investors do eliminate it, either by holding very large portfolios or by buying shares in a mutual fund. We are left, then, with market risk, which is caused by general movements in the stock market and reflects the fact that most stocks are systematically affected by events such as wars, recessions, and inflation. Market risk is the only risk that should matter to a rational, diversified investor.

3. Investors must be compensated for bearing risk—the greater the risk of a stock, the higher its required return. However, compensation is required only for risk that cannot be eliminated by diversification. If risk premiums existed on a stock due to its diversifiable risk, that stock would be a bargain to well-diversified investors. They would start buying it and bid up its price, and the stock's final (equilibrium) price would be consistent with an expected return that reflected only its market risk.

    To illustrate this point, suppose half of Stock B's risk is market risk (it occurs because the stock moves up and down with the market), while the other half is diversifiable. You are thinking of buying Stock B and holding it in a one-stock portfolio, so you would be exposed to all of its risk. As compensation for bearing so much risk, you want a risk premium of 8% over the 6% T-bond rate; so your required return is $r_B = 6\% + 8\% = 14\%$. But other investors, including your professor, are well diversified. They are also looking at Stock B; but they would hold it in diversified portfolios, eliminate its diversifiable risk, and thus be exposed to only half as much risk as you are. Therefore, their required risk premium would be half as large as yours, and their required rate of return would be $r_B = 6\% + 4\% = 10\%$.

    If the stock was priced to yield the 14% you require, those diversified investors, including your professor, would buy it, push its price up and its yield down, and prevent you from purchasing the stock at a price low enough to provide the 14% return. In the end, you would have to accept a 10% return or keep your money in the bank.

4. The market risk of a stock is measured by its beta coefficient, which is an index of the stock's relative volatility. Here are some benchmark betas:

    $b = 0.5$: Stock is only half as volatile, or risky, as an average stock.
    $b = 1.0$: Stock is of average risk.
    $b = 2.0$: Stock is twice as risky as an average stock.

5. A portfolio consisting of low-beta stocks will also have a low beta because the beta of a portfolio is a weighted average of its individual securities' betas, found using this equation:

$$b_p = w_1 b_1 + w_2 b_2 + \ldots + w_N b_N$$

$$= \sum_{i=1}^{N} w_i b_i$$

8.5

Here b_p is the beta of the portfolio, and it shows how volatile the portfolio is relative to the market; w_i is the fraction of the portfolio invested in the

i^{th} stock; and b_i is the beta coefficient of the ith stock. To illustrate, if an investor holds a $100,000 portfolio consisting of $33,333.33 invested in each of three stocks and if each of the stocks has a beta of 0.70, the portfolio's beta will be $b_p = 0.70$:

$$b_p = 0.333(0.70) + 0.333(0.70) + 0.333(0.70) = 0.70$$

Such a portfolio would be less risky than the market, so it should experience relatively narrow price swings and have relatively small rate-of-return fluctuations. In terms of Figure 8.7, the slope of its regression line would be 0.70, which is less than that for a portfolio of average stocks.

Now suppose one of the existing stocks is sold and replaced by a stock with $b_i = 2.00$. This action will increase the portfolio's beta from $b_{p1} = 0.70$ to $b_{p2} = 1.13$:

$$b_{p2} = 0.333(0.70) + 0.333(0.70) + 0.333(2.00) = 1.13$$

Had a stock with $b_i = 0.20$ been added, the portfolio's beta would have declined from 0.70 to 0.53. Adding a low-beta stock would therefore reduce the portfolio's riskiness. Consequently, changing the stocks in a portfolio can change the riskiness of that portfolio.

6. Because a stock's beta coefficient determines how the stock affects the riskiness of a diversified portfolio, beta is, in theory, the most relevant measure of a stock's risk.

 QUICK QUESTION

QUESTION:
Portfolio P consists of two stocks: 50% is invested in Stock A and 50% is invested in Stock B. Stock A has a standard deviation of 25% and a beta of 1.2, while Stock B has a standard deviation of 35% and a beta of 0.80. The correlation between these stocks is 0.4.

a. What is the standard deviation of Portfolio P?
  1. Less than 30%
  2. 30%
  3. More than 30%
b. What is the beta of Portfolio P?
c. Which stock is riskier to a diversified investor?

ANSWER:
a. No calculation is needed to answer this question. Remember that the standard deviation of a portfolio of two stocks is less than the weighted average of the individual stocks' standard deviations, as long as the correlation between the stocks is less than 1.0. So, in this case because the correlation is 0.4, we know that the standard deviation of Portfolio P is less than 30%.

b. $b_p = 0.5(1.2) + 0.5(0.8)$

   $b_p = 1.0$.

   The beta of a portfolio is equal to the weighted average of the individual stocks' betas.

c. The relevant measure of risk to a diversified investor is beta. It follows that a diversified investor would view the higher beta stock (Stock A) as being more risky.

GLOBAL PERSPECTIVES

The Benefits of Diversifying Overseas

The increasing availability of international securities is making it possible to achieve a better risk-return trade-off than could be obtained by investing only in U.S. securities. So investing overseas might result in a portfolio with less risk but a higher expected return. This result occurs because of low correlations between the returns on U.S. and international securities, along with potentially high returns on overseas stocks.

Figure 8.6, presented earlier, demonstrated that an investor can reduce the risk of his or her portfolio by holding a number of stocks. The figure below suggests that investors may be able to reduce risk even further by holding a portfolio of stocks from all around the world, given the fact that the returns on domestic and international stocks are not perfectly correlated.

Even though foreign stocks represent roughly 60% of the worldwide equity market and despite the apparent benefits from investing overseas, the typical U.S. investor still puts less than 10% of his or her money in foreign stocks. One possible explanation for this reluctance to invest overseas is that investors prefer domestic stocks because of lower transactions costs. However, this explanation is questionable because recent studies reveal that investors buy and sell overseas stocks more frequently than they trade their domestic stocks.

Other explanations for the domestic bias include the additional risks from investing overseas (for example, exchange rate risk) and the fact that the typical U.S. investor is uninformed about international investments and/or thinks that international investments are extremely risky. It has been argued that world capital markets have become more integrated, causing the correlation of returns between different countries to increase, which reduces the benefits from international diversification. In addition, U.S. corporations are investing more internationally, providing U.S. investors with international diversification even if they purchase only U.S. stocks.

Given the benefits of global diversification, many analysts recommend that U.S. investors hold a large percentage of foreign assets in their portfolio. For example, Mohamed El-Erian, a noted investor who is CEO of the investment management firm PIMCO and who appears regularly on CNBC, recently recommended that for long-term investors, U.S. stocks should be only 15% of their portfolio. While different analysts have different views and El-Erian's recommendations may seem extreme to some, our guess is that in the future U.S. investors will shift more of their assets to overseas investments.

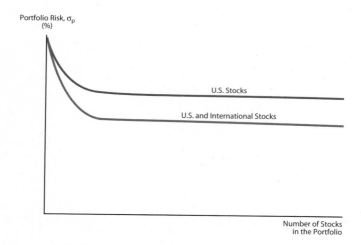

Sources: Geoff Colvin, "Mohamed El-Erian: Tough Times Ahead," *CNNMoney.com* (money.cnn.com), December 10, 2009; and Kenneth Kasa, "Measuring the Gains from International Portfolio Diversification," *Federal Reserve Bank of San Francisco Weekly Letter*, no. 94–14, April 8, 1994.

Explain the following statement: An asset held as part of a portfolio is generally less risky than the same asset held in isolation.

What is meant by *perfect positive correlation, perfect negative correlation,* and *zero correlation*?

In general, can the riskiness of a portfolio be reduced to zero by increasing the number of stocks in the portfolio? Explain.

What is an average-risk stock? What is the beta of such a stock?

Why is it argued that beta is the best measure of a stock's risk?

An investor has a two-stock portfolio with $25,000 invested in Stock X and $50,000 invested in Stock Y. X's beta is 1.50, and Y's beta is 0.60. What is the beta of the investor's portfolio? **(0.90)**

8-4 THE RELATIONSHIP BETWEEN RISK AND RATES OF RETURN

The preceding section demonstrated that under the CAPM theory, beta is the most appropriate measure of a stock's relevant risk. The next issue is this: For a given level of risk as measured by beta, what rate of return is required to compensate investors for bearing that risk? To begin, let us define the following terms:

$\hat{r}_i$ = *expected* rate of return on the ith stock.

r_i = *required* rate of return on the ith stock. Note that if $\hat{r}_i$ is less than r_i, the typical investor will not purchase this stock or will sell it if he or she owns it. If $\hat{r}_i$ is greater than r_i, the investor will purchase the stock because it looks like a bargain. Investors will be indifferent if $\hat{r}_i = r_i$. Buying and selling by investors tends to force the expected return to equal the required return, although the two can differ from time to time before the adjustment is completed.

$\bar{r}_i$ = realized, after-the-fact return. A person obviously does not know $\bar{r}_i$ at the time he or she is considering the purchase of a stock.

r_{RF} = risk-free rate of return. In this context, r_{RF} is generally measured by the return on U.S. Treasury securities. Some analysts recommend that short-term T-bills be used; others recommend long-term T-bonds. We generally use T-bonds because their maturity is closer to the average investor's holding period for stocks.

b_i = beta coefficient of the ith stock. The beta of an average stock is $b_A = 1.0$.

r_M = required rate of return on a portfolio consisting of all stocks, which is called the *market portfolio*. r_M is also the required rate of return on an average ($b_A = 1.0$) stock.

$RP_M = (r_M - r_F)$ = risk premium on "the market" and the premium on an average stock. This is the additional return over the risk-free rate required to compensate an average investor for assuming an average amount of risk. Average risk means a stock where $b_i = b_A = 1.0$.

$RP_i = (r_M - r_{RF})b_i = (RP_M)b_i$ = risk premium on the ith stock. A stock's risk premium will be less than, equal to, or greater than the premium on an average stock, RP_M, depending on whether its beta is less than, equal to, or greater than 1.0. If $b_i = b_A = 1.0$, then $RP_i = RP_M$.

Market Risk Premium, RP$_M$

The additional return over the risk-free rate needed to compensate investors for assuming an average amount of risk.

The **market risk premium, RP$_M$**, shows the premium that investors require for bearing the risk of an average stock. The size of this premium depends on how risky investors think the stock market is and on their degree of risk aversion. Let us assume that at the current time, Treasury bonds yield $r_{RF} = 6\%$ and an average share of stock has a required rate of return of $r_M = 11\%$. Therefore, the market risk premium is 5%, calculated as follows:

$$RP_M = r_M - r_{RF} = 11\% - 6\% = 5\%$$

It should be noted that the risk premium of an average stock, $r_M - r_{RF}$, is hard to measure because it is impossible to obtain a precise estimate of the expected future return of the market, r_M.[20] Given the difficulty of estimating future market returns, analysts often look to historical data to estimate the market risk premium. Historical data suggest that the market risk premium varies somewhat from year to year due to changes in investors' risk aversion but that it has generally ranged from 4% to 8%.

While historical estimates might be a good starting point for estimating the market risk premium, those estimates would be misleading if investors' attitudes toward risk changed considerably over time. (See "Estimating the Market Risk Premium" box on page 283.) Indeed, many analysts have argued that the market risk premium has fallen in recent years. If this claim is correct, the market risk premium is considerably lower than one based on historical data.

The risk premium on individual stocks varies in a systematic manner from the market risk premium. For example, if one stock is twice as risky as another stock as measured by their beta coefficients, its risk premium should be twice as high. Therefore, if we know the market risk premium, RP$_M$, and the stock's beta, b_i, we can find its risk premium as the product $(RP_M)b_i$. For example, if beta for Stock L = 0.5 and RP$_M$ = 5%, RP$_L$ will be 2.5%:

$$\begin{aligned}
\text{Risk premium for Stock L} = RP_L &= (RP_M)b_L \\
&= (5\%)(0.5) \\
&= 2.5\%
\end{aligned}$$

8.6

As the discussion in Chapter 6 implied, the required return for any stock can be found as follows:

Required return on a stock = Risk-free return + Premium for the stock's risk

Here the risk-free return includes a premium for expected inflation; and if we assume that the stocks under consideration have similar maturities and liquidity, the required return on Stock L can be found using the **Security Market Line (SML) equation**:

Security Market Line (SML) Equation

An equation that shows the relationship between risk as measured by beta and the required rates of return on individual securities.

$$\begin{aligned}
\genfrac{}{}{0pt}{}{\text{Required return}}{\text{on Stock L}} &= \genfrac{}{}{0pt}{}{\text{Risk-free}}{\text{return}} + \left(\genfrac{}{}{0pt}{}{\text{Market risk}}{\text{premium}}\right)\left(\genfrac{}{}{0pt}{}{\text{Stock L's}}{\text{beta}}\right) \\
r_L &= r_{RF} + (r_M - r_{RF})b_L \\
&= r_{RF} + (RP_M)b_L \\
&= 6\% + (11\% - 6\%)(0.5) \\
&= 6\% + 2.5\% \\
&= 8.5\%
\end{aligned}$$

8.7

---

[20]This concept, as well as other aspects of the CAPM, is discussed in more detail in Chapter 3 of Eugene F. Brigham and Phillip R. Daves, *Intermediate Financial Management*, 11th edition Mason, OH: (South-Western/Cengage Learning, 2013). That chapter also discusses the assumptions embodied in the CAPM framework. Some of those assumptions are unrealistic; and because of this, the theory does not hold exactly.

ESTIMATING THE MARKET RISK PREMIUM

The Capital Asset Pricing Model (CAPM) is more than a theory describing the trade-off between risk and return—it is also widely used in practice. As we will see later, investors use the CAPM to determine the discount rate for valuing stocks and corporate managers use it to estimate the cost of equity capital.

The market risk premium is a key component of the CAPM, and it should be the difference between the *expected future return on the overall stock market and the expected future return on a riskless investment*. However, we cannot obtain investors' expectations; instead, academicians and practitioners often use a historical risk premium as a proxy for the expected risk premium. The historical premium is found by taking the difference between the actual return on the overall stock market and the risk-free rate during a number of different years and then averaging the annual results. Morningstar (through its recent purchase of Ibbotson Associates) may provide the most comprehensive estimates of historical risk premiums. It reports that the annual premiums have averaged 6.7% over the past 87 years.

There are three potential problems with historical risk premiums. First, what is the proper number of years over which to compute the average? Morningstar goes back to 1926, when good data first became available; but that is an arbitrary choice, and the starting and ending points make a major difference in the calculated premium.

Second, historical premiums are likely to be misleading at times when the market risk premium is changing. To illustrate, the stock market was very strong from 1995 through 1999, *in part because investors were becoming less risk-averse, which*

means that they applied a lower risk premium when they valued stocks. The strong market resulted in stock returns of about 30% per year; and when bond yields were subtracted from the high stock returns, the calculated risk premiums averaged 22.3% a year. When those high numbers were added to data from prior years, they caused the long-run historical risk premium as reported by Morningstar to increase. Thus, a declining "true" risk premium led to very high stock returns, which, in turn, led to an increase in the calculated historical risk premium. That's a worrisome result, to say the least.

The third concern is that historical estimates may be biased upward because they include only the returns of firms that have survived—they do not reflect the losses incurred on investments in failed firms. Stephen Brown, William Goetzmann, and Stephen Ross discussed the implications of this *"survivorship bias"* in a 1995 *Journal of Finance* article. Putting these ideas into practice, Tim Koller, Marc Goedhart, and David Wessels recently suggested that survivorship bias increases historical returns by 1% to 2% a year. Therefore, they suggest that practitioners subtract 1% to 2% from the historical estimates to obtain the risk premium for use in the CAPM.

A 2012 survey of more than 7,000 academics, analysts, and practitioners in 82 countries provides further insights into the techniques they use to estimate the market risk premium. For the United States, the academics on average estimated that the market risk premium was 5.6%, which was somewhat higher than the estimates reported by analysts and practitioners (5.0% and 5.5% respectively). Similar estimates were reported in many of the other leading developed countries.

Sources: *Ibbotson Stocks, Bonds, Bills, and Inflation: 2013 Valuation Yearbook* (Chicago: Morningstar, Inc., 2013); John R. Graham and Campbell R. Harvey, "The Equity Risk Premium in 2013," *Social Science Research Network*, January 28, 2013, ssrn.com/abstract=2206538; Pablo Fernandez, Javier Aguirreamalloa, and Luis Corres, "Market Risk Premium Used in 82 Countries in 2012: A Survey with 7,192 Answers," *Social Science Research Network*, January 29, 2013, ssrn.com/abstract=2084213; Stephen J. Brown, William N. Goetzmann, and Stephen A. Ross, "Survival," *Journal of Finance*, vol. 50, no. 3 (July 1995), pp. 853–873; and Tim Koller, Marc Goedhart, and David Wessels, *Valuation: Measuring and Managing the Value of Companies*, 4th ed. (New York: McKinsey & Company, 2005).

Stock H had $b_H = 2.0$, so its required rate of return is 16%:

$$r_H = 6\% + (5\%)2.0 = 16\%$$

An average stock, with $b = 1.0$, would have a required return of 11%, the same as the market return:

$$r_A = 6\% + (5\%)1.0 = 11\% = r_M$$

The SML equation is plotted in Figure 8.8 using the data shown below the graph on Stocks L, A, and H and assuming that $r_{RF} = 6\%$ and $r_M = 11\%$. Note the following points:

1. Required rates of return are shown on the vertical axis, while risk as measured by beta is shown on the horizontal axis. This graph is quite

different from the one shown in Figure 8.7, where we calculated betas. In the earlier graph, the returns on individual stocks were plotted on the vertical axis and returns on the market index were shown on the horizontal axis. The betas found in Figure 8.7 were then plotted as points on the horizontal axis of Figure 8.8.

2. Riskless securities have $b_i = 0$; so the return on the riskless asset, $r_{RF} = 6.0\%$, is shown as the vertical axis intercept in Figure 8.8.

3. The slope of the SML in Figure 8.8 can be found using the rise-over-run procedure. When beta goes from 0 to 1.0, the required return goes from 6% to 11%, or 5%; so the slope is 5%/1.0 = 5%. Thus, a 1-unit increase in beta causes a 5% increase in the required rate of return.

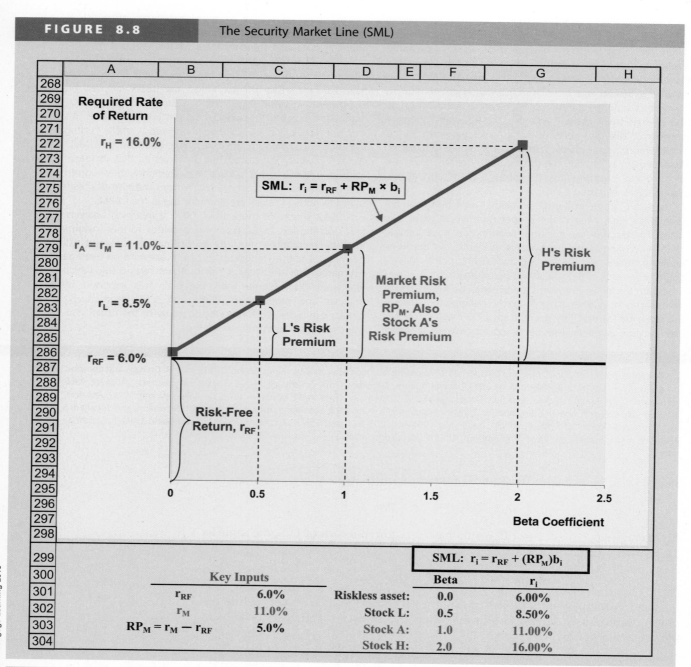

FIGURE 8.8 The Security Market Line (SML)

4. The slope of the SML reflects the degree of risk aversion in the economy—the greater the average investor's risk aversion, (a) the steeper the slope of the line and (b) the greater the risk premium for all stocks—hence, the higher the required rate of return on all stocks.

Both the SML and a company's position on it change over time due to changes in interest rates, investors' risk aversion, and individual companies' betas. Such changes are discussed in the following sections.

8-4a THE IMPACT OF EXPECTED INFLATION

As we discussed in Chapter 6, interest amounts to "rent" on borrowed money, or the price of money. Thus, r_{RF} is the price of money to a riskless borrower. We also saw that the risk-free rate as measured by the rate on U.S. Treasury securities is called the *nominal, or quoted, rate;* and it consists of two elements: (1) a *real inflation-free rate of return, r^*,* and (2) an *inflation premium, IP,* equal to the anticipated rate of inflation.[21] Thus, $r_{RF} = r^* + IP$. The real rate on long-term Treasury bonds has historically ranged from 2% to 4%, with a mean of about 3%. Therefore, if no inflation were expected, long-term Treasury bonds would yield about 3%. However, as the expected rate of inflation increases, a premium must be added to the real risk-free rate of return to compensate investors for the loss of purchasing power that results from inflation. Therefore, the 6% r_{RF} shown in Figure 8.8 might be thought of as consisting of a 3% real risk-free rate of return plus a 3% inflation premium: $r_{RF} = r^* + IP = 3\% + 3\% = 6\%$.

If the expected inflation rate rose by 2%, to $3\% + 2\% = 5\%$, r_{RF} would rise to 8%. Such a change is shown in Figure 8.9. Notice that the increase in r_{RF} leads

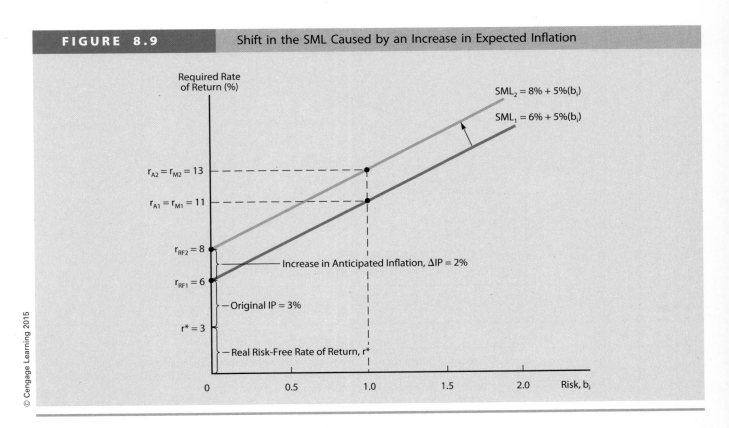

| FIGURE 8.9 | Shift in the SML Caused by an Increase in Expected Inflation |

© Cengage Learning 2015

---

[21]Long-term Treasury bonds also contain a maturity risk premium, MRP. We include the MRP in r^* to simplify the discussion.

to an equal increase in the rates of return on all risky assets because the same inflation premium is built into required rates of return on both riskless and risky assets.[22] Therefore, the rate of return on our illustrative average stock, r_A, increases from 11% to 13%. Other risky securities' returns also rise by two percentage points.

8-4B CHANGES IN RISK AVERSION

The slope of the SML reflects the extent to which investors are averse to risk—the steeper the slope of the line, the more the average investor requires as compensation for bearing risk. Suppose investors were indifferent to risk; that is, they were not at all risk-averse. If r_{RF} was 6%, risky assets would also have a required return of 6% because if there were no risk aversion, there would be no risk premium. In that case, the SML would plot as a horizontal line. However, because investors are risk-averse, there is a risk premium; and the greater the risk aversion, the steeper the slope of the SML.

Figure 8.10 illustrates an increase in risk aversion. The market risk premium rises from 5% to 7.5%, causing r_M to rise from $r_{M1} = 11\%$ to $r_{M2} = 13.5\%$. The returns on other risky assets also rise, and the effect of this shift in risk aversion is

| FIGURE 8.10 | Shift in the SML Caused by Increased Risk Aversion |

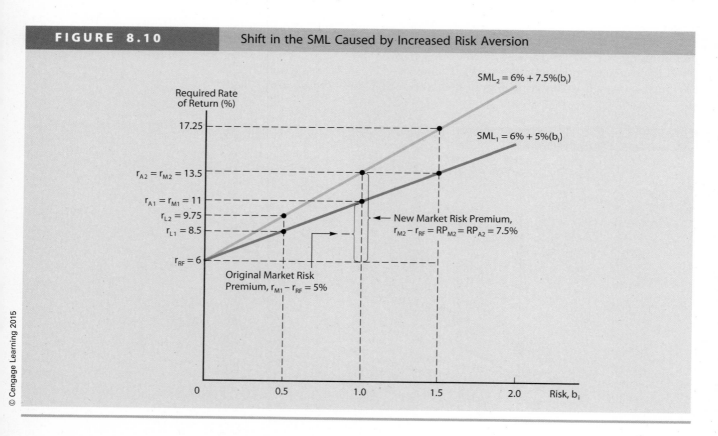

[22]Recall that the inflation premium for any asset is the average expected rate of inflation over the asset's life. Thus, in this analysis, we must assume that all securities plotted on the SML graph have the same life or that the expected rate of future inflation is constant.

It should also be noted that r in a CAPM analysis can be proxied by either a long-term rate (the T-bond rate) or a short-term rate (the T-bill rate). Traditionally, the T-bill rate was used; but in recent years, there has been a movement toward use of the T-bond rate because there is a closer relationship between T-bond yields and stocks' returns than between T-bill yields and stocks' returns. See *Ibbotson Stocks, Bonds, Bills, and Inflation: 2013 Valuation Yearbook* (Chicago: Morningstar, Inc., 2013), p. 44, for a discussion.

more pronounced on riskier securities. For example, the required return on Stock L with $b = 0.5$ increases by only 1.25 percentage points, from 8.5% to 9.75%, whereas the required return on a stock with a beta of 1.5 increases by 3.75 percentage points, from 13.5% to 17.25%.

 QUICK QUESTION

QUESTION:
The risk-free rate is 3% and the market risk premium ($r_M - r_{RF}$) is 4%. Stock A has a beta of 1.2 and Stock B has a beta of 0.8.

a. What is the required rate of return on each stock?
b. Assume that investors become less willing to take on risk (that is, they become more risk averse) so the market risk premium rises from 4% to 6%. Assume that the risk-free rate remains constant. What effect will this have on the required rates of return on the two stocks?

ANSWER:
a. $RP_M = r_M - r_{RF} = 4\%$

$$r_A = r_{RF} + RP_M(b_A)$$
$$= 3\% + 4\%(1.2)$$
$$= 7.8\%$$
$$r_B = r_{RF} + RP_M(b_B)$$
$$= 3\% + 4\%(0.8)$$
$$= 6.2\%$$

b. RP_M rises from 4% to 6% but r_{RF} remains at 3%.

$$r_A = 3\% + 6\%(1.2)$$
$$= 10.2\%$$
$$r_B = 3\% + 6\%(0.8)$$
$$= 7.8\%$$

Thus, the required rate of return on Stock A increases from 7.8% to 10.2%, while the required rate of return on Stock B increases from 6.2% to 7.8%. Note that Stock A's required return has increased more than Stock B's required return because Stock A has a higher beta. Shifts in the risk premium have a more pronounced effect on riskier stocks (i.e., those stocks with higher betas).

8-4c CHANGES IN A STOCK'S BETA COEFFICIENT

As we see later in the book, a firm can influence its market risk (hence, its beta) through changes in the composition of its assets and through changes in the amount of debt it uses. A company's beta can also change as a result of external factors such as increased competition in its industry and expiration of basic patents. When such changes occur, the firm's required rate of return also changes; and as we see in Chapter 9, this change will affect its stock price. For example, consider Allied Food Products, with a beta of 1.48. Now suppose some action occurred that caused Allied's beta to increase from 1.48 to 2.0. If the conditions depicted in Figure 8.8 held, Allied's required rate of return would increase from 13.4% to 16%:

$$r_1 = r_{RF} + (r_M - r_{RF})b_i$$
$$= 6\% + (11\% - 6\%)1.48$$
$$= 13.4\%$$

to

$$r_2 = 6\% + (11\% - 6\%)2.0$$
$$= 16.0\%$$

As we see in Chapter 9, this change will have a negative effect on Allied's stock price.[23]

SELF TEST

Differentiate between a stock's expected rate of return ($\hat{r}$); required rate of return (r); and realized, after-the-fact historical return ($\bar{r}$). Which would have to be larger to induce you to buy the stock, $\hat{r}$ or r? At a given point in time, would $\hat{r}$, r, and $\bar{r}$ typically be the same or different? Explain.

What are the differences between the relative volatility graph (Figure 8.7), where "betas are made," and the SML graph (Figure 8.8), where "betas are used"? Explain how both graphs are constructed and what information they convey.

What would happen to the SML graph in Figure 8.8 if expected inflation increased or decreased?

What happens to the SML graph when risk aversion increases or decreases?

What would the SML look like if investors were indifferent to risk, that is, if they had zero risk aversion?

How can a firm influence the size of its beta?

A stock has a beta of 1.2. Assume that the risk-free rate is 4.5% and the market risk premium is 5%. What is the stock's required rate of return? **(10.5%)**

8-5 SOME CONCERNS ABOUT BETA AND THE CAPM

The Capital Asset Pricing Model (CAPM) is more than just an abstract theory described in textbooks—it has great intuitive appeal and is widely used by analysts, investors, and corporations. However, a number of recent studies have raised concerns about its validity. For example, a study by Eugene Fama of the University of Chicago and Kenneth French of Dartmouth found no historical relationship between stocks' returns and their market betas, confirming a position long held by some professors and stock market analysts.[24]

As an alternative to the traditional CAPM, researchers and practitioners are developing models with more explanatory variables than just beta. These multivariable models represent an attractive generalization of the traditional

*Kenneth French's website, **mba.tuck.dartmouth.edu/ pages/faculty/ken.french/ index.html**, is an excellent resource for information regarding factors related to stock returns.*

---

[23]The concepts covered in this chapter are obviously important to investors, but they are also important for managers in two key ways. First, as we see in the next chapter, the risk of a stock affects the required rate of return on equity capital, and that feeds directly into the important subject of capital budgeting. Second, and also related to capital budgeting, the "true" risk of individual projects is impacted by their correlation with the firm's other projects and with other assets that the firm's stockholders might hold. We discuss these topics in later chapters.

[24]See Eugene F. Fama and Kenneth R. French, "The Cross-Section of Expected Stock Returns," *Journal of Finance*, vol. 47, no. 2 (June 1992), pp. 427–465; and Eugene F. Fama and Kenneth R. French, "Common Risk Factors in the Returns on Stocks and Bonds," *Journal of Financial Economics*, vol. 33, no. 1 (February 1993), pp. 3–56. They found that stock returns are related to firm size and market/book ratios. Small firms and firms with low market/book ratios had higher returns; however, they found no relationship between returns and beta.

CAPM model's insight that market risk—risk that cannot be diversified away—underlies the pricing of assets. In the multivariable models, risk is assumed to be caused by a number of different factors, whereas the CAPM gauges risk only relative to returns on the market portfolio. These multi-variable models represent a potentially important step forward in finance theory; however, they also have some deficiencies when applied in practice. As a result, the basic CAPM is still the most widely used method for estimating required rates of return on stocks.

SELF TEST

Have there been any studies that question the validity of the CAPM? Explain.

8-6 SOME CONCLUDING THOUGHTS: IMPLICATIONS FOR CORPORATE MANAGERS AND INVESTORS

The connection between risk and return is an important concept, and it has numerous implications for both corporate managers and investors. As we will see in later chapters, corporate managers spend a great deal of time assessing the risk and returns on individual projects. Indeed, given their concerns about the risk of individual projects, it might be fair to ask why we spend so much time discussing the riskiness of stocks. Why not begin by looking at the riskiness of such business assets as plant and equipment? *The reason is that for management whose primary goal is stock price maximization, the overriding consideration is the riskiness of the firm's stock, and the relevant risk of any physical asset must be measured in terms of its effect on the stock's risk as seen by investors.* For example, suppose Goodyear, the tire company, is considering a major investment in a new product, recapped tires. Sales of recaps (hence, earnings on the new operation) are highly uncertain; so on a stand-alone basis, the new venture appears to be quite risky. However, suppose returns in the recap business are negatively correlated with Goodyear's other operations—when times are good and people have plenty of money, they buy new cars with new tires; but when times are bad, they tend to keep their old cars and buy recaps for them. Therefore, returns would be high on regular operations and low on the recap division during good times, but the opposite would be true during recessions. The result might be a pattern like that shown earlier in Figure 8.4 for Stocks W and M. Thus, what appears to be a risky investment when viewed on a stand-alone basis might not be very risky when viewed within the context of the company as a whole.

This analysis can be extended to the corporation's stockholders. Because Goodyear's stock is owned by diversified stockholders, the real issue each time management makes an investment decision is this: How will this investment affect the risk of our stockholders? Again, the stand-alone risk of an individual project may look quite high; however, viewed in the context of the project's effect on stockholder risk, it may not be very large. We address this issue again in Chapter 12, where we examine the effects of capital budgeting on companies' beta coefficients and thus on stockholders' risks.

While these concepts are obviously important for individual investors, they are also important for corporate managers. We summarize some key ideas that all investors should consider:

1. There is a trade-off between risk and return. The average investor likes higher returns but dislikes risk. It follows that higher-risk investments need to offer investors higher expected returns. Put another way—if you are seeking higher returns, you must be willing to assume higher risks.

2. Diversification is crucial. By diversifying wisely, investors can dramatically reduce risk without reducing their expected returns. Don't put all of your money in one or two stocks or in one or two industries. A huge mistake that many people make is to invest a high percentage of their funds in their employer's stock. If the company goes bankrupt, they not only lose their job but also their invested capital. While no stock is completely riskless, you can smooth out the bumps by holding a well-diversified portfolio.

3. Real returns are what matters. All investors should understand the difference between nominal and real returns. When assessing performance, the real return (what remains after inflation) is what matters. It follows that as expected inflation increases, investors need to receive higher nominal returns.

4. The risk of an investment often depends on how long you plan to hold the investment. Common stocks, for example, can be extremely risky for short-term investors. However, over the long haul, the bumps tend to even out; thus, stocks are less risky when held as part of a long-term portfolio. Indeed, in his best-selling book *Stocks for the Long Run,* Jeremy Siegel of the University of Pennsylvania concludes that "[t]he safest long-term investment for the preservation of purchasing power has clearly been stocks, not bonds."

5. While the past gives us insights into the risk and returns on various investments, there is no guarantee that the future will repeat the past. Stocks that have performed well in recent years might tumble, while stocks that have struggled may rebound. The same thing may hold true for the stock market as a whole. Even Jeremy Siegel, who has preached that stocks have historically been good long-term investments, also has argued that there is no assurance that returns in the future will be as strong as they have been in the past. More importantly, when purchasing a stock, you always need to ask, "Is this stock fairly valued, or is it currently priced too high?" We discuss this issue more completely in the next chapter.

SELF TEST

Explain the following statement: The stand-alone risk of an individual corporate project may be quite high; but viewed in the context of its effect on stockholders' risk, the project's true risk may not be very large.

How does the correlation between returns on a project and returns on the firm's other assets affect the project's risk?

What are some important concepts for individual investors to consider when evaluating the risk and returns of various investments?

TYING IT ALL TOGETHER

In this chapter, we described the relationship between risk and return. We discussed how to calculate risk and return for individual assets and for portfolios. In particular, we differentiated between stand-alone risk and risk in a portfolio context and we explained the benefits of diversification. We also discussed the CAPM, which describes how risk should be measured and how risk affects rates of return. In the chapters that follow, we give you the tools needed to estimate the required rates of return on a firm's common stock and explain how that return and the yield on its bonds are used to develop the firm's cost of capital. As you will see, the cost of capital is a key element in the capital budgeting process.

SELF-TEST QUESTIONS AND PROBLEMS

(Solutions Appear in Appendix A)

ST-1   **KEY TERMS**   Define each of the following terms using graphs or equations to illustrate your answers whenever feasible:

a.   Risk; stand-alone risk; probability distribution

b.   Expected rate of return, $\hat{r}$

c.   Standard deviation, σ; coefficient of variation (CV)

d.   Risk aversion; risk premium (RP); realized rate of return, $\bar{r}$

e.   Risk premium for Stock i, RP_i; market risk premium, RP_M

f.   Expected return on a portfolio, $\hat{r}_p$; market portfolio

g.   Correlation; correlation coefficient, ρ

h.   Market risk; diversifiable risk; relevant risk

i.   Capital Asset Pricing Model (CAPM)

j.   Beta coefficient, b; average stock's beta, b_A

k.   Security Market Line (SML) equation

ST-2   **REALIZED RATES OF RETURN**   Stocks A and B have the following historical returns:

Year	Stock A's Returns, r_A	Stock B's Returns, r_B
2009	(24.25%)	5.50%
2010	18.50	26.73
2011	38.67	48.25
2012	14.33	(4.50)
2013	39.13	43.86

a.   Calculate the average rate of return for each stock during the period 2009 through 2013. Assume that someone held a portfolio consisting of 50% of Stock A and 50% of Stock B. What would the realized rate of return on the portfolio have been in each year from 2009 through 2013? What would the average return on the portfolio have been during that period?

b. Calculate the standard deviation of returns for each stock and for the portfolio. Use Equation 8.2a.

c. Looking at the annual returns on the two stocks, would you guess that the correlation coefficient between the two stocks is closer to $+0.8$ or to -0.8?

d. If more randomly selected stocks had been included in the portfolio, which of the following is the most accurate statement of what would have happened to σ_p?

1. σ_p would have remained constant.

2. σ_p would have been in the vicinity of 20%.

3. σ_p would have declined to zero if enough stocks had been included.

ST-3 **BETA AND THE REQUIRED RATE OF RETURN** ECRI Corporation is a holding company with four main subsidiaries. The percentage of its capital invested in each of the subsidiaries (and their respective betas) are as follows:

Subsidiary	Percentage of Capital	Beta
Electric utility	60%	0.70
Cable company	25	0.90
Real estate development	10	1.30
International/special projects	5	1.50

a. What is the holding company's beta?

b. If the risk-free rate is 6% and the market risk premium is 5%, what is the holding company's required rate of return?

c. ECRI is considering a change in its strategic focus; it will reduce its reliance on the electric utility subsidiary, so the percentage of its capital in this subsidiary will be reduced to 50%. At the same time, it will increase its reliance on the international/special projects division, so the percentage of its capital in that subsidiary will rise to 15%. What will the company's required rate of return be after these changes?

QUESTIONS

8-1 Suppose you owned a portfolio consisting of $250,000 of long-term U.S. government bonds.

a. Would your portfolio be riskless? Explain.

b. Now suppose the portfolio consists of $250,000 of 30-day Treasury bills. Every 30 days your bills mature, and you will reinvest the principal ($250,000) in a new batch of bills. You plan to live on the investment income from your portfolio, and you want to maintain a constant standard of living. Is the T-bill portfolio truly riskless? Explain.

c. What is the least risky security you can think of? Explain.

8-2 The probability distribution of a less risky expected return is more peaked than that of a riskier return. What shape would the probability distribution be for (a) completely certain returns and (b) completely uncertain returns?

8-3 A life insurance policy is a financial asset, with the premiums paid representing the investment's cost.

a. How would you calculate the expected return on a 1-year life insurance policy?

b. Suppose the owner of a life insurance policy has no other financial assets—the person's only other asset is "human capital," or earnings capacity. What is the correlation coefficient between the return on the insurance policy and the return on the human capital?

c. Life insurance companies must pay administrative costs and sales representatives' commissions; hence, the expected rate of return on insurance premiums is generally low or even negative. Use portfolio concepts to explain why people buy life insurance in spite of low expected returns.

8-4 Is it possible to construct a portfolio of real-world stocks that has a required return equal to the risk-free rate? Explain.

8-5 Stock A has an expected return of 7%, a standard deviation of expected returns of 35%, a correlation coefficient with the market of −0.3, and a beta coefficient of −0.5. Stock B has an expected return of 12%, a standard deviation of returns of 10%, a 0.7 correlation with the market, and a beta coefficient of 1.0. Which security is riskier? Why?

8-6 A stock had a 12% return last year, a year when the overall stock market declined. Does this mean that the stock has a negative beta and thus very little risk if held in a portfolio? Explain.

8-7 If investors' aversion to risk increased, would the risk premium on a high-beta stock increase by more or less than that on a low-beta stock? Explain.

8-8 If a company's beta were to double, would its required return also double?

8-9 In Chapter 7, we saw that if the market interest rate, r_d, for a given bond increased, the price of the bond would decline. Applying this same logic to stocks, explain (a) how a decrease in risk aversion would affect stocks' prices and earned rates of return, (b) how this would affect risk premiums as measured by the historical difference between returns on stocks and returns on bonds, and (c) what the implications of this would be for the use of historical risk premiums when applying the SML equation.

PROBLEMS

Easy Problems 1–5

8-1 **EXPECTED RETURN** A stock's returns have the following distribution:

Demand for the Company's Products	Probability of This Demand Occurring	Rate of Return if This Demand Occurs
Weak	0.1	(50%)
Below average	0.2	(5)
Average	0.4	16
Above average	0.2	25
Strong	0.1	60
	1.0	

Calculate the stock's expected return, standard deviation, and coefficient of variation.

8-2 **PORTFOLIO BETA** An individual has $35,000 invested in a stock with a beta of 0.8 and another $40,000 invested in a stock with a beta of 1.4. If these are the only two investments in her portfolio, what is her portfolio's beta?

8-3 **REQUIRED RATE OF RETURN** Assume that the risk-free rate is 6% and the required return on the market is 13%. What is the required rate of return on a stock with a beta of 0.7?

8-4 **EXPECTED AND REQUIRED RATES OF RETURN** Assume that the risk-free rate is 5% and the market risk premium is 6%. What is the required return for the overall stock market? What is the required rate of return on a stock with a beta of 1.2?

8-5 **BETA AND REQUIRED RATE OF RETURN** A stock has a required return of 11%, the risk-free rate is 7%, and the market risk premium is 4%.

a. What is the stock's beta?

b. If the market risk premium increased to 6%, what would happen to the stock's required rate of return? Assume that the risk-free rate and the beta remain unchanged.

Intermediate
Problems
6–12

8-6   **EXPECTED RETURNS**   Stocks X and Y have the following probability distributions of expected future returns:

Probability	X	Y
0.1	(10%)	(35%)
0.2	2	0
0.4	12	20
0.2	20	25
0.1	38	45

a.   Calculate the expected rate of return, $\hat{r}_Y$, for Stock Y ($\hat{r}_X = 12\%$).

b.   Calculate the standard deviation of expected returns, σ_X, for Stock X ($\sigma_Y = 20.35\%$). Now calculate the coefficient of variation for Stock Y. Is it possible that most investors will regard Stock Y as being less risky than Stock X? Explain.

8-7   **PORTFOLIO REQUIRED RETURN**   Suppose you are the money manager of a $4 million investment fund. The fund consists of four stocks with the following investments and betas:

Stock	Investment	Beta
A	$ 400,000	1.50
B	600,000	(0.50)
C	1,000,000	1.25
D	2,000,000	0.75

If the market's required rate of return is 14% and the risk-free rate is 6%, what is the fund's required rate of return?

8-8   **BETA COEFFICIENT**   Given the following information, determine the beta coefficient for Stock J that is consistent with equilibrium: $\hat{r}_J = 12.5\%$; $r_{RF} = 4.5\%$; $r_M = 10.5\%$.

8-9   **REQUIRED RATE OF RETURN**   Stock R has a beta of 1.5, Stock S has a beta of 0.75, the required return on an average stock is 13%, and the risk-free rate of return is 7%. By how much does the required return on the riskier stock exceed the required return on the less risky stock?

8-10   **CAPM AND REQUIRED RETURN**   Bradford Manufacturing Company has a beta of 1.45, while Farley Industries has a beta of 0.85. The required return on an index fund that holds the entire stock market is 12.0%. The risk-free rate of interest is 5%. By how much does Bradford's required return exceed Farley's required return?

8-11   **CAPM AND REQUIRED RETURN**   Calculate the required rate of return for Manning Enterprises assuming that investors expect a 3.5% rate of inflation in the future. The real risk-free rate is 2.5%, and the market risk premium is 6.5%. Manning has a beta of 1.7, and its realized rate of return has averaged 13.5% over the past 5 years.

8-12   **REQUIRED RATE OF RETURN**   Suppose $r_{RF} = 9\%$, $r_M = 14\%$, and $b_i = 1.3$.

a.   What is r_i, the required rate of return on Stock i?

b.   Now suppose that r_{RF} (1) increases to 10% or (2) decreases to 8%. The slope of the SML remains constant. How would this affect r_M and r_i?

c.   Now assume that r_{RF} remains at 9% but r_M (1) increases to 16% or (2) falls to 13%. The slope of the SML does not remain constant. How would these changes affect r_i?

Challenging
Problems
13–21

8-13   **CAPM, PORTFOLIO RISK, AND RETURN**   Consider the following information for Stocks X, Y, and Z. The returns on the three stocks are positively correlated, but they are not perfectly correlated. (That is, each of the correlation coefficients is between 0 and 1.)

Stock	Expected Return	Standard Deviation	Beta
X	9.00%	15%	0.8
Y	10.75	15	1.2
Z	12.50	15	1.6

Fund Q has one-third of its funds invested in each of the three stocks. The risk-free rate is 5.5%, and the market is in equilibrium. (That is, required returns equal expected returns.)

a.   What is the market risk premium($r_M - r_{RF}$)?
b.   What is the beta of Fund Q?
c.   What is the required return of Fund Q?
d.   Would you expect the standard deviation of Fund Q to be less than 15%, equal to 15%, or greater than 15%? Explain.

8-14   **PORTFOLIO BETA**   Suppose you held a diversified portfolio consisting of a $7,500 investment in each of 20 different common stocks. The portfolio's beta is 1.12. Now suppose you decided to sell one of the stocks in your portfolio with a beta of 1.0 for $7,500 and use the proceeds to buy another stock with a beta of 1.75. What would your portfolio's new beta be?

8-15   **CAPM AND REQUIRED RETURN**   HR Industries (HRI) has a beta of 1.8, while LR Industries' (LRI) beta is 0.6. The risk-free rate is 6%, and the required rate of return on an average stock is 13%. The expected rate of inflation built into r_{RF} falls by 1.5 percentage points, the real risk-free rate remains constant, the required return on the market falls to 10.5%, and all betas remain constant. After all of these changes, what will be the difference in the required returns for HRI and LRI?

8-16   **CAPM AND PORTFOLIO RETURN**   You have been managing a $5 million portfolio that has a beta of 1.25 and a required rate of return of 12%. The current risk-free rate is 5.25%. Assume that you receive another $500,000. If you invest the money in a stock with a beta of 0.75, what will be the required return on your $5.5 million portfolio?

8-17   **PORTFOLIO BETA**   A mutual fund manager has a $20 million portfolio with a beta of 1.5. The risk-free rate is 4.5%, and the market risk premium is 5.5%. The manager expects to receive an additional $5 million, which she plans to invest in a number of stocks. After investing the additional funds, she wants the fund's required return to be 13%. What should be the average beta of the new stocks added to the portfolio?

8-18   **EXPECTED RETURNS**   Suppose you won the lottery and had two options: (1) receiving $0.5 million or (2) taking a gamble in which at the flip of a coin you receive $1 million if a head comes up but receive zero if a tail comes up.

a.   What is the expected value of the gamble?
b.   Would you take the sure $0.5 million or the gamble?
c.   If you chose the sure $0.5 million, would that indicate that you are a risk averter or a risk seeker?
d.   Suppose the payoff was actually $0.5 million—that was the only choice. You now face the choice of investing it in a U.S. Treasury bond that will return $537,500 at the end of a year or a common stock that has a 50-50 chance of being worthless or worth $1,150,000 at the end of the year.

1.   The expected profit on the T-bond investment is $37,500. What is the expected dollar profit on the stock investment?
2.   The expected rate of return on the T-bond investment is 7.5%. What is the expected rate of return on the stock investment?
3.   Would you invest in the bond or the stock? Why?
4.   Exactly how large would the expected profit (or the expected rate of return) have to be on the stock investment to make you invest in the stock, given the 7.5% return on the bond?
5.   How might your decision be affected if, rather than buying one stock for $0.5 million, you could construct a portfolio consisting of 100 stocks with $5,000 invested in each? Each of these stocks has the same return characteristics as the one stock—that is, a 50-50 chance of being worth zero or $11,500 at year-end. Would the correlation between returns on these stocks matter? Explain.

8-19 **EVALUATING RISK AND RETURN**   Stock X has a 10% expected return, a beta coefficient of 0.9, and a 35% standard deviation of expected returns. Stock Y has a 12.5% expected return, a beta coefficient of 1.2, and a 25% standard deviation. The risk-free rate is 6%, and the market risk premium is 5%.

   a. Calculate each stock's coefficient of variation.
   b. Which stock is riskier for a diversified investor?
   c. Calculate each stock's required rate of return.
   d. On the basis of the two stocks' expected and required returns, which stock would be more attractive to a diversified investor?
   e. Calculate the required return of a portfolio that has $7,500 invested in Stock X and $2,500 invested in Stock Y.
   f. If the market risk premium increased to 6%, which of the two stocks would have the larger increase in its required return?

8-20 **REALIZED RATES OF RETURN**   Stocks A and B have the following historical returns:

Year	Stock A's Returns, r_A	Stock B's Returns, r_B
2009	(18.00%)	(14.50%)
2010	33.00	21.80
2011	15.00	30.50
2012	(0.50)	(7.60)
2013	27.00	26.30

   a. Calculate the average rate of return for each stock during the period 2009 through 2013.
   b. Assume that someone held a portfolio consisting of 50% of Stock A and 50% of Stock B. What would the realized rate of return on the portfolio have been each year? What would the average return on the portfolio have been during this period?
   c. Calculate the standard deviation of returns for each stock and for the portfolio.
   d. Calculate the coefficient of variation for each stock and for the portfolio.
   e. Assuming you are a risk-averse investor, would you prefer to hold Stock A, Stock B, or the portfolio? Why?

8-21 **SECURITY MARKET LINE**   You plan to invest in the Kish Hedge Fund, which has total capital of $500 million invested in five stocks:

Stock	Investment	Stock's Beta Coefficient
A	$160 million	0.5
B	120 million	1.2
C	80 million	1.8
D	80 million	1.0
E	60 million	1.6

Kish's beta coefficient can be found as a weighted average of its stocks' betas. The risk-free rate is 6%, and you believe the following probability distribution for future market returns is realistic:

Probability	Market Return
0.1	−28%
0.2	0
0.4	12
0.2	30
0.1	50

   a. What is the equation for the Security Market Line (SML)? (Hint: First, determine the expected market return.)
   b. Calculate Kish's required rate of return.

c. Suppose Rick Kish, the president, receives a proposal from a company seeking new capital. The amount needed to take a position in the stock is $50 million, it has an expected return of 15%, and its estimated beta is 1.5. Should Kish invest in the new company? At what expected rate of return should Kish be indifferent to purchasing the stock?

COMPREHENSIVE/SPREADSHEET PROBLEM

8-22 **EVALUATING RISK AND RETURN** Bartman Industries' and Reynolds Inc.'s stock prices and dividends, along with the Winslow 5000 Index, are shown here for the period 2008–2013. The Winslow 5000 data are adjusted to include dividends.

	Bartman Industries		Reynolds Inc.		Winslow 5000
Year	Stock Price	Dividend	Stock Price	Dividend	Includes Dividends
2013	$17.25	$1.15	$48.75	$3.00	$11,663.98
2012	14.75	1.06	52.30	2.90	8,785.70
2011	16.50	1.00	48.75	2.75	8,679.98
2010	10.75	0.95	57.25	2.50	6,434.03
2009	11.37	0.90	60.00	2.25	5,602.28
2008	7.62	0.85	55.75	2.00	4,705.97

a. Use the data to calculate annual rates of return for Bartman, Reynolds, and the Winslow 5000 Index. Then calculate each entity's average return over the 5-year period. (Hint: Remember, returns are calculated by subtracting the beginning price from the ending price to get the capital gain or loss, adding the dividend to the capital gain or loss, and dividing the result by the beginning price. Assume that dividends are already included in the index. Also, you cannot calculate the rate of return for 2008 because you do not have 2007 data.)

b. Calculate the standard deviations of the returns for Bartman, Reynolds, and the Winslow 5000. (Hint: Use the sample standard deviation formula, Equation 8.2a in this chapter, which corresponds to the STDEV function in Excel.)

c. Calculate the coefficients of variation for Bartman, Reynolds, and the Winslow 5000.

d. Construct a scatter diagram that shows Bartman's and Reynolds' returns on the vertical axis and the Winslow 5000 Index's returns on the horizontal axis.

e. Estimate Bartman's and Reynolds' betas by running regressions of their returns against the index's returns. (Hint: Refer to Web Appendix 8A.) Are these betas consistent with your graph?

f. Assume that the risk-free rate on long-term Treasury bonds is 6.04%. Assume also that the average annual return on the Winslow 5000 is *not* a good estimate of the market's required return—it is too high. So use 11% as the expected return on the market. Use the SML equation to calculate the two companies' required returns.

g. If you formed a portfolio that consisted of 50% Bartman and 50% Reynolds, what would the portfolio's beta and required return be?

h. Suppose an investor wants to include Bartman Industries' stock in his portfolio. Stocks A, B, and C are currently in the portfolio; and their betas are 0.769, 0.985, and 1.423, respectively. Calculate the new portfolio's required return if it consists of 25% of Bartman, 15% of Stock A, 40% of Stock B, and 20% of Stock C.

INTEGRATED CASE

MERRILL FINCH INC.

8-23 **RISK AND RETURN**   Assume that you recently graduated with a major in finance. You just landed a job as a financial planner with Merrill Finch Inc., a large financial services corporation. Your first assignment is to invest $100,000 for a client. Because the funds are to be invested in a business at the end of 1 year, you have been instructed to plan for a 1-year holding period. Further, your boss has restricted you to the investment alternatives in the following table, shown with their probabilities and associated outcomes. (For now, disregard the items at the bottom of the data; you will fill in the blanks later.)

Returns on Alternative Investments

					Estimated Rate of Return		
State of the Economy	**Probability**	**T-Bills**	**High Tech**	**Collections**	**U.S. Rubber**	**Market Portfolio**	**2-Stock Portfolio**
Recession	0.1	5.5%	(27.0%)	27.0%	6.0%[a]	(17.0%)	0.0%
Below average	0.2	5.5	(7.0)	13.0	(14.0)	(3.0)	
Average	0.4	5.5	15.0	0.0	3.0	10.0	7.5
Above average	0.2	5.5	30.0	(11.0)	41.0	25.0	
Boom	0.1	5.5	45.0	(21.0)	26.0	38.0	12.0
r̂				1.0%	9.8%	10.5%	
σ		0.0		13.2	18.8	15.2	3.4
CV				13.2	1.9	1.4	0.5
b				−0.87	0.88		

Note:

[a]The estimated returns of U.S. Rubber do not always move in the same direction as the overall economy. For example, when the economy is below average, consumers purchase fewer tires than they would if the economy was stronger. However, if the economy is in a flat-out recession, a large number of consumers who were planning to purchase a new car may choose to wait and instead purchase new tires for the car they currently own. Under these circumstances, we would expect U.S. Rubber's stock price to be higher if there is a recession than if the economy was just below average.

Merrill Finch's economic forecasting staff has developed probability estimates for the state of the economy; and its security analysts developed a sophisticated computer program to estimate the rate of return on each alternative under each state of the economy. High Tech Inc. is an electronics firm, Collections Inc. collects past-due debts, and U.S. Rubber manufactures tires and various other rubber and plastics products. Merrill Finch also maintains a "market portfolio" that owns a market-weighted fraction of all publicly traded stocks; you can invest in that portfolio and thus obtain average stock market results. Given the situation described, answer the following questions:

a. 1. Why is the T-bill's return independent of the state of the economy? Do T-bills promise a completely risk-free return? Explain.

2. Why are High Tech's returns expected to move with the economy, whereas Collections' are expected to move counter to the economy?

b. Calculate the expected rate of return on each alternative and fill in the blanks on the row for r̂ in the previous table.

c. You should recognize that basing a decision solely on expected returns is appropriate only for risk-neutral individuals. Because your client, like most people, is risk-averse, the riskiness of each alternative is an important aspect of the decision. One possible measure of risk is the standard deviation of returns.

1. Calculate this value for each alternative and fill in the blank on the row for σ in the table.

2. What type of risk is measured by the standard deviation?

3. Draw a graph that shows *roughly* the shape of the probability distributions for High Tech, U.S. Rubber, and T-bills.

d. Suppose you suddenly remembered that the coefficient of variation (CV) is generally regarded as being a better measure of stand-alone risk than the standard deviation when the alternatives being considered have widely differing expected returns. Calculate the missing CVs and fill in the blanks on the row for CV in the table. Does the CV produce the same risk rankings as the standard deviation? Explain.

e. Suppose you created a two-stock portfolio by investing $50,000 in High Tech and $50,000 in Collections.

1. Calculate the expected return$(\hat{r}_p)$, the standard deviation(σ_p), and the coefficient of variation (CV_p) for this portfolio and fill in the appropriate blanks in the table.

2. How does the riskiness of this two-stock portfolio compare with the riskiness of the individual stocks if they were held in isolation?

f. Suppose an investor starts with a portfolio consisting of one randomly selected stock.

1. What would happen to the riskiness and to the expected return of the portfolio as more randomly selected stocks were added to the portfolio?

2. What is the implication for investors? Draw a graph of the two portfolios to illustrate your answer.

g. 1. Should the effects of a portfolio impact the way investors think about the riskiness of individual stocks?

2. If you decided to hold a one-stock portfolio (and consequently were exposed to more risk than diversified investors), could you expect to be compensated for all of your risk; that is, could you earn a risk premium on the part of your risk that you could have eliminated by diversifying?

h. The expected rates of return and the beta coefficients of the alternatives supplied by Merrill Finch's computer program are as follows:

Security	Return, $\hat{r}$	Risk (Beta)
High Tech	12.4%	1.32
Market	10.5	1.00
U.S. Rubber	9.8	0.88
T-bills	5.5	0.00
Collections	1.0	(0.87)

1. What is a beta coefficient, and how are betas used in risk analysis?

2. Do the expected returns appear to be related to each alternative's market risk?

3. Is it possible to choose among the alternatives on the basis of the information developed thus far? Use the data given at the start of the problem to construct a graph that shows how the T-bill's, High Tech's, and the market's beta coefficients are calculated. Then discuss what betas measure and how they are used in risk analysis.

i. The yield curve is currently flat; that is, long-term Treasury bonds also have a 5.5% yield. Consequently, Merrill Finch assumes that the risk-free rate is 5.5%.

1. Write out the Security Market Line (SML) equation, use it to calculate the required rate of return on each alternative, and graph the relationship between the expected and required rates of return.

2. How do the expected rates of return compare with the required rates of return?

3. Does the fact that Collections has an expected return that is less than the T-bill rate make any sense? Explain.

4. What would be the market risk and the required return of a 50-50 portfolio of High Tech and Collections? Of High Tech and U.S. Rubber?

j. 1. Suppose investors raised their inflation expectations by 3 percentage points over current estimates as reflected in the 5.5% risk-free rate. What effect would higher inflation have on the SML and on the returns required on high- and low-risk securities?

2. Suppose instead that investors' risk aversion increased enough to cause the market risk premium to increase by 3 percentage points. (Inflation remains constant.) What effect would this have on the SML and on returns of high- and low-risk securities?

THOMSON REUTERS

Use the Thomson ONE—Business School Edition online database to work this chapter's questions.

Using Past Information to Estimate Required Returns

Chapter 8 discussed the basic trade-off between risk and return. In the Capital Asset Pricing Model (CAPM) discussion, beta was identified as the correct measure of risk for diversified shareholders. Recall that beta measures the extent to which the returns of a given stock move with the stock market. When using the CAPM to estimate required returns, we would like to know how the stock will move with the market in the future; but because we don't have a crystal ball, we generally use historical data to estimate this relationship with beta.

As mentioned in Web Appendix 8A, beta can be estimated by regressing the individual stock's returns against the returns of the overall market. As an alternative to running our own regressions, we can rely on reported betas from a variety of sources. These published sources make it easy for us to readily obtain beta estimates for most large publicly traded corporations. However, a word of caution is in order. Beta estimates can often be quite sensitive to the time period in which the data are estimated, the market index used, and the frequency of the data used. Therefore, it is not uncommon to find a wide range of beta estimates among the various published sources. Indeed, Thomson One reports multiple beta estimates. These multiple estimates reflect the fact that Thomson One puts together data from a variety of sources.

Discussion Questions

1. Begin by looking at the historical performance of the overall stock market. If you want to see, for example, the performance of the S&P 500, select "INDICES" (near bottom left of your screen), enter S&PCOMP, and click "GO." Click on "OVERVIEW." You will see a quick summary of the market's performance over the past 1, 3, and 12 months. How has the market performed over the past year?
2. Now click on "PRICES" on the left-hand side of the screen. From the next screen you should see the interactive price chart with the S&P 500 index's performance during the past year. You can also change the time frame graphed and view the data from which the chart is drawn.
3. Now let's take a closer look at the stocks of four companies: Colgate Palmolive (Ticker = CL), Campbell Soup (CPB), Motorola Solutions (MSI), and Tiffany & Co (TIF). Before looking at the data, which of these companies would you expect to have a relatively high beta (greater than 1.0) and which of these companies would you expect to have a relatively low beta (less than 1.0)?
4. Select one of the four stocks listed in Question 3 by selecting "COMPANY ANALYSIS," entering the company's ticker symbol in the blank companies box, and clicking "GO." On the company overview page, you should see a chart that summarizes how the stock has done relative to the S&P 500 over the past 6 months. Has the stock outperformed or underperformed the overall market during this time period?
5. If you scroll down the company overview page, you should see an estimate of the company's beta. What is the company's beta? What was the source of the estimated beta?
6. Click on "PRICES" on the left-hand side of the screen. What is the company's current dividend yield? What has been its total return to investors over the past 6 months? Over the past year? Over the past 3 years? (Remember that total return includes the dividend yield plus any capital gains or losses.)
7. Assume that the risk-free rate is 4% and the market risk premium is 5%. What is the required return on the company's stock?
8. Repeat the same exercise for each of the three remaining companies. Do the reported betas confirm your earlier intuition? In general, do you find that the higher-beta stocks tend to do better in up markets and worse in down markets? Explain.

© newphotoservice/Shutterstock.com

Stocks and Their Valuation

Searching for the Right Stock

Over the long run, returns in the U.S. stock market have been quite strong, averaging approximately 12% per year. However, these returns are far from certain, and there is considerable variation in the market's performance from year to year. Indeed, as the chart below indicates, the S&P 500 index has been on a real roller coaster ride since early 2000, where there have been a series of sharp peaks and valleys. Most notably, we see the dramatic collapse of the market in 2008 and early 2009. Since then, the S&P 500 has dramatically rebounded from a value of 811 in April 2009 to 1697.60 in September 2013.

As we discussed in Chapter 8, the returns of individual stocks are even more volatile than the returns of the overall market. For example, in 2012, Lumber Liquidators' stock price rose 199.2%, Regeneron Pharmaceutical's stock price jumped 208.6%, and, most impressively, 3D Systems' stock price soared 270.5%. On the down side, Lone Pine Resources' stock price declined 82.5%, Dynegy's stock price dropped 89.3%, and Houston American Energy's stock price plummeted 98.2%. This wide range in individual stocks' performance shows, first, that diversification is important and, second, that when it comes to picking stocks, it is not enough to simply pick a good company—the stock must also be "fairly" priced.

To determine whether a stock is fairly priced, you first need to estimate the stock's true value, or "intrinsic value," a concept first discussed in Chapter 1. With this objective in mind, in this chapter we describe some models that analysts have used to estimate intrinsic values. As you will see, while it is difficult to predict stock prices, we are not completely in the dark. Indeed, after studying this chapter, you should have a reasonably good understanding of the factors that influence stock prices; and with that knowledge—plus a little luck—you should be able to successfully navigate the market's often-treacherous ups and downs.

Week of Sep 9, 2013: ▪ ^GSPC1687.99

Source: Finance.yahoo.com, September 16, 2013.

Sources: Matt Jarzemsky, "Wall Street Aims to Move Past Glitchy Year," *The Wall Street Journal*, January 2, 2013, p. R6; Allan Sloan, "The Incredible Shrinking Bull," *Fortune*, March 17, 2008, p. 24; and Alexandra Twin, "Best and Worst Stocks of 2007," *CNNMoney.com*, December 31, 2007.

PUTTING THINGS IN PERSPECTIVE

*Key trends in the securities industry are listed and explained at **sifma.org/ research/statistics.aspx**.*

In Chapter 7, we examined bonds and their valuation. We now turn to stocks, both common and preferred. Because the cash flows provided by bonds are set by contract, it is generally easy to predict their cash flows. Preferred stock dividends are also set by contract, which makes them similar to bonds; and they are valued in much the same way. However, common stock dividends are not contractual—they depend on the firm's earnings, which in turn depend on many random factors, making their valuation more difficult. Two fairly straightforward models are used to estimate stocks' intrinsic (or "true") values: (1) the discounted dividend model and (2) the corporate valuation model. A stock should, of course, be bought if its price is less than its estimated intrinsic value and sold if its price exceeds its intrinsic value.

By the time you finish this chapter, you should be able to:

- Discuss the legal rights of stockholders.
- Explain the distinction between a stock's price and its intrinsic value.
- Identify the two models that can be used to estimate a stock's intrinsic value: the discounted dividend model and the corporate valuation model.
- List the key characteristics of preferred stock, and describe how to estimate the value of preferred stock.

Stock valuation is interesting in its own right; but you also need to understand valuation when estimating a firm's cost of capital for use in its capital budgeting analysis, which is probably a firm's most important task.

9-1 LEGAL RIGHTS AND PRIVILEGES OF COMMON STOCKHOLDERS

A corporation's common stockholders are the owners of the corporation; and as such, they have certain rights and privileges, as discussed in this section.

9-1A CONTROL OF THE FIRM

A firm's common stockholders have the right to elect its directors, who, in turn, elect the officers who manage the business. In a small firm, usually the major stockholder is also the president and chair of the board of directors. In large, publicly owned firms, the managers typically have some stock, but their personal holdings are generally insufficient to give them voting control. Thus, the managements of most publicly owned firms can be removed by the stockholders if the management team is not effective.

State and federal laws stipulate how stockholder control is to be exercised. First, corporations must hold elections of directors periodically, usually once a year, with the vote taken at the annual meeting. Each share of stock has one vote; thus, the owner of 1,000 shares has 1,000 votes for each director.[1] Stockholders can appear at the annual meeting and vote in person, but typically they transfer their right to vote to another person by means of a **proxy**. Management always solicits stockholders' proxies and usually receives them. However, if earnings are poor and stockholders are dissatisfied, an outside group may solicit the proxies in an effort to overthrow management and take control of the business. This is known as a **proxy fight**.

The question of control has become a central issue in finance in recent years. The frequency of proxy fights has increased, as have attempts by one corporation to take over another by purchasing a majority of the outstanding stock. These actions are called **takeovers**. Some well-known examples of takeover battles in past years include KKR's acquisition of RJR Nabisco, Chevron's acquisition of Gulf Oil, and the QVC/Viacom fight to take over Paramount. More recently, in November 2009, Kraft Foods made a hostile takeover bid of $16.7 billion for Cadbury, the British chocolate and gum manufacturer. On January 19, 2010, Cadbury's management accepted Kraft's revised $21.8 billion buyout offer and agreed to recommend the offer to its shareholders.

Managers without more than 50% of their firms' stock are very concerned about proxy fights and takeovers, and many of them have attempted to obtain stockholder approval for changes in their corporate charters that would make takeovers more difficult. For example, a number of companies have persuaded their stockholders to agree (1) to elect only one-third of the directors each year (rather than electing all directors each year), (2) to require 75% of the stockholders (rather than 50%) to approve a merger, and (3) to vote in a "poison pill" provision that would allow the stockholders of a firm that is taken over by another firm to buy shares in the second firm at a reduced price. The poison pill makes the acquisition unattractive and thus helps ward off hostile takeover attempts. Managers seeking such changes generally cite a fear that the firm will be picked up at a bargain price, but it often appears that the managers' concern about their own positions is the primary consideration.

Managers' moves to make takeovers more difficult have been countered by stockholders, especially large institutional stockholders, who do not like barriers erected to protect incompetent managers. To illustrate, the California Public Employees Retirement System (CalPERS), which is one of the largest institutional investors, has led proxy fights with several corporations whose

Proxy

A document giving one person the authority to act for another, typically the power to vote shares of common stock.

Proxy Fight

An attempt by a person or group to gain control of a firm by getting its stockholders to grant that person or group the authority to vote its shares to replace the current management.

Takeover

An action whereby a person or group succeeds in ousting a firm's management and taking control of the company.

---

[1]In the situation described, a 1,000-share stockholder could cast 1,000 votes for each of three directors if there were three contested seats on the board. An alternative procedure that may be prescribed in the corporate charter calls for *cumulative voting*. There the 1,000-share stockholder would get 3,000 votes if there were three vacancies, and he or she could cast all of them for one director. Cumulative voting helps small groups obtain representation on the board.

financial performances were poor in CalPERS' judgment. CalPERS wants companies to increase outside (nonmanagement) directors' ability to force managers to be more responsive to stockholder complaints.

Managers' pay is another contentious issue. It has been asserted, with considerable support, that CEOs tend to pick other CEOs to serve on their boards, with "you-scratch-my-back-and-I'll-scratch-yours" behavior resulting in excessive compensation packages to top managers. Boards have tried to conceal the facts by making it extremely difficult for stockholders to know top managers' salaries and bonuses. CalPERS and other institutional investors have weighed in on this issue, and most firms today have been forced to make their compensation packages more transparent. Similarly, the Dodd–Frank bill imposed a Say-on-Pay provision, which provides shareholders the ability to vote on executive compensation. While this provision is non-binding, it imposes some pressure on managers who don't want to see shareholders voting to disapprove of their pay package.

For many years, SEC rules prohibited large investors such as CalPERS from getting together to force corporate managers to institute policy changes. However, the SEC began changing its rules in 1993, and now large investors can work together to force management changes. These rulings have helped keep managers focused on stockholder concerns, which means the maximization of stock prices.

9-1b THE PREEMPTIVE RIGHT

Preemptive Right
A provision in the corporate charter or bylaws that gives common stockholders the right to purchase on a pro rata basis new issues of common stock (or convertible securities).

Common stockholders often have the right, called the **preemptive right**, to purchase on a pro rata basis any additional shares sold by the firm. In some states, the preemptive right is automatically included in every corporate charter; in other states, it must be specifically inserted into the charter.

The purpose of the preemptive right is twofold. First, it prevents the management of a corporation from issuing a large number of additional shares and purchasing those shares itself. Management could use this tactic to seize control of the corporation and frustrate the will of the current stockholders. The second, and far more important, reason for the preemptive right is to protect stockholders from a dilution of value. For example, suppose 1,000 shares of common stock, each with a price of $100, were outstanding, making the total market value of the firm $100,000. If an additional 1,000 shares were sold at $50 a share, or for $50,000, this would raise the firm's total market value to $150,000. When the new total market value is divided by the 2,000 total shares now outstanding, a value of $75 a share is obtained. The old stockholders would thus lose $25 per share, and the new stockholders would have an instant profit of $25 per share. Thus, selling common stock at a price below the market value would dilute a firm's price and transfer wealth from its present stockholders to those who were allowed to purchase the new shares. The preemptive right prevents this.

SELF TEST

Identify some actions that companies have taken to make takeovers more difficult.

What is the preemptive right, and what are the two primary reasons for its existence?

Classified Stock
Common stock that is given a special designation such as Class A or Class B to meet special needs of the company.

9-2 TYPES OF COMMON STOCK

Although most firms have only one type of common stock, in some instances, **classified stock** is used to meet special needs. Generally, when special classifications are used, one type is designated *Class A,* another *Class B,* and so forth. Small, new companies seeking funds from outside sources frequently use different types of common stock. For example, when Google went public, it sold Class A stock to the public while its Class B stock was retained by the company's insiders. The key difference is that the Class B stock has 10 votes per share while the Class A stock has 1 vote per share. Google's Class B shares are predominantly held by the company's two founders and its current CEO. The use of classified stock thus enables the company's founders to maintain control over the company without having to own a majority of the common stock. For this reason, Class B stock of this type is sometimes called **founders' shares**. Because *dual-class* share structures of this type give special voting privileges to key insiders, these structures are sometimes criticized because they may enable insiders to make decisions that are counter to the interests of the majority of stockholders.

Founders' Shares
Stock owned by the firm's founders that enables them to maintain control over the company without having to own a majority of stock.

Note that "Class A," "Class B," and so forth, have no standard meanings. Most firms have no classified shares; but a firm that does could designate its Class B shares as founders' shares and its Class A shares as those sold to the public, while another could reverse those designations. Still other firms could use stock classifications for entirely different purposes. For example, when General Motors acquired Hughes Aircraft for $5 billion, it paid in part with a new Class H common, GMH, which had limited voting rights and whose dividends were tied to Hughes's performance as a GM subsidiary. The reasons for the new stock were that (1) GM wanted to limit voting privileges on the new classified stock because of management's concern about a possible takeover and (2) Hughes's employees wanted to be rewarded more directly on Hughes's own performance than would have been possible through regular GM stock. These Class H shares disappeared in 2003 when GM decided to sell off the Hughes unit.

SELF TEST

What are some reasons a company might use classified stock?

9-3 STOCK PRICE VERSUS INTRINSIC VALUE

We saw in Chapter 1 that a manager should seek to maximize the value of his or her firm's stock. In that chapter, we also emphasized the difference between stock price and intrinsic value. The stock price is simply the current market price, and it is easily observed for publicly traded companies. By contrast, intrinsic value, which represents the "true" value of the company's stock, cannot be directly observed and must instead be estimated. Figure 9.1 illustrates once again the connection between stock price and intrinsic value.

As the figure suggests, market equilibrium occurs when the stock's price equals its intrinsic value. If the stock market is reasonably efficient, gaps between the stock price and intrinsic value should not be very large and they should not persist for very long. However, in some cases, an individual company's stock price may be much higher or lower than its intrinsic value. During several years leading up to the credit crunch of 2007–2008, most of the large investment banks were reporting record profits and selling at record prices. However, much of those earnings were illusory because they did not reflect the huge risks that existed in the mortgage-backed securities that these firms were purchasing. So with hindsight, we now know that the market prices of most financial firms' stocks

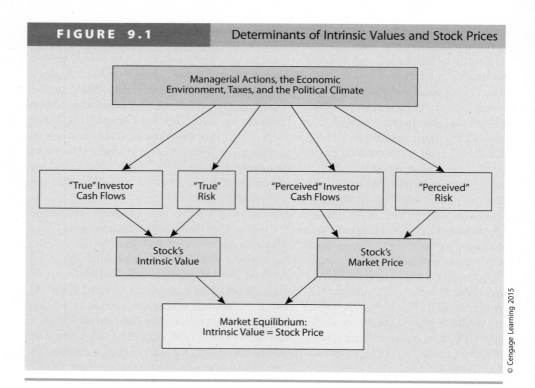

FIGURE 9.1   Determinants of Intrinsic Values and Stock Prices

Managerial Actions, the Economic Environment, Taxes, and the Political Climate

"True" Investor Cash Flows

"True" Risk

"Perceived" Investor Cash Flows

"Perceived" Risk

Stock's Intrinsic Value

Stock's Market Price

Market Equilibrium: Intrinsic Value = Stock Price

exceeded their intrinsic values just prior to 2007. Then when the market realized what was happening, those stock prices crashed. Citigroup, Merrill Lynch, and others lost more than 60% of their value in a few short months; and Bear Stearns, the fifth-largest investment bank, saw its stock price drop from $171 in 2007 to $2 just before its ultimate collapse in mid-March 2008. It clearly pays to question market prices at times!

9-3a WHY DO INVESTORS AND COMPANIES CARE ABOUT INTRINSIC VALUE?

The remainder of this chapter focuses primarily on different approaches for estimating a stock's intrinsic value. Before these approaches are described, it is worth asking why it is important for investors and companies to understand how to calculate intrinsic value.

When investing in common stocks, one's goal is to purchase stocks that are undervalued (i.e., the price is below the stock's intrinsic value) and avoid stocks that are overvalued. Consequently, Wall Street analysts, institutional investors who control mutual funds and pension funds, and many individual investors are interested in finding reliable models that help predict a stock's intrinsic value.

Investors obviously care about intrinsic value, but managers also need to understand how intrinsic value is estimated. First, managers need to know how alternative actions are likely to affect stock prices; and the models of intrinsic value that we cover help demonstrate the connection between managerial decisions and firm value. Second, managers should consider whether their stock is significantly undervalued or overvalued before making certain decisions. For example, firms should consider carefully the decision to issue new shares if they believe their stock is undervalued; and an estimate of their stock's intrinsic value is the key to such decisions.

Two basic models are used to estimate intrinsic values: the *discounted dividend model* and the *corporate valuation model*. The dividend model focuses on dividends, while the corporate model goes beyond dividends and focuses on sales, costs, and free cash flows. In the following sections, we describe these approaches in more detail.

9-4 THE DISCOUNTED DIVIDEND MODEL

The value of a share of common stock depends on the cash flows it is expected to provide, and those flows consist of two elements: (1) the dividends the investor receives each year while he or she holds the stock and (2) the price received when the stock is sold. The final price includes the original price paid plus an expected capital gain. Keep in mind that there are many different investors in the market and thus many different sets of expectations. Therefore, investors will have different opinions about a stock's true intrinsic value and thus its proper price. The analysis as performed by the **marginal investor**, whose actions actually determine the equilibrium stock price, is critical; but every investor, marginal or not, implicitly goes through the same type of analysis.

The following terms are used in our analysis:[2]

Marginal Investor
A representative investor whose actions reflect the beliefs of those people who are currently trading a stock. It is the marginal investor who determines a stock's price.

D_t = the dividend a stockholder expects to receive at the end of each Year t. D_0 is the last dividend the company paid. Because it has already been paid, a buyer of the stock will not receive D_0. The first dividend a new buyer will receive is D_1, which is paid at the end of Year 1. D_2 is the dividend expected at the end of Year 2; D_3, at the end of Year 3; and so forth. D_0 is known with certainty; but D_1, D_2, and all other future dividends are *expected values*; and different investors can have different expectations.[3] Our primary concern is with D_t as forecasted by the *marginal investor*.

P_0 = actual **market price** of the stock today. P_0 is known with certainty, but predicted future prices are subject to uncertainty.

$\hat{P}_t$ = both the expected price and the expected intrinsic value of the stock at the end of each Year t (pronounced "P hat t") as seen by the investor doing the

Market Price, P_0
The price at which a stock sells in the market.

---

[2]Many terms are described here, and students sometimes get concerned about having to memorize all of them. We tell our students that we will provide formula sheets for use on exams, so they don't have to try to memorize everything. With their minds thus eased, they end up learning what the terms are rather than memorizing them.

[3]Stocks generally pay dividends quarterly, so theoretically we should evaluate them on a quarterly basis. However, most analysts actually work with annual data because forecasted stock data are not precise enough to warrant the use of a quarterly model. For additional information on the quarterly model, see Charles M. Linke and J. Kenton Zumwalt, "Estimation Biases in Discounted Cash Flow Analysis of Equity Capital Costs in Rate Regulation," *Financial Management*, vol. 13, no. 3 (Autumn 1984), pp. 15–21.

analysis. $\hat{P}_t$ is based on the investor's estimates of the dividend stream and the riskiness of that stream. There are many investors in the market, so there can be many estimates for $\hat{P}_t$. However, for the marginal investor, P_0 must equal $\hat{P}_0$. Otherwise, a disequilibrium would exist, and buying and selling in the market would soon result in P_0 equaling $\hat{P}_0$ as seen by the marginal investor.

Growth Rate, g

The expected rate of growth in dividends per share.

g = expected **growth rate** in dividends as predicted by an investor. If dividends are expected to grow at a constant rate, g should also equal the expected growth rate in earnings and the stock's price. Different investors use different g's to evaluate a firm's stock; but the market price, P_0, is based on g as estimated by the marginal investor.

Required Rate of Return, r_s

The minimum rate of return on a common stock that a stockholder considers acceptable.

r_s = **required**, or minimum acceptable, **rate of return** on the stock considering its riskiness and the returns available on other investments. Different investors typically have different opinions, but the key is again the marginal investor. The determinants of r_s include factors discussed in Chapter 8, including the real rate of return, expected inflation, and risk.

Expected Rate of Return, $\hat{r}_s$

The rate of return on a common stock that a stockholder expects to receive in the future.

$\hat{r}_s$ = **expected rate of return** (pronounced "r hat s") that an investor believes the stock will provide in the future. The expected return can be above or below the required return; but a rational investor will buy the stock if $\hat{r}_s$ exceeds r_s, sell the stock if $\hat{r}_s$ is less than r_s, and simply hold the stock if these returns are equal. Again, the key is the marginal investor, whose views determine the actual stock price.

Actual (Realized) Rate of Return, $\bar{r}_s$

The rate of return on a common stock actually received by stockholders in some past period; $\bar{r}_s$ may be greater or less than $\hat{r}_s$ and/or r_s.

$\bar{r}_s$ = **actual, or realized,** *after-the-fact* **rate of return,** pronounced "r bar s." You can *expect* to obtain a return of $\bar{r}_s$ = 10% if you buy a stock today; but if the market declines, you may end up with an actual realized return that is much lower, perhaps even negative.

Dividend Yield

The expected dividend divided by the current price of a share of stock.

D_1/P_0 = **dividend yield** expected during the coming year. If Company X's stock is expected to pay a dividend of D_1 = \$1 during the next 12 months and if X's current price is P_0 = \$20, the expected dividend yield will be \$1/\$20 = 0.05 = 5%. Different investors could have different expectations for D_1; but again, the marginal investor is the key.

Capital Gains Yield

The capital gain during a given year divided by the beginning price.

$(\hat{P}_1 - P_0)/P_0$ = expected **capital gains yield** on the stock during the coming year. If the stock sells for \$20.00 today and if it is expected to rise to \$21.00 by the end of the year, the expected capital gain will be $\hat{P}_1 - P_0$ = \$21.00 − \$20.00 = \$1.00 and the expected capital gains yield will be \$1.00/\$20.00 = 0.05 = 5%. Different investors can have different expectations for $\hat{P}_1$, but the marginal investor is key.

Expected Total Return

The sum of the expected dividend yield and the expected capital gains yield.

Expected total return = $\hat{r}_s$ = expected dividend yield (D_1/P_0) plus expected capital gains yield $[(\hat{P}_1 - P_0)/P_0]$. In our example, the **expected total return** = 5% + 5% = 10%.

All active investors hope to achieve better-than-average returns—they hope to identify stocks whose intrinsic values exceed their current prices and whose expected returns (expected by this investor) exceed their required rates of return. Note, though, that about half of all investors are likely to be disappointed. A good understanding of the points made in this chapter can help you avoid being disappointed.

9-4A EXPECTED DIVIDENDS AS THE BASIS FOR STOCK VALUES

In our discussion of bonds, we used Equation 7.1 to find the value of a bond; the equation is the present value of interest payments over the bond's life plus the present value of its maturity (or par) value:

$$V_B = \frac{INT}{(1 + r_d)^1} + \frac{INT}{(1 + r_d)^2} + \cdots + \frac{INT}{(1 + r_d)^N} + \frac{M}{(1 + r_d)^N}$$

Stock prices are likewise determined as the present value of a stream of cash flows, and the basic stock valuation equation is similar to the one for bonds. What are the cash flows that a corporation will provide to its stockholders? To answer that question, think of yourself as an investor who purchases the stock of a company that is expected to exist indefinitely (for example, GE). You intend to hold it (in your family) forever. In this case, all you (and your heirs) will receive is a stream of dividends; and the value of the stock today can be calculated as the present value of an infinite stream of dividends:

$$\text{Value of stock} = \hat{P}_0 = \text{PV of expected future dividends}$$

$$= \frac{D_1}{(1 + r_s)^1} + \frac{D_2}{(1 + r_s)^2} + \cdots + \frac{D_\infty}{(1 + r_s)^\infty}$$

$$= \sum_{t=1}^{\infty} \frac{D_t}{(1 + r_s)^t}$$

9.1

What about the more typical case, where you expect to hold the stock for a finite period and then sell it—what will be the value of $\hat{P}_0$ in this case? Unless the company is likely to be liquidated or sold and thus disappears, *the value of the stock is again determined by Equation 9.1.* To see this, recognize that for any individual investor, the expected cash flows consist of expected dividends plus the expected sale price of the stock. However, the sale price to the current investor depends on the dividends some future investor expects, and that investor's expected sale price is also dependent on some future dividends, and so forth. Therefore, for all present and future investors in total, expected cash flows must be based on expected future dividends. Put another way, unless a firm is liquidated or sold to another concern, the cash flows it provides to its stockholders will consist only of a stream of dividends. Therefore, the value of a share of stock must be established as the present value of the stock's expected dividend stream.[4]

---

[4]The general validity of Equation 9.1 can also be confirmed by asking yourself the following question: Suppose I buy a stock and expect to hold it for 1 year. I will receive dividends during the year plus the value $\hat{P}_1$ when I sell it at the end of the year. But what will determine the value of $\hat{P}_1$? The answer is that it will be determined as the present value of the dividends expected during Year 2 plus the stock price at the end of that year, which, in turn, will be determined as the present value of another set of future dividends and an even more distant stock price. This process can be continued ad infinitum, and the ultimate result is Equation 9.1.

We should note that investors periodically lose sight of the long-run nature of stocks as investments and forget that in order to sell a stock at a profit, one must find a buyer who will pay the higher price. If you analyze a stock's value in accordance with Equation 9.1, conclude that the stock's market price exceeds a reasonable value, and buy the stock anyway, you would be following the *"bigger fool" theory of investment*—you think you may be a fool to buy the stock at its excessive price; but you also believe that when you get ready to sell it, you can find someone who is an even bigger fool. The bigger fool theory was widely followed in the summer of 2000, just before the stock market crashed.

SELF TEST

Explain the following statement: Whereas a bond contains a promise to pay interest, a share of common stock typically provides an expectation of, but no promise of, dividends plus capital gains.

What are the two parts of most stocks' expected total return?

If $D_1 = \$2.00$, $g = 6\%$, and $P_0 = \$40.00$, what are the stock's expected dividend yield, capital gains yield, and total expected return for the coming year? **(5%, 6%, 11%)**

Is it necessary for all investors to have the same expectations regarding a stock for the stock to be in equilibrium?

What would happen to a stock's price if the "marginal investor" examined a stock and concluded that its intrinsic value was greater than its current market price?

9-5 Constant Growth Stocks

Equation 9.1 is a generalized stock valuation model in the sense that the time pattern of D_t can be anything: D_t can be rising, falling, or fluctuating randomly; or it can be zero for several years. Equation 9.1 can be applied in any of these situations; and with a computer spreadsheet, we can easily use the equation to find a stock's intrinsic value—provided we have an estimate of the future dividends. However, it is not easy to obtain accurate estimates of future dividends.

Still, for many companies it is reasonable to predict that dividends will grow at a constant rate. In this case, Equation 9.1 may be rewritten as follows:

$$\hat{P}_0 = \frac{D_0(1+g)^1}{(1+r_s)^1} + \frac{D_0(1+g)^2}{(1+r_s)^2} + \cdots + \frac{D_0(1+g)^\infty}{(1+r_s)^\infty}$$

$$= \frac{D_0(1+g)}{r_s - g} = \frac{D_1}{r_s - g} \qquad \textbf{9.2}$$

Constant Growth (Gordon) Model
Used to find the value of a constant growth stock.

The last term of Equation 9.2 is the **constant growth model,** or **Gordon model,** named after Myron J. Gordon, who did much to develop and popularize it.[5]

The term r_s in Equation 9.2 is the *required rate of return,* which is a riskless rate plus a risk premium. However, we know that if the stock is in equilibrium, the required rate of return must equal the expected rate of return, which is the expected dividend yield plus an expected capital gains yield. So we can solve Equation 9.2 for r_s, but now using the hat to indicate that we are dealing with an expected rate of return:[6]

$$
\begin{array}{ccccc}
\text{Expected rate} & = & \text{Expected} & + & \text{Expected growth rate, or} \\
\text{of return} & & \text{dividend yield} & & \text{capital gains yield} \\
\hat{r}_s & = & \dfrac{D_1}{P_0} & + & g
\end{array}
\qquad \textbf{9.3}
$$

We illustrate Equations 9.2 and 9.3 in the following section.

---

[5]The last term in Equation 9.2 is derived in the Web Extension of Chapter 5 of Eugene F. Brigham and Phillip R. Daves, *Intermediate Financial Management*, 11th edition (Mason, OH: South-Western/Cengage Learning, 2013). In essence, Equation 9.2 is the sum of a geometric progression, and the final result is the solution value of the progression.

[6]The r_s value in Equation 9.2 is a *required* rate of return; but when we transform Equation 9.2 to obtain Equation 9.3, we are finding an *expected* rate of return. Obviously, the transformation requires that $r_s = \hat{r}_s$. This equality must hold if the stock is in equilibrium, as most normally are.

Analysis of a Constant Growth Stock   **TABLE 9.1**

	A	B	C	D	E	F	G	H	I
3									
4	**I. Basic Information:**			**II. Formulas Used in the Analysis:**					
5	D_0 =	$1.15		Dividend in Year t , D_t, in Column 2				$D_{t-1}(1 + g)$	
6	P_0 =	$23.06		Intrinsic value (and price) in Year t, P_t, in Column 3				$D_{t+1} / (r_s - g)$	
7	g =	8.30%		Dividend yield (constant) in Column 4				D_t / P_{t-1}	
8	r_s =	13.70%		Capital gains yield (constant) in Column 5				$(P_t - P_{t-1}) / P_{t-1}$	
9				Total return (constant) in Column 6				Div. yield + CG yield	
10				PV of dividends discounted at 13.7% in Column 7				$D_t / (1 + r_s)^t$	
11	**III. Examples:**								
12		Column 2		D_1 = $1.1500(1.083)				$1.25	
13		Column 3		P_0 = $1.25 / (0.137 - 0.083)				$23.06	
14		Column 4		Dividend yield, Year 1: $1.25 / $23.06				5.4%	
15		Column 5		Cap gains yield, Year 1: ($24.98 - $23.06) / $23.06				8.3%	
16		Column 6		Total return, Year 1: 5.4 % + 8.3 %				13.7%	
17		Column 7		PV of D_1 discounted at 13.7%				$1.10	
18									
19	**IV. Forecasted Results over Time:**						PV of		
20	At end			Dividend	Capital	Total	dividend		
21	of year:	Dividend	Price *	yield	gains yield	return	at 13.7%		
22	(1)	(2)	(3)	(4)	(5)	(6)	(7)		
23	2014	$1.15	$23.06						
24	2015	$1.25	$24.98	5.4%	8.3%	13.7%	$1.10		
25	2016	$1.35	$27.05	5.4%	8.3%	13.7%	$1.04		
26	2017	$1.46	$29.30	5.4%	8.3%	13.7%	$0.99		
27	2018	$1.58	$31.73	5.4%	8.3%	13.7%	$0.95		
28	2019	$1.71	$34.36	5.4%	8.3%	13.7%	$0.90		
29	2020	$1.86	$37.21	5.4%	8.3%	13.7%	$0.86		
30	2021	$2.01	$40.30	5.4%	8.3%	13.7%	$0.82		
31	2022	$2.18	$43.65	5.4%	8.3%	13.7%	$0.78		
32	2023	$2.36	$47.27	5.4%	8.3%	13.7%	$0.74		
33	2024	$2.55	$51.19	5.4%	8.3%	13.7%	$0.71		
34	↓						↓		
35	∞					Sum of PVs from 1 to ∞ = P_0 =	$23.06	= Value on 1/1/2015	
36									
37	* Because this is a constant growth stock, we could have found the value for P_t as $P_{t-1}(1 + g)$. For example, P_1 = $23.06(1.083) = $24.97. This value differs from the one in the table due to a rounding difference. You shouldn't worry about rounding differences.								

9-5A ILLUSTRATION OF A CONSTANT GROWTH STOCK

Table 9.1 presents an analysis of Allied Food Products' stock as performed by a security analyst after a meeting for analysts and other investors presided over by Allied's CFO. The table looks complicated, but it is really quite straightforward.[7] Part I, in the upper left corner, provides some basic data. The last dividend, which was just paid, was $1.15; the stock's last closing price was $23.06; and it is in equilibrium. Based on an analysis of Allied's history and likely future, the analyst forecasts that earnings and dividends will grow at a constant rate of 8.3% per year and that the stock's price will grow at this same rate. Moreover, the analyst believes that the most appropriate required rate of return is 13.7%. Different analysts might use different inputs; but we assume for now that because this analyst is widely followed, her results represent those of the marginal investor.

---

[7]You may notice some minor "errors" in the table. These are not errors—they are simply differences caused by rounding.

Look at Part IV, where we show the predicted stream of dividends and stock prices along with annual values for the dividend yield, the capital gains yield, and the expected total return. Notice that the total return shown in Column 6 is equal to the required rate of return shown in Part I. This indicates that the stock analyst thinks that the stock is fairly priced; hence, it is in equilibrium. She forecasted data for 10 years, but she could have forecasted out to infinity.

Part II shows the formulas used to calculate the data in Part IV, and Part III gives examples of the calculations. For example, D_1, the first dividend a purchaser would receive, is forecasted to be $D_1 = \$1.15(1.083) = \$1.25$, and the other forecasted dividends in Column 2 were calculated similarly. The estimated intrinsic values shown in Column 3 are based on Equation 9.2, the constant growth model: $P_0 = D_1/(r_s - g) = \$1.25/(0.137 - 0.083) = \$23.06$ (corrected for rounding), $\hat{P}_1 = \$24.98$, and so forth.

Column 4 shows the dividend yield, which for 2015 is $D_1/P_0 = 5.40\%$; and this number is constant thereafter. The capital gain expected during 2015 is $\hat{P}_1 - P_0 = \$24.98 - \$23.06 = \$1.92$, which when divided by P_0 gives the expected capital gains yield, $\$1.92/\$23.06 = 8.3\%$, again corrected for rounding. The total return is found as the dividend yield plus the capital gains yield, 13.7%; and it is both constant and equal to the required rate of return given in Part I.

Finally, look at Column 7 in the table. Here we find the present value of each of the dividends shown in Column 2, discounted at the required rate of return. For example, the PV of $D_1 = \$1.25/(1.137)^1 = \$1.10$, the PV of $D_2 = \$1.35/(1.137)^2 = \$1.04$, and so forth. If you extended the table out to about 170 years (with Excel, this is easy), then summed the PVs of the dividends, you would obtain the same value as that found using Equation 9.2, $\$23.06$.[8] Figure 9.2 shows graphically what's happening. We extended the table out 20 years and then plotted dividends from Column 2 in the upper step function curve and the PV of those dividends in the lower curve. The sum of the PVs is an estimate of the stock's forecasted intrinsic value.

Note that in Table 9.1, the forecasted intrinsic value is equal to the current stock price and the expected total return is equal to the required rate of return. In this situation, the analyst would call the stock a "Hold" and would recommend that investors not buy or sell it. However, if the analyst were somewhat more optimistic and thought the growth rate would be 10.0% rather than 8.3%, the forecasted intrinsic value would be (by Equation 9.2) $34.19 and the analyst would call it a "Buy." At $g = 6\%$, the intrinsic value would be $15.83 and the stock would be a "Sell." Changes in the required rate of return would produce similar changes in the forecasted intrinsic value and thus the equilibrium current price.

9-5b Dividends Versus Growth

The discounted dividend model as expressed in Equation 9.2 shows that, other things held constant, a higher value for D_1 increases a stock's price. However, Equation 9.2 shows that a higher growth rate also increases the stock's price. But now recognize the following:

- Dividends are paid out of earnings.
- Therefore, growth in dividends requires growth in earnings.

---

[8]The dividends get quite large, but the discount rate exceeds the growth rate; so the PVs of the dividends become quite small. In theory, you would have to go out to infinity to find the exact price of a constant growth stock, but the difference between the Equation 9.2 value and the sum of the PVs can't be seen out to 2 decimal places if you extend the analysis to 170 periods.

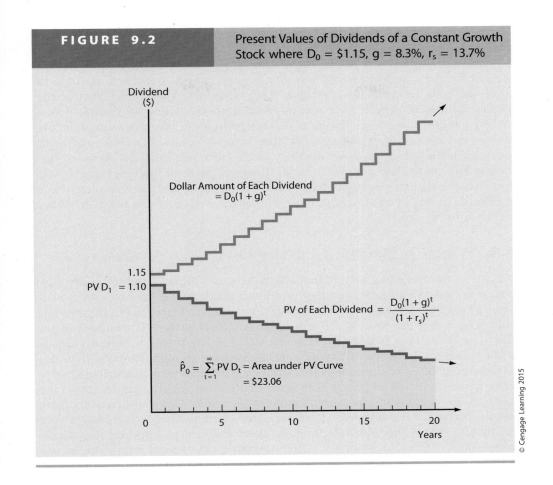

| FIGURE 9.2 | Present Values of Dividends of a Constant Growth Stock where $D_0 = \$1.15$, $g = 8.3\%$, $r_s = 13.7\%$ |

Dividend ($)

Dollar Amount of Each Dividend $= D_0(1 + g)^t$

1.15
PV D_1 = 1.10

PV of Each Dividend $= \dfrac{D_0(1 + g)^t}{(1 + r_s)^t}$

$\hat{P}_0 = \displaystyle\sum_{t=1}^{\infty} \text{PV } D_t = $ Area under PV Curve $= \$23.06$

0   5   10   15   20
Years

© Cengage Learning 2015

- Earnings growth in the long run occurs primarily because firms retain earnings and reinvest them in the business.
- Therefore, the higher the percentage of earnings retained, the higher the growth rate.

To illustrate this, suppose you inherit a business that has $1,000,000 of assets and no debt, thus $1,000,000 of equity. The expected return on equity (ROE) equals 10.0%, so its expected earnings for the coming year are (0.10)($1,000,000) = $100,000. You could take out the entire $100,000 of earnings in dividends, or you could reinvest some or all of the $100,000 in the business. If you pay out all the earnings, you will have $100,000 of dividend income this year, but dividends will not grow because assets, and therefore earnings, will not grow.

However, suppose you decide to have the firm pay out 40% and retain 60%. Now your dividend income in Year 1 will be $40,000; but assets will rise by $60,000, and earnings and dividends will likewise increase:

$$\text{Next year's earnings} = \text{Prior earnings} + \text{ROE(Retained earnings)}$$
$$= \$100,000 + 0.1(\$60,000)$$
$$= \$106,000$$
$$\text{Next year's dividends} = 0.4(\$106,000) = \$42,400$$

Moreover, your dividend income will continue to grow by 6% per year thereafter:

$$\text{Growth rate} = (1 - \text{Payout ratio})\text{ROE}$$
$$= (1 - 0.4)10.0\%$$
$$= 0.6(10.0\%) = 6.0\%$$

9.4

This demonstrates that in the long run, growth in dividends depends primarily on the firm's payout ratio and its ROE.

In our example, we assumed that other things remain constant. This is often but not always a logical assumption. For example, suppose the firm develops a successful new product, hires a better CEO, or makes some other change that increased the ROE. Any of these actions could cause the ROE to increase and thus the growth rate to increase. Also note that the earnings of new firms are often low or even negative for several years, and then begin to rise rapidly; finally, growth levels off as the firm approaches maturity. Such a firm might pay no dividends for its first few years, then pay a low initial dividend but let it increase rapidly, and finally make regular payments that grow at a constant rate once earnings have stabilized. In any such situation, the nonconstant model as discussed in a later section must be used.

9-5c WHICH IS BETTER: CURRENT DIVIDENDS OR GROWTH?

We saw in the preceding section that a firm can pay a higher current dividend by increasing its payout ratio, but that will lower its dividend growth rate. So the firm can provide a relatively high current dividend or a high growth rate but not both. This being the case, which would stockholders prefer? The answer is not clear. As we will see in Chapter 14, some stockholders prefer current dividends while others prefer a lower payout ratio and future growth. Empirical studies have been unable to determine which strategy is optimal for maximizing a firm's stock price. So dividend policy is an issue that management must decide on the basis of its judgment, not a mathematical formula. Logically, shareholders should prefer for the company to retain more earnings (hence pay less current dividends) if the firm has exceptionally good investment opportunities; however, shareholders should prefer a high payout if investment opportunities are poor. In spite of this, taxes and other factors complicate the situation. We will discuss all this in detail in Chapter 14; but for now, just assume that the firm's management has decided on a payout policy and uses that policy to determine the actual dividend.

9-5d REQUIRED CONDITIONS FOR THE CONSTANT GROWTH MODEL

Several conditions are necessary for Equation 9.2 to be used. First, the required rate of return, r_s, must be greater than the long-run growth rate, g. *If the equation is used in situations where g is greater than r_s, the results will be wrong, meaningless, and misleading.* For example, if the forecasted growth rate in our example was 15% and thus exceeded the 13.7% required rate of return, stock price as calculated by Equation 9.2 would be a *negative* $101.73. That would be nonsense—stocks can't have negative prices. Moreover, in Table 9.1, the PV of each future dividend would exceed that of the prior year. If this situation was graphed in Figure 9.2, the step-function curve for the PV of dividends would be increasing, not decreasing; so the sum would be infinitely high, which would indicate an infinitely high stock price. Obviously, stock prices cannot be either infinite or negative, so Equation 9.2 cannot be used unless $r_s > g$.

Second, the constant growth model as expressed in Equation 9.2 is not appropriate unless a company's growth rate is expected to remain constant in the future. This condition almost never holds for new start-up firms, but it does exist for many mature companies. Indeed, mature firms such as Allied and GE are generally expected to grow at about the same rate as nominal gross domestic product (that is, real GDP plus inflation). On this basis, one might expect the dividends of an average, or "normal," company to grow at a rate of 5% to 8% a year.

Note too that Equation 9.2 is sufficiently general to handle the case of a **zero growth stock**, where the dividend is expected to remain constant over time. If $g = 0$, Equation 9.2 reduces to Equation 9.5:

Zero Growth Stock
A common stock whose future dividends are not expected to grow at all; that is, g = 0.

$$\hat{P}_0 = \frac{D}{r_s}$$

 9.5

This is the same equation as the one we developed in Chapter 5 for a perpetuity, and it is simply the current dividend divided by the required rate of return.

Finally, as we discuss later in the chapter, most firms, even rapidly growing start-ups and others that pay no dividends at present, can be expected to pay dividends at some point in the future, at which time the constant growth model will be appropriate. For such firms, Equation 9.2 is used as one part of a more complicated valuation equation that we discuss next.

SELF TEST

Write out and explain the valuation formula for a constant growth stock.

Describe how the formula for a zero growth stock can be derived from the formula for a normal constant growth stock.

Firm A is expected to pay a dividend of $1.00 at the end of the year. The required rate of return is $r_s = 11\%$. Other things held constant, what would the stock's price be if the growth rate was 5%? What if g was 0%? **($16.67, $9.09)**

Firm B has a 12% ROE. Other things held constant, what would its expected growth rate be if it paid out 25% of its earnings as dividends? 75%? **(9%, 3%)**

If Firm B had a 75% payout ratio but then lowered it to 25%, causing its growth rate to rise from 3% to 9%, would that action necessarily increase the price of its stock? Why or why not?

9-6 VALUING NONCONSTANT GROWTH STOCKS

For many companies, it is not appropriate to assume that dividends will grow at a constant rate. Indeed, most firms go through *life cycles* where they experience different growth rates during different parts of the cycle. In their early years, most firms grow much faster than the economy as a whole; then they match the economy's growth; and finally they grow at a slower rate than the economy.[9] Automobile manufacturers in the 1920s, computer software firms such as Microsoft in the 1990s, and Google in the 2000s are examples of firms in the early part of their cycle. These firms are defined as **supernormal,** or **nonconstant growth,**

Supernormal (Nonconstant) Growth
The part of the firm's life cycle in which it grows much faster than the economy as a whole.

---

[9]The concept of life cycles could be broadened to *product cycle*, which would include both small start-up companies and large companies such as Microsoft and Procter & Gamble, which periodically introduce new products that give sales and earnings a boost. We should also mention *business cycles*, which alternately depress and boost sales and profits. The growth rate just after a major new product has been introduced (or just after a firm emerges from the depths of a recession) is likely to be much higher than the "expected long-run average growth rate," which is the proper number for use in the discounted dividend model.

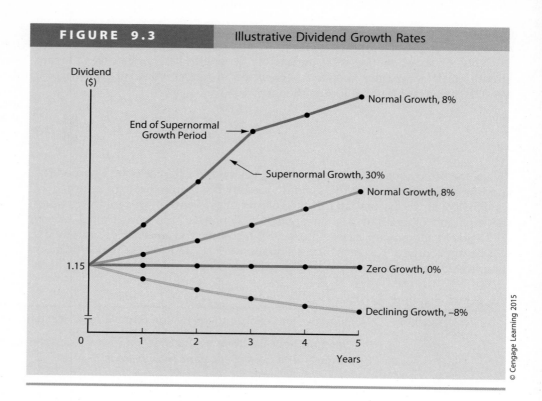

FIGURE 9.3 Illustrative Dividend Growth Rates

Dividend ($)

End of Supernormal Growth Period

Normal Growth, 8%

Supernormal Growth, 30%

Normal Growth, 8%

1.15

Zero Growth, 0%

Declining Growth, −8%

0 1 2 3 4 5

Years

© Cengage Learning 2015

firms. Figure 9.3 illustrates nonconstant growth and compares it with normal growth, zero growth, and negative (or declining) growth.[10]

In the figure, the dividends of the supernormal growth firm are expected to grow at a 30% rate for three years, after which the growth rate is expected to fall to 8%, the assumed average for the economy. The value of this firm's stock, like any other asset, is the present value of its expected future dividends as determined by Equation 9.1. When D_t is growing at a constant rate, we can simplify Equation 9.1 to Equation 9.2, $\hat{P}_0 = D_1/(r_s - g)$. In the supernormal case, however, the expected growth rate is not a constant. In our example, there are two distinctly different rates.

Because Equation 9.2 requires a constant growth rate, we obviously cannot use it to value stocks that are not growing at a constant rate. However, assuming that a company currently enjoying supernormal growth will eventually slow down and become a constant growth stock, we can combine Equations 9.1 and 9.2 to construct a new formula, Equation 9.6, for valuing the stock.

First, we assume that the dividend will grow at a nonconstant rate (generally a relatively high rate) for N periods, after which it will grow at a constant rate, g. N is often called the **horizon,** or **terminal, date.** Second, we can use the constant growth formula, Equation 9.2, to determine what the stock's **horizon,** or **continuing, value** will be N periods from today:

Horizon (Terminal) Date

The date when the growth rate becomes constant. At this date, it is no longer necessary to forecast the individual dividends.

Horizon (Continuing) Value

The value at the horizon date of all dividends expected thereafter.

---

[10]A negative growth rate indicates a declining company. A mining company whose profits are falling because of a declining ore body is an example. Someone purchasing stock in such a company would expect its earnings (and consequently its dividends and stock price) to decline each year, which would lead to capital losses rather than capital gains. Obviously, a declining company's stock price is relatively low, and its dividend yield must be high enough to offset the expected capital loss and still produce a competitive total return. Students sometimes argue that they would never be willing to buy a stock whose price was expected to decline. However, if the present value of the expected dividends exceeds the stock price, the stock is still a good investment that would provide a good return.

$$\text{Horizon value} = \hat{P}_N = \frac{D_{N+1}}{r_s - g}$$

The stock's intrinsic value today, $\hat{P}_0$, is the present value of the dividends during the nonconstant growth period plus the present value of the horizon value:

$$\hat{P}_0 = \underbrace{\frac{D_1}{(1+r_s)^1} + \frac{D_2}{(1+r_s)^2} + \cdots + \frac{D_N}{(1+r_s)^N}}_{\substack{\text{PV of dividends during the} \\ \text{nonconstant growth} \\ \text{period, } t = 1, \cdots N}} + \underbrace{\frac{D_{N+1}}{(1+r_s)^{N+1}} + \cdots + \frac{D_\infty}{(1+r_s)^\infty}}_{\substack{\text{Horizon value} = \text{PV of dividends} \\ \text{during the constant growth} \\ \text{period, } t = N+1, \cdots \infty}}$$

$$\hat{P}_0 = \underbrace{\frac{D_1}{(1+r_s)^1} + \frac{D_2}{(1+r_s)^2} + \cdots + \frac{D_N}{(1+r_s)^N}}_{\substack{\text{PV of dividends during the} \\ \text{nonconstant growth period} \\ t = 1, \cdots N}} + \underbrace{\frac{\hat{P}_N}{(1+r_s)^N}}_{\substack{\text{PV of horizon} \\ \text{value, } \hat{P}_N: \\ \frac{[(D_{N+1})/(r_s - g)]}{(1+r_s)^N}}}$$

9.6

To implement Equation 9.6, we go through the following three steps:

1. Find the PV of each dividend during the period of nonconstant growth and sum them.

2. Find the expected stock price at the end of the nonconstant growth period. At this point it has become a constant growth stock, so it can be valued with the constant growth model. Discount this price back to the present.

3. Add these two components to find the stock's intrinsic value, $\hat{P}_0$.

Figure 9.4 illustrates the process for valuing nonconstant growth stocks. Here we use a new company, Firm M, and we assume the following information:

r_s = stockholders' required rate of return = 13.4%. This rate is used to discount the cash flows.

N = years of nonconstant growth = 3.

g_s = rate of growth in both earnings and dividends during the nonconstant growth period = 30%. This rate is shown directly on the time line. (Note: The growth rate during the nonconstant growth period could vary from year to year. Also, there could be several different nonconstant growth periods—for example, 30% for three years, 20% for the next three years, and a constant 8% thereafter).

g_n = rate of normal, constant growth after the nonconstant period = 8.0%. This rate is also shown on the time line, after Year 3, when it is in effect.

D_0 = last dividend the company paid = $1.15.

The valuation process diagrammed in Figure 9.4 is explained in the steps set forth below the time line. The value of the nonconstant growth stock is calculated as $39.21.

Note that in this example, we assumed a relatively short 3-year horizon to keep things simple. When evaluating stocks, most analysts use a longer horizon (for example, 10 years) to estimate intrinsic values. This requires a few more

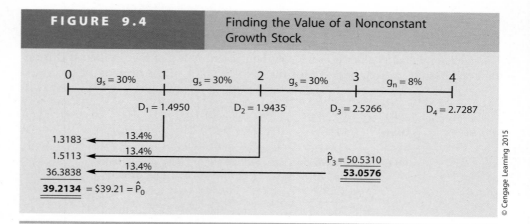

FIGURE 9.4   Finding the Value of a Nonconstant Growth Stock

© Cengage Learning 2015

Notes:

Step 1. Calculate the dividends expected at the end of each year during the nonconstant growth period. Calculate the first dividend, $D_1 = D_0(1 + g_s) = \$1.15(1.30) = \$1.4950$. Here g_s is the growth rate during the 3-year nonconstant growth period, 30%. Show the \$1.4950 on the time line as the cash flow at Time 1. Calculate $D_2 = D_1(1 + g_s) = \$1.4950(1.30) = \$1.9435$, then $D_3 = D_2(1 + g_s) = \$1.9435(1.30) = \$2.5266$. Show these values on the time line as the cash flows at Time 2 and Time 3. Note that D_0 is used only to calculate D_1.

Step 2. The price of the stock is the PV of dividends from Time 1 to infinity; so in theory, we could project each future dividend, with the normal growth rate, $g_n = 8\%$, used to calculate D_4 and subsequent dividends. However, we know that after D_3 has been paid at Time 3, the stock becomes a constant growth stock. Therefore, we can use the constant growth formula to find $\hat{P}_3$ which is the PV of the dividends from Time 4 to infinity as evaluated at Time 3.

First, we determine $D_4 = \$2.5266(1.08) = \$2.7287$ for use in the formula; then we calculate $\hat{P}_3$ as follows:

$$\hat{P}_3 = \frac{D_4}{r_s - g_n} = \frac{\$2.7287}{0.134 - 0.08} = \$50.5310.$$

We show this \$50.5310 on the time line as a second cash flow at Time 3. The \$50.5310 is a Time 3 cash flow in the sense that the stockholder could sell the stock for \$50.5310 at Time 3 and in the sense that \$50.5310 is the present value of the dividend cash flows from Time 4 to infinity. Note that the total cash flow at Time 3 consists of the sum of $D_3 + \hat{P}_3 = \$2.5266 + \$50.5310 = \$53.0576$.

Step 3. Now that the cash flows have been placed on the time line, we can discount each cash flow at the required rate of return, $r_s = 13.4\%$. We could discount each cash flow by dividing by $(1.134)^t$, where $t = 1$ for Time 1, $t = 2$ for Time 2, and $t = 3$ for Time 3. This produces the PVs shown to the left below the time line; and the sum of the PVs is the value of the nonconstant growth stock, \$39.21.

With a financial calculator, you can find the PV of the cash flows as shown on the time line with the cash flow (CFLO) register of your calculator. Enter 0 for CF_0 because you receive no cash flow at Time 0, $CF_1 = 1.495$, $CF_2 = 1.9435$, and $CF_3 = 2.5266 + 50.5310 = 53.0576$. Then enter $I/YR = 13.4$ and press the NPV key to find the value of the stock, \$39.21.

calculations; but because analysts use spreadsheets, the arithmetic is not a problem. In practice, the real limitation is obtaining reliable forecasts for future growth.

SELF TEST

Explain how one would find the value of a nonconstant growth stock.

Explain what is meant by horizon (terminal) date and horizon (continuing) value.

EVALUATING STOCKS THAT DON'T PAY DIVIDENDS

The discounted dividend model assumes that the firm is currently paying a dividend. However, many firms, even highly profitable ones, including Google and Dell, have never paid a dividend. If a firm is expected to begin paying dividends in the future, we can modify the equations presented in the chapter and use them to determine the value of the stock.

A new business often expects to have low sales during its first few years of operation as it develops its product. Then if the product catches on, sales will grow rapidly for several years. Sales growth brings with it the need for additional assets—a firm cannot increase sales without also increasing its assets, and asset growth requires an increase in liability and/or equity accounts. Small firms can generally obtain some bank credit, but they must maintain a reasonable balance between debt and equity. Thus, additional bank borrowings require increases in equity, and getting the equity capital needed to support growth can be difficult for small firms. They have limited access to the capital markets; and even when they can sell common stock, their owners are reluctant to do so for fear of losing voting control. Therefore, the best source of equity for most small businesses is retained earnings; for this reason most small firms pay no dividends during their rapid growth years. Eventually, though, successful small firms do pay dividends, and those dividends generally grow rapidly at first but slow down to a sustainable constant rate once the firm reaches maturity.

If a firm currently pays no dividends but is expected to pay future dividends, the value of its stock can be found as follows:

1. Estimate at what point dividends will be paid, the amount of the first dividend, the growth rate during the supernormal growth period, the length of the supernormal period, the long-run (constant) growth rate, and the rate of return required by investors.

2. Use the constant growth model to determine the stock price after the firm reaches a stable growth situation.

3. Set out on a time line the cash flows (dividends during the supernormal growth period and the stock price once the constant growth state is reached); then find the present value of these cash flows. That present value represents the value of the stock today.

To illustrate this process, consider the situation for Marvel-Lure Inc., a company that was set up in 2013 to produce and market a new high-tech fishing lure. Marvel-Lure's sales are currently growing at a rate of 200% per year. The company expects to experience a high but declining rate of growth in sales and earnings during the next 10 years, after which analysts estimate that it will grow at a steady 10% per year. The firm's management has announced that it will pay no dividends for 5 years but that if earnings materialize as forecasted, it will pay a dividend of $0.20 per share at the end of Year 6, $0.30 in Year 7, $0.40 in Year 8, $0.45 in Year 9, and $0.50 in Year 10. After Year 10, current plans are to increase dividends by 10% per year.

Marvel-Lure's investment bankers estimate that investors require a 15% return on similar stocks. Therefore, we find the value of a share of Marvel-Lure's stock as follows:

$$\hat{P}_0 = \frac{\$0}{(1.15)^1} + \cdots + \frac{\$0}{(1.15)^5} + \frac{\$0.20}{(1.15)^6} + \frac{\$0.30}{(1.15)^7} + \frac{\$0.40}{(1.15)^8}$$
$$+ \frac{\$0.45}{(1.15)^9} + \frac{\$0.50}{(1.15)^{10}} + \left(\frac{\$0.50(1.10)}{0.15 - 0.10}\right)\left(\frac{1}{(1.15)^{10}}\right)$$
$$= \$3.30$$

The last term finds the expected stock price in Year 10 and then finds the present value of that price. Thus, we see that the discounted dividend model can be applied to firms that currently pay no dividends, provided we can estimate future dividends with a fair degree of confidence. However, in many cases, we can have more confidence in the forecasts of free cash flows; and in these situations, it is better to use the corporate valuation model.

9-7 ENTERPRISE-BASED APPROACH TO VALUATION[11]

Thus far we have discussed the discounted dividend model for valuing a firm's common stock. This procedure is widely used, but it is based on the assumption that the analyst can forecast future dividends reasonably well. This is often true for mature companies that have a history of steadily growing dividends. However, dividends are dependent on earnings; so a reliable dividend forecast must be based on an underlying forecast of the firm's future sales, costs, and capital

---

[11]The corporate valuation model presented in this section is widely used by analysts, and it is in many respects superior to the discounted dividend model. However, it is rather involved as it requires the estimation of future sales, costs, and cash flows before the discounting process is begun. Therefore, in the introductory course, some instructors may prefer to omit Section 9-7 and skip to Section 9-8.

Corporate Valuation Model

A valuation model used as an alternative to the discounted dividend model to determine a firm's value, especially one with no history of dividends, or the value of a division of a larger firm. The corporate model first calculates the firm's free cash flows, then finds their present values to determine the firm's value.

requirements. This recognition has led to an alternative stock valuation approach, the **corporate valuation model**.

Rather than starting with a forecast of dividends, the corporate valuation model focuses on the firm's future free cash flows. We discussed free cash flow (FCF) in Chapter 3, where we developed the following equation:

$$\text{FCF} = \left[\text{EBIT}(1 - \text{T}) + \begin{array}{c} \text{Depreciation} \\ \text{and amortization} \end{array} \right] - \left[\begin{array}{c} \text{Capital} \\ \text{expenditures} \end{array} + \begin{array}{c} \Delta\text{Net operating} \\ \text{working capital} \end{array} \right]$$

EBIT is earnings before interest and taxes, and free cash flow represents the cash generated from current operations less the cash that must be spent on investments in fixed assets and working capital to support future growth.

Consider the case of Home Depot (HD). The first term in brackets in the preceding equation represents the amount of cash that HD is generating from its existing stores. The second term represents the amount of cash the company plans to spend this period to construct new stores. To open a new store, HD must spend cash to purchase the land and construct the building—these are the capital expenditures, and they lead to a corresponding increase in the firm's fixed assets as shown on the balance sheet. But HD also needs to increase its working capital, especially inventory. Putting everything together, HD generates positive free cash flow for its investors if and only if the money from its existing stores exceeds the money required to build and equip its new stores.

9-7a THE CORPORATE VALUATION MODEL

In Chapter 3, we explained that a firm's value is determined by its ability to generate cash flow both now and in the future. Therefore, its market value can be expressed as follows:

$$\begin{array}{c} \text{Market value} \\ \text{of company} \end{array} = V_{\text{Company}} = \text{PV of expected future free cash flows}$$

$$= \frac{\text{FCF}_1}{(1 + \text{WACC})^1} + \frac{\text{FCF}_2}{(1 + \text{WACC})^2} + \cdots + \frac{\text{FCF}_\infty}{(1 + \text{WACC})^\infty} \qquad \textbf{9.7}$$

Here FCF_t is the free cash flow in Year t; and the discount rate, the WACC, is the weighted average cost of all the firm's capital. When thinking about the WACC, note these two points:

1. The firm finances with debt, preferred stock, and common equity. The WACC is the weighted average of these three types of capital, and we discuss it in detail in Chapter 10.

2. Free cash flow is the cash generated *before any payments are made to any investors; so it must be used to compensate common stockholders, preferred stockholders, and bondholders.* Moreover, each type of investor has a required rate of return; and the weighted average of those returns is the WACC, which is used to discount the free cash flows.

Free cash flows are generally forecasted for 5 to 10 years, after which it is assumed that the final explicitly forecasted FCF will grow at some long-run constant rate. Once the company reaches its horizon date, when cash flows begin to grow at a constant rate, we can use the following formula to calculate the market value of the company as of that date:

$$\text{Horizon value} = V_{\text{Company at } t = N} = \text{FCF}_{N+1}/(\text{WACC} - g_{\text{FCF}}) \qquad \textbf{9.8}$$

Allied Food Products: Free Cash Flow Valuation   **TABLE 9.2**

	A	B	C	D	E	F	G	H	I
135	Part 1. Key Inputs					Forecasted Years			
136				2015	2016	2017	2018	2019	
137	Sales growth rate			10.0%	9.0%	9.0%	9.0%	8.0%	
138	Operating costs as a % of sales			87.0%	87.0%	86.0%	85.0%	85.0%	
139	Growth in net fixed assets			8.0%	8.0%	8.0%	8.0%	8.0%	
140	Growth in NOWC			8.0%	8.0%	8.0%	8.0%	8.0%	
141	Depr'n as a % of operating capital			6.0%	8.0%	7.0%	7.0%	7.0%	
142	Tax rate			40%					
143	WACC			10%					
144	Long-run FCF growth, g_{FCF}			6.0%					
145									
146	Part 2. Forecast of Cash Flows During Period of Nonconstant Growth								
147			Historical			Forecasted Years			
148			2014	2015	2016	2017	2018	2019	
149									
150	Sales		$3,000.0	$3,300.0	$3,597.0	$3,920.7	$4,273.6	$4,615.5	
151	Operating costs		2,616.2	2,871.0	3,129.4	3,371.8	3,632.6	3,923.2	
152	DEP = Depreciation		100.0	116.6	168.0	158.7	171.4	185.1	
153	EBIT		$283.8	$312.4	$299.6	$390.2	$469.6	$507.2	
154	EBIT x (1 − T)		170.3	187.4	179.8	234.1	281.8	304.3	
155	EBIT x (1 − T) + DEP		270.3	304.1	347.8	392.8	453.2	489.4	
156									
157	Net fixed assets		$1,000.0	$1,080.0	$1,166.4	$1,259.7	$1,360.5	$1,469.3	
158	Net oper. working capital (NOWC)		800.0	864.0	933.1	1,007.8	1,088.4	1,175.5	
159	Total operating capital		$1,800.0	$1,944.0	$2,099.5	$2,267.5	$2,448.9	$2,644.8	
160	Net CAPEX = Change in net fixed assets		130.0	80.0	86.4	93.3	100.8	108.8	
161	CAPEX = Gross capital expenditures = Net CAPEX + DEP		230.0	196.6	254.4	252.0	272.2	294.0	
162	ΔNOWC		150.0	64.0	69.1	74.6	80.6	87.1	
163									
164	Free Cash Flow, FCF = EBIT(1 − T) + DEP − CAPEX − ΔNOWC		−$109.7	$43.4	$24.3	$66.1	$100.4	$108.4	
165	PV of FCFs		N.A.	$39.5	$20.1	$49.7	$68.6	$67.3	
166									
167	Part 3. Horizon Value and Intrinsic Value Estimation								
168	Estimated Value at the Horizon, 2019								
169	Free Cash Flow (2020)			$114.9					
170	Horizon Value at 2019, HV_{2019}			$2,872.7					
171	PV of HV_{2019}			$1,783.7					
172									
173	Calculation of Firm's Intrinsic Value								
174	Sum of PVs of FCFs, 2015–2019			$245.1					
175	PV of HV_{2019}			1,783.7					
176	Total corporate value			$2,028.8					
177	Less: market value of debt and preferred			860.0					
178	Intrinsic value of common equity			$1,168.8					
179	Shares outstanding (millions)			50.0					
180									
181	Intrinsic Value Per Share			$23.38					

$$HV_{2019} = \frac{FCF_{2019}(1+g_{FCF})}{WACC - g_{FCF}} = \frac{FCF_{2020}}{WACC - g_{FCF}}$$

$$HV_{2019} / (1+WACC)^N$$

The corporate model is applied internally by the firm's financial staff and by outside security analysts. For illustrative purposes, we discuss an analysis conducted by Susan Buskirk, senior food analyst for the investment banking firm Morton Staley and Company. Her analysis is summarized in Table 9.2, which was reproduced from the chapter Excel model.

- Based on Allied's history and Buskirk's knowledge of the firm's business plan, she estimated sales, costs, and cash flows on an annual basis for 5 years. Growth will vary during those years, but she assumes that things will stabilize and growth will be constant after the fifth year. She would have made explicit forecasts for more years if she thought it would take longer to reach a steady-state, constant growth situation.

- For each of the first five years, Buskirk paid particular attention to the key variables that influence free cash flow. Specifically, she focused on EBIT, required capital expenditures, and the anticipated changes in net operating working capital (NOWC).

- Buskirk next calculated the expected free cash flows (FCFs) for each of the 5 nonconstant growth years, and she found the PV of those cash flows discounted at the WACC.

- After Year 5, she assumed that FCF growth would be constant; hence, the constant growth model could be used to find Allied's total market value at Year 5. This "horizon, or continuing, value" is the sum of the PVs of the FCFs from Year 6 on out into the future, discounted back to Year 5 at the WACC. It follows that: Horizon Value$_{t=5}$ = FCF$_6$/(WACC–g$_{FCF}$), where g$_{FCF}$ represents the long-run growth rate of the free cash flow.

- Next, she discounted the Year 5 horizon value back to the present to find its PV at Year 0.

- She then summed all the PVs, the annual cash flows during the nonconstant period plus the PV of the horizon value, to find the firm's estimated total market value.

- Then she subtracted the current market value of the debt and preferred stock to find the value of Allied's common equity.

Finally, she divided the equity value by the number of shares outstanding, and the result was her estimate of Allied's intrinsic value per share. This value was quite close to the stock's market price, so she concluded that Allied's stock is priced at its equilibrium level. Consequently, she issued a "Hold" recommendation on the stock. If the estimated intrinsic value had been significantly below the market price, she would have issued a "Sell" recommendation; if the estimated intrinsic value had been well above the market price, she would have called the stock a "Buy."

9-7b Comparing the Corporate Valuation and Discounted Dividend Models

Analysts use both the discounted dividend model and the corporate valuation model when valuing mature, dividend-paying firms; and they generally use the corporate model when valuing divisions and firms that do not pay dividends. In principle, we should find the same intrinsic value using either model, but differences are often observed. When a conflict exists, the assumptions embedded in the corporate model can be reexamined; and once the analyst is convinced they are reasonable, the results of that model are used. In our Allied example, the estimates were extremely close—the discounted dividend model predicted a price of $23.06 per share versus $23.38 using the corporate model; both are essentially equal to Allied's actual $23.06 price.

In practice, intrinsic value estimates based on the two models normally deviate from one another and from actual stock prices, leading different analysts to reach different conclusions about the attractiveness of a given stock. The better the analyst, the more often his or her valuations turn out to be correct; but no one can make perfect predictions because too many things can change randomly and

OTHER APPROACHES TO VALUING COMMON STOCKS

While the dividend growth and the corporate valuation models presented in this chapter are the most widely used methods for valuing common stocks, they are by no means the only approaches. Analysts often use a number of different techniques to value stocks. Two of these alternative approaches are described here.

The P/E Multiple Approach

Investors have long looked for simple rules of thumb to determine whether a stock is fairly valued. One such approach is to look at the stock's price-to-earnings (P/E) ratio. Recall from Chapter 4 that a company's P/E ratio shows how much investors are willing to pay for each dollar of reported earnings. As a starting point, you might conclude that stocks with low P/E ratios are undervalued because their price is "low" given current earnings, while stocks with high P/E ratios are overvalued.

Unfortunately, however, valuing stocks is not that simple. We should not expect all companies to have the same P/E ratio. P/E ratios are affected by risk—investors discount the earnings of riskier stocks at a higher rate. Thus, all else equal, riskier stocks should have lower P/E ratios. In addition, when you buy a stock, you have a claim not only on current earnings but also on all future earnings. All else equal, companies with stronger growth opportunities will generate larger future earnings and thus should trade at higher P/E ratios. Therefore, Chipotle Mexican Grill is not necessarily overvalued just because its P/E ratio is 39.2 at a time when the median firm in its industry has a P/E of 23.5. Investors believe that Chipotle's growth potential is well above average. Whether the stock's future prospects justify its P/E ratio remains to be seen; but in and of itself, a high P/E ratio does not mean that a stock is overvalued.

Nevertheless, P/E ratios can provide a useful starting point in stock valuation. If a stock's P/E ratio is well above its industry average and if the stock's growth potential and risk are similar to other firms in the industry, the stock's price may be too high. Likewise, if a company's P/E ratio falls well below its historical average, the stock may be undervalued—particularly if the company's growth prospects and risk are unchanged and if the overall P/E for the market has remained constant or increased.

One obvious drawback of the P/E approach is that it depends on reported accounting earnings. For this reason, some analysts choose to rely on other multiples to value stocks. For example, some analysts look at a company's price-to-cash-flow ratio, while others look at the price-to-sales ratio.

The EVA Approach

In recent years, analysts have looked for more rigorous alternatives to the discounted dividend model. More than a quarter of all stocks listed on the NYSE pay no dividends. This proportion is even higher on NASDAQ. While the discounted dividend model can still be used for these stocks (see "Evaluating Stocks That Don't Pay Dividends"), this approach requires that analysts forecast when the stock will begin paying dividends, what the dividend will be once it is established, and what the future dividend growth rate will be. In many cases, these forecasts contain considerable errors.

An alternative approach is based on the concept of Economic Value Added (EVA), which we discussed in Chapter 3 and in the Chapter 4 box "Economic Value Added (EVA) versus Net Income," that can be written as follows:

$$\text{EVA} = (\text{Equity capital})(\text{ROE} - \text{Cost of equity capital})$$

This equation suggests that companies can increase their EVA by investing in projects that provide shareholders with returns that are above their cost of equity capital, which is the return they could expect to earn on alternative investments with the same level of risk. When you purchase stock in a company, you receive more than just the book value of equity—you also receive a claim on all future value that is created by the firm's managers (the present value of all future EVAs). It follows that a company's market value of equity can be written as follows:

$$\text{Market value of equity} = \text{Book value} + \text{PV of all future EVAs}$$

We can find the "fundamental" value of the stock, P_0, by simply dividing the preceding expression by the number of shares outstanding.

As is the case with the discounted dividend model, we can simplify the expression by assuming that at some point in time, annual EVA becomes a perpetuity, or grows at some constant rate over time. Presented here is a simplified version of what is often referred to as the Edwards-Bell-Ohlson (EBO) model. For a more complete description of this technique and an excellent summary of how it can be used in practice, read the article "Measuring Wealth," by Charles M. C. Lee, in *CA Magazine*, April 1996, pp. 32–37.

unpredictably in the future. Given all this, does it matter whether you use the corporate model or the dividend model to value stocks? We would argue that it does. If we had to value, for example, 100 mature companies whose dividends were expected to grow steadily in the future, we would probably use the discounted dividend model. Here we would estimate only the growth rate in dividends, not the entire set of pro forma financial statements; hence, it would be more feasible to use the dividend model.

However, if we were studying just one company or a few companies, especially companies still in the high-growth stage of their life cycles, we would want to project future financial statements before estimating future dividends. Because we would already have projected future financial statements, we would go ahead and apply the corporate model. Intel, which pays a dividend of $0.90 versus earnings of about $2.01, is an example of a company where either model could be used; but we believe the corporate model is better.

Now suppose you were trying to estimate the value of a company such as eBay that, to date (2013), has never paid a dividend or a new firm that is about to go public. In either situation, you would be better off using the corporate valuation model. Actually, even if a company is paying steady dividends, much can be learned from the corporate model; so analysts today use it for all types of valuations. The process of projecting future financial statements can reveal a great deal about a company's operations and financing needs. Also, such an analysis can provide insights into actions that might be taken to increase the company's value; and for this reason, it is integral to the planning and forecasting process, as we discuss in a later chapter.

SELF TEST

Write out the equation for free cash flows and explain it.

Why might someone use the corporate valuation model for companies that have a history of paying dividends?

What steps are taken to find a stock price using the corporate model?

Why might the calculated intrinsic value differ from the stock's current market price? Which would be "correct," and what does "correct" mean?

9-8 PREFERRED STOCK[12]

Preferred stock is a *hybrid*—it is similar to a bond in some respects and to common stock in others. This hybrid nature becomes apparent when we try to classify preferred stock in relation to bonds and common stock. Like bonds, preferred stock has a par value and a fixed dividend that must be paid before dividends can be paid on the common stock. However, the directors can omit (or "pass") the preferred dividend without throwing the company into bankruptcy. So although preferred stock calls for a fixed payment like bonds, skipping the payment will not lead to bankruptcy.

As noted earlier, a preferred stock entitles its owners to regular, fixed dividend payments. If the payments last forever, the issue is a *perpetuity* whose value, V_p, is found as follows:

$$V_p = \frac{D_p}{r_p}$$

 9.9

---

[12]Preferred stock is discussed in more detail in Chapter 20 of Brigham and Daves, *Intermediate Financial Management*, 11th edition (Mason, OH: South-Western/Cengage Learning, 2013).

V_p is the value of the preferred stock, D_p is the preferred dividend, and r_p is the required rate of return on the preferred. Allied Food has no preferred outstanding, but discussions about such an issue suggested that its preferred should pay a dividend of $10 per year. If its required return was 10.3%, the preferred's value would be $97.09, found as follows:

$$V_p = \frac{\$10.00}{0.103} = \$97.09$$

In equilibrium, the expected return, $\hat{r}_s$, must be equal to the required return, r_p. Thus, if we know the preferred's current price and dividend, we can solve for the expected rate of return as follows:

$$\hat{r}_p = \frac{D_p}{V_p}$$

9.9a

Some preferreds have a stated maturity, often 50 years. Assume that our illustrative preferred matured in 50 years, paid a $10 annual dividend, and had a required return of 8%. We could then find its price as follows: Enter $N = 50$, $I/YR = 8$, $PMT = 10$, and $FV = 100$. Then press PV to find the price, $V_p = \$124.47$. If r_p rose to 10%, change I/YR to 10, in which case $V_p = PV = \$100$. If you know the price of a share of preferred stock, you can solve for I/YR to find the expected rate of return, $\hat{r}_p$.

SELF TEST

Explain the following statement: Preferred stock is a hybrid security.

Is the equation used to value preferred stock more like the one used to value a bond or the one used to value a "normal" constant growth common stock? Explain.

TYING IT ALL TOGETHER

Corporate decisions should be analyzed in terms of how alternative courses of action are likely to affect a firm's value. However, it is necessary to know how stock prices are established before attempting to measure how a given decision will affect a specific firm's value. This chapter discussed the rights and privileges of common stockholders, showed how stock values are determined, and explained how investors estimate stocks' intrinsic values and expected rates of return.

Two types of stock valuation models were discussed: the discounted dividend model and the corporate valuation model. The discounted dividend model is useful for mature, stable companies. It is easier to use, but the corporate valuation model is more flexible and better for use with companies that do not pay dividends or whose dividends would be especially hard to predict.

We also discussed preferred stock, which is a hybrid security that has some characteristics of a common stock and some of a bond. Preferreds are valued using models similar to those for perpetual and "regular" bonds.

SELF-TEST QUESTIONS AND PROBLEMS

(Solutions Appear in Appendix A)

ST-1 KEY TERMS Define the following terms:

a. Proxy; proxy fight; takeover

b. Preemptive right

c. Classified stock; founders' shares

d. Marginal investor; intrinsic value ($\hat{P}_0$); market price (P_0)

e. Required rate of return, r_s; expected rate of return, $\hat{r}_s$; actual (realized) rate of return, $\bar{r}_s$

f. Capital gains yield; dividend yield; expected total return; growth rate, g

g. Zero growth stock

h. Constant growth (Gordon) model; supernormal (nonconstant) growth

i. Corporate valuation model

j. Horizon (terminal) date; horizon (continuing) value

k. Preferred stock

ST-2 STOCK GROWTH RATES AND VALUATION You are considering buying the stocks of two companies that operate in the same industry. They have very similar characteristics except for their dividend payout policies. Both companies are expected to earn $3 per share this year; but Company D (for "dividend") is expected to pay out all of its earnings as dividends, while Company G (for "growth") is expected to pay out only one-third of its earnings, or $1 per share. D's stock price is $25. G and D are equally risky. Which of the following statements is most likely to be true?

a. Company G will have a faster growth rate than Company D. Therefore, G's stock price should be greater than $25.

b. Although G's growth rate should exceed D's, D's current dividend exceeds that of G, which should cause D's price to exceed G's.

c. A long-term investor in Stock D will get his or her money back faster because D pays out more of its earnings as dividends. Thus, in a sense, D is like a short-term bond and G is like a long-term bond. Therefore, if economic shifts cause r_d and r_s to increase, and if the expected dividend streams from D and G remain constant, both Stocks D and G will decline, but D's price should decline further.

d. D's expected and required rate of return is $\hat{r}_s = r_s = 12\%$. G's expected return will be higher because of its higher expected growth rate.

e. If we observe that G's price is also $25, the best estimate of G's growth rate is 8%.

ST-3 CONSTANT GROWTH STOCK VALUATION Fletcher Company's current stock price is $36.00, its last dividend was $2.40, and its required rate of return is 12%. If dividends are expected to grow at a constant rate, g, in the future and if r_s is expected to remain at 12%, what is Fletcher's expected stock price 5 years from now?

ST-4 NONCONSTANT GROWTH STOCK VALUATION Snyder Computers Inc. is experiencing rapid growth. Earnings and dividends are expected to grow at a rate of 15% during the next 2 years, at 13% the following year, and at a constant rate of 6% during Year 4 and thereafter. Its last dividend was $1.15, and its required rate of return is 12%.

a. Calculate the value of the stock today.

b. Calculate $\hat{P}_1$ and $\hat{P}_2$.

c. Calculate the dividend and capital gains yields for Years 1, 2, and 3.

QUESTIONS

9-1 It is frequently stated that the one purpose of the preemptive right is to allow individuals to maintain their proportionate share of the ownership and control of a corporation.

    a. How important do you suppose control is for the average stockholder of a firm whose shares are traded on the New York Stock Exchange?

    b. Is the control issue likely to be of more importance to stockholders of publicly owned or closely held (private) firms? Explain.

9-2 Is the following equation correct for finding the value of a constant growth stock? Explain.

$$\hat{P}_0 = \frac{D_0}{r_s + g}$$

9-3 If you bought a share of common stock, you would probably expect to receive dividends plus an eventual capital gain. Would the distribution between the dividend yield and the capital gains yield be influenced by the firm's decision to pay more dividends rather than to retain and reinvest more of its earnings? Explain.

9-4 Two investors are evaluating GE's stock for possible purchase. They agree on the expected value of D_1 and on the expected future dividend growth rate. Further, they agree on the riskiness of the stock. However, one investor normally holds stocks for 2 years, while the other holds stocks for 10 years. On the basis of the type of analysis done in this chapter, should they both be willing to pay the same price for GE's stock? Explain.

9-5 A bond that pays interest forever and has no maturity is a perpetual bond. In what respect is a perpetual bond similar to a no-growth common stock? Are there preferred stocks that are evaluated similarly to perpetual bonds and other preferred issues that are more like bonds with finite lives? Explain.

9-6 Discuss the similarities and differences between the discounted dividend and corporate valuation models.

9-7 This chapter discusses the discounted dividend and corporate valuation models for valuing common stocks. Two alternative approaches, the P/E multiple and EVA approaches, were presented. Explain each approach and how you might use each one to value a common stock.

PROBLEMS

Easy Problems 1–6

9-1 **DPS CALCULATION** Warr Corporation just paid a dividend of $1.50 a share (that is, $D_0 = \$1.50$). The dividend is expected to grow 7% a year for the next 3 years and then at 5% a year thereafter. What is the expected dividend per share for each of the next 5 years?

9-2 **CONSTANT GROWTH VALUATION** Thomas Brothers is expected to pay a $0.50 per share dividend at the end of the year (that is, $D_1 = \$0.50$). The dividend is expected to grow at a constant rate of 7% a year. The required rate of return on the stock, r_s, is 15%. What is the stock's current value per share?

9-3 **CONSTANT GROWTH VALUATION** Harrison Clothiers' stock currently sells for $20.00 a share. It just paid a dividend of $1.00 a share (that is, $D_0 = \$1.00$). The dividend is expected to grow at a constant rate of 6% a year. What stock price is expected 1 year from now? What is the required rate of return?

9-4 **NONCONSTANT GROWTH VALUATION** Hart Enterprises recently paid a dividend, D_0, of $1.25. It expects to have nonconstant growth of 20% for 2 years followed by a constant rate of 5% thereafter. The firm's required return is 10%.

    a. How far away is the horizon date?

    b. What is the firm's horizon, or continuing, value?

    c. What is the firm's intrinsic value today, $\hat{P}_0$?

9-5 **CORPORATE VALUATION** Smith Technologies is expected to generate $150 million in free cash flow next year, and FCF is expected to grow at a constant rate of 5% per year indefinitely. Smith has no debt or preferred stock, and its WACC is 10%. If Smith has 50 million shares of stock outstanding, what is the stock's value per share?

9-6 **PREFERRED STOCK VALUATION** Fee Founders has perpetual preferred stock outstanding that sells for $60 a share and pays a dividend of $5 at the end of each year. What is the required rate of return?

Intermediate
Problems
7–15

9-7 **PREFERRED STOCK RATE OF RETURN** What will be the nominal rate of return on a perpetual preferred stock with a $100 par value, a stated dividend of 8% of par, and a current market price of (a) $60, (b) $80, (c) $100, and (d) $140?

9-8 **PREFERRED STOCK VALUATION** Ezzell Corporation issued perpetual preferred stock with a 10% annual dividend. The stock currently yields 8%, and its par value is $100.

a. What is the stock's value?

b. Suppose interest rates rise and pull the preferred stock's yield up to 12%. What is its new market value?

9-9 **PREFERRED STOCK RETURNS** Bruner Aeronautics has perpetual preferred stock outstanding with a par value of $100. The stock pays a quarterly dividend of $2, and its current price is $80.

a. What is its nominal annual rate of return?

b. What is its effective annual rate of return?

9-10 **VALUATION OF A DECLINING GROWTH STOCK** Martell Mining Company's ore reserves are being depleted, so its sales are falling. Also, because its pit is getting deeper each year, its costs are rising. As a result, the company's earnings and dividends are declining at the constant rate of 5% per year. If $D_0 = \$5$ and $r_s = 15\%$, what is the value of Martell Mining's stock?

9-11 **VALUATION OF A CONSTANT GROWTH STOCK** A stock is expected to pay a dividend of $0.50 at the end of the year (that is, $D_1 = 0.50$), and it should continue to grow at a constant rate of 7% a year. If its required return is 12%, what is the stock's expected price 4 years from today?

9-12 **VALUATION OF A CONSTANT GROWTH STOCK** Investors require a 15% rate of return on Levine Company's stock (that is, $r_s = 15\%$).

a. What is its value if the previous dividend was $D_0 = \$2$ and investors expect dividends to grow at a constant annual rate of (1) –5%, (2) 0%, (3) 5%, or (4) 10%?

b. Using data from Part a, what would the Gordon (constant growth) model value be if the required rate of return was 15% and the expected growth rate was (1) 15% or (2) 20%? Are these reasonable results? Explain.

c. Is it reasonable to think that a constant growth stock could have $g > r_s$? Why or why not?

9-13 **CONSTANT GROWTH** You are considering an investment in Keller Corporation's stock, which is expected to pay a dividend of $2.00 a share at the end of the year ($D_1 = \$2.00$) and has a beta of 0.9. The risk-free rate is 5.6%, and the market risk premium is 6%. Keller currently sells for $25.00 a share, and its dividend is expected to grow at some constant rate g. Assuming the market is in equilibrium, what does the market believe will be the stock price at the end of 3 years? (That is, what is $\hat{P}_3$?)

9-14 **NONCONSTANT GROWTH** Microtech Corporation is expanding rapidly and currently needs to retain all of its earnings; hence, it does not pay dividends. However, investors expect Microtech to begin paying dividends, beginning with a dividend of $1.00 coming 3 years from today. The dividend should grow rapidly—at a rate of 50% per year—during Years 4 and 5; but after Year 5, growth should be a constant 8% per year. If the required return on Microtech is 15%, what is the value of the stock today?

9-15 **CORPORATE VALUATION** Dozier Corporation is a fast-growing supplier of office products. Analysts project the following free cash flows (FCFs) during the next 3 years, after which FCF is expected to grow at a constant 7% rate. Dozier's WACC is 13%.

Year	0	1	2	3
FCF ($ millions)		−$20	$30	$40

a. What is Dozier's horizon, or continuing, value? (Hint: Find the value of all free cash flows beyond Year 3 discounted back to Year 3.)

b. What is the firm's value today?

c. Suppose Dozier has $100 million of debt and 10 million shares of stock outstanding. What is your estimate of the current price per share?

9-16 **NONCONSTANT GROWTH** Mitts Cosmetics Co.'s stock price is $58.88, and it recently paid a $2.00 dividend. This dividend is expected to grow by 25% for the next 3 years, then grow forever at a constant rate, g; and $r_s = 12\%$. At what constant rate is the stock expected to grow after Year 3?

9-17 **CONSTANT GROWTH** Your broker offers to sell you some shares of Bahnsen & Co. common stock that paid a dividend of $2.00 *yesterday*. Bahnsen's dividend is expected to grow at 5% per year for the next 3 years. If you buy the stock, you plan to hold it for 3 years and then sell it. The appropriate discount rate is 12%.

a. Find the expected dividend for each of the next 3 years; that is, calculate D_1, D_2, and D_3. Note that $D_0 = \$2.00$.

b. Given that the first dividend payment will occur 1 year from now, find the present value of the dividend stream; that is, calculate the PVs of D_1, D_2, and D_3 and then sum these PVs.

c. You expect the price of the stock 3 years from now to be $34.73; that is, you expect $\hat{P}_3$ to equal $34.73. Discounted at a 12% rate, what is the present value of this expected future stock price? In other words, calculate the PV of $34.73.

d. If you plan to buy the stock, hold it for 3 years, and then sell it for $34.73, what is the most you should pay for it today?

e. Use Equation 9.2 to calculate the present value of this stock. Assume that $g = 5\%$ and that it is constant.

f. Is the value of this stock dependent upon how long you plan to hold it? In other words, if your planned holding period was 2 years or 5 years rather than 3 years, would this affect the value of the stock today, $\hat{P}_0$? Explain.

9-18 **NONCONSTANT GROWTH STOCK VALUATION** Taussig Technologies Corporation (TTC) has been growing at a rate of 20% per year in recent years. This same growth rate is expected to last for another 2 years, then decline to $g_n = 6\%$.

a. If $D_0 = \$1.60$ and $r_s = 10\%$, what is TTC's stock worth today? What are its expected dividend and capital gains yields at this time, that is, during Year 1?

b. Now assume that TTC's period of supernormal growth is to last for 5 years rather than 2 years. How would this affect the price, dividend yield, and capital gains yield? Answer in words only.

c. What will TTC's dividend and capital gains yields be once its period of supernormal growth ends? (Hint: These values will be the same regardless of whether you examine the case of 2 or 5 years of supernormal growth; the calculations are very easy.)

d. Explain why investors are interested in the changing relationship between dividend and capital gains yields over time.

9-19 **CORPORATE VALUATION** Barrett Industries invests a large sum of money in R&D; as a result, it retains and reinvests all of its earnings. In other words, Barrett does not pay any dividends and it has no plans to pay dividends in the near future. A major pension fund is interested in purchasing Barrett's stock. The pension fund manager has estimated Barrett's free cash flows for the next 4 years as follows: $3 million, $6 million, $10 million, and $15 million. After the fourth year, free cash flow is projected to grow at a constant 7%. Barrett's WACC is 12%, the market value of its debt and preferred stock totals $60 million, and it has 10 million shares of common stock outstanding.

a. What is the present value of the free cash flows projected during the next 4 years?

b. What is the firm's horizon, or continuing, value?

c. What is the firm's total value today?

d. What is an estimate of Barrett's price per share?

9-20 **CORPORATE VALUE MODEL** Assume that today is December 31, 2014, and that the following information applies to Vermeil Airlines:

- After-tax operating income [EBIT$(1 - T)$] for 2015 is expected to be $500 million.
- The depreciation expense for 2015 is expected to be $100 million.
- The capital expenditures for 2015 are expected to be $200 million.
- No change is expected in net operating working capital.
- The free cash flow is expected to grow at a constant rate of 6% per year.

- The required return on equity is 14%.
- The WACC is 10%.
- The market value of the company's debt is $3 billion.
- 200 million shares of stock are outstanding.

Using the corporate valuation model approach, what should be the company's stock price today?

9-21 **NONCONSTANT GROWTH** Assume that it is now January 1, 2015. Wayne-Martin Electric Inc. (WME) has developed a solar panel capable of generating 200% more electricity than any other solar panel currently on the market. As a result, WME is expected to experience a 15% annual growth rate for the next 5 years. Other firms will have developed comparable technology at the end of 5 years, and WME's growth rate will slow to 5% per year indefinitely. Stockholders require a return of 12% on WME's stock. The most recent annual dividend (D_0), which was paid yesterday, was $1.75 per share.

a. Calculate WME's expected dividends for 2015, 2016, 2017, 2018, and 2019.

b. Calculate the value of the stock today, $\hat{P}_0$. Proceed by finding the present value of the dividends expected at the end of 2015, 2016, 2017, 2018, and 2019 plus the present value of the stock price that should exist at the end of 2019. The year-end 2019 stock price can be found by using the constant growth equation. Notice that to find the December 31, 2019, price, you must use the dividend expected in 2020, which is 5% greater than the 2019 dividend.

c. Calculate the expected dividend yield (D_1/P_0), capital gains yield, and total return (dividend yield plus capital gains yield) expected for 2015. (Assume that $\hat{P}_0 = P_0$ and recognize that the capital gains yield is equal to the total return minus the dividend yield.) Then calculate these same three yields for 2020.

d. How might an investor's tax situation affect his or her decision to purchase stocks of companies in the early stages of their lives, when they are growing rapidly, versus stocks of older, more mature firms? When does WME's stock become "mature" for purposes of this question?

e. Suppose your boss tells you she believes that WME's annual growth rate will be only 12% during the next 5 years and that the firm's long-run growth rate will be only 4%. Without doing any calculations, what general effect would these growth rate changes have on the price of WME's stock?

f. Suppose your boss also tells you that she regards WME as being quite risky and that she believes the required rate of return should be 14%, not 12%. Without doing any calculations, determine how the higher required rate of return would affect the price of the stock, the capital gains yield, and the dividend yield. Again, assume that the long-run growth rate is 4%.

COMPREHENSIVE/SPREADSHEET PROBLEM

9-22 **NONCONSTANT GROWTH AND CORPORATE VALUATION** Rework Problem 9-18, Parts a, b, and c, using a spreadsheet model. For Part b, calculate the price, dividend yield, and capital gains yield as called for in the problem. After completing Parts a through c, answer the following additional question using the spreadsheet model.

d. TTC recently introduced a new line of products that has been wildly successful. On the basis of this success and anticipated future success, the following free cash flows were projected:

Year	1	2	3	4	5	6	7	8	9	10
FCF	$5.5	$12.1	$23.8	$44.1	$69.0	$88.8	$107.5	$128.9	$147.1	$161.3

After the tenth year, TTC's financial planners anticipate that its free cash flow will grow at a constant rate of 6%. Also, the firm concluded that the new product caused the WACC to fall to 9%. The market value of TTC's debt is $1,200 million, it uses no preferred stock, and there are 20 million shares of common stock outstanding. Use the corporate valuation model to value the stock.

INTEGRATED CASE

MUTUAL OF CHICAGO INSURANCE COMPANY

9-23 **STOCK VALUATION** Robert Balik and Carol Kiefer are senior vice presidents of the Mutual of Chicago Insurance Company. They are co-directors of the company's pension fund management division, with Balik having responsibility for fixed-income securities (primarily bonds) and Kiefer being responsible for equity investments. A major new client, the California League of Cities, has requested that Mutual of Chicago present an investment seminar to the mayors of the represented cities; and Balik and Kiefer, who will make the actual presentation, have asked you to help them.

To illustrate the common stock valuation process, Balik and Kiefer have asked you to analyze the Bon Temps Company, an employment agency that supplies word-processor operators and computer programmers to businesses with temporarily heavy workloads. You are to answer the following questions:

a. Describe briefly the legal rights and privileges of common stockholders.

b. 1. Write a formula that can be used to value any stock, regardless of its dividend pattern.

   2. What is a constant growth stock? How are constant growth stocks valued?

   3. What are the implications if a company forecasts a constant g that exceeds its r_s? Will many stocks have expected $g > r_s$ in the short run (that is, for the next few years)? In the long run (that is, forever)?

c. Assume that Bon Temps has a beta coefficient of 1.2, that the risk-free rate (the yield on T-bonds) is 7%, and that the required rate of return on the market is 12%. What is Bon Temps's required rate of return?

d. Assume that Bon Temps is a constant growth company whose last dividend (D_0, which was paid yesterday) was $2.00 and whose dividend is expected to grow indefinitely at a 6% rate.

   1. What is the firm's expected dividend stream over the next 3 years?

   2. What is its current stock price?

   3. What is the stock's expected value 1 year from now?

   4. What are the expected dividend yield, capital gains yield, and total return during the first year?

e. Now assume that the stock is currently selling at $30.29. What is its expected rate of return?

f. What would the stock price be if its dividends were expected to have zero growth?

g. Now assume that Bon Temps is expected to experience nonconstant growth of 30% for the next 3 years, then return to its long-run constant growth rate of 6%. What is the stock's value under these conditions? What are its expected dividend and capital gains yields in Year 1? Year 4?

h. Suppose Bon Temps is expected to experience zero growth during the first 3 years and then resume its steady-state growth of 6% in the fourth year. What would be its value then? What would be its expected dividend and capital gains yields in Year 1? In Year 4?

i. Finally, assume that Bon Temps's earnings and dividends are expected to decline at a constant rate of 6% per year, that is, $g = -6\%$. Why would anyone be willing to buy such a stock, and at what price should it sell? What would be its dividend and capital gains yields in each year?

j. Suppose Bon Temps embarked on an aggressive expansion that requires additional capital. Management decided to finance the expansion by borrowing $40 million and by halting dividend payments to increase retained earnings. Its WACC is now 10%, and the projected free cash flows for the next 3 years are −$5 million, $10 million, and $20 million. After Year 3, free cash flow is projected to grow at a constant 6%. What is Bon Temps's total value? If it has 10 million shares of stock and $40 million of debt and preferred stock combined, what is the price per share?

k. Suppose Bon Temps decided to issue preferred stock that would pay an annual dividend of $5.00 and that the issue price was $50.00 per share. What would be the stock's expected return? Would the expected rate of return be the same if the preferred was a perpetual issue or if it had a 20-year maturity?

THOMSON REUTERS

Use the Thomson ONE—Business School Edition online database to work this chapter's questions.

ESTIMATING EXXON MOBIL CORPORATION'S INTRINSIC STOCK VALUE

In this chapter, we described the various factors that influence stock prices and the approaches that analysts use to estimate a stock's intrinsic value. By comparing these intrinsic value estimates to the current price, an investor can assess whether it makes sense to buy or sell a particular stock. Stocks trading at a price far below their estimated intrinsic values may be good candidates for purchase, whereas stocks trading at prices far in excess of their intrinsic value may be good stocks to avoid or sell. While estimating a stock's intrinsic value is a complex exercise that requires reliable data and good judgment, we can use the data available in Thomson ONE to arrive at a quick "back-of-the-envelope" calculation of intrinsic value.

Discussion Questions

1. For purposes of this exercise, let's take a closer look at the stock of Exxon Mobil Corporation (XOM). Looking at the COMPANY ANALYSIS OVERVIEW, we can see the company's current stock price and its performance relative to the overall market in recent months. What is Exxon Mobil's current stock price? How has the stock performed relative to the market over the past few months?

2. Click on "NEWS & EVENTS" on the left-hand side of your screen to see the company's recent news stories. Have there been any recent events impacting the company's stock price, or have things been relatively quiet?

3. To provide a starting point for gauging a company's relative valuation, analysts often look at a company's price-to-earnings (P/E) ratio. Return to the COMPANY OVERVIEW page. Here you can see XOM's forward P/E ratio, which uses XOM's next 12-month estimate of earnings in the calculation. To see its current P/E ratio, click on "FINANCIALS" (on the left-hand side of your screen), scroll down to "WORLDSCOPE" (under Financial Ratios on the left-hand side of your screen), and click on "ANNUAL INCOME STATEMENT RATIOS." The firm's current P/E ratio is shown at the top right of your screen. What is the firm's current P/E ratio?

4. To put XOM's P/E ratio in perspective, it is useful to see how this ratio has varied over time. Scroll down to the Stock Performance section of this screen. The first two lines of this section show the firm's P/E ratio using the end-of-year closing price and the 5-year average over time. Is XOM's current P/E ratio well above or well below its latest 5-year average? Explain why the current P/E deviates from its historical trend. On the basis of this information, does XOM's current P/E suggest that the stock is undervalued or overvalued? Explain.

5. To put the firm's current P/E ratio in perspective, it is useful to compare this ratio with that of other companies in the same industry. To see how XOM's P/E ratio stacks up to its peers, click on "COMPARABLES" (left-hand side of your screen). Scroll down and select "KEY FINANCIAL RATIOS." At the bottom of the table, you should see information on the P/E ratio of each comparable company in the section titled "Market Value Ratios." For the most part, is XOM's P/E ratio above or below that of its peers? In Chapter 4, we discussed the various factors that may influence P/E ratios. Can any of these factors explain why XOM's P/E ratio differs from its peers? Explain. If you want to compare XOM to a different set of firms, click on "CLICK TO SELECT NEW PEER SET." (This appears toward the top of the screen.)

6. In the text, we discussed using the discounted dividend model to estimate a stock's intrinsic value. To keep things as simple as possible, let's assume at first that XOM's dividend is expected to grow at a constant rate of 5% annually over time. So, $g = 5\%$. If so, the intrinsic value equals $D_1/(r_s-g)$, where D_1 is the expected annual dividend 1 year from now, r_s is the stock's required rate of return, and g is the dividend's constant growth rate.

   Go back to the COMPANY OVERVIEW page. Select "FINANCIALS"; and under "FINANCIAL RATIOS," select "WORLDSCOPE" and "ANNUAL INCOME STATEMENT RATIOS." On your screen at the bottom of the Per Share Data section, you should see the firm's annual dividend over the past several years. Multiply the prior year's dividend by $1 + g$ to arrive at an estimate of D_1.

7. The required return on equity, r_s, is the final input needed to estimate intrinsic value. For our purposes, you can assume a number (say, 9% or 10%) or you can use the CAPM to calculate an estimate of the cost of equity using the data available in Thomson ONE. (For more details, look at the Thomson ONE exercise for Chapter 8.) Having decided on your best estimates for D_1, r_s, and g, you can calculate XOM's intrinsic value. Be careful to make sure that the long-run growth rate is less than the required rate of return. How does this estimate compare with the current stock price? Does your preliminary analysis suggest that XOM is undervalued or overvalued? Explain.

8. It is often useful to perform a sensitivity analysis, where you show how your estimate of intrinsic value varies according to different estimates of D_1, r_s, and g. To do so, recalculate your intrinsic value estimate for a range of different estimates for each of these key inputs. One convenient way to do this is to set up a simple data table in Excel. Refer to the Excel tutorial accessed through the student companion website for instructions on data tables. On the basis of this analysis, what inputs justify the current stock price?

9. Until now, we have assumed that XOM's dividend will grow at a long-run constant rate of 5% annually. To gauge whether this is a reasonable assumption, it's helpful to look at XOM's dividend history. Go back to the "Worldscope, Annual Income Statement Ratios" screen. At the bottom of the Per Share Data section, you should see the firm's annual dividend over the past several years. On the basis of this information, what has been the average annual dividend growth rate?

   Another way to obtain estimates of dividend growth rates is to look at analysts' forecasts for future dividends, which can be found under "ESTIMATES" (on the left-hand side of your screen). Near the top of that screen, you should see an area marked "Consensus Estimates." Use the scroll bar to change from EPS estimates to DPS estimates. What is the median year-end dividend forecast? Also notice that the last line of this area shows the long-term growth rate (LTG). What is the median forecast of the company's long-term growth rate? On the basis of the dividend history you uncovered in Question 6 and your assessment of XOM's future dividend payout policies, do you think it is reasonable to assume that the constant growth model is a good proxy for intrinsic value? If not, how would you use the available data in Thomson ONE to estimate intrinsic value using the nonconstant growth model?

10. Finally, you can also use the information in Thomson ONE to value the entire corporation. This approach requires that you estimate XOM's annual free cash flows. Once you estimate the value of the entire corporation, you subtract the value of debt and preferred stock to arrive at an estimate of the company's equity value. By dividing this value by the number of shares of common stock outstanding, you calculate an alternative estimate of the stock's intrinsic value. While this approach may take additional time and involves more judgment concerning forecasts of future free cash flows, you can use the financial statements and growth forecasts in Thomson ONE as useful starting points.

    Go to Worldscope's Cash Flow Ratios Report (which you find by clicking on "FINANCIALS" under "FINAN-CIAL RATIOS" click on "WORLDSCOPE" and "ANNUAL CASH FLOW RATIOS"). There you will find historical annual free cash flow per share values. While these numbers are useful as a starting point to arrive at an estimate for the next year, Worldscope's definition of free cash flow subtracts out dividends per share. Therefore, to make it comparable to the measure in this text, you must add back dividends. To see Worldscope's definition of free cash flow (or any term), go to the top of your screen and click on "GLOSSARY." A dialog box will appear on the screen. Here, you can select the appropriate database (Worldscope is shown here now), and then either enter the term or scroll down to find the term for which you are looking for the definition.

Stock Market Equilibrium

Recall that r_x, the required return on Stock X, can be found using the Security Market Line (SML) equation from the Capital Asset Pricing Model (CAPM) as discussed in Chapter 8:

$$r_X = r_{RF} + (r_M - r_{RF})b_X = r_{RF} + (RP_M)b_X$$

If the risk-free rate is 6%, the market risk premium is 5%, and Stock X has a beta of 2, the marginal investor will require a return of 16% on the stock:

$$r_X = 6\% + (5\%)2.0$$
$$= 16\%$$

This 16% required return is shown as the point on the SML in Figure 9A.1 associated with beta = 2.0. A marginal investor will purchase Stock X if its expected return is more than 16%, will sell it if the expected return is less than 16%, and will be indifferent (will hold it but not buy or sell it) if the expected return is exactly 16%.

9A-1 AN ILLUSTRATION

Now suppose the investor's portfolio contains Stock X; he or she analyzes its prospects and concludes that its earnings, dividends, and price can be expected to grow at a constant rate of 5% per year. The last dividend was $D_0 = \$2.8571$, so the next expected dividend is as follows:

$$D_1 = \$2.8571(1.05) = \$3.00$$

The investor observes that the stock price, P_0, is $30. Should he or she buy more of Stock X, sell the stock, or maintain the present position?

The investor can calculate Stock X's *expected rate of return* as follows:

$$\hat{r}_X = \frac{D_1}{P_0} + g = \frac{\$3}{\$30} + 5\% = 15\%$$

FIGURE 9A.1	Expected and Required Returns on Stock X

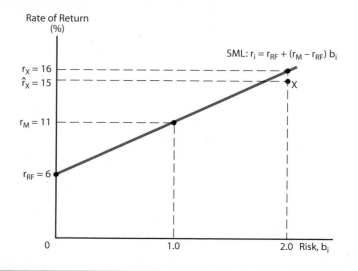

This value is plotted on Figure 9A.1 as Point X, which is below the SML. Because the expected rate of return is less than the required return, he or she (and many other investors) would want to sell the stock. However, few people would want to buy at the $30 price; so the present owners would be unable to find buyers unless they cut the stock price. Thus, the price would decline, and the decline would continue until the price hit $27.27. At that point, the stock would be in **equilibrium**, defined as the price at which the expected rate of return, 16%, is equal to the required rate of return:

$$\hat{r}_X = \frac{\$3.00}{\$27.27} + 5\% = 11\% + 5\% = 16\% = r_X$$

Had the stock initially sold for less than $27.27 (say, $25), events would have been reversed. Investors would have wanted to purchase the stock because its expected rate of return would have exceeded its required rate of return, buy orders would have come in, and the stock's price would have been driven up to $27.27.

To summarize, in equilibrium, two related conditions must hold:

1. A stock's expected rate of return as seen by the marginal investor must equal its required rate of return: $\hat{r}_i = r_i$.

2. The actual market price of the stock must equal its intrinsic value as estimated by the marginal investor: $P_0 = \hat{P}_0$.

Of course, some individual investors may believe that $\hat{r}_i > r_i$ and $\hat{P}_0 > P_0$ (hence, they would invest most of their funds in the stock), while other investors might have an opposite view and sell all of their shares. However, investors at the margin establish the actual market price; and for these investors, we must have $\hat{r}_i = r_i$ and $\hat{P}_0 = P_0$. If these conditions do not hold, trading will occur until they do.

Equilibrium
The condition under which the expected return on a security is just equal to its required return, $\hat{r}_i = r_i$. Also, $P_0 = \hat{P}_0$, and the price is stable.

9A-2 CHANGES IN EQUILIBRIUM STOCK PRICES

Stock prices are not constant—they undergo violent changes at times. For example, during the week of October 6, 2008, through October 10, 2008, the Dow Jones Industrial Average fell more than 1,874 points representing an 18% decline. On October 27, 1997, the Dow Jones Industrials fell 554 points, a 7.18% drop in value. Even worse, on October 19, 1987, the Dow lost 508 points, causing an average stock to lose 23% of its value on that one day, and some individual stocks lost more than 70%. More recently, on August 8, 2011, the Dow lost 634 points, representing a 5.55% drop in value.

To see what could cause such changes to occur, assume that Stock X is in equilibrium, selling at a price of $27.27 per share. If all expectations were met exactly, during the next year the price would gradually rise to $28.63, or by 5%. However, suppose conditions changed as indicated in the second column of the following table:

	Variable Value	
	Original	**New**
Risk-free rate, r_{RF}	6%	5%
Market risk premium, $r_M - r_{RF}$	5%	4%
Stock X's beta coefficient, b_x	2.0	1.25
Stock X's expected growth rate, g_x	5%	6%
D_0	$2.8571	$2.8571
Price of Stock X	$27.27	?

Now give yourself a test: How would the change in each variable, by itself, affect the price; and what new price would result?

Every change, taken alone, would lead to an *increase* in the price. The first three changes together lower r_X, which declines from 16% to 10%:

$$\text{Original } r_X = 6\% + 5\%(2.0) = 16\%$$
$$\text{New } r_X = 5\% + 4\%(1.25) = 10\%$$

Using these values, together with the new g, we find that $\hat{P}_0$ rises from $27.27 to $75.71, or by approximately 178%:[1]

$$\text{Original } \hat{P}_0 = \frac{\$2.8571(1.05)}{0.16 - 0.05} = \frac{\$3.00}{0.11} = \$27.27$$

$$\text{New } \hat{P}_0 = \frac{\$2.8571(1.06)}{0.10 - 0.06} = \frac{\$3.0285}{0.04} = \$75.71$$

Note too that at the new price, the expected and required rates of return will be equal:[2]

$$\hat{r}_X = \frac{\$3.0285}{\$75.71} + 6\% = 10\% = r_X$$

Evidence suggests that stocks, especially those of large companies, adjust rapidly when their fundamental positions change. Such stocks are followed closely by a number of security analysts; so as soon as things change, so does the stock price. Consequently, equilibrium ordinarily exists for any given stock, and required and expected returns are generally close to equal. Stock prices certainly change, sometimes violently and rapidly; but this simply reflects changing conditions and expectations. There are, of course, times when a stock will continue to react for several months to unfolding favorable or unfavorable developments. However, this does not signify a long adjustment period, it simply indicates that as more new information about the situation becomes available, the market adjusts to it.

QUESTIONS

9A-1 For a stock to be in equilibrium, what two conditions must hold?

9A-2 If a stock is not in equilibrium, explain how financial markets adjust to bring it into equilibrium.

PROBLEMS

9A-1 **RATES OF RETURN AND EQUILIBRIUM** Stock C's beta coefficient is $b_C = 0.4$, while Stock D's is $b_D = -0.5$. (Stock D's beta is negative, indicating that its return rises when returns on most other stocks fall. There are very few negative beta stocks, although collection agency stocks are sometimes cited as an example.)

---

[1]A price change of this magnitude is by no means rare. The prices of *many* stocks double or halve during a year. For example, in 2012, Lumber Liquidators' stock price increased by 199.2%. On the other hand, Houston American Energy's stock price declined by 98.2%.

[2]It should be obvious by now that actual realized rates of return are not necessarily equal to expected and required returns. Thus, an investor might have expected to receive a return of 15% if he or she had purchased Lumber Liquidators' or Houston American Energy's stock in 2012; but after the fact, the realized return on Lumber Liquidators was far above 15%, whereas the return on Houston American Energy was far below 15%.

a. If the risk-free rate is 7% and the required rate of return on an average stock is 11%, what are the required rates of return on Stocks C and D?

b. For Stock C, suppose the current price, P_0, is $25.00; the next expected dividend, D_1 is $1.50; and the stock's expected constant growth rate is 4%. Is the stock in equilibrium? Explain and describe what will happen if the stock is not in equilibrium.

9A-2   **EQUILIBRIUM STOCK PRICE**   The risk-free rate of return, r_{RF}, is 6%; the required rate of return on the market, r_M, is 10%; and Upton Company's stock has a beta coefficient of 1.5.

a. If the dividend expected during the coming year, D_1, is $2.25 and if g = a constant 5%, at what price should Upton's stock sell?

b. Now suppose the Federal Reserve Board increases the money supply, causing the risk-free rate to drop to 5% and r_M to fall to 9%. What would happen to Upton's price?

c. In addition to the change in Part b, suppose investors' risk aversion declines and this, combined with the decline in r_{RF}, causes r_M to fall to 8%. Now what is Upton's price?

d. Suppose Upton has a change in management. The new group institutes policies that increase the expected constant growth rate from 5% to 6%. Also, the new management smoothes out fluctuations in sales and profits, causing beta to decline from 1.5 to 1.3. Assume that r_{RF} and r_M are equal to the values in Part c. After all these changes, what is its new equilibrium price? (Note: D_1 is now $2.27.)

9A-3   **BETA COEFFICIENTS**   Suppose Chance Chemical Company's management conducted a study and concluded that if it expands its consumer products division (which is less risky than its primary business, industrial chemicals), its beta will decline from 1.2 to 0.9. However, consumer products have a somewhat lower profit margin, and this would cause its constant growth rate in earnings and dividends to fall from 6% to 4%. The following also apply: r_M = 9%, r_{RF} = 6%, and D_0 = $2.00.

a. Should management expand the consumer products division? Explain.

b. Assume all the facts given except the change in the beta coefficient. How low would the beta have to fall to cause the expansion to be a good one? (Hint: Set $\hat{P}_0$ under the new policy equal to $\hat{P}_0$ under the old one and find the new beta that will produce this equality.)

retaining earnings

issuing new stock

CHAPTER 10

The Cost of Capital

Creating Value at Disney

Walt Disney Co. (DIS) is one of the world's most successful companies. Despite a tough economic environment over the past few years, Disney's managers have worked hard to create value for shareholders by investing in assets that earn more than the cost of the capital used to acquire them. For example, if a project earns 20% but the capital invested in it costs only 10%, taking on the project will increase the firm's value and thus its stock price.

Capital is obtained in three primary forms: debt, preferred stock, and common equity, with equity acquired by retaining earnings and issuing new stock. The investors who provide

{ retaining earnings
issuing new stock.

capital to Disney expect to earn at least their required rate of return on that capital, and the required return represents the firm's cost of capital.[1] A variety of factors influence the cost of capital. Some—including interest rates, state and federal tax policies, and general economic conditions—are outside the firm's control. However, the firm's decisions regarding how it raises capital and how it invests those funds also have a profound effect on its cost of capital.

Estimating the cost of capital for a company such as Disney is conceptually straightforward. Disney's capital comes from debt plus common equity, so its cost of capital

---

[1]Recall from earlier chapters that expected and required returns as seen by the marginal investor must be equal; otherwise, the security will not be in equilibrium. Therefore, buying and selling will force this equality to hold, except for short periods immediately following the release of new information. Because expected and required returns are normally equal, we use the two terms interchangeably.

depends largely on the level of interest rates in the economy and the marginal stockholder's required rate of return on equity. However, Disney operates many different divisions throughout the world; so the corporation is similar to a portfolio that contains a number of different stocks, each with a different risk. Recall that portfolio risk is a weighted average of the relevant risks of the different stocks in the portfolio.

Similarly, each of Disney's divisions has its own level of risk, and hence, its own cost of capital. Therefore, Disney's overall cost of capital is a weighted average of its divisions'

costs. For example, Disney's Media Networks' segment (which includes ABC and ESPN) probably has a different cost of capital than its Parks and Resorts unit (which includes Disney World Resort, Disneyland, and the Disney Cruise Line); and even projects within divisions have different costs because some projects are riskier than others. Moreover, its overseas projects may have different risks and thus different costs of capital than similar domestic projects. As we will see in this chapter, the cost of capital is an essential element in a firm's capital budgeting process. This process is the primary determinant of the firm's long-run stock price.

PUTTING THINGS IN PERSPECTIVE

In the last four chapters, we explained how risk influences prices and required rates of return on bonds and stocks. A firm's primary objective is to maximize its shareholders' value. The principal way value is increased is by investing in projects that earn more than their cost of capital. In the next two chapters, we will see that a project's future cash flows can be forecasted and that those cash flows can be discounted to find their present value. Then if the PV of the future cash flows exceeds the project's cost, the firm's value will increase if the project is accepted. However, we need a discount rate to find the PV of these future cash flows, and that discount rate is the firm's cost of capital. Finding the cost of the capital required to take on new projects is the primary focus of this chapter.[2]

Most formulas used in this chapter were developed earlier, when we examined the required rates of return on bonds and stocks in Chapters 7 and 9. *Indeed, the rates of return that investors require on bonds and stocks represent the costs of those securities to the firm.* As we shall see, companies estimate the required returns on their securities, calculate a weighted average of the costs of their different types of capital, and use this average cost for capital budgeting purposes.

When you finish this chapter, you should be able to:

· Explain why the weighted average cost of capital (WACC) is used in capital budgeting.
· Estimate the costs of different capital components—debt, preferred stock, retained earnings, and common stock.
· Combine the different component costs to determine the firm's WACC.

These concepts are necessary to understand the firm's capital budgeting process.

---

[2]If projects differ in risk, risk-adjusted costs of capital should be used, not one single corporate cost of capital. We discuss this point later in Section 10-9.

10-1 An Overview of the Weighted Average Cost of Capital (WACC)

Table 10.1 shows Allied Food Products' balance sheet as presented in Chapter 3, with three additions: (1) the actual capital supplied by investors (banks, bond-holders, and stockholders) calculated using the accounting-based book values; (2) the market values of the investor-supplied capital; and (3) the target capital structure that Allied plans to use in the future.

When calculating the WACC, our concern is with capital that must be provided by *investors*—interest-bearing debt, preferred stock, and common equity. Accounts payable and accruals, which arise spontaneously when capital budgeting projects are undertaken, are not included as part of investor-supplied capital because they do not come directly from investors. Looking at Column 1 of Table 10.1, we see that using the accounting-based book values, Allied's capital consists of 47.8% debt and 52.2% equity.

While these accounting-based measures are important, Allied's investors are more concerned about the current market value of the company's debt and equity, which are shown in Column 2 of Table 10.1. To keep things relatively simple, we assume that the market value of Allied's debt is equal to its book value (i.e., we assume that its average outstanding debt is trading at its par value).[3] The

Allied Food Products: Capital Structure Used to Calculate the WACC (Dollars in Millions)   **TABLE 10.1**

Assets and Claims Against Assets at Book Value on 12/31/14

Assets		Claims			Investor-Supplied Capital: Payables and Accruals are excluded because they come from operations, not from investors					
					Book Value (1)		**Market Value (2)**		**Target (3)**	
Cash	$ 10	Accounts payable	$ 60	3.0%						
Receivables	375	Accruals	140	7.0%						
Inventories	615	Notes payable	110	5.5%	$ 110		$ 110			
Total C.A.	$ 1,000	Total C.L.	$ 310	15.5%						
Net fixed assets	$ 1,000	Long-term debt	750	37.5%	750		750			
		Total liabilities	$ 1,060	53.0%	$ 860	47.8%	$ 860	42.7%	45.0%	
		Preferred stock	-	0.0%	-	0.0%	-	0.0%	2.0%	
		Common stock	130	6.5%	130					
		Retained earnings	810	40.5%	810					
		Total common equity	$ 940	47.0%	$ 940	52.2%	$ 1,153	57.3%	53.0%	
Total	$ 2,000	Total	$ 2,000	100.0%	$ 1,800	100.0%	$ 2,013	100.0%	100.0%	

© Cengage Learning 2015

Notes:

1. The market value calculations assume that the company's debt is trading at par, so the market value of debt equals the book value of debt.

2. The market value of equity is the share price of common stock multiplied by the number of shares outstanding. At 12/31/14, the firm has 50 million shares outstanding and its stock sold for $23.06 per share.

---

[3]In practice, the market value of debt may be somewhat higher or lower than its book value, depending on whether the outstanding bonds are trading at a premium or at a discount. Again, to keep things simple, for our purposes we will generally assume that the market value of debt equals the book value of debt when calculating the WACC.

# of shares of stock outstanding × the current stock price.

market value of equity is the number of shares of stock outstanding multiplied by the current stock price. Recall from Chapter 3, that Allied has 50 million shares of common stock outstanding, and the company's stock currently trades at $23.06 per share, which means that the market value of its equity is $1.153 billion. Because the market value of its equity exceeds the book value of its equity, we see that Allied's market-based capital structure has a higher percentage of equity (57.3%) than the capital structure that was calculated using its accounting-based book values (52.2%).

While these market-based numbers are a useful starting point, what ultimately matters is the **target capital structure** which refers to how Allied plans to raise capital to fund its future projects. In Chapter 13, we explore in more detail how companies determine their target capital structure. As we will see, there is an optimal capital structure—one where the percentages of debt, preferred stock, and common equity maximize the firm's value. As shown in Column 3 of Table 10.1, Allied Food has concluded that its target capital structure should include 45% debt, 2% preferred stock, and 53% common equity; and in the future it plans to raise capital in those proportions. Therefore, we use those target weights when we calculate Allied's weighted average cost of capital. It follows that Allied's overall cost of capital is a weighted average of the costs of the various types of capital it uses, where the weights correspond to the company's target capital structure.

Target Capital Structure

The mix of debt, preferred stock, and common equity the firm plans to raise to fund its future projects.

SELF TEST

When calculating WACC, what capital is excluded and why?

When calculating a company's WACC, should book value, market value, or target weights be used? Explain.

Why might the weights of capital be different depending on whether book values, market values, or target values are used?

10-2 BASIC DEFINITIONS

The investor-supplied items—debt, preferred stock, and common equity—are called **capital components.** Increases in assets must be financed by increases in these capital components. The cost of each component is called its *component cost;* for example, Allied can borrow money at 10%, so its component cost of debt is 10%.[4] These costs are then combined to form a weighted average cost of capital, which is used in the firm's capital budgeting analysis. Throughout this chapter, we concentrate on the three major capital components. The following symbols identify the cost and weight of each:

Capital Components

One of the types of capital used by firms to raise funds.

r_d = interest rate on the firm's new debt = before-tax component cost of debt. It can be found in several ways, including calculating the yield to maturity on the firm's currently outstanding bonds.

---

[4]We will see shortly that there is a before-tax and an after-tax cost of debt; for now, it is sufficient to know that 10% is the before-tax component cost of debt. Also, for simplicity, we assume that long- and short-term debt have the same cost; hence, we deal with just one type of debt.

$r_d(1 - T)$ = after-tax component cost of debt, where T is the firm's marginal tax rate. $r_d(1 - T)$ *is the debt cost used to calculate the weighted average cost of capital.* As we shall see, the after-tax cost of debt is lower than its before-tax cost because interest is tax deductible.

r_p = component cost of preferred stock, found as the yield investors expect to earn on the preferred stock. Preferred dividends are not tax deductible; hence, the before- and after-tax costs of preferred are equal.

r_s = component cost of common equity raised by retaining earnings, or *internal equity.* It is the r_s developed in Chapters 8 and 9 and defined there as the rate of return that investors require on a firm's common stock. Most firms, once they have become well established, obtain all of their new equity as retained earnings; hence, r_s is their cost of all new equity.

r_e = component cost of *external equity,* or common equity raised by issuing new stock. As we will see, r_e is equal to r_s plus a factor that reflects the cost of issuing new stock. Note, though, that established firms such as Allied Food rarely issue new stock; hence, r_e is rarely a relevant consideration except for very young, rapidly growing firms.

w_d, w_p, w_c = target weights of debt, preferred stock, and common equity (which includes retained earnings, internal equity, and new common stock, external equity). The weights are the percentages of the different types of capital the firm plans to use when it raises capital in the future. Target weights may differ from actual current weights.[5]

WACC = the firm's weighted average, or overall, cost of capital.

The target proportions of debt (w_d), preferred stock (w_p), and common equity (w_c), along with the costs of those components, are used to calculate the firm's **weighted average cost of capital, WACC.** We assume at this point that all new common equity is raised as retained earnings, as is true for most companies; hence, the cost of common equity is r_s.

Weighted Average Cost of Capital (WACC)

A weighted average of the component costs of debt, preferred stock, and common equity.

$$\text{WACC} = \binom{\% \text{ of debt}}{} \binom{\text{After-tax cost of debt}}{} + \binom{\% \text{ of preferred stock}}{} \binom{\text{Cost of preferred stock}}{} + \binom{\% \text{ of common equity}}{} \binom{\text{Cost of common equity}}{}$$

$$= \quad w_d r_d(1-T) \quad + \quad w_p r_p \quad + \quad w_c r_s \qquad \text{10.1}$$

Note that only debt has a tax adjustment factor, $(1 - T)$. As discussed in the next section, this is because interest on debt is tax deductible but preferred dividends and the returns on common stock (dividends and capital gains) are not.

These definitions and concepts are discussed in the remainder of the chapter, using Allied Food for illustrative purposes. Later in Chapter 13, we extend the discussion to show how the optimal mix of securities minimizes the firm's cost of capital and maximizes its value.

---

[5]We should also note that the weights could be based on the book values of the capital components or on their market values. The market value of the equity is found by multiplying the stock's price by the number of shares outstanding. Market-value weights are theoretically superior; but accountants show assets on a book-value basis; bond rating agencies and security analysts generally focus on book values, and market-value weights are quite unstable because stock prices fluctuate widely. If a firm's book and market values differ widely, the firm may set its *target* weights as a blend of book and market weights. We discuss this at greater length in Chapter 13; but for now, just take the target weights provided in this chapter as management determined.

Identify the firm's three major capital structure components and give their respective component cost and weight symbols.

Why might there be two different component costs for common equity? Which one is generally relevant, and for what type of firm is the second one likely to be relevant?

If a firm now has a debt ratio of 50% but plans to finance with only 40% debt in the future, what should it use as w_d when it calculates its WACC? Explain.

10-3 COST OF DEBT, $r_d(1-T)$

The interest rate a firm must pay on its *new* debt is defined as its **before-tax cost of debt, r_d.** Firms can estimate r_d by asking their bankers what it will cost to borrow or by finding the yield to maturity on their currently outstanding debt (as we illustrated in Chapter 7). *However, the **after-tax cost of debt**, should be used to calculate the weighted average cost of capital.* This is the interest rate on new debt, r_d, less the tax savings that result because interest is tax deductible:[6]

Before-Tax Cost of Debt, r_d
The interest rate the firm must pay on new debt.

After-Tax Cost of Debt, $r_d(1-T)$
The relevant cost of new debt, taking into account the tax deductibility of interest; used to calculate the WACC.

$$\text{After-tax cost of debt} = \text{Interest rate on new debt} - \text{Tax savings}$$
$$= r_d - r_d T$$
$$= r_d(1-T)$$

 10.2

In effect, the government pays part of the cost of debt because interest is tax deductible. Therefore, if Allied can borrow at an interest rate of 10% and its marginal federal-plus-state tax rate is 40%, its after-tax cost of debt will be 6%.[7]

$$\text{After-tax cost of debt} = r_d(1-T) = 10\%(1.0-0.4)$$
$$= 10\%(0.6)$$
$$= 6.0\%$$

We use the after-tax cost of debt in calculating the WACC because we are interested in maximizing the value of the firm's stock, and the stock price depends on *after-tax* cash flows. Because we are concerned with after-tax cash flows and because cash flows and rates of return should be calculated on a comparable basis, we adjust the interest rate downward due to debt's preferential tax treatment.[8]

It is important to emphasize that the cost of debt is the interest rate on *new* debt, not outstanding debt. We are interested in the cost of new debt because our

---

[6]If Allied borrowed $100,000 at 10%, it would have to write a check for $10,000 to pay annual interest charges. However, that $10,000 would be a tax deduction, which at a 40% tax rate would save $4,000 annually in taxes. The tax rate is *zero* for a firm with losses. Therefore, for a company that does not pay taxes, the cost of debt is not reduced. In Equation 10.2, if the tax rate is zero, the after-tax cost of debt is not reduced and is simply equal to the before-tax cost of debt.

[7]Note that in 2013, the federal tax rate for most large corporations is 35%. However, most corporations are also subject to state income taxes; so for illustrative purposes, we assume that the effective federal-plus-state tax rate on marginal income is 40%.

[8]Strictly speaking, the after-tax cost of debt should reflect the *expected* cost of debt. While Allied's bonds have a promised return of 10%, there is some chance of default, so its bondholders' expected return (and consequently Allied's cost) is a bit less than 10%. For a relatively strong company such as Allied, this difference is quite small. As we discuss later in the chapter, Allied must also incur flotation costs when it issues debt, but like the difference between the promised and the expected rates of return, flotation costs for debt are generally small. Finally, note that these two factors tend to offset one another—not including the possibility of default leads to an overstatement of the cost of debt, but not including flotation costs leads to an understatement. For all these reasons, r_d is generally a good approximation of the before-tax cost of debt capital and $r_d(1-T)$ of the after-tax cost.

primary concern with the cost of capital is its use in capital budgeting decisions. For example, would a new machine earn a return greater than the cost of the capital needed to acquire the machine? The rate at which the firm has borrowed in the past is irrelevant when answering this question because we need to know the cost of *new capital. For these reasons, the yield to maturity on outstanding debt (which reflects current market conditions) is a better measure of the cost of debt than the coupon rate.* Note that if the yield curve is upward- or downward-sloping, the cost of long- and short-term debt will differ. In these cases, the yield to maturity on the company's long-term debt is generally used to calculate the cost of debt because, more often than not, the capital is being raised to fund long-term projects.[9] However, as we see in Chapter 15, some companies regularly use a mix of short-term and long-term debt to finance their projects. When calculating their costs of debt, these companies may choose to calculate an average of their debt costs based on the proportion of long- and short-term debt that they plan to use.

SELF TEST

Why is the after-tax cost of debt rather than the before-tax cost used to calculate the WACC?

Why is the relevant cost of debt the interest rate on *new* debt, not that on already outstanding, or *old*, debt?

How can the yield to maturity on a firm's outstanding debt be used to estimate its before-tax cost of debt?

A company has outstanding 20-year noncallable bonds with a face value of $1,000, an 11% annual coupon, and a market price of $1,294.54. If the company was to issue new debt, what would be a reasonable estimate of the interest rate on that debt? If the company's tax rate is 40%, what is its after-tax cost of debt? **(8.0%; 4.8%)**

10-4 COST OF PREFERRED STOCK, r_p

Cost of Preferred Stock, r_p
The rate of return investors require on the firm's preferred stock; r_p is calculated as the preferred dividend, D_p, divided by the current price, P_p.

The component **cost of preferred stock, r_p,** used to calculate the weighted average cost of capital is the preferred dividend, D_p, divided by the current price of the preferred stock, P_p.

$$\text{Component cost of preferred stock} = r_p = \frac{D_p}{P_p}$$

10.3

Allied does not have any preferred stock outstanding, but the company plans to issue some in the future and therefore has included it in its target capital structure. Allied would sell this stock to a few large hedge funds, the stock would have a $10.00 dividend per share, and it would be priced at $97.50 a share. Therefore, Allied's cost of preferred stock would be 10.3%:[10]

$$r_p = \$10.00/\$97.50 = 10.3\%$$

---

[9]To get a true measure of the cost of debt, you should use the yield to maturity on outstanding debt that is noncallable and not convertible to common stock.
[10]This preferred stock would be sold directly to a group of hedge funds, so no flotation costs would be incurred. If significant flotation costs were involved, the cost of the preferred should be adjusted upward, as we explain in a later section.

As we can see from Equation 10.3, calculating the cost of preferred stock is easy. This is particularly true for traditional "plain vanilla" preferred that pays a fixed dividend in perpetuity. However, in Chapter 9, we noted that some preferred issues have a specified maturity date and we described how to calculate the expected return on these issues. Also, preferred stock may include an option to convert to common stock, which adds another layer of complexity. We leave these more complicated situations for advanced classes. Finally, note that no tax adjustments are made when calculating r_p because preferred dividends, unlike interest on debt, are *not* tax deductible; so no tax savings are associated with preferred stock.

SELF TEST

Is a tax adjustment made to the cost of preferred stock? Why or why not?

A company's preferred stock currently trades at $80 per share and pays a $6 annual dividend per share. Ignoring flotation costs, what is the firm's cost of preferred stock? **(7.50%)**

10-5 THE COST OF RETAINED EARNINGS, r_s

The costs of debt and preferred stock are based on the returns that investors require on these securities. Similarly, the cost of common equity is based on the rate of return that investors require on the company's common stock. Note, though, that new common equity is raised in two ways: (1) by retaining some of the current year's earnings and (2) by issuing new common stock.[11] We use the symbol r_s to designate the **cost of retained earnings** and r_e to designate the **cost of new common stock**, or external equity. Equity raised by issuing stock has a higher cost than equity from retained earnings due to the flotation costs required to sell new common stock. Therefore, once firms get beyond the start-up stage, they normally obtain all of their new equity by retaining earnings.

Some have argued that retained earnings should be "free" because they represent money that is "left over" after dividends are paid. While it is true that no direct costs are associated with retained earnings, this capital still has a cost, an *opportunity cost*. The firm's after-tax earnings belong to its stockholders. Bondholders are compensated by interest payments; preferred stockholders, by preferred dividends. But the net earnings remaining after paying interest and preferred dividends belong to the common stockholders, and these earnings serve to compensate them for the use of their capital. The managers, who work for the stockholders, can either pay out earnings in the form of dividends or retain earnings for reinvestment in the business. When managers make this decision, they should recognize that there is an opportunity cost involved—stockholders

Cost of Retained Earnings, r_s
The rate of return required by stockholders on a firm's common stock.

Cost of New Common Stock, r_e
The cost of external equity; based on the cost of retained earnings, but increased for flotation costs necessary to issue new common stock.

---

[11]The term *retained earnings* can be interpreted to mean the balance sheet account *retained earnings,* consisting of all the earnings retained in the business throughout its history or the income statement item *addition to retained earnings*. The income statement item is relevant in this chapter. For our purpose, *retained earnings* refers to that part of the current year's earnings not paid as dividends (hence, available for reinvestment in the business this year). If this is not clear, look back at Allied's balance sheet shown in Table 3.1 and note that at the end of 2013, Allied had $750 million of retained earnings; but that figure rose to $810 million by the end of 2014. Then look at the 2014 income statement, where you will see that Allied retained $60 million of its 2014 income. This $60 million was the new equity from retained earnings that was used, along with some additional debt, to fund the 2014 capital budgeting projects. Also, you can see from the 2013 and 2014 balance sheets that Allied had $130 million of common stock at the end of both years. This indicates that it did not issue (sell) any new common stock to raise capital during 2014.

could have received the earnings as dividends and invested this money in other stocks, in bonds, in real estate, or in anything else. *Therefore, the firm needs to earn at least as much on any earnings retained as the stockholders could earn on alternative investments of comparable risk.*

What rate of return can stockholders expect to earn on equivalent-risk investments? First, recall from Chapter 9 that stocks are normally in equilibrium, with expected and required rates of return equal: $\hat{r}_s = r_s$. Thus, Allied's stockholders expect to be able to earn r_s on their money. *Therefore, if the firm cannot invest retained earnings to earn at least r_s, it should pay those funds to its stockholders and let them invest directly in stocks or other assets that will provide that return.*

Whereas debt and preferred stocks are contractual obligations whose costs are clearly stated within the contracts, stocks have no comparable stated cost rate. That makes it difficult to measure r_s. However, we can employ the techniques developed in Chapters 8 and 9 to produce reasonably good estimates of the cost of equity from retained earnings. To begin, recall that if a stock is in equilibrium, its *required rate of return, r_s,* must be equal to its *expected rate of return, $\hat{r}_s$.* Further, its *required return* is equal to a risk-free rate, r_{RF}, plus a risk premium, RP, whereas the *expected return* on the stock is its expected dividend yield, D_1/P_0, plus its expected growth rate, g. Thus, we can write the following equation and estimate r_s using the left term, the right term, or both terms:

$$\text{Required rate of return} = \text{Expected rate of return}$$
$$r_s = r_{RF} + RP = D_1/P_0 + g = \hat{r}_s$$

10.4

The left term is based on the Capital Asset Pricing Model (CAPM) as discussed in Chapter 8, and the right term is based on the discounted dividend model as developed in Chapter 9. We discuss these two procedures, in addition to one based on the firm's own cost of debt, in the following sections.

10-5A THE CAPM APPROACH

The most widely used method for estimating the cost of common equity is the Capital Asset Pricing Model (CAPM) as developed in Chapter 8.[12] Here are the steps used to find r_s:

Step 1: Estimate the risk-free rate, r_{RF}. We generally use the 10-year Treasury bond rate as the measure of the risk-free rate, but some analysts use the short-term Treasury bill rate.

Step 2: Estimate the stock's beta coefficient, b_i, and use it as an index of the stock's risk. The *i* signifies the *i*th company's beta.

Step 3: Estimate the market risk premium. Recall that the market risk premium is the difference between the return that investors require on an average stock and the risk-free rate.[13]

---

[12]A recent survey by John Graham and Campbell Harvey indicates that the CAPM approach is most often used to estimate the cost of equity. More than 70% of the surveyed firms used the CAPM approach. In some cases, they used beta from the CAPM as one determinant of r_s, but they also added other factors thought to improve the estimate. For more details, see John R. Graham and Campbell R. Harvey, "The Theory and Practice of Corporate Finance: Evidence from the Field," *Journal of Financial Economics*, vol. 60, nos. 2 and 3 (May–June 2001), pp. 187–243, for the survey, and Eugene F. Fama and Kenneth R. French, "Common Risk Factors in the Return on Stocks and Bonds," *Journal of Financial Economics*, vol. 33, no. 1 (1993), pp. 3–56.

[13]It is important to be consistent in the use of a long-term versus a short-term rate for r_{RF} and for the market risk premium. The market risk premium ($RP_M = r_M - r_{RF}$) depends on the measure used for the risk-free rate. The yield curve is normally upward-sloping, so the 10-year Treasury bond rate normally exceeds the short-term Treasury bill rate. In this case, it follows that one will obtain a lower estimate of the market risk premium if the higher longer-term bond rate is used as the risk-free rate. At any rate, the r_{RF} used to find the market risk premium should be the same as the r_{RF} used as the first term in the CAPM equation.

Step 4: Substitute the preceding values in the CAPM equation to estimate the
required rate of return on the stock in question:

$$r_s = r_{RF} + (RP_M)b_i$$
$$= r_{RF} + (r_M - r_{RF})b_i$$

10.5

Thus, the CAPM estimate of r_s is equal to the risk-free rate, r_{RF}, plus a risk premium
that is equal to the risk premium on an average stock, $(r_M - r_{RF})$, scaled up or down
to reflect the particular stock's risk as measured by its beta coefficient, b_i.

Assume that in today's market, $r_{RF} = 5.6\%$, the market risk premium is
$RP_M = 5.0\%$, and Allied's beta is 1.48. Using the CAPM approach, Allied's cost
of equity is estimated to be 13.0%:

$$r_s = 5.6\% + (5.0\%)(1.48)$$
$$= 13.0\%$$

Although the CAPM appears to produce an accurate, precise estimate of r_s,
several potential problems exist. First, as we saw in Chapter 8, if a firm's stockholders are not well diversified, they may be concerned with *stand-alone risk* rather
than just market risk. In that case, the firm's true investment risk would not be
measured by its beta and the CAPM estimate would understate the correct value
of r_s. Further, even if the CAPM theory is valid, it is hard to obtain accurate
estimates of the required inputs because (1) there is controversy about whether
to use long-term or short-term Treasury yields for r_{RF}, (2) it is hard to estimate
the beta that investors expect the company to have in the future, and (3) it is
difficult to estimate the proper market risk premium. As we indicated earlier, the
CAPM approach is used most often; but because of the just-noted problems,
analysts also estimate the cost of equity using the other approaches discussed in
the following sections.

10-5B BOND-YIELD-PLUS-RISK-PREMIUM APPROACH

In situations where reliable inputs for the CAPM approach are not available,
as would be true for a closely held company, analysts often use a somewhat
subjective procedure to estimate the cost of equity. Empirical studies suggest
that the risk premium on a firm's stock over its own bonds generally ranges from
3 to 5 percentage points.[14] Based on this evidence, one might simply add a
judgmental risk premium of 3% to 5% to the interest rate on the firm's own
long-term debt to estimate its cost of equity. Firms with risky, low-rated, and
consequently high-interest-rate debt also have risky, high-cost equity; and the
procedure of basing the cost of equity on the firm's own readily observable debt
cost utilizes this logic. For example, given that Allied's bonds yield 10%, its cost of
equity might be estimated as follows:

$$r_s = \text{Bond yield} + \text{Risk premium} = 10.0\% + 4.0\% = 14.0\%$$

The bonds of a riskier company might have a higher yield, 12%, in which case the
estimated cost of equity would be 16%:

$$r_s = 12.0\% + 4.0\% = 16.0\%$$

---

[14]Ibbotson Associates, a well-known research firm, has calculated the historical returns on common
stocks and on corporate bonds and used the differential as an estimate of the *historical risk premium* of
stocks over corporate bonds. Historical risk premiums vary from year to year, but a range of 3% to 5%
is common. Also, analysts have calculated the CAPM-required return on equity for publicly traded
firms in a given industry, averaged them, subtracted those firms' average bond yield, and used the
differential as an *expected risk premium*. Again, these risk premium estimates are often generally in the
3% to 5% range.

Because the 4% risk premium is an estimate based on judgment, the estimated value of r_s is also judgmental. Therefore, one might use a range of 3% to 5% for the risk premium and obtain a range of 13% to 15% for Allied. While this method does not produce a precise cost of equity, it should "get us in the right ballpark."

10-5c DIVIDEND-YIELD-PLUS-GROWTH-RATE, OR DISCOUNTED CASH FLOW (DCF), APPROACH

In Chapter 9, we saw that both the price and the expected rate of return on a share of common stock depend, ultimately, on the stock's expected cash flows. For companies that are expected to remain in business indefinitely, the cash flows are the dividends; on the other hand, if investors expect the firm to be acquired by some other company or to be liquidated, the cash flows will be dividends for some number of years plus a price at the horizon date when the firm is expected to be acquired or liquidated. Like most firms, Allied is expected to continue indefinitely, in which case the following equation applies:

$$P_0 = \frac{D_1}{(1 + r_s)^1} + \frac{D_2}{(1 + r_s)^2} + \ldots + \frac{D_\infty}{(1 + r_s)^\infty}$$
$$= \sum_{t=1}^{\infty} \frac{D_t}{(1 + r_s)^t}$$

10.6

Here P_0 is the current stock price, D_t is the dividend expected to be paid at the end of Year t, and r_s is the required rate of return. If dividends are expected to grow at a constant rate, as we saw in Chapter 9, Equation 10.6 reduces to this important formula:[15]

$$P_0 = \frac{D_1}{r_s - g}$$

 10.7

We can solve for r_s to obtain the required rate of return on common equity, which for the marginal investor is also equal to the expected rate of return:

$$r_s = \hat{r}_s = \frac{D_1}{P_0} + \text{Expected g}$$

 10.8

Thus, investors expect to receive a dividend yield, D_1/P_0, plus a capital gain, g, for a total expected return of $\hat{r}_s$; and in equilibrium, this expected return is also equal to the required return, r_s. This method of estimating the cost of equity is called the *discounted cash flow*, or *DCF, method*. Henceforth, we will assume that equilibrium exists, which permits us to use the terms r_s and $\hat{r}_s$ interchangeably.

It is easy to calculate the dividend yield; but because stock prices fluctuate, the yield varies from day to day, which leads to fluctuations in the DCF cost of equity. Also, it is difficult to determine the proper growth rate. If past growth rates in earnings and dividends have been relatively stable and if investors expect a continuation of past trends, g may be based on the firm's historic growth rate. *However, if the company's past growth has been abnormally high or low due to a unique situation or because of general economic fluctuations, investors will not project historical growth rates into the future.* In this case, which applies to Allied, g must be obtained in some other manner.

Security analysts regularly forecast growth rates for earnings and dividends, looking at such factors as projected sales, profit margins, and competition. For example, *Value Line Investment Survey,* which is available in most libraries,

---

[15]If the growth rate is not expected to be constant, the DCF procedure can still be used to estimate r_s; but in this case, it is necessary to calculate an average growth rate using the procedures described in this chapter's Excel model.

provides growth rate forecasts for 1,700 companies; Citigroup, UBS, Credit Suisse, Morgan Stanley, and other organizations make similar forecasts. Averages of these forecasts are available on Yahoo! Finance and other websites. Therefore, someone estimating a firm's cost of equity can obtain analysts' forecasts and use them as a proxy for the growth expectations of investors in general. Then they can combine this g with the current dividend yield to estimate $\hat{r}_s$:

$$\hat{r}_s = \frac{D_1}{P_0} + \text{Growth rate as projected by security analysts}$$

Again, note that this estimate of $\hat{r}_s$ is based on the assumption that g is expected to remain constant in the future. Otherwise, we must use an average of expected future rates.[16]

To illustrate the DCF approach, Allied's stock sells for $23.06, its next expected dividend is $1.25, and analysts expect its growth rate to be 8.3%. Thus, Allied's expected and required rates of return (hence, its cost of retained earnings) are estimated to be 13.7%:

$$\hat{r}_s = r_s = \frac{\$1.25}{\$23.06} + 8.3\%$$
$$= 5.4\% + 8.3\%$$
$$= 13.7\%$$

Based on the DCF method, 13.7% is the minimum rate of return that should be earned on retained earnings to justify plowing earnings back into the business rather than paying them out to shareholders as dividends. Put another way, because investors are thought to have an *opportunity* to earn 13.7% if earnings are paid out as dividends, the *opportunity cost* of equity from retained earnings is 13.7%.

10-5D AVERAGING THE ALTERNATIVE ESTIMATES

In our examples, Allied's estimated cost of equity was 13.0% by the CAPM, 14.0% by the bond-yield-plus-risk premium method, and 13.7% by the DCF method. Which method should the firm use? If management has confidence in one method, it would probably use that method's estimate alone. Otherwise, it might use some weighted average of the three methods.

As consultants, we have estimated companies' costs of capital on numerous occasions. We generally take into account all three methods, but we rely most heavily on the method that seems best under the circumstances. Judgment is important and comes into play here, as is true for most decisions in finance. Also, we recognize that our final estimate will almost certainly be incorrect to some extent.[17] Therefore, we always provide a range and state that in our judgment, the

[16]Analysts' growth rate forecasts are usually for 5 years into the future, and the rates provided represent the average growth rate over that 5-year horizon. Studies have shown that analysts' forecasts represent the best source of growth rate data for DCF cost of capital estimates. See Robert Harris, "Using Analysts' Growth Rate Forecasts to Estimate Shareholder Required Rates of Return," *Financial Management* (Spring 1986), pp. 58–67.

Two organizations—IBES and Zacks—collect the forecasts of leading analysts for most larger companies, average these forecasts, and publish the averages. The IBES and Zacks data are available through online computer data services.

[17]Investment bankers are generally regarded as experts on concepts such as the cost of capital, and they are paid big salaries for their analyses. But those investment bankers aren't always accurate. To illustrate, the stock price of the fifth-largest investment bank, Bear Stearns, closed on Friday, March 14, 2008, at $30. Its employees owned 33% of the stock. On Sunday, in a special meeting, its board of directors agreed to sell the company to JPMorgan for $2 per share. Bear Stearns was eventually sold to JPMorgan for $10 per share in 2008, and it has since discontinued the use of the Bear Stearns name. As you can see, even investment bankers don't always get it right, so don't expect precision unless you are given a set of numbers and told to do some relatively simple calculations.

cost of equity is within that range. For Allied, we used a range of 13% to 14%; the company then used 13.5% as the estimate of its cost of retained earnings when it calculated its WACC:

Final estimate of r_s used to calculate Allied's WACC: 13.5%

SELF TEST

Why must a cost be assigned to retained earnings?

What three approaches are used to estimate the cost of common equity? Which approach is most commonly used in practice?

Identify some potential problems with the CAPM.

Which of the two components of the DCF formula, the dividend yield or the growth rate, do you think is more difficult to estimate? Why?

What's the logic behind the bond-yield-plus-risk-premium approach?

Suppose you are an analyst with the following data: r_{RF} = 5.5%, $r_M - r_{RF}$ = 6%, b = 0.8, D_1 = $1.00, P_0 = $25.00, g = 6%, and r_d = firm's bond yield = 6.5%. What is this firm's cost of equity using the CAPM, DCF, and bond-yield-plus-risk-premium approaches? Use the midrange of the judgmental risk premium for the bond-yield-plus-risk-premium approach. (**CAPM = 10.3%; DCF = 10%; Bond yield + RP = 10.5%**)

10-6 Cost of New Common Stock, r_e

Companies generally use an investment banker when they issue new common stock and sometimes when they issue preferred stock or bonds. In return for a fee, investment bankers help the company structure the terms, set a price for the issue, and sell the issue to investors. The bankers' fees are called *flotation costs,* and the total cost of the capital raised is the investors' required return plus the flotation cost.

For most firms at most times, equity flotation costs are not an issue because most equity comes from retained earnings. Therefore, in our discussion to this point, we have ignored flotation costs. However, flotation costs can often be substantial. So if a firm does plan to issue new stock, these costs should not be ignored. When firms use investment bankers to raise capital, two approaches can be used to account for flotation costs.[18] We describe them in the next two sections.

10-6a Add Flotation Costs to a Project's Cost

In the next chapter, we show that capital budgeting projects typically involve an initial cash outlay followed by a series of cash inflows. One approach to handling flotation costs, found as the sum of the flotation costs for the debt, preferred, and common stock used to finance the project, is to add this sum to the initial investment cost. Because the investment cost is increased, the project's expected rate of return is reduced. For example, consider a 1-year project with an initial cost (not including flotation costs) of $100 million. After 1 year, the project is expected to produce an inflow of $115 million. Therefore, its expected rate of return is $115/$100 − 1 = 0.15 = 15.0%. However, if the project requires the company to

---

[18]A more complete discussion of flotation cost adjustments can be found in Chapter 10 of Brigham and Daves, *Intermediate Financial Management,* 11th edition Mason, OH: (South-Western/Cengage Learning, 2013), and other advanced texts.

raise $100 million of new capital and incur $2 million of flotation costs, the total up-front cost will rise to $102 million, which will lower the expected rate of return to $115/$102 − 1 = 0.1275 = 12.75%.

10-6B INCREASE THE COST OF CAPITAL

The second approach involves adjusting the cost of capital rather than increasing the project's investment cost. If the firm plans to continue using the capital in the future, as is generally true for equity, this second approach theoretically will be better. The adjustment process is based on the following logic. If there are flotation costs, the issuing firm receives only a portion of the capital provided by investors, with the remainder going to the underwriter. To provide investors with their required rate of return on the capital they contributed, each dollar the firm actually receives must "work harder"; that is, each dollar must earn a higher rate of return than the investors' required rate of return. For example, suppose investors require a 13.7% return on their investment, but flotation costs represent 10% of the funds raised. Therefore, the firm actually keeps and invests only 90% of the amount that investors supplied. In that case, the firm must earn about 14.3% on the available funds in order to provide investors with a 13.7% return on their investment. This higher rate of return is the flotation-adjusted cost of equity.

The DCF approach can be used to estimate the effects of flotation costs. Here is the equation for the *cost of new common stock, r_e*:

$$\text{Cost of equity from new stock} = r_e = \frac{D_1}{P_0(1 - F)} + g \qquad \text{ 10.9}$$

Here **F** is the percentage **flotation cost** required to sell the new stock, so $P_0(1 - F)$ is the net price per share received by the company.

Assuming that Allied has a flotation cost of 10%, its cost of new common equity, r_e, would be calculated as follows:

$$r_e = \frac{\$1.25}{\$23.06(1 - 0.10)} + 8.3\%$$

$$= \frac{\$1.25}{\$20.75} + 8.3\%$$

$$= 6.0\% + 8.3\% = 14.3\%$$

Flotation Cost, F
The percentage cost of issuing new common stock.

This is 0.6% higher than the previously estimated 13.7% DCF cost of equity, so the **flotation cost adjustment** is 0.6%:

$$\frac{\text{Flotation cost}}{\text{adjustment}} = \frac{\text{Adjusted}}{\text{DCF cost}} - \frac{\text{Pure}}{\text{DCF cost}} = 14.3\% - 13.7\% = 0.6\%$$

Flotation Cost Adjustment
The amount that must be added to r_s to account for flotation costs to find r_e.

The 0.6% flotation cost adjustment can be added to the previously estimated $r_s = 13.5\%$ (Allied management's estimate of its cost of equity considering all three approaches), resulting in a cost of equity from new common stock, or external equity, of 14.1%:

$$\frac{\text{Cost of}}{\text{external equity}} = r_s + \frac{\text{Flotation cost}}{\text{adjustment}} = 13.5\% + 0.6\% = 14.1\%$$

If Allied earns 14.1% on funds obtained from selling new stock, the investors who purchased that stock will end up earning 13.5%, their required rate of return, on the money they invested. If Allied earns more than 14.1%, its stock price should rise; but the price should fall if Allied earns less than 14.1%.[19]

---

[19]Flotation costs for preferred stock and bonds are handled similarly to common stock. In both cases, the dollars of flotation costs are deducted from the price of the security, P_P for preferred stock and $1,000 for bonds issued at par. Then for preferred, the cost is found using Equation 10.9 with $g = 0$. For bonds, we find the YTM based on the net proceeds received, $1,000 − Flotation costs. (For example, the net proceeds would be $970 if flotation costs are 3% of the issue price.)

10-6c WHEN MUST EXTERNAL EQUITY BE USED?

Because of flotation costs, dollars raised by selling new stock must "work harder" than dollars raised by retaining earnings. Moreover, because no flotation costs are involved, retained earnings cost less than new stock. Therefore, firms should utilize retained earnings to the greatest extent possible. However, if a firm has more good investment opportunities than can be financed with retained earnings plus the debt and preferred stock supported by those retained earnings, it may need to issue new common stock. The total amount of capital that can be raised before new stock must be issued is defined as the **retained earnings breakpoint**, and it can be calculated as follows:

Retained Earnings Breakpoint

The amount of capital raised beyond which new common stock must be issued.

$$\text{Retained earnings breakpoint} = \frac{\text{Addition to retained earnings for the year}}{\text{Equity fraction}}$$

10.10

Allied's addition to retained earnings in 2015 is expected to be $66 million (as we will see later in Chapter 16); and its target capital structure consists of 45% debt, 2% preferred, and 53% equity. Therefore, its retained earnings breakpoint for 2015 is as follows:

Retained earnings breakpoint = $66/0.53 = $124.5 million

To prove that this is correct, note that a capital budget of $124.5 million could be financed as 0.45($124.5) = $56 million of debt, 0.02($124.5) = $2.5 million of preferred stock, and 0.53($124.5) = $66 million of equity raised from retained earnings. Up to a total of $124.5 million of new capital raised for the capital budget will not exhaust the addition to retained earnings, so equity would have a cost of $r_s = 13.5\%$. However, if the capital budget exceeded $124.5 million the addition to retained earnings would be exhausted, and Allied would have to obtain equity by issuing new common stock at a cost of $r_e = 14.1\%$.[20]

SELF TEST

What are the two approaches that can be used to adjust for flotation costs?

Would a firm that has many good investment opportunities be likely to have a higher or a lower dividend payout ratio than a firm with few good investment opportunities? Explain.

A firm's common stock has $D_1 = \$1.50$, $P_0 = \$30.00$, $g = 5\%$, and $F = 4\%$. If the firm must issue new stock, what is its cost of new external equity? **(10.21%)**

Suppose Firm A plans to retain $100 million of earnings for the year. It wants to finance its capital budget using a target capital structure of 46% debt, 3% preferred, and 51% common equity. How large could its capital budget be before it must issue new common stock? **($196.08 million)**

[20]This breakpoint is only suggested—it is not written in stone. For example, rather than issuing new common stock, the company could use more debt (hence, increase its debt ratio) or it could increase its addition to retained earnings by reducing its dividend payout ratio. Both actions would change the retained earnings breakpoint. Also, breakpoints could occur due to increases in the costs of debt and preferred. Indeed, a number of changes could occur; and the end result would be a large number of potential breakpoints.

10-7 COMPOSITE, OR WEIGHTED AVERAGE, COST OF CAPITAL, WACC

Allied's target capital structure calls for 45% debt, 2% preferred stock, and 53% common equity. Earlier we saw that its before-tax cost of debt is 10.0%, its after-tax cost of debt is $r_d(1 - T) = 10\%(0.6) = 6.0\%$, its cost of preferred stock is 10.3%, its cost of common equity from retained earnings is 13.5%, and its marginal tax rate is 40%. Equation 10.1, presented earlier, can be used to calculate its WACC when all of the new common equity comes from retained earnings:

$$\begin{aligned} \text{WACC} &= w_d r_d (1 - T) && + && w_p r_p && + w_c r_s \\ &= 0.45(10\%)(0.6) + 0.02(10.3\%) + 0.53(13.5\%) \\ &= 10.1\% \text{ if equity comes from retained earnings} \end{aligned}$$

Under these conditions, every dollar of new capital that Allied raises would consist of 45 cents of debt with an after-tax cost of 6%, 2 cents of preferred stock with a cost of 10.3%, and 53 cents of common equity from additions to retained earnings with a cost of 13.5%. The average cost of each whole dollar, or the WACC, would be 10.1%.

This estimate of Allied's WACC assumes that common equity comes exclusively from retained earnings. If, instead, Allied had to issue new common stock, its WACC would be slightly higher because of the additional flotation costs.

$$\begin{aligned} \text{WACC} &= w_d r_d (1 - T) && + w_p r_p && + w_c r_e \\ &= 0.45(10\%)(0.6) + 0.02(10.3\%) + 0.53(14.1\%) \\ &= 10.4\% \text{ with equity raised by selling new stock} \end{aligned}$$

In Web Appendix 10A, we discuss in more detail the connection between the firm's WACC and the costs of issuing new common stock.

SELF TEST

Write the equation for the WACC.

Firm A has the following data: Target capital structure of 46% debt, 3% preferred, and 51% common equity; Tax rate = 40%; r_d = 7%; r_p = 7.5%; r_s = 11.5%; and r_e = 12.5%. What is the firm's WACC if it does not issue any new stock? **(8.02%)**

What is Firm A's WACC if it issues new common stock? **(8.53%)**

Firm A has 11 equally risky capital budgeting projects, each costing $19,608 million and each having an expected rate of return of 8.25%. Firm A's retained earnings breakpoint is $196.08 million. The firm's WACC using retained earnings is 8.2% but increases to 8.5% if new equity must be issued. The company invests in projects where the expected return exceeds the cost of capital. How much capital should Firm A raise and invest? Why? **($196.08 million; the 11th project would have a higher WACC than its expected rate of return.)**

10-8 FACTORS THAT AFFECT THE WACC

The cost of capital is affected by a number of factors. Some are beyond the firm's control, but others can be influenced by its financing and investment decisions.

10-8A FACTORS THE FIRM CANNOT CONTROL

The three most important factors that the firm cannot directly control are *interest rates in the economy, the general level of stock prices,* and *tax rates.* If interest rates in the economy rise, the cost of debt increases because the firm must pay bondholders more when it borrows. Similarly, if stock prices in general decline, pulling the firm's stock price down, its cost of equity will rise. Also, because tax rates are used in the calculation of the component cost of debt, they have an important effect on the firm's cost of capital. Taxes also affect the cost of capital in other less apparent ways. For example, when tax rates on dividends and capital gains were lowered relative to rates on interest income, stocks became relatively more attractive than debt; consequently, the cost of equity and WACC declined.

10-8b FACTORS THE FIRM CAN CONTROL

A firm can directly affect its cost of capital in three primary ways: (1) by changing its *capital structure,* (2) by changing its *dividend payout ratio,* and (3) by *altering its capital budgeting decision rules* to accept projects with more or less risk than projects previously undertaken.

SOME REAL-WORLD ESTIMATES OF THE WACC

In the table below, we have summarized quick estimates (done in May 2013) of the WACC for some leading companies. Our calculations were based on the following assumptions:

1. We did not have access to the company's internal target capital structure forecasts, so we used the current market-value weights for debt and equity as the capital structure weights. For simplicity, we assumed that the market value of the company's debt equaled the book value of debt (as estimated by *Value Line Investment Survey*). The market value of equity is the company's stock price multiplied by the number of shares outstanding. The market equity weight and the market debt weight are the percentage of capital (on a market basis) coming from equity and debt respectively. Note that the firms in this table do not use preferred stock, so we can eliminate the preferred stock term in the WACC equation.

2. The yield to maturity of the company's debt was compiled from the Financial Industry Regulatory Authority (FINRA), which is the largest independent securities regulator in the United States. Where available, we selected an outstanding bond issue with a maturity of 10 years or more. The income tax rate was

obtained from *Value Line Investment Survey*. The after-tax cost of debt is the yield to maturity multiplied by one minus the company's tax rate.

3. The risk-free rate approximates the yield to maturity on 10-year government debt. We assumed a market risk premium of 6.0%, and we used the CAPM to estimate the cost of equity. The stock's betas were obtained from *Value Line Investment Survey*.

4. The WACC was calculated as follows:

$$\text{WACC} = (\textbf{Market debt weight}) \times (\textbf{After-tax cost of debt})$$
$$+ (\textbf{Market equity weight}) \times (\textbf{CAPM cost of equity})$$

As expected, companies in more stable businesses (Campbell Soup, Walmart, and Coca-Cola) have the lowest WACC estimates, whereas companies in riskier industries (Boeing, Disney, Apple, and Marriott) have higher WACC estimates. While these quick estimates can give you a broad sense of the WACC for each of these companies, you should recognize that these calculations are very sensitive to changes in the underlying assumptions. For example, if we assume a higher or lower market risk premium, or use a different source to estimate betas, we can often arrive at significantly different estimates for these WACCs.

Company	Market Equity Weight	Market Debt Weight	Yield to Maturity on Existing Debt	Income Tax Rate	After-Tax Cost of Debt	Risk-free Rate	Market Risk Premium	Value Line Beta	CAPM Cost of Equity	WACC
Campbell Soup	87.46%	12.54%	3.56%	31.04%	2.45%	2.00%	6.00%	0.50	5.00%	4.68%
Walmart	86.26	13.74	2.65	31.01	1.83	2.00	6.00	0.60	5.60	5.08
Coca-Cola	92.81	7.19	2.10	23.06	1.61	2.00	6.00	0.60	5.60	5.31
Merck & Co.	89.23	10.77	3.10	23.40	2.38	2.00	6.00	0.80	6.80	6.32
Exxon Mobil Corp.	98.05	1.95	1.95	43.59	1.10	2.00	6.00	0.75	6.50	6.39
Southwest Airlines	77.40	22.60	5.09	38.54	3.13	2.00	6.00	1.00	8.00	6.90
Microsoft Corp.	96.40	3.60	3.94	18.58	3.21	2.00	6.00	0.85	7.10	6.96
Home Depot	91.23	8.77	3.99	36.01	2.55	2.00	6.00	0.90	7.40	6.98
Boeing	89.94	10.06	3.08	33.96	2.04	2.00	6.00	1.05	8.30	7.67
Disney (Walt)	90.63	9.37	3.70	33.34	2.47	2.00	6.00	1.05	8.30	7.75
Apple Inc.	100.00	0.00	—	25.16	—	2.00	6.00	1.00	8.00	8.00
Marriott Int'l	84.05	15.95	1.92	32.74	1.29	2.00	6.00	1.30	9.80	8.44

Capital structure impacts a firm's cost of capital. So far we have assumed that Allied has a given target capital structure, and we used the target weights to calculate its WACC. However, if the firm changes its target capital structure, the weights used to calculate the WACC will change. Other things held constant, an increase in the target debt ratio tends to lower the WACC (and vice versa if the debt ratio is lowered) because the after-tax cost of debt is lower than the cost of equity. However, other things are not likely to remain constant. An increase in the use of debt will increase the riskiness of both the debt and the equity, and these increases in component costs might more than offset the effects of the changes in the weights and raise the WACC. In Chapter 13, we will discuss how a firm can try to balance these effects to reach its optimal capital structure.

Dividend policy affects the amount of retained earnings available to the firm and thus the need to sell new stock and incur flotation costs. This suggests that the higher the dividend payout ratio, the smaller the addition to retained earnings, the higher the cost of equity, and therefore the higher the firm's WACC will be. However, investors may prefer dividends to retained earnings, in which case reducing dividends might lead to an increase in both r_s and r_e. As we will see in Chapter 14, the optimal dividend policy is a complicated issue, but one that can have an important effect on the cost of capital.

The firm's capital budgeting decisions can also affect its cost of capital. When we estimate the firm's cost of capital, we use as the starting point the required rates of return on its outstanding stock and bonds. These cost rates reflect the riskiness of the firm's existing assets. Therefore, we have been implicitly assuming that new capital will be invested in assets that have the same risk as existing assets. This assumption is generally correct, as most firms do invest in assets similar to ones they currently operate. However, if the firm decides to invest in an entirely new and risky line of business, its component costs of debt and equity (and thus its WACC) will increase.

SELF TEST

Name three factors that affect the cost of capital and that are beyond the firm's control.

What are three factors under the firm's control that can affect its cost of capital?

Suppose interest rates in the economy increase. How would such a change affect the costs of both debt and common equity based on the CAPM?

10-9 ADJUSTING THE COST OF CAPITAL FOR RISK

As you will see in Chapters 11 and 12, the cost of capital is a key element in the capital budgeting process. Projects should be accepted if and only if their estimated returns exceed their costs of capital. Thus, the cost of capital is a "hurdle rate"—a project's expected rate of return must "jump the hurdle" for it to be accepted. Moreover, investors require higher returns on riskier investments. Consequently, companies that are raising capital to take on risky projects will have higher costs of capital than companies that are investing in safer projects.

Figure 10.1 illustrates the trade-off between risk and the cost of capital. Firm L is in a low-risk business and has a WACC of 8%. Firm A is an average-risk business with a WACC of 10%, while Firm H's business is exposed to greater risk and consequently has a WACC of 12%. Thus, Firm L will accept a typical project if

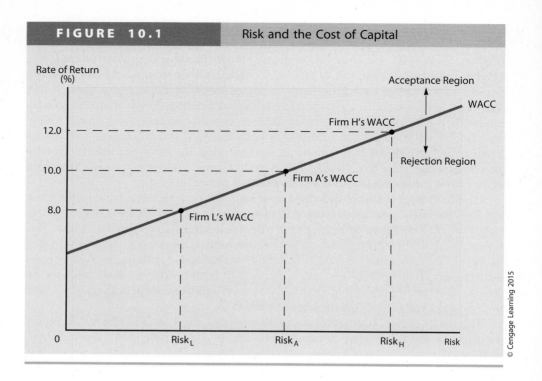

FIGURE 10.1   Risk and the Cost of Capital

its expected return is above 8%. Firm A's hurdle rate is 10%, while the corresponding hurdle rate for Firm H is 12%.

It's important to remember that the costs of capital for Firms L, A, and H in Figure 10.1 represent the overall, or composite, WACCs for the three firms and thus apply only to "typical" projects for each firm. However, different projects often have different risks, even for a given firm. *Therefore, each project's hurdle rate should reflect the risk of the project, not the risk associated with the firm's average project as reflected in its composite WACC.* Empirical studies do indicate that firms consider the risks of individual projects, but the studies also indicate that most firms regard most projects as having about the same risk as the firm's average existing assets. Therefore, the WACC is used to evaluate most projects; but if a project has an especially high or low risk, the WACC will be adjusted up or down to account for the risk differential.

For example, assume that Firm A (the average-risk firm with a composite WACC of 10%) has two divisions, L and H. Division L has relatively little risk; and if it were operated as a separate firm, its WACC would be 7%. Division H has higher risk, and its divisional cost of capital is 13%. Because the two divisions are of equal size, Firm A's composite WACC is calculated as 0.50(7%) + 0.50(13%) = 10%. However, it would be a mistake to use this 10% WACC for either division. To see this point, assume that Division L is considering a relatively low-risk project with an expected return of 9%, while Division H is considering a higher-risk project with an expected return of 11%. As shown in Figure 10.2, Division L's project should be accepted because its return is above its risk-based cost of capital, whereas Division H's project should be rejected. If the 10% corporate WACC was used by each division, the decision would be reversed: Division H would incorrectly accept its project, and Division L would incorrectly reject its project. In general, failing to adjust for differences in risk would lead the firm to accept too many risky projects and reject too many safe ones. Over time, the firm would become riskier, its WACC would increase, and its shareholder value would suffer. We return to these issues in Chapter 12, when we consider different approaches for measuring project risk.

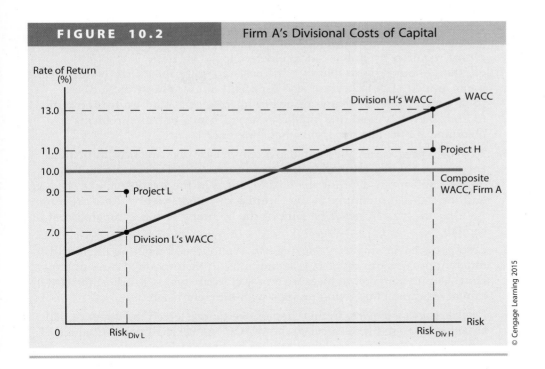

FIGURE 10.2   Firm A's Divisional Costs of Capital

© Cengage Learning 2015

SELF TEST

Why is the cost of capital sometimes referred to as a "hurdle rate"?

How should firms evaluate projects with different risks?

Should all divisions within the same firm use the firm's composite WACC for evaluating all capital budgeting projects? Explain.

10-10 SOME OTHER PROBLEMS WITH COST OF CAPITAL ESTIMATES

A number of issues related to the cost of capital have not been mentioned or were glossed over in this chapter. These topics are covered in advanced finance courses, but they deserve mention now to alert you to potential dangers and to provide a preview of some matters covered in advanced courses.

1. *Depreciation-generated funds.*[21] The largest single source of capital for many firms is depreciation, yet we have not discussed how the cost of this capital is determined. In brief, depreciation cash flows can either be reinvested or returned to investors (stockholders *and* creditors). The cost of depreciation-generated funds is thus an opportunity cost; and it is approximately equal to the WACC from retained earnings, preferred stock, and debt. Therefore, we can ignore it in our estimate of the WACC.

---

[21]See Table 3.3, the statement of cash flows, for an illustration of the cash flows provided from depreciation. Refer to advanced finance textbooks for a discussion on the treatment of depreciation-generated funds.

2. *Privately owned firms.* Our discussion of the cost of equity focused on publicly owned corporations, and we have concentrated on the rate of return required by public stockholders. However, there is a serious question about how to measure the cost of equity for a firm whose stock is not traded. Tax issues are also especially important in these cases. As a general rule, the same principles of cost of capital estimation apply to both privately held and publicly owned firms, but the problems of obtaining input data are somewhat different.

3. *Measurement problems.* We cannot overemphasize the practical difficulties encountered when estimating the cost of equity. It is very difficult to obtain good input data for the CAPM, for g in the formula $\hat{r}_s = D_1/P_0 + g$, and for the risk premium in the formula r_s = Bond yield + Risk premium. As a result, we can never be sure of the accuracy of our estimated cost of capital.

4. *Costs of capital for projects of differing risk.* We touched briefly on the fact that different projects can differ in risk and, thus, in their required rates of return. However, it is difficult to measure a project's risk (hence, to adjust the cost of capital for capital budgeting projects with different risks).

5. *Capital structure weights.* In this chapter, we took as given the target capital structure and used it to calculate the WACC. As we shall see in Chapter 13, establishing the target capital structure is a major task in itself.

Although this list of problems appears formidable, the state of the art in cost of capital estimation is not in bad shape. The procedures outlined in this chapter can be used to obtain costs of capital estimates that are sufficiently accurate for practical purposes, so the problems listed previously merely indicate the desirability of refinements. The refinements are not unimportant, but the problems noted do not invalidate the usefulness of the procedures outlined in this chapter.

SELF TEST

Identify some problem areas in cost of capital analysis. Do these problems invalidate the cost of capital procedures discussed in this chapter? Explain.

TYING IT ALL TOGETHER

We began this chapter by discussing the concept of the weighted average cost of capital. We then discussed the three major capital components (debt, preferred stock, and common equity) and the procedures used to estimate each component's cost. Next, we calculated the WACC, which is a key element in capital budgeting. A key issue here is the weights that should be used to find the WACC. In general, companies consider a number of factors and then establish a target capital structure that is used to calculate the WACC. We discuss the target capital structure and its affect on the WACC in more detail in Chapter 13.

The cost of capital is a key element in capital budgeting decisions, our focus in the following chapters. Indeed, capital budgeting as it should be done is impossible without a good estimate of the cost of capital; so you need to have a good understanding of cost of capital concepts before you continue to the next chapter, where we discuss capital budgeting basics.

SELF-TEST QUESTIONS AND PROBLEMS

(Solutions Appear in Appendix A)

ST-1 **KEY TERMS**   Define each of the following terms:

a. Target capital structure; capital components

b. Before-tax cost of debt, r_d; after-tax cost of debt, $r_d(1-T)$

c. Cost of preferred stock, r_p

d. Cost of retained earnings, r_s; cost of new common stock, r_e

e. Weighted average cost of capital, WACC

f. Flotation cost, F; flotation cost adjustment; retained earnings breakpoint

ST-2 **WACC**   Lancaster Engineering Inc. (LEI) has the following capital structure, which it considers to be optimal:

Debt	25%
Preferred stock	15
Common equity	60
	100%

LEI's expected net income this year is $34,285.72; its established dividend payout ratio is 30%; its federal-plus-state tax rate is 40%; and investors expect future earnings and dividends to grow at a constant rate of 9%. LEI paid a dividend of $3.60 per share last year, and its stock currently sells for $54.00 per share. LEI can obtain new capital in the following ways:

● New preferred stock with a dividend of $11.00 can be sold to the public at a price of $95.00 per share.

● Debt can be sold at an interest rate of 12%.

a. Determine the cost of each capital component.

b. Calculate the WACC.

c. LEI has the following investment opportunities that are average-risk projects:

Project	Cost at t = 0	Rate of Return
A	$10,000	17.4%
B	20,000	16.0
C	10,000	14.2
D	20,000	13.2
E	10,000	12.0

Which projects should LEI accept? Why? Assume that LEI does not want to issue any new common stock.

QUESTIONS

10-1 How would each of the following scenarios affect a firm's cost of debt, $r_d(1-T)$; its cost of equity, r_s; and its WACC? Indicate with a plus (+), a minus (−), or a zero (0) if the factor would raise, lower, or have an indeterminate effect on the item in question. Assume for each answer that other things are held constant even though in some instances this would probably not be true. Be prepared to justify your answer but recognize that several of the parts have no single correct answer. These questions are designed to stimulate thought and discussion.

	Effect on		
	$r_d(1-T)$	r_s	WACC
a. The corporate tax rate is lowered.	_____	_____	_____
b. The Federal Reserve tightens credit.	_____	_____	_____
c. The firm uses more debt; that is, it increases its debt ratio.	_____	_____	_____
d. The dividend payout ratio is increased.	_____	_____	_____
e. The firm doubles the amount of capital it raises during the year.	_____	_____	_____
f. The firm expands into a risky new area.	_____	_____	_____
g. The firm merges with another firm whose earnings are countercyclical both to those of the first firm and to the stock market.	_____	_____	_____
h. The stock market falls drastically, and the firm's stock price falls along with the rest.	_____	_____	_____
i. Investors become more risk averse.	_____	_____	_____
j. The firm is an electric utility with a large investment in nuclear plants. Several states are considering a ban on nuclear power generation.	_____	_____	_____

10-2 Assume that the risk-free rate increases but the market risk premium remains constant. What impact would this have on the cost of debt? What impact would it have on the cost of equity?

10-3 How should the capital structure weights used to calculate the WACC be determined?

10-4 Suppose a firm estimates its WACC to be 10%. Should the WACC be used to evaluate all of its potential projects, even if they vary in risk? If not, what might be "reasonable" costs of capital for average-, high-, and low-risk projects?

10-5 The WACC is a weighted average of the costs of debt, preferred stock, and common equity. Would the WACC be different if the equity for the coming year came solely in the form of retained earnings versus some equity from the sale of new common stock? Would the calculated WACC depend in any way on the size of the capital budget? How might dividend policy affect the WACC?

PROBLEMS

Easy Problems 1–5

10-1 **AFTER-TAX COST OF DEBT** The Heuser Company's currently outstanding bonds have a 10% coupon and a 12% yield to maturity. Heuser believes it could issue new bonds at par that would provide a similar yield to maturity. If its marginal tax rate is 35%, what is Heuser's after-tax cost of debt?

10-2 **COST OF PREFERRED STOCK** Tunney Industries can issue perpetual preferred stock at a price of $47.50 a share. The stock would pay a constant annual dividend of $3.80 a share. What is the company's cost of preferred stock, r_p?

10-3 **COST OF COMMON EQUITY** Percy Motors has a target capital structure of 40% debt and 60% common equity, with no preferred stock. The yield to maturity on the company's outstanding bonds is 9%, and its tax rate is 40%. Percy's CFO estimates that the company's WACC is 9.96%. What is Percy's cost of common equity?

10-4 **COST OF EQUITY WITH AND WITHOUT FLOTATION** Javits & Sons' common stock currently trades at $30.00 a share. It is expected to pay an annual dividend of $3.00 a share at the end of the year ($D_1 = \$3.00$), and the constant growth rate is 5% a year.

a. What is the company's cost of common equity if all of its equity comes from retained earnings?

b. If the company issued new stock, it would incur a 10% flotation cost. What would be the cost of equity from new stock?

10-5 **PROJECT SELECTION** Midwest Water Works estimates that its WACC is 10.5%. The company is considering the following capital budgeting projects:

Project	Size	Rate of Return
A	$1 million	12.0%
B	2 million	11.5
C	2 million	11.2
D	2 million	11.0
E	1 million	10.7
F	1 million	10.3
G	1 million	10.2

Assume that each of these projects is just as risky as the firm's existing assets and that the firm may accept all the projects or only some of them. Which set of projects should be accepted? Explain.

Intermediate Problems 6–13

10-6 **COST OF COMMON EQUITY** The future earnings, dividends, and common stock price of Carpetto Technologies Inc. are expected to grow 7% per year. Carpetto's common stock currently sells for $23.00 per share; its last dividend was $2.00; and it will pay a $2.14 dividend at the end of the current year.

a. Using the DCF approach, what is its cost of common equity?

b. If the firm's beta is 1.6, the risk-free rate is 9%, and the average return on the market is 13%, what will be the firm's cost of common equity using the CAPM approach?

c. If the firm's bonds earn a return of 12%, based on the bond-yield-plus-risk-premium approach, what will be r_s? Use the midpoint of the risk premium range discussed in Section 10-5 in your calculations.

d. If you have equal confidence in the inputs used for the three approaches, what is your estimate of Carpetto's cost of common equity?

10-7 **COST OF COMMON EQUITY WITH AND WITHOUT FLOTATION** The Evanec Company's next expected dividend, D_1, is $3.18; its growth rate is 6%; and its common stock now sells for $36.00. New stock (external equity) can be sold to net $32.40 per share.

a. What is Evanec's cost of retained earnings, r_s?

b. What is Evanec's percentage flotation cost, F?

c. What is Evanec's cost of new common stock, r_e?

10-8 **COST OF COMMON EQUITY AND WACC** Patton Paints Corporation has a target capital structure of 40% debt and 60% common equity, with no preferred stock. Its before-tax cost of debt is 12%, and its marginal tax rate is 40%. The current stock price is $P_0 = \$22.50$. The last dividend was $D_0 = \$2.00$, and it is expected to grow at a 7% constant rate. What is its cost of common equity and its WACC?

10-9 **WACC** The Patrick Company's year-end balance sheet is shown below. Its cost of common equity is 16%, its before-tax cost of debt is 13%, and its marginal tax rate is 40%. Assume that the firm's long-term debt sells at par value. The firm's total debt, which is the sum of the company's short-term debt and long-term debt, equals $1,152. The firm has 576 shares of common stock outstanding that sell for $4.00 per share. Calculate Patrick's WACC using market-value weights.

Assets		Liabilities and Equity	
Cash	$ 130	Accounts payable and accruals	$ 10
Accounts receivable	240	Short-term debt	52
Inventories	360	Long-term debt	1,100
Plant and equipment, net	2,160	Common equity	1,728
Total assets	$2,890	Total liabilities and equity	$2,890

10-10 **WACC** Klose Outfitters Inc. believes that its optimal capital structure consists of 60% common equity and 40% debt, and its tax rate is 40%. Klose must raise additional capital to fund its upcoming expansion. The firm will have $2 million of retained earnings with a cost of $r_s = 12\%$. New common stock in an amount up to $6 million would have a cost of $r_e = 15\%$. Furthermore, Klose can raise up to $3 million of debt at an interest rate of $r_d = 10\%$ and an additional $4 million of debt at $r_d = 12\%$. The CFO estimates that a proposed expansion would require an investment of $5.9 million. What is the WACC for the last dollar raised to complete the expansion?

10-11 **WACC AND PERCENTAGE OF DEBT FINANCING** Hook Industries' capital structure consists solely of debt and common equity. It can issue debt at $r_d = 11\%$, and its common stock currently pays a $2.00 dividend per share ($D_0 = \$2.00$). The stock's price is currently $24.75, its dividend is expected to grow at a constant rate of 7% per year, its tax rate is 35%, and its WACC is 13.95%. What percentage of the company's capital structure consists of debt?

10-12 **WACC** Midwest Electric Company (MEC) uses only debt and common equity. It can borrow unlimited amounts at an interest rate of $r_d = 10\%$ as long as it finances at its target capital structure, which calls for 45% debt and 55% common equity. Its last dividend (D_0) was $2, its expected constant growth rate is 4%, and its common stock sells for $20. MEC's tax rate is 40%. Two projects are available: Project A has a rate of return of 13%, while Project B's return is 10%. These two projects are equally risky and about as risky as the firm's existing assets.

a. What is its cost of common equity?
b. What is the WACC?
c. Which projects should Midwest accept?

10-13 **COST OF COMMON EQUITY WITH FLOTATION** Ballack Co.'s common stock currently sells for $46.75 per share. The growth rate is a constant 12%, and the company has an expected dividend yield of 5%. The expected long-run dividend payout ratio is 25%, and the expected return on equity (ROE) is 16%. New stock can be sold to the public at the current price, but a flotation cost of 5% would be incurred. What would be the cost of new equity?

Challenging Problems 14–20

10-14 **COST OF PREFERRED STOCK INCLUDING FLOTATION** Trivoli Industries plans to issue perpetual preferred stock with an $11.00 dividend. The stock is currently selling for $97.00; but flotation costs will be 5% of the market price, so the net price will be $92.15 per share. What is the cost of the preferred stock, including flotation?

10-15 **WACC AND COST OF COMMON EQUITY** Kahn Inc. has a target capital structure of 60% common equity and 40% debt to fund its $10 billion in operating assets. Furthermore, Kahn Inc. has a WACC of 13%, a before-tax cost of debt of 10%, and a tax rate of 40%. The company's retained earnings are adequate to provide the common equity portion of its capital budget. Its expected dividend next year (D_1) is $3, and the current stock price is $35.

a. What is the company's expected growth rate?
b. If the firm's net income is expected to be $1.1 billion, what portion of its net income is the firm expected to pay out as dividends? (Hint: Refer to Equation 9.4 in Chapter 9.)

10-16 **COST OF COMMON EQUITY** The Bouchard Company's EPS was $6.50 in 2014, up from $4.42 in 2009. The company pays out 40% of its earnings as dividends, and its common stock sells for $36.00.

a. Calculate the past growth rate in earnings. (Hint: This is a 5-year growth period.)

b. The last dividend was $D_0 = 0.4(\$6.50) = \$2.60$. Calculate the next expected dividend, D_1, assuming that the past growth rate continues.

c. What is Bouchard's cost of retained earnings, r_s?

10-17 **CALCULATION OF g AND EPS** Sidman Products' common stock currently sells for $60.00 a share. The firm is expected to earn $5.40 per share this year and to pay a year-end dividend of $3.60, and it finances only with common equity.

a. If investors require a 9% return, what is the expected growth rate?

b. If Sidman reinvests retained earnings in projects whose average return is equal to the stock's expected rate of return, what will be next year's EPS? (Hint: Refer to Equation 9.4 in Chapter 9.)

10-18 **WACC AND OPTIMAL CAPITAL BUDGET** Adams Corporation is considering four average-risk projects with the following costs and rates of return:

Project	Cost	Expected Rate of Return
1	$2,000	16.00%
2	3,000	15.00
3	5,000	13.75
4	2,000	12.50

The company estimates that it can issue debt at a rate of $r_d = 10\%$, and its tax rate is 30%. It can issue preferred stock that pays a constant dividend of $5.00 per year at $49.00 per share. Also, its common stock currently sells for $36.00 per share; the next expected dividend, D_1 is $3.50; and the dividend is expected to grow at a constant rate of 6% per year. The target capital structure consists of 75% common stock, 15% debt, and 10% preferred stock.

a. What is the cost of each of the capital components?

b. What is Adams' WACC?

c. Only projects with expected returns that exceed WACC will be accepted. Which projects should Adams accept?

10-19 **ADJUSTING COST OF CAPITAL FOR RISK** Ziege Systems is considering the following independent projects for the coming year:

Project	Required Investment	Rate of Return	Risk
A	$4 million	14.0%	High
B	5 million	11.5	High
C	3 million	9.5	Low
D	2 million	9.0	Average
E	6 million	12.5	High
F	5 million	12.5	Average
G	6 million	7.0	Low
H	3 million	11.5	Low

Ziege's WACC is 10%, but it adjusts for risk by adding 2% to the WACC for high-risk projects and subtracting 2% for low-risk projects.

a. Which projects should Ziege accept if it faces no capital constraints?
b. If Ziege can only invest a total of $13 million, which projects should it accept and what would be the dollar size of its capital budget?
c. Suppose Ziege can raise additional funds beyond the $13 million, but each new increment (or partial increment) of $5 million of new capital will cause the WACC to increase by 1%. Assuming that Ziege uses the same method of risk adjustment, which projects should it now accept and what would be the dollar size of its capital budget?

10-20 **WACC** The following table gives Foust Company's earnings per share for the last 10 years. The common stock, 7.8 million shares outstanding, is now (1/1/15) selling for $65.00 per share. The expected dividend at the end of the current year (12/31/15) is 55% of the 2014 EPS. Because investors expect past trends to continue, g may be based on the historical earnings growth rate. (Note that 9 years of growth are reflected in the 10 years of data.)

Year	EPS	Year	EPS
2005	$3.90	2010	$5.73
2006	4.21	2011	6.19
2007	4.55	2012	6.68
2008	4.91	2013	7.22
2009	5.31	2014	7.80

The current interest rate on new debt is 9%; Foust's marginal tax rate is 40%; and its target capital structure is 40% debt and 60% equity.

a. Calculate Foust's after-tax cost of debt and common equity. Calculate the cost of equity as $r_s = D_1/P_0 + g$.
b. Find Foust's WACC.

COMPREHENSIVE/SPREADSHEET PROBLEM

10-21 **CALCULATING THE WACC** Here is the condensed 2014 balance sheet for Skye Computer Company (in thousands of dollars):

	2014
Current assets	$2,000
Net fixed assets	3,000
Total assets	$5,000
Accounts payable and accruals	$ 900
Short-term debt	100
Long-term debt	1,100
Preferred stock (10,000 shares)	250
Common stock (50,000 shares)	1,300
Retained earnings	1,350
Total common equity	$2,650
Total liabilities and equity	$5,000

Skye's earnings per share last year were $3.20. The common stock sells for $55.00, last year's dividend (D_0) was $2.10, and a flotation cost of 10% would be required to sell new common stock. Security analysts are projecting that the common dividend will grow at an annual rate of 9%. Skye's preferred stock pays a dividend of $3.30 per share, and its preferred stock sells for $30.00 per share. The firm's before-tax cost of debt is 10%, and its marginal tax rate is 35%. The firm's currently outstanding 10% annual coupon rate long-term debt sells at par value. The market risk premium is 5%, the risk-free rate is 6%, and Skye's beta is 1.516. The firm's total debt, which is the sum of the company's short-term debt and long-term debt, equals $1.2 million.

a. Calculate the cost of each capital component, that is, the after-tax cost of debt, the cost of preferred stock, the cost of equity from retained earnings, and the cost of newly issued common stock. Use the DCF method to find the cost of common equity.

b. Now calculate the cost of common equity from retained earnings using the CAPM method.

c. What is the cost of new common stock based on the CAPM? (Hint: Find the difference between r_e and r_s as determined by the DCF method and add that differential to the CAPM value for r_s.)

d. If Skye continues to use the same market-value capital structure, what is the firm's WACC assuming that (1) it uses only retained earnings for equity? (2) it expands so rapidly that it must issue new common stock?

INTEGRATED CASE

COLEMAN TECHNOLOGIES INC.

10-22 COST OF CAPITAL Coleman Technologies is considering a major expansion program that has been proposed by the company's information technology group. Before proceeding with the expansion, the company must estimate its cost of capital. Suppose you are an assistant to Jerry Lehman, the financial vice president. Your first task is to estimate Coleman's cost of capital. Lehman has provided you with the following data, which he believes may be relevant to your task.

● The firm's tax rate is 40%.

● The current price of Coleman's 12% coupon, semiannual payment, noncallable bonds with 15 years remaining to maturity is $1,153.72. Coleman does not use short-term interest-bearing debt on a permanent basis. New bonds would be privately placed with no flotation cost.

● The current price of the firm's 10%, $100.00 par value, quarterly dividend, perpetual preferred stock is $111.10.

● Coleman's common stock is currently selling for $50.00 per share. Its last dividend (D_0) was $4.19, and dividends are expected to grow at a constant annual rate of 5% in the foreseeable future. Coleman's beta is 1.2, the yield on T-bonds is 7%, and the market risk premium is estimated to be 6%. For the bond-yield-plus-risk-premium approach, the firm uses a risk premium of 4%.

● Coleman's target capital structure is 30% debt, 10% preferred stock, and 60% common equity.

To structure the task somewhat, Lehman has asked you to answer the following questions.

a. 1. What sources of capital should be included when you estimate Coleman's WACC?

2. Should the component costs be figured on a before-tax or an after-tax basis?

3. Should the costs be historical (embedded) costs or new (marginal) costs?

b. What is the market interest rate on Coleman's debt and its component cost of debt?

c. 1. What is the firm's cost of preferred stock?

2. Coleman's preferred stock is riskier to investors than its debt, yet the preferred's yield to investors is lower than the yield to maturity on the debt. Does this suggest that you have made a mistake? (Hint: Think about taxes.)

d. 1. Why is there a cost associated with retained earnings?

2. What is Coleman's estimated cost of common equity using the CAPM approach?

e. What is the estimated cost of common equity using the DCF approach?

f. What is the bond-yield-plus-risk-premium estimate for Coleman's cost of common equity?

g. What is your final estimate for r_s?

h. Explain in words why new common stock has a higher cost than retained earnings.

i. 1. What are two approaches that can be used to adjust for flotation costs?

2. Coleman estimates that if it issues new common stock, the flotation cost will be 15%. Coleman incorporates the flotation costs into the DCF approach. What is the estimated cost of newly issued common stock, considering the flotation cost?

j. What is Coleman's overall, or weighted average, cost of capital (WACC)? Ignore flotation costs.

k. What factors influence Coleman's composite WACC?

l. Should the company use the composite WACC as the hurdle rate for each of its projects? Explain.

 THOMSON REUTERS

Use the Thomson ONE—Business School Edition online database to answer this chapter's questions.

CALCULATING 3M'S COST OF CAPITAL

In this chapter, we described how to estimate a company's WACC, which is the weighted average of its costs of debt, preferred stock, and common equity. Most of the data we need to do this can be found in Thomson ONE. Here we walk through the steps used to calculate Minnesota Mining & Manufacturing's (MMM) WACC.

Discussion Questions

1. As a first step, we need to estimate what percentage of MMM's capital comes from debt, preferred stock, and common equity. If we click on "FINANCIALS," we can see from the balance sheet the amount of MMM's short-term debt, long-term debt, and common equity. (As of year-end 2012, MMM had no preferred stock.) Alternatively, under "Financial Ratios," you can click on "WORLDSCOPE" and "ANNUAL BALANCE SHEET RATIOS." Here you will find a recent measure of total debt as a percentage of total capital. Here, total debt includes all interest-bearing debt and is the sum of short-term debt and long-term debt.

    a. Recall that the weights used in the WACC are based on the company's target capital structure. If we assume that the company wants to maintain the same mix of capital that it currently has on its balance sheet, what weights should you use to estimate the WACC for MMM?

    b. From the COMPANY OVERVIEW screen, you can find MMM's market capitalization, which is the market value of its common equity. Using the sum of its short-term debt and long-term debt from the balance sheet (we assume that the market value of its debt equals its book value) and its market capitalization, recalculate the firm's debt and common equity weights to be used in the WACC equation. These weights are approximations of market-value weights. Be sure not to include accruals in the debt calculation.

2. Once again we can use the CAPM to estimate MMM's cost of equity. Thomson ONE provides various estimates of beta—select the measure that you think is best and combine this with your estimates of the risk-free rate and the market risk premium to obtain an estimate of its cost of equity. (See the Thomson ONE exercise in Chapter 8 for more details.) What is your estimate for MMM's cost of equity? Why might it not make much sense to use the DCF approach to estimate MMM's cost of equity?

3. Next, we need to calculate MMM's cost of debt. Unfortunately, Thomson ONE doesn't provide a direct measure of the cost of debt. However, we can use different approaches to estimate it. One approach is to take the company's interest expense and divide it by total debt (which is the sum of short-term debt and long-term debt). This approach only works if the historical cost of debt equals the yield to maturity in today's market (that is, if MMM's outstanding bonds are trading at close to par). This approach may produce misleading estimates in years in which MMM issues a significant amount of new debt. For example, if a company issues a great deal of debt at the end of the year, the full amount of debt will appear on the year-end balance sheet, yet we still may not see a sharp increase in interest expense on the annual income statement because the debt was outstanding for only a small portion of the entire year. When this situation occurs, the estimated cost of debt will likely understate the true cost of debt. Another approach is to try to find this number in the notes to the company's annual report by accessing the company's home page and its Investor Relations section. Alternatively, you can go to other external sources, such as bondsonline.com, for corporate bond spreads, which can be used to find estimates of the cost of debt. Remember that you need the after-tax cost of debt to calculate a firm's WACC, so you will need MMM's tax rate (which has averaged about 30% in recent years). What is your estimate of MMM's after-tax cost of debt?

4. a. What is your estimate of MMM's WACC using the book-value weights calculated in Question 1a?

   b. What is your estimate of MMM's WACC using the market-value weights calculated in Question 1b?

   c. Explain the difference between the two WACC estimates. Which estimate do you prefer? Explain your answer.

   d. How confident are you in the estimate chosen in Part c? Explain your answer.

The Basics of Capital Budgeting

Competition in the Aircraft Industry: Airbus vs. Boeing

For the last several years, Boeing has been involved in a titanic struggle with European consortium Airbus (a unit of the European Aeronautic Defence & Space Co., EADS) for dominance in the commercial aircraft industry.[1] Recently, the battle has centered on what a correspondent for Airchive.com has characterized as the "War of the Wide Bodies." Boeing's entry in this battle is its 787 Dreamliner. To compete with the Dreamliner, Airbus is expected to soon unveil the A350 XWB (where XWB stands for extra-wide body).

As you might expect, these projects require billions of dollars of capital to develop, and along the way, the companies make many detailed calculations when forecasting crucial factors such as development costs, operating costs, and anticipated demand. Typically in these types of projects, Boeing and Airbus project negative cash flows for the first 5 or 6 years, and then positive cash flows for the following 20 years. Given their forecasted cash flows, both managements decided that taking on the projects would increase each company's intrinsic value. But given the inherent risks in this business and the fact that the planes will compete with one another, both Boeing's and Airbus's financial analysts recognized that their forecasts were subject to considerable errors.

In the past, both companies have struggled with production issues, and it is not

---

[1]Airbus SAS is owned by European Aeronautic Defence & Space Company (EADS), which is owned by the French government and several large European companies. Airbus was formed because the Europeans wanted to create an organization large enough to compete with Boeing.

unusual for their planes to be over budget and behind schedule. In a recent high-profile example, Boeing was forced to temporarily ground its Dreamliner planes because in two instances a key battery produced by one of its suppliers had caught on fire. To its credit, the company was able to quickly provide a fix to the problem, and it has maintained strong orders along the way. At the same time, Boeing and Airbus are facing new competition from other companies, such as Bombardier of Canada and Embraer of Brazil who have focused on smaller more energy-efficient jets that are increasingly in demand. This shift in the com-petitive environment has forced Boeing and Airbus to rethink the types of projects they want to invest in during the next decade.

Projects such as the Dreamliner and A350 XWB receive a great deal of attention; but Boeing, Airbus, and other compa-nies make a great many routine investment decisions every year, ranging from buying new trucks or machinery to pur-chasing computers and software to optimize inventory man-agement. While each project has its own unique character-istics, the same techniques described in this chapter are used to analyze projects of all types and sizes.

Sources: Christopher Drew and Jad Mouawad, "Boeing Fix for Battery Is Approved by F.A.A.," *The New York Times*, April 20, 2013, p. B1; Jack Harty, "Countdown to Launch: The Airbus A350 XWB," airchive.com, http://airchive.com/blog/2013/03/18/countdown-to-launch-the-airbus-a350-xwb/, March 18, 2013; and Peter Sanders and Daniel Michaels, "Winds of Change for Boeing, Airbus," *The Wall Street Journal* (online.wsj.com), March 16, 2010.

PUTTING THINGS IN PERSPECTIVE

In the last chapter, we discussed the cost of capital. Now we turn to investment decisions involving fixed assets, or *capital budgeting.* Here *capital* refers to long-term assets used in production, while a *budget* is a plan that outlines projected expenditures during some future period. Thus, the *capital budget* is a summary of planned investments in long-term assets, and **capital budgeting** is the whole process of analyzing projects and deciding which ones to include in the capital budget. Boeing, Airbus, and other companies use the techniques in this chapter when deciding to accept or reject proposed capital expenditures.

Capital Budgeting
The process of planning expenditures on assets with cash flows that are expected to extend beyond one year.

When you finish this chapter, you should be able to:

- Discuss capital budgeting.
- Calculate and use the major capital budgeting decision criteria, which are NPV, IRR, MIRR, and payback.
- Explain why NPV is the best criterion and how it overcomes problems inherent in the other methods.

With an understanding of the theory of capital budgeting developed in this chapter, which uses simplified examples, you will be ready for the next chapter, where we discuss how cash flows are estimated, how risk is measured, and how capital budgeting decisions are made.

11-1 An Overview of Capital Budgeting

The same concepts used in security valuation are also used in capital budgeting, but there are two major differences. First, stocks and bonds exist in the security markets, and investors select from the available set; firms, however, create capital budgeting projects.

Second, for most securities, investors have no influence on the cash flows produced by their investments, whereas corporations have a major influence on projects' results. Still, in both security valuation and capital budgeting, we forecast a set of cash flows, find the present value of those flows, and make the investment only if the PV of the inflows exceeds the investment's cost.

A firm's growth, and even its ability to remain competitive and to survive, depends on a constant flow of ideas relating to new products, to improvements in existing products, and to ways of operating more efficiently. Accordingly, well-managed firms go to great lengths to develop good capital budgeting proposals. For example, the executive vice president of one successful corporation said that his company takes the following steps to generate projects:

> *Our R&D department constantly searches for new products and ways to improve existing products. In addition, our Executive Committee, which consists of senior executives in marketing, production, and finance, identifies the products and markets in which our company should compete, and the Committee sets long-run targets for each division. These targets, which are spelled out in the corporation's* **strategic business plan***, provide a general guide to the operating executives who must meet them. The operating executives then seek new products, set expansion plans for existing products, and look for ways to reduce production and distribution costs. Because bonuses and promotions are based on each unit's ability to meet or exceed its targets, these economic incentives encourage our operating executives to seek out profitable investment opportunities.*
>
> *While our senior executives are judged and rewarded on the basis of how well their units perform, people further down the line are given bonuses and stock options for suggestions that lead to profitable investments. Additionally, a percentage of our corporate profit is set aside for distribution to nonexecutive employees, and we have an Employees' Stock Ownership Plan (ESOP) to provide further incentives. Our objective is to encourage employees at all levels to keep an eye out for good ideas, especially those that lead to capital investments.*

Strategic Business Plan

A long-run plan that outlines in broad terms the firm's basic strategy for the next 5 to 10 years.

Analyzing capital expenditure proposals is not costless—benefits can be gained, but analysis does have a cost. For certain types of projects, an extremely detailed analysis may be warranted, while for other projects, simpler procedures are adequate. Accordingly, firms generally categorize projects and then analyze them in each category somewhat differently:

1. *Replacement: needed to continue current operations.* One category consists of expenditures to replace worn-out or damaged equipment required in the production of profitable products. The only questions here are should the operation be continued and if so, should the firm continue to use the same production processes? If the answers are yes, the project will be approved without going through an elaborate decision process.

2. *Replacement: cost reduction.* This category includes expenditures to replace serviceable but obsolete equipment and thereby to lower costs. These decisions are discretionary, and a fairly detailed analysis is generally required.

3. *Expansion of existing products or markets.* These are expenditures to increase output of existing products or to expand retail outlets or distribution facilities in markets now being served. Expansion decisions are more complex because they require an explicit forecast of growth in demand, so a more detailed analysis is required. The go/no-go decision is generally made at a higher level within the firm.

4. *Expansion into new products or markets.* These investments relate to new products or geographic areas, and they involve strategic decisions that could change the fundamental nature of the business. Invariably, a detailed analysis

is required, and the final decision is generally made at the top level of management.

5. *Safety and/or environmental projects.* Expenditures necessary to comply with government orders, labor agreements, or insurance policy terms fall into this category. How these projects are handled depends on their size, with small ones being treated much like the Category 1 projects.

6. *Other projects.* This catch-all includes items such as office buildings, parking lots, and executive aircraft. How they are handled varies among companies.

7. *Mergers.* In a merger, one firm buys another one. Buying a whole firm is different from buying an asset such as a machine or investing in a new airplane, but the same principles are involved. The concepts of capital budgeting underlie merger analysis.

In general, relatively simple calculations, and only a few supporting documents, are required for replacement decisions, especially maintenance investments in profitable plants. More detailed analyses are required for cost-reduction projects, for expansion of existing product lines, and especially for investments in new products or areas. Also, within each category, projects are grouped by their dollar costs: Larger investments require increasingly detailed analysis and approval at higher levels. Thus, a plant manager might be authorized to approve maintenance expenditures up to $10,000 using a relatively unsophisticated analysis, but the full board of directors might have to approve decisions that involve amounts greater than $1 million or expansions into new products or markets.

If a firm has capable and imaginative executives and employees and if its incentive system is working properly, many ideas for capital investment will be advanced. Some ideas will be good ones, but others will not. Therefore, procedures must be established for screening projects. Companies use, and we discuss, the following criteria for deciding to accept or reject projects:[2]

1. Net Present Value (NPV)
2. Internal Rate of Return (IRR)
3. Modified Internal Rate of Return (MIRR)
4. Regular Payback
5. Discounted Payback

The NPV is the best method, primarily because it addresses directly the central goal of financial management—maximizing shareholder wealth. However, all of the methods provide useful information, and all are used in practice at least to some extent.

SELF TEST

How is capital budgeting similar to security valuation? How is it different?

What are some ways that firms generate ideas for capital projects?

Identify the major project classification categories and explain how and why they are used.

What is the single best capital budgeting decision criterion? Explain.

---

[2]Two other rarely used criteria, the Profitability Index and the Accounting Rate of Return, are covered in Chapter 12 and Web Extension 12A of Eugene F. Brigham and Phillip R. Daves, *Intermediate Financial Management*, 11th edition (Mason, OH: South-Western/Cengage Learning, 2013).

11-2 NET PRESENT VALUE (NPV)

We saw in Chapter 3 that there is a difference between cash flows and accounting income, and we noted that investors are particularly concerned with *free cash flow*. Recall that free cash flow represents the net amount of cash that is available for all investors after taking into account the necessary investments in fixed assets (capital expenditures) and net operating working capital.

Net Present Value (NPV)
A method of ranking investment proposals using the NPV, which is equal to the present value of the project's free cash flows discounted at the cost of capital.

In Chapter 9, we demonstrated that the value of the firm is equal to the present value of the free cash flows the firm produces for its investors over time. Similarly, the value of a project is equal to its **net present value (NPV)**, which is simply the present value of the project's free cash flows discounted at the cost of capital. The net present value (NPV) tells us how much a project contributes to shareholder wealth—the larger the NPV, the more value the project adds; and added value means a higher stock price.[3] Thus, NPV is the best selection criterion.

The most difficult aspect of capital budgeting is estimating the relevant cash flows. For simplicity, the cash flows are treated as a given in this chapter, which allows us to focus on the rules for making capital budgeting decisions. However, in Chapter 12, we discuss cash flow estimation in detail.

We use the data for Projects S and L shown in Table 11.1 to illustrate the calculation. The S stands for *Short*; the L, for *Long*. Project S is a short-term project in the sense that more of its cash inflows come early, while L has more total cash inflows but they come in later in its life. The projects are equally risky, and they both have a 10% cost of capital. Furthermore, the cash flows have been adjusted to reflect depreciation, taxes, and salvage values. The investment outlays shown as CF_0 include fixed assets and any necessary investments in working capital, and cash flows come in at the end of the year. Finally, we show the table with an "Excel look," which simply means adding row and column headings to a "regular" table. All of the calculations can be done easily with a financial calculator; but because some students may want to work with Excel, we show how problems would be set up in Excel. Do keep in mind, though, that Excel is not necessary.

We find the NPVs as follows:

1. The present value of each cash flow is calculated and discounted at the project's risk-adjusted cost of capital, r = 10% in our example.

2. The sum of the discounted cash flows is defined as the project's NPV.

The equation for the NPV, set up with input data for Project S, is as follows:

$$NPV = CF_0 + \frac{CF_1}{(1+r)^1} + \frac{CF_2}{(1+r)^2} + \cdots + \frac{CF_N}{(1+r)^N}$$

$$= \sum_{t=0}^{N} \frac{CF_t}{(1+r)^t}$$

11.1

$$NPV_S = -\$1,000 + \frac{\$500}{(1.10)^1} + \frac{\$400}{(1.10)^2} + \frac{\$300}{(1.10)^3} + \frac{\$100}{(1.10)^4}$$

$$= -\$1,000 + \$454.55 + \$330.58 + \$225.39 + \$68.30$$

$$= \$78.82$$

Here CF_t is the expected cash flow at Time t, r is the project's risk-adjusted cost of capital (or WACC), and N is its life. Projects generally require an initial investment— for example, developing the product, buying the equipment needed to manufacture it, building a factory, and stocking inventory. The initial investment is a

---

[3]We could divide the NPV by the number of shares outstanding to estimate a project's effect on the stock price. However, given the lag between project acceptance and visible effects on earnings, this is rarely done for routine projects. However, for major projects, this procedure is useful.

	A	B	C	D	E	F	G
13	WACC for both projects =		10%				
14		Initial Cost	After-Tax, End-of-Year Cash Inflows, CF$_t$				Total
15	Year	0	1	2	3	4	Inflows
16	Project S	-$1,000	$500	$400	$300	$100	$1,300
17	Project L	-$1,000	$100	$300	$400	$675	$1,475

Data on Projects S and L **TABLE 11.1**

negative cash flow. For Projects S and L, only CF$_0$ is negative; but for large projects such as Boeing's Dreamliner or Airbus's A350 XWB, outflows occur for several years before cash inflows ever begin.

Figure 11.1 shows the cash flow time line for Project S; the PV of each cash flow; and the sum of the PVs, which is by definition the NPV. The cost, at t = 0, is −$1,000. The first positive cash flow is $500; and with a regular calculator, you could find its PV as $500/(1.10)^1 = $454.55. You could also find the PV of the $500 with a financial calculator. Other PVs could be found similarly, and the end result would be the numbers in the left column of the diagram. When we sum those numbers, the result is $78.82, which is NPV$_S$. Note that the initial cost, the −$1,000, is not discounted because it occurs at Time 0. The NPV for Project L, $100.40, could be found similarly.

The step-by-step procedure shown in Figure 11.1 is useful for illustrating how the NPV is calculated; but in practice (and on exams), it is far more efficient to use a financial calculator or Excel. Different calculators are set up somewhat differently; but as we discussed in Chapter 5, they all have a "cash flow register" that can be used to evaluate uneven cash flows such as those for Projects S and L. Equation 11.1 is programmed into these calculators, and all you must do is enter the cash flows (with the correct signs) along with r = I/YR = 10. Once the data have been entered and you press the NPV key, the answer, 78.82, appears on the screen.[4]

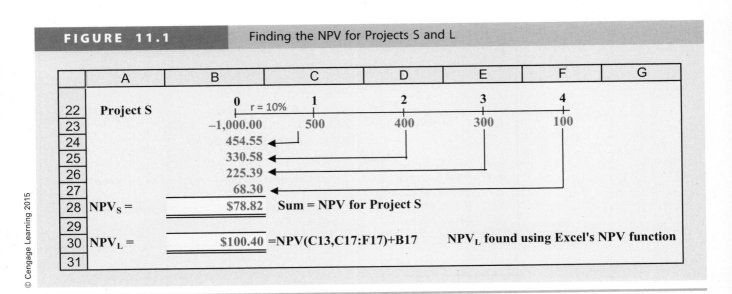

FIGURE 11.1 Finding the NPV for Projects S and L

[4]The keystrokes for finding the NPV are shown for several calculators in the calculator tutorials provided on the text's website, www.cengagebrain.com.

If you are familiar with Excel, you can use Excel's NPV function to find the NPVs for S and L:[5]

$$NPV_S = \$78.82$$
$$NPV_L = \$100.40$$

The calculations used to obtain these values are provided in the chapter's Excel model, as shown in Figure 11.1. If you want to know something about Excel, you should review the model because this is the way most people in practice find NPVs.

Before using these NPVs in the decision process, we need to know whether Projects S and L are **independent** or **mutually exclusive**. Independent projects are projects whose cash flows are not affected by one another. If Walmart was considering a new store in Boise and another in Atlanta, the projects would be independent; and if both had positive NPVs, Walmart should accept both. Mutually exclusive projects, on the other hand, are projects where if one project is accepted, the other must be rejected. A conveyor belt system to move goods in a warehouse and a fleet of forklifts used for the same purpose would be mutually exclusive—accepting one implies rejecting the other.

Independent Projects
Projects with cash flows that are not affected by the acceptance or non-acceptance of other projects.

Mutually Exclusive Projects
A set of projects where only one can be accepted.

 QUICK QUESTION

Projects X and Y have the following cash flows:

End-of-Year Cash Flows

	0	1	2	3	WACC $= r = 10\%$
X	−$700	$500	$300	$100	
Y	−$700	$100	$300	$600	

QUESTIONS:
a. If a 10% cost of capital is appropriate for both projects, what are their NPVs?
b. Which project(s) would you accept if X and Y are (1) independent or (2) mutually exclusive?

ANSWERS:

a.
$$NPV_X = -\$700 + \$500/(1.10)^1 + \$300/(1.10)^2 + \$100/(1.10)^3$$
$$= -\$700 + \$454.55 + \$247.93 + \$75.13$$
$$= \mathbf{\$77.61}$$

$$NPV_Y = -\$700 + \$100/(1.10)^1 + \$300/(1.10)^2 + \$600/(1.10)^3$$
$$= -\$700 + \$90.91 + \$247.93 + \$450.79$$
$$= \mathbf{\$89.63}$$

b. (1) If the two projects are independent, then both projects would be accepted because both have positive NPVs.
(2) If the two projects are mutually exclusive, then Project Y would be accepted because it has the larger positive NPV.

---

[5]Excel's NPV function has the following format : =NPV(rate, CF$_1$ to CF$_N$). Notice that the NPV function (shown in Figure 11.1) does not include the initial outlay at Time 0. Excel's NPV function assumes that the first cell reference in the cash flow range given refers to the cash flow at Time 1. Thus, the initial outlay must be subtracted from the value obtained using Excel's NPV function to calculate the project's NPV.

What should be the decision if Projects S and L are independent? In this case, both should be accepted because both have positive NPVs and thus add value to the firm. However, if they are mutually exclusive, Project L should be chosen because it has the higher positive NPV and thus adds more value than S. Here is a summary of the NPV decision rules:

- *Independent projects.* If NPV exceeds zero, accept the project.
- *Mutually exclusive projects.* Accept the project with the highest positive NPV. If no project has a positive NPV, reject them all.

Because projects must be either independent or mutually exclusive, one or the other of these rules applies to every project.

SELF TEST

Why is the NPV the primary capital budgeting decision criterion?

Differentiate between independent and mutually exclusive projects.

11-3 INTERNAL RATE OF RETURN (IRR)

In Chapter 7, we discussed the yield to maturity on a bond and we explained that if you hold it to maturity, you will earn the YTM on your investment. The YTM is found as the discount rate that forces the PV of the cash inflows to equal the price of the bond. This same concept is involved in capital budgeting when we calculate a project's **internal rate of return (IRR)**:

> *A project's IRR is the discount rate that forces the PV of its inflows to equal its cost. This is equivalent to forcing the NPV to equal zero. The IRR is an estimate of the project's rate of return, and it is comparable to the YTM on a bond.*

Internal Rate of Return (IRR)
The discount rate that forces a project's NPV to equal zero.

To calculate the IRR, we begin with Equation 11.1 for the NPV, replace r in the denominator with the term IRR, and set the NPV equal to zero. This transforms Equation 11.1 into Equation 11.2, the one used to find the IRR. The rate that forces NPV to equal zero is the IRR.[6]

$$NPV = CF_0 + \frac{CF_1}{(1+IRR)^1} + \frac{CF_2}{(1+IRR)^2} + \cdots + \frac{CF_N}{(1+IRR)^N} = 0$$

$$0 = \sum_{t=0}^{N} \frac{CF_t}{(1+IRR)^t}$$

11.2

$$NPV_s = 0 = -\$1,000 + \frac{\$500}{(1+IRR)^1} + \frac{\$400}{(1+IRR)^2} + \frac{\$300}{(1+IRR)^3} = \frac{\$100}{(1+IRR)^4}$$

Figure 11.2 illustrates the process of finding the IRR for Project S. Three procedures can be used:

1. *Trial and Error.* We could use a trial-and-error procedure—try a discount rate; see if the equation solves to zero; and if it doesn't, try a different rate. We could then continue until we found the rate that forces the NPV to zero; that rate would be the IRR. For Project S, the IRR is 14.489%. Note, though, that the

---

[6]For a large, complex project like Boeing's Dreamliner, costs are incurred for several years before cash inflows begin. That means that we have a number of negative cash flows before the positive cash flows start.

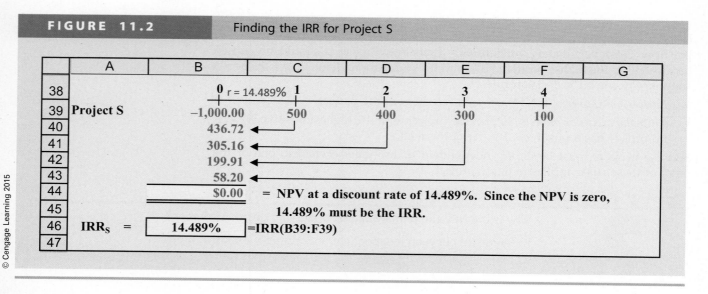

FIGURE 11.2		Finding the IRR for Project S				

FIGURE 11.2   Finding the IRR for Project S

	A	B	C	D	E	F	G
38		**0** r = 14.489%	**1**	**2**	**3**	**4**	
39	**Project S**	−1,000.00	500	400	300	100	
40		436.72					
41		305.16					
42		199.91					
43		58.20					
44		\$0.00	= NPV at a discount rate of 14.489%. Since the NPV is zero,				
45			14.489% must be the IRR.				
46	**IRR$_S$** =	14.489%	=IRR(B39:F39)				
47							

trial-and-error procedure is so time-consuming that before computers and financial calculators were available, the IRR was rarely used. It's useful to think about the trial-and-error procedure, but it's far better to use a calculator or Excel to do the actual calculations.

2. *Calculator Solution.* Enter the cash flows in the calculator's cash flow register just as we did to find the NPV; then press the button labeled "IRR." Instantly, you get the IRR. Here are the values for Projects S and L:[7]

$$IRR_S = 14.489\%$$
$$IRR_L = 13.549\%$$

3. *Excel Solution.* It is even easier to find IRRs using Excel's IRR function, as we demonstrate in the chapter model and illustrate in Figure 11.2.

QUICK QUESTION

The cash flows for Projects X and Y are as follows:

	End-of-Year Cash Flows				
	0	**1**	**2**	**3**	**WACC = r = 10%**
X	−\$700	\$500	\$300	\$100	
Y	−\$700	\$100	\$300	\$600	

QUESTIONS:

a. What are the projects' IRRs?

b. Which project(s) would the IRR method select if the firm had a 10% cost of capital and the projects were (1) independent or (2) mutually exclusive?

---

[7]See the calculator tutorials on the text's website, www.cengagebrain.com. Note that once the cash flows have been entered in the cash flow register, you can find the NPV and the IRR. To find the NPV, enter the interest rate (I/YR) and then press the NPV key. Then with no further entries, press the IRR key to find the IRR. Thus, once you set up the calculator to find the NPV, it is easy to find the IRR. This is one reason most firms calculate both the NPV and the IRR. If you calculate one, it is easy to calculate the other; and both provide information that decision makers find useful. The same is true with Excel.

ANSWERS:

a. Using a financial calculator, you would enter each cash flow into the calculator's cash flow register and press the IRR key to find the answer.

Project X
Enter the data in your financial calculator as follows: $CF_0 = -700$; $CF_1 = 500$; $CF_2 = 300$; $CF_3 = 100$; ■ IRR = **18.01%**.

Project Y
Enter the data in your financial calculator as follows, making sure to clear your registers first: $CF_0 = -700$; $CF_1 = 100$; $CF_2 = 300$; $CF_3 = 600$; ■ IRR = **15.56%**.

b. (1) If both projects were independent, both projects would be accepted because both IRRs are greater than the firm's WACC.

(2) If both projects were mutually exclusive, using the IRR method Project X would be chosen because its IRR is greater than the IRR of Project Y, and it is greater than the firm's WACC.

Why is the discount rate that causes a project's NPV to equal zero so special? The reason is that the IRR is an estimate of the project's rate of return. If this return exceeds the cost of the funds used to finance the project, the difference will be an additional return (in a sense a "bonus") that goes to the firm's stockholders and causes the stock price to rise. Project S has an estimated return of 14.489% versus a 10% cost of capital, so it provides an additional return of 4.489% above its cost of capital. On the other hand, if the IRR is less than the cost of capital, stockholders must make up the shortfall, which will hurt the stock price.

Note again that the IRR formula, Equation 11.2, is simply the NPV formula, Equation 11.1, solved for the particular discount rate that forces the NPV to equal zero. Thus, the same basic equation is used for both methods. The only difference is that with the NPV method the discount rate is given and we find the NPV; while with the IRR method the NPV is set equal to zero and we find the interest rate that produces this equality.

As we noted earlier, projects should be accepted or rejected depending on whether their NPVs are positive. However, the IRR is sometimes used (improperly we believe) to rank projects and make capital budgeting decisions. When this is done, here are the decision rules:

- *Independent projects.* If IRR exceeds the project's WACC, accept the project. If IRR is less than the project's WACC, reject it.

- *Mutually exclusive projects.* Accept the project with the highest IRR, provided that IRR is greater than WACC. Reject all projects if the best IRR does not exceed WACC.

The IRR is logically appealing—it is useful to know the rates of return on proposed investments. However, as we demonstrate in Section 11-7, NPV and IRR can produce conflicting conclusions when a choice is being made between mutually exclusive projects; and when conflicts occur, the NPV is generally better.

SELF TEST

In what sense is a project's IRR similar to the YTM on a bond?

WHY NPV IS BETTER THAN IRR

Buffett University recently hosted a seminar on business methods for managers. A finance professor covered capital budgeting, explaining how to calculate the NPV and stating that it should be used to screen potential projects. In the Q&A session, Ed Wilson, the treasurer of an electronics firm, said that his firm used the IRR primarily because the CFO and the directors understood the selection of projects based on their rates of return but didn't understand the NPV. Ed had tried to explain why the NPV was better, but he simply confused everyone; so the company stuck with the IRR. Now a meeting on the firm's capital budget is approaching, and Ed asked the professor for a simple way to explain why the NPV is better.

The professor recommended the following extreme example. A firm with adequate access to capital and a 10% WACC is choosing between two equally risky, mutually exclusive projects. Project Large calls for investing $100,000 and then receiving $50,000 per year for 10 years, while Project Small calls for investing $1 and receiving $0.60 per year for 10 years. Here is each project's NPV and IRR:

Project Large (L)	Project Small (S)
$CF_0 = -\$100,000$	$CF_0 = -\$1.00$
$CF_{1-10} = \$50,000$	$CF_{1-10} = \$0.60$
$I/YR = 10$	$I/YR = 10$
NPV = $207,228.36	NPV = $2.69
IRR = 49.1%	IRR = 59.4%

The IRR says choose S, but the NPV says take L. Intuitively, it's obvious that the firm would be better off choosing the large project in spite of its lower IRR. With a cost of capital of only 10%, a 49% rate of return on a $100,000 investment is more profitable than a 59% return on a $1 investment.

When Ed gave this example in his firm's executive meeting on the capital budget, the CFO argued that this example was extreme and unrealistic, and that no one would choose S in spite of its higher IRR. Ed agreed, but he asked the CFO where the line should be drawn between realistic and unrealistic examples. When Ed received no answer, he went on to say that (1) it's hard to draw this line and (2) the NPV is always better because it tells us how much value each project will add to the firm, and value is what the firm should maximize. The president was listening, and he declared Ed the winner. The company switched from using IRR to NPV, and Ed is now the CFO.

11-4 MULTIPLE INTERNAL RATES OF RETURN[8]

A problem with the IRR is that under certain conditions, a project may have more than one IRR. First, note that a project is said to have *normal* cash flows if it has one or more cash outflows (costs) followed by a series of cash inflows. If, however, a cash *outflow* occurs sometime after the inflows have commenced, meaning that the signs of the cash flows change *more than once*, the project is said to have *nonnormal* cash flows. Examples follow:

Normal: − + + + + +   or   − − − + + + + +
Nonnormal: − + + + + −   or   − + + + − + + +

An example of a project with nonnormal cash flows would be a strip coal mine where the company spends money to purchase the property and prepare the site for mining, has positive inflows for several years, and then the company spends more money to return the land to its original condition. In such a case, the project might have two IRRs, that is, **multiple IRRs**.[9]

Multiple IRRs

The situation where a project has two or more IRRs.

To illustrate multiple IRRs, suppose a firm is considering a potential strip mine (Project M) that has a cost of $1.6 million and will produce a cash flow of

---

[8]This section is relatively technical, but it can be omitted without loss of continuity.
[9]Equation 11.2 is a polynomial of degree n; so it has n different roots, or solutions. All except one of the roots is an imaginary number when investments have normal cash flows (one or more cash outflows followed by cash inflows). So in the normal case, only one value of IRR appears. However, the possibility of multiple real roots (hence multiple IRRs) arises when negative cash flows occur after the project has been placed in operation.

$10 million at the end of Year 1. Then at the end of Year 2, the firm must spend $10 million to restore the land to its original condition. Therefore, the project's expected cash flows (in millions) are as follows:

	Year 0	End of Year 1	End of Year 2
Cash flows	−$1.6	+$10	−$10

We can substitute these values into Equation 11.2 and solve for the IRR:

$$NPV = \frac{-\$1.6 \text{ million}}{(1 + IRR)^0} + \frac{\$10 \text{ million}}{(1 + IRR)^1} + \frac{-\$10 \text{ million}}{(1 + IRR)^2} = 0$$

NPV equals 0 when IRR = 25%, but it also equals 0 when IRR = 400%.[10] Therefore, Project M has an IRR of 25% and another of 400%, and we don't know which one to use. This relationship is depicted graphically in Figure 11.3.[11] The graph is constructed by plotting the project's NPV at different discount rates.

Note that no dilemma regarding Project M would arise if the NPV method was used; we would simply find the NPV and use it to evaluate the project. We would see that if Project M's cost of capital was 10%, its NPV would be −$0.7736 million, and the project should be rejected. However, if r was between 25% and 400%, NPV would be positive, but those numbers would not be realistic or useful for anything.

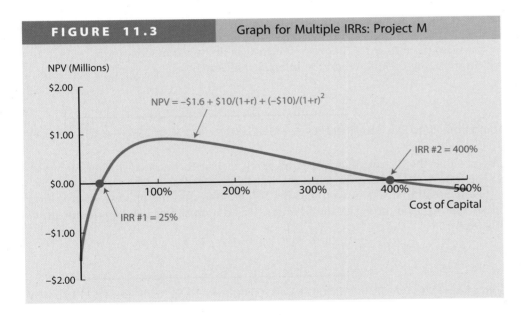

FIGURE 11.3 Graph for Multiple IRRs: Project M

WACC = 10%

Discount Rate	NPV	
0%	−$1.6000	
10	−0.7736	
25	0.0000	= IRR #1
110	0.8943	
400	0.0000	= IRR #2
500	−0.2111	

---

[10]If you attempt to find Project M's IRR with an HP calculator, you will get an error message, while TI calculators give only the IRR that's closest to zero. When you encounter either situation, you can find the approximate IRRs by calculating NPVs using several different values for r = I/YR, plotting NPV on the vertical axis with the corresponding discount rate on the horizontal axis of a graph, and seeing about where NPV = 0. The intersection with the X-axis provides a rough idea of the IRRs' values. With some calculators and with Excel, you can find both IRRs by entering guesses, as explained in the calculator and Excel tutorials on the text's website, www.cengagebrain.com.

[11]Figure 11.3 is called an NPV profile. Profiles are discussed in more detail in section 11-7.

What condition regarding cash flows would cause more than one IRR to exist?

Project MM has the following cash flows:

	End-of-Year Cash Flows		
0	1	2	3
−$1,000	$2,000	$2,000	−$3,350

Calculate MM's NPV at discount rates of 0%, 10%, 12.2258%, 25%, 122.1470%, and 150%. What are MM's IRRs? If the cost of capital is 10%, should the project be accepted or rejected? **(NPVs range from −$350 to +$164 and then back down to −$94; the IRRs are 12.23% and 122.15%. At a 10% WACC, the project's NPV is negative so reject the project.)**

11-5 REINVESTMENT RATE ASSUMPTIONS[12]

The NPV calculation is based on the assumption that cash inflows can be reinvested at the project's risk-adjusted WACC, whereas the IRR calculation is based on the assumption that cash flows can be reinvested at the IRR. To see why this is so, consider the following diagram, which was first used in Chapter 5 to illustrate the future value of $100 when the interest rate was 5%.

```
        0        5%      1       5%      2       5%      3
        |----------------|----------------|----------------|
Going from PV to FV:  PV = $100.00 ──→ $105.00 ──→ $110.25 ──→ $115.76 = FV
```

Observe that the FV calculation assumes that the interest earned during each year can be reinvested to earn the same 5% in each succeeding year.

Now recall that when we found the PV, we reversed the process, discounting rather than compounding at the 5% rate. This diagram was used to demonstrate this point:

```
        0        5%      1       5%      2       5%      3
        |----------------|----------------|----------------|
Going from FV to PV:  PV = $100.00 ◄── $105.00 ◄── $110.25 ◄── $115.76 = FV
```

This led to the following conclusion: *When we calculate a present value, we are implicitly assuming that cash flows can be reinvested at a specified interest rate, 5% in our example.* This applies to Projects S and L: When we calculated their NPVs, we discounted at the WACC, 10%, which means that we were assuming that their cash flows could be reinvested at 10%.

Now consider the IRR. In Section 11-3 we presented a cash flow diagram set up to show the PVs of the cash flows when discounted at the IRR. We saw that for Project S the sum of the PVs is equal to the cost at a discount rate of 14.489%; so by definition, 14.489% is the IRR for Project S. Now we can ask this question: What reinvestment rate is built into the IRR?

---

[12]This section gives a theoretical explanation of the key difference between NPV and IRR. However, it is relatively technical; so if time is a constraint, professors may decide to have students skip it and just read the box titled, "Why NPV Is Better than IRR," which appears in Section 11-3.

Because discounting at a given rate assumes that cash flows can be reinvested at that same rate, the IRR assumes that cash flows are reinvested at the IRR.

The NPV assumes reinvestment at the WACC, while the IRR assumes reinvestment at the IRR. Which assumption is more reasonable? For most firms, assuming reinvestment at the WACC is more reasonable for the following reasons:

- If a firm has reasonably good access to the capital markets, it can raise all the capital it needs at the going rate, which in our example is 10%.

- Because the firm can obtain capital at 10%, if it has investment opportunities with positive NPVs, it should take them on and it can finance them at a 10% cost.

- If the firm uses internally generated cash flows from past projects rather than external capital, this will save it the 10% cost of capital. Thus, 10% is the *opportunity cost* of the cash flows, and that is the effective return on reinvested funds.

To illustrate, suppose a project's IRR is 50%, the firm's WACC is 10%, and the firm has adequate access to the capital markets. Thus, the firm can raise the capital it needs at the 10% rate. Unless the firm is a monopoly, the 50% return would attract competition, which would make it difficult to find new projects with similar high returns, which is what the IRR assumes. Moreover, even if the firm does find such projects, it could take them on with external capital that costs 10%. The logical conclusion is that the original project's cash flows will save the 10% cost of the external capital, and that is the effective return on those flows.

If a firm does not have good access to external capital and if it has many potential projects with high IRRs, it might be reasonable to assume that a project's cash flows could be reinvested at a rate close to its IRR. However, that situation rarely exists: Firms with good investment opportunities generally *do* have good access to debt and equity markets.

Our conclusion is that the assumption built into the IRR—that cash flows can be reinvested at the IRR—is flawed, whereas the assumption built into the NPV—that cash flows can be reinvested at the WACC—is generally correct. Moreover, if the true reinvestment rate is less than the IRR, the true rate of return on the investment must be less than the calculated IRR; thus, the IRR is misleading as a measure of a project's profitability. This point is discussed further in the next section.

SELF TEST

Why is it true that a reinvestment rate is implicitly assumed whenever we find the present value of a future cash flow? Would it be possible to find the PV of a FV without specifying an implicit reinvestment rate?

What reinvestment rate is built into the NPV calculation? The IRR calculation?

For a firm that has adequate access to capital markets, is it more reasonable to assume reinvestment at the WACC or the IRR? Explain.

11-6 Modified Internal Rate of Return (MIRR)[13]

It is logical for managers to want to know the expected rate of return on investments, and this is what the IRR is supposed to tell them. However, the IRR is based on the assumption that projects' cash flows can be reinvested at the IRR.

---

[13] Again, this section is relatively technical, but it too can be omitted without loss of continuity.

This assumption is generally incorrect, and this causes the IRR to overstate the project's true return.[14] Given this fundamental flaw, is there a percentage evaluator that is better than the regular IRR? The answer is yes—we can modify the IRR to make it a better measure of profitability.

This new measure, the **modified IRR (MIRR)**, is illustrated for Project S in Figure 11.4. It is similar to the regular IRR except that it is based on the assumption that cash flows are reinvested at the WACC (or some other explicit rate if that is a more reasonable assumption). Refer to Figure 11.4 as you read about its construction.

Modified IRR (MIRR)

The discount rate at which the present value of a project's cost is equal to the present value of its terminal value, where the terminal value is found as the sum of the future values of the cash inflows, compounded at the firm's cost of capital.

1. Project S has just one outflow, a negative $1,000 at t = 0. Because it occurs at Time 0, it is not discounted and its PV is –$1,000. If the project had additional outflows, we would find the PV at t = 0 for each one and sum them to arrive at the PV of total costs for use in the MIRR calculation.

2. Next, we find the future value of each *inflow* compounded at the WACC out to the "terminal year," which is the year the last inflow is received. We assume that cash flows are reinvested at the WACC. For Project S, the first cash flow, $500, is compounded at WACC = 10% for 3 years and it grows to $665.50. The second inflow, $400, grows to $484.00; the third inflow grows to $330.00. The last inflow is received at the end, so it is not compounded at all. The sum of the future values, $1,579.50, is called the "terminal value," or TV.

3. We now have the cost at t = 0, –$1,000, and the TV at Year 4, $1,579.50. There is some discount rate that will cause the PV of the terminal value to equal the cost. *That interest rate is defined as the MIRR.* In a calculator, enter N = 4, PV = –1000, PMT = 0, and FV = 1579.50. Then when you press the I/YR key, you get the MIRR, 12.11%.

4. The MIRR can be found in a number of ways. Figure 11.4 illustrates how the MIRR is calculated: We compound each cash inflow, sum them to determine the TV, and then find the rate that causes the PV of the TV to equal the cost. That rate is 12.11%. However, some of the better calculators have a built-in MIRR function that streamlines the process. In Excel, you can use either the RATE or MIRR function to calculate the MIRR as shown in Figure 11.4.[15] We explain how to use the calculator function in the calculator tutorials, and we explain how to find MIRR with Excel in the chapter Excel model.[16]

---

[14]The IRR overstates the expected return for accepted projects because cash flows cannot generally be reinvested at the IRR. Therefore, the average IRR for accepted projects is greater than the true expected rate of return. This imparts an upward bias on corporate projections based on IRRs.

[15]Excel's MIRR function allows you to enter a different reinvestment rate from the WACC for the cash inflows. However, we assume reinvestment at the WACC, so the WACC is entered twice in the Excel MIRR function, shown in Figure 11.4.

[16]Equation 11.2a summarizes these steps.

$$\sum_{t=0}^{N} \frac{COF_t}{(1+r)^t} = \frac{\sum_{t=0}^{N} CIF_t(1+r)^{N-t}}{(1+MIRR)^N}$$

$$PV\ costs = \frac{TV}{(1+MIRR)^N}$$

11.2a

COF_t is the cash outflow at time t, and CIF_t is the cash inflow at time t. The left term is the PV of the investment outlays when discounted at the cost of capital; the numerator of the second term is the compounded value of the inflows, assuming the inflows are reinvested at the cost of capital. The MIRR is the discount rate that forces the PV of the TV to equal the PV of the costs.

Also note that there are alternative definitions for the MIRR. One difference relates to whether negative cash flows, after the positive cash flows begin, should be compounded and treated as part of the TV or discounted and treated as a cost. A related issue is whether negative and positive flows in a given year should be netted or treated separately. For a complete discussion, see William R. McDaniel, Daniel E. McCarty, and Kenneth A. Jessell, "Discounted Cash Flow with Explicit Reinvestment Rates: Tutorial and Extension," *The Financial Review*, vol. 23, no. 3 (August 1988), pp. 369–385; and David M. Shull, "Interpreting Rates of Return: A Modified Rate of Return Approach," *Financial Practice and Education*, vol. 10 (Fall 1993), pp. 67–71.

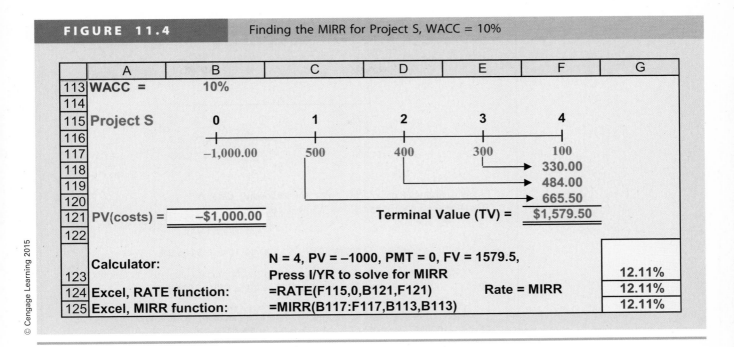

FIGURE 11.4   Finding the MIRR for Project S, WACC = 10%

The MIRR has two significant advantages over the regular IRR. First, whereas the regular IRR assumes that the cash flows from each project are reinvested at the IRR, the MIRR assumes that cash flows are reinvested at the cost of capital (or some other explicit rate). Because reinvestment at the IRR is generally not correct, the MIRR is generally a better indicator of a project's true profitability. Second, the MIRR eliminates the multiple IRR problem—there can never be more than one MIRR, and it can be compared with the cost of capital when deciding to accept or reject projects.

QUICK QUESTION

Projects A and B have the following cash flows:

	End-of-Year Cash Flows		
	0	**1**	**2**
Project A	−$1,000	$1,150	$ 100
Project B	−$1,000	$ 100	$1,300

Their cost of capital is 10%.

QUESTIONS:
a. What are the projects' NPVs, IRRs, and MIRRs?
b. Which project would each method select if the projects were mutually exclusive?

ANSWERS:
a. *Project A*

$$NPV: -\$1,000 + \$1,150/(1.10)^1 + \$100/(1.10)^2 = \textbf{\$128.10}$$

Alternatively, enter the cash flows into the financial calculator as follows:
$CF_0 = -1000$; $CF_1 = 1150$; $CF_2 = 100$; $I/YR = 10$; ■ NPV = **$128.10**.

IRR: Enter the cash flows into the financial calculator as follows:

$CF_0 = -1000$; $CF_1 = 1150$; $CF_2 = 100$; ■ IRR = **23.12%**.

MIRR:

Using a financial calculator, enter the following data: N = 2; PV = −1000; PMT = 0; FV = 1365; and solve for I/YR = MIRR = **16.83%**.

Project B

NPV : $-\$1,000 + \$100/(1.10)^1 + \$1,300/(1.10)^2 = \textbf{\$165.29}$.

Alternatively, enter the cash flows into the financial calculator as follows: $CF_0 = -1000$; $CF_1 = 100$; $CF_2 = 1300$; I/YR = 10; ■ NPV = **$165.29**.

IRR: Enter the cash flows into the financial calculator as follows: $CF_0 = -1000$; $CF_1 = 100$; $CF_2 = 1300$; ■ IRR = **19.13%**.

MIRR:

Using a financial calculator, enter the following data: N = 2; PV = −1000; PMT = 0; FV = 1410; and solve for I/YR = MIRR = **18.74%**.

b. Here's a summary of the results. The project chosen under each method is highlighted.

	Project A	**Project B**
NPV	$128.10	$165.29
IRR	23.12%	19.13%
MIRR	16.83%	18.74%

Using the NPV and MIRR criteria, you would select Project B; however, if you use the IRR criteria you would select Project A. Because Project B adds the most value to the firm, B should be chosen.

Our conclusion is that the MIRR is better than the regular IRR; however, this question remains: Is MIRR as good as the NPV? Here are our conclusions:

- For *independent* projects, the NPV, IRR, and MIRR always reach the same accept/reject conclusion; so the three criteria are equally good when evaluating independent projects.

- However, if projects are *mutually exclusive* and they differ in size, conflicts can arise. In such cases, the NPV is best because it selects the project that maximizes value.[17]
- Our overall conclusions are that (1) the MIRR is superior to the regular IRR as an indicator of a project's "true" rate of return but that (2) NPV is better than IRR and MIRR when choosing among competing projects.

SELF TEST

What's the primary difference between the MIRR and the regular IRR?

Which provides a better estimate of a project's "true" rate of return, the MIRR or the regular IRR? Explain.

11-7 NPV PROFILES

Figure 11.5 presents the **net present value profile** for Project S. To make the profile, we find the project's NPV at a number of different discount rates and then plot those values to create a graph. Note that at a zero cost of capital, the NPV is simply the net total of the undiscounted cash flows, $1,300 - $1,000 = 300. This value is plotted as the vertical axis intercept. Also recall that the IRR is the discount rate that causes the NPV to equal zero, so the discount rate at which the profile line crosses the horizontal axis is the project's IRR. When we connect the data points, we have the NPV profile.[18]

Now consider Figure 11.6, which shows two NPV profiles—one for Project S and one for L—and note the following points:

- The IRRs are fixed, and S has the higher IRR regardless of the cost of capital.
- However, the NPVs vary depending on the actual cost of capital.
- The two NPV profile lines cross at a cost of capital of 11.975%, which is called the **crossover rate**. The crossover rate can be found by calculating the IRR of the differences in the projects' cash flows, as demonstrated below:

	0	1	2	3	4
Project S	−$1,000	$500	$400	$300	$100
−Project L	−$1,000	$100	$300	$400	$675
$\Delta = CF_S - CF_L$	$ 0	$400	$100	−$100	−$575
IRR Δ =	11.975% = Crossover rate				

- Project L has the higher NPV if the cost of capital is less than the crossover rate, but S has the higher NPV if the cost of capital is greater than that rate.

Net Present Value Profile
A graph showing the relationship between a project's NPV and the firm's cost of capital.

Crossover Rate
The cost of capital at which the NPV profiles of two projects cross and, thus, at which the projects' NPVs are equal.

---

[17]See Brigham and Daves, *Intermediate Financial Management*, 11th edition (Mason, OH: South-Western/ Cengage Learning, 2013), pp. 466–468.
[18]Notice that the NPV profile is curved—it is *not* a straight line. NPV approaches CF_0, which is the −$1,000 project cost, as the discount rate increases toward infinity. At an infinitely high cost of capital, all the PVs of the inflows would be zero; so NPV at r = ∞ must be CF_0. We should also note that under certain conditions, the NPV profiles can cross the horizontal axis several times or never cross it. This point was discussed in Section 11-4.

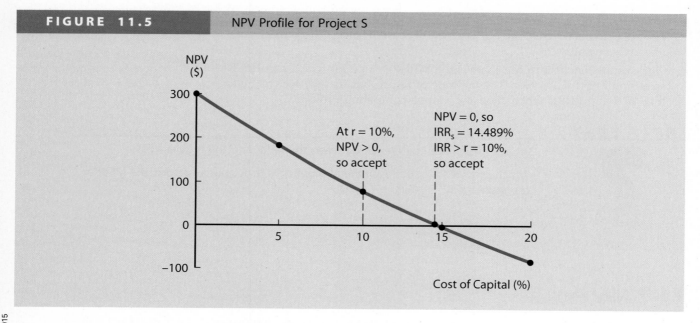

| FIGURE 11.5 | NPV Profile for Project S |

Cost of Capital	NPV$_S$
0%	$300.00
5	180.42
10	78.82
14.489	0.00 NPV = $0, so IRR = 14.489%
15	−8.33
20	−83.72

Notice that Project L has the steeper slope, indicating that a given increase in the cost of capital causes a larger decline in NPV$_L$ than in NPV$_S$. To see why this is so, recall that L's cash flows come in later than those of S. Therefore, L is a long-term project and S is a short-term project. Next, recall the equation for the NPV:

$$NPV = CF_0 + \frac{CF_1}{(1+r)^1} + \frac{CF_2}{(1+r)^2} + \cdots + \frac{CF_N}{(1+r)^N}$$

Now recognize that the impact of an increase in the cost of capital is much greater on distant than near-term cash flows, as we demonstrate here:

Effect of doubling r on a Year 1 cash flow:

$$\text{PV of \$100 due in 1 year @ } r = 5\%: \frac{\$100}{(1.05)^1} = \$95.24$$

$$\text{PV of \$100 due in 1 year @ } r = 10\%: \frac{\$100}{(1.10)^1} = \$90.91$$

$$\text{Percentage decline due to higher } r = \frac{\$95.24 - \$90.91}{\$95.24} = 4.5\%$$

Effect of doubling r on a Year 20 cash flow:

$$\text{PV of \$100 due in 20 years @ } r = 5\%: \frac{\$100}{(1.05)^{20}} = \$37.69$$

$$\text{PV of \$100 due in 20 years @ } r = 10\%: \frac{\$100}{(1.10)^{20}} = \$14.86$$

$$\text{Percentage decline due to higher } r = \frac{\$37.69 - \$14.86}{\$37.69} = 60.6\%$$

FIGURE 11.6	NPV Profiles for Projects S and L

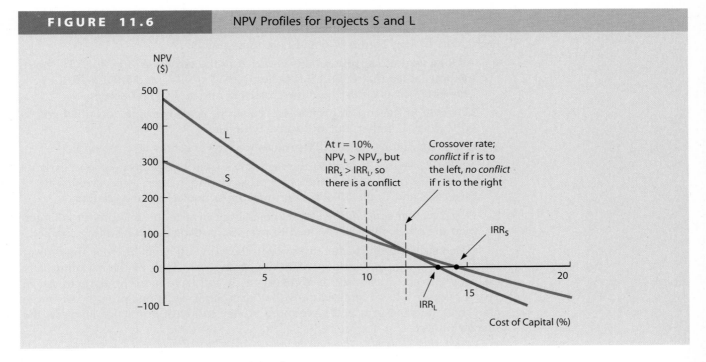

Cost of Capital	NPV_S	NPV_L
0%	$300.00	$475.00
5	180.42	268.21
10	78.82	100.40
Crossover = 11.97	42.84	42.84
IRR_L = 13.55	15.64	0.00
IRR_S = 14.49	0.00	−24.37
15	−8.33	−37.26
20	−83.72	−151.33

Thus, a doubling of the discount rate results in only a 4.5% decline in the PV of a Year 1 cash flow, but the same discount rate increase causes the PV of a Year 20 cash flow to fall by more than 60%. *Therefore, if a project has most of its cash flows coming in the later years, its NPV will decline sharply if the cost of capital increases; but a project whose cash flows come earlier will not be severely penalized by high capital costs.* Most of Project L's cash flows come in its later years; so if the cost of capital is high, L is hurt much worse than Project S. Therefore, Project L's NPV profile has the steeper slope.

Sometimes the NPV and IRR methods produce conflicting results. We can use NPV profiles to see when conflicts can and cannot arise.

If an independent project with normal cash flows is being evaluated, the NPV and IRR criteria always lead to the same accept/reject decision: If NPV says accept, IRR also says accept, and vice versa. To see why this is so, look at Figure 11.5 and notice that (1) the IRR says accept if the project's cost of capital is less than (or to the left of) the IRR and (2) if the cost of capital is less than the IRR, the NPV will be positive. Thus, at any cost of capital less than 14.489%, Project S will be recommended by both the NPV and IRR criteria; but both methods reject the project if the cost of capital is greater than 14.489%. A similar graph could be used for Project L or any other normal project, and we would always reach the same conclusion: *For normal, independent projects, if the IRR says accept, so will the NPV.*

Assume that Projects S and L are mutually exclusive rather than independent. Therefore, we can choose either S or L, or we can reject both; but we can't accept both. Now look at Figure 11.6 and note these points:

- As long as the cost of capital is *greater than* the crossover rate, 11.975%, both methods agree that Project S is better: $NPV_S > NPV_L$ and $IRR_S > IRR_L$. Therefore, if r is *greater* than the crossover rate, no conflict occurs.

- However, if the cost of capital is *less than* the crossover rate, a conflict arises: NPV ranks L higher, but IRR ranks S higher.

Two basic conditions cause NPV profiles to cross and thus lead to conflicts:[19]

1. *Timing differences.* If most of the cash flows from one project come in early while most of those from the other project come in later, as occurred with Projects S and L, the NPV profiles may cross and result in a conflict.

2. *Project size (or scale) differences.* If the amount invested in one project is larger than the other, this too can lead to profiles crossing and a resulting conflict.

When size or timing differences occur, the firm will have different amounts of funds to invest in the various years depending on which of the two mutually exclusive projects it chooses. If it chooses S, it will have more funds to invest in Year 1 because S has a higher inflow that year. Similarly, if one project costs more than the other, the firm will have more money to invest at $t = 0$ if it selects the smaller project.

Given this situation, the rate of return at which differential cash flows can be reinvested is a critical issue. We saw earlier that the NPV assumes reinvestment at the cost of capital and that this is generally the best assumption. Therefore, *when conflicts exist between mutually exclusive projects, use the NPV method.*

11-8 PAYBACK PERIOD

Payback Period

The length of time required for an investment's cash flows to cover its cost.

NPV is the most commonly used method for capital budgeting today; but historically, the first selection criterion used was the **payback period**, defined as the number of years required to recover the funds invested in a project from its cash flows. Equation 11.3 is used for the calculation, and the process is diagrammed in Figure 11.7. We start with the project's cost, a negative value, and then add the cash inflow for each year until the cumulative cash flow turns positive. The payback year is the year prior to full recovery plus a fraction equal to the shortfall at the end of that year divided by the cash flow during the full recovery year:[20]

---

[19]Of course, mutually exclusive projects can differ with respect to both scale and timing. Also, if mutually exclusive projects have different lives (as opposed to different cash flow patterns over a common life), this introduces further complications; and for meaningful comparisons, some mutually exclusive projects must be evaluated over a common life. This point is discussed later in Chapter 12 and in Web Appendix 12E on the text's website, www.cengagebrain.com.

[20]Equation 11.3 assumes that cash flows come in uniformly during the full recovery year.

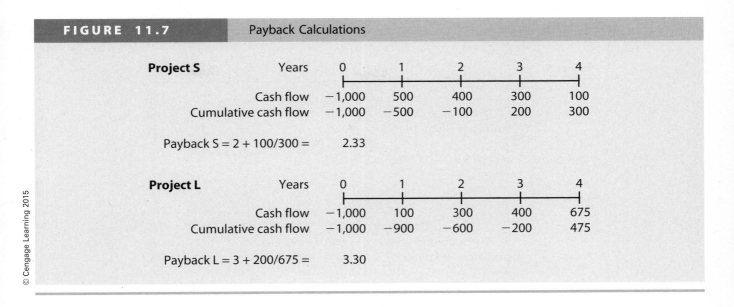

FIGURE 11.7	Payback Calculations

Project S

Years	0	1	2	3	4
Cash flow	−1,000	500	400	300	100
Cumulative cash flow	−1,000	−500	−100	200	300

Payback S = 2 + 100/300 =   2.33

Project L

Years	0	1	2	3	4
Cash flow	−1,000	100	300	400	675
Cumulative cash flow	−1,000	−900	−600	−200	475

Payback L = 3 + 200/675 =   3.30

$$\text{Payback} = \begin{array}{c}\text{Number of}\\\text{years prior to}\\\text{full recovery}\end{array} + \dfrac{\begin{array}{c}\text{Unrecovered cost}\\\text{at start of year}\end{array}}{\begin{array}{c}\text{Cash flow during}\\\text{full recovery year}\end{array}} \qquad \textbf{11.3}$$

The shorter the payback, the better the project. Therefore, if the firm requires a payback of three years or less, S would be accepted, but L would be rejected. If the projects were mutually exclusive, S would be ranked over L because of its shorter payback.

The payback has three flaws: (1) All dollars received in different years are given the same weight (i.e., the time value of money is ignored). (2) Cash flows beyond the payback year are given no consideration regardless of how large they might be. (3) Unlike the NPV, which tells us how much wealth a project adds, and the IRR, which tells us how much a project yields over the cost of capital, the payback merely tells us when we will recover our investment. There is no necessary relationship between a given payback and investor wealth maximization, so we do not know what an acceptable payback is. The firm might use 2 years, 3 years, or any other number as the minimum acceptable payback; but the choice is arbitrary.

To counter the first criticism, analysts developed the **discounted payback**. Here cash flows are discounted at the WACC; then those discounted cash flows are used to find the payback. In Figure 11.8, we calculate the discounted paybacks for S and L assuming that both have a 10% cost of capital. Each inflow is divided by $(1 + r)^t = (1.10)^t$, where t is the year in which the cash flow occurs and r is the project's cost of capital; and those PVs are used to find the payback. Project S's discounted payback is 2.95, while L's is 3.78.

Note that the payback is a "break-even" calculation in the sense that if cash flows come in at the expected rate, the project will break even. However, because the regular payback doesn't consider the cost of capital, it doesn't specify the true break-even year. The discounted payback does consider capital costs; but it still disregards cash flows beyond the payback year, which is a serious flaw. Further, if mutually exclusive projects vary in size, both payback methods can conflict with the NPV, which might lead to a poor choice. Finally, there is no way of telling how low the paybacks must be to justify project acceptance.

Although the payback methods have faults as ranking criteria, they do provide information about *liquidity* and *risk.* The shorter the payback, other things held constant, the greater the project's liquidity. This factor is often important for

Discounted Payback
The length of time required for an investment's cash flows, discounted at the investment's cost of capital, to cover its cost.

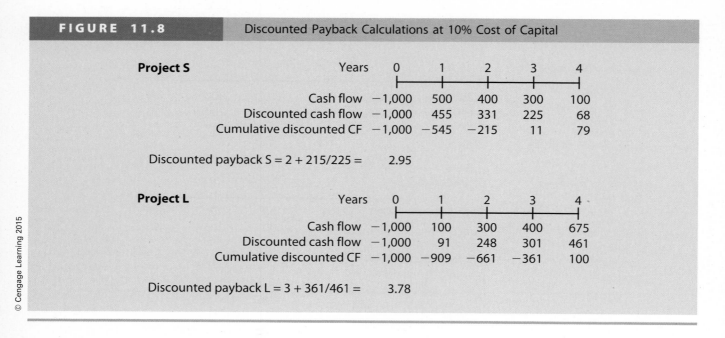

FIGURE 11.8	Discounted Payback Calculations at 10% Cost of Capital

Project S

	Years	0	1	2	3	4
Cash flow		−1,000	500	400	300	100
Discounted cash flow		−1,000	455	331	225	68
Cumulative discounted CF		−1,000	−545	−215	11	79

Discounted payback S = 2 + 215/225 =   2.95

Project L

	Years	0	1	2	3	4
Cash flow		−1,000	100	300	400	675
Discounted cash flow		−1,000	91	248	301	461
Cumulative discounted CF		−1,000	−909	−661	−361	100

Discounted payback L = 3 + 361/461 =   3.78

smaller firms that don't have ready access to the capital markets. Also, cash flows expected in the distant future are generally riskier than near-term cash flows, so the payback is used as one *risk indicator*.

SELF TEST

What information does the payback convey that is absent from the other capital budgeting decision methods?

What three flaws does the regular payback have? Does the discounted payback correct all of these flaws? Explain.

Project P has a cost of $1,000 and cash flows of $300 per year for three years plus another $1,000 in Year 4. The project's cost of capital is 15%. What are Project P's regular and discounted paybacks? **(3.10, 3.55)** If the company requires a payback of three years or less, would the project be accepted? Would this be a good accept/reject decision considering the NPV and/or the IRR? **(NPV = $256.72, IRR = 24.78%)**

11-9 CONCLUSIONS ON CAPITAL BUDGETING METHODS

We have discussed five capital budgeting decision criteria—NPV, IRR, MIRR, payback, and discounted payback. We compared these methods with one another and highlighted their strengths and weaknesses. In the process, we may have created the impression that "sophisticated" firms should use only one method, the NPV. However, virtually all capital budgeting decisions are analyzed by computer, so it is easy to calculate all five decision criteria. In making the accept/reject decision, large, sophisticated firms such as Boeing and Airbus generally calculate and consider all five measures because each provides a somewhat different piece of information about the decision.

NPV is the single best criterion because it provides a direct measure of value the project adds to shareholder wealth. IRR and MIRR measure profitability expressed as a percentage rate of return, which is useful to decision makers. Further, IRR and MIRR contain information concerning a project's "safety margin." To illustrate, consider a firm whose WACC is 10% that must choose between these two mutually exclusive projects: SS (for small), which costs $10,000 and is expected to return $16,500 at the end of one year, and LL (for large), which costs $100,000 and has an expected payoff of $115,550 after one year. SS has a huge IRR, 65%, while LL's IRR is a more modest 15.6%. The NPV paints a somewhat different picture—at the 10% cost of capital, SS's NPV is $5,000 while LL's is $5,045. By the NPV rule, we would choose LL. However, SS's IRR indicates that it has a much larger margin for error: Even if its cash flow was 39% below the $16,500 forecast, the firm would still recover its $10,000 investment. On the other hand, if LL's inflows fell by only 13.5% from its forecasted $115,550, the firm would not recover its investment. Further, if neither project generated any cash flows, the firm would lose only $10,000 on SS but $100,000 if it accepted LL.

The modified IRR has all the virtues of the IRR, but it incorporates a better reinvestment rate assumption and avoids the multiple rate of return problem. So if decision makers want to know projects' rates of return, the MIRR is a better indicator than the regular IRR.

Payback and discounted payback provide indications of a project's *liquidity* and *risk*. A long payback means that investment dollars will be locked up for a long time; hence, the project is relatively illiquid. In addition, a long payback means that cash flows must be forecasted far out into the future, and that probably makes the project riskier than one with a shorter payback. A good analogy for this is bond valuation. An investor should never compare the yields to maturity on two bonds without also considering their terms to maturity because a bond's risk is significantly influenced by the number of years remaining until its maturity. The same holds true for capital projects.

In summary, the different measures provide different types of information. Because it is easy to calculate all of them, all should be considered when capital budgeting decisions are being made. For most decisions, the greatest weight should be given to the NPV, but it would be foolish to ignore the information provided by the other criteria.

SELF TEST

Describe the advantages and disadvantages of the five capital budgeting methods discussed in this chapter.

Should capital budgeting decisions be made solely on the basis of a project's NPV? Explain.

11-10 Decision Criteria Used in Practice

Surveys designed to find out which of the criteria managers actually use have been taken over the years. Surveys prior to 1999 asked companies to indicate which method they gave the most weight, while the most recent survey, in 1999, asked what method(s) managers actually calculated and used. A summary of all these surveys is shown in Table 11.2, and it reveals some interesting trends.

First, the NPV criterion was not used significantly before 1980; but by 1999, it was close to the top in usage. Moreover, informal discussions with companies suggest that if a survey were to be taken in 2013, NPV would be at the top of this

TABLE 11.2 Capital Budgeting Methods Used in Practice

	Primary Criterion			Calculate and Use
	1960	**1970**	**1980**	**1999**
NPV	0%	0%	15%	75%
IRR	20	60	65	76
Payback	35	15	5	57
Discounted Payback	NA	NA	NA	29
Other	45	25	15	NA
Totals	100%	100%	100%	

Sources: The 1999 data are from John R. Graham and Campbell R. Harvey, "The Theory and Practice of Corporate Finance: Evidence from the Field," *Journal of Financial Economics*, vol. 60, nos. 2 and 3 (2001), pp. 187–244. Data from prior years are our estimates based on averaging data from these studies: J. S. Moore and A. K. Reichert, "An Analysis of the Financial Management Techniques Currently Employed by Large U.S. Corporations," *Journal of Business Finance and Accounting*, vol. 10, no. 4 (Winter 1983), pp. 623–645; and M. T. Stanley and S. R. Block, "A Survey of Multinational Capital Budgeting," *The Financial Review*, vol. 19, no. 1 (March 1984), pp. 36–51.

list. Second, the IRR method is widely used, but its recent growth is less dramatic than that of NPV. Third, payback was the most important criterion years ago, but its use as the primary criterion had fallen drastically by 1980. Companies still use payback because it is easy to calculate and it does provide some information, but it is rarely used today as the primary criterion. Fourth, "other methods," primarily the accounting rate of return and the profitability index, have been fading due to the increased use of IRR and especially NPV.

These trends are consistent with our evaluation of the various methods. NPV is the best single criterion, but all of the methods provide useful information and all are easy to calculate; thus, all are used, along with judgment and common sense. We will have more to say about all this in the next chapter.

SELF TEST

What trends in capital budgeting methodology can be seen from Table 11.2?

TYING IT ALL TOGETHER

In this chapter, we described five techniques—NPV, IRR, MIRR, payback, and discounted payback—that are used to evaluate proposed capital budgeting projects. NPV is the best single measure as it tells us how much value each project contributes to shareholder wealth. Therefore, NPV is the method that should be given the greatest weight in capital budgeting decisions. However, the other approaches provide useful information; and in this age of computers, it is easy to calculate all of them. Therefore, managers generally look at all five criteria when deciding to accept or reject projects and when choosing among mutually exclusive projects.

In this chapter, we took the cash flows given and used them to illustrate the different capital budgeting methods. As you will see in the next chapter, estimating cash flows is a major task. Still, the framework established in this chapter is critically important for sound capital budgeting analyses; and at this point, you should:

- Understand capital budgeting.
- Know how to calculate and use the major capital budgeting decision criteria, which are NPV, IRR, MIRR, and payback.
- Understand why NPV is the best criterion and how it overcomes problems inherent in the other methods.
- Recognize that while NPV is the best method, the other methods do provide information that decision makers find useful.

SELF-TEST QUESTIONS AND PROBLEMS

(Solutions Appear in Appendix A)

ST-1 **KEY TERMS** Define the following terms:
  a. Capital budgeting; strategic business plan
  b. Net present value (NPV)
  c. Internal rate of return (IRR)
  d. NPV profile; crossover rate
  e. Mutually exclusive projects; independent projects
  f. Nonnormal cash flows; normal cash flows; multiple IRRs
  g. Modified internal rate of return (MIRR)
  h. Payback period; discounted payback

ST-2 **CAPITAL BUDGETING CRITERIA** You must analyze two projects, X and Y. Each project costs $10,000, and the firm's WACC is 12%. The expected cash flows are as follows:

	0	1	2	3	4
Project X	−$10,000	$6,500	$3,000	$3,000	$1,000
Project Y	−$10,000	$3,500	$3,500	$3,500	$3,500

  a. Calculate each project's NPV, IRR, MIRR, payback, and discounted payback.
  b. Which project(s) should be accepted if they are independent?
  c. Which project(s) should be accepted if they are mutually exclusive?
  d. How might a change in the WACC produce a conflict between the NPV and IRR rankings of the two projects? Would there be a conflict if WACC were 5%? (Hint: Plot the NPV profiles. The crossover rate is 6.21875%.)
  e. Why does the conflict exist?

QUESTIONS

11-1   How are project classifications used in the capital budgeting process?

11-2   What are three potential flaws with the regular payback method? Does the discounted payback method correct all three flaws? Explain.

11-3   Why is the NPV of a relatively long-term project (one for which a high percentage of its cash flows occurs in the distant future) more sensitive to changes in the WACC than that of a short-term project?

11-4   What is a mutually exclusive project? How should managers rank mutually exclusive projects?

11-5   If two mutually exclusive projects were being compared, would a high cost of capital favor the longer-term or the shorter-term project? Why? If the cost of capital declined, would that lead firms to invest more in longer-term projects or shorter-term projects? Would a decline (or an increase) in the WACC cause changes in the IRR ranking of mutually exclusive projects? Explain.

11-6   Discuss the following statement: If a firm has only independent projects, a constant WACC, and projects with normal cash flows, the NPV and IRR methods will always lead to identical capital budgeting decisions. What does this imply about the choice between IRR and NPV? If each of the assumptions were changed (one by one), how would your answer change?

11-7   Why might it be rational for a small firm that does not have access to the capital markets to use the payback method rather than the NPV method?

11-8   Project X is very risky and has an NPV of $3 million. Project Y is very safe and has an NPV of $2.5 million. They are mutually exclusive, and project risk has been properly considered in the NPV analyses. Which project should be chosen? Explain.

11-9   What reinvestment rate assumptions are built into the NPV, IRR, and MIRR methods? Give an explanation for your answer.

11-10 A firm has a $100 million capital budget. It is considering two projects, each costing $100 million. Project A has an IRR of 20% and an NPV of $9 million; it will be terminated after 1 year at a profit of $20 million, resulting in an immediate increase in EPS. Project B, which cannot be postponed, has an IRR of 30% and an NPV of $50 million. However, the firm's short-run EPS will be reduced if it accepts Project B because no revenues will be generated for several years.

   a.   Should the short-run effects on EPS influence the choice between the two projects?

   b.   How might situations like this influence a firm's decision to use payback?

PROBLEMS

Easy Problems 1–6

11-1   **NPV**   Project K costs $52,125, its expected cash inflows are $12,000 per year for 8 years, and its WACC is 12%. What is the project's NPV?

11-2   **IRR**   Refer to Problem 11-1. What is the project's IRR?

11-3   **MIRR**   Refer to Problem 11-1. What is the project's MIRR?

11-4   **PAYBACK PERIOD**   Refer to Problem 11-1. What is the project's payback?

11-5   **DISCOUNTED PAYBACK**   Refer to Problem 11-1. What is the project's discounted payback?

11-6   **NPV**   Your division is considering two projects with the following cash flows (in millions):

	0	1	2	3
Project A	−$25	$5	$10	$17
Project B	−$20	$10	$9	$6

   a.   What are the projects' NPVs assuming the WACC is 5%? 10%? 15%?

   b.   What are the projects' IRRs at each of these WACCs?

   c.   If the WACC was 5% and A and B were mutually exclusive, which project would you choose? What if the WACC was 10%? 15%? (Hint: The crossover rate is 7.81%.)

11-7 **CAPITAL BUDGETING CRITERIA** A firm with a 14% WACC is evaluating two projects for this year's capital budget. After-tax cash flows, including depreciation, are as follows:

	0	1	2	3	4	5
Project A	−$6,000	$2,000	$2,000	$2,000	$2,000	$2,000
Project B	−$18,000	$5,600	$5,600	$5,600	$5,600	$5,600

a. Calculate NPV, IRR, MIRR, payback, and discounted payback for each project.
b. Assuming the projects are independent, which one(s) would you recommend?
c. If the projects are mutually exclusive, which would you recommend?
d. Notice that the projects have the same cash flow timing pattern. Why is there a conflict between NPV and IRR?

11-8 **CAPITAL BUDGETING CRITERIA: ETHICAL CONSIDERATIONS** A mining company is considering a new project. Because the mine has received a permit, the project would be legal; but it would cause significant harm to a nearby river. The firm could spend an additional $10 million at Year 0 to mitigate the environmental problem, but it would not be required to do so. Developing the mine (without mitigation) would cost $60 million, and the expected cash inflows would be $20 million per year for 5 years. If the firm does invest in mitigation, the annual inflows would be $21 million. The risk-adjusted WACC is 12%.

a. Calculate the NPV and IRR with and without mitigation.
b. How should the environmental effects be dealt with when this project is evaluated?
c. Should this project be undertaken? If so, should the firm do the mitigation?

11-9 **CAPITAL BUDGETING CRITERIA: ETHICAL CONSIDERATIONS** An electric utility is considering a new power plant in northern Arizona. Power from the plant would be sold in the Phoenix area, where it is badly needed. Because the firm has received a permit, the plant would be legal; but it would cause some air pollution. The company could spend an additional $40 million at Year 0 to mitigate the environmental problem, but it would not be required to do so. The plant without mitigation would cost $240 million, and the expected cash inflows would be $80 million per year for 5 years. If the firm does invest in mitigation, the annual inflows would be $84 million. Unemployment in the area where the plant would be built is high, and the plant would provide about 350 good jobs. The risk-adjusted WACC is 17%.

a. Calculate the NPV and IRR with and without mitigation.
b. How should the environmental effects be dealt with when evaluating this project?
c. Should this project be undertaken? If so, should the firm do the mitigation? Why or why not?

11-10 **CAPITAL BUDGETING CRITERIA: MUTUALLY EXCLUSIVE PROJECTS** A firm with a WACC of 10% is considering the following mutually exclusive projects:

	0	1	2	3	4	5
Project A	−$400	$55	$55	$55	$225	$225
Project B	−$600	$300	$300	$50	$50	$49

Which project would you recommend? Explain.

11-11 **CAPITAL BUDGETING CRITERIA: MUTUALLY EXCLUSIVE PROJECTS** Project S costs $15,000, and its expected cash flows would be $4,500 per year for 5 years. Mutually exclusive Project L costs $37,500, and its expected cash flows would be $11,100 per year for 5 years. If both projects have a WACC of 14%, which project would you recommend? Explain.

11-12 **IRR AND NPV** A company is analyzing two mutually exclusive projects, S and L, with the following cash flows:

	0	1	2	3	4
Project S	−$1,000	$900	$250	$10	$10
Project L	−$1,000	$0	$250	$400	$800

The company's WACC is 10%. What is the IRR of the *better* project? (Hint: The better project may or may not be the one with the higher IRR.)

11-13 **MIRR**   A firm is considering two mutually exclusive projects, X and Y, with the following cash flows:

	0	1	2	3	4
Project X	−$1,000	$100	$300	$400	$700
Project Y	−$1,000	$1,000	$100	$50	$50

The projects are equally risky, and their WACC is 12%. What is the MIRR of the project that maximizes shareholder value?

Challenging Problems 14–22

11-14 **CHOOSING MANDATORY PROJECTS ON THE BASIS OF LEAST COST**   Kim Inc. must install a new air conditioning unit in its main plant. Kim must install one or the other of the units; otherwise, the highly profitable plant would have to shut down. Two units are available, HCC and LCC (for high and low capital costs, respectively). HCC has a high capital cost but relatively low operating costs, while LCC has a low capital cost but higher operating costs because it uses more electricity. The costs of the units are shown here. Kim's WACC is 7%.

	0	1	2	3	4	5
HCC	−$600,000	−$50,000	−$50,000	−$50,000	−$50,000	−$50,000
LCC	−$100,000	−$175,000	−$175,000	−$175,000	−$175,000	−$175,000

a.   Which unit would you recommend? Explain.

b.   If Kim's controller wanted to know the IRRs of the two projects, what would you tell him?

c.   If the WACC rose to 15% would this affect your recommendation? Explain your answer and the reason this result occurred.

11-15 **NPV PROFILES: TIMING DIFFERENCES**   An oil-drilling company must choose between two mutually exclusive extraction projects, and each costs $12 million. Under Plan A, all the oil would be extracted in 1 year, producing a cash flow at $t = 1$ of $14.4 million. Under Plan B, cash flows would be $2.1 million per year for 20 years. The firm's WACC is 12%.

a.   Construct NPV profiles for Plans A and B, identify each project's IRR, and show the approximate crossover rate.

b.   Is it logical to assume that the firm would take on all available independent, average-risk projects with returns greater than 12%? If all available projects with returns greater than 12% have been undertaken, does this mean that cash flows from past investments have an opportunity cost of only 12% because all the company can do with these cash flows is to replace money that has a cost of 12%? Does this imply that the WACC is the correct reinvestment rate assumption for a project's cash flows? Why or why not?

11-16 **NPV PROFILES: SCALE DIFFERENCES**   A company is considering two mutually exclusive expansion plans. Plan A requires a $40 million expenditure on a large-scale integrated plant that would provide expected cash flows of $6.4 million per year for 20 years. Plan B requires a $12 million expenditure to build a somewhat less efficient, more labor-intensive plant with expected cash flows of $2.72 million per year for 20 years. The firm's WACC is 10%.

a.   Calculate each project's NPV and IRR.

b.   Graph the NPV profiles for Plan A and Plan B and approximate the crossover rate.

c.   Calculate the crossover rate where the two projects' NPVs are equal.

d.   Why is NPV better than IRR for making capital budgeting decisions that add to shareholder value?

11-17 **CAPITAL BUDGETING CRITERIA**   A company has a 12% WACC and is considering two mutually exclusive investments (that cannot be repeated) with the following cash flows:

	0	1	2	3	4	5	6	7
Project A	−$300	−$387	−$193	−$100	$600	$600	$850	−$180
Project B	−$405	$134	$134	$134	$134	$134	$134	$0

    a.   What is each project's NPV?

    b.   What is each project's IRR?

    c.   What is each project's MIRR? (Hint: Consider Period 7 as the end of Project B's life.)

    d.   From your answers to Parts a, b, and c, which project would be selected? If the WACC was 18%, which project would be selected?

    e.   Construct NPV profiles for Projects A and B.

    f.   Calculate the crossover rate where the two projects' NPVs are equal.

    g.   What is each project's MIRR at a WACC of 18%?

11-18   **NPV AND IRR**   A store has 5 years remaining on its lease in a mall. Rent is $2,000 per month, 60 payments remain, and the next payment is due in 1 month. The mall's owner plans to sell the property in a year and wants rent at that time to be high so that the property will appear more valuable. Therefore, the store has been offered a "great deal" (owner's words) on a new 5-year lease. The new lease calls for no rent for 9 months, then payments of $2,600 per month for the next 51 months. The lease cannot be broken, and the store's WACC is 12% (or 1% per month).

    a.   Should the new lease be accepted? (Hint: Make sure you use 1% per month.)

    b.   If the store owner decided to bargain with the mall's owner over the new lease payment, what new lease payment would make the store owner indifferent between the new and old leases? (Hint: Find FV of the old lease's original cost at t = 9; then treat this as the PV of a 51-period annuity whose payments represent the rent during months 10 to 60.)

    c.   The store owner is not sure of the 12% WACC—it could be higher or lower. At what *nominal* WACC would the store owner be indifferent between the two leases? (Hint: Calculate the differences between the two payment streams; then find its IRR.)

11-19   **MULTIPLE IRRS AND MIRR**   A mining company is deciding whether to open a strip mine, which costs $2 million. Cash inflows of $13 million would occur at the end of Year 1. The land must be returned to its natural state at a cost of $12 million, payable at the end of Year 2.

    a.   Plot the project's NPV profile.

    b.   Should the project be accepted if WACC = 10%? if WACC = 20%? Explain your reasoning.

    c.   Think of some other capital budgeting situations in which negative cash flows during or at the end of the project's life might lead to multiple IRRs.

    d.   What is the project's MIRR at WACC = 10%? At WACC = 20%? Does MIRR lead to the same accept/reject decision for this project as the NPV method? Does the MIRR method *always* lead to the same accept/reject decision as NPV? (Hint: Consider mutually exclusive projects that differ in size.)

11-20   **NPV**   A project has annual cash flows of $7,500 for the next 10 years and then $10,000 each year for the following 10 years. The IRR of this 20-year project is 10.98%. If the firm's WACC is 9%, what is the project's NPV?

11-21   **MIRR**   Project X costs $1,000, and its cash flows are the same in Years 1 through 10. Its IRR is 12%, and its WACC is 10%. What is the project's MIRR?

11-22   **MIRR**   A project has the following cash flows:

This project requires two outflows at Years 0 and 2, but the remaining cash flows are positive. Its WACC is 10%, and its MIRR is 14.14%. What is the Year 2 cash outflow?

COMPREHENSIVE/SPREADSHEET PROBLEM

11-23 **CAPITAL BUDGETING CRITERIA** Your division is considering two projects. Its WACC is 10%, and the projects' after-tax cash flows (in millions of dollars) would be as follows:

	0	1	2	3	4
Project A	−$30	$5	$10	$15	$20
Project B	−$30	$20	$10	$8	$6

a. Calculate the projects' NPVs, IRRs, MIRRs, regular paybacks, and discounted paybacks.

b. If the two projects are independent, which project(s) should be chosen?

c. If the two projects are mutually exclusive and the WACC is 10%, which project(s) should be chosen?

d. Plot NPV profiles for the two projects. Identify the projects' IRRs on the graph.

e. If the WACC was 5%, would this change your recommendation if the projects were mutually exclusive? If the WACC was 15%, would this change your recommendation? Explain your answers.

f. The crossover rate is 13.5252%. Explain what this rate is and how it affects the choice between mutually exclusive projects.

g. Is it possible for conflicts to exist between the NPV and the IRR when *independent* projects are being evaluated? Explain your answer.

h. Now look at the regular and discounted paybacks. Which project looks better when judged by the paybacks?

i. If the payback was the only method a firm used to accept or reject projects, what payback should it choose as the cutoff point, that is, reject projects if their paybacks are not below the chosen cutoff? Is your selected cutoff based on some economic criteria, or is it more or less arbitrary? Are the cutoff criteria equally arbitrary when firms use the NPV and/or the IRR as the criteria? Explain.

j. Define the MIRR. What's the difference between the IRR and the MIRR, and which generally gives a better idea of the rate of return on the investment in a project? Explain.

k. Why do most academics and financial executives regard the NPV as being the single best criterion and better than the IRR? Why do companies still calculate IRRs?

INTEGRATED CASE

ALLIED COMPONENTS COMPANY

11-24 **BASICS OF CAPITAL BUDGETING** You recently went to work for Allied Components Company, a supplier of auto repair parts used in the after-market with products from Daimler AG, Ford, Toyota, and other automakers. Your boss, the chief financial officer (CFO), has just handed you the estimated cash flows for two proposed projects. Project L involves adding a new item to the firm's ignition system line; it would take some time to build up the market for this product, so the cash inflows would increase over time. Project S involves an add-on to an existing line, and its cash flows would decrease over time. Both projects have 3-year lives because Allied is planning to introduce entirely new models after 3 years.

Here are the projects' after-tax cash flows (in thousands of dollars):

	0	1	2	3
Project L	−$100	$10	$60	$80
Project S	−$100	$70	$50	$20

Depreciation, salvage values, net operating working capital requirements, and tax effects are all included in these cash flows. The CFO also made subjective risk assessments of each project, and he concluded that both projects have risk characteristics that are similar to the firm's average project. Allied's WACC is 10%. You must determine whether one or both of the projects should be accepted.

a. What is capital budgeting? Are there any similarities between a firm's capital budgeting decisions and an individual's investment decisions?

b. What is the difference between independent and mutually exclusive projects? Between projects with normal and nonnormal cash flows?

c. 1. Define the term *net present value (NPV)*. What is each project's NPV?

    2. What is the rationale behind the NPV method? According to NPV, which project(s) should be accepted if they are independent? Mutually exclusive?

    3. Would the NPVs change if the WACC changed? Explain.

d. 1. Define the term *internal rate of return (IRR)*. What is each project's IRR?

    2. How is the IRR on a project related to the YTM on a bond?

    3. What is the logic behind the IRR method? According to IRR, which project(s) should be accepted if they are independent? Mutually exclusive?

    4. Would the projects' IRRs change if the WACC changed?

e. 1. Draw NPV profiles for Projects L and S. At what discount rate do the profiles cross?

    2. Look at your NPV profile graph without referring to the actual NPVs and IRRs. Which project(s) should be accepted if they are independent? Mutually exclusive? Explain. Are your answers correct at any WACC less than 23.6%?

f. 1. What is the underlying cause of ranking conflicts between NPV and IRR?

    2. What is the reinvestment rate assumption, and how does it affect the NPV versus IRR conflict?

    3. Which method is best? Why?

g. 1. Define the term *modified IRR (MIRR)*. Find the MIRRs for Projects L and S.

    2. What are the MIRR's advantages and disadvantages as compared to the NPV?

h. 1. What is the payback period? Find the paybacks for Projects L and S.

    2. What is the rationale for the payback method? According to the payback criterion, which project(s) should be accepted if the firm's maximum acceptable payback is 2 years, if Projects L and S are independent? If Projects L and S are mutually exclusive?

    3. What is the difference between the regular and discounted payback methods?

    4. What are the two main disadvantages of discounted payback? Is the payback method useful in capital budgeting decisions? Explain.

i. As a separate project (Project P), the firm is considering sponsoring a pavilion at the upcoming World's Fair. The pavilion would cost $800,000, and it is expected to result in $5 million of incremental cash inflows during its 1 year of operation. However, it would then take another year, and $5 million of costs, to demolish the site and return it to its original condition. Thus, Project P's expected cash flows (in millions of dollars) look like this:

The project is estimated to be of average risk, so its WACC is 10%.

    1. What is Project P's NPV? What is its IRR? Its MIRR?

    2. Draw Project P's NPV profile. Does Project P have normal or nonnormal cash flows? Should this project be accepted? Explain.

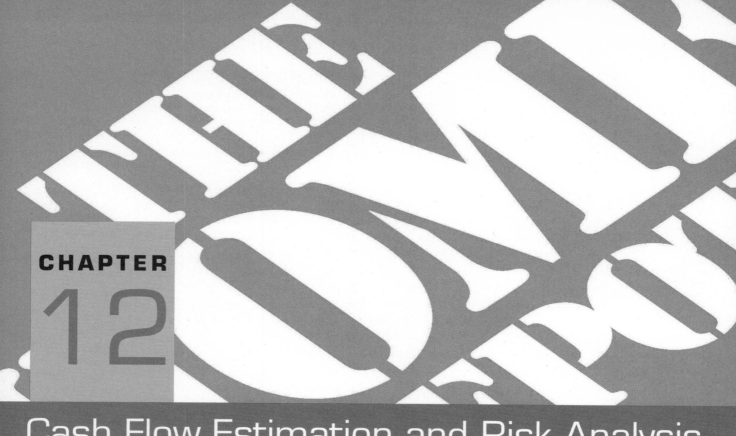

CHAPTER 12

Cash Flow Estimation and Risk Analysis

Home Depot Carefully Evaluates New Investments

Home Depot (HD) has grown phenomenally over the past two decades. At the beginning of 1990, HD had 118 stores with annual sales of $2.8 billion. By early 2013, it had 2,256 stores and annual sales of $75 billion. Stockholders have benefited mightily from this growth as the stock's price has increased from a split-adjusted $1.87 in 1990 to $73 in May 2013.

However, during this time period, the news has not always been good. As you might expect, the company struggled in 2008 and 2009 in the midst of the financial crisis and a declining housing market. Discussing its struggles in its 2009 Annual Report, the company's management made the following observations:

> In fiscal 2008, the Company reduced its square footage growth plans to improve free cash flow, provide stronger returns for the

Company, and invest in its existing stores to continue improving the customer experience. As a result of this store rationalization plan, the Company determined that it would no longer pursue the opening of approximately 50 U.S. stores that had been in its new store pipeline. The Company expects to dispose of or sublet these pipeline locations over varying periods. The Company also closed 15 underperforming U.S. stores in the second quarter of fiscal 2008, and the Company expects to dispose of or sublet those locations over varying periods.

In the years since this annual report was released, the company slowly continues to open new stores in areas it thinks the stores will thrive. For example in 2012, it opened three new stores in the United States (one of which was a relocation), it opened nine stores in

Mexico, and it closed seven stores in China. So it is clear that Home Depot is being very careful when it comes to evaluating new investments. This caution is understandable: It costs several million dollars to purchase land, construct a new store, and stock it with inventory. Therefore, it is critical that the company perform a financial analysis to determine whether a potential store's expected cash flows will cover its costs.

Home Depot uses information from its existing stores to forecast the new stores' expected cash flows. Thus far, its forecasts have been outstanding, but there are always risks. First, a store's sales might be less than projected, especially if the economy weakens. Second, some of HD's customers might bypass the store altogether and buy directly from manufacturers through the Internet. Third, its new stores could "cannibalize," or take sales away from, its existing stores.

Rational expansion decisions require detailed assessments of the forecasted cash flows, along with a measure of the risk that forecasted sales might not be realized. That information can then be used to determine the risk-adjusted NPV associated with each potential project. In this chapter, we describe techniques for estimating projects' cash flows, as well as projects' risks. Companies such as Home Depot use these techniques on a regular basis when making capital budgeting decisions.

PUTTING THINGS IN PERSPECTIVE

The basic principles of capital budgeting were covered in Chapter 11. Given a project's expected cash flows, it is easy to calculate the primary decision criterion—the NPV—as well as the supplemental criteria, IRR, MIRR, payback, and discounted payback. However, in the real world, cash flow values are not just handed to you—rather, they must be estimated based on information from various sources. Moreover, uncertainty surrounds the forecasted cash flows, and some projects are more uncertain and thus riskier than others. In this chapter, we review examples that illustrate how project cash flows are estimated, discuss techniques for measuring and then dealing with risk, and discuss how projects are evaluated once they begin operation.

When you finish this chapter, you should be able to:

- Identify "relevant" cash flows that should and should not be included in a capital budgeting analysis.
- Estimate a project's relevant cash flows and put them into a time line format that can be used to calculate a project's NPV, IRR, and other capital budgeting metrics.
- Explain how risk is measured, and use this measure to adjust the firm's WACC to account for differential project riskiness.
- Discuss how some projects can be altered after they have been accepted, and how these alterations can change a project's cash flows and thus its realized NPV.
- Describe the post-audit, which is an important part of the capital budgeting process, and discuss its relevance in capital budgeting decisions.

12-1 CONCEPTUAL ISSUES IN CASH FLOW ESTIMATION

Before the cash flow estimation process is illustrated, we need to discuss several important conceptual issues. A failure to handle these issues properly can lead to calculating incorrect project NPVs, which will lead to bad capital budgeting decisions.

12-1A FREE CASH FLOW VERSUS ACCOUNTING INCOME

In the last chapter, we showed that a project's NPV is equal to the present value of its discounted free cash flows. Recall from Chapters 3 and 9 that free cash flow is defined as:

$$\text{FCF} = \left[\text{EBIT}(1-T) + \begin{array}{c} \text{Depreciation} \\ \text{and amortization} \end{array} \right] - \left[\begin{array}{c} \text{Capital} \\ \text{expenditures} \end{array} + \begin{array}{c} \Delta\text{Net operating} \\ \text{working capital} \end{array} \right]$$

A typical project will require the firm to spend money up-front at $t = 0$ to make the necessary investments in fixed assets and net operating working capital. In some cases, the firm may also need to make continued investments throughout the life of the project, particularly for a growing project where the company needs to steadily add fixed assets and inventory over time. For simplicity, unless otherwise stated, we will assume that investments in fixed assets and net operating working capital will occur only at $t = 0$.

After the initial investments are made, the project will hopefully produce positive cash flows over its operating life. The first bracketed term in the free cash flow equation [EBIT(1 − T) + Depreciation and amortization] represents the project's operating cash flows. In most cases, these cash flows will vary over the life of the project.

Once the project is completed, the company sells the project's fixed assets and inventory and receives cash.[1] In some respects, we can think of the sale of fixed assets at the end of the project as a negative capital expenditure—instead of using cash to purchase fixed assets, the company is selling the assets to generate cash.

The price that the company receives for a fixed asset at the end of the project is often referred to as its *salvage value.* The company will also have to pay taxes if the asset's salvage value exceeds its book value. More specifically:

Taxes paid on salvaged assets = Tax rate × (Salvage value − Book value)

Here the book value equals the initial price for the asset minus the asset's total accumulated depreciation. While depreciation is not a cash expense, it does affect the company's taxes. For this reason, what matters is the depreciation rate that the firm's accountants use for tax purposes. In many cases, these depreciation rates and salvage values may be considerably different from the values used in GAAP accounting to report accounting income in the firm's financial statements. Note, that the equation above indicates that the taxes paid would be negative (i.e., the firm would receive a tax credit) if the company sold the asset for less than its book value.

As we mentioned above, a project will generally require an initial increase in NOWC. Assume that Home Depot is considering a project to open a new store. The company estimates that it will need $5 million in new inventory to stock the store, $3 million of that inventory will be financed through new accounts payable, and the remaining $2 million will be paid in cash. If all other working capital components remain constant, the project will increase the company's current operating assets by $5 million and increase the company's current operating liabilities by $3 million. The resulting change in NOWC is the $2 million in cash that is necessary to open the store. If the amount of inventory and accounts payable remain constant over time, there will be no additional changes in NOWC over the life of the project. Once the project is completed (the store is closed), the final $5 million in inventory will be sold and the company will pay off its remaining $3 million in accounts payable. The firm will receive the remaining

---

[1]In many cases, these fixed assets and inventory are "sold" within the company for use in other projects. In these instances, the company would establish the price that the old project would charge the new project. These "transfer prices" are important, and well-run companies work hard to make sure that they are fairly set to insure that assets are efficiently transferred within the company.

$2 million in cash, which corresponds to the investment made for the change in NOWC that was required when the project began.

12-1b TIMING OF CASH FLOWS

In theory, capital budgeting analyses should deal with cash flows exactly when they occur; hence, daily cash flows theoretically would be better than annual flows. However, it would be costly to estimate and analyze daily cash flows, and they would probably be no more accurate than annual estimates because we simply cannot accurately forecast at a daily level out 10 years or so into the future. Therefore, we generally assume that all cash flows occur at the end of the year. Note, however, for projects with highly predictable cash flows, it might be useful to assume that cash flows occur at midyear (or even quarterly or monthly); but for most purposes, we assume end-of-year flows.

12-1c INCREMENTAL CASH FLOWS

Incremental cash flows are flows that will occur *if and only if* some specific event occurs. In capital budgeting, the event is the firm's acceptance of a project and the project's incremental cash flows are ones that occur as a result of this decision. Cash flows such as investments in buildings, equipment, and working capital needed for the project are obviously incremental, as are sales revenues and operating costs associated with the project. However, some items are not so obvious, as we explain later in this section.

Incremental Cash Flow
A cash flow that will occur if and only if the firm takes on a project.

12-1d REPLACEMENT PROJECTS

Two types of projects can be distinguished: expansion projects, where the firm makes an investment, such as a new Home Depot store, and replacement projects, where the firm replaces existing assets, generally to reduce costs. For example, suppose Home Depot is considering replacing some of its delivery trucks. The benefit would be lower fuel and maintenance expenses, and the shiny new trucks also might improve the company's image and reduce pollution. Replacement analysis is complicated by the fact that almost all of the cash flows are incremental, found by subtracting the new cost numbers from the old numbers. Thus, the fuel bill for a more efficient new truck might be $10,000 per year versus $15,000 for the old truck. The $5,000 savings is the incremental cash flow that would be used in the replacement analysis. Similarly, we would need to find the difference in depreciation and other factors that affect cash flows. Once we have found the incremental cash flows, we use them in a "regular" NPV analysis to decide whether to replace the asset or to continue using it.

12-1e SUNK COSTS

A **sunk cost** is an outlay that was incurred in the past and cannot be recovered in the future regardless of whether the project under consideration is accepted. In capital budgeting, we are concerned with *future incremental cash flows*—we want to know if the *new* investment will produce enough incremental cash flow to justify the incremental investment. *Because sunk costs were incurred in the past and cannot be recovered regardless of whether the project is accepted or rejected, they are not relevant in the capital budgeting analysis.*

Sunk Cost
A cash outlay that has already been incurred and that cannot be recovered regardless of whether the project is accepted or rejected.

To illustrate this concept, suppose Home Depot spent $2 million to investigate a potential new store and obtain the permits required to build it. That $2 million would be a sunk cost—the money is gone, and it won't come back regardless of whether or not the new store is built.

Not handling sunk costs properly can lead to incorrect decisions. For example, suppose Home Depot completed the analysis and found that it must spend an additional $17 million, on top of the $2 million site study, to open the store.

Suppose it then used as the required investment $19 million and calculated the new store's projected NPV as *negative* $1 million. This would indicate that HD should reject the new store. *However, that would be a bad decision.* The real issue is whether the *incremental* $17 million would result in *incremental* cash inflows sufficient to produce a positive NPV. If the $2 million sunk cost is disregarded, as it should be, the new store's true NPV will be a *positive* $1 million. Therefore, the failure to deal properly with the sunk cost would lead to turning down a project that would add $1 million to stockholders' value.

12-1F OPPORTUNITY COSTS ASSOCIATED WITH ASSETS THE FIRM OWNS

Opportunity Costs
The best return that could be earned on assets the firm already owns if those assets are not used for the new project.

Another issue relates to **opportunity costs** associated with assets the firm already owns. For example, suppose Home Depot owns land with a market value of $2 million and that land will be used for the new store if HD decides to build it. If HD decides to go forward with the project, only another $15 million will be required, not the typical $17 million because HD would not need to buy the required land. Does this mean that HD should use $15 million as the cost of the new store? The answer is no. If the new store is not built, HD could sell the land and receive a cash flow of $2 million. This $2 million is an *opportunity cost*—something that HD would not receive if the land was used for the new store. Therefore, the $2 million must be charged to the new project, and a failure to do so would artificially and incorrectly increase the new project's NPV.

Consider further the following example. Assume that a firm owns a building and equipment with a market (resale) value of $10 million. The property is not being used, and the firm is considering using it for a new project. The only required additional investment would be $100,000 for working capital, and the new project would produce a cash inflow of $50,000 forever. If the firm has a WACC of 10% and evaluates the project using only the $100,000 of working capital as the required investment, it would find an NPV of $50,000/0.10 = $500,000. Does this mean that the project is a good one? The answer is no. The firm can sell the property for $10 million, which is a much larger amount than $500,000.

12-1G EXTERNALITIES

Externality
An effect on the firm or the environment that is not reflected in the project's cash flows.

Another potential problem involves **externalities**, which are defined as the effects of a project on other parts of the firm or the environment. The three types of externalities—negative within-firm externalities, positive within-firm externalities, and environmental externalities—are explained next.

Negative Within-Firm Externalities

Cannibalization
The situation when a new project reduces cash flows that the firm would otherwise have had.

As noted earlier, when retailers, such as Home Depot, open new stores that are too close to their existing stores, this takes customers away from their existing stores. In this case, even though the new store has positive cash flows, its existence reduces some of the firm's current cash flows. This type of externality is called **cannibalization** because the new business eats into the company's existing business. Manufacturers also can experience cannibalization. Thus, if Cengage Learning, the publisher of this book, decides to publish another introductory finance text, that new book will presumably reduce sales of this one. Those lost cash flows should be taken into account, and that means charging them as a cost when analyzing the proposed new book.

Dealing properly with negative externalities can be tricky. If Cengage decides not to publish the new book because of its cannibalization effects, might another publisher publish it, causing our book to lose sales regardless of what Cengage does? Logically, Cengage must examine the total situation, which is more than a simple mechanical analysis. Experience and knowledge of the industry is required to make good decisions.

One of the best examples of a company's misstep from dealing incorrectly with cannibalization effects was IBM's response when transistors made personal computers possible in the 1970s. IBM's mainframe computers were the biggest game in town, and they generated huge profits. But IBM also had the technology for PCs, entered the PC market, and for a time was the leading PC company. However, top management decided to rein back the PC division because managers were afraid it would hurt the more profitable mainframe business. That decision opened the door for Microsoft, Intel, Dell, Hewlett-Packard, and others; and IBM went from being the most profitable firm in the world to one whose very survival was threatened. To its credit, IBM has been able to successfully shift its emphasis to where it now focuses on a broad range of technology and business services. Nevertheless, this experience highlights the fact that while it is essential to understand the theory of finance, it is equally important to understand the business environment, including how competitors are likely to react to a firm's actions. A great deal of judgment goes into making good financial decisions.

Positive Within-Firm Externalities

Cannibalization occurs when new products compete with old ones. However, a new project also can be *complementary* to an old one, in which case cash flows in the old operation will be *increased* when the new one is introduced. For example, Apple's iPod was a profitable product; but when Apple made an investment in another project, its iTunes music store, that investment boosted sales of the iPod. So if an analysis of the proposed music store indicated a negative NPV, the analysis would not have been complete unless the incremental cash flows that would occur in the iPod division were credited to the music store. That might well change the project's NPV from negative to positive.

Environmental Externalities

The most common type of negative externality is a project's impact on the environment. Government rules and regulations constrain what companies can do, but firms have some flexibility in dealing with the environment. For example, suppose a manufacturer is studying a proposed new plant. The company could meet the environmental regulations at a cost of $1 million, but the plant would still emit fumes that might cause ill feelings in its neighborhood. Those ill feelings would not show up in the cash flow analysis, but they still should be considered. Perhaps a relatively small additional expenditure would reduce the emissions substantially, make the plant look good relative to other plants in the area, and provide goodwill that in the future would help the firm's sales and negotiations with governmental agencies.

Of course, everyone's profits depend on the earth remaining healthy, so companies have an incentive to do things to protect the environment even though those actions are not required. However, if one firm decides to take actions that are good for the environment but costly, its products must reflect those higher costs. If its competitors decide to get by with less costly but less environmentally friendly processes, they can price their products lower and make more money. Of course, more environmentally friendly companies can advertise their environmental efforts, and this might—or might not—offset their higher costs. All of this illustrates why government regulations are necessary, both nationally and internationally. Finance, politics, and the environment are all interconnected.

12-2 ANALYSIS OF AN EXPANSION PROJECT

In Chapter 11, we analyzed two projects, S and L. We were given the cash flows and used them to illustrate how the NPV, IRR, MIRR, and payback are calculated. In the real world, a project's cash flows are rarely just given to you; instead the finance staff will need to assemble the relevant information. Frequently, this information comes from a variety of sources within the company. For example, the marketing department may provide sales projections, the company's engineers may estimate costs, and the accounting staff may provide information about taxes and depreciation.

To illustrate, let's assume that Allied is considering a new expansion project, which is Project S that we introduced in Chapter 11. Project S is a new health-food product that Allied is considering introducing to the market. Along the way, Allied's finance staff has received a lot of information, the highlights of which are summarized below.

- Project S will require Allied to purchase $900,000 of equipment in 2015 (t = 0).
- Inventory will increase by $175,000 and accounts payable will rise by $75,000. All other working capital components will stay the same, so the change in net operating working capital (NOWC) is $100,000 at t = 0.
- The project will last for four years. The company forecasts the following sales: 2,685,000 units in 2016; 2,600,000 units in 2017; 2,525,000 units in 2018; and 2,450,000 units in 2019. Each unit will sell for $2.
- The fixed cost of producing the product is $2 million each year, and the variable cost of producing each unit will rise from $1.018 in 2016 to $1.221 in 2019.
- The company will use accelerated depreciation, however the CFO is also interested in seeing how the project's value would change if it instead used straight-line depreciation.
- When the project is completed in 2019 (t = 4), the company expects that it will be able to salvage the equipment for $50,000 and that it will fully recover the NOWC of $100,000.
- The estimated tax rate is 40%.
- Based on the perceived risk, the project's WACC is estimated to be 10%.

To keep things straight, the finance staff has organized all of the key data in a spreadsheet, which is shown in Table 12.1. Note that unit sales and dollars (except for unit sales price and variable cost per unit) are in thousands; we omitted three zeros to streamline the presentation.

Table 12.1 divides the project's cash flows into three components:

1. The initial investments that are required at t = 0. These include capital expenditures and changes in net operating working capital (ΔNOWC).
2. The operating cash flows the company receives over the life of the project.
3. The terminal cash flows that are realized when the project is completed. These cash flows include the after-tax salvage value of the equipment and the recovery of the NOWC.

| | Cash Flow Estimation and Analysis for Expansion Project S | | | | **TABLE 12.1** | | | |

	A	B	C	D	E	F	G	H	I
12					0	1	2	3	4
13	*Investment Outlays at Time = 0*								
14	CAPEX = Building and Equipment				−$900				
15	ΔNOWC = Additional net operating working capital needed				−100				
16	*Operating Cash Flows Over the Project's Life (Time = 1 − 4)*								
17	Unit sales					2,685	2,600	2,525	2,450
18	Sales price					$2.00	$2.00	$2.00	$2.00
19	Variable cost per unit					$1.018	$1.078	$1.046	$1.221
20	Sales revenues = Units × Price					$5,370	$5,200	$5,050	$4,900
21	Variable costs = Units × Cost/unit					2,735	2,803	2,640	2,992
22	Fixed operating costs except depr'n					2,000	2,000	2,000	2,000
23	Depreciation: <u>Accelerated</u> from table below					297	405	135	63
24	Total operating costs					$5,032	$5,208	$4,775	$5,055
25	EBIT (or Operating income)					$338	−$8	$275	−$155
26	Taxes on operating income		40%			135	−3	110	−62
27	EBIT (1 − T) = After-tax project operating income					$203	−$5	$165	−$93
28	Add back depreciation					297	405	135	63
29	EBIT (1 − T) + Depreciation					$500	$400	$300	-$30
30	*Terminal Cash Flows at Time = 4*								
31	Salvage value (taxed as ordinary income)								50
32	Tax on salvage value = 0.4 × (SV − BV of equipment at t = 4)								20
33	After-tax salvage value								30
34	ΔNOWC = Recovery of net operating working capital								100
35	Project free cash flows = EBIT(1 − T) + DEP − CAPEX − ΔNOWC				−$1,000	$500	$400	$300	$100
36									
37	*Depreciation*			Accelerated		1	2	3	4
38		Cost:	$900	Rate		33%	45%	15%	7%
39				Depreciation		$297	$405	$135	$63
40	*Alternative depreciation*			Straight line		1	2	3	4
41		Cost:	$900	Rate		25%	25%	25%	25%
42				Depreciation		$225	$225	$225	$225
43	*Project Evaluation @ WACC =*			10%					
44			Accelerated		Formulas		Straight line		
45		NPV	$78.82		=NPV(D43,F35:I35)+E35		$64.44		
46		IRR	14.489%		=IRR(E35:I35)		13.437%		
47		MIRR	12.106%		=MIRR(E35:I35,D43,D43)		11.731%		
48		Payback	2.33		=G12+(−E35−F35−G35)/H35		2.60		

© Cengage Learning 2015

Notes:

1. Accelerated depreciation rates are set by Congress. We show the approximate rates for a 4-year asset in 2013. Companies also have the option of using straight-line depreciation. Under IRS rules, salvage value is not deducted when establishing the depreciable basis. However, if a salvage payment is received, it is called a *recapture of depreciation* and is taxed at the 40% rate.

2. If the firm owned assets that would be used for the project but would be sold if the project is not accepted, the after-tax value of those assets would be shown as an "opportunity cost" in the "Investment Outlays" section.

3. If this project would reduce sales and cash flows from one of the firm's other divisions, then the after-tax cannibalization effect, or "externality," would be deducted from the operating cash flows shown on Row 29.

4. If the firm had previously incurred costs associated with this project, but those costs could not be recovered regardless of whether this project is accepted, then they are "sunk costs" and should not enter the analysis.

The column headers in the table, A through I, and the row headers, 12 through 48, designate cells, which contain the project data. For example, the equipment needed for Project S will cost $900, and that number is shown in Cell E14 as a negative number. The equipment is expected to have a salvage value of $50 at the end of the project's 4-year life; this is shown in Cell I31.[2] The new project will require $100 of net operating working capital; this is shown in Cell E15 as a negative number because it is a cost, and then it is shown as a positive number in Cell I34 because it is recovered at the end of Year 4. The total investment at Time 0 is $1,000, which is shown in Cell E35.

Unit sales of Project S are shown on Row 17; they are expected to decline somewhat over the project's 4-year life. The sales price, a constant $2, is shown on Row 18. The projected variable cost per unit is given on Row 19; it generally increases over time due to expected increases in materials and labor. Sales revenues, which are calculated as units multiplied by price, are given on Row 20. Variable costs, equal to units multiplied by VC/unit, are given on Row 21; and fixed costs excluding depreciation, which are a constant $2,000, are shown on Row 22.

Depreciation is found as the annual rate allowed by the IRS times the depreciable basis. As noted in Chapter 3, Congress sets the depreciation rates that can be used for tax purposes and these are the tax rates used in the capital budgeting analysis. Congress permits firms to depreciate assets by the straight-line method or by an accelerated method. As we will see, profitable firms are better off using accelerated depreciation. We discuss depreciation more fully in Appendix 12A; but to simplify things for this chapter, we assume that the applicable accelerated rates for a project with a 4-year life are as given on Row 38 of the depreciation section of the table and that straight-line rates are as given on Row 41. Thus, we assume that if the firm uses accelerated depreciation, it will write off 33% of the basis during Year 1, another 45% in Year 2, and so forth. These are the rates used to obtain the cash flows shown in the table.

The depreciable basis is the cost of the equipment including any shipping or installation costs, or $900 as shown in Cells E14, C38, and C41. The total depreciation over the 4 years equals the cost of the equipment.

If for some reason the firm decided to use straight-line depreciation, it could write off a constant $225 per year. Its total cash flows over the entire 4 years would be the same as under accelerated depreciation; but under straight line, those cash flows would come in a bit slower than under accelerated depreciation because the firm would have higher tax payments in the early years and lower tax payments in later years.

We calculate the annual cash flows for Project S over the 4 years in Columns F, G, H, and I, with operating cash flows shown on Row 29. On Rows 31–34, we include the terminal cash flows in Year 4 to arrive at the project's free cash flows on Row 35. These numbers are identical to the cash flows used in Chapter 11 for Project S. Because the numbers are the same, the NPV, IRR, MIRR, and payback shown in Cells C45 through C48 are identical to those we calculated in Chapter 11.

The Excel model used to create Table 12.1 is part of the chapter Excel model available on the text's website, www.cengagebrain.com. We recommend that anyone with a computer and some familiarity with Excel access the model and work through it to see how the table was generated. Anyone doing real-world capital budgeting today would use such a model; and our model provides a good template, or starting point, if and when you need to analyze an actual project.

12-2A EFFECT OF DIFFERENT DEPRECIATION RATES

If we replaced the accelerated depreciation numbers in Table 12.1 with the constant $225 values that would exist under the straight line method, the result would be a free cash flow time line on Row 35 that has the same total flows. However, in

---

[2]The equipment will be fully depreciated after 4 years. Therefore, the $50 estimated salvage value will exceed the book value, which will be zero. This $50 gain is classified as a recapture of depreciation, and it is taxed at the same rate as ordinary income.

the early years, the cash flows resulting from straight-line depreciation would be lower than those now in the table; and the later years' cash flows would show higher numbers. Because of the time value of money, dollars received earlier have a higher present value than dollars received later. Therefore, Project S's NPV is higher if the firm uses accelerated depreciation. The exact effect is shown in the Project Evaluation section of Table 12.1—the NPV is $78.82 under accelerated depreciation and $64.44, or 18% less, with straight line.

Now suppose Congress wants to encourage companies to increase their capital expenditures to boost economic growth and employment. What change in depreciation would have the desired effect? The answer is to make accelerated depreciation even more accelerated. For example, if the firm could write off this 4-year equipment at rates of 50%, 35%, 10%, and 5%, its early tax payments would be lower, early cash flows would be higher, and the project's NPV would be higher than that shown in Table 12.1.

12-2B CANNIBALIZATION

Project S does not involve any cannibalization effects. Suppose, however, that Project S would reduce the after-tax cash flows of another division by $50 per year. No other firm would take on this project if our firm turns it down. In this case, we would add a row at about Row 28 and deduct $50 for each year. If this were done, Project S would now have a negative NPV; hence, it would be rejected. On the other hand, if Project S would cause additional flows in some other division (a positive externality), those after-tax inflows should be attributed to Project S.

12-2C OPPORTUNITY COSTS

Now suppose the $900 initial cost shown in Table 12.1 was based on the assumption that the project would save money by using some equipment the company now owns and that equipment would be sold for $100, after taxes, if the project is rejected. The $100 is an opportunity cost, and it should be reflected in our calculations. We would add $100 to the project's cost. The result would be an NPV of $78.82 − $100 = −$21.18, so the project would now be rejected.

12-2D SUNK COSTS

Now suppose the firm had spent $150 on a marketing study to estimate potential sales. This $150 could not be recovered regardless of whether the project is accepted or rejected. Should the $150 be charged to Project S when determining its NPV for capital budgeting purposes? The answer is no. We are interested only in *incremental costs*. The $150 is not an incremental cost; it is a *sunk cost*. Therefore, it should not enter into the analysis.

One additional point should be made about sunk costs. If the $150 expenditure was actually made, in the final analysis, Project S would turn out to be a loser: Its NPV would be $78.82 − $150 = −$71.18. If we could somehow back up and reconsider the project *before* the $150 had been spent, we would see that the project should be rejected. However, we can't back up—at this point, we can either abandon the project or spend $1,000 and go forward with it. If we go forward, we will receive an incremental NPV of $78.82, which would reduce the loss from −$150 to −$71.18.

12-2E OTHER CHANGES TO THE INPUTS

Variables other than depreciation also could be varied, and these changes would alter the calculated cash flows and thus NPV and IRR. For example, we could increase or decrease the projected unit sales, the sales price, the variable and/or the fixed costs, the initial investment cost, the working capital requirements, the salvage value, and even the tax rate if we thought Congress was likely to raise or lower taxes. Such changes could be made easily in an Excel model, making it possible to see the resulting changes in NPV and IRR immediately. This is called *sensitivity analysis,* and we discuss it in Section 12-5 when we take up procedures for measuring projects' risks.

SELF TEST

In what ways is the setup for finding a project's cash flows similar to the projected income statements for a new single-product firm? In what ways would the two statements be different?

Would a project's NPV for a typical firm be higher or lower if the firm used accelerated rather than straight-line depreciation? Explain.

How could the analysis in Table 12.1 be modified to consider cannibalization, opportunity costs, and sunk costs?

Why does net operating working capital (NOWC) appear as both a negative and a positive number in Table 12.1?

12-3 REPLACEMENT ANALYSIS[3]

In the last section, we assumed that Project S was an entirely new project. So all of its cash flows were incremental—they occurred only if the firm accepted the project. This is true for expansion projects; but for replacement projects, we must find cash flow *differentials* between the new and old projects and these differentials are the incremental cash flows that we analyze.

We evaluate a replacement decision in Table 12.2, which is set up much like Table 12.1, but with data on both a new, highly efficient machine (which will be depreciated on an accelerated basis) and the old machine (which is depreciated on a straight-line basis). Here we find the firm's cash flows when it continues using the old machine and the cash flows when it decides to purchase a new machine. Finally, we subtract the old flows from the new to arrive at the *incremental cash flows.* We used Excel in our analysis; but again, we could have used a calculator or pencil and paper. Here are the key inputs used in the analysis. No additional operating working capital is needed.

Data applicable to both machines:

Sales revenues, which would remain constant	$ 2,500
Expected life of the new and old machines	4 years
WACC for the analysis	10%
Tax rate	40%

Data for old machine:

Market (salvage) value of the old machine today	$ 400
Old labor, materials, and other costs per year	$ 1,000
Old machine's annual depreciation	$ 100

Data for new machine:

Cost of new machine	$ 2,000
New labor, materials, and other costs per year	$ 400

---

[3]This section is somewhat technical, but it can be omitted without a loss of continuity.

Replacement Project R   **TABLE 12.2**

	A	B	C	D	E	F	G	H	I
12					**0**	**1**	**2**	**3**	**4**
13	*Part I. Free Cash Flows Before Replacement:*								
	Old Machine (CAPEX and ∆NOWC = 0)								
14	Sales revenues					$2,500	$2,500	$2,500	$2,500
15	Costs except depreciation					1,000	1,000	1,000	1,000
16	Depreciation					100	100	100	100
17	Total operating costs					$1,100	$1,100	$1,100	$1,100
18	EBIT (or Operating income)					$1,400	$1,400	$1,400	$1,400
19	Taxes 40%					560	560	560	560
20	EBIT (1 — T) = After-tax operating income					$840	$840	$840	$840
21	Add back depreciation					100	100	100	100
22	Free cash flows before replacement EBIT(1 — T) + DEP — CAPEX — ∆NOWC					$940	$940	$940	$940
23	*Part II. Free Cash Flows After Replacement:* *New Machine (∆NOWC = 0)*								
24	New machine cost				−$2,000				
25	After-tax salvage value, old machine				400				
26	CAPEX				−$1,600				
27	Sales revenues					$2,500	$2,500	$2,500	$2,500
28	Costs except depreciation					400	400	400	400
29	Depreciation					660	900	300	140
30	Total operating costs					$1,060	$1,300	$700	$540
31	EBIT (or Operating income)					$1,440	$1,200	$1,800	$1,960
32	Taxes 40%					576	480	720	784
33	EBIT(1 — T) = After-tax operating income					$864	$720	$1,080	$1,176
34	Add back depreciation					660	900	300	140
35	Free cash flows after replacement EBIT(1 — T) + DEP — CAPEX — ∆NOWC				−$1,600	$1,524	$1,620	$1,380	$1,316
36	Part III. Incremental Cash Flows and Evaluation								
37	*Incremental CFs = CF After — CF Before*				−$1,600	$584	$680	$440	$376
38									
39	*Project Evaluation @ WACC =*		*10%*						
40			NPV =		$80.28				
41			IRR =		12.51%				
42			MIRR =		11.35%				
43			Payback =		2.76				
44	Part IV. Alternative (Streamlined) Calculation for Incremental CFs								
45		New machine cost			−$2,000				
46		Salvage value, old machine			400				
47		Net cost of new machine			−$1,600				
48	Cost savings = Old — New					$600	$600	$600	$600
49	A-T savings = Cost savings × (1 — Tax rate)					360	360	360	360
50	∆ Depreciation = (New — Old)					560	800	200	40
51	Depr'n tax savings = ∆ Depreciation × Tax rate					224	320	80	16
52	Incremental CFs = A-T cost savings + Depr'n tax savings				−$1,600	$584	$680	$440	$376
53									

The key here is to find the *incremental* cash flows. As noted previously, we find the cash flows from the operation with the old machine, then find the cash flows with the new machine, then find the differences in the cash flows. This is what we do in Parts I, II, and III of Table 12.2. Because there will be an additional expenditure to purchase the new machine, that cost is shown in Cell E24. However, we can sell the old machine for $400, so that is shown as an inflow in Cell E25. The cash outlay at Time 0 is $1,600, as shown in Cell E35.

The cash flows based on the old machine are shown on Row 22, and those for the new one are on Row 35. Then on Row 37, we show the differences in the cash flows with and without replacement—these are the incremental cash flows used to find the replacement NPV. When we evaluate the incremental cash flows, we see that the replacement has an NPV of $80.28, so the old machine should be replaced.[4]

In some instances, replacements add capacity as well as lower operating costs. When this is the case, sales revenues in Part II would be increased; and if that led to an increase in net operating working capital, that number would be shown as a Time 0 expenditure along with its recovery at the end of the project's life. These changes would, of course, be reflected in the differential cash flows on Row 37.

SELF TEST

What role do incremental cash flows play in a replacement analysis?

If you were analyzing a replacement project and you suddenly learned that the old equipment could be sold for $1,000 rather than $100, would this new information make the replacement look better or worse?

In Table 12.2, we assumed that output would not change if the old machine was replaced. Suppose output would actually double. How would this change be dealt with in the framework of Table 12.2?

12-4 Risk Analysis in Capital Budgeting[5]

Projects differ in risk, and risk should be reflected in capital budgeting decisions. However, it is difficult to measure risk, especially for new projects where no history exists. For this reason, managers deal with risk in many different ways, ranging from almost totally subjective adjustments to highly sophisticated analyses that involve computer simulation and complex statistics.

Three separate and distinct types of risk are involved:

1. **Stand-alone risk**, which is a project's risk assuming (a) that it is the only asset the firm has and (b) that the firm is the only stock in each investor's portfolio. Stand-alone risk is measured by the variability of the project's expected returns. *Diversification is totally ignored.*

2. **Corporate,** or **within-firm, risk**, which is a project's risk to the corporation as opposed to its investors. Within-firm risk takes account of the fact that the

Stand-Alone Risk

The risk an asset would have if it were a firm's only asset and if investors owned only one stock. It is measured by the variability of the asset's expected returns.

Corporate (Within-Firm) Risk

Risk considering the firm's diversification but not stockholder diversification. It is measured by a project's effect on uncertainty about the firm's expected future returns.

---

[4]We could have found the incremental cash flows by calculating the differences in the only factors that change, the net cost of the new machine, operating cost savings reduced for the taxes, and the differences in depreciation, which save some taxes. This procedure is shown in Part IV of the table. The two procedures produce the same incremental cash flows and NPV, as they must.

[5]Some professors may choose to cover some of the risk sections (12-4 through 12-6) and skip others. We offer a range of choices, and we tried to make the exposition clear enough that interested and self-motivated students can read these sections on their own even if the sections are not assigned.

project is only one asset in the firm's portfolio of assets; hence, some of its risk will be eliminated by diversification within the firm. This type of risk is measured by the project's impact on uncertainty about the firm's future returns.

3. **Market**, or **beta, risk**, which is the riskiness of the project as seen by a well-diversified stockholder who recognizes (a) that the project is only one of the firm's assets and (b) that the firm's stock is but one part of his or her stock portfolio. The project's market risk is measured by its effect on the firm's beta coefficient.

Market (Beta) Risk
Considers both firm and stockholder diversification. It is measured by the project's beta coefficient.

Taking on a project with a great deal of stand-alone or corporate risk will not necessarily affect the firm's beta. However, if the project has high stand-alone risk and if its returns are highly correlated with returns on the firm's other assets and with returns on most other stocks in the economy, the project will have a high degree of all three types of risk. Market risk is theoretically the most relevant of the three because it is the one reflected in stock prices. Unfortunately, market risk is also the most difficult to estimate, primarily because new projects don't have "market prices" that can be related to stock market returns. Therefore, most decision makers do a *quantitative* analysis of stand-alone risk and then consider the other two risk measures in a *qualitative* manner.

Projects are generally classified into several categories. Then with the firm's overall WACC as a starting point, a **risk-adjusted cost of capital** is assigned to each category. For example, a firm might establish three risk classes, assign the corporate WACC to average-risk projects, add a 5% risk premium for higher-risk projects, and subtract 2% for low-risk projects. Under this setup, if the company's overall WACC was 10%, 10% would be used to evaluate average-risk projects, 15% for high-risk projects, and 8% for low-risk projects. While this approach is probably better than not making any risk adjustments, these adjustments are highly subjective and difficult to justify. Unfortunately, there's no perfect way to specify how high or low the adjustments should be.[6]

Risk-Adjusted Cost of Capital
The cost of capital appropriate for a given project, given the riskiness of that project. The greater the risk, the higher the cost of capital.

SELF TEST

What are the three types of project risk?

Which type is theoretically the most relevant? Why?

What is one classification scheme that firms often use to obtain risk-adjusted costs of capital?

12-5 MEASURING STAND-ALONE RISK

A project's stand-alone risk reflects uncertainty about its cash flows. The required investment, unit sales, sales prices, and operating costs shown in Table 12.1 for Project S are subject to uncertainty. First-year sales were projected at 2,685 units (actually, 2,685,000, but we shortened it to 2,685 to streamline the analysis) to be sold at a price of $2 per unit. However, unit sales would almost certainly be somewhat higher or lower than 2,685, and the price would probably turn out to

---

[6]We should note that the CAPM approach can be used for projects provided there are specialized publicly traded firms in the same business as that of the project under consideration. For further information on estimating the risk-adjusted cost of capital, see Web Appendix 12C; and for more information on measuring market (or beta) risk, see Web Appendix 12D.

be different from the projected $2 per unit. Similarly, the other variables would probably differ from their indicated values. *Indeed, all the inputs are expected values, and actual values can vary from expected values.*

Three techniques are used to assess stand-alone risk: (1) sensitivity analysis, (2) scenario analysis, and (3) Monte Carlo simulation. We discuss them in the following sections.

12-5a SENSITIVITY ANALYSIS

Sensitivity Analysis

Percentage change in NPV resulting from a given percentage change in an input variable, other things held constant.

Intuitively, we know that a change in a key input variable such as units sold or sales price will cause the NPV to change. **Sensitivity analysis** *measures the percentage change in NPV that results from a given percentage change in an input, other variables held at their expected values.* This is by far the most commonly used type of risk analysis, and it is used by most firms. It begins with a *base-case* situation, where the project's NPV is found using the base-case value for each input variable. Here's a list of the key inputs for Project S:

- Equipment cost
- Change in net operating working capital
- Unit sales
- Sales price
- Variable cost per unit
- Fixed operating costs
- Tax rate
- WACC

Base-Case NPV

The NPV when sales and other input variables are set equal to their most likely (or base-case) values.

The data we used back in Table 12.1 were the *most likely,* or *base-case,* values; and the resulting NPV, $78.82, is the **base-case NPV**. It's easy to imagine changes in the inputs, and those changes would result in different NPVs.

When senior managers review capital budgeting studies, they are interested in the base-case NPV, but they always go on to ask the financial analyst a series of "what if" questions: What if unit sales turn out to be 25% below the base-case level? What if market conditions force us to price the product at $1.80, not $2? What if variable costs are higher than we forecasted? Sensitivity analysis is designed to provide answers to such questions. Each variable is increased or decreased from its expected value, holding other variables constant at their base-case levels. Then the NPV is calculated using the changed input. Finally, the resulting set of NPVs is plotted to show how sensitive NPV is to changes in each variable.

Figure 12.1 shows Project S's sensitivity graph for six key variables. The table below the graph gives the NPVs based on different values of the inputs, and those NPVs were then plotted to make the graph. Figure 12.1 shows that as unit sales and price increase, the project's NPV increases, whereas the opposite is true for the other four input variables. An increase in variable costs, fixed costs, equipment costs, and WACC lowers the project's NPV. The ranges shown at the bottom of the table and the slopes of the lines in the graph indicate how sensitive NPV is to changes in each input. When the data are plotted in Figure 12.1, the slopes of the lines in the graph indicate how sensitive NPV is to each input: *The larger the range, the steeper the variable's slope and the more sensitive the NPV is to changes in this variable.* We see that NPV is very sensitive to changes in the sales price, fairly sensitive to changes in variable costs, a bit less sensitive to units sold and fixed costs, but not very sensitive to changes in the equipment cost or the WACC.

If we were comparing two projects, the one with the steeper sensitivity lines would be riskier, other things held constant, because relatively small changes in

FIGURE 12.1	Sensitivity Graph for Project S

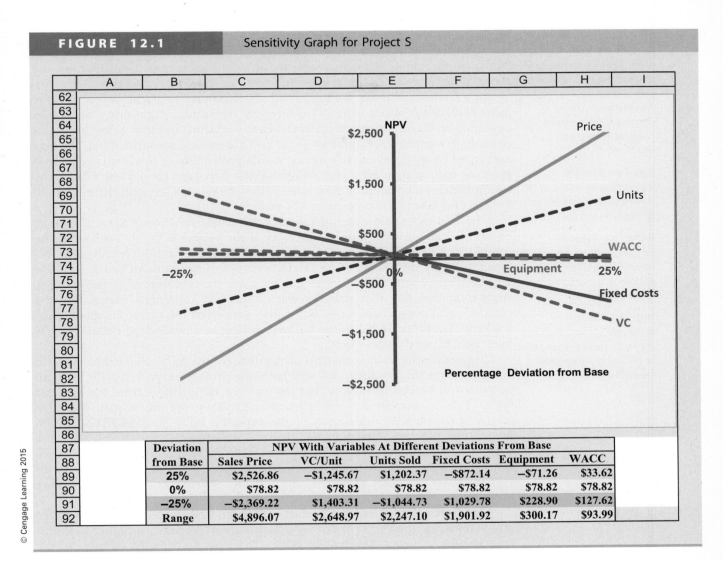

	Deviation from Base	NPV With Variables At Different Deviations From Base					
		Sales Price	VC/Unit	Units Sold	Fixed Costs	Equipment	WACC
	25%	$2,526.86	−$1,245.67	$1,202.37	−$872.14	−$71.26	$33.62
	0%	$78.82	$78.82	$78.82	$78.82	$78.82	$78.82
	−25%	−$2,369.22	$1,403.31	−$1,044.73	$1,029.78	$228.90	$127.62
	Range	$4,896.07	$2,648.97	$2,247.10	$1,901.92	$300.17	$93.99

Notes:

1. When all of the inputs are set at their base-case levels, their deviations from base are all zero, and the NPV is $78.82. So, the vertical axis intercept is at $78.82.

2. If the sales price is set 25% above its expected $2 price and all other variables are set at their expected values, then the NPV would be +$2,526.86. If the price is set 25% below its expected $2 price, then the NPV would be −$2,369.22. All the other NPVs shown in the table were found similarly. Excel Data Tables were used to streamline the calculations.

3. Note that the best- and worst-case NPVs are different from those in the next section, which shows scenario analysis. In scenario analysis, all the variables are 25% above or below their expected levels, so the best- and worst-case NPVs are much higher or lower than those in the sensitivity analysis, where only one variable is set at its best or worst level.

the input variables would produce large changes in the NPV. Thus, sensitivity analysis provides useful insights into a project's risk.[7]

12-5b Scenario Analysis

In sensitivity analysis, we change one variable at a time. However, it is useful to know what would happen to the project's NPV if all of the inputs turned out to be better or worse than expected. Also, we can assign probabilities to the good, bad,

---

[7]Sensitivity analysis is tedious using a regular calculator but easy using a spreadsheet. We used the chapter's Excel model to calculate the NPVs and to draw the graph in Figure 12.1. To conduct such an analysis by hand would be quite time-consuming, and if the basic data were changed even slightly—say the cost of the equipment was increased slightly—all of the calculations would have to be redone. With a spreadsheet, by simply typing over the old input with the new one, the analysis is changed instantaneously.

Scenario Analysis

A risk analysis technique in which "bad" and "good" sets of financial circumstances are compared with a most likely, or base-case, situation.

and most likely (or base-case) scenarios, then find the expected value and the standard deviation of the NPV. **Scenario analysis** allows for these extensions—it allows us to change more than one variable at a time, and it incorporates the probabilities of changes in the key variables.

In a scenario analysis, we begin with the **base-case scenario**, which uses the most likely set of input values. We then ask marketing, engineering, and other operating managers to specify a **worst-case scenario** (low unit sales, low sales price, high variable costs, and so forth) and a **best-case scenario**. Often the best and worst cases are defined as having a 25% probability of conditions being that good or bad, with a 50% probability for the base-case conditions. Obviously, conditions can take on more than three values, but such a scenario setup is useful to help understand the project's riskiness.

Base-Case Scenario

An analysis in which all of the input variables are set at their most likely values.

The best-case, base-case, and worst-case values for Project S are shown in Figure 12.2, along with plots of the data. If the project is highly successful, the combination of a high sales price, low production costs, and high unit sales will result in a very high NPV, $7,450.38. However, if things turn out badly, the NPV will be a negative $4,782.40. The graphs show the wide range of possibilities, suggesting that this is a risky project. If the bad conditions materialize, the company will not go bankrupt—this is just one project for a large company. Still, losing $4,782.40 (or $4,782,400 as we are working in thousands of dollars) would hurt the company's stock price.

Worst-Case Scenario

An analysis in which all of the input variables are set at their worst reasonably forecasted values.

If we multiply each scenario's probability by the NPV under that scenario and then sum the products, we will have the project's expected NPV, $706.40 as shown in Figure 12.2. Note that the *expected* NPV differs from the *base-case* NPV. This is not an error—mathematically, they are not equal. We also calculate the standard deviation of the expected NPV; it is $4,370.24. When we divide the standard deviation by the expected NPV, we calculate the coefficient of variation, 6.19, which is a measure of stand-alone risk. The firm's average-risk project has a coefficient of variation of about 2.0, so the CV of 6.19 indicates that this project is much riskier than most of the firm's other projects.

Best-Case Scenario

An analysis in which all of the input variables are set at their best reasonably forecasted values.

Our firm's WACC is 10%, so that rate should be used to find the NPV of an average-risk project. Project S is riskier than average, so a higher discount rate should be used to find its NPV. There is no way to determine the "correct" discount rate—this is a judgment call. However, some firms increase the corporate WACC when they evaluate projects deemed to be relatively risky and reduce it for low-risk projects. When the NPV was recalculated using a 12.5% WACC, the base-case NPV fell from $78.82 to $33.62; so the project still had a positive NPV when its expected cash flows were discounted at the risk-adjusted WACC.

Note that the base-case results are the same in our sensitivity and scenario analyses; but in the scenario analysis, the worst case is much worse than in the sensitivity analysis and the best case is much better. In scenario analysis, all of the variables are set at their best or worst values, while in sensitivity analysis, only one variable is adjusted and all the others are left at their base-case values.

12-5c MONTE CARLO SIMULATION

Monte Carlo Simulation

A risk analysis technique in which probable future events are simulated on a computer, generating estimated rates of return and risk indexes.

Monte Carlo simulation, so named because this type of analysis grew out of work on the mathematics of casino gambling, is a sophisticated version of scenario analysis. Here the project is analyzed under a large number of scenarios, or "runs." In the first run, the computer randomly picks a value for each variable—units sold, sales price, variable costs per unit, and so forth. Those values are then used to calculate an NPV, and that NPV is stored in the computer's memory. Next, a second set of input values is selected at random

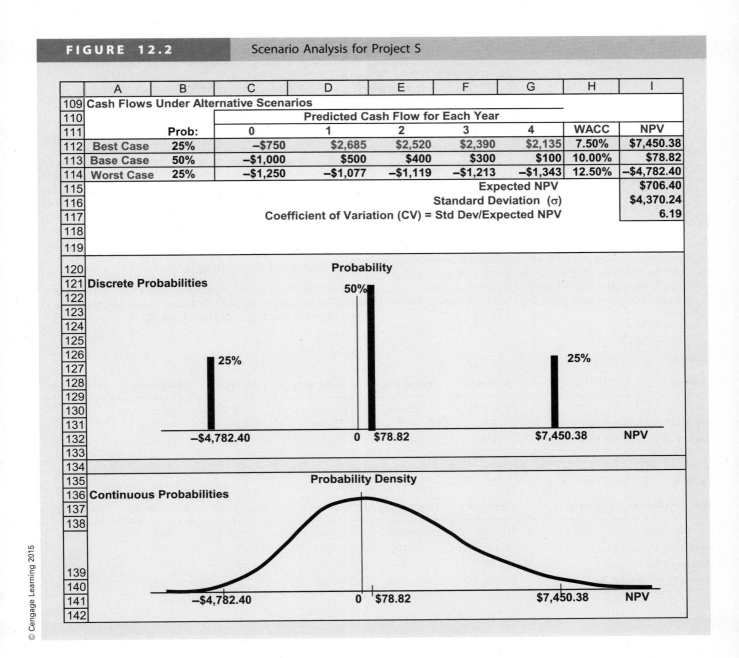

FIGURE 12.2 Scenario Analysis for Project S

	A	B	C	D	E	F	G	H	I
109	**Cash Flows Under Alternative Scenarios**								
110				**Predicted Cash Flow for Each Year**					
111		**Prob:**	**0**	**1**	**2**	**3**	**4**	**WACC**	**NPV**
112	Best Case	25%	−$750	$2,685	$2,520	$2,390	$2,135	7.50%	$7,450.38
113	Base Case	50%	−$1,000	$500	$400	$300	$100	10.00%	$78.82
114	Worst Case	25%	−$1,250	−$1,077	−$1,119	−$1,213	−$1,343	12.50%	−$4,782.40
115							Expected NPV		$706.40
116							Standard Deviation (σ)		$4,370.24
117						Coefficient of Variation (CV) = Std Dev/Expected NPV			6.19
118									
119									

and a second NPV is calculated. This process is repeated perhaps 1,000 times, generating 1,000 NPVs. The mean of the 1,000 NPVs is determined and used as a measure of the project's expected profitability, and the standard deviation (or perhaps the coefficient of variation) of the NPVs is used as a measure of risk.

Monte Carlo simulation is technically more complex than scenario analysis, but simulation software makes the process manageable. Simulation is useful; but because of its complexity, a detailed discussion is best left for advanced finance courses.[8]

---

[8]To use Monte Carlo simulation, one needs probability distributions for the inputs and correlation coefficients between each pair of inputs. It is often difficult to obtain "reasonable" values for the correlations, especially for new projects where no historical data are available. This limits the use of simulation analysis.

GLOBAL PERSPECTIVES

Capital Budgeting Practices in the Asian/Pacific Region

A 1999 survey of executives in Australia, Hong Kong, Indonesia, Malaysia, the Philippines, and Singapore asked several questions about companies' capital budgeting practices. The study yielded the results summarized here.

Techniques for Evaluating Corporate Projects

Consistent with U.S. companies, most companies in this region evaluate projects using IRR, NPV, and payback. IRR usage ranged from 96% (in Australia) to 86% (in Hong Kong). NPV usage ranged from 96% (in Australia) to 81% (in the Philippines). Payback usage ranged from 100% (in Hong Kong and the Philippines) to 81% (in Indonesia).

Techniques for Estimating the Cost of Equity Capital

Recall from Chapter 10 that three basic approaches can be used to estimate the cost of equity: CAPM, dividend yield plus growth rate (DCF), and cost of debt plus a risk premium. The use of these methods varied considerably from country to country (see Table A). The CAPM is used most often by U.S. firms. This is also true for Australian firms, but not for the other Asian/Pacific firms, which instead more often use the DCF and risk premium approaches.

Techniques for Assessing Risk

Firms in the Asian/Pacific region rely heavily on scenario and sensitivity analyses. They also use decision trees and Monte Carlo simulation, but less frequently (see Table B).

Table A

Method	Australia	Hong Kong	Indonesia	Malaysia	Philippines	Singapore
CAPM	72.7%	26.9%	0.0%	6.2%	24.1%	17.0%
Dividend yield plus growth rate	16.4	53.8	33.3	50.0	34.5	42.6
Cost of debt plus risk premium	10.9	23.1	53.4	37.5	58.6	42.6

Table B

Risk Assessment Technique	Australia	Hong Kong	Indonesia	Malaysia	Philippines	Singapore
Scenario analysis	96%	100%	94%	80%	97%	90%
Sensitivity analysis	100	100	88	83	94	79
Decision tree analysis	44	58	50	37	33	46
Monte Carlo simulation	38	35	25	9	24	35

Source: Adapted from George W. Kester et al., "Capital Budgeting Practices in the Asia-Pacific Region: Australia, Hong Kong, Indonesia, Malaysia, Philippines, and Singapore," *Financial Practice and Education*, vol. 9, no. 1 (Spring–Summer 1999), pp. 25–33.

SELF TEST

Explain briefly how a sensitivity analysis is done and what the analysis is designed to show.

What is a scenario analysis, what is it designed to show, and how does it differ from a sensitivity analysis?

What is Monte Carlo simulation? How does a simulation analysis differ from a regular scenario analysis?

12-6 Within-Firm and Beta Risk[9]

Sensitivity analysis, scenario analysis, and Monte Carlo simulation as described in the preceding section dealt with stand-alone risk. They provide useful information about a project's risk; but if the project is negatively correlated with the firm's other projects, it might stabilize the firm's total earnings and thus be relatively safe. Similarly, if a project is negatively correlated with returns on most stocks, it might reduce the firm's beta and thus be correctly evaluated with a relatively low WACC. So in theory, we should be more concerned with within-firm and beta risk than with stand-alone risk.

Although managers recognize the importance of within-firm and beta risk, they generally end up dealing with these risks subjectively, or judgmentally, rather than quantitatively. The problem is that to measure diversification's effects on risk, we need the *correlation coefficient between a project's returns and returns on the firm's other assets,* which requires historical data that obviously do not exist for new projects. Experienced managers generally have a "feel" for how a project's returns will relate to returns on the firm's other assets. Generally, positive correlation is expected; and if the correlation is high, stand-alone risk will be a good proxy for within-firm risk. Similarly, managers can make judgmental estimates about whether a project's returns will be high when the economy and the stock market are strong (hence, what the project's beta should be). But for the most part, those estimates are subjective, not based on actual data.

However, projects occasionally involve an entirely new product line, such as a steel company going into iron ore mining. In such cases, the firm may be able to obtain betas for *"pure-play"* companies in the new area. For example, this steel company might get the average beta for a group of mining companies such as Rio Tinto and BHP Billiton, assume that its mining subsidiary has similar characteristics, and use the average beta of the "comparables" to calculate a WACC for the mining subsidiary. While the pure-play approach makes sense for some projects, its use is rare. Just think about it. How would you find a pure-play proxy for a new inventory control system, machine tool, truck, or most other projects? The answer is, you couldn't.

Our conclusions regarding risk analysis are as follows:

- It is very difficult, if not impossible, to quantitatively measure projects' within-firm and beta risks.

- Most projects' returns are positively correlated with returns on the firm's other assets and with returns on the stock market. This being the case, because stand-alone risk is correlated with within-firm and market risk, not much is lost by focusing just on stand-alone risk.

- Experienced managers make many judgmental assessments, including those related to risk; and they work them into the capital budgeting process. Introductory students like neat, precise answers; and they want to make decisions on the basis of calculated NPVs. Experienced managers consider quantitative NPVs, but they also bring subjective judgment into the decision process.

- If a firm does not use the types of analyses covered in this book, it will have trouble. On the other hand, if a firm tries to quantify everything and let a computer make its decisions, it too will have trouble. Good managers understand and use the theory of finance, but they apply it with judgment.

---

[9]This section is relatively technical, but it can be omitted without a loss of continuity.

12-7 REAL OPTIONS[10]

Traditional discounted cash flow (DCF) analysis—where cash flows are estimated and then discounted to obtain the expected NPV—has been the cornerstone of capital budgeting since the 1950s. However, in recent years it has been shown that DCF techniques do not always lead to proper capital budgeting decisions.

DCF techniques were originally developed to value securities such as stocks and bonds. These are *passive* investments—once the investment has been made, most investors can take no actions that influence the cash flows they produce.[11] However, capital budgeting projects are not passive investments—managers can often take *positive actions* after the investment has been made that alter the cash flow stream. Opportunities for such actions are called **real options**—"real" to distinguish them from financial options like an option to purchase shares of Boeing stock, and "options" because they offer the right but not the obligation to take the future action to increase cash flows. Real options are valuable, but this value is not captured by conventional NPV analysis. Therefore, a project's real options must be considered separately.

Real Options

The right but not the obligation to take some future action.

12-7A TYPES OF REAL OPTIONS

There are several types of real options, including (1) *abandonment*, where the project can be shut down if its cash flows are low; (2) *timing*, where a project can be delayed until more information about demand and/or costs can be obtained; (3) *expansion*, where the project can be expanded if demand turns out to be stronger than expected; (4) *output flexibility*, where the output can be changed if market conditions change; and (5) *input flexibility*, where the inputs used in the production process (say, coal versus natural gas for generating electricity) can be changed if input prices and/or availability change. We illustrate abandonment options here in the text and we cover other types of options in Web Appendix 12F.

12-7B ABANDONMENT OPTIONS

Abandonment Option

The option to shut down a project if operating cash flows turn out to be lower than expected. This option can both raise expected profitability and lower project risk.

In capital budgeting we generally assume that a project will be operated for its full physical life. However, this is not always the best course of action. If the firm has the **option to abandon** a project during its operating life, this can lower its risk, increase its expected profitability, and raise its calculated NPV.

---

[10]This section is relatively technical, but it can be omitted without a loss of continuity if there is insufficient time to cover it.

[11]Large investors such as Warren Buffett and some hedge fund operators can purchase stock in companies and then influence the firms' operations and cash flows. However, the average stockholder does not have this influence.

Table 12.3 gives a picture of the **decision tree** for Project S. In the scenario analysis in Section 12-5 we examined Project S under the Best Case, Base Case, and Worst Case assumptions. In the worst-case situation, the project has negative cash flows for its full 4-year life. However, if the company can abandon the project after Year 1, when it sees that it is not a success, then its expected NPV can be improved. The earlier analysis is reproduced in the top section of Table 12.3, labeled "No Abandonment." In Column C, which is Time 0, we see that the firm must invest between $750 and $1,250. Columns D through G show the annual cash flows under each scenario, and in Column H we show the WACCs for each scenario. Then, in Column I, we show the NPV under each scenario when the cash flows are discounted at their respective WACCs. The sum of the products obtained by multiplying each probability times each branch NPV is the expected NPV, which is $706.40. The standard deviation and the coefficient of variation are also calculated to provide an idea of the project's risk. This project has a positive expected NPV; hence, by the NPV criterion it should be accepted.

Now suppose the company could make a second decision, at t = 1, to abandon (or shut down) the project if things go badly during Year 1. To see what would happen then, we add another branch to the tree, as shown in the Worst #2 row in Table 12.3 under the "Can Abandon" situation. Here we assume that the company abandons the project at the end of Year 1, when information about the actual production costs and demand conditions become available. If things were

Decision Tree

A diagram that lays out different branches that are the result of different decisions made or the result of different economic situations.

| | | | Decision Tree for Abandonment Option (Dollars in Thousands) | | | | | | **TABLE 12.3** | |

	A	B	C	D	E	F	G	H	I	J
21	**Situation 1. No Abandonment**									
22			**Predicted Cash Flow for Each Year**							
23		**Prob.**	**0**	**1**	**2**	**3**	**4**	**WACC**	**NPV**	
24	**Best Case**	**25%**	-$750	$2,685	$2,520	$2,390	$2,135	7.50%	$7,450.38	
25	**Base**	**50%**	−$1,000	$500	$400	$300	$100	10.00%	$78.82	
26	**Worst Case**	**25%**	−$1,250	−$1,077	−$1,119	−$1,213	−$1,343	12.50%	−$4,782.40	
27					**Expected NPV**				$706.40	
28					**Standard Deviation (σ)**				$4,370.24	
29				**Coefficient of Variation (CV) = Std Dev/Expected NPV**					6.19	
30										
31	**Situation 2. Can Abandon**									
32			**Predicted Cash Flow for Each Year**							
33		**Prob.**	**0**	**1**	**2**	**3**	**4**	**WACC**	**NPV**	
34	**Best Case**	**25%**	−$750	$2,685	$2,520	$2,390	$2,135	7.50%	$7,450.38	
35	**Base**	**50%**	−$1,000	$500	$400	$300	$100	10.00%	$78.82	
36	**Worst #1**	**0%**	−$1,250	−$1,077	−$1,119	−$1,213	−$1,343	12.50%	−$4,782.40	Don't use
37	**Worst #2**	**25%**	−$1,250	−$1,077	$0	$0	$0	12.50%	−$2,207.67	Use
38				**Expected NPV (includes #2, excludes #1)**					$1,350.09	
39					**Standard Deviation (σ)**				$3,643.60	
40				**Coefficient of Variation (CV) = Std Dev/Expected NPV**					2.70	
41										
42				**Value of the Real Option to Abandon**						
43				**Expected NPV with Abandonment**					$1,350.09	
44				**Expected NPV without Abandonment**					$706.40	
45				**Difference = Value of the Option**					$643.68	
46										

going well, the project would be continued. However, if things were going badly, the firm would close the operation and not suffer the indicated losses during the next 3 years.[12]

Given the "Can Abandon" option, the firm would clearly prefer to abandon the project than to continue it under the worst-case scenario. Therefore, we assign a zero probability to continuing after a bad start. Therefore, the 25% probability associated with the worst case is used for "Worst #2" and a 0% probability is assigned to "Worst #1."

The option to abandon raises the expected NPV from $706.40 to $1,350.09, and it also lowers the standard deviation. Those changes combine to lower the coefficient of variation from 6.19 to 2.70. The coefficient of variation is still above the company's average CV of 2.0, which indicates that the project is still more risky than most, even after the abandonment option has been considered. Therefore, the 12.50% WACC is still appropriate for discounting this project's free cash flows. Also, note that the difference between the expected NPVs with and without abandonment represents the **option value** to abandon this project. As shown in the lower part of Table 12.3, this option is worth $643.68. If the NPV of the "No Abandonment" situation had been negative, then the value of the option would simply have been the NPV of the "Can Abandon" situation.

With this project, the ability to abandon it makes the NPV look better, but it does not reverse the accept/reject decision. However, it often turns out that if we fail to consider abandonment, the bad case is so bad that the expected NPV is negative, but when abandonment is considered, the expected NPV becomes positive. Clearly, abandonment must be considered to obtain valid assessments for different projects, and the opportunity to abandon a project is an important way to limit downside losses.

Note too that it might be necessary for the firm to arrange things so that it has the possibility of abandonment when it is making the initial decision about a project. This might require contractual arrangements with suppliers, customers, and its union, and there might be some costs to obtaining these advance permissions. Any such costs could be compared with the value of the option as we calculated it, and this could enter into the initial decision.

Option Value

The difference between the expected NPVs with and without the relevant option. It is the value that is not accounted for in a traditional NPV analysis. A positive option value expands the firm's opportunities.

SELF TEST

Why might DCF techniques not always lead to proper capital budgeting decisions?

What is a real option?

What are some types of real options? Briefly explain each one.

Would you expect an abandonment option to increase or decrease a project's NPV and its risk as measured by the coefficient of variation? Why?

How can the value of an option be estimated?

12-8 THE OPTIMAL CAPITAL BUDGET

Thus far, we have described various factors that managers consider when they evaluate individual projects. For planning purposes, managers must also forecast the total capital budget, because the amount of capital raised affects

---

[12]If the assets devoted to the project could be sold, then this after-tax amount would be a cash inflow at the time of the sale, presumably at the end of Year 1.

the WACC and thus influences projects' NPVs. We use Data Devices Inc. (DDI), a manufacturer and distributor of storage devices, to illustrate how this process works.

Step 1. The treasurer obtains an estimate of the firm's overall composite WACC. As we discussed in Chapter 10, this composite WACC is based on market conditions, the firm's capital structure, and the riskiness of its assets. DDI's projects are roughly similar from year to year in terms of their risks.

Step 2. The corporate WACC is scaled up or down for each of the firm's divisions to reflect the division's risk. DDI, for example, assigns a factor of 0.9 to its stable, low-risk replacement battery division, but a factor of 1.1 to its large disk drives, which it sells to computer manufacturers and whose business is extremely competitive. Therefore, if the corporate cost of capital is determined to be 10.50%, the cost of capital for the battery division is 0.9(10.50%) = 9.45%, while that for the disk-drive division is 1.1(10.50%) = 11.55%.

Step 3. Financial managers within each of the firm's divisions estimate the relevant cash flows and risks of each of their potential projects. The estimated cash flows should explicitly consider any embedded real options. Then, within each division, projects are classified into one of three groups—high risk, average risk, and low risk—and the same 0.9 and 1.1 factors are used to adjust the divisional cost of capital estimates. (A factor of 1.0 would be used for an average-risk project.) For example, a low-risk project in the battery division would be assigned a cost of capital of 0.9(9.45%) = 8.51%, while a high-risk project in the disk-drive division would have a cost of 1.1(11.55%) = 12.71%.

Step 4. Each project's NPV is then determined, using its risk-adjusted cost of capital. The optimal capital budget consists of all independent projects with positive NPVs plus those mutually exclusive projects with the highest positive NPVs.

In estimating its **optimal capital budget**, we assumed that DDI can obtain financing for all of its profitable projects. This assumption is reasonable for large, mature firms with good track records. However, smaller firms, new firms, and firms with dubious track records, may have difficulties raising capital, even for projects that the firm concludes would have highly positive NPVs. In such circumstances, the size of the capital budget may be constrained, a situation called **capital rationing**. If capital is limited, it should be used in the most efficient way possible. Procedures have been developed for allocating capital so as to maximize the aggregate NPV subject to the constraint that the capital rationing ceiling is not exceeded. However, these procedures are extremely complicated, so they are best left for advanced finance courses.

The procedures discussed in this section cannot be implemented with precision. However, they do force the firm to think carefully about each division's relative risk, about the risk of each project within the divisions, and about the relationship between the total amount of capital raised and the cost of that capital. Further, the process forces the firm to adjust its capital budget to reflect capital market conditions. If the costs of debt and equity rise, this fact will be reflected in the cost of capital used to evaluate projects, and projects that would be marginally acceptable when capital costs were low would (correctly) be ruled unacceptable when capital costs become high.

Optimal Capital Budget
The annual investment in long-term assets that maximizes the firm's value.

Capital Rationing
The situation in which a firm can raise only a specified, limited amount of capital regardless of how many good projects it has.

12-9 THE POST-AUDIT

A final aspect of the capital budgeting process is the post-audit, which involves (1) comparing actual results with those predicted by the project's sponsors and (2) explaining why any differences occurred. For example, many firms require that the operating divisions send a monthly report for the first six months after a project goes into operation and a quarterly report thereafter, until the project's results meet expectations. From then on, reports on the operation are reviewed on a regular basis like those of other operations. The post-audit has two main purposes:

1. *Improve forecasts.* When decision makers are forced to compare their projections with actual outcomes, there is a tendency for estimates to improve. Conscious or unconscious biases are observed and eliminated; new forecasting methods are sought as the need for them becomes apparent; and people simply tend to do everything better, including forecasting, if they know that their actions are being monitored.

2. *Improve operations.* Businesses are run by people, and people can perform at higher or lower levels of efficiency. When a divisional team has made a forecast about an investment, the team members are, in a sense, putting their reputations on the line. Accordingly, if costs are above and sales below predicted levels, then executives in production, marketing, and other areas will strive to improve operations and to bring results into line with forecasts. In a discussion related to this point, one executive made this statement: "You academicians only worry about making good decisions. In business, we also worry about making decisions good."

The post-audit is not a simple process. First, we must recognize that each element of the cash flow forecast is subject to uncertainty, so a percentage of all projects undertaken by any reasonably aggressive firm will necessarily go awry. This fact must be considered when appraising the performances of the operating executives who sponsor projects. Second, projects sometimes fail to meet expectations for reasons beyond the control of their sponsors and for reasons that no one could be expected to anticipate. Third, it is often difficult to separate the operating results of one investment from those of a larger system. Although some projects stand alone and permit ready identification of costs and revenues, the cost savings that result from assets like new computers may be very hard to measure. Fourth, it is often hard to hand out blame or praise because the executives who were responsible for launching a given investment have moved on by the time the results are known.

Because of these difficulties, some firms tend to play down the importance of the post-audit. However, observations of both businesses and governmental units suggest that the best-run and most successful organizations put a lot of emphasis on post-audits. Accordingly, we regard the post-audit as an important element in a good capital budgeting system.

SELF TEST

What is done in the post-audit?

Identify several benefits of the post-audit.

What are some factors that complicate the post-audit process?

TYING IT ALL TOGETHER

This chapter focused on estimating the free cash flows that are used in a capital budgeting analysis, appraising the riskiness of those flows, finding NPVs when risk is present, and calculating the NPVs of mutually exclusive projects having unequal lives. Here is a summary of our primary conclusions:

- Some cash flows are *relevant* (hence, should be included in a capital budgeting analysis), while others should not be included. The key question is this: Is the cash flow *incremental* in the sense that it will occur if and only if the project is accepted?
- *Sunk costs* are not incremental costs—they are not affected by accepting or rejecting the project. *Cannibalization* and other *externalities,* on the other hand, are incremental—they will occur if and only if the project is accepted.
- The cash flows used to analyze a project are different from a project's *net income.* One important factor is that *depreciation* is deducted when accountants calculate net income, but because it is a noncash charge, it must be added back to find cash flows.
- Many projects require additional *net operating working capital.* An increase in net operating working capital is an additional outlay when the project is started but is an inflow at the end of the project's life, when the capital is recovered (i.e., the investment in operating working capital is reduced when the project is completed).
- We considered two types of projects, expansion and replacement. For a replacement project, we find the difference in the free cash flows when the firm continues to use the old asset versus the new asset. If the NPV of the differential flows is positive, the replacement should be made.
- The forecasted free cash flows (and hence NPV and other outputs) are only estimates—they may turn out to be incorrect, and this means *risk.*
- There are three types of risk: *stand-alone, within-firm,* and *market* (or *beta) risk.* In theory, market risk is most relevant; but because it cannot be measured for

most projects, stand-alone risk is the one on which we generally focus. However, firms subjectively consider within-firm and market risk, which they definitely should not ignore. Note, though, that because the three types of risk are generally positively correlated, stand-alone risk is often a good proxy for the other risks.

- Stand-alone risk can be analyzed using *sensitivity analysis, scenario analysis,* and/or *Monte Carlo simulation.*
- Once a decision has been made about a project's relative risk, we determine a *risk-adjusted WACC* for evaluating it.
- *Real options* enable firms to take actions to alter the originally forecasted cash flows after a project is in operation. These options can increase NPVs and reduce risk.
- The *post-audit*, which compares the project's actual performance to its expected results, is an important part of the capital budgeting process.

SELF-TEST QUESTIONS AND PROBLEMS

(Solutions Appear in Appendix A)

ST-1 **KEY TERMS** Define the following terms:

a. Incremental cash flow; sunk cost; opportunity cost; externality; cannibalization

b. Stand-alone risk; corporate (within-firm) risk; market (beta) risk

c. Risk-adjusted cost of capital

d. Sensitivity analysis; base-case NPV

e. Scenario analysis; base-case scenario; worst-case scenario; best-case scenario

f. Monte Carlo simulation

g. Real option; abandonment option; decision tree

h. Option value

i. Optimal capital budget; capital rationing

j. Post-audit

ST-2 **PROJECT AND RISK ANALYSIS** As a financial analyst, you must evaluate a proposed project to produce printer cartridges. The equipment would cost $55,000, plus $10,000 for installation. Annual sales would be 4,000 units at a price of $50 per cartridge, and the project's life would be 3 years. Current assets would increase by $5,000 and payables by $3,000. At the end of 3 years the equipment could be sold for $10,000. Depreciation would be based on the MACRS 3-year class, so the applicable rates would be 33%, 45%, 15%, and 7%. Variable costs would be 70% of sales revenues, fixed costs excluding depreciation would be $30,000 per year, the marginal tax rate is 40%, and the corporate WACC is 11%.

a. What is the required investment, that is, the Year 0 project cash flow?

b. What are the annual depreciation charges?

c. What are the project's annual cash flows?

d. If the project is of average risk, what is its NPV? Should it be accepted?

e. Management is uncertain about the exact unit sales. What would the project's NPV be if unit sales turned out to be 20% below forecast but other inputs were as forecasted? Would this change the decision? Explain.

f. The CFO asks you to do a scenario analysis using these inputs:

	Probability	Unit Sales	VC%
Best case	25%	4,800	65%
Base case	50	4,000	70
Worst case	25	3,200	75

Other variables are unchanged. What are the expected NPV, its standard deviation, and the coefficient of variation? [Hint: To do the scenario analysis, you must change unit sales and VC% to the values specified for each scenario, get the scenario cash flows, and then find each scenario's NPV. Then you must calculate the project's expected NPV, standard deviation(σ), and coefficient of variation (CV). This is not difficult, but it would require a lot of calculations. You might want to look at the answer in Appendix A at the back of the text, but make sure you understand how it was calculated.]

g. The firm's project CVs generally range from 1.0 to 1.5. A 3% risk premium is added to the WACC if the initial CV exceeds 1.5, and the WACC is reduced by 0.5% if the CV is 0.75 or less. Then a revised NPV is calculated. What WACC should be used for this project when project risk has been properly considered? What are the revised values for the NPV, standard deviation, and coefficient of variation? Would you recommend that the project be accepted? Why or why not?

QUESTIONS

12-1 Operating cash flows rather than accounting income are listed in Table 12.1. Why do we focus on cash flows as opposed to net income in capital budgeting?

12-2 Explain why sunk costs should not be included in a capital budgeting analysis but opportunity costs and externalities should be included. Give an example of each.

12-3 Explain why net operating working capital is included in a capital budgeting analysis and how it is recovered at the end of a project's life.

12-4 Why are interest charges not deducted when a project's cash flows for use in a capital budgeting analysis are calculated?

12-5 Most firms generate cash inflows every day, not just once at the end of the year. In capital budgeting, should we recognize this fact by estimating daily project cash flows and then using them in the analysis? If we do not, are our results biased? If so, would the NPV be biased up or down? Explain.

12-6 What are some differences in the analysis for a replacement project versus that for a new expansion project?

12-7 Distinguish among beta (or market) risk, within-firm (or corporate) risk, and stand-alone risk for a project being considered for inclusion in the capital budget.

12-8 In theory, market risk should be the only "relevant" risk. However, companies focus as much on stand-alone risk as on market risk. What are the reasons for the focus on stand-alone risk?

12-9 Define (a) sensitivity analysis, (b) scenario analysis, and (c) simulation analysis. If GE were considering two projects (one for $500 million to develop a satellite communications system and the other for $30,000 for a new truck), on which would the company be more likely to use a simulation analysis?

12-10 If you were the CFO of a company that had to decide on hundreds of potential projects every year, would you want to use sensitivity analysis and scenario analysis as described in the chapter, or would the amount of arithmetic required take too much time and thus not be cost-effective? What involvement would nonfinancial people such as those in marketing, accounting, and production have in the analysis?

PROBLEMS

**Easy Problems
1–5**

12-1 **REQUIRED INVESTMENT** Truman Industries is considering an expansion. The necessary equipment would be purchased for $9 million, and the expansion would require an additional $3 million investment in net operating working capital. The tax rate is 40%.

a. What is the initial investment outlay?

b. The company spent and expensed $50,000 on research related to the project last year. Would this change your answer? Explain.

c. The company plans to use a building that it owns to house the project. The building could be sold for $1 million after taxes and real estate commissions. How would that fact affect your answer?

12-2 **PROJECT CASH FLOW** Eisenhower Communications is trying to estimate the first-year cash flow (at Year 1) for a proposed project. The financial staff has collected the following information on the project:

Sales revenues	$10 million
Operating costs (excluding depreciation)	7 million
Depreciation	2 million
Interest expense	2 million

The company has a 40% tax rate, and its WACC is 10%.

a. What is the project's cash flow for the first year ($t = 1$)?

b. If this project would cannibalize other projects by $1 million of cash flow before taxes per year, how would this change your answer to Part a?

c. Ignore Part b. If the tax rate dropped to 30%, how would that change your answer to Part a?

12-3 **AFTER-TAX SALVAGE VALUE** Kennedy Air Services is now in the final year of a project. The equipment originally cost $20 million, of which 80% has been depreciated. Kennedy can sell the used equipment today for $5 million, and its tax rate is 40%. What is the equipment's after-tax salvage value?

12-4 **REPLACEMENT ANALYSIS** The Chang Company is considering the purchase of a new machine to replace an obsolete one. The machine being used for the operation has a book value and a market value of zero. However, the machine is in good working order and will last at least another 10 years. The proposed replacement machine will perform the operation so much more efficiently that Chang's engineers estimate that it will produce after-tax cash flows (labor savings and depreciation) of $9,000 per year. The new machine will cost $40,000 delivered and installed, and its economic life is estimated to be 10 years. It has zero salvage value. The firm's WACC is 10%, and its marginal tax rate is 35%. Should Chang buy the new machine?

12-5 **OPTIMAL CAPITAL BUDGET** Marble Construction estimates that its WACC is 10% if equity comes from retained earnings. However, if the company issues new stock to raise new equity, it estimates that its WACC will rise to 10.8%. The company believes that it will exhaust its retained earnings at $2,500,000 of capital due to the number of highly profitable projects available to the firm and its limited earnings. The company is considering the following seven investment projects:

Project	Size	IRR
A	$ 650,000	14.0%
B	1,050,000	13.5
C	1,000,000	11.2
D	1,200,000	11.0
E	500,000	10.7
F	650,000	10.3
G	700,000	10.2

Assume that each of these projects is independent and that each is just as risky as the firm's existing assets. Which set of projects should be accepted, and what is the firm's optimal capital budget?

Intermediate
Problems
6–12

12-6   **DEPRECIATION METHODS**   Kristin is evaluating a capital budgeting project that should last for 4 years. The project requires $800,000 of equipment. She is unsure what depreciation method to use in her analysis, straight-line or the 3-year MACRS accelerated method. Under straight-line depreciation, the cost of the equipment would be depreciated evenly over its 4-year life (ignore the half-year convention for the straight-line method). The applicable MACRS depreciation rates are 33%, 45%, 15%, and 7% as discussed in Appendix 12A. The company's WACC is 10%, and its tax rate is 40%.

a.   What would the depreciation expense be each year under each method?

b.   Which depreciation method would produce the higher NPV, and how much higher would it be?

12-7   **SCENARIO ANALYSIS**   Huang Industries is considering a proposed project whose estimated NPV is $12 million. This estimate assumes that economic conditions will be "average." However, the CFO realizes that conditions could be better or worse, so she performed a scenario analysis and obtained these results:

Economic Scenario	Probability of Outcome	NPV
Recession	0.05	($70 million)
Below average	0.20	(25 million)
Average	0.50	12 million
Above average	0.20	20 million
Boom	0.05	30 million

Calculate the project's expected NPV, standard deviation, and coefficient of variation.

12-8   **NEW PROJECT ANALYSIS**   You must evaluate the purchase of a proposed spectrometer for the R&D department. The base price is $140,000, and it would cost another $30,000 to modify the equipment for special use by the firm. The equipment falls into the MACRS 3-year class and would be sold after 3 years for $60,000. The applicable depreciation rates are 33%, 45%, 15%, and 7% as discussed in Appendix 12A. The equipment would require an $8,000 increase in net operating working capital (spare parts inventory). The project would have no effect on revenues, but it should save the firm $50,000 per year in before-tax labor costs. The firm's marginal federal-plus-state tax rate is 40%.

a.   What is the initial investment outlay for the spectrometer, that is, what is the Year 0 project cash flow?

b.   What are the project's annual cash flows in Years 1, 2, and 3?

c.   If the WACC is 12%, should the spectrometer be purchased? Explain.

12-9   **NEW PROJECT ANALYSIS**   You must evaluate a proposal to buy a new milling machine. The base price is $108,000, and shipping and installation costs would add another $12,500. The machine falls into the MACRS 3-year class, and it would be sold after 3 years for $65,000. The applicable depreciation rates are 33%, 45%, 15%, and 7% as discussed in Appendix 12A. The machine would require a $5,500 increase in net operating working capital (increased inventory less increased accounts payable). There would be no effect on revenues, but pretax labor costs would decline by $44,000 per year. The marginal tax rate is 35%, and the WACC is 12%. Also, the firm spent $5,000 last year investigating the feasibility of using the machine.

a.   How should the $5,000 spent last year be handled?

b.   What is the initial investment outlay for the machine for capital budgeting purposes, that is, what is the Year 0 project cash flow?

c.   What are the project's annual cash flows during Years 1, 2, and 3?

d.   Should the machine be purchased? Explain your answer.

12-10   **REPLACEMENT ANALYSIS**   The Dauten Toy Corporation currently uses an injection molding machine that was purchased 2 years ago. This machine is being depreciated on a straight-line basis, and it has 6 years of remaining life. Its current book value is $2,100, and it can be sold for $2,500 at this time. Thus, the annual depreciation expense is $2,100/6 = $350 per year. If the old machine is not replaced, it can be sold for $500 at the end of its useful life.

Dauten is offered a replacement machine which has a cost of $8,000, an estimated useful life of 6 years, and an estimated salvage value of $800. This machine falls into the MACRS 5-year class so the applicable depreciation rates are 20%, 32%, 19%, 12%, 11%, and 6%. The replacement machine would permit an output expansion, so sales would rise by $1,000 per year; even so, the new machine's much greater efficiency would cause operating expenses to decline by $1,500 per year. The new machine would require that inventories be increased by $2,000, but accounts payable would simultaneously increase by $500. Dauten's marginal federal-plus-state tax rate is 40%, and its WACC is 15%. Should it replace the old machine?

12-11 **REPLACEMENT ANALYSIS** Mississippi River Shipyards is considering the replacement of an 8-year-old riveting machine with a new one that will increase earnings before depreciation from $27,000 to $54,000 per year. The new machine will cost $82,500, and it will have an estimated life of 8 years and no salvage value. The new machine will be depreciated over its 5-year MACRS recovery period; so the applicable depreciation rates are 20%, 32%, 19%, 12%, 11%, and 6%. The applicable corporate tax rate is 40%, and the firm's WACC is 12%. The old machine has been fully depreciated and has no salvage value. Should the old riveting machine be replaced by the new one? Explain your answer.

12-12 **PROJECT RISK ANALYSIS** The Butler-Perkins Company (BPC) must decide between two mutually exclusive projects. Each costs $6,750 and has an expected life of 3 years. Annual project cash flows begin 1 year after the initial investment and are subject to the following probability distributions:

Project A		Project B	
Probability	Cash Flows	Probability	Cash Flows
0.2	$6,000	0.2	$ 0
0.6	6,750	0.6	6,750
0.2	7,500	0.2	18,000

BPC has decided to evaluate the riskier project at 12% and the less-risky project at 10%.

a. What is each project's expected annual cash flow? Project B's standard deviation (σ_B) is $5,798, and its coefficient of variation (CV$_B$) is 0.76. What are the values of σ_A and CV$_A$?

b. Based on the risk-adjusted NPVs, which project should BPC choose?

c. If you knew that Project B's cash flows were negatively correlated with the firm's other cash flows whereas Project A's flows were positively correlated, how might this affect the decision? If Project B's cash flows were negatively correlated with gross domestic product (GDP), while A's flows were positively correlated, would that influence your risk assessment?

Challenging Problems 13–18

12-13 **SCENARIO ANALYSIS** Your firm, Agrico Products, is considering a tractor that would have a cost of $36,000, would increase pretax operating cash flows before taking account of depreciation by $12,000 per year, and would be depreciated on a straight-line basis to zero over 5 years at the rate of $7,200 per year beginning the first year. (Thus, annual cash flows would be $12,000 before taxes plus the tax savings that result from $7,200 of depreciation.) The managers disagree about whether the tractor would last 5 years. The controller insists that she knows of tractors that have lasted only 4 years. The treasurer agrees with the controller, but he argues that most tractors do give 5 years of service. The service manager then states that some last for as long as 8 years.

Given this discussion, the CFO asks you to prepare a scenario analysis to determine the importance of the tractor's life on the NPV. Use a 40% marginal federal-plus-state tax rate, a zero salvage value, and a 10% WACC. Assuming each of the indicated lives has the same probability of occurring (probability = 1/3), what is the tractor's expected NPV? (Hint: Use the 5-year straight-line depreciation for all analyses and ignore the MACRS half-year convention for this problem.)

12-14 **NEW PROJECT ANALYSIS** Holmes Manufacturing is considering a new machine that costs $250,000 and would reduce pretax manufacturing costs by $90,000 annually. Holmes would use the 3-year MACRS method to depreciate the machine, and management thinks the machine would have a value of $23,000 at the end of its 5-year operating life. The applicable depreciation rates are 33%, 45%, 15%, and 7% as discussed in Appendix 12A. Net operating working capital would increase by $25,000 initially, but it would be recovered at the end of the project's 5-year life. Holmes's marginal tax rate is 40%, and a 10% WACC is appropriate for the project.

a. Calculate the project's NPV, IRR, MIRR, and payback.

b. Assume management is unsure about the $90,000 cost savings—this figure could deviate by as much as plus or minus 20%. What would the NPV be under each of these situations?

c. Suppose the CFO wants you to do a scenario analysis with different values for the cost savings, the machine's salvage value, and the net operating working capital (NOWC) requirement. She asks you to use the following probabilities and values in the scenario analysis:

Scenario	Probability	Cost Savings	Salvage Value	NOWC
Worst case	0.35	$ 72,000	$18,000	$30,000
Base case	0.35	90,000	23,000	25,000
Best case	0.30	108,000	28,000	20,000

Calculate the project's expected NPV, its standard deviation, and its coefficient of variation. Would you recommend that the project be accepted? Why or why not?

12-15 **REPLACEMENT ANALYSIS** The Erley Equipment Company purchased a machine 5 years ago at a cost of $90,000. The machine had an expected life of 10 years at the time of purchase, and it is being depreciated by the straight-line method by $9,000 per year. If the machine is not replaced, it can be sold for $10,000 at the end of its useful life.

A new machine can be purchased for $150,000, including installation costs. During its 5-year life, it will reduce cash operating expenses by $50,000 per year. Sales are not expected to change. At the end of its useful life, the machine is estimated to be worthless. MACRS depreciation will be used, and the machine will be depreciated over its 3-year class life rather than its 5-year economic life; so the applicable depreciation rates are 33%, 45%, 15%, and 7%.

The old machine can be sold today for $55,000. The firm's tax rate is 35%. The appropriate WACC is 16%.

a. If the new machine is purchased, what is the amount of the initial cash flow at Year 0?

b. What are the incremental cash flows that will occur at the end of Years 1 through 5?

c. What is the NPV of this project? Should Erley replace the old machine? Explain.

12-16 **REPLACEMENT ANALYSIS** The Bigbee Bottling Company is contemplating the replacement of one of its bottling machines with a newer and more efficient one. The old machine has a book value of $600,000 and a remaining useful life of 5 years. The firm does not expect to realize any return from scrapping the old machine in 5 years, but it can sell it now to another firm in the industry for $265,000. The old machine is being depreciated by $120,000 per year, using the straight-line method.

The new machine has a purchase price of $1,175,000, an estimated useful life and MACRS class life of 5 years, and an estimated salvage value of $145,000. The applicable depreciation rates are 20%, 32%, 19%, 12%, 11%, and 6%. It is expected to economize on electric power usage, labor, and repair costs, as well as to reduce the number of defective bottles. In total, an annual savings of $255,000 will be realized if the new machine is installed. The company's marginal tax rate is 35% and it has a 12% WACC.

a. What initial cash outlay is required for the new machine?

b. Calculate the annual depreciation allowances for both machines and compute the change in the annual depreciation expense if the replacement is made.

   c. What are the incremental cash flows in Years 1 through 5?

   d. Should the firm purchase the new machine? Support your answer.

   e. In general, how would each of the following factors affect the investment decision, and how should each be treated?

     1. The expected life of the existing machine decreases.

     2. The WACC is not constant but is increasing as Bigbee adds more projects into its capital budget for the year.

12-17 **ABANDONMENT OPTION** The Scampini Supplies Company recently purchased a new delivery truck. The new truck costs $22,500; and it is expected to generate after-tax cash flows, including depreciation, of $6,250 per year. The truck has a 5-year expected life. The expected year-end abandonment values (salvage values after tax adjustments) for the truck are given here. The company's WACC is 10%.

Year	Annual After-Tax Cash Flow	Abandonment Value
0	($22,500)	—
1	6,250	$17,500
2	6,250	14,000
3	6,250	11,000
4	6,250	5,000
5	6,250	0

   a. Should the firm operate the truck until the end of its 5-year physical life; if not, what is the truck's optimal economic life?

   b. Would the introduction of abandonment values, in addition to operating cash flows, ever *reduce* the expected NPV and/or IRR of a project? Explain.

12-18 **OPTIMAL CAPITAL BUDGET** Hampton Manufacturing estimates that its WACC is 12.5%. The company is considering the following seven investment projects:

Project	Size	IRR
A	$ 750,000	14.0%
B	1,250,000	13.5
C	1,250,000	13.2
D	1,250,000	13.0
E	750,000	12.7
F	750,000	12.3
G	750,000	12.2

   a. Assume that each of these projects is independent and that each is just as risky as the firm's existing assets. Which set of projects should be accepted, and what is the firm's optimal capital budget?

   b. Now assume that Projects C and D are mutually exclusive. Project D has an NPV of $400,000, whereas Project C has an NPV of $350,000. Which set of projects should be accepted, and what is the firm's optimal capital budget?

   c. Ignore Part b and assume that each of the projects is independent but that management decides to incorporate project risk differentials. Management judges Projects B, C, D, and E to have average risk; Project A to have high risk; and Projects F and G to have low risk. The company adds 2% to the WACC of those projects that are significantly more risky than average, and it subtracts 2% from the WACC of those projects that are substantially less risky than average. Which set of projects should be accepted, and what is the firm's optimal capital budget?

Comprehensive/Spreadsheet Problem

12-19   **NEW PROJECT ANALYSIS**   You must analyze a potential new product—a caulking compound that Cory Materials' R&D people developed for use in the residential construction industry. Cory's marketing manager thinks the company can sell 115,000 tubes per year at a price of $3.25 each for 3 years, after which the product will be obsolete. The required equipment would cost $150,000, plus another $25,000 for shipping and installation. Current assets (receivables and inventories) would increase by $35,000, while current liabilities (accounts payable and accruals) would rise by $15,000. Variable cost per unit is $1.95, fixed costs (exclusive of depreciation) would be $70,000 per year, and fixed assets would be depreciated under MACRS with a 3-year life. (Refer to Appendix 12A for MACRS depreciation rates.) When production ceases after 3 years, the equipment should have a market value of $15,000. Cory's tax rate is 40%, and it uses a 10% WACC for average-risk projects.

a. Find the required Year 0 investment and the project's annual cash flows. Then calculate the project's NPV, IRR, MIRR, and payback. Assume at this point that the project is of average risk.

b. Suppose you now learn that R&D costs for the new product were $30,000 and that those costs were incurred and expensed for tax purposes last year. How would this affect your estimate of NPV and the other profitability measures?

c. If the new project would reduce cash flows from Cory's other projects and if the new project would be housed in an empty building that Cory owns and could sell, how would those factors affect the project's NPV?

d. Are this project's cash flows likely to be positively or negatively correlated with returns on Cory's other projects and with the economy, and should this matter in your analysis? Explain.

e. **Spreadsheet assignment: at instructor's option**   Construct a spreadsheet that calculates the cash flows, NPV, IRR, payback, and MIRR.

f. The CEO expressed concern that some of the base-case inputs for the caulking compound might be too optimistic or too pessimistic, and he wants to know how the NPV would be affected if these six variables were 20% above or 20% below the base-case levels: unit sales, sales price, variable cost, fixed costs, WACC, and equipment cost. Hold other things constant when you consider each variable and construct a sensitivity graph to illustrate your results.

g. Do a scenario analysis based on the assumption that there is a 25% probability that each of the six variables itemized in Part f will turn out to have their best-case values as calculated in Part f, a 50% probability that all will have their base-case values, and a 25% probability that all will have their worst-case values. The other variables remain at base-case levels. Calculate the expected NPV, the standard deviation of NPV, and the coefficient of variation.

h. Does Cory's management use the risk-adjusted discount rate to adjust for project risk? Explain.

INTEGRATED CASE

ALLIED FOOD PRODUCTS

12-20   **CAPITAL BUDGETING AND CASH FLOW ESTIMATION**   Allied Food Products is considering expanding into the fruit juice business with a new fresh lemon juice product. Assume that you were recently hired as assistant to the director of capital budgeting and you must evaluate the new project.

The lemon juice would be produced in an unused building adjacent to Allied's Fort Myers plant; Allied owns the building, which is fully depreciated. The required equipment would cost $200,000, plus an additional $40,000 for shipping and installation. In addition, inventories would rise by $25,000, while accounts payable would increase by $5,000. All of these costs would be incurred at t = 0. By a special ruling, the machinery could be depreciated under the MACRS system as 3-year property. The applicable depreciation rates are 33%, 45%, 15%, and 7%.

The project is expected to operate for 4 years, at which time it will be terminated. The cash inflows are assumed to begin 1 year after the project is undertaken, or at t = 1, and to continue out to t = 4. At the end of the project's life (t = 4), the equipment is expected to have a salvage value of $25,000.

Unit sales are expected to total 100,000 units per year, and the expected sales price is $2.00 per unit. Cash operating costs for the project (total operating costs less depreciation) are expected to total 60% of dollar sales. Allied's tax rate is 40%, and its WACC is 10%. Tentatively, the lemon juice project is assumed to be of equal risk to Allied's other assets.

You have been asked to evaluate the project and to make a recommendation as to whether it should be accepted or rejected. To guide you in your analysis, your boss gave you the following set of tasks/questions:

a. Allied has a standard form that is used in the capital budgeting process. (See Table IC 12.1.) Part of the table has been completed, but you must replace the blanks with the missing numbers. Complete the table using the following steps:

1. Fill in the blanks under Year 0 for the initial investment outlays: CAPEX and ΔNOWC.

2. Complete the table for unit sales, sales price, total revenues, and operating costs excluding depreciation.

3. Complete the depreciation data.

4. Complete the table down to after-tax operating income and then down to the project's operating cash flows, EBIT(1 − T) + DEP.

5. Fill in the blanks under Year 4 for the terminal cash flows and complete the project free cash flow line. Discuss the recovery of net operating working capital. What would have happened if the machinery were sold for less than its book value?

b. 1. Allied uses debt in its capital structure, so some of the money used to finance the project will be debt. Given this fact, should the projected cash flows be revised to show projected interest charges? Explain.

2. Suppose you learned that Allied had spent $50,000 to renovate the building last year, expensing these costs. Should this cost be reflected in the analysis? Explain.

3. Suppose you learned that Allied could lease its building to another party and earn $25,000 per year. Should that fact be reflected in the analysis? If so, how?

4. Assume that the lemon juice project would take profitable sales away from Allied's fresh orange juice business. Should that fact be reflected in your analysis? If so, how?

c. Disregard all the assumptions made in Part b and assume there is no alternative use for the building over the next 4 years. Now calculate the project's NPV, IRR, MIRR, and payback. Do these indicators suggest that the project should be accepted? Explain.

d. If this project had been a replacement rather than an expansion project, how would the analysis have changed? Think about the changes that would have to occur in the cash flow table.

e. 1. What three levels, or types, of project risk are normally considered?

2. Which type is most relevant?

3. Which type is easiest to measure?

4. Are the three types of risk generally highly correlated?

f. 1. What is sensitivity analysis?

2. How would you perform a sensitivity analysis on the unit sales, salvage value, and WACC for the project? Assume that each of these variables deviates from its base-case, or expected, value by plus or minus 10%, 20%, and 30%. Explain how you would calculate the NPV, IRR, MIRR, and payback for each case; but don't do the analysis unless your instructor asks you to.

3. What is the primary weakness of sensitivity analysis? What are its primary advantages?

Calculate the answers to the remaining questions only if your instructor asks you to. Also note that it will take a *long time* to do the calculations unless you are using an Excel model.

Allied's Lemon Juice Project (in Thousands)					**TABLE IC 12.1**
End of Year:	0	1	2	3	4
I. Investment Outlays					
Equipment cost					
Installation	___				
CAPEX					
Increase in inventory					
Increase in accounts payable	___				
ΔNOWC					
II. Project Operating Cash Flows					
Unit sales (thousands)			100		
Price/unit		$ 2.00	$ 2.00	___	___
Total revenues		___	___	___	$200.0
Operating costs excluding depreciation			$120.0		
Depreciation				36.0	16.8
Total costs		$ 199.2	$228.0	___	___
EBIT (or operating income)				$44.0	
Taxes on operating income		0.3	___		25.3
EBIT (1 – T) = After-tax operating income				$ 26.4	
Add back depreciation		79.2		36.0	
EBIT (1 – T) + DEP	$ 0.0	$ 79.7	___	___	$ 54.7
III. Project Termination Cash Flows					
Salvage value (taxed as ordinary income)					
Tax on salvage value					
After-tax salvage value					___
ΔNOWC = Recovery of net operating working capital	___	___	___	___	___
Project free cash flows = EBIT(1 – T) + DEP – CAPEX – ΔNOWC	($260.0)	___	___	___	$ 89.7
IV. Results					
NPV =					
IRR =					
MIRR =					

g. Assume that inflation is expected to average 5% over the next 4 years and that this expectation is reflected in the WACC. Moreover, inflation is expected to increase revenues and variable costs by this same 5%. Does it appear that inflation has been dealt with properly in the initial analysis to this point? If not, what should be done and how would the required adjustment affect the decision?

h. The expected cash flows, considering inflation (in thousands of dollars), are given in Table IC 12.2. Allied's WACC is 10%. Assume that you are confident about the estimates of all the variables that affect the cash flows except unit sales. If product acceptance is poor, sales would be only 75,000 units a year, while a strong consumer response would produce sales of 125,000 units. In either case, cash costs would still amount to 60% of revenues. You believe that there is a

TABLE IC 12.2 Allied's Lemon Juice Project Considering 5% Inflation (in Thousands)

	Year				
	0	1	2	3	4
Investment Outlays:					
CAPEX	($240)				
ΔNOWC	(20)				
Project Operating Cash Flows:					
Units sales (thousands)		100	100	100	100
Sales price (dollars)		$ 2.100	$2.205	$ 2.315	$ 2.431
Total revenues		$210.0	$220.5	$231.5	$243.1
Cash operating costs (60%)		126.0	132.3	138.9	145.9
Depreciation		79.2	108.0	36.0	16.8
EBIT (or operating income)		$ 4.8	($ 19.8)	$ 56.6	$ 80.4
Taxes on operating income (40%)		1.9	(7.9)	22.6	32.1
EBIT(1 – T) = After-tax operating income		$ 2.9	($ 11.9)	$ 34.0	$ 48.3
Plus depreciation		79.2	108.0	36.0	16.8
EBIT(1 – T) + DEP		$ 82.1	$ 96.1	$ 70.0	$ 65.1
Terminal Cash Flows:					
Salvage value					25.0
Tax on SV (40%)					10.0
After-tax salvage value					15.0
ΔNOWC					20.0
Project free cash flows	($ 260)	$ 82.1	$ 96.1	$ 70.0	$100.1
Cumulative cash flows for payback:	(260.0)	(177.9)	(81.8)	(11.8)	88.3
Compounded inflows for MIRR:		109.2	116.3	77.0	100.1
Sum of compounded inflows:					402.6
NPV = $15.0					
IRR = 12.6%					
MIRR = 11.6%					

© Cengage Learning 2015

25% chance of poor acceptance, a 25% chance of excellent acceptance, and a 50% chance of average acceptance (the base case). Provide numbers only if you are using a computer model.

1. What is the worst-case NPV? The best-case NPV?

2. Use the worst-case, most likely case (or base-case), and best-case NPVs with their probabilities of occurrence, to find the project's expected NPV, standard deviation, and coefficient of variation.

i. Assume that Allied's average project has a coefficient of variation (CV) in the range of 1.25 to 1.75. Would the lemon juice project be classified as high risk, average risk, or low risk? What type of risk is being measured here?

j. Based on common sense, how highly correlated do you think the project would be with the firm's other assets? (Give a correlation coefficient or range of coefficients, based on your judgment.)

k. How would the correlation coefficient and the previously calculated σ combine to affect the project's contribution to corporate, or within-firm, risk? Explain.

l. Based on your judgment, what do you think the project's correlation coefficient would be with respect to the general economy and thus with returns on "the market"? How would correlation with the economy affect the project's market risk?

m. Allied typically adds or subtracts 3% to its WACC to adjust for risk. After adjusting for risk, should the lemon juice project be accepted? Should any subjective risk factors be considered before the final decision is made? Explain.

n. In recent months, Allied's group has begun to focus on real option analysis.

   1. What is real option analysis?

   2. What are some examples of projects with embedded real options?

Tax Depreciation

Depreciation is covered in detail in accounting courses, so here we provide only some basic information that is needed for capital budgeting. First, note that accountants generally calculate each asset's depreciation in two ways—they generally use straight line to figure the depreciation used for reporting profits to investors, but they use depreciation rates provided by the Internal Revenue Service (IRS) and called MACRS (Modified Accelerated Cost Recovery System) rates when they calculate depreciation for tax purposes. In capital budgeting, we are concerned with tax depreciation, so the relevant rates are the MACRS rates.

Under MACRS, each type of fixed asset is assigned to a "class" and is then depreciated over the asset's **class life**. Table 12A.1 provides class lives for different types of assets as they existed in 2013. Next, as we show in Table 12A.2, MACRS specifies **annual depreciation rates** for assets in each class life. Real properties (buildings) are depreciated on a straight-line basis over 27.5 or 39 years, but all other assets are depreciated over shorter periods and on an accelerated basis, with high depreciation charges in the early years and less depreciation in the later years. The IRS tables are based on the **half-year convention**, where it is assumed that the asset is placed in service halfway through the first year and is taken out of service halfway through the year after its class life.

In the following example, we calculate depreciation on equipment that would be classified as a 5-year asset with a cost of $8 million. In developing the tables, the IRS assumes that the machinery would be used for only six months of the year in which it is acquired, for 12 months in each of the next four years, and then for six months of the sixth year. Here are the depreciation charges, in thousands, that could be deducted for tax purposes based on MACRS:

Class Life
The specified life of assets under the MACRS system.

Annual Depreciation Rates
The annual expense accountants charge against income for "wear and tear" of an asset. For tax purposes, the IRS provides that appropriate MACRS rates be used that are dependent on an asset's class life.

Half-Year Convention
Assumes assets are used for half of the first year and half of the last year.

Year	1	2	3	4	5	6
Rate	20%	32%	19%	12%	11%	6%
Depreciation	$1,600	$2,560	$1,520	$960	$880	$480

The total of the annual depreciation charges equals the $8 million cost of the asset, but it would be taken over six years and thus would affect cash flows over those six years.

TABLE 12A.1 Major Classes and Asset Lives for MACRS

Class	Type of Property
3-year	Certain special manufacturing tools
5-year	Automobiles, light-duty trucks, computers, and certain special manufacturing equipment
7-year	Most industrial equipment, office furniture, and fixtures
10-year	Certain longer-lived types of equipment
27.5-year	Residential rental real property such as apartment buildings
39-year	All nonresidential real property, including commercial and industrial buildings

© Cengage Learning 2015

| | Recovery Allowance Percentage for Personal Property | | | **TABLE 12A.2** |

	Class of Investment			
Ownership Year	**3-year**	**5-year**	**7-year**	**10-year**
1	33%	20%	14%	10%
2	45	32	25	18
3	15	19	17	14
4	7	12	13	12
5		11	9	9
6		6	9	7
7			9	7
8			4	7
9				7
10				6
11				3
	100%	100%	100%	100%

© Cengage Learning 2015

Notes:

1. We developed these recovery allowance percentages based on the 200% declining balance method prescribed by MACRS, with a switch to straight-line depreciation at some point in the asset's life. For example, consider the 5-year recovery allowance percentages. The straight-line percentage would be 20% per year, so the 200% declining balance multiplier is $2.0(20\%) = 40\% = 0.4$. However, because the half-year convention applies, the MACRS percentage for Year 1 is 20%. For Year 2, there is 80% of the depreciable basis remaining to be depreciated, so the recovery allowance percentage is $0.40(80\%) = 32\%$. In Year 3, $20\% + 32\% = 52\%$ of the depreciation has been taken, leaving 48%, so the percentage is $0.4(48\%) = 19\%$. In Year 4, the percentage is $0.4(29\%) = 12\%$. After 4 years, straight-line depreciation exceeds the declining balance depreciation, so a switch is made to straight-line (this is permitted under the law). However, the half-year convention must also be applied at the end of the class life, and the remaining 17% of depreciation must be taken (amortized) over 1.5 years. Thus, the percentage in Year 5 is $17\%/1.5 \approx 11\%$, and in Year 6, $17\% - 11\% = 6\%$. Although the tax tables carry the allowance percentages out to two decimal places, we have rounded to the nearest whole number for ease of illustration.

2. Residential rental property (apartments) is depreciated over a 27.5-year life, whereas commercial and industrial structures are depreciated over 39 years. In both cases, straight-line depreciation must be used. The depreciation allowance for the first year is based, pro rata, on the month the asset was placed in service, with the remainder of the first year's depreciation being taken in the 28th or 40th year.

PART 5

CAPITAL STRUCTURE AND DIVIDEND POLICY

CHAPTER

CHAPTER 13

Capital Structure and Leverage

Debt: Rocket Booster or Anchor? Caterpillar Inc.

If it is to grow, a firm needs capital, and capital comes primarily in the form of debt or equity. Debt financing has two important advantages: (1) Interest paid is tax deductible, whereas dividends are not deductible, and this lowers debt's relative cost to equity. (2) The return on debt is fixed, so stockholders do not have to share the firm's profits if the company turns out to be extremely successful.

However, debt also has disadvantages: (1) Using more debt increases the firm's risk, and that raises the costs of both its debt and equity. (2) If the company falls on hard times and its operating income is not sufficient to cover interest charges, then the firm may go bankrupt. Good times may be just around the corner, but too much debt can bankrupt the company before it reaches that corner.

Because of the additional risk from using debt, companies with volatile earnings and operating cash flows tend to limit its use. On the other hand, companies with low business risk and stable operating cash flows can benefit from taking on more debt. Firms realize that when bad times hit, interest must be paid so they must become "leaner" to strengthen their financial position and keep their credit rating from declining. In 2009, Caterpillar Inc. (CAT), the world's largest producer of earthmoving equipment, found itself in this precise situation.

At year-end 2008, Caterpillar's book value capital structure (debt over capital) consisted of 89% debt and 11% equity. An 89% debt ratio is quite high, and Caterpillar's management was well aware that excessive debt can push an otherwise well-regarded company into bankruptcy. Indeed, the country was in the middle of a recession that spilled over into global markets. Because Caterpillar's foreign sales made up 67% of its revenues, the company was hit hard. As a result, the firm's sales fell in 2009.

Accordingly, Caterpillar's management began to get its "financial house in order" by lowering its working capital, reducing overhead costs, and paying down its investor-supplied debt. In fact, from the first quarter of 2009 through the end of 2012, Caterpillar steadily reduced its reliance on debt financing. As a result of these actions, its debt-to-capital ratio had declined to 76%, despite a sluggish economy. For many companies, a 76% debt ratio would still be too high.

However, if we examine Caterpillar's capital structure in more detail, it soon becomes apparent that there is more here than meets the eye. At year-end, on a book-value basis, Caterpillar had about $54.5 billion of investor-supplied debt versus equity of $17.5 billion, but its market capitalization

(stock price times the number of shares outstanding) was approximately $58.7 billion. From a market-value perspective, Caterpillar's debt-to-capital ratio was only $54.5/($54.5 + $58.7) ≈ 48%, which was considerably lower than 76% calculated on a book-value basis. This helps explain why the company continued to have an A bond rating.

Indeed, in early 2013 there were some indications that the company was beginning to reverse its course. Caterpillar announced plans to reinstitute its stock buy-back program. By reducing its outstanding equity, this plan would once again push up the company's debt ratio on a book-value basis.

Caterpillar and other companies can finance with either debt or equity. Is one better than the other? If so, should firms finance either with all debt or all equity? Or, if the best solution is some mix of debt and equity, what is the optimal mix? As you read this chapter, think about these questions and consider how you would answer them.

PUTTING THINGS IN PERSPECTIVE

When we calculated the weighted average cost of capital (WACC) in Chapter 10, we assumed that the firm had a specific target capital structure. However, target capital structures often change over time, such changes affect the risk and cost of each type of capital, and all this can change the WACC. Moreover, a change in the WACC will affect capital budgeting decisions and, ultimately, the stock price.

Many factors influence capital structure decisions; and, as we will see, determining the optimal capital structure is not an exact science. Therefore, even firms in the same industry often have dramatically different capital structures. In this chapter, we consider the effects of debt on risk and on the optimal capital structure.

When you finish this chapter, you should be able to:

- Explain why there may be differences in a firm's capital structure when measured on a book-value basis, a market-value basis, or a target basis.
- Distinguish between business risk and financial risk, and explain the effects that debt financing has on the firm's expected return and risk.
- Discuss the analytical framework used when determining the optimal capital structure.
- Discuss capital structure theory, and use it to explain why firms in different industries tend to have different capital structures.

13-1 Book, Market, or "Target" Weights?

Capital

Investor-supplied funds such as long- and short-term loans from individuals and institutions, preferred stock, common stock, and retained earnings.

Capital Structure

The mix of debt, preferred stock, and common equity that is used to finance the firm's assets.

Optimal Capital Structure

The capital structure that maximizes a stock's intrinsic value.

The term **capital** refers to *investor-supplied funds*—debt, preferred stock, common stock, and retained earnings.[1] Accounts payable and accruals are *not* included in our definition of capital because they are not provided by investors—they come from suppliers, workers, and taxing authorities as a result of normal operations, not as investments by investors. A firm's **capital structure** is typically defined as the percentage of each type of investor-supplied capital, with the total being 100%. The **optimal capital structure** is the mix of debt, preferred stock, and common equity that maximizes the stock's intrinsic value. As we will see, the capital structure that maximizes the intrinsic value also minimizes the WACC.

13-1A Measuring the Capital Structure

To begin, we must answer this question: How should the capital structure be measured? Should we work with book values as provided by accountants and shown on the balance sheet; with the market values of the debt, preferred stock, and common equity; or with some other set of numbers? To see what's involved, consider Table 13.1, which compares the book and market values for Caterpillar (CAT) from a recent financial statement.[2]

TABLE 13.1   "Snapshot" of 12/31/12 Caterpillar Inc.'s Book Value, Market Value, and Target Capital Structure (Billions of Dollars)

	Condensed Balance Sheet Assets and Claims Against Assets At Book Values					Investor supplied capital: Payables and accruals are excluded because they come from operations, not from investors				
	Assets			**Claims**		**Book Value**		**Market Value**		**Target %**
Cash	$ 5.5	Accounts payable		$15.3	17.1%	–	–	–	–	–
Receivables	20.5	Accruals		2.0	2.2%	–	–	–	–	–
Inventories	15.5									
Other C.A.	1.0	Notes payable (ST debt)		12.4	13.9%	$12.4	17%	$ 12.4	11%	5%
Total C.A.	$42.5	Total C.L.		$29.7	33.3%					
		Long-term debt		42.1	47.1%	42.1	58%	42.1	37%	45%
Fixed assets	$46.8	Total liabilities		$71.8	80.4%	$54.5	**76%**	$ 54.5	**48%**	**50%**
		Common stock		$4.5	5.0%	$4.5				
		Retained earnings		13.0	14.6%	13.0				
		Total common equity		$17.5	19.6%	$17.5	**24%**	$ 58.7	**52%**	**50%**
Total assets	$89.3	Total claims		$89.3	100%	$72.0	100%	$113.2	100%	100%

Note: At the time of this analysis, CAT had 655 million shares outstanding, its book value per share was $26.76, and its market price was $89.61 per share. *We do not know its management-determined target capital structure. The 50% debt ratio is just our estimate of what a reasonable target might be.* The procedure illustrated in Section 13-3 shows how CAT *might* go about establishing its target capital structure.

[1]Capital is frequently defined to include only long-term debt, that is, debt due in more than a year. However, many companies use short-term loans from banks on a permanent basis, and for this reason we include short-term debt that is *provided by investors* in our definition of "capital."

[2]CAT's actual balance sheet is broken down into so many elements that it is several pages long. For convenience, we compress it into the categories shown in Table 13.1. The data used in the table are from its December 31, 2012, balance sheet.

1. In this case, as is generally true, the market value of the debt was fairly close to its book value; so, for simplicity, we show the same dollars of debt in both the book and market columns.

2. However at the time of this analysis, the common stock sold for $89.61 per share versus its $26.76 book value. There were 655 million shares outstanding, so the market value of the equity was $58.7 billion, calculated as $89.61(655,000,000) = $58.7 billion, versus a $17.5 billion book value.

3. For capital structure purposes, no distinction is made between common equity raised by issuing stock versus retaining earnings. Stockholders provided both components, either by purchasing newly issued shares or by allowing management to retain earnings rather than to distribute them as dividends.

4. Caterpillar does not use preferred stock, but if it did, the market value of preferred would be calculated in the same way as we calculated the market value of its common equity.

5. According to most financial theorists, it is better to use market values than book values. However, most financial analysts report data on a book-value basis, and bond rating agencies report book values and seem to give them at least as much weight as market values. Also, stock prices are quite volatile; so, if we use market values, then the weights used to calculate the WACC will also be volatile. For all these reasons, some analysts argue for the use of book values.

6. In a perfect world, a firm would identify its optimal capital structure based on market values, raise capital so as to maintain that structure, and use the optimal percentages to calculate its WACC. However, the world is not perfect. It is impossible to identify a precisely optimal structure, and given the volatility inherent in financial markets, it would be impossible to remain on target over time even if the optimal structure could be identified. As a result, most firms focus on a *target debt ratio range* as opposed to a single number.[3]

7. Generally, a firm's CFO considers the capital structures of the firms against which it benchmarks and performs an analysis similar to what we do in the remainder of this chapter.

8. Assume that Caterpillar's management concluded that the firm's optimal capital structure has 50% debt and set its target debt range at 45% to 55%. The equity range is thus (1 − % Debt), or between 45% and 55% equity. Now, for simplicity, assume that the average interest rate on both short-term and long-term debt is 5%, the cost of equity is 11%, and its corporate tax rate is approximately 30%. Using weights from Table 13.1, the following calculations show that the choice of capital structure makes a significant difference in the WACC estimates:

$$\text{WACC}_{\text{Book}} = w_{d(\text{Book})}(r_d)(1 - T) + w_{c(\text{Book})}(r_s)$$
$$= 0.76(5\%)(1 - 0.3) + 0.24(11\%) = 0.0266 + 0.0264 = 5.30\%$$

$$\text{WACC}_{\text{Market}} = w_{d(\text{Market})}(r_d)(1 - T) + w_{c(\text{Market})}(r_s)$$
$$= 0.48(5\%)(1 - 0.3) + 0.52(11\%) = 0.0168 + 0.0572 = 7.40\%$$

$$\text{WACC}_{\text{Target}} = w_{d(\text{Target})}(r_d)(1 - T) + w_{c(\text{Target})}(r_s)$$
$$= 0.5(5\%)(1 - 0.3) + 0.5(11\%) = 0.0175 + 0.055 = 7.25\%$$

The greater the difference between the stock's book value and market value, the greater the difference between the alternative WACCs.

---

[3] A study by Graham and Harvey surveyed corporate managers and asked whether their firms established a target capital structure. Eighty-one percent of the respondents indicated that their firms did have target capital structures. Ten percent said that they had strict target debt ratios, 34% indicated that they had a somewhat tight range for their target debt ratios, and 37% indicated that they had flexible targets. See John R. Graham and Campbell R. Harvey, "The Theory and Practice of Corporate Finance: Evidence from the Field," *Journal of Financial Economics*, vol. 60, nos. 2 & 3 (May–June 2001), pp. 187–243.

9. Using the 50% midpoint target debt ratio, our estimate of CAT's WACC for an average-risk project would be 7.25%, or approximately 7.3%.

If the actual debt ratio were significantly below the target range, the firm would probably raise capital by issuing debt, whereas if the debt ratio were above the target range, equity would probably be used. Note also that the target range is likely to change over time as conditions change. As discussed in the opening vignette, Caterpillar has initiated a stock buy-back program so it appears that the company's target debt ratio is somewhere in the higher part of the 45%–55% range.

13-1B CAPITAL STRUCTURE CHANGES OVER TIME

Firms' actual capital structures change over time, and for two quite different reasons:

- *Deliberate actions:* If a firm is not currently at its target, it may deliberately raise new money in a manner that moves the actual structure toward the target.

- *Market actions:* The firm could incur high profits or losses that lead to significant changes in book value equity as shown on its balance sheet and to a decline in its stock price. Similarly, while the book value of its debt would probably not change, interest rate changes due to changes in the general level of rates and/or changes in the firm's default risk could cause significant changes in its debt's market value. Such changes in the market value of the debt and/or equity could result in large changes in its measured capital structure.

Still, at any given moment, most firms have a specific target range in mind.[4] If the actual debt ratio has surpassed the target, a firm can sell a large stock issue and use the proceeds to retire debt. Or, if the stock price has increased and pushed the debt ratio below the target, it can issue bonds and use the proceeds to repurchase stock. And, of course, a firm can gradually move toward its target through its annual financings to support its capital budget.[5]

SELF TEST

Define the terms "book-value capital structure," "market-value capital structure," and "target capital structure," and explain why they differ from one another.

Would the market-value debt ratio tend to be higher than the book-value debt ratio during a stock market boom or a recession? Explain.

Why would the WACC based on market values tend to be higher than the one based on book values if the stock price exceeded its book value?

Which would you expect to be more stable over time, a firm's book-value or market-value capital structure? Explain.

---

[4]Even if the firm concluded that its debt ratio was below the lower limit—then it could finance its entire capital budget for the year with debt—it should still use a WACC based on the target capital structure when evaluating projects for inclusion in the firm's capital budget.

[5]Firms face costs when they adjust their capital structure, and this is particularly the case if the firm has to pay an investment banker to help it raise new debt or equity. Consequently, if the benefits of moving toward their target capital structure (a lower WACC) are less than the costs of adjusting their capital structure, firms may decide not to immediately adjust their capital structure to its target level. If you are interested in more details about capital structure adjustments, see the following article which looks at the connection between transactions costs and the speed at which firms adjust to their target capital structure: Michael W. Faulkender, Mark J. Flannery, Kristine Watson Hankins, and Jason M. Smith, "Cash Flows and Leverage Adjustments," *Journal of Financial Economics*, vol. 103, no. 3 (March 2012), pp. 632–646.

13-2 BUSINESS AND FINANCIAL RISK

In Chapter 8, we examined risk from the viewpoint of an individual investor and we distinguished between *risk on a stand-alone basis,* where an asset's cash flows are analyzed by themselves, and *risk in a portfolio context,* where cash flows from a number of assets are combined and consolidated cash flows are analyzed. In a portfolio context, we saw that an asset's risk can be divided into two components: *diversifiable risk,* which can be diversified away and hence is of little concern to most investors, and *market risk,* which is measured by the beta coefficient and reflects broad market movements that cannot be eliminated by diversification and therefore is of concern to investors. Then in Chapter 12, we examined risk from the viewpoint of the corporation and we considered how capital budgeting decisions affect the firm's riskiness.

Now we introduce two new dimensions of risk:

1. *Business risk,* which is the riskiness of the firm's assets if no debt is used.
2. *Financial risk,* which is the additional risk placed on the common stockholders as a result of using debt.

13-2A BUSINESS RISK

Business risk is the single most important determinant of capital structure, and it represents the amount of risk that is inherent in the firm's operations even if it uses no debt financing. A commonly used measure of business risk is the standard deviation of the firm's return on invested capital, or ROIC. Recall from Chapter 4 that ROIC is defined as follows:[6]

Business Risk
The riskiness inherent in the firm's operations if it uses no debt.

$$\text{ROIC} = \text{EBIT}(1 - T)/\text{Total invested capital}$$

ROIC measures the after-tax return that the company provides for all of its investors. Because ROIC does not vary with changes in capital structure, the standard deviation of ROIC (σ_{ROIC}) measures the underlying risk of the firm before considering the effects of debt financing, thereby providing a good measure of business risk.[7]

We use Bigbee Electronics, a *debt-free (unlevered)* firm, to illustrate business risk. The top graph in Figure 13.1 shows the trend in Bigbee's return on invested capital, or ROIC, from 2005 through 2013. Graphs like this show security analysts and managers how much ROIC has varied in the past and thus might vary in the future. The lower graph shows the probability distribution of Bigbee's ROIC, based on the 2005–2013 data given in the top section.

Bigbee's ROIC fluctuations were caused by many factors—booms and recessions in the economy, successful new products introduced by Bigbee and its competitors, labor strikes, a fire in Bigbee's main plant, and so on. Similar events will doubtless occur in the future, and when they do, the realized ROIC will be higher or lower than the expected 9.0%. Further, there is always the possibility that a long-term disaster will strike, permanently depressing the company's earning power. For example, a competitor might introduce a new product that makes Bigbee's products totally obsolete and puts the company out of business—much like what happened to buggy manufacturers when automobiles were invented.

---

[6]Also note that EBIT(1 − T) is the after-tax income the firm would have if it used no debt. Similarly, ROIC is the ROE the firm would have if it were debt-free.

[7]At the outset, we assume that changes in capital structure have no effect on the firm's operating performance. Later in the chapter, we discuss some circumstances when the level of debt financing may affect the company's operating performance (EBIT); in these circumstances, ROIC would vary with different debt levels.

FIGURE 13.1   Return on Invested Capital (ROIC), 2005–2013

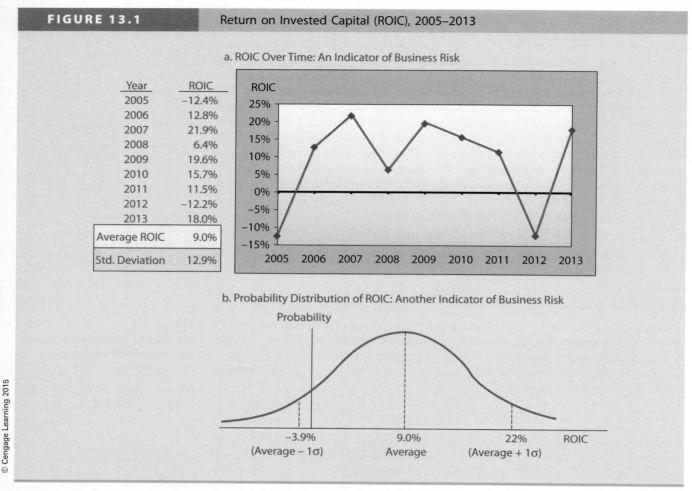

a. ROIC Over Time: An Indicator of Business Risk

Year	ROIC
2005	−12.4%
2006	12.8%
2007	21.9%
2008	6.4%
2009	19.6%
2010	15.7%
2011	11.5%
2012	−12.2%
2013	18.0%
Average ROIC	9.0%
Std. Deviation	12.9%

b. Probability Distribution of ROIC: Another Indicator of Business Risk

Note: Because Bigbee has no debt, its ROIC is equal to its ROE, hence we could replace the term ROIC with ROE. Note, though, that as soon as debt is issued, ROE and ROIC will differ.

The more uncertainty there is about future EBIT and thus ROIC, the greater the company's *business risk.* Bigbee uses no debt, so its stockholders currently face only business risk. However, if it issues debt, its stockholders would face the existing business risk plus some additional financial risk. Business risk varies from industry to industry and also among firms in a given industry. Further, a firm's business risk can change over time. For example, the electric utilities were for many years regarded as having little business risk, but over the past few decades, utilities have faced increased competition and greater uncertainty regarding potential environmental regulations, both of which have somewhat increased the industry's risk. Today, food processors like Kraft and Pillsbury illustrate companies with low business risk, while cyclical manufacturers such as steel companies, as well as new start-up companies, have high business risk.[8]

---

[8]We have avoided any discussion of market versus company-specific risk in this section. We note now (1) that any action that increases business risk in the sense of stand-alone risk will generally increase a firm's beta coefficient and (2) that a part of business risk as we define it will generally be company-specific and hence subject to elimination as a result of diversification by the firm's stockholders.

13-2B FACTORS THAT AFFECT BUSINESS RISK

Business risk depends on a number of factors, including the following:

1. *Competition.* If a firm has a monopoly on a necessary product, it will have little risk from competition and thus have stable sales and sales prices. However, monopolistic firms' prices are often regulated, and they may not be able to raise prices enough to cover rising costs. Still, other things held constant, less competition lowers business risk.

2. *Demand variability.* The more stable the demand for a firm's products, other things held constant, the lower its business risk.

3. *Sales price variability.* Firms whose products are sold in volatile markets are exposed to more business risk than firms whose output prices are stable, other things held constant.

4. *Input cost variability.* Firms whose input costs are uncertain have higher business risk.

5. *Product obsolescence.* Firms in high-tech industries like pharmaceuticals and computers depend on a constant stream of new products. The faster its products become obsolete, the greater a firm's business risk.

6. *Foreign risk exposure.* Firms that generate a high percentage of their earnings overseas are subject to earnings declines due to exchange rate fluctuations. They are also exposed to political risk.

7. *Regulatory risk and legal exposure.* Firms that operate in highly regulated industries such as financial services and utilities are subject to changes in the regulatory environment which may have a profound effect on the company's current and future profitability. Other companies face significant legal exposure that could damage the company if they are forced to pay large settlements. For example, in the aftermath of the Deepwater Horizon oil spill in the Gulf of Mexico, BP still faces huge cleanup costs and future legal costs for lost wages, damages to area tourism, and possible legal violations. Tobacco companies and pharmaceutical companies have also incurred huge legal costs after being sued for damages created by their products.

8. *The extent to which costs are fixed: operating leverage.* If a high percentage of its costs are fixed and thus do not decline when demand falls, this increases the firm's business risk. This factor is called *operating leverage,* and it is discussed in the next section.

Each of these factors is determined partly by industry characteristics and partly by managerial decisions. For example, Bigbee could reduce input cost volatility by negotiating long-term labor and supply contracts, but it might have to pay more than the current spot price to obtain such contracts.[9]

13-2C OPERATING LEVERAGE

As noted earlier, business risk depends in part on the extent to which a firm builds fixed costs into its operations—if fixed costs are high, even a small decline in sales can lead to a large decline in ROIC. So other things held constant, the higher a firm's fixed costs, the greater its business risk. Higher fixed costs are generally associated with more highly automated, capital-intensive firms and industries. However, businesses that employ highly skilled workers who must be retained and paid even during recessions also have relatively high fixed costs, as do firms

---

[9]*Hedging,* which involves actions that lock in future costs or prices, can also be used to reduce business risk. For example, a jewelry company like Tiffany might buy gold futures to freeze the price it must pay for gold, while a gold mining firm like Newmont Mining might *sell* gold futures to lock in the price it will earn on the gold it produces.

with high product development costs, because the amortization of development costs is a fixed cost.

Operating Leverage
The extent to which fixed costs are used in a firm's operations.

When a high percentage of total costs are fixed, the firm is said to have a high degree of **operating leverage**. In physics, leverage implies the use of a lever to raise a heavy object with a small force. In politics, if people have leverage, their smallest word or action can accomplish a great deal. *In business terminology, a high degree of operating leverage, other factors held constant, implies that a relatively small change in sales results in a large change in ROIC.*

Figure 13.2 illustrates the concept of operating leverage by comparing the results that Bigbee could expect if it used different degrees of operating leverage. Plan A calls for a relatively small amount of fixed costs, $25,000. Here the firm would not have much automated equipment; so its depreciation, maintenance, property taxes, and so forth, would be low. However, the total operating costs line has a relatively steep slope, indicating that variable costs per unit are higher than they would be if the firm used more operating leverage. Plan B calls for a higher level of fixed costs, $70,000. Here the firm uses automated equipment (with which one operator can turn out a few or many units at the same labor cost) to a much larger extent. The break-even point is higher under Plan B—breakeven occurs at 70,000 units under Plan B versus only 50,000 units under Plan A.

Operating Breakeven
The output quantity at which EBIT = 0.

We can calculate the break-even quantity by recognizing that **operating breakeven** occurs when earnings before interest and taxes (EBIT) = 0:[10]

$$EBIT = PQ - VQ - F = 0$$

 13.1

Here P is average sales price per unit of output, Q is units of output, V is variable cost per unit, and F is fixed operating costs. If we solve for the break-even quantity, Q_{BE} we get this expression:

$$Q_{BE} = \frac{F}{P - V}$$

13.1a

Thus, for Plan A,

$$Q_{BE} = \frac{\$25,000}{\$2.00 - \$1.50} = 50,000 \text{ units}$$

And for Plan B,

$$Q_{BE} = \frac{\$70,000}{\$2.00 - \$1.00} = 70,000 \text{ units}$$

How does operating leverage affect business risk? *Other things held constant, the higher a firm's operating leverage, the higher its business risk.* This point is demonstrated in Figure 13.3, where we develop probability distributions for ROIC under Plans A and B.

The top section of Figure 13.3 graphs the probability distribution of sales that was presented in tabular form in Figure 13.2. The sales probability distribution depends on how demand for the product varies, not on whether the product is manufactured by Plan A or by Plan B. Therefore, the same sales probability distribution applies to both production plans. This distribution has expected sales of $200,000; it ranges from zero to about $400,000, with a standard deviation of $\sigma_{Sales} = \$98,793$.

---

[10]This definition of breakeven does not include any fixed financial costs. If there were fixed financial costs, the firm would suffer an accounting loss at the operating break-even point. We introduce financial costs shortly.

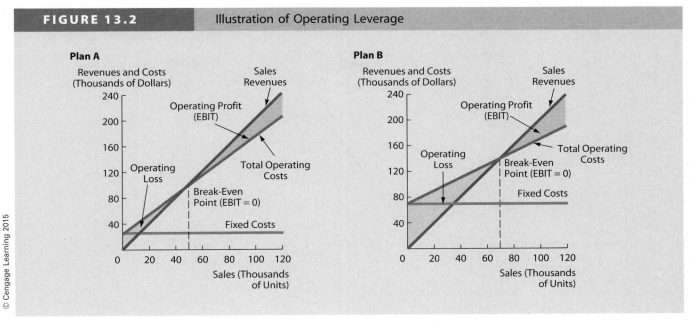

| **FIGURE 13.2** | Illustration of Operating Leverage |

	Plan A	**Plan B**
Price	$ 2.00	$ 2.00
Variable costs	$ 1.50	$ 1.00
Fixed costs	$ 25,000	$ 70,000
Invested capital	$200,000	$200,000
Tax rate	40%	40%

| | | | | **Plan A** | | | | | **Plan B** | | |
Demand	**Probability**	**Units Sold**	**Dollar Sales**	**Operating Costs**	**Operating Profit (EBIT)**	**EBIT(1 − T)**	**ROIC**	**Operating Costs**	**Operating Profit (EBIT)**	**EBIT(1 − T)**	**ROIC**
Terrible	0.05	0	$ 0	$ 25,000	($25,000)	($15,000)	(7.50)%	$ 70,000	($ 70,000)	($42,000)	(21.00)%
Poor	0.20	40,000	80,000	85,000	(5,000)	(3,000)	(1.50)	110,000	(30,000)	(18,000)	(9.00)
Normal	0.50	100,000	200,000	175,000	25,000	15,000	7.50	170,000	30,000	18,000	9.00
Good	0.20	160,000	320,000	265,000	55,000	33,000	16.50	230,000	90,000	54,000	27.00
Wonderful	0.05	200,000	400,000	325,000	75,000	45,000	22.50	270,000	130,000	78,000	39.00
Expected value		100,000	$200,000	$175,000	$25,000	$15,000	7.50%	$170,000	$ 30,000	$18,000	9.00%
Standard deviation					$24,698		7.41%		$ 49,396		14.82%
Coefficient of variation					0.99		0.99		1.65		1.65

Notes:

a. Operating costs = Variable costs + Fixed costs

b. Because the company has no debt, Net Income = EBIT(1 − T) and ROE = ROIC, but these equations would no longer hold once the company had outstanding debt.

c. The break-even sales levels for Plans A and B are not shown in the table, but it is 50,000 units or $100,000 for A and 70,000 units or $140,000 for B.

d. The expected values, standard deviations, and coefficients of variation were found using procedures discussed in Chapter 8.

We use the sales probability distribution, together with the operating costs at each sales level, to develop graphs of the ROIC probability distributions under Plans A and B. These are shown in the lower section of Figure 13.3. Plan B has a higher expected ROIC, but this plan also entails a much higher probability of losses. Plan B, the one with more fixed costs and a higher degree of operating leverage, is clearly riskier. *In general, holding other factors constant, the higher the degree of operating leverage, the greater the firm's business risk.* In the discussion that follows, we assume that Bigbee has decided to go ahead with Plan B because its

FIGURE 13.3	Analysis of Business Risk

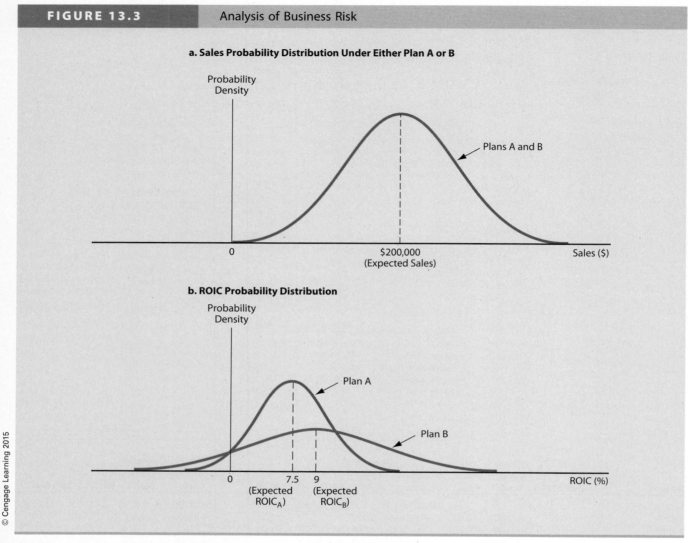

a. Sales Probability Distribution Under Either Plan A or B

Probability Density

Plans A and B

0      $200,000   Sales ($)
       (Expected Sales)

b. ROIC Probability Distribution

Probability Density

Plan A

Plan B

0   7.5   9   ROIC (%)
     (Expected   (Expected
      ROIC$_A$)   ROIC$_B$)

Note: We are using continuous distributions to approximate the discrete distributions contained in Figure 13.2.

management believes that the higher expected return is sufficient to compensate for the higher risk.

To what extent can firms control their operating leverage? To a large extent, operating leverage is determined by technology. Electric utilities, telephone companies, airlines, steel mills, and chemical companies must have large investments in fixed assets; and this results in high fixed costs and operating leverage. Similarly, pharmaceutical, auto, computer, and other companies must spend heavily to develop new products; and product-development costs increase operating leverage. Grocery stores and service businesses such as accounting and consulting firms, on the other hand, generally have significantly lower fixed costs and, therefore, lower operating leverage. Still, although industry factors do exert a major influence, all firms have some control over their operating leverage. For example, an electric utility can expand its generating capacity by building either gas-fired or nuclear plants. Nuclear plants would require larger investments and would have higher fixed costs, but their variable operating costs would be relatively low. Gas-fired plants, on the other hand, would require smaller investments and would have lower fixed costs; but the variable costs (for gas) would be high. So, by its capital budgeting decisions, a utility (or any other company) can influence its operating leverage and hence its business risk.

The concept of operating leverage was originally developed for use in capital budgeting. Mutually exclusive projects that involve alternative production methods for a given product often have different degrees of operating leverage and thus different break-even points and different degrees of risk. Bigbee Electronics and many other companies regularly undertake a type of break-even analysis (the sensitivity analysis discussed in Chapter 12) for each proposed project as a part of their regular capital budgeting process. Still, once a corporation's operating leverage has been established, this factor exerts a major influence on its capital structure decision.

13-2d FINANCIAL RISK

Financial risk is the additional risk placed on the common stockholders as a result of the decision to finance with debt. Conceptually, stockholders face a certain amount of risk that is inherent in the firm's operations—this is its business risk, defined as the uncertainty inherent in projections of future operating income. If a firm uses debt (financial leverage), this concentrates the business risk on common stockholders. To illustrate, suppose 10 people decide to form a corporation to own and operate a large apartment complex. There is a certain amount of business risk in the operation. If the firm is capitalized only with common equity and if each person buys 10% of the stock, each investor will share equally in the business risk. However, suppose the firm is capitalized with 50% debt and 50% equity, with 5 of the investors putting up their capital as debt and the other 5 putting up their money as equity. The debtholders will receive a fixed payment, and it will come before the stockholders receive anything. Also, if the firm goes bankrupt, the debtholders must be paid off before the stockholders receive anything. In this case, the 5 investors who put up the equity will have to bear all of the business risk; so the common stock will be twice as risky as it would have been had the firm been financed only with equity. *Thus, the use of debt, or* **financial leverage**, *concentrates the firm's business risk on the stockholders.* (In Web Appendix 13A, we describe in more detail the interaction between operating leverage and financial leverage.)

To illustrate the business risk concentration, we can extend the Bigbee Electronics example. To date, the company has never used debt, but the treasurer is now considering a possible change in its capital structure. As we mentioned earlier, changes in debt will not affect ROIC, but it will affect the proportion of risk borne by the firm's stockholders. More specifically, changes in the use of debt would cause changes in earnings per share (EPS) as well as changes in risk—both would affect the stock price. To understand the relationship between financial leverage and EPS, first consider Table 13.2, which shows how Bigbee's cost of debt would vary if it used different amounts of

Financial Risk

An increase in stockholders' risk, over and above the firm's basic business risk, resulting from the use of financial leverage.

Financial Leverage

The extent to which fixed-income securities (debt and preferred stock) are used in a firm's capital structure.

	Interest Rates for Bigbee with Different Debt/Capital Ratios	**TABLE 13.2**

Amount Borrowed[a]	Debt/Capital Ratio	Interest Rate, r_d, on All Debt
$20,000	10%	4.0%
40,000	20	4.3
60,000	30	5.0
80,000	40	5.8
100,000	50	7.2
120,000	60	10.0

Note:
[a]We assume that the firm must borrow in increments of $20,000. We also assume that Bigbee is unable to borrow more than $120,000, which is 60% of its total capital, due to restrictions in its corporate charter.

debt to finance a fixed amount of capital. The higher the percentage of debt in the capital structure, the riskier the debt and, for that reason, the higher the interest rate lenders would charge.

For now, assume that only two financing choices are being considered—remain at 100% equity or shift to 50% debt and 50% equity. We also assume that with no debt, Bigbee has 10,000 shares of common stock outstanding and if it decides to change its capital structure, common stock would be repurchased at the $20 current stock price. Now consider Table 13.3, which shows how the financing choice would affect Bigbee's profitability and risk.

First, focus on Section I, which assumes that Bigbee uses no debt. Because debt is zero, interest is also zero; hence net income is equal to $EBIT(1 - T)$. ROIC is calculated as $EBIT(1 - T)$ divided by invested capital. Bigbee's invested capital, which is $200,000, equals equity because it has no debt. Net income is then divided by the $200,000 of equity to calculate ROE. Note that Bigbee will receive a tax credit if net income is negative (when demand is terrible or poor). Here we assume that Bigbee's losses can be carried back to offset income earned in the prior year, thus resulting in a tax credit. The ROE at each sales level is then multiplied by the probability of that sales level to calculate the 9% expected ROE. Note that this 9% is the same as that found in Figure 13.2 for Plan B. Finally, because there is no debt, the percentages calculated in the ROIC column are identical to those in the ROE column.

Section I of the table also calculates Bigbee's earnings per share (EPS) for each scenario under the assumption that the company continues to use no debt. Net income is divided by the 10,000 common shares outstanding to obtain EPS. If demand is terrible, the EPS will be −$4.20; but if demand is wonderful, the EPS will rise to $7.80. The EPS at each sales level is then multiplied by the probability of that level to calculate the expected EPS, which is $1.80 if Bigbee uses no debt. We also calculate the standard deviation of EPS and the coefficient of variation as indicators of the firm's risk at a zero debt ratio: $\sigma_{EPS} = \$2.96$ and $CV_{EPS} = 1.65$.

Now look at Section II, the situation if Bigbee decides to use 50% debt with an interest rate of 7.2%. Neither sales nor operating costs will be affected—the EBIT, the $EBIT(1 - T)$, and the ROIC columns are the same, whether Bigbee has zero debt or 50% debt. However, the company now has $100,000 of debt with a cost of 7.2%; thus, its interest expense is $7,200. This interest must be paid regardless of the state of the economy—if it is not paid, the company will be forced into bankruptcy and stockholders will be wiped out. Therefore, we show a $7,200 cost in Column 6 as a fixed number for all sales levels. Column 7 shows the resulting net income. When net income is divided by the equity investment—which now is only $100,000 because $100,000 of the $200,000 invested capital was financed with debt—we find the ROE under each demand state. If demand is terrible and sales are zero, a very large loss will be incurred and the ROE will be −46.32%. However, if demand is wonderful, ROE will be 73.68%. The expected ROE is the probability-weighted average, which is 13.68% if the company uses 50% debt. Note that when debt is added to the firm's capital structure, ROE and ROIC are no longer equal.

Typically, using debt increases the expected rate of return for an investment. However, debt also increases risk to the common stockholders. This situation holds with our example—financial leverage raises the expected ROE from 9% to 13.68%, but it also increases the risk of the investment as measured by the coefficient of variation of ROE, which rises from 1.65 to 2.17. Figure 13.4 graphs the data in Table 13.3. It demonstrates that using financial leverage increases the expected ROE but that it also flattens out the probability distribution, increases the probability of a large loss, and thus increases the risk borne by stockholders.

Effects of Financial Leverage: Bigbee Electronics Financed with Zero Debt or 50% Debt   **TABLE 13.3**

Section 1. Zero Debt

Debt/Capital ratio	0%
Tax rate	40%
Invested capital	$200,000
Debt	$ 0
Equity	$200,000
Shares outstanding	10,000

Demand for Product (1)	Probability (2)	EBIT (3)	EBIT(1 − T) (4)	ROIC (5)	Interest (6)	Net Income= (EBIT − I)(1 − T) (7)	ROE (8)	EPS[a] (9)
Terrible	0.05	($ 70,000)	($42,000)	(21.00)%	$0	($42,000)	(21.00)%	($4.20)
Poor	0.20	(30,000)	(18,000)	(9.00)	0	(18,000)	(9.00)	(1.80)
Normal	0.50	30,000	18,000	9.00	0	18,000	9.00	1.80
Good	0.20	90,000	54,000	27.00	0	54,000	27.00	5.40
Wonderful	0.05	130,000	78,000	39.00	0	78,000	39.00	7.80
Expected value		$ 30,000	$18,000	9.00%	$0	$18,000	9.00%	$1.80
Standard deviation							14.82%	$2.96
Coefficient of variation							1.65	1.65

Section II. 50% Debt

Debt/Capital ratio	50%
Tax rate	40%
Invested capital	$200,000
Debt	$100,000
Interest rate	7.2%
Equity	$100,000
Shares outstanding	5,000

Demand for Product (1)	Probability (2)	EBIT (3)	EBIT(1 − T) (4)	ROIC (5)	Interest (6)	Net Income= (EBIT − I)(1 − T) (7)	ROE (8)	EPS[a] (9)
Terrible	0.05	($ 70,000)	($42,000)	(21.00)%	$7,200	($46,320)	(46.32)%	($ 9.26)
Poor	0.20	(30,000)	(18,000)	(9.00)	7,200	(22,320)	(22.32)	(4.46)
Normal	0.50	30,000	18,000	9.00	7,200	13,680	13.68	2.74
Good	0.20	90,000	54,000	27.00	7,200	49,680	49.68	9.94
Wonderful	0.05	130,000	78,000	39.00	7,200	73,680	73.68	14.74
Expected value		$ 30,000	$18,000	9.00%	$7,200	$13,680	13.68%	$ 2.74
Standard deviation							29.64%	$ 5.93
Coefficient of variation							2.17	2.17

Assumptions:

1. In terms of its operating leverage, Bigbee has chosen Plan B. The probability distribution and EBIT are obtained from Figure 13.2.
2. Sales and operating costs (and thus EBIT) are not affected by the financing decision. Therefore, EBIT, EBIT(1−T), and ROIC under both financing plans are identical and are taken from Figure 13.2.
3. All losses can be carried back to offset income in the prior year.

[a]The EPS figures can also be obtained using the following formula in which the numerator amounts to an income statement at a given sales level displayed horizontally:

$$EPS = \frac{(Sales - Fixed\ costs - Variable\ costs - Interest)(1 - Tax\ rate)}{Shares\ outstanding} = \frac{(EBIT - I)(1 - T)}{Shares\ outstanding}$$

For example, with zero debt and sales = $200,000, EPS is $1.80:

$$EPS_{D/(D+E)=0\%} = \frac{(\$200,000 - \$70,000 - \$100,000 - \$0)(0.6)}{10,000} = \$1.80$$

With 50% debt and sales = $200,000, EPS is $2.74:

$$EPS_{D/(D+E)=50\%} = \frac{(\$200,000 - \$70,000 - \$100,000 - \$7,200)(0.6)}{5,000} = \$2.74$$

Refer to the tabular data given in Figure 13.2 to arrive at sales, fixed costs, and variable costs that are used in the preceding equations.

Note: Because the demand for the product has a normal distribution, the probability distribution is symmetrical. Consequently, the expected values equal the values under normal demand. This would not occur under an asymmetrical probability distribution.

| FIGURE 13.4 | ROE Probability Distributions for Bigbee Electronics, with and without Financial Leverage |

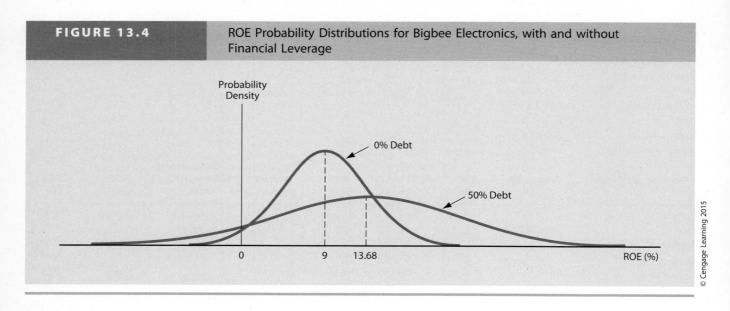

We can also calculate Bigbee's EPS if it uses 50% debt. With Debt = $0, 10,000 shares would be outstanding; but if half the equity was replaced by debt (Debt = $100,000), only 5,000 shares would be outstanding. We can determine the EPS that would result at each of the possible demand levels under the different capital structures.[11] With no debt, EPS would be −$4.20 if demand was terrible, $1.80 if demand was normal, and $7.80 if demand was wonderful. With 50% debt, EPS would be −$9.26 if demand was terrible, $2.74 if demand was normal, and $14.74 if demand was wonderful. Expected EPS would be $1.80 with no debt but $2.74 with 50% financial leverage. Although expected EPS would be much higher if financial leverage was employed, the risk of low, or even negative, EPS would also be higher if debt was used.

Another view of the relationships among expected EPS, risk, and financial leverage is presented in Figure 13.5. The tabular data in the lower section were calculated in the manner set forth in Table 13.3, and the graphs plot these data. Here we see that expected EPS rises until the firm is financed with 50% debt. Interest charges rise, but this effect is more than offset by the declining number of shares outstanding as debt is substituted for equity. However, EPS peaks at a debt ratio of 50%, beyond which interest rates rise so rapidly that EPS falls in spite of the falling number of shares outstanding.[12] The right graph in Figure 13.5 shows that risk, as measured by the coefficient of variation of EPS, rises continuously and at an increasing rate as debt is substituted for equity.

These examples make it clear that using leverage has both positive and negative effects: Higher leverage increases expected EPS (in this example, until the Debt/Capital ratio equals 50%), but it also increases risk. When determining its optimal capital structure, Bigbee needs to balance these positive and negative effects of leverage. This issue is discussed in the following sections.

---

[11]We assume in this example that the firm could change its capital structure by repurchasing common stock at its book value of $100,000/5,000 shares = $20 per share. However, the firm may have to pay a higher price to repurchase its stock on the open market. If Bigbee had to pay $22 per share, it could repurchase only $100,000/$22 = 4,545 shares; and in this case, expected EPS would be only $13,680/(10,000 − 4,545) = $13,680/5,455 = $2.51 rather than $2.74.

[12]In this context and in the remainder of this chapter, the debt ratio we are referring to is the Debt/Capital ratio.

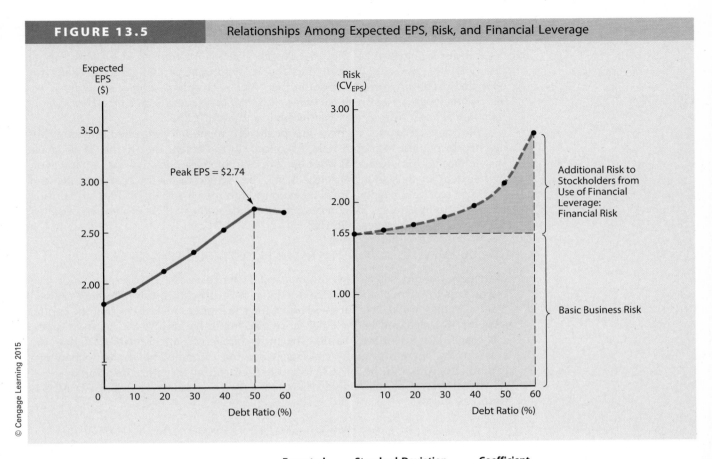

| FIGURE 13.5 | Relationships Among Expected EPS, Risk, and Financial Leverage |

Debt/Capital	Expected EPS	Standard Deviation of EPS	Coefficient of Variation
0%[a]	$1.80[a]	$2.96[a]	1.65[a]
10	1.95	3.29	1.69
20	2.12	3.70	1.75
30	2.31	4.23	1.83
40	2.54	4.94	1.95
50[a]	2.74[a]	5.93[a]	2.17[a]
60	2.70	7.41	2.74

Note:
[a]Values for Debt/Capital = 0% and 50% are taken from Table 13.3. Values at other Debt/Capital ratios were calculated similarly.

SELF TEST

What is business risk, and how can it be measured?

What are some determinants of business risk?

Why does business risk vary from industry to industry?

What is operating leverage?

How does operating leverage affect business risk?

What is financial risk, and how does it arise?

Explain this statement: Using financial leverage has both good and bad effects.

© Cengage Learning 2015

13-3 Determining the Optimal Capital Structure

As we saw in Figure 13.5, Bigbee's expected EPS is maximized at a Debt/Capital ratio of 50%. Does that mean that Bigbee's optimal capital structure calls for 50% debt? The answer is a resounding "No!" *The optimal capital structure is the one that maximizes the price of the firm's stock, and this generally calls for a Debt/Capital ratio that is lower than the one that maximizes expected EPS.*

We know that stock prices are positively related to expected earnings but negatively related to higher risk. Therefore, to the extent that higher debt levels raise expected EPS, financial leverage works to increase the stock price. However, higher debt levels also increase the firm's risk, which raises the cost of equity and works to reduce the stock price. So even though increasing the Debt/Capital ratio from 40% to 50% raises EPS, in our example, the higher EPS is more than offset by the corresponding increase in risk.

13-3A WACC and Capital Structure Changes

Managers should set as the target capital structure the debt–equity mix that maximizes the firm's stock price. However, it is difficult to estimate how a given change in the capital structure will affect the stock price. As it turns out, the capital structure that maximizes the stock price also minimizes the WACC; and at times, it is easier to predict how a capital structure change will affect the WACC than the stock price. Therefore, many managers use the estimated relationship between capital structure and the WACC to guide their capital structure decisions.

Recall from Chapter 10 that when a firm uses no preferred stock, the WACC is found as follows:

$$\text{WACC} = w_d(r_d)(1 - T) + w_c(r_s)$$

In this expression, w_d and w_c represent the percentage of debt and equity in the firm's capital structure, respectively, and they must sum to 1.0. Note that in Table 13.4 an increase in the Debt/Capital ratio increases the costs of both debt and equity. [The cost of debt, r_d, is taken from Table 13.2 but multiplied by $(1 - T)$ to put it on an after-tax basis.] Bondholders recognize that if a firm has a higher Debt/Capital ratio, this increases the risk of financial distress, which leads to higher interest rates.

In practice, financial managers use financial statement forecasting models to determine how changes in the debt-to-capital ratio will affect the current ratio, times-interest-earned ratio, and EBITDA coverage ratio.[13] They then discuss their projected ratios with bankers and bond rating agencies, which ask probing questions and may make their own adjustments to the firm's forecasts. The bankers and rating agencies compare the firm's ratios with those of other firms in its industry and arrive at a "what if" rating and corresponding interest rate. Moreover, if the company plans to issue bonds to the public, the SEC requires that it inform investors what the coverages will be after the new bonds have been sold. Recognizing all this, sophisticated financial managers use their forecasted ratios to predict how bankers and other lenders will judge their firms' risks and thus their costs of debt. Experienced financial managers and investment bankers can judge quite accurately the effects of capital structure on the cost of debt.

13-3B The Hamada Equation

Increasing the debt ratio increases the risk that bondholders face and thus the cost of debt. More debt also raises the risk borne by stockholders, which raises the cost of equity, r_s. It is harder to quantify leverage's effects on the cost of equity, but a theoretical formula can help measure the effect.

---

[13]We discuss financial statement forecasts in Chapter 16.

Bigbee's Stock Price and WACC Estimates with Different Debt/Capital Ratios								TABLE 13.4
$w_d=$ Debt/Capital (1)	Debt/ Equity[a] (2)	$r_d(1-T)$ (3)	Expected EPS (and DPS)[b] (4)	Estimated Beta[c] (5)	$r_s = [r_{RF} + (RP_M)b]^d$ (6)	Estimated Price[e] (7)	Resulting P/E Ratio (8)	WACC[f] (9)
0%	0.00%	2.40%	$1.80	1.00	9.00%	$20.00	11.11×	9.00%
10	11.11	2.40	1.95	1.07	9.40	20.71	10.64	8.70
20	25.00	2.58	2.12	1.15	9.90	21.42	10.10	8.44
30	42.86	3.00	2.31	1.26	10.54	21.95	9.49	8.28
40	66.67	3.48	2.54	1.40	11.40	22.25	8.77	8.23
50	100.00	4.32	2.74	1.60	12.60	21.71	7.94	8.46
60	150.00	6.00	2.70	1.90	14.40	18.75	6.94	9.36

Notes:

[a] $D/E = \dfrac{w_d}{1 - w_d}$, where w_d = Debt/(Debt + Equity) = Debt/Capital.

[b] Bigbee pays all of its earnings out as dividends, so EPS = DPS.

[c] The firm's unlevered beta, b_U, is 1.0. The remaining betas were calculated using the Hamada equation, given the unlevered beta, tax rate, and D/E ratio as inputs.

[d] We assume that r_{RF} = 3% and RP_M = 6%. Therefore, at Debt/Capital = 0, r_s = 3% + (6%)1.0 = 9%. Other values of r_s are calculated similarly.

[e] Because all earnings are paid out as dividends, no retained earnings will be reinvested in the business and growth in EPS and DPS will be zero. Hence, the zero growth stock price model developed in Chapter 9 can be used to estimate the price of Bigbee's stock. For example, at Debt/Capital = 0,

$$P_0 = \frac{DPS}{r_s} = \frac{\$1.80}{0.09} = \$20$$

Other prices were calculated similarly.

[f] Column 9 values are found with the weighted average cost of capital (WACC) equation developed in Chapter 10:

$$WACC = w_d(r_d)(1 - T) + w_c(r_s)$$

For example, at Debt/Capital = 40%,

$$WACC = 0.4(5.8\%)(0.6) + 0.6(11.40\%) = 8.23\%$$

To begin, recall from Chapter 8 that a stock's beta is the relevant measure of risk for a diversified investor. Moreover, beta increases with financial leverage. Robert Hamada formulated the following equation to quantify this effect.[14]

$$b_L = b_U[1 + (1 - T)(D/E)]$$

 13.2

Here b_L is the firm's current beta, which we now assume is based on the existence of some financial leverage, and b_U is the firm's beta if the firm were debt-free, or unlevered.[15] If the firm were debt-free, its beta would depend entirely on its business risk and thus would be a measure of the firm's "basic business risk."

---

[14] See Robert S. Hamada, "Portfolio Analysis, Market Equilibrium, and Corporation Finance," *Journal of Finance*, vol. 24, no. 1 (March 1969), pp. 13–31.

[15] Note that Equation 13.2 is the original equation that Hamada put forward, and it was based on a set of assumptions. The most notable were (a) that the beta of the company's debt is zero, (b) that the level of debt is constant, and (c) that the values of the company's interest tax shields are discounted at the before-tax cost of debt. Other researchers have derived alternative equations that are based on different assumptions. For example, one commonly used alternative assumes that the company's debt ratio remains constant and that the interest tax shields are discounted at the unlevered cost of equity. In this case, the resulting equation is as follows:

$$b_L = b_U(1 + D/E)$$

D/E is the measure of financial leverage as used in the Hamada equation, and T is the corporate tax rate.[16]

Now recall the CAPM version of the cost of equity:

$$r_s = r_{RF} + (RP_M)b_i$$

Note that beta is the only variable in the equity cost equation that is under management's control. The other two variables, r_{RF} and RP_M are determined by market forces that are beyond the firm's control; but b_L is determined by the firm's operating decisions, which as we saw earlier, affect its basic business risk, and by its capital structure decisions as reflected in its debt (or D/E) ratio.

Unlevered Beta, b_U

The firm's beta coefficient if it has no debt.

We can solve Equation 13.2 to find the **unlevered beta**, b_U, obtaining Equation 13.2a:

$$b_U = b_L/[1 + (1-T)(D/E)]$$

13.2a

Because the current (levered) beta is known, as are the tax rate and the debt/equity ratio, we can insert values for these known variables and find the unlevered beta. The unlevered beta can then be used in Equation 13.2 with different debt levels to find the levered betas that would exist at those different debt levels. The resulting betas can be used to find the cost of equity at different debt levels.

We can illustrate this with Bigbee Electronics. First, assume that the risk-free rate of return, r_{RF}, is 3% and that the market risk premium, RP_M, is 6%. Next, we need the unlevered beta, b_U. Because Bigbee has no debt, its D/E = 0. Therefore, its current 1.0 beta is also its unlevered beta; hence, $b_U = 1.0$. With b_U, r_{RF}, and RP_M specified, we can use Equation 13.2 to estimate Bigbee's betas at different degrees of financial leverage and its resulting cost of equity at each debt ratio.

Bigbee's betas at different debt/equity ratios are shown in Column 5 of Table 13.4. The current cost of equity is 9% as shown on the first line of Column 6:

$$r_s = r_{RF} + \text{Risk premium}$$
$$= 3\% + (6\%)(1.0)$$
$$= 3\% + 6\% = 9\%$$

From this equation, we see that 3% is the risk-free rate and 6% is the firm's risk premium. Because Bigbee currently uses no debt, it has no financial risk. Therefore, the 6% risk premium is attributable entirely to business risk.

If Bigbee changes its capital structure by adding debt, this would increase the risk stockholders would have to bear. That, in turn, would result in a higher risk premium. Conceptually, a firm's cost of equity consists of the following components:

$$r_s = r_{RF} + \text{Premium for business risk} + \text{Premium for financial risk}$$

Figure 13.6, which is based on data shown in Column 6 of Table 13.4, graphs Bigbee's costs of equity at different debt ratios. As the figure shows, r_s consists of the 3% risk-free rate, a constant 6% premium for business risk, and a premium for financial risk that starts at zero but rises at an increasing rate as the firm's debt ratio increases.

---

[16]Note that w_d is equal to the percentage of debt in the firm's capital structure, and it is equal to Debt/Capital = D/(D + E). So it follows that

$$\frac{D}{E} = \frac{w_d}{1 - w_d}$$

For example, if the firm has $40 of debt and $60 of equity, w_d = D/(D + E) = $40/($40 + $60) = 0.4. Therefore,

$$\frac{D}{E} = \frac{0.4}{1 - 0.4} = \frac{0.4}{0.6} = 0.6667$$

Note also that Hamada's equation assumes that debt and equity are reported at market values rather than accounting book values. This point is discussed at length in Chapter 15 of Eugene F. Brigham and Phillip R. Daves, *Intermediate Financial Management*, 11th edition (Mason, OH: South-Western/Cengage Learning, 2013), where feedbacks among capital structure, stock prices, and capital costs are examined.

FIGURE 13.6	Bigbee's Required Rates of Return on Equity at Different Debt Levels

 QUICK QUESTION

QUESTION:

Barnes Co. currently has a capital structure that consists of 40% debt and 60% common equity. The company has a 40% tax rate. Currently the levered beta (b_L) on the company's stock is 1.4.

a. What is the company's unlevered beta (b_U)?

b. What would be the company's levered beta (b_L) if Barnes changed its capital structure to 20% debt and 80% common equity?

ANSWER:

a. The company's unlevered beta is calculated as follows:

$$b_U = b_L / [1 + (1 - T)(D/E)]$$
$$b_U = 1.4 / [1 + (0.6)(0.4/0.6)]$$
$$b_U = 1.0$$

Notice that $b_U < b_L$. b_U is the firm's beta if it had no debt. Beta is a measure of risk, so with no debt one would anticipate $b_U < b_L$.

b. Using the unlevered beta calculated in Part a, the company's new levered beta under the changed capital structure of 20% debt and 80% equity is calculated as follows:

$$b_L = b_U [1 + (1 - T)(D/E)]$$
$$b_L = 1.0 [1 + (0.6)(0.2/0.8)]$$
$$b_L = 1.15$$

Again, notice that the new $b_L <$ original b_L. This result is consistent with the reduction in debt level. The risk is lower, and this is reflected in the new lower levered beta.

13-3c THE OPTIMAL CAPITAL STRUCTURE

Column 9 of Table 13.4 also shows Bigbee's WACCs at different capital structures. Currently, it has no debt; so its debt ratio is zero and its WACC is $r_s = 9\%$. As Bigbee begins to substitute lower-cost debt for higher-cost equity, its WACC declines. However, as the debt ratio rises, the costs of both debt and equity rise, at first slowly but then at a faster and faster rate. Eventually, the increasing costs of the two components offset the fact that more low-cost debt is being used. Indeed, at 40% debt, the WACC hits a minimum of 8.23%; after that, it rises with further increases in the debt ratio.

Another way of looking at this is to note that even though the component cost of equity is higher than that of debt, using only lower-cost debt would not maximize value because of the feedback effects of debt on the costs of debt and equity. For example, if Bigbee used more than 40% debt (say, 50%), it would have more of the less expensive capital component in its capital structure; but this benefit would be more than offset by the fact that the additional debt increases the costs of debt and equity.

Finally, and very importantly, recall that the capital structure that minimizes the WACC is also the capital structure that maximizes the firm's stock price. Bigbee distributes all of its earnings as dividends, so it reinvests no earnings in the business, which leads to an expected growth rate in earnings and dividends of zero. Thus, in Bigbee's case, we can use the zero growth stock price model developed in Chapter 9 to estimate the stock price at each different capital structure. These estimates are shown in Column 7 of Table 13.4. Here we see that the stock price first rises with financial leverage, hits a peak of $22.25 at a debt ratio of 40%, and then begins to decline. *Thus, Bigbee's optimal capital structure occurs at a debt ratio of 40%, and that debt ratio both maximizes its stock price and minimizes its WACC.*[17]

The EPS, cost of capital, and stock price data shown in Table 13.4 are plotted in Figure 13.7. As the graph shows, the debt ratio that maximizes Bigbee's expected EPS is 50%. However, the expected stock price is maximized, and the WACC is minimized at a 40% debt ratio. Thus, Bigbee's optimal capital structure calls for 40% debt and 60% equity. Management should set its target capital structure at these ratios; and if the existing ratios are off target, it should move toward that target when new securities are issued.

SELF TEST

What happens to the component costs of debt and equity when the debt ratio is increased? Why does this occur?

Using the Hamada equation, explain the effects of financial leverage on beta.

What is the equation for calculating a firm's unlevered beta?

Use the Hamada equation to calculate the unlevered beta for Firm X with the following data: $b_L = 1.25$, T = 40%, Debt/Capital = 0.42, and Equity/Capital = 0.58. **($b_U = 0.8714$)**

What would be the cost of equity for Firm X at Equity/Capital ratios of 1.0 (no debt) and 0.58 assuming that $r_{RF} = 5\%$ and $RP_M = 4\%$? **(8.49%, 10%)**

Using a graph and illustrative data, discuss the premiums for financial risk and business risk at different debt levels. Do these premiums vary depending on the debt level? Explain.

Is expected EPS generally maximized at the optimal capital structure? Explain.

---

[17]We could also estimate the stock price if some earnings were retained and the expected growth rate were positive. However, this would complicate the analysis, and it is another reason we generally analyze the optimal capital structure decision using the WACC rather than the stock price.

FIGURE 13.7	Effects of Capital Structure on EPS, Cost of Capital, and Stock Price

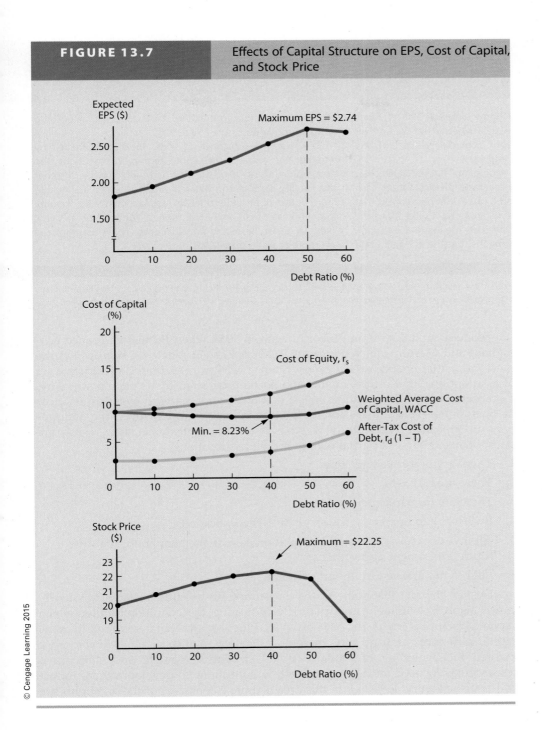

13-4 CAPITAL STRUCTURE THEORY

Business risk is an important determinant of the optimal capital structure. More-over, firms in different industries have different business risks. So we would expect capital structures to vary considerably across industries, and this is the case. For example, biotechnology companies generally have very different capital structures than food processors. In addition, capital structures vary among firms within a given industry, which is a bit harder to explain. What factors can explain these differences? In an attempt to answer that question, academics and practitioners have developed a number of theories.

YOGI BERRA ON THE MM PROPOSITION

When a waitress asked Yogi Berra (Baseball Hall of Fame catcher for the New York Yankees) whether he wanted his pizza cut into four pieces or eight, Yogi replied: "Better make it four. I don't think I can eat eight."

Yogi's quip helps convey Modigliani and Miller's basic insight. The firm's choice of leverage divides future cash flows in a way that's like slicing a pizza. MM recognized that if a company's future investments are fixed, it's like fixing the size of the pizza: No information costs means that everyone sees the same pizza; no taxes means that the IRS gets none

of the pie; and no "contracting" costs means that nothing sticks to the knife.

So just as the substance of Yogi's meal is unaffected by whether the pizza is sliced into four pieces or eight, the economic substance of the firm is unaffected by whether the liability side of the balance sheet is sliced to include more or less debt under the MM assumptions. Note, though, that whereas the IRS may get none of Yogi's pizza, it is very likely to get some of the firm's income. Yogi's assumptions are more realistic than MM's.

Sources: Lee Green, *Sportswit* (New York: Fawcett Crest, 1984), p. 228; and Michael J. Barclay, Clifford W. Smith, and Ross L. Watts, "The Determinants of Corporate Leverage and Dividend Policies," *Journal of Applied Corporate Finance*, vol. 7, no. 4 (Winter 1995), pp. 4–19. Used by permission.

Modern capital structure theory began in 1958 when Professors Franco Modigliani and Merton Miller (hereafter, MM) published what has been called the most influential finance article ever written.[18] MM proved, under a restrictive set of assumptions, that a firm's value should be unaffected by its capital structure. Put another way, MM's results suggest that it does not matter how a firm finances its operations—hence, that capital structure is irrelevant. However, the assumptions upon which MM's study was based are not realistic, so their results are questionable. Here is a partial listing of their assumptions:

1. There are no brokerage costs.
2. There are no taxes.
3. There are no bankruptcy costs.
4. Investors can borrow at the same rate as corporations.
5. All investors have the same information as management about the firm's future investment opportunities.
6. EBIT is not affected by the use of debt.

Despite the fact that some of these assumptions are unrealistic, MM's irrelevance result is extremely important. By indicating the conditions under which capital structure is irrelevant, MM provided clues about what is required to make capital structure relevant and, therefore, to affect a firm's value. MM's work marked the beginning of modern capital structure research, and subsequent research has focused on relaxing the MM assumptions to develop a more robust and realistic theory. Research in this area is quite extensive, but the highlights are summarized in the following sections.

13-4A THE EFFECT OF TAXES[19]

MM's original 1958 paper was criticized harshly, and they published a follow-up in 1963 that relaxed the assumption of no corporate taxes.[20] They recognized that the Tax Code allows corporations to deduct interest payments as an expense, but

---

[18]Franco Modigliani and Merton H. Miller, "The Cost of Capital, Corporation Finance, and the Theory of Investment," *American Economic Review*, vol. 48, no. 3 (June 1958), pp. 261–297. Both Modigliani and Miller won Nobel Prizes for their work.

[19]This section is relatively technical, and it can be omitted without a loss of continuity.

[20]Franco Modigliani and Merton H. Miller, "Corporate Income Taxes and the Cost of Capital: A Correction," *American Economic Review*, vol. 53, no. 3 (June 1963), pp. 433–443.

dividend payments to stockholders are not deductible. This differential treatment encourages corporations to use debt in their capital structures. Indeed, MM demonstrated that if all their other assumptions hold, this differential treatment leads to an optimal capital structure of 100% debt.

MM's 1963 work was modified several years later by Merton Miller (this time without Modigliani), when he brought in the effects of personal taxes.[21] Miller noted that bonds pay interest, which is taxed as personal income at rates going up to 35% (39.6% in 2013), while income from stocks comes partly from dividends and partly from capital gains. Further, long-term capital gains are taxed at a maximum rate of 15% (20% in 2013 for high-income taxpayers), and this tax can be deferred until the stock is sold and the gain realized. If a stock is held until the owner dies, no capital gains tax must be paid. So on balance, returns on common stocks are taxed at lower effective rates than returns on debt.[22]

Because of the tax situation, Miller argued that investors are willing to accept relatively low before-tax returns on stocks as compared to the before-tax returns on bonds. For example, an investor in the 39.6% tax bracket might require a 10% pretax return on Bigbee's bonds, which would result in a $10\%(1 - T) = 10\%(0.604) = 6.04\%$ after-tax return. Bigbee's stock is riskier than its bonds, so the investor would require a higher after-tax return (say, 8%) on the stock. Because the stock's returns (either dividends or capital gains) would be taxed at 20%, a pretax return of $8\%/(1 - T) = 8.0\%/0.80 = 10.0\%$ would provide the required 8.0% after-tax return. In this example, the interest rate on the bonds would be 10%, the same as the required return on the stock, r_s. Thus, the more favorable treatment of income on the stock would cause investors to accept the same before-tax returns on the stock and on the bond.[23]

As Miller pointed out, (1) the *deductibility of interest* favors the use of debt financing, but (2) the *more favorable tax treatment of income from stocks* lowers the required rates of return on stocks and thus favors the use of equity. It is difficult to specify the net effect of these two factors. However, most observers believe that interest deductibility has a stronger effect and hence that our tax system favors the corporate use of debt. Still, that effect is certainly reduced by the lower taxes on stock income. Indeed, Duke University professor John Graham estimated the overall tax benefits of debt financing.[24] He concluded that the tax benefits associated with debt financing represent about 7% of the average firm's value; so if a leverage-free firm decided to use an average amount of debt, its value would rise by 7%.

13-4B THE EFFECT OF POTENTIAL BANKRUPTCY

MM's irrelevance results also depend on the assumption that firms don't go bankrupt and hence that bankruptcy costs are irrelevant. However, in practice, bankruptcy exists, and it can be quite costly. Firms in bankruptcy have high legal and accounting expenses, and they have a hard time retaining customers, suppliers, and employees. Moreover, bankruptcy often forces a firm to liquidate assets for less than they would be worth if the firm continued to operate. Assets such as

---

[21]Merton H. Miller, "Debt and Taxes," *Journal of Finance*, vol. 32, no. 2 (May 1977), pp. 261–275.

[22]When Miller wrote his article, dividends were taxed at a maximum rate of 70% and capital gains at a much lower rate. Today (2013) dividends and capital gains are taxed at a maximum rate of 20% for high-income taxpayers, but interest is taxed at a maximum rate of 39.6%. [Capital gains can be caught by the Alternative Minimum Tax (AMT), in which case they are taxed at either 26% or 28% depending on one's income bracket.] These tax law changes would not affect Miller's final conclusion.

[23]The situation here is similar to that involving tax-exempt municipal bonds versus taxable bonds.

[24]John R. Graham, "How Big Are the Tax Benefits of Debt?" *Journal of Finance*, vol. 55, no. 5 (October 2000), pp. 1901–1941; and John R. Graham, "Estimating the Tax Benefits of Debt," *Journal of Applied Corporate Finance*, vol. 14, no. 1 (Spring 2001), pp. 42–54.

plant and equipment are often illiquid because they are configured to a company's individual needs and because they are difficult to disassemble and move.

Note too that the *threat of bankruptcy*, not just bankruptcy per se, brings about these problems. If they become concerned about the firm's future, key employees start "jumping ship," suppliers start refusing to grant credit, customers begin seeking more stable suppliers, and lenders start demanding higher interest rates and imposing stricter loan covenants.

Bankruptcy-related problems are likely to increase the more debt a firm has in its capital structure. Therefore, bankruptcy costs discourage firms from pushing their use of debt to excessive levels. Note too that bankruptcy-related costs have two components: (1) the probability of their occurrence and (2) the costs that will be incurred if financial distress arises. A firm whose earnings are relatively volatile, all else equal, faces a greater chance of bankruptcy and thus should use less debt than a more stable firm. This is consistent with our earlier point that firms with high operating leverage (and thus greater business risk) should limit their use of financial leverage. Likewise, firms whose assets are illiquid and would have to be sold at "fire sale" prices should limit their use of debt financing.

13-4c TRADE-OFF THEORY

Trade-Off Theory

The capital structure theory that states that firms trade off the tax benefits of debt financing against problems caused by potential bankruptcy.

The preceding arguments led to the development of what is called "the trade-off theory of leverage." This theory states that firms trade off the tax benefits of debt financing against problems caused by potential bankruptcy. A summary of the **trade-off theory** is expressed graphically in Figure 13.8. Here are some observations about the figure:

1. The fact that interest paid is a deductible expense makes debt less expensive than common or preferred stock. In effect, the government pays part of the cost of debt—or to put it another way, debt provides *tax shelter benefits*. As a result, using more debt reduces taxes and thus allows more of the firm's operating income (EBIT) to flow through to investors. This factor, on which

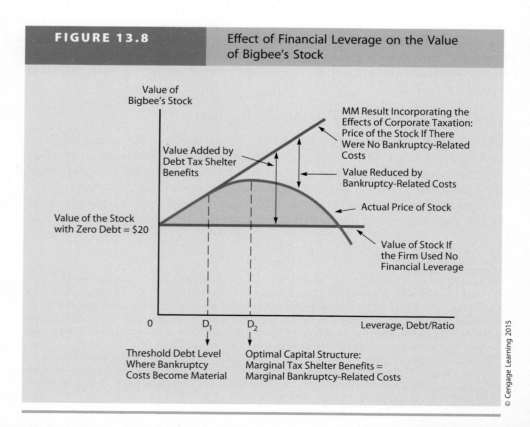

FIGURE 13.8 Effect of Financial Leverage on the Value of Bigbee's Stock

MM focused, tends to raise the stock's price. Indeed, under the assumptions of MM's original paper, the stock price would be maximized at 100% debt. The line labeled "MM Result Incorporating the Effects of Corporate Taxation" in Figure 13.8 expresses the relationship between stock prices and debt under their assumptions.

2. In the real world, firms have target debt ratios that call for less than 100% debt to limit the adverse effects of potential bankruptcy.

3. There is some threshold level of debt, labeled D_1 in Figure 13.8, below which the probability of bankruptcy is so low as to be immaterial. Beyond D_1, however, bankruptcy-related costs become increasingly important and they begin to offset the tax benefits of debt. In the range from D_1 to D_2, bankruptcy-related costs reduce but do not completely offset the tax benefits of debt; so the firm's stock price continues to rise (but at a decreasing rate) as its debt ratio increases. However, beyond D_2, bankruptcy-related costs exceed the tax benefits; so from this point on, increasing the debt ratio lowers the stock price. Therefore, D_2 is the optimal capital structure, the one where the stock price is maximized. Of course, D_1 and D_2 vary from firm to firm depending on business risk and bankruptcy costs, and they can change for a given firm over time.

4. While theoretical and empirical work supports the general shape of the curves in Figures 13.7 and 13.8, these graphs must be taken as approximations, not as precisely defined functions. The numbers in Figure 13.7 are rounded to two decimal places, but that is merely for illustrative purposes—the numbers are not nearly that accurate because the graph is based on estimates.

5. Another disturbing aspect of capital structure theory expressed in Figure 13.8 is the fact that many large, successful firms such as Intel and Microsoft use far less debt than the theory suggests. This point led to the development of signaling theory, which is discussed in the next section.

13-4D SIGNALING THEORY

MM assumed that everyone—investors and managers alike—has the same information about a firm's prospects. This is called **symmetric information**. However, in fact, managers often have better information than outside investors. This is called **asymmetric information**, and it has an important effect on the optimal capital structure. To see why, consider two situations, one where the company's managers know that its prospects are extremely favorable (Firm F) and one where the managers know that the future looks unfavorable (Firm U).

Now suppose Firm F's R&D labs have just discovered a nonpatentable cure for the common cold. They want to keep the new product a secret as long as possible to delay competitors' entry into the market. New plants must be built to make the new product, so capital must be raised. But how should Firm F raise the needed capital? If it sells stock, when profits from the new product start flowing in, the price of the stock will rise sharply and purchasers of the new stock will make a bonanza. The current stockholders (including the managers) also will do well, but not as well as they would have done if the company had not sold stock before the price increased. In that case, they would not have had to share the benefits of the new product with the new stockholders. *Therefore, we would expect a firm with very favorable prospects to avoid selling stock, and instead raise any required new capital by using new debt, even if this moved its debt ratio beyond the target level.*[25]

Symmetric Information
The situation where investors and managers have identical information about firms' prospects.

Asymmetric Information
The situation where managers have different (better) information about firms' prospects than do investors.

---

[25]It would be illegal for Firm F's managers to personally purchase more shares on the basis of their inside knowledge of the new product. They could be sent to jail if they did.

Now consider Firm U. Suppose its managers have information that new orders are off sharply because a competitor has installed new technology that improved the quality of its products. Firm U must upgrade its own facilities at a high cost just to maintain current sales. As a result, its return on investment will fall (but not by as much as if it took no action, which would lead to a 100% loss through bankruptcy). How should Firm U raise the needed capital? Here the situation is just the reverse of that facing Firm F—Firm U will want to sell stock so that some of the adverse consequences will be borne by new investors. *Therefore, a firm with unfavorable prospects would want to finance with stock, which would mean bringing in new investors to share the losses.*[26]

The conclusion from all this is that firms with extremely bright prospects prefer not to finance through new stock offerings, whereas firms with poor prospects do like to finance with outside equity. How should you, as an investor, react to this conclusion? You ought to say, "If I see that a company plans to issue new stock, I should worry because I know that management would not want to issue stock if future prospects looked good. However, management would want to issue stock if things looked bad. Therefore, I should lower my estimate of the firm's value, other things held constant, if it plans to issue new stock."

If you gave that answer, your views are consistent with those of sophisticated portfolio managers. *In a nutshell, the announcement of a stock offering is generally taken as a* **signal** *that the firm's prospects as seen by its management are not bright.* This, in turn, suggests that when a firm announces a new stock offering, more often than not, the price of its stock will decline.[27] Empirical studies have shown that this situation does exist.[28]

What are the implications of all this for capital structure decisions? Issuing stock emits a negative signal and thus tends to depress the stock price; so even if the company's prospects are bright, a firm should, in normal times, maintain a **reserve borrowing capacity** that can be used in the event that some especially good investment opportunity comes along. *This means that firms should, in normal times, use more equity and less debt than is suggested by the tax benefit/bankruptcy cost trade-off model illustrated in Figure 13.8.*

13-4E USING DEBT FINANCING TO CONSTRAIN MANAGERS

In Chapter 1, we stated that conflicts of interest may arise if managers and shareholders have different objectives. Such conflicts are particularly likely when the firm has more cash than is needed to support its core operations. Managers often use excess cash to finance their pet projects or for perquisites such as plush offices, corporate jets, and skyboxes at sports arenas, all of which may do little to benefit stock prices.[29] By contrast, managers with more limited free cash flow are less able to make wasteful expenditures.

Firms can reduce excess cash flow in a variety of ways. One way is to funnel some of it back to shareholders through higher dividends or stock repurchases. Another alternative is to tilt the target capital structure toward more debt in the hope that higher debt service requirements will force managers to become more disciplined. If debt is not serviced as required, the

Signal

An action taken by a firm's management that provides clues to investors about how management views the firm's prospects.

Reserve Borrowing Capacity

The ability to borrow money at a reasonable cost when good investment opportunities arise. Firms often use less debt than specified by the MM optimal capital structure in "normal" times to ensure that they can obtain debt capital later if necessary.

---

[26]Of course, Firm U would have to make certain disclosures when it offered new shares to the public, but it might be able to meet the legal requirements without fully disclosing management's worst fears.

[27]Stock issues are more of a negative signal for mature companies than for new, rapidly growing firms, where investors expect rapid growth to require additional equity.

[28]See Paul Asquith and David W. Mullins, Jr., "The Impact of Initiating Dividend Payments on Shareholders' Wealth," *Journal of Business*, vol. 56, no. 1 (January 1983), pp. 77–96.

[29]If you don't believe that corporate managers can waste money, read Bryan Burrough, *Barbarians at the Gate: The Fall of RJR Nabisco* (New York: Harper & Row, 1990), the story of the takeover of RJR-Nabisco.

firm will be forced into bankruptcy, in which case its managers would lose their jobs. Therefore, a manager is less likely to buy an expensive corporate jet if the firm has large debt service requirements.

A leveraged buyout (LBO) is a good way to reduce excess cash flow. In an LBO, debt is used to finance the purchase of a high percentage of the company's shares. Indeed, the projected savings from reducing frivolous waste has motivated quite a few leveraged buyouts. As noted, high debt payments after the LBO force managers to conserve cash by eliminating unnecessary expenditures.

Of course, increasing debt and reducing free cash flow has its downside: It increases the risk of bankruptcy. A former professor (who is currently the Federal Reserve chairman) has argued that adding debt to a firm's capital structure is like putting a dagger into the steering wheel of a car.[30] The dagger—which points toward your chest—motivates you to drive more carefully; but you may get stabbed if someone runs into you, even if you are being careful. The analogy applies to corporations in the following sense: Higher debt forces managers to be more careful with shareholders' money; but even well-run firms can face bankruptcy (get stabbed) if some event beyond their control, such as a war, an earthquake, a strike, or a recession, occurs. To complete the analogy, the capital structure decision comes down to deciding how big a dagger stockholders should use to keep managers in line.

If you find the discussion of capital structure theory imprecise and somewhat confusing, you're not alone. In truth, not even the chairman of the Federal Reserve Board knows how to identify a firm's precise optimal capital structure or how to measure the effects of capital structure changes on stock prices and the cost of capital. In practice, capital structure decisions must be made using a combination of judgment and numerical analysis. Still, an understanding of the theoretical issues presented here can help you make better judgments about capital structure issues.

13-4f PECKING ORDER HYPOTHESIS

Yet another factor that may influence capital structures is the idea that managers have a preferred **pecking order** when it comes to raising capital and that this pecking order affects capital structure decisions.[31] We know that firms often finance in the following order: Their first source of funds is accounts payable and accruals. Retained earnings generated during the current year would be the next source. Then, if the amount of retained earnings is not sufficient to cover capital requirements, firms issue debt. Finally, and only as a last resort, they issue new common stock.

Pecking Order
The sequence in which firms prefer to raise capital: first spontaneous credit, then retained earnings, then other debt, and finally new common stock.

Why might it be logical for a firm to follow this pecking order? First, no flotation costs are incurred to raise capital as spontaneous credit or retained earnings, and costs are relatively low when issuing new debt. However, flotation costs for new stock issues are quite high, and the existence of asymmetric information/signaling effects makes it even more undesirable to finance with new common stock. So, the pecking order theory is logical, and it can influence a firm's capital structure, although there is still some debate about its relative importance.[32]

---

[30]Ben Bernanke, "Is There Too Much Corporate Debt?" Federal Reserve Bank of Philadelphia, *Business Review* (September/October 1989), pp. 3–13.
[31]See Jonathan Baskin, "An Empirical Investigation of the Pecking Order Hypothesis," *Financial Management*, vol. 18 (Spring 1989), pp. 26–35.
[32]See Murray Frank and V.K. Goyal, "Testing the Pecking Order Theory of Capital Structure," *Journal of Financial Economics*, vol. 67, no. 2 (February 2003), pp. 217–248.

13-4G WINDOWS OF OPPORTUNITY

Windows of Opportunity
The occasion where a company's managers adjust its firm's capital structure to take advantage of certain market situations.

If a company's stock is selling for a price different than its intrinsic value, the company's managers can adjust the firm's capital structure to take advantage of this mispricing. When a company's stock is overvalued (trading for more than its intrinsic value), its managers can take the opportunity to issue new equity at a time when its market value is relatively high. Likewise, managers may choose to repurchase stock when the firm's stock is undervalued. A study by Malcolm Baker and Jeffrey Wurgler documents that many companies take advantage of these **"windows of opportunity,"** and they argue that these attempts to time the market have had a profound effect on these companies' capital structures.[33]

SELF TEST

Why does MM's theory with taxes lead to 100% debt?

How would an increase in corporate taxes tend to affect an average firm's capital structure? What about an increase in the personal tax rate?

Explain what asymmetric information means and how signals affect capital structure decisions.

What is meant by reserve borrowing capacity, and why is it important to firms?

How can the use of debt serve to discipline managers?

What is the pecking order hypothesis, and how does it influence firms' capital structures?

How do "windows of opportunity" impact a firm's capital structure?

13-5 CHECKLIST FOR CAPITAL STRUCTURE DECISIONS

In addition to the types of analyses discussed previously, firms generally consider the following factors when making capital structure decisions:

1. *Sales stability.* A firm whose sales are relatively stable can safely take on more debt and incur higher fixed charges than a company with unstable sales. Utility companies, because of their stable demand, historically have been able to use more financial leverage than can industrial firms.

2. *Asset structure.* Many companies also take their desired cash holdings into account when setting their target capital structure. Holding other factors constant, a company is able to take on more debt if it has more cash on the balance sheet. For this reason, some analysts also evaluate an alternative measure, **net debt**, which subtracts cash and equivalent securities from the company's total debt:

Net Debt
Equal to short-term debt plus long-term debt less cash and equivalents. Companies often look at this measure when setting their target capital structure.

$$\text{Net debt} = \text{Short-term debt} + \text{Long-term debt} - \text{Cash and equivalents}$$

Looking at Table 13.1, we see that Caterpillar has $49 billion in net debt ($54.5 billion in total debt minus $5.5 billion in cash and equivalents). Holding other factors constant, firms that have more cash or other assets

---

[33]See Malcolm Baker and Jeffrey Wurgler, "Market Timing and Capital Structure," *The Journal of Finance*, vol. 57, no. 1 (February 2002), pp. 1–32.

that are suitable as security for loans tend to use debt relatively heavily. General-purpose assets that can be used by many businesses make good collateral, whereas special-purpose assets do not. Thus, real estate companies are usually highly leveraged, whereas companies involved in technological research are not.[34]

3. *Operating leverage.* Other things the same, a firm with less operating leverage is better able to employ financial leverage because it will have less business risk.

4. *Growth rate.* Other things the same, faster-growing firms must rely more heavily on external capital. Further, the flotation cost involved in selling common stock exceeds that incurred when selling debt, which encourages rapidly growing firms to rely more heavily on debt. At the same time, however, those firms often face higher uncertainty, which tends to reduce their willingness to use debt.

5. *Profitability.* It is often observed that firms with very high rates of return on investment use relatively little debt. Although there is no theoretical justification for this fact, one practical explanation is that very profitable firms such as Intel, Microsoft, and Google do not need to do much debt financing. Their high rates of return enable them to do most of their financing with internally generated funds.

6. *Taxes.* Interest is a deductible expense, and deductions are most valuable to firms with high tax rates. Therefore, the higher a firm's tax rate, the greater the advantage of debt.

7. *Control.* The effect of debt versus stock on a management's control position can influence capital structure. If management currently has voting control (more than 50% of the stock) but is not in a position to buy any more stock, it may choose debt for new financings. On the other hand, management may decide to use equity if the firm's financial situation is so weak that the use of debt might subject it to serious risk of default. The reason? If the firm goes into default, managers will probably lose their jobs. However, if too little debt is used, management runs the risk of a takeover. Thus, control considerations can lead to the use of debt or equity because the type of capital that best protects management varies from situation to situation. In any event, if management is at all insecure, it will consider the control situation.

8. *Management attitudes.* No one can prove that one capital structure will lead to higher stock prices than another. Management, then, can exercise its own judgment about the proper capital structure. Some managers tend to be relatively conservative and thus use less debt than an average firm in the industry, whereas aggressive managers use a relatively high percentage of debt in their quest for higher profits.

9. *Lender and rating agency attitudes.* Regardless of a manager's analysis of the proper leverage factors for his or her firm, the attitudes of lenders and rating agencies frequently influence financial structure decisions. Corporations often discuss their capital structures with lenders and rating agencies and give much weight to their advice. For example, Moody's and Standard & Poor's

---

[34]Two capital structure issues that we do not address in this chapter relate to how long-term leases and convertible securities impact the financing mix. Leases are de facto a substitute for debt, so it would be appropriate to determine the present value of the firm's future lease payments and treat them as debt. Thus, if we were examining two firms with debt ratios of 50%, but one leases many of its assets and does not reflect those transactions on its balance sheet, then it is really more leveraged than the other firm. Convertibles are bonds (or preferred stocks) that can be converted into common stock at the option of the holder. Before conversion, these securities technically increase the firm's financial leverage, but immediately after conversion leverage declines. For a precise examination of a firm's leverage, it would be useful to estimate the likely timing of conversion and take it into account. However, such an analysis goes beyond the scope of an introductory text.

recently told one large utility that its bonds would be downgraded if it issued more bonds. This influenced its decision, and its next financing was with common equity.

10. *Market conditions.* Conditions in the stock and bond markets undergo long- and short-run changes that can have an important bearing on a firm's optimal capital structure. For example, during a recent credit crunch, the junk bond market dried up and there simply was no market at a "reasonable" interest rate for any new long-term bonds rated below BBB. Therefore, low-rated companies in need of capital were forced to go to the stock market or to the short-term debt market, regardless of their target capital structures. When conditions eased, however, these companies sold long-term bonds to get their capital structures back on target.

11. *The firm's internal condition.* A firm's own internal condition can also have a bearing on its target capital structure. For example, suppose a firm just successfully completed an R&D program and forecasts higher earnings in the immediate future. However, the new earnings are not yet anticipated by investors and are not reflected in the stock price. This company would not want to issue stock—it would prefer to finance with debt until the higher earnings materialize and are reflected in the stock price. Then it could sell an issue of common stock, use the proceeds to retire the debt, and return to its target capital structure. This point was discussed earlier in connection with asymmetric information and signaling.

12. *Financial flexibility.* An astute corporate treasurer made this statement to the authors:

> *Our company can earn a lot more money from good capital budgeting and operating decisions than from good financing decisions. Indeed, we are not sure exactly how financing decisions affect our stock price, but we know for sure that having to turn down promising ventures because funds are not available will reduce our long-run profitability. For this reason, my primary goal as treasurer is to always be in a position to raise the capital needed to support operations.*
>
> *We also know that when times are good, we can raise capital with either stocks or bonds, but when times are bad, suppliers of capital are much more willing to make funds available if we give them a stronger position, and this means debt. Further, when we sell a new issue of stock, this sends a negative "signal" to investors, so stock sales by a mature company such as ours are not desirable.*

Combining these thoughts gives rise to the goal of maintaining financial flexibility, which from an operational viewpoint means maintaining adequate "reserve borrowing capacity." Determining the "adequate" reserve is based on judgment; but it clearly depends on the firm's forecasted need for funds, predicted capital market conditions, management's confidence in its forecasts, and the consequences of a capital shortage.

SELF TEST

How does sales stability affect the target capital structure?

How do the types of assets used affect a firm's capital structure?

How do taxes affect the target capital structure?

How do the attitudes of lenders and rating agencies affect capital structure?

How does the firm's internal condition affect its actual capital structure?

What is financial flexibility, and is it increased or decreased by a high debt ratio? Explain.

13-6 VARIATIONS IN CAPITAL STRUCTURES

As might be expected, wide variations in the use of financial leverage occur across industries and among the individual firms in each industry. Table 13.5 illustrates differences for selected companies in different industries; the ranking is in ascending order of the company's long-term debt ratio.[35]

Petroleum, aerospace, biotechnology, and steel companies use relatively little debt because their industries tend to be cyclical, oriented toward research, or subject to huge product liability suits. On the other hand, grocery stores, utility companies, and airlines use debt relatively heavily because their fixed assets make good security for mortgage bonds and their relatively stable sales make it safe to carry more than average debt.

The times-interest-earned (TIE) ratio gives an indication of how vulnerable the company is to financial distress. This ratio depends on three factors: (1) the percentage of debt, (2) the interest rate on the debt, and (3) the company's profitability. Generally, low-leveraged companies such as Exxon Mobil and Eli Lilly have high coverage ratios, whereas companies like ConAgra, Kroger, and U.S. Airways, which have financed heavily with debt, have lower coverage ratios.

Wide variations in capital structures also exist among firms in given industries. This can be seen from Table 13.5. For example, although the average ratio of long-term debt to total capital in 2013 for the petroleum industry was 22.48%, Exxon Mobil had a ratio of 7.41%. Thus, factors unique to individual firms, including managerial attitudes, play an important role in setting target capital structures.

Capital Structure Percentages, 2013: Selected Companies Ranked by Company Long-Term Debt Ratios[a] **TABLE 13.5**

	Company			Industry	
Name	**Long-Term Debt Ratio**	**Times-Interest-Earned Ratio**	**Description**	**Long-Term Debt Ratio**	**Times-Interest-Earned Ratio**
Exxon Mobil[b]	7.41%	—	Petroleum	22.48%	11.6×
Schnitzer Steel	27.01	4.7×	Steel	26.47	37.3
Eli Lilly	27.01	90.7	Pharmaceuticals	49.75	37.9
CSX	50.25	6.1	Railroads	40.48	11.2
Rockwell Collins	50.74	85.5	Aerospace	81.13	30.0
Hewlett Packard	53.27	11.4	Computers	48.98	9.3
Amgen	55.16	10.1	Biotechnology	37.50	15.3
TECO Energy	56.52	3.1	Electric Utilities	57.45	3.6
Darden Restaurants	58.68	5.4	Restaurants	58.51	17.5
ConAgra Foods	67.74	4.5	Food Processing	73.54	10.1
Kroger	67.85	5.7	Grocery Stores	45.36	7.2
U.S. Airways	85.34	2.8	Airlines	97.09	3.6

Notes:
[a]Long-term debt ratios are calculated as a percentage of total capital, where total capital is defined as long-term debt plus equity, with both measured at book value. Note that this measure of the debt ratio does not include short-term debt.
[b]Exxon Mobil's interest expense as measured in millions is zero, so its TIE ratio is undefined.

Source: *MSN Money* (money.msn.com), May 29, 2013.

---

[35]Information on capital structures and financial strength is available from a multitude of sources. We used *MSN Money* (money.msn.com) to develop Table 13.5, but published sources include *The Value Line Investment Survey, Risk Management Association Annual Statement Studies,* and *Dun & Bradstreet Key Business Ratios.*

Why do wide variations in the use of financial leverage occur across industries and among individual firms in each industry?

TYING IT ALL TOGETHER

When we studied the cost of capital in Chapter 10, we took the firm's capital structure as given and calculated the cost of capital based on that structure. Then in Chapters 11 and 12, we described capital budgeting techniques, which use the cost of capital as input. Capital budgeting decisions determine the types of projects that a firm accepts, which affect the nature of the firm's assets and its business risk. In this chapter, we reverse the process, taking the firm's assets and business risk as given and then seeking to determine the best way to finance those assets. More specifically, in this chapter, we examined the effects of financial leverage on earnings per share, stock prices, and the cost of capital and we discussed various capital structure theories.

The different theories lead to different conclusions about the optimal capital structure, and no one has been able to prove that one theory is better than the others. Therefore, we cannot estimate a firm's optimal capital structure with much precision. Accordingly, financial executives generally treat the optimal capital structure as a range—for example, 40% to 50% debt—rather than as a precise point, such as 45% debt. The concepts discussed in this chapter are used as a guide, and they help managers understand the factors to consider when they are setting the target capital structures of their firms.

SELF-TEST QUESTIONS AND PROBLEMS

(Solutions Appear in Appendix A)

ST-1   **KEY TERMS**   Define each of the following terms:
   a. Capital; capital structure; optimal capital structure
   b. Business risk; financial risk
   c. Financial leverage; operating leverage; operating breakeven
   d. Hamada equation; unlevered beta
   e. Symmetric information; asymmetric information
   f. Modigliani–Miller theories
   g. Trade-off theory; signaling theory
   h. Reserve borrowing capacity; pecking order
   i. Windows of opportunity; net debt

ST-2 **OPERATING LEVERAGE AND BREAK-EVEN ANALYSIS** Olinde Electronics Inc. produces stereo components that sell at P = $100 per unit. Olinde's fixed costs are $200,000, variable costs are $50 per unit, 5,000 components are produced and sold each year, EBIT is currently $50,000, and Olinde's assets (all equity-financed) are $500,000. Olinde can change its production process by adding $400,000 to assets and $50,000 to fixed operating costs. This change would (1) reduce variable costs per unit by $10 and (2) increase output by 2,000 units, but (3) the sales price on all units would have to be lowered to $95 to permit sales of the additional output. Olinde has tax loss carry-forwards that cause its tax rate to be zero, it uses no debt, and its average cost of capital is 10%.

a. Should Olinde make the change? Why or why not?

b. Would Olinde's break-even point increase or decrease if it made the change?

c. Suppose Olinde was unable to raise additional equity financing and had to borrow the $400,000 at an interest rate of 10% to make the investment. Use the DuPont equation to find the expected ROA of the investment. Should Olinde make the change if debt financing must be used? Explain.

ST-3 **OPTIMAL CAPITAL STRUCTURE** Carlisle Industries is trying to determine its optimal capital structure, which now consists of only common equity. The firm will add debt to its capital structure if it minimizes its WACC, but the firm has no plans to use preferred stock in its capital structure. In addition, the firm's size will remain the same, so funds obtained from debt issued will be used to repurchase stock. The percentage of shares repurchased will be equal to the percentage of debt added to the firm's capital structure. (In other words, if the firm's debt-to-capital ratio increases from 0 to 25%, then 25% of the shares outstanding will be repurchased.)

Its treasury staff has consulted with investment bankers. On the basis of those discussions, the staff has created the following table showing the firm's debt cost at different debt levels:

Debt-to-Capital Ratio (w_d)	Equity-to-Capital Ratio (w_c)	Debt-to-Equity Ratio (D/E)	Bond Rating	Before-Tax Cost of Debt (r_d)
0.00	1.00	0.0000	AA	5.0%
0.25	0.75	0.3333	A	6.0
0.50	0.50	1.0000	BBB	8.3
0.75	0.25	3.0000	BB	11.0

The firm has total capital of $5 million and 200,000 shares of common stock outstanding. Its EBIT is $500,000 and will not change if debt, at any of the levels shown in the table above, is added to the firm's capital structure. Carlisle uses the CAPM to estimate its cost of common equity, r_s. It estimates that the risk-free rate is 3.5%, the market risk premium is 4.5%, and its tax rate is 35%. Carlisle's current beta, which is b_U because it has no debt, is 1.25.

a. Calculate the firm's interest expense, net income, shares outstanding, and EPS for each of the capital structures shown in the table above.

b. At what capital structure is EPS maximized, and what is the firm's EPS at this capital structure?

c. Calculate the after-tax cost of debt $[r_d(1 - T)]$, beta (b_L), cost of equity (r_s), and WACC for each of the capital structures shown in the table above.

d. Considering only the capital structures shown, at what capital structure is WACC minimized and what is the WACC at this capital structure?

e. At what capital structure does the firm maximize shareholder value? Is this the same capital structure selected in Parts b and d? Explain why it is, or why it isn't the same.

f. As an analyst, what is your recommendation to the firm's management regarding Carlisle's capital structure?

QUESTIONS

13-1 Changes in sales cause changes in profits. Would the profit change associated with sales changes be larger or smaller if a firm increased its operating leverage? Explain your answer.

13-2 Would each of the following increase, decrease, or have an indeterminant effect on a firm's break-even point (unit sales)?

a. The sales price increases with no change in unit costs.

b. An increase in fixed costs is accompanied by a decrease in variable costs.

c. A new firm decides to use MACRS depreciation for both book and tax purposes rather than the straight-line depreciation method.

d. Variable labor costs decline; other things are held constant.

13-3 Discuss the following statement: All else equal, firms with relatively stable sales are able to carry relatively high debt ratios. Is the statement true or false? Why?

13-4 If Congress increased the personal tax rate on interest, dividends, and capital gains but simultaneously reduced the rate on corporate income, what effect would this have on the average company's capital structure?

13-5 Which of the following would likely encourage a firm to increase the debt in its capital structure?

a. The corporate tax rate increases.

b. The personal tax rate increases.

c. Due to market changes, the firm's assets become less liquid.

d. Changes in the bankruptcy code make bankruptcy less costly to the firm.

e. The firm's sales and earnings become more volatile.

13-6 Why do public utilities generally use different capital structures than biotechnology companies?

13-7 Why is EBIT generally considered independent of financial leverage? Why might EBIT actually be affected by financial leverage at high debt levels?

13-8 Is the debt level that maximizes a firm's expected EPS the same as the debt level that maximizes its stock price? Explain.

13-9 If a firm goes from zero debt to successively higher levels of debt, why would you expect its stock price to rise first, then hit a peak, and then begin to decline?

13-10 When the Bell System was broken up, the old AT&T was split into a new AT&T and seven regional telephone companies. The specific reason for forcing the breakup was to increase the degree of competition in the telephone industry. AT&T had a monopoly on local service, long distance, and the manufacture of all equipment used by telephone companies; and the breakup was expected to open most of those markets to competition. In the court order that set the terms of the breakup, the capital structures of the surviving companies were specified and much attention was given to the increased competition telephone companies could expect in the future. Do you think the optimal capital structure after the breakup was the same as the pre-breakup optimal capital structure? Explain your position.

13-11 A firm is about to double its assets to serve its rapidly growing market. It must choose between a highly automated production process and a less automated one. It also must choose a capital structure for financing the expansion. Should the asset investment and financing decisions be jointly determined, or should each decision be made separately? How would these decisions affect one another? How could the leverage concept be used to help management analyze the situation?

PROBLEMS

**Easy Problems
1–5**

13-1   **BREAK-EVEN ANALYSIS**   A company's fixed operating costs are $500,000, its variable costs are $3.00 per unit, and the product's sales price is $4.00. What is the company's break-even point; that is, at what unit sales volume will its income equal its costs?

13-2   **OPTIMAL CAPITAL STRUCTURE**   Jackson Trucking Company is in the process of setting its target capital structure. The CFO believes that the optimal debt-to-capital ratio is somewhere between 20% and 50%, and her staff has compiled the following projections for EPS and the stock price at various debt levels:

Debt/Capital Ratio	Projected EPS	Projected Stock Price
20%	$3.20	$35.00
30	3.45	36.50
40	3.75	36.25
50	3.50	35.50

Assuming that the firm uses only debt and common equity, what is Jackson's optimal capital structure? At what debt-to-capital ratio is the company's WACC minimized?

13-3   **RISK ANALYSIS**

a.   Given the following information, calculate the expected value for Firm C's EPS. Data for Firms A and B are as follows: $E(EPS_A) = \$5.10$, $\sigma_A = \$3.61$, $E(EPS_B) = \$4.20$, and $\sigma_B = \$2.96$.

	Probability				
	0.1	**0.2**	**0.4**	**0.2**	**0.1**
Firm A: EPS_A	($1.50)	$1.80	$5.10	$8.40	$11.70
Firm B: EPS_B	(1.20)	1.50	4.20	6.90	9.60
Firm C: EPS_C	(2.40)	1.35	5.10	8.85	12.60

b.   You are given that $\sigma_C = \$4.11$. Discuss the relative riskiness of the three firms' earnings.

13-4   **UNLEVERED BETA**   Harley Motors has $10 million in assets, which were financed with $2 million of debt and $8 million in equity. Harley's beta is currently 1.2, and its tax rate is 40%. Use the Hamada equation to find Harley's unlevered beta, b_U.

13-5   **FINANCIAL LEVERAGE EFFECTS**   Firms HL and LL are identical except for their financial leverage ratios and the interest rates they pay on debt. Each has $20 million in invested capital, has $4 million of EBIT, and is in the 40% federal-plus-state tax bracket. Firm HL, however, has a debt-to-capital ratio of 50% and pays 12% interest on its debt, whereas LL has a 30% debt-to-capital ratio and pays only 10% interest on its debt. Neither firm uses preferred stock in its capital structure.

a.   Calculate the return on invested capital (ROIC) for each firm.

b.   Calculate the return on equity (ROE) for each firm.

c.   Observing that HL has a higher ROE, LL's treasurer is thinking of raising the debt-to-capital ratio from 30% to 60% even though that would increase LL's interest rate on all debt to 15%. Calculate the new ROE for LL.

**Intermediate
Problems
6–9**

13-6   **BREAK-EVEN ANALYSIS**   The Weaver Watch Company sells watches for $25, fixed costs are $140,000, and variable costs are $15 per watch.

a.   What is the firm's gain or loss at sales of 8,000 watches? At 18,000 watches?

b.   What is the break-even point? Illustrate by means of a chart.

c.   What would happen to the break-even point if the selling price was raised to $31? What is the significance of this analysis?

d.   What would happen to the break-even point if the selling price was raised to $31 but variable costs rose to $23 a unit?

13-7   **FINANCIAL LEVERAGE EFFECTS**   The Neal Company wants to estimate next year's return on equity (ROE) under different financial leverage ratios. Neal's total capital is $14 million, it currently uses only common equity, it has no future plans to use preferred stock in its capital structure, and its federal-plus-state tax rate is 40%. The CFO has estimated next year's EBIT for three possible states of the world: $4.2 million with a 0.2 probability, $2.8 million with a 0.5 probability, and $700,000 with a 0.3 probability. Calculate Neal's expected ROE, standard deviation, and coefficient of variation for each of the following debt-to-capital ratios; then evaluate the results:

Debt/Capital Ratio	Interest Rate
0%	—
10	9%
50	11
60	14

13-8   HAMADA EQUATION   Cyclone Software Co. is trying to establish its optimal capital structure. Its current capital structure consists of 25% debt and 75% equity; however, the CEO believes that the firm should use more debt. The risk-free rate, r_{RF}, is 5%; the market risk premium, RP_M, is 6%; and the firm's tax rate is 40%. Currently, Cyclone's cost of equity is 14%, which is determined by the CAPM. What would be Cyclone's estimated cost of equity if it changed its capital structure to 50% debt and 50% equity?

13-9   RECAPITALIZATION   Tapley Inc. currently has total capital equal to $5 million, has zero debt, is in the 40% federal-plus-state tax bracket, has a net income of $1 million, and distributes 40% of its earnings as dividends. Net income is expected to grow at a constant rate of 5% per year, 200,000 shares of stock are outstanding, and the current WACC is 13.40%.

The company is considering a recapitalization where it will issue $1 million in debt and use the proceeds to repurchase stock. Investment bankers have estimated that if the company goes through with the recapitalization, its before-tax cost of debt will be 11% and its cost of equity will rise to 14.5%.

a.   What is the stock's current price per share (before the recapitalization)?

b.   Assuming that the company maintains the same payout ratio, what will be its stock price following the recapitalization? Assume that shares are repurchased at the price calculated in Part a.

Challenging Problems 10–13

13-10   BREAKEVEN AND OPERATING LEVERAGE

a.   Given the following graphs, calculate the total fixed costs, variable costs per unit, and sales price for Firm A. Firm B's fixed costs are $120,000, its variable costs per unit are $4, and its sales price is $8 per unit.

b.   Which firm has the higher operating leverage at any given level of sales? Explain.

c.   At what sales level, in units, do both firms earn the same operating profit?

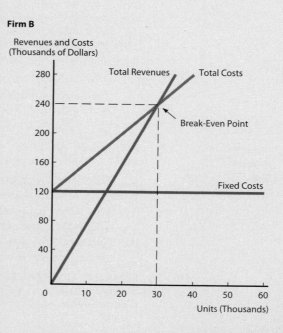

13-11 **RECAPITALIZATION** Currently, Bloom Flowers Inc. has a capital structure consisting of 20% debt and 80% equity. Bloom's debt currently has an 8% yield to maturity. The risk-free rate (r_{RF}) is 5%, and the market risk premium ($r_M - r_{RF}$) is 6%. Using the CAPM, Bloom estimates that its cost of equity is currently 12.5%. The company has a 40% tax rate.

    a.   What is Bloom's current WACC?

    b.   What is the current beta on Bloom's common stock?

    c.   What would Bloom's beta be if the company had no debt in its capital structure? (That is, what is Bloom's unlevered beta, b_U?)

Bloom's financial staff is considering changing its capital structure to 40% debt and 60% equity. If the company went ahead with the proposed change, the yield to maturity on the company's bonds would rise to 9.5%. The proposed change will have no effect on the company's tax rate.

    d.   What would be the company's new cost of equity if it adopted the proposed change in capital structure?

    e.   What would be the company's new WACC if it adopted the proposed change in capital structure?

    f.   Based on your answer to Part e, would you advise Bloom to adopt the proposed change in capital structure? Explain.

13-12 **BREAKEVEN AND LEVERAGE** Wingler Communications Corporation (WCC) produces premium stereo headphones that sell for $28.80 per set, and this year's sales are expected to be 450,000 units. Variable production costs for the expected sales under present production methods are estimated at $10,200,000, and fixed production (operating) costs at present are $1,560,000. WCC has $4,800,000 of debt outstanding at an interest rate of 8%. There are 240,000 shares of common stock outstanding, and there is no preferred stock. The dividend payout ratio is 70%, and WCC is in the 40% federal-plus-state tax bracket.

The company is considering investing $7,200,000 in new equipment. Sales would not increase, but variable costs per unit would decline by 20%. Also, fixed operating costs would increase from $1,560,000 to $1,800,000. WCC could raise the required capital by borrowing $7,200,000 at 10% or by selling 240,000 additional shares of common stock at $30 per share.

    a.   What would be WCC's EPS (1) under the old production process, (2) under the new process if it uses debt, and (3) under the new process if it uses common stock?

    b.   At what unit sales level would WCC have the same EPS assuming it undertakes the investment and finances it with debt or with stock? {Hint: V = variable cost per unit = $8,160,000/450,000, and EPS = $[(PQ - VQ - F - I)(1 - T)]/N$. Set $EPS_{Stock} = EPS_{Debt}$ and solve for Q.}

    c.   At what unit sales level would EPS = 0 under the three production/financing setups— that is, under the old plan, the new plan with debt financing, and the new plan with stock financing? (Hint: Note that $V_{old} = $10,200,000/450,000$ and use the hints for Part b, setting the EPS equation equal to zero.)

    d.   On the basis of the analysis in Parts a through c and given that operating leverage is lower under the new setup, which plan is the riskiest, which has the highest expected EPS, and which would you recommend? Assume that there is a fairly high probability of sales falling as low as 250,000 units. Determine EPS_{Debt} and EPS_{Stock} at that sales level to help assess the riskiness of the two financing plans.

13-13 **FINANCING ALTERNATIVES** The Severn Company plans to raise a net amount of $270 million to finance new equipment in early 2015. Two alternatives are being considered: Common stock may be sold to net $60 per share, or bonds yielding 12% may be issued. The balance sheet and income statement of the Severn Company prior to financing are as follows:

The Severn Company: Balance Sheet as of December 31, 2014
(Millions of Dollars)

Current assets	$ 900.00	Notes payable	$ 255.00
Net fixed assets	450.00	Long-term debt (10%)	697.50
		Common stock, $3 par	60.00
		Retained earnings	337.50
Total assets	$1,350.00	Total liabilities and equity	$1,350.00

**The Severn Company: Income Statement for Year Ended
December 31, 2014 (Millions of Dollars)**

Sales	$2,475.00
Operating costs	2,227.50
Earnings before interest and taxes (10%)	$ 247.50
Interest on short-term debt	15.00
Interest on long-term debt	69.75
Earnings before taxes	$ 162.75
Federal-plus-state taxes (40%)	65.10
Net income	$ 97.65

The probability distribution for annual sales is as follows:

Probability	Annual Sales (Millions of Dollars)
0.30	$2,250
0.40	2,700
0.30	3,150

Assuming that EBIT equals 10% of sales, calculate earnings per share (EPS) under the debt financing and the stock financing alternatives at each possible sales level. Then calculate expected EPS and σ_{EPS} under both debt and stock financing alternatives. Also calculate the debt-to-capital ratio and the times-interest-earned (TIE) ratio at the expected sales level under each alternative. The old debt will remain outstanding. Which financing method do you recommend? [Hint: Notes payable should be included in both the numerator and the denominator of the debt-to-capital ratio.]

COMPREHENSIVE/SPREADSHEET PROBLEM

13-14   **WACC AND OPTIMAL CAPITAL STRUCTURE** Elliott Athletics is trying to determine its optimal capital structure, which now consists of only debt and common equity. The firm does not currently use preferred stock in its capital structure, and it does not plan to do so in the future. Its treasury staff has consulted with investment bankers. On the basis of those discussions, the staff has created the following table showing the firm's debt cost at different debt levels:

Debt-to-Capital Ratio (w_d)	Equity-to-Capital Ratio (w_c)	Debt-to-Equity Ratio (D/E)	Bond Rating	Before-Tax Cost of Debt (r_d)
0.0	1.0	0.00	A	7.0%
0.2	0.8	0.25	BBB	8.0
0.4	0.6	0.67	BB	10.0
0.6	0.4	1.50	C	12.0
0.8	0.2	4.00	D	15.0

Elliott uses the CAPM to estimate its cost of common equity, r_s, and estimates that the risk-free rate is 5%, the market risk premium is 6%, and its tax rate is 40%. Elliott estimates that if it had no debt, its "unlevered" beta, b_U, would be 1.2.

a. What is the firm's optimal capital structure, and what would be its WACC at the optimal capital structure?

b. If Elliott's managers anticipate that the company's business risk will increase in the future, what effect would this likely have on the firm's target capital structure?

c. If Congress were to dramatically increase the corporate tax rate, what effect would this likely have on Elliott's target capital structure?

d. Plot a graph of the after-tax cost of debt, the cost of equity, and the WACC versus (1) the debt/capital ratio and (2) the debt/equity ratio.

INTEGRATED CASE

CAMPUS DELI INC.

13-15 **OPTIMAL CAPITAL STRUCTURE**   Assume that you have just been hired as business manager of Campus Deli (CD), which is located adjacent to the campus. Sales were $1,100,000 last year, variable costs were 60% of sales, and fixed costs were $40,000. Therefore, EBIT totaled $400,000. Because the university's enrollment is capped, EBIT is expected to be constant over time. Because no expansion capital is required, CD distributes all earnings as dividends. Invested capital is $2 million, and 80,000 shares are outstanding. The management group owns about 50% of the stock, which is traded in the over-the-counter market.

CD currently has no debt—it is an all-equity firm—and its 80,000 shares outstanding sell at a price of $25 per share, which is also the book value. The firm's federal-plus-state tax rate is 40%. On the basis of statements made in your finance text, you believe that CD's shareholders would be better off if some debt financing were used. When you suggested this to your new boss, she encouraged you to pursue the idea but to provide support for the suggestion.

In today's market, the risk-free rate, r_{RF}, is 6% and the market risk premium, RP_M, is 6%. CD's unlevered beta, b_U is 1.0. CD currently has no debt, so its cost of equity (and WACC) is 12%. If the firm was recapitalized, debt would be issued and the borrowed funds would be used to repurchase stock. Stockholders, in turn, would use funds provided by the repurchase to buy equities in other fast-food companies similar to CD. You plan to complete your report by asking and then answering the following questions.

a. 1. What is business risk? What factors influence a firm's business risk?

  2. What is operating leverage, and how does it affect a firm's business risk?

  3. What is the firm's return on invested capital (ROIC)?

b. 1. What do the terms *financial leverage* and *financial risk* mean?

  2. How does financial risk differ from business risk?

c. To develop an example that can be presented to CD's management as an illustration, consider two hypothetical firms: Firm U with zero debt financing and Firm L with $10,000 of 12% debt. Both firms have $20,000 in invested capital and a 40% federal-plus-state tax rate, and they have the following EBIT probability distribution for next year:

Probability	EBIT
0.25	$2,000
0.50	3,000
0.25	4,000

  1. Complete the partial income statements and the firms' ratios in Table IC 13.1.

  2. Be prepared to discuss each entry in the table and to explain how this example illustrates the effect of financial leverage on expected rate of return and risk.

d. After speaking with a local investment banker, you obtain the following estimates of the cost of debt at different debt levels (in thousands of dollars):

Amount Borrowed	Debt/Capital Ratio	D/E Ratio	Bond Rating	r_d
$ 0	0	0	—	—
250	0.125	0.1429	AA	8.0%
500	0.250	0.3333	A	9.0
750	0.375	0.6000	BBB	11.5
1,000	0.500	1.0000	BB	14.0

Now consider the optimal capital structure for CD.

  1. To begin, define the terms *optimal capital structure* and *target capital structure*.

  2. Why does CD's bond rating and cost of debt depend on the amount of money borrowed?

TABLE IC 13.1   Income Statements and Ratios

	Firm U			Firm L		
Total capital	$20,000	$20,000	$20,000	$20,000	$20,000	$20,000
Equity	$20,000	$20,000	$20,000	$10,000	$10,000	$10,000
Probability	0.25	0.50	0.25	0.25	0.50	0.25
Sales	$ 6,000	$ 9,000	$12,000	$ 6,000	$ 9,000	$12,000
Operating costs	4,000	6,000	8,000	4,000	6,000	8,000
Earnings before interest and taxes	$ 2,000	$ 3,000	$ 4,000	$ 2,000	$ 3,000	$ 4,000
Interest (12%)	0	0	0	1,200		1,200
Earnings before taxes	$ 2,000	$ 3,000	$ 4,000	$ 800	$	$ 2,800
Taxes (40%)	800	1,200	1,600	320		1,120
Net income	$ 1,200	$ 1,800	$ 2,400	$ 480	$	$ 1,680
ROIC	6.0%	9.0%	12.0%	%	%	%
ROE	6.0%	9.0%	12.0%	4.8%	%	16.8%
TIE	∞	∞	∞	1.7×	×	3.3×
Expected ROIC		9.0%			%	
Expected ROE		9.0%			10.8%	
Expected TIE		∞			2.5×	
σ_{ROIC}		2.1%			%	
σ_{ROE}		2.1%			4.2%	
σ_{TIE}		0			0.6×	

3. Assume that shares could be repurchased at the current market price of $25 per share. Calculate CD's expected EPS and TIE at debt levels of $0, $250,000, $500,000, $750,000, and $1,000,000. How many shares would remain after recapitalization under each scenario?

4. Using the Hamada equation, what is the cost of equity if CD recapitalizes with $250,000 of debt? $500,000? $750,000? $1,000,000?

5. Considering only the levels of debt discussed, what is the capital structure that minimizes CD's WACC?

6. What would be the new stock price if CD recapitalizes with $250,000 of debt? $500,000? $750,000? $1,000,000? Recall that the payout ratio is 100%, so $g = 0$.

7. Is EPS maximized at the debt level that maximizes share price? Why or why not?

8. Considering only the levels of debt discussed, what is CD's optimal capital structure?

9. What is the WACC at the optimal capital structure?

e. Suppose you discovered that CD had more business risk than you originally estimated. Describe how this would affect the analysis. How would the analysis be affected if the firm had less business risk than originally estimated?

f. What are some factors a manager should consider when establishing his or her firm's target capital structure?

g. Put labels on Figure IC 13.1 and then discuss the graph as you might use it to explain to your boss why CD might want to use some debt.

h. How does the existence of asymmetric information and signaling affect capital structure?

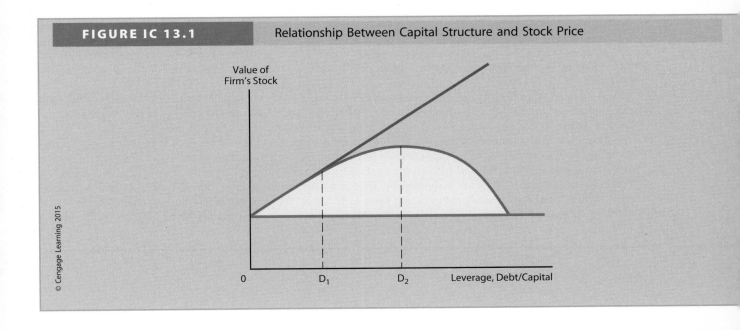

FIGURE IC 13.1 Relationship Between Capital Structure and Stock Price

THOMSON REUTERS

Use the Thomson ONE—Business School Edition online database to work this chapter's questions.

Exploring the Capital Structures for Four Restaurant Companies

This chapter provides an overview of the effects of leverage and describes the process that firms use to determine their optimal capital structure. The chapter also indicates that capital structures tend to vary across industries and across countries. If you are interested in exploring these differences in more detail, Thomson ONE provides information about the capital structures of each of the companies it follows. The following discussion questions demonstrate how we can use this information to evaluate the capital structures for four restaurant companies: Cheesecake Factory (CAKE), Chipotle Mexican Grill (CMG), Ruby Tuesday (RT), and O'Charley's Inc. (CHUX).

Discussion Questions

1. To get an overall picture of each company's capital structure, it is helpful to look at a chart that summarizes the company's capital structure over the past decade. To obtain this chart, choose a company to start with and select FINANCIALS. Next, select MORE>THOMSON REPORTS & CHARTS>CAPITAL STRUCTURE. This should generate a chart that plots the company's total long-term debt, total common equity, and total current liabilities over the past decade. What, if any, are the major trends that emerge when you're looking at these charts? Do these companies tend to have relatively high or relatively low levels of debt? Do these companies have significant levels of current liabilities? Have their capital structures changed over time?

2. To get more details about the companies' capital structures over the past 5 years, select FINANCIALS>FINANCIAL RATIOS>THOMSON RATIOS. From here, you can select ANNUAL RATIOS and/or 5 YEAR AVERAGE RATIOS REPORT. In each case, you can scroll down and look for "Leverage Ratios." Here you will find a variety of leverage ratios for the past 5 years. (Notice that these two pages offer different information. The ANNUAL RATIOS page offers year-end leverage ratios, while the 5 YEAR AVERAGE RATIOS REPORT offers the average ratio over the previous 5 years for each calendar date. In other words, the 5 YEAR AVERAGE RATIOS REPORT

smoothes the changes in capital structure over the reporting period.) Do these ratios suggest that the company has significantly changed its capital structure over the past 5 years? If so, what factors could possibly explain this shift? (Financial statements might be useful to detect any shifts that may have led to the company's changing capital structure. You may also consult the company's annual report to see if there is any discussion and/or explanation for these changes. Both the historical financial statements and annual report information can be found via Thomson ONE.)

3. Repeat this procedure for the other three companies. Do you find similar capital structures for each of the four companies? Do you find that the capital structures have moved in the same direction over the past 5 years, or have the different companies changed their capital structures in different ways over the past 5 years?

4. The financial ratios investigated thus far are based on book values of debt and equity. Determine whether using the market value of equity (market capitalization is found on the OVERVIEW page) makes a significant difference in the most recent year's "LT Debt Pct Common Equity," "Total Debt Pct Common Equity," and "LT Debt Pct Total Capital." (Note: "LT Debt" is defined by Thomson ONE as the "Long Term Debt" listed on the balance sheet, while "Total Debt" is defined as "Long Term Debt" plus "ST Debt & Current Portion Due LT Debt.") Are there big differences between the capital structures measured on a book or market basis? Explain your answer.

© Sergio Azenha/Alamy

Distributions to Shareholders: Dividends and Share Repurchases

Apple Shifts Gears and Begins to Unload Part of Its Vast Cash Hoard

Profitable companies regularly face three important questions: (1) How much of our free cash flow should we pass on to shareholders? (2) Should we provide this cash to stockholders by raising the dividend or by repurchasing stock? (3) Should we maintain a stable, consistent payment policy; or should we let the payments vary as conditions change?

In this chapter, we discuss many of the issues that affect firms' cash distribution policies. As we will see, mature companies with stable cash flows and limited growth opportunities tend to return a significant amount of their cash to shareholders either by paying dividends or by repurchasing common stock. By contrast, rapidly growing companies with good investment opportunities are prone to invest most of their available cash in new projects rather than paying dividends or repurchasing stock. Apple

Inc., which has been regarded over the past decade as the epitome of a growth company, illustrates this tendency. Its sales grew from $6.2 billion in 2003 to $156.5 billion in 2012, which translates to an annual growth rate of more than 40%. Much of this growth came from large, long-term investments in new products and technology; given the firm's emphasis on growth, it had long been reluctant to pay dividends.

Demonstrating this viewpoint at a shareholders' meeting in early 2010, Apple's legendary co-founder and CEO Steve Jobs strongly reaffirmed that the company had no intentions to start paying a dividend, even though Apple had more than $50 billion in cash and short-term securities on its balance sheet. According to The Wall Street Journal, Jobs said "that he preferred 'to leave the powder dry' for future acquisitions, though none were in the offing. He added that the cash 'will come in handy'."

However, after Steve Jobs died in late 2011, the company faced increased pressure to return some of its cash to shareholders. Since then, the company's cash holdings have continued to balloon, while at the same time there are growing concerns that Apple's growth engine may be slowing down. Reflecting these concerns, the company's stock fell sharply from $700 in October 2012 to below $400 per share just six months later in April 2013.

Well aware of the new environment, the company's new CEO Tim Cook shifted gears; in early 2012, Apple established a dividend and also announced a plan to repurchase shares of its common stock. However, despite these efforts to return cash to its shareholders, the cash kept pouring in, and by early 2013 the company still had a staggering $137 billion of cash and securities on its balance sheet.

In response, the company took even more dramatic steps. In April 2013, it announced a 15% increase in its quarterly dividend and plans to raise its share repurchases from $10 billion to $60 billion. So while Apple continues to generate a great deal of cash, its aggressive use of dividends and share repurchases to return cash to shareholders recently represents an important shift in policy.

When managers decide how and when to distribute cash to shareholders, they face a fundamental question: Could we earn more on the available cash if we kept it in the firm and used it to invest in new projects, or would shareholders earn more if they received the cash and invested it in alternative investments with the same risk? If the company could earn more, it would make sense to retain the cash. However, if investors could earn more, the company would increase shareholder value by paying out more dividends and/or by repurchasing more shares.

Sources: Ben Charny, "Jobs Defends Apple's Cash Hoard," *The Wall Street Journal* (online.wsj.com), February 25, 2010; and Steven Russolillo, "Apple Announces Massive Cash Plans," *The Wall Street Journal* (online.wsj.com), April 23, 2013.

PUTTING THINGS IN PERSPECTIVE

Successful companies earn income. That income can be reinvested in operating assets, used to retire debt, or distributed to stockholders. If the decision is made to distribute income to stockholders, three key issues arise: (1) How much should be distributed? (2) Should the distribution be in the form of dividends, or should the cash be passed on to shareholders by buying back stock? (3) How stable should the distribution be? That is, should the funds paid out from year to year be stable and dependable, which stockholders like; or should they be varied depending on the firms' cash flows and investment requirements, which managers tend to like?

Those three issues are the primary focus of this chapter. By the time you complete it, you should be able to:

- **Explain why some investors like the firm to pay more dividends while other investors prefer reinvestment and the resulting capital gains.**
- **Discuss the various trade-offs that companies face when trying to establish their optimal dividend policy.**
- **Differentiate between stock splits and stock dividends.**
- **List the advantages and disadvantages of stock repurchases vis-à-vis dividends from both investors' and companies' perspectives.**

14-1 DIVIDENDS VERSUS CAPITAL GAINS: WHAT DO INVESTORS PREFER?

When deciding how much cash to distribute, financial managers must keep in mind that the firm's objective is to maximize shareholder value. Consequently, the **target payout ratio**—defined as the percentage of net income to be paid out as cash dividends—should be based in large part on investors' preferences for dividends versus capital gains: Do investors prefer to receive dividends; or would they rather have the firm plow the cash back into the business, which presumably will produce capital gains? This preference can be considered in terms of the constant growth stock valuation model.

Target Payout Ratio
The target percentage of net income paid out as cash dividends.

$$\hat{P}_0 = \frac{D_1}{r_s - g}$$

If the company increases the payout ratio, this will raise D_1, which, taken alone, will cause the stock price to rise. However, if D_1 is raised, less money will be available for reinvestment, which will cause the expected growth rate to decline; and that will tend to lower the stock's price. Therefore, any change in the payout policy will have two opposing effects. As a result, the **optimal dividend policy** must strike the balance between current dividends and future growth that maximizes the stock price. In the following sections, we discuss the major theories that have been advanced to explain how investors regard current dividends versus future growth.

Optimal Dividend Policy
The dividend policy that strikes a balance between current dividends and future growth and maximizes the firm's stock price.

14-1A DIVIDEND IRRELEVANCE THEORY

Professors Merton Miller and Franco Modigliani (MM) advanced the **dividend irrelevance theory**, which stated that dividend policy has no effect on either the price of a firm's stock or its cost of capital.[1] MM developed their theory under a stringent set of assumptions; and under those assumptions, they proved that a firm's value is determined only by its basic earning power and its business risk. In other words, the value of the firm depends only on the income produced by its assets, not on how that income is split between dividends and retained earnings. Note, though, that MM assumed, among other things, that no taxes are paid on dividends, that stocks can be bought and sold with no transactions costs, and that everyone—investors and managers alike—has the same information regarding firms' future earnings.

Dividend Irrelevance Theory
The theory that a firm's dividend policy has no effect on either its value or its cost of capital.

Given their assumptions, MM argued that each shareholder can construct his or her own dividend policy. For example, if a firm does not pay dividends, a shareholder who wants a 5% dividend can "create" it by selling 5% of his or her stock. Conversely, if a company pays a higher dividend than an investor wants, the investor can use the unwanted dividends to buy additional shares of the company's stock. Note, though, that in the real world, individual investors who want additional dividends would have to incur transactions costs to sell shares, and investors who do not want dividends would have to pay taxes on the unwanted dividends and then incur transactions costs to purchase shares with the after-tax dividends. Because taxes and transactions costs do exist, dividend policy may well be relevant and investors may prefer policies that help them reduce taxes and transactions costs.

---

[1]Merton H. Miller and Franco Modigliani, "Dividend Policy, Growth, and the Valuation of Shares," *Journal of Business*, October 1961, pp. 411–433.

In defense of their theory, MM noted that many stocks are owned by institutional investors who pay no taxes and who can buy and sell stocks with very low transactions costs. For such investors, dividend policy might well be irrelevant; and if these investors dominate the market and represent the "marginal investor," MM's theory could be valid in spite of its unrealistic assumptions. Note too that for tax-paying investors, the taxes and transactions costs depend on what the individual investor's income is and how long he or she plans to hold the stock. As a result, when it comes to investors' preferences for dividends, one size does not fit all. Next, we discuss why some investors prefer dividends whereas others prefer capital gains.

14-1b REASONS SOME INVESTORS PREFER DIVIDENDS

The principal conclusion of MM's dividend irrelevance theory is that dividend policy does not affect either stock prices or the required rate of return on equity, r_s. Early critics of MM's theory suggested that investors preferred a sure dividend today to an uncertain future capital gain. In particular, Myron Gordon and John Lintner argued that r_s declines as the dividend payout is increased because investors are less certain of receiving the capital gains that should result from retaining earnings than they are of receiving dividend payments.[2]

Bird-in-the-Hand Fallacy
MM's name for the Gordon–Lintner theory that a firm's value will be maximized by setting a high dividend payout ratio.

MM disagreed. They argued that r_s is independent of dividend policy, which implies that investors are indifferent between dividends and capital gains, that is, between D_1/P_0 and g. MM called the Gordon-Lintner argument the **bird-in-the-hand fallacy** because in MM's view, most investors plan to reinvest their dividends in the stock of the same or similar firms and, in any event, the riskiness of the firm's cash flows to investors in the long run is determined by the riskiness of operating cash flows, not by dividend payout policy.

Keep in mind, however, that MM's theory relied on the assumption that there are no taxes or transactions costs, which means that investors who prefer dividends could simply create their own dividend policy by selling a percentage of their stock each year. In reality, most investors face transactions costs when they sell stock; so investors who are looking for a steady stream of income would logically prefer that companies pay regular dividends. For example, retirees who have accumulated wealth over time and now want annual income from their investments probably prefer dividend-paying stocks.

14-1c REASONS SOME INVESTORS PREFER CAPITAL GAINS

While dividends reduce transactions costs for investors who are looking for steady income from their investments, dividends increase transactions costs for other investors who are less interested in income and more interested in saving money for the long-term future. These long-term investors want to reinvest their dividends, and that creates transactions costs. Given this concern, a number of companies have established dividend reinvestment plans that help investors automatically reinvest their dividends. (We discuss dividend reinvestment plans in Section 14-4.)

In addition (and perhaps more importantly), the Tax Code encourages many individual investors to prefer capital gains to dividends. One key advantage is that taxes must be paid on dividends the year they are received; whereas taxes on

---

[2]Myron J. Gordon, "Optimal Investment and Financing Policy," *Journal of Finance*, vol. 18, no. 2 (May 1963), pp. 264–272; and John Lintner, "Dividends, Earnings, Leverage, Stock Prices, and the Supply of Capital to Corporations," *Review of Economics and Statistics*, vol. 44, no. 3 (August 1962), pp. 243–269.

capital gains are not paid until the stock is sold. Due to time value effects, a dollar of taxes paid in the future has a lower effective cost than a dollar of taxes paid today.[3] Apart from this advantage, the tax rate on dividends has often been higher than the tax rate on capital gains. For example, prior to 2003, dividends were taxed at the ordinary income tax rate, which went up to 38.6% versus a rate of 20% on long-term capital gains. These differential rates were eliminated in 2003, when the maximum tax rate on dividends and long-term capital gains was set at 15%.[4] However, in early 2013, Congress increased the maximum tax rate on dividends and long-term capital gains to 20% for high-income taxpayers.[5]

SELF TEST

Explain briefly the ideas behind the dividend irrelevance theory.

What did Modigliani and Miller assume about taxes and brokerage costs when they developed their dividend irrelevance theory?

Why did MM refer to the Gordon-Lintner dividend argument as the bird-in-the-hand fallacy?

Why do some investors prefer high-dividend-paying stocks?

Why might other investors prefer low-dividend-paying stocks?

14-2 OTHER DIVIDEND POLICY ISSUES

Before we discuss how dividend policy is set in practice, we need to examine two other issues that affect dividend policy: (1) the *information content,* or *signaling, hypothesis* and (2) the *clientele effect.*

14-2A INFORMATION CONTENT, OR SIGNALING, HYPOTHESIS

An increase in the dividend is often accompanied by an increase in the stock price, while a dividend cut generally leads to a stock price decline. This observation was used to refute MM's irrelevance theory—their opponents argued that stock price actions after changes in dividend payouts demonstrate that investors prefer dividends to capital gains. However, MM argued differently. They noted that corporations are reluctant to cut dividends and hence that corporations do not raise dividends unless they anticipate higher earnings in the future to support the higher dividends. Thus, MM argued that a higher-than-expected dividend increase

---

[3]Moreover, if a stock is held by someone until he or she dies, there is no capital gains tax at all—the beneficiaries who receive the stock can use the stock's value on the date of death as their cost basis, which permits them to escape the capital gains tax completely.

[4]However, long-term capital gains are classified as income subject to the Alternative Minimum Tax (AMT), and the AMT rate in 2013 was 26% or 28% depending on your income bracket. The AMT was supposed to hit only the very wealthy, but prior to 2013 it was not indexed for inflation. So by 2012, many not-so-wealthy individuals were being hit. However, Congress fixed this problem with new tax legislation and beginning in 2013 the AMT exemption amounts are indexed to inflation.

[5]Effective January 1, 2013, long-term capital gains and dividend tax rates increased to 20% for single taxpayers earning more than $400,000 and for married persons filing jointly earning more than $450,000. Short-term capital gains on assets held for one year or less are taxed as ordinary income. Effective January 1, 2013, the top tax rate on ordinary income was 39.6% for single taxpayers earning more than $400,000 and married persons filing jointly earning more than $450,000.

is a signal to investors that management forecasts good future earnings.[6] Conversely, a dividend reduction, or a smaller-than-expected increase, is a signal that management forecasts poor future earnings. If the MM position is correct, stock price changes after dividend increases or decreases do not demonstrate a preference for dividends over retained earnings. Rather, such price changes simply indicate that dividend announcements have **information (signaling) content**, about future earnings.

Information (Signaling) Content

The theory that investors regard dividend changes as signals of management's earnings forecasts.

Managers often have better information about future prospects for dividends than public stockholders, so there is clearly some information content in dividend announcements. However, it is difficult to tell whether the stock price changes that follow dividend increases or decreases reflect only signaling effects (as MM argue) or both signaling and dividend preference. Still, a firm should consider signaling effects when it is contemplating a change in dividend policy. For example, if a firm has good long-term prospects but also has a need for cash to fund current investments, it might be tempted to cut the dividend to increase funds available for investment. However, this action might cause the stock price to decline because the dividend reduction is taken as a signal that future earnings are likely to decline, when just the reverse is actually true. So managers should consider signaling effects when they set dividend policy.

14-2b CLIENTELE EFFECT

Clienteles

Different groups of stockholders who prefer different dividend payout policies.

As we indicated earlier, different groups, or **clienteles**, of stockholders prefer different dividend payout policies. For example, retired individuals, pension funds, and university endowment funds generally prefer cash income; so they often want the firm to distribute a high percentage of its earnings. Such investors are frequently in low or even zero tax brackets, so taxes are of little concern. On the other hand, stockholders in their peak earning years might prefer reinvestment because they have less need for current investment income and simply reinvest dividends received after incurring income taxes and brokerage costs.

If a firm retains and reinvests income rather than paying dividends, those stockholders who need current income will be disadvantaged. The value of their stock might increase, but they will be forced to go to the trouble and expense of selling some of their shares to obtain cash. Also, some institutional investors (or trustees for individuals) might be legally precluded from selling stock and then "spending capital." On the other hand, stockholders who are saving rather than spending dividends favor the low-dividend policy: The less the firm pays out in dividends, the less these stockholders have to pay in current taxes and the less trouble and expense they must go through to reinvest their after-tax dividends. Therefore, investors who want current investment income should own shares in high-dividend-payout firms, while investors with no need for current investment income should own shares in low-dividend-payout firms. For example, investors seeking high cash income might invest in Duke Energy, an electric utility that paid a dividend of $3.06 for a dividend payout of 95% in mid-2013, while investors favoring growth could invest in Adobe Systems, a computer software company that had no dividend payout.

Clientele Effect

The tendency of a firm to attract a set of investors who like its dividend policy.

All of this suggests that a **clientele effect** exists, which means that firms have different clienteles and that the clienteles have different preferences; hence, a

---

[6]Stephen Ross has suggested that managers can use capital structure as well as dividends to give signals concerning a firm's future prospects. For example, a firm with good earnings prospects can carry more debt than a similar firm with poor earnings prospects. This theory, called *incentive signaling*, rests on the premise that signals with cash-based variables (either debt interest or dividends) cannot be mimicked by unsuccessful firms because those firms do not have the future cash-generating power to maintain the announced interest or dividend payment. Thus, investors are more likely to believe a glowing verbal report when it is accompanied by a dividend increase or a debt-financed expansion program. See Stephen A. Ross, "The Determination of Financial Structure: The Incentive-Signaling Approach," *The Bell Journal of Economics*, vol. 8, no. 1 (Spring 1977), pp. 23–40.

change in dividend policy might upset the majority clientele and have a negative effect on the stock's price.[7] This suggests that a company should follow a stable, dependable dividend policy so as to avoid upsetting its clientele.

Borrowing from the ideas of *behavioral finance,* some recent research suggests that investors' preferences for dividends vary over time. Malcolm Baker and Jeffrey Wurgler have proposed a **catering theory** for dividends where investors sometimes have strong preferences for safety and high-dividend-paying stocks, whereas at other times they are more aggressive and seek low-dividend-paying stocks with greater potential for capital gains. Baker and Wurgler argue that corporate managers accommodate the shifting preferences of investors, and are more likely to initiate dividends when dividend-paying stocks are in favor with investors, and are more likely to omit dividends when investors demonstrate a greater preference for capital gains.[8]

Catering Theory

A theory that suggests investors' preference for dividends varies over time and that corporations adapt their dividend policy to cater to the current desires of investors.

SELF TEST

Define (1) information content and (2) the clientele effect, and explain how they affect dividend policy.

What is "catering theory," and how does it impact a firm's dividend policy?

14-3 ESTABLISHING THE DIVIDEND POLICY IN PRACTICE

Investors may or may not prefer dividends to capital gains; however, because of the clientele effect, they almost certainly prefer *predictable* dividends. Given this situation, how should firms set their basic dividend policies? In particular, how should a company establish the specific percentage of earnings it will distribute, the form of that distribution, and the stability of its distributions over time? In this section, we describe how most firms answer those questions.

14-3A SETTING THE TARGET PAYOUT RATIO: THE RESIDUAL DIVIDEND MODEL[9]

When a firm is deciding how much cash to distribute to stockholders, it should consider two points: (1) The overriding objective is to maximize shareholder value; and (2) the firm's cash flows really belong to its shareholders, so management should not retain income unless they can reinvest those earnings at higher rates of return than shareholders can earn themselves. On the other hand, recall from Chapter 10 that internal equity (retained earnings) is less expensive than external equity (new common stock); so if good investments are available, it is better to finance them with retained earnings than with new stock.

---

[7]For example, see R. Richardson Pettit, "Taxes, Transactions Costs and the Clientele Effect of Dividends," *The Journal of Financial Economics,* vol. 5, no. 3 (December 1977), pp. 419–436.

[8]See Malcolm Baker and Jeffrey Wurgler, "A Catering Theory of Dividends," *The Journal of Finance,* vol. 59, no. 3 (June 2004), pp. 1125–1165.

[9]The term *payout ratio* can be interpreted two ways: (1) in the conventional way, as the percentage of net income paid out as *cash dividends* or (2) as the percentage of net income distributed to stockholders *through dividends and share repurchases.* In this section, we assume that no repurchases occur. Increasingly, though, firms are using the residual model to determine "distributions to shareholders" and then making a separate decision as to the form of those distributions. Further, over time, an increasing percentage of the total distribution has been in the form of share repurchases.

When a dividend policy is established, one size does not fit all. Some firms produce a large amount of cash but have limited investment opportunities—this is true for firms in profitable but mature industries where few growth opportunities exist. Such firms typically distribute a large percentage of their cash to shareholders, thereby attracting investor clienteles who prefer high dividends. Other firms have many good investment opportunities but currently generate little or no excess cash. Such firms generally distribute few or no cash dividends but enjoy rising earnings and stock prices, thereby attracting investors who prefer capital gains.

The past few decades have seen increasing numbers of young, high-growth firms trading on the stock exchanges. A study by Eugene Fama and Kenneth French showed that the proportion of firms paying dividends has fallen sharply over time. In 1978, 66.5% of firms on the major stock exchanges paid dividends. By 1999, that proportion had fallen to 20.8%. Fama and French's analysis suggested that part of this decline was due to the changing composition of firms on the exchanges. However, their analysis also indicated that all firms, new and old, have become less likely to pay dividends.[10]

As a result of the 2003 tax changes, which lowered the tax rate on dividends, many companies initiated dividends or increased their payouts. For example, in 2002, only 113 companies raised or initiated dividends; however, in 2003 that number doubled to 229. Previously, those companies would have been more inclined to repurchase shares. As of June 2013, 413 companies in the S&P 500 paid dividends.

As Table 14.1 suggests, dividend payouts and dividend yields for large corporations vary considerably. Generally, firms in stable, cash-producing industries such as utilities, food, and tobacco pay relatively high dividends, whereas companies in rapidly growing industries such as computer software and biotechnology tend to pay lower dividends. Average dividends also differ significantly across countries. Higher payout ratios in some countries can be partially explained by lower tax rates on earnings distributed as cash dividends relative to applicable rates on reinvested income. This biases the dividend policy toward higher payouts.

For a given firm, the optimal payout ratio is a function of four factors: (1) management's opinion about its investors' preferences for dividends versus

TABLE 14.1   Dividend Payouts in 2013

Company	Industry	Dividend Payout	Dividend Yield
I. Companies That Pay High Dividends			
Windstream	Telecommunications	281.00%	12.63%
AT&T	Telecommunications	137.00	5.10
Great Northern Iron Ore	Metals	118.00	19.90
Reynolds American	Tobacco	88.00	5.24
Pitney Bowes	Business Equipment	83.00	5.18
II. Companies That Pay No Dividends			
Adobe Systems	Computer Software	0.00%	0.00%
Amazon.com	Online Retail	"	"
Biogen Idec Inc	Biotechnology	"	"
eBay	Internet Services	"	"
Unisys Corp.	Computers	"	"

Source: *MSN Money* (money.msn.com), June 6, 2013.

[10]Eugene F. Fama and Kenneth R. French, "Disappearing Dividends: Changing Firm Characteristics or Lower Propensity to Pay?" *Journal of Applied Corporate Finance*, vol. 14, no. 1 (Spring 2001), pp. 67–79; and "Disappearing Dividends: Changing Firm Characteristics or Lower Propensity to Pay?" *Journal of Financial Economics*, vol. 60, no. 1 (April 2001), pp. 3–43. The latter citation is a longer and more technical version of the first paper cited.

capital gains, (2) the firm's investment opportunities, (3) the firm's target capital structure, and (4) the availability and cost of external capital. These factors are combined in what we call the **residual dividend model**. First, under this model, we assume that investors are indifferent between dividends and capital gains. Then the firm follows these four steps to establish its target payout ratio: (1) It determines the optimal capital budget; (2) given its target capital structure, it determines the amount of equity needed to finance that budget; (3) it uses retained earnings to meet equity requirements to the extent possible; and (4) it pays dividends only if more earnings are available than are needed to support the optimal capital budget. The word *residual* implies "leftover," and the residual policy implies that dividends are paid out of "leftover" earnings.

> **Residual Dividend Model**
> *A model in which the dividend paid is set equal to net income minus the amount of retained earnings necessary to finance the firm's optimal capital budget.*

If a firm rigidly follows the residual dividend policy, dividends paid in any given year can be expressed in the following equation:

$$\text{Dividends} = \text{Net income} - \frac{\text{Retained earnings required to help}}{\text{finance new investments}}$$

$$= \text{Net income} - [(\text{Target equity ratio})(\text{Total capital budget})]$$

For example, suppose the company has $100 million of earnings, it has a target equity ratio of 60%, and it plans to spend $50 million on capital projects. In that case, it would need $50(0.6) = $30 million of common equity plus $20 million of new debt to finance the capital budget. That would leave $100 − $30 = $70 million available for dividends, which would result in a 70% payout ratio.

Note that the amount of equity needed to finance the capital budget might exceed net income. In the preceding example, if the capital budget was $100/Equity percentage = $100/0.6 = $166.67 million, no dividends would be paid. If the capital budget exceeded $166.67, the company would have to issue new common stock in order to maintain its target capital structure.

Most firms have a target capital structure that calls for at least some debt, so new financing is done partly with debt and partly with equity. As long as a firm finances with the optimal mix of debt and equity and uses only internally generated equity (retained earnings), the marginal cost of each new dollar of capital will be minimized. So internally generated equity is available for financing a certain amount of new investment; but beyond that amount, the firm must turn to more expensive new common stock. At the point where new stock must be sold, the cost of equity (and consequently the marginal cost of capital) rises.

To illustrate these points, consider the case of Texas and Western (T&W) Transport Company. T&W's overall composite cost of capital is 10%. However, this cost assumes that all new equity comes from retained earnings. If the company must issue new stock, its cost of capital will be higher. T&W has $60 million of net income and a target capital structure with 60% equity and 40% debt. Provided it does not pay any cash dividends, T&W could make net investments (investments in addition to asset replacements from depreciation) of $100 million, consisting of $60 million from retained earnings plus $40 million of new debt supported by the retained earnings, at a 10% marginal cost of capital. If the capital budget exceeded $100 million, the required equity component would exceed net income, which is, of course, the maximum possible amount of retained earnings. In this case, T&W would have to issue new common stock, thereby pushing its cost of capital above 10%.[11]

---

[11]If T&W does not retain all of its earnings, its cost of capital will rise above 10% before its capital budget reaches $100 million. For example, if T&W chose to retain $36 million, its cost of capital would increase once the capital budget exceeded $36/0.6 = $60 million. To understand this point, note that a capital budget of $60 million would require $36 million of equity. If the capital budget rose above $60 million, the company's required equity capital would exceed its retained earnings, thereby requiring it to issue new common stock.

At the beginning of its planning period, T&W's financial staff considers all proposed projects for the upcoming period. All independent projects are accepted if their estimated IRRs exceed their risk-adjusted costs of capital. In choosing among mutually exclusive projects, the project with the highest positive NPV is accepted. The capital budget represents the amount of capital that is required to finance all accepted projects. If T&W follows a strict residual dividend policy, we can see from Table 14.2 that the estimated capital budget will have a profound effect on its dividend payout ratio. If investment opportunities are poor, the capital budget will be only $40 million. To maintain the target capital structure, 0.6($40) = $24 million must be equity, with the remaining $16 million as debt. If T&W followed a strict residual policy, it would pay out $60 − $24 = $36 million as dividends; hence, its payout ratio would be $36/$60 = 0.6 = 60%.

If the company's investment opportunities were average, its capital budget would be $70 million. This would require $42 million of equity; so dividends would be $60 − $42 = $18 million, for a payout of $18/$60 = 30%. Finally, if investment opportunities were good, the capital budget would be $150 million and 0.6($150) = $90 million of equity would be required. Therefore, all of the net income would be retained, dividends would be zero, and the company would have to issue some new common stock to maintain the target capital structure.

We see then that under the residual model, dividends and the payout ratio would vary with investment opportunities. Dividend variations would also occur if earnings fluctuated. Because investment opportunities and earnings vary from year to year, strict adherence to the residual dividend policy would result in unstable dividends. One year the firm might pay zero dividends because it needed the money to finance good investment opportunities, but the next year it might pay high dividends because investment opportunities were poor and it didn't need to retain as much. Similarly, fluctuating earnings would also lead to variable dividends, even if investment opportunities were stable. *Therefore, following the residual dividend policy would almost certainly lead to fluctuating, unstable dividends.* This would not be bad if investors were not bothered by fluctuating dividends; but because investors prefer stable, dependable dividends, it would not be optimal to strictly follow the residual model each year. One possible strategy that firms could use to balance these concerns is to:

1. Estimate earnings and investment opportunities, on average, over the next 5 or so years.

TABLE 14.2   T&W's Dividend Payout Ratio with $60 Million of Net Income When Faced with Different Investment Opportunities (Dollars in Millions)

	Investment Opportunities		
	Poor	**Average**	**Good**
Capital budget	$40	$70	$150
Net income (NI)	60	60	60
Required equity (0.6 × Capital budget)	24	42	90
Dividends paid (NI − Required equity)	$36	$18	($ 30)[a]
Dividend payout ratio (Dividends/NI)	60%	30%	0%

© Cengage Learning 2015

Note:
[a]With a $150 million capital budget, T&W would retain all of its earnings and also issue $30 million of new common stock.

2. Use the forecasted information to find the average dividends that would be paid using the residual model (and the corresponding payout ratio) during the planning period.

3. Set a target payout policy based on the projected data.

Thus, firms should use the residual policy to help set their long-run target payout ratios, but not as a guide to the payout in any one year.

Most large companies use the residual dividend model in a conceptual sense and then implement it with a computerized financial forecasting model. Information on projected capital expenditures and working capital requirements is entered into the model, along with sales forecasts, profit margins, depreciation, and the other elements required to forecast cash flows. The target capital structure is also specified; the model then generates the amount of debt and equity that will be required to meet the capital budgeting requirements while maintaining the target capital structure.

Dividend payments are introduced; and the higher the payout ratio, the greater the required external equity. Most companies use the model to find a dividend payout over the forecast period (generally 5 years) that will provide sufficient equity to support the capital budget without having to sell new common stock or taking the capital structure ratios outside the optimal range. This chapter's Excel model includes an illustration of this process. In addition, Web Appendix 14A discusses this approach in more detail. The end result might be a memo such as the following from the CFO to the chairperson of the board:

> We forecasted the total market demand for our products, what our share of the market is likely to be, and our required investments in capital assets and working capital. Using this information, we developed projected balance sheets and income statements for the period 2015–2019.
>
> Our 2014 dividends totaled $50 million, or $2.00 per share. On the basis of projected earnings, cash flows, and capital requirements, we can increase the dividend by 6% per year. This would be consistent with a payout ratio of 42%, on average, over the forecast period. Any faster dividend growth rate would require us to sell common stock, cut the capital budget, or raise the debt ratio. Any slower growth rate would lead to increases in the common equity ratio. Therefore, I recommend that the Board increase the dividend for 2015 by 6%, to $2.12, and that it plan for similar increases in the future.
>
> Events over the next 5 years will undoubtedly lead to differences between our forecasts and actual results. If and when such events occur, we should reexamine our position. However, I am confident that we can meet random cash shortfalls by increasing our borrowings—we have unused debt capacity that gives us flexibility in this regard.
>
> We ran the corporate model under several scenarios. If the economy totally collapses, our earnings will not cover the dividend. However, in all likely scenarios our cash flows would cover the recommended dividend. I know the Board does not want to push the dividend up to a level where we would have to cut it under poor economic conditions. Our model runs indicate, though, that the $2.12 dividend could be maintained under any reasonable set of forecasts. Only if we increased the dividend to more than $3.00 would we be seriously exposed to the danger of having to reduce it.
>
> I might also note that most analysts' reports are forecasting that our dividends will grow in the 5% to 6% range. Thus, if we go to $2.12, we will be at the high end of the forecast range, which should give our stock a boost. With takeover rumors so widespread, getting the stock price up a bit would make us all breathe a little easier.
>
> Finally, we considered distributing cash to shareholders through a stock repurchase program. Here we would reduce the dividend payout ratio and use the funds generated to buy our stock on the open market. Such a program has several advantages, but it would also have drawbacks. I do not recommend that we institute a stock repurchase program at this time. However, if our free cash flows exceed our forecasts, I would recommend that we use these surpluses to buy back stock. Also, I plan to continue looking into a regular repurchase program, and I may recommend such a program in the future.

GLOBAL PERSPECTIVES

Dividend Yields Around the World

Average dividend yields have varied over time, and they vary considerably in different countries around the world. The accompanying graph, obtained from a study by Elroy Dimson, Paul Marsh, and Mike Staunton of the London Business School, shows how the average dividend yield for 16 different countries has changed over the past century. In both 1900 and 1950, dividend yields varied from nation to nation, but the average around the world was about 5%. However, by 2004, the yield in most coun-

tries had declined significantly and the average had fallen to about 3%. For the United States, the average dividend yield was 4.3% in 1900, 7.2% in 1950, and 1.7% in 2004. Thus, U.S. stocks went from having one of the highest yields in 1900 to the second lowest in 2004. Since then, the average dividend yield for U.S. stocks has increased somewhat. In June 2013, the dividend yield on the S&P 500 stood just above 2%, a level that is still below the average yield found in many other countries.

Dividend Yields Around the World: 1900, 1950, and 2004

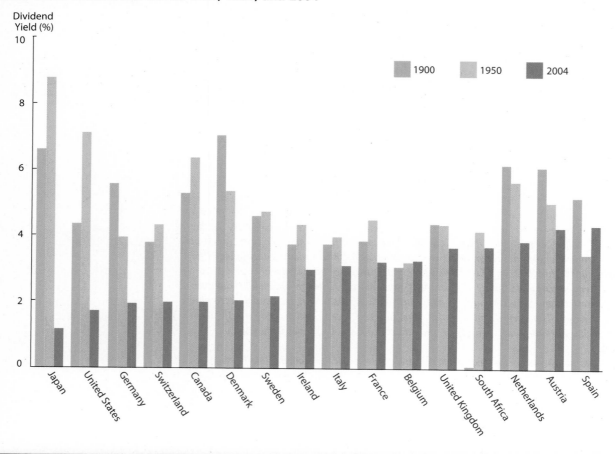

Source: Elroy Dimson, Paul Marsh, and Mike Staunton, *Triumph of the Optimists*, Princeton University Press, 2002. Reprinted with permission of the authors.

This company has very stable operations, so it can plan its dividends with a fairly high degree of confidence. Other companies, especially those in cyclical industries, have difficulty maintaining a dividend in bad times that would be too low in good times. Such companies often set a very low "regular" dividend and then supplement it with an "extra" dividend when times are good, which is known as a **low-regular-dividend-plus-extras** dividend policy. The company announces a low regular dividend that it is confident it can maintain "come hell or high water," one that stockholders could count on under all conditions. Then when times are good and profits and cash flows are high, the company pays a clearly designated extra dividend. Because investors recognize that the extras might not be maintained in the future, they don't interpret them as a signal that the companies' earnings are permanently higher nor do they take the elimination of the extra as a negative signal.

Alternately, companies may temporarily suspend paying dividends because of a short-run need for cash, but the hope is that they will be able to restore the dividend when its situation returns to normal. For example, during the Deepwater Horizon oil spill crisis, BP bowed to political pressure and suspended a series of dividend payments for the first three quarters of 2010, using the cash to pay for part of its clean-up operations. BP resumed paying dividends in the fourth quarter of 2010 (although at a smaller amount than it had been paying prior to the oil spill).

Low-Regular-Dividend-Plus-Extras

The policy of announcing a low, regular dividend that can be maintained no matter what and then, when times are good, paying a designated "extra" dividend.

14-3B EARNINGS, CASH FLOWS, AND DIVIDENDS

We normally think of earnings as being the primary determinant of dividends, but cash flows are actually more important. This is demonstrated in Figure 14.1, which plots data for Chevron Corporation from 1985 through 2012. Panel A shows that Chevron's dividends per share (DPS) rose slowly but steadily from 1985 to 2012. Earnings per share (EPS) also grew slowly; but they were more volatile, rising and falling with the price of oil. The earnings payout ratio (defined as DPS/EPS) averaged 63% over the entire 28 years, but it exceeded 100% on several occasions.

Cash flow per share (CFPS) tracked EPS very closely—the two were correlated at 0.99. However, CFPS was always higher than EPS, and it always exceeded the dividend by a substantial margin. Moreover, cash dividends are paid in cash; so even when earnings were insufficient to cover the dividend, cash flows took up the slack and enabled the company to maintain a stable dividend policy.

Now look at Panel B. Here we see that the earnings payout is extremely volatile, but the cash flow payout (defined as DPS/CFPS) is relatively stable and always below 100%. Those stable (and high) cash flows indicate that Chevron's dividend is relatively safe, and investors can count on receiving it going forward. Indeed, given the very high cash flows per share, continued substantial dividend increases (or large share repurchases) are likely—provided something bad doesn't happen in the oil market.

Chevron is typical of most large, strong companies. Its dividend is dependable, and it grows at a steady rate. Earnings are relatively volatile; but cash flows are more stable, and those stable cash flows are responsible for the steady dividends. When earnings change dramatically, either up or down, dividends are likely to follow with a lag while management determines whether the earnings change is likely to continue. Thus, the dip in Chevron's earnings in 2001 and 2002 turned out to be temporary, so the dividend was maintained and even increased during those years. The huge earnings and cash flow gains after 2002 continued into 2008. However, earnings and cash flows declined in 2009 during the economic slowdown but have returned to even higher levels during 2010 through 2012. Chevron's DPS is still well below its CFPS and EPS, which suggests that dividends, repurchases, and profitable new investments will continue on into the future. But Chevron does deal with oil; and with that commodity, strange things can happen!

14-3C PAYMENT PROCEDURES

Companies normally pay dividends quarterly; and if conditions permit, the dividend is increased once each year. For example, Katz Corporation paid $0.50 per quarter in 2014, an annual rate of $2.00. In common financial parlance, we say that Katz's 2014 *regular quarterly dividend* was $0.50 and its *annual dividend* was $2.00. In late 2014,

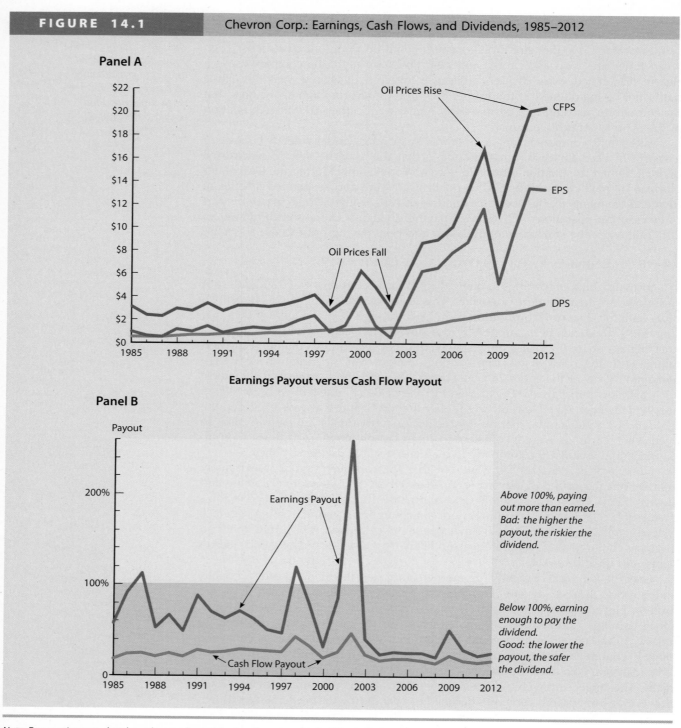

FIGURE 14.1   Chevron Corp.: Earnings, Cash Flows, and Dividends, 1985–2012

Note: For consistency, data have been adjusted for two-for-one splits in 1994 and 2004.

Source: Adapted from *Value Line Investment Survey*, various issues.

Katz's board of directors met, reviewed projections for 2015, and decided to keep the 2015 dividend at $2.00. The directors announced the $2.00 rate, so stockholders can count on receiving it unless unanticipated operating problems arise.

The actual payment procedure is as follows:

1. *Declaration date.* On the **declaration date**—say, November 7—the directors meet and declare the regular dividend, issuing a statement similar to the following: "On November 7, 2014, the directors of Katz Corporation met and

Declaration Date

The date on which a firm's directors issue a statement declaring a dividend.

declared the regular quarterly dividend of 50 cents per share, payable to holders of record at the close of business on December 4, payment to be made on January 2, 2015." For accounting purposes, the declared dividend becomes an actual liability on the declaration date. If a balance sheet was constructed, the amount ($0.50 × Number of shares outstanding) would appear as a current liability and retained earnings would be reduced by a like amount.

2. *Holder-of-record date.* At the close of business on the **holder-of-record date**, December 4, the company closes its stock transfer books and makes up a list of shareholders as of that date. If Katz Corporation is notified of the sale before the close of business on December 4, the new owner will receive the dividend. However, if notification is received on or after December 5, the previous owner will receive the dividend check.

3. *Ex-dividend date.* Suppose Jean Buyer buys 100 shares of stock from John Seller on December 1. Will the company be notified of the transfer in time to list Buyer as the new owner and thus pay the dividend to her? To avoid conflict, the securities industry has set up a convention under which the right to the dividend remains with the stock until 2 business days prior to the holder-of-record date; on the second business day before that date, the right to the dividend no longer goes with the shares. The date when the right to the dividend leaves the stock is called the **ex-dividend date**. In this case, the ex-dividend date is 2 business days prior to December 4, or December 2:

Dividend goes with stock if it is bought on or before this date	December 1
Ex-dividend date: Buyer does not receive the dividend	December 2
Buyer does not receive the dividend	December 3
Holder-of-record date; not normally of concern to stockholder	December 4

Therefore, if Buyer is to receive the dividend, Buyer must buy the stock on or before December 1. If Buyer buys it on December 2 or later, Seller will receive the dividend because he or she will be the official holder of record.

Katz's dividend amounts to $0.50, so the ex-dividend date is important. Barring fluctuations in the stock market, we would normally expect the price of a stock to drop by approximately the amount of the dividend on the ex-dividend date. Thus, if Katz closed at $30.50 on December 1, it would probably open at about $30 on December 2.[12]

4. *Payment date.* The company actually mails the checks to the holders of record on January 2, the **payment date**.

Holder-of-Record Date
If the company lists the stockholder as an owner on this date, then the stockholder receives the dividend.

Ex-Dividend Date
The date on which the right to the current dividend no longer accompanies a stock; it is usually two business days prior to the holder-of-record date.

Payment Date
The date on which a firm actually mails dividend checks.

---

[12]Tax effects cause the price decline, on average, to be less than the full amount of the dividend. If you bought Katz's stock on December 1, you would receive the dividend, but you would almost immediately pay 15% (20% if you were a high-income bracket taxpayer) of it in taxes. Thus, you would want to wait until December 2 to buy the stock if you thought you could get it for $0.50 less per share. Your reaction (and that of others) would influence stock prices around dividend payment dates. Here is what would happen:

1. Other things held constant, a stock's price should rise during the quarter, with the daily price increase (for Katz) equal to $0.50/90 = $0.005556. Therefore, if the price started at $30 just after its last ex-dividend date, it would rise to $30.50 on December 1.
2. In the absence of taxes, the stock's price would fall to $30 on December 2 and then start up as the next dividend accrual period began. Thus, over time, if everything else was held constant, the stock's price would follow a sawtooth pattern if it was plotted on a graph.
3. Because of taxes, the stock's price would neither rise by the full amount of the dividend nor fall by the full dividend amount when it goes ex-dividend.
4. The amount of the rise and subsequent fall would be the Dividend (1 − T), where generally T = 15%, the tax rate on individual dividends (unless you are a high-income bracket taxpayer then T = 20%).

See Edwin J. Elton and Martin J. Gruber, "Marginal Stockholder Tax Rates and the Clientele Effect," *Review of Economics and Statistics,* vol. 5, no. 3 (February 1970), pp. 68–74, for an interesting discussion of the subject.

SELF TEST

Explain the logic of the residual dividend model, the steps a firm would take to implement it, and the reason it is more likely to be used to establish a long-run payout target than to set the actual year-by-year payout ratio.

How do firms use long-run planning models to help set dividend policy?

Which are more critical to the dividend decision, earnings or cash flow? Explain.

Explain the procedures used to actually pay the dividend.

What is the ex-dividend date, and why is it important to investors?

A firm has a capital budget of $30 million, net income of $35 million, and a target capital structure of 45% debt and 55% equity. If the residual dividend policy is used, what is the firm's dividend payout ratio? **(52.86%)**

14-4 Dividend Reinvestment Plans

Dividend Reinvestment Plans (DRIP)

A plan that enables a stockholder to automatically reinvest dividends received back into the stock of the paying firm.

During the 1970s, most large companies instituted **dividend reinvestment plans (DRIPs)**, under which stockholders can automatically reinvest their dividends in the stock of the paying corporation.[13] Today most large companies offer DRIPs, but participation rates vary considerably. There are two types of DRIPs: (1) plans that involve only old, already-outstanding stock and (2) plans that involve newly issued stock. In either case, the stockholder must pay taxes on the amount of the dividends even though stock rather than cash is received.

Under both types of DRIPs, stockholders choose between continuing to receive dividend checks versus having the company use the dividends to buy more stock in the corporation for the investor. Under an "old stock" plan, the company gives the money that stockholders who elect to use the DRIP would have received to a bank, which acts as a trustee. The bank then uses the money to purchase the corporation's stock on the open market and allocates the shares purchased to the participating stockholders' accounts on a pro rata basis. The transaction costs of buying shares (brokerage costs) are low because of volume purchases, so these plans benefit small stockholders who do not need current cash dividends.

A "new stock" DRIP invests the dividends in newly issued stock; hence, these plans raise new capital for the firm. AT&T, Xerox, and many other companies have used new stock plans to raise substantial amounts of equity. No fees are charged to stockholders, and some companies have offered stock at discounts of 1% to 10% below the actual market price. The companies offer discounts because they would have incurred flotation costs if the new stock had been raised through investment banks.

One interesting aspect of DRIPs is that they are forcing corporations to reexamine their basic dividend policies. A high participation rate in a DRIP suggests that stockholders might be better served if the firm simply reduced cash dividends, which would save stockholders some personal income taxes. Quite a few firms have surveyed their stockholders to learn more about their preferences and to find out how they would react to a change in dividend policy. A more rational approach to basic dividend policy decisions may emerge from this

---

[13]See Richard H. Pettway and R. Phil Malone, "Automatic Dividend Reinvestment Plans," *Financial Management*, vol. 2, no. 4 (Winter 1973), pp. 11–18, for an old but still excellent discussion of the subject.

research. Companies switch from old stock to new stock DRIPs depending on their need for equity capital.

Many companies offering DRIPs have expanded their programs by moving to "open enrollment," whereby anyone can purchase the firm's stock directly and thus bypass brokers' commissions. Exxon Mobil not only allows investors to buy their initial shares at no fee but also lets them pick up additional shares through automatic bank account withdrawals. Several plans, including Exxon Mobil's, offer dividend reinvestment for individual retirement accounts; and some allow participants to invest weekly or monthly rather than on the quarterly dividend schedule. With all of these plans (and many others), stockholders can invest more than the dividends they are forgoing—they simply send a check to the company and buy shares without a brokerage commission.

SELF TEST

What are dividend reinvestment plans?

What are their advantages and disadvantages from both stockholders' and firms' perspectives?

14-5 SUMMARY OF FACTORS INFLUENCING DIVIDEND POLICY

In earlier sections, we described the theories of investor preference for dividends and the potential effects of dividend policy on the value of a firm. We also discussed the residual dividend model for setting a firm's long-run target payout ratio. In this section, we discuss several other factors that affect the dividend decision. These factors may be grouped into four broad categories: (1) constraints on dividend payments, (2) investment opportunities, (3) availability and cost of alternative sources of capital, and (4) effects of dividend policy on r_s. We discuss these factors next.

14-5A CONSTRAINTS

1. *Bond indentures.* Debt contracts often limit dividend payments to earnings generated after the loan was granted. Also, debt contracts often stipulate that no dividends can be paid unless the current ratio, times-interest-earned ratio, and other safety ratios exceed stated minimums.

2. *Preferred stock restrictions.* Typically, common dividends cannot be paid if the company has omitted its preferred dividend. The preferred arrearages must be satisfied before common dividends can be resumed.

3. *Impairment of capital rule.* Dividend payments cannot exceed the balance sheet item "retained earnings." This legal restriction, known as the impairment of capital rule, is designed to protect creditors. Without the rule, a company that is in trouble might distribute most of its assets to stockholders and leave its debtholders out in the cold. (Liquidating dividends can be paid out of capital; but they must be indicated as such, and they must not reduce capital below the limits stated in debt contracts.)

4. *Availability of cash.* Cash dividends can be paid only with cash. Thus, a shortage of cash in the bank can restrict dividend payments. However, the ability to borrow can offset this factor.

5. *Penalty tax on improperly accumulated earnings.* To prevent wealthy individuals from using corporations to avoid personal taxes, the Tax Code provides for a special surtax on improperly accumulated income. Thus, if the IRS can demonstrate that a firm's dividend payout ratio is deliberately being held down to help its stockholders avoid personal taxes, the firm is subject to heavy penalties. This factor is relevant primarily to privately owned firms.

14-5b INVESTMENT OPPORTUNITIES

1. *Number of profitable investment opportunities.* As we saw in our discussion of the residual dividend model, if a firm has a large number of profitable investment opportunities, this will tend to produce a low target payout ratio and vice versa if the firm has few good investment opportunities.

2. *Possibility of accelerating or delaying projects.* The ability to accelerate or postpone projects permits a firm to adhere more closely to a stable dividend policy.

14-5c ALTERNATIVE SOURCES OF CAPITAL

1. *Cost of selling new stock.* If a firm needs to finance a given level of investment, it can obtain equity by retaining earnings or by issuing new common stock. If flotation costs (including any negative signaling effects of a stock offering) are high, r_e will be well above r_s, making it better to set a low payout ratio and to finance through retention rather than through the sale of new common stock. On the other hand, a high dividend payout ratio is more feasible for a firm whose flotation costs are low. Flotation costs differ among firms—for example, the flotation percentage is especially high for small firms, so they tend to set low payout ratios.

2. *Ability to substitute debt for equity.* A firm can finance a given level of investment with debt or equity. As noted, low stock flotation costs permit a more flexible dividend policy because equity can be raised by retaining earnings or by selling new stock. A similar situation holds for debt policy: If the firm can adjust its debt ratio without raising its WACC sharply, it can pay the expected dividend, even if earnings fluctuate, by additional borrowing.

3. *Control.* If management is concerned about maintaining control, it may be reluctant to sell new stock; hence, the company may retain more earnings than it otherwise would. However, if stockholders want higher dividends and a proxy fight looms, the dividend might be increased.

14-5d EFFECTS OF DIVIDEND POLICY ON r_s

The effects of dividend policy on r_s may be considered in terms of four factors: (1) stockholders' desire for current versus future income, (2) the perceived riskiness of dividends versus capital gains, (3) the tax advantage of capital gains, and (4) the information (signaling) content of dividends. We discussed each of those factors earlier, so we only note here that the importance of each factor varies from firm to firm depending on the makeup of its current and possible future stockholders.

It should be apparent that dividend policy decisions are based more on informed judgment than on quantitative analysis. Even so, to make rational dividend decisions, financial managers must take into account all the points discussed in the preceding sections.

SELF TEST

Identify the four broad sets of factors that affect dividend policy.

What constraints affect dividend policy?

How do investment opportunities affect dividend policy?

How does the availability and cost of outside capital affect dividend policy?

14-6 STOCK DIVIDENDS AND STOCK SPLITS

Stock dividends were originally used in lieu of regular cash dividends by firms that were short of cash. Today, though, the primary purpose of stock dividends is to increase the number of shares outstanding and thus to lower the stock's price in the market. Stock splits have a similar purpose.

Up-to-date information about changes in stock splits and stock buybacks is now just a few clicks away. A good place to get started is The Online Investor at **theonlineinvestor.com**.

Stock dividends and splits can be explained best through an example. We use Porter Electronic Controls Inc., a $700 million electronic components manufacturer, for this purpose. Since its inception, Porter's markets have been expanding and the company has enjoyed growth in sales and earnings. Some of its earnings have been paid out in dividends; but some also were retained each year, causing its earnings per share and the stock price to grow. The company began its life with only a few thousand shares outstanding; and, after some years of growth, each of Porter's shares had a very high EPS and DPS. When a "normal" P/E ratio was applied, the resulting market price was so high that few people could afford to buy a "round lot" of 100 shares. This limited demand for the stock and thus kept the firm's total market value below what it would have been if more shares at a lower price had been outstanding. To correct this situation, Porter "split its stock," as described in the next section.

14-6A STOCK SPLITS

Although there is little empirical evidence to support the contention, there is nevertheless a widespread belief in financial circles that an *optimal price range* exists for stocks. *Optimal* means that if the price is within this range, the price/earnings ratio (and hence the firm's value) will be maximized. Many observers, including Porter's management, believe that the best range for most stocks is from $20 to $80 per share. Accordingly, if the price of Porter's stock rose to $80, management would probably declare a two-for-one **stock split**, thus doubling the number of shares outstanding, halving the earnings and dividends per share, and thereby lowering the stock price. Each stockholder would have more shares, but each share would be worth less. In Yogi Berra's terms (refer to the feature box "Yogi Berra on the MM Proposition" in Chapter 13), a stock split just divides the corporate value pie into more slices. If the post-split price was $40, Porter's stockholders would be exactly as well off as they were before the split. However, if the stock price stabilized above $40, stockholders would be better off. Stock splits can be split in varying proportions—for example, the stock can be split two-for-one, three-for-one, one-and-a-half-for-one, or any other way.[14]

Stock Split

An action taken by a firm to increase the number of shares outstanding, such as doubling the number of shares outstanding by giving each stockholder two new shares for each one formerly held.

---

[14]*Reverse splits*, which reduce the shares outstanding, also can be used. For example, a company whose stock sells for $5 might employ a one-for-five reverse split, exchanging one new share for five old ones and raising the value of the shares to about $25, which is within the optimal price range. LTV Corporation did this after several years of losses had driven its stock price below the optimal range.

14-6B Stock Dividends

Stock dividends are similar to stock splits because they "divide the pie into smaller slices" without affecting the fundamental position of the current stockholders. On a 5% stock dividend, the holder of 100 shares would receive an additional 5 shares (without cost); on a 20% stock dividend, the same holder would receive 20 new shares; and so forth. Again, the total number of shares is increased; so, holding all other things constant, earnings, dividends, and price per share all decline.

If a firm wants to reduce its stock price, should it use a stock split or a stock dividend? Stock splits are generally used after a sharp price run-up to produce a large price reduction. Stock dividends used on a regular annual basis keep the stock price more or less constrained. For example, if a firm's earnings and dividends were growing at about 10% per year, its stock price would tend to increase at about that same rate and it would soon be outside the desired trading range. A 10% annual stock dividend would maintain the stock price within the optimal trading range. Note, however, that because small stock dividends create bookkeeping problems and unnecessary expenses, firms use stock splits far more often than stock dividends.[15]

14-6C Effect on Stock Prices

If a company splits its stock or declares a stock dividend, will this increase the market value of its stock? Several empirical studies have addressed this question. Here is a summary of their findings.[16]

1. On average, the price of a company's stock rises shortly after it announces a stock split or dividend.

2. One reason that stock splits and stock dividends may lead to higher prices is that investors often take stock splits and dividends as signals of higher future earnings. Because only companies whose managements believe that things look good tend to split their stocks, the announcement of a stock split is taken as a signal that earnings and cash dividends are likely to rise. Thus, the price increases associated with stock splits and dividends may be the result of a favorable signal for earnings and dividends.

3. If a company announces a stock split or dividend, its price will tend to rise. However, if during the next few months it does not announce an increase in earnings and dividends, the stock price generally will drop back to the earlier level. This supports the signaling effect discussed earlier.

4. By creating more shares and lowering the stock price, stock splits may also increase the stock's liquidity. This tends to increase the firm's value.

---

[15]Accountants treat stock splits and stock dividends somewhat differently. For example, in a two-for-one stock split, the number of shares outstanding is doubled and the par value is halved, and that is about all there is to it. With a stock dividend, a bookkeeping entry is made transferring "retained earnings" to "common stock." For example, if a firm had 1,000,000 shares outstanding, if the stock price was $10, and if it wanted to pay a 10% stock dividend, (1) each stockholder would be given 1 new share of stock for each 10 shares held and (2) the accounting entries would involve showing 100,000 more shares outstanding and transferring 100,000($10) = $1,000,000 from "retained earnings" to "common stock." The retained earnings transfer limits the size of stock dividends, but that is not important because companies can split their stock any way they choose.

[16]See Eugene F. Fama, Lawrence Fisher, Michael C. Jensen, and Richard Roll, "The Adjustment of Stock Prices to New Information," *International Economic Review*, vol. 10, no. 1 (February 1969), pp. 1–21; Mark S. Grinblatt, Ronald M. Masulis, and Sheridan Titman, "The Valuation Effects of Stock Splits and Stock Dividends," *Journal of Financial Economics*, vol. 13, no. 4 (December 1984), pp. 461–490; Ravi Dahr, William N. Goetzmann, and Ning Zhu, "The Impact of Clientele Changes: Evidence from Stock Splits," Yale International Center for Finance Working Paper No. 03-14, European Finance Association 2005 Moscow Meetings Paper, American Finance Association 2005 Philadelphia Meetings Paper (a copy is available at Social Science Research Network: papers.ssrn.com/abstract=410104); and Thomas E. Copeland, "Liquidity Changes Following Stock Splits," *Journal of Finance*, vol. 34, no. 1 (March 1979), pp. 115–141.

5. There is evidence that stock splits change the mix of shareholders. The proportion of trades made by individual investors tends to increase after a stock split, whereas the proportion of trades made by institutional investors tends to fall. We are not sure how this affects the stock's value.

What do we conclude from these findings? From a pure economic standpoint, stock dividends and splits are just additional pieces of paper. However, they provide management with a relatively low-cost way of signaling that the firm's prospects look good. Further, we should note that few large, publicly owned stocks sell at prices above several hundred dollars; therefore, we simply do not know what the effect would be if, for example, Chevron, Microsoft, Xerox, Hewlett-Packard, and other highly successful firms had never split their stocks and consequently sold at prices in the thousands or even millions of dollars per share.

A recent *Bloomberg Businessweek* article notes that stock splits have become a lot less popular in recent years. The article suggests that one possible reason for this shift is that individual investors have increasingly moved from buying shares of individual companies and have instead navigated towards mutual funds. Consequently, institutional investors (such as mutual funds) have become relatively more important. These institutional investors are less concerned about whether a stock's price is above or below a particular range, and they are less likely to value stock splits.[17]

Finally, it is worth pointing out that Warren Buffett, Chairman and CEO of Berkshire Hathaway, had long resisted the use of stock splits but he shifted gears in early 2010. After Berkshire Hathaway acquired Burlington Northern Santa Fe, the company announced a 50-for-one split for its Class B shares. Prior to the announcement, the stock traded around $3,500 per share. After the split, the stock traded around $70 per share.

SELF TEST

What are stock dividends and stock splits?

How do stock dividends and splits affect stock prices?

In what situation should a firm pay a stock dividend?

In what situation should a firm split its stock?

Suppose you have 100 common shares of Tillman Industries. The EPS is $4.00, the DPS is $2.00, and the stock sells for $60 per share. Now Tillman announces a two-for-one split. Immediately after the split, how many shares will you have, what will be the adjusted EPS and DPS, and what would you expect the stock price to be? **(200 shares; $2.00; $1.00; probably a little over $30)**

14-7 STOCK REPURCHASES

Several years ago, a *Fortune* article entitled "Beating the Market by Buying Back Stock" reported that during a one-year period, more than 600 major corporations repurchased significant amounts of their own stock. It also gave illustrations of some specific companies' repurchase programs and the effects of these programs

---

[17]Refer to Whitney Kisling and Alex Barinka, "Stock Splits Lose Their Allure for Companies Trading Above $100," *Bloomberg Businessweek* (businessweek.com), August 22, 2013.

on stock prices. The article's conclusion was that "buybacks have made a mint for shareholders who stay with the companies carrying them out."

More recently, as we noted in the opening vignette, Apple Inc. has established a quarterly dividend and has repurchased shares of its common stock. Apple's recent actions are part of a larger trend in which many leading companies have repurchased stock. How do stock repurchase programs work, and why have they become so prevalent over the past several years? We discuss these questions in the remainder of this section.

Stock Repurchases

Transactions in which a firm buys back shares of its own stock, thereby decreasing shares outstanding, increasing EPS, and, often, increasing the stock price.

There are three principal types of **stock repurchases**: (1) situations where the firm has cash available for distribution to its stockholders, and it distributes this cash by repurchasing shares rather than by paying cash dividends, (2) situations where the firm concludes that its capital structure is too heavily weighted with equity, and it sells debt and uses the proceeds to buy back its stock, and (3) situations where the firm has issued options to employees, and it uses open market repurchases to obtain stock for use when the options are exercised.

Stock that has been repurchased by a firm is called *treasury stock.* If some of the outstanding stock is repurchased, fewer shares will remain outstanding. Assuming that the repurchase does not adversely affect the firm's future earnings, the earnings per share on the remaining shares will increase, resulting in a higher market price per share. As a result, capital gains will have been substituted for dividends.

14-7A THE EFFECTS OF STOCK REPURCHASES

Many companies have been repurchasing their stock in recent years. As mentioned in the opening vignette, in 2013, Apple announced plans for a $60 billion stock repurchase that would take place over a number of years. *The Wall Street Journal* recently reported that between 2006 and early 2013, DirecTV has repurchased 57% of its shares, which is the highest proportion of shares repurchased among the stocks in the S&P 500 over this time period.[18] In the past, other large repurchases have been made by Procter & Gamble, Dell, Home Depot, Texas Instruments, IBM, Coca-Cola, Teledyne, Atlantic Richfield, Goodyear, and Xerox. In fact, share repurchases in 2012 totaled $384.3 billion for S&P 500 companies.

The effects of a repurchase can be illustrated with data on American Development Corporation (ADC). The company expects to earn $4.4 million in 2014, and it plans to use 50% of this amount (or $2.2 million) to repurchase shares of its common stock. There are 1.1 million shares outstanding, and the market price is $20 a share. ADC believes that it can use the $2.2 million to repurchase 110,000 of its shares at the current price of $20 per share.[19]

The effect of the repurchase on the EPS and market price per share of the remaining stock can be analyzed as follows:

---

[18]Refer to Vipal Monga, "DirecTV Tops in Buying Back Stock Since 2006," *The Wall Street Journal* (online.wsj.com), May 9, 2013.

[19]Stock repurchases are generally made in one of three ways: (1) A publicly owned firm can simply buy its own stock through a broker on the open market. (2) It can make a *tender offer,* under which it permits stockholders to send in (that is, "tender") their shares to the firm in exchange for a specified price per share. In this case, the firm generally indicates that it will buy up to a specified number of shares within a particular time period (usually about 2 weeks); if more shares are tendered than the company wants to purchase, purchases are made on a pro rata basis. (3) The firm can purchase a block of shares from one large holder on a negotiated basis. If a negotiated purchase is employed, care must be taken to ensure that this one stockholder does not receive preferential treatment over other stockholders, or that any preference given can be justified by "sound business reasons." A number of years ago Texaco's management was sued by stockholders who were unhappy over the company's repurchase of about $600 million of stock from the Bass Brothers at a substantial premium over the market price. The suit charged that Texaco's management, afraid the Bass Brothers would attempt a takeover, used the buyback to "get them off its back." Such payments have been dubbed *greenmail.*

1. Current EPS $= \dfrac{\text{Total earnings}}{\text{Number of shares}} = \dfrac{\$4.4 \text{ million}}{1.1 \text{ million}} = \$4.00$ per share

2. P/E ratio $= \dfrac{\$20}{\$4} = 5\times$

3. EPS after repurchasing 110,000 shares $= \dfrac{\$4.4 \text{ million}}{0.99 \text{ million}} = \$4.44$ per share

4. P/E ratio after repurchase $= \dfrac{\$20}{\$4.44} = 4.50\times$

It should be noted from this example that we assumed that the shares were repurchased at the current stock price of $20 per share. In this example, the company's EPS increased, but there was a corresponding drop in its P/E ratio. One reason the P/E ratio may drop is that the repurchase works to increase the company's debt ratio (as there are now fewer shares of stock outstanding). Because of the higher debt ratio, shareholders may consider the stock to be riskier. As a result, the future earnings are discounted at a higher rate, which reduces the P/E ratio.

In reality, companies often have to pay a premium in order to get shareholders to sell their shares back to the company. If instead, ADC had to pay $22 per share to repurchase the stock, it would only be able to repurchase 100,000 shares. In this case, the EPS would be somewhat lower ($4.40 = $4.4 million/1 million shares), and the P/E ratio would again be 5.0×. (This assumes that the market price of the stock remains at $22 following the repurchase.)

For a variety of reasons, the stock's price might change as a result of the repurchase operation, rising if investors viewed it favorably and falling if they viewed it unfavorably. Some of these factors are considered next.

14-7B ADVANTAGES OF REPURCHASES

The advantages of repurchases are as follows:

1. A repurchase announcement may be viewed as a positive signal by investors because repurchases are often motivated by managements' belief that their firms' shares are undervalued.

2. The stockholders have a choice when the firm distributes cash by repurchasing stock—they can sell or not sell. With a cash dividend, on the other hand, stockholders must accept a dividend payment and pay the tax. Thus, those stockholders who need cash can sell back some of their shares, while those who do not want additional cash can simply retain their stock. From a tax standpoint, a repurchase permits both types of stockholders to get what they want.

3. A repurchase can remove a large block of stock that is "overhanging" the market and keeping the price per share down.

4. Dividends are "sticky" in the short run because managements are reluctant to raise the dividend if the increase cannot be maintained in the future—managements dislike cutting cash dividends because of the negative signal a cut gives. Therefore, if excess cash flows are expected to be temporary, managements may prefer to make distributions as share repurchases rather than to declare increased cash dividends that cannot be maintained.

5. Companies can use the residual dividend model to set a target cash distribution level, then divide the distribution into a *dividend component* and a *repurchase component*. The dividend payout ratio will be relatively low; but the dividend itself will be relatively secure, and it will grow as a result of the declining number of shares outstanding. This gives the company more flexibility in adjusting the total distribution than if the entire distribution were in the form of cash dividends because repurchases can be varied from year to year without sending adverse signals. This procedure has much to recommend it, and it is an important reason for the dramatic increase in the

volume of share repurchases. IBM, NextEra Energy (formerly FPL Group), Walmart, and most other large companies use repurchases in this manner.

6. Repurchases can be used to produce large-scale changes in capital structure. For example, a number of years ago Consolidated Edison decided that its debt ratio was so low that it was not minimizing its WACC. It then borrowed $400 million and used the funds to repurchase shares of its common stock. This resulted in an immediate shift from a nonoptimal to an optimal capital structure.

7. Companies that use stock options as an important component of employee compensation can repurchase shares and then reissue those shares when employees exercise their options. This avoids having to issue new shares, which dilutes earnings per share. Microsoft and other high-tech companies have used this procedure in recent years.

14-7c DISADVANTAGES OF REPURCHASES

Disadvantages of repurchases include the following:

1. Stockholders may not be indifferent between dividends and capital gains, and the stock price might benefit more from cash dividends than from repurchases. Cash dividends are generally dependable, but repurchases are not.

2. The *selling* stockholders may not be fully aware of all the implications of a repurchase, or they may not have all the pertinent information about the corporation's present and future activities. This is especially true in situations where management has good reason to believe that the stock price is well below its intrinsic value. However, firms generally announce repurchase programs before embarking on them to avoid potential stockholder suits.

3. The corporation may pay too high a price for the repurchased stock, to the disadvantage of remaining stockholders. If its shares are not actively traded and if the firm seeks to acquire a relatively large number of shares of its stock, the price may be bid above its intrinsic value and then fall after the firm ceases its repurchase operations.

14-7d CONCLUSIONS ON STOCK REPURCHASES

When all the pros and cons on stock repurchases have been totaled, where do we stand? Our conclusions may be summarized as follows:

1. Because of the deferred tax on capital gains, repurchases have a tax advantage over dividends as a way to distribute income to stockholders. This advantage is reinforced by the fact that repurchases provide cash to stockholders who want cash but also allow those who do not need current cash to delay its receipt. On the other hand, dividends are more dependable and are thus better suited for those who need a steady source of income.

2. Because of signaling effects, companies should not pay fluctuating dividends—that would lower investors' confidence in the company and adversely affect its cost of equity and its stock price. However, cash flows vary over time, as do investment opportunities; so the "proper" dividend in the residual dividend model sense varies. To get around this problem, a company can set its dividend at a level low enough to keep dividend payments from constraining operations and then use repurchases on a more or less regular basis to distribute excess cash. Such a procedure would provide regular, dependable dividends in addition to supplemental cash flows to those stockholders who want it.

3. Repurchases are also useful when a firm wants to make a large, rapid shift in its capital structure, to distribute cash from a one-time event such as the sale of a division, or to obtain shares for use in an employee stock option plan.

In earlier editions of this book, we argued that companies ought to be doing more repurchasing and distributing less cash as dividends. Increases in the size and frequency of repurchases in recent years suggest that companies have finally reached this same conclusion.

SELF TEST

Explain how repurchases can (1) help stockholders limit taxes and (2) help firms change their capital structures.

What is treasury stock?

What are three procedures a firm can use to repurchase its stock?

What are some advantages and disadvantages of stock repurchases?

How can stock repurchases help a company operate in accordance with the residual dividend model?

TYING IT ALL TOGETHER

Once a company becomes profitable, it must decide what to do with the cash it generates. It may choose to retain cash and use it to purchase additional operating assets, to repay outstanding debt, or to acquire other companies. Alternatively, it may choose to return cash to shareholders. Keep in mind that every dollar that management chooses to retain is a dollar that shareholders could have received and invested elsewhere. Therefore, managers should retain earnings if and only if they can invest the money within the firm, and earn more than stockholders can earn outside the firm. Consequently, high-growth companies with many good projects tend to retain a high percentage of their earnings, whereas mature companies with a great deal of cash but limited investment opportunities tend to have generous cash distribution policies.

SELF-TEST QUESTIONS AND PROBLEMS

(Solutions Appear in Appendix A)

ST-1 **KEY TERMS** Define each of the following terms:

a. Target payout ratio; optimal dividend policy

b. Dividend irrelevance theory; bird-in-the-hand fallacy

c. Information content (signaling) hypothesis; clienteles; clientele effect

d. Catering theory; residual dividend model

e. Low-regular-dividend-plus-extras

f. Declaration date; holder-of-record date; ex-dividend date; payment date

g. Dividend reinvestment plan (DRIP)

h. Stock split; stock dividend

i. Stock repurchase

ST-2 **ALTERNATIVE DIVIDEND POLICIES** Components Manufacturing Corporation (CMC) has an all-common-equity capital structure. It has 200,000 shares of $2 par value common stock outstanding. When CMC's founder, who was also its research director and most successful inventor, retired unexpectedly to the South Pacific in late 2014, CMC was left suddenly and permanently with materially lower growth expectations and relatively few attractive new investment opportunities. Unfortunately, there was no way to replace the founder's contributions to the firm. Previously, CMC found it necessary to reinvest most of its earnings to finance growth, which averaged 12% per year. Future growth at a 6% rate is considered realistic, but that level would call for an increase in the dividend payout. Further, it now appears that new investment projects, with at least the 14% rate of return required by CMC's stockholders ($r_s = 14\%$), would total only $800,000 for 2015, compared to a projected net income of $2,000,000. If the existing 20% dividend payout was continued, retained earnings would be $1.6 million in 2015; but as noted, only $800,000 of investments would yield the 14% cost of capital.

The one encouraging point is that the high earnings from existing assets are expected to continue, and net income of $2 million is still expected for 2015. Given the dramatically changed circumstances, CMC's management is reviewing the firm's dividend policy.

a. Assuming that the acceptable 2015 investment projects would be financed entirely by earnings retained during the year, and assuming that CMC uses the residual dividend model, calculate DPS in 2015.

b. What payout ratio does your answer to Part a imply for 2015?

c. If a 60% payout ratio is maintained for the foreseeable future, what is your estimate of the present market price for the common stock? How does this compare with the market price that should have prevailed under the assumptions existing just before the news about the founder's retirement? If the two values of P_0 are different, comment on why they are different.

d. What would happen to the stock price if the old 20% payout was continued? Assume that if this payout is maintained, the average rate of return on the retained earnings will fall to 7.5% and the new growth rate will be as follows:

$$g = (1.0 - \textbf{Payout ratio})(\textbf{ROE})$$
$$= (1.0 - 0.2)(7.5\%)$$
$$= (0.8)(7.5\%) = 6.0\%$$

QUESTIONS

14-1 Discuss the pros and cons of having the directors formally announce a firm's future dividend policy.

14-2 The cost of retained earnings is less than the cost of new outside equity capital. Consequently, it is totally irrational for a firm to sell a new issue of stock and to pay cash dividends during the same year. Discuss the meaning of those statements.

14-3 Would it ever be rational for a firm to borrow money in order to pay cash dividends? Explain.

14-4 Modigliani and Miller (MM) on the one hand and Gordon and Lintner (GL) on the other hand have expressed strong views regarding the effect of dividend policy on a firm's cost of capital and value.

a. In essence, what are MM's and GL's views regarding the effect of dividend policy on the cost of capital and stock prices?

b. How could MM use the information content, or signaling, hypothesis to counter their opponents' arguments? If you were debating MM, how would you counter them?

c. How could MM use the clientele effect concept to counter their opponents' arguments? If you were debating MM, how would you counter them?

14-5 How would each of the following changes tend to affect aggregate (that is, the average for all corporations) payout ratios, other things held constant? Explain your answers.

a. An increase in the personal income tax rate

b. A liberalization of depreciation for federal income tax purposes—that is, faster tax write-offs

c. An increase in interest rates

d. An increase in corporate profits

e. A decline in investment opportunities

f. Permission for corporations to deduct dividends for tax purposes as they now deduct interest expense

g. A change in the Tax Code so that realized and unrealized long-term capital gains in any year are taxed at the same rate as ordinary income

14-6 One position expressed in the financial literature is that firms set their dividends as a residual after using income to support new investment.

a. Explain what a residual dividend policy implies, illustrating your answer with a table showing how different investment opportunities can lead to different dividend payout ratios.

b. Think back to Chapter 13 where we considered the relationship between capital structure and the cost of capital. If the WACC-versus-debt-ratio plot was shaped like a sharp V, would this have a different implication for the importance of setting dividends according to the residual policy than if the plot was shaped like a shallow bowl (a flattened U)?

14-7 Executive salaries have been shown to be more closely correlated to the size of the firm than to its profitability. If a firm's board of directors is controlled by management rather than outside directors, this might result in the firm's retaining more earnings than can be justified from the stockholders' point of view. Discuss those statements, being sure (1) to discuss the interrelationships among cost of capital, investment opportunities, and new investment and (2) to explain the implied relationship between dividend policy and stock prices.

14-8 What is the difference between a stock dividend and a stock split? As a stockholder, would you prefer to see your company declare a 100% stock dividend or a two-for-one split? Assume that either action is feasible.

14-9 Most firms like to have their stock selling at a high P/E ratio, and they also like to have extensive public ownership (many different shareholders). Explain how stock dividends or stock splits may help achieve those goals.

14-10 Indicate whether the following statements are true or false. If the statement is false, explain why.

a. If a firm repurchases its stock in the open market, the shareholders who tender the stock are subject to capital gains taxes.

b. If you own 100 shares in a company's stock and the company's stock splits 2-for-l, you will own 200 shares in the company following the split.

c. Some dividend reinvestment plans increase the amount of equity capital available to the firm.

d. The Tax Code encourages companies to pay a large percentage of their net income in the form of dividends.

e. If your company has established a clientele of investors who prefer large dividends, the company is unlikely to adopt a residual dividend policy.

f. If a firm follows a residual dividend policy, holding all else constant, its dividend payout will tend to rise whenever the firm's investment opportunities improve.

14-11 What is meant by catering theory, and how might it impact a firm's dividend policy?

PROBLEMS

Easy
Problems
1–3

14-1 **RESIDUAL DIVIDEND MODEL** Axel Telecommunications has a target capital structure that consists of 70% debt and 30% equity. The company anticipates that its capital budget for the upcoming year will be $3,000,000. If Axel reports net income of $2,000,000 and it follows a residual dividend payout policy, what will be its dividend payout ratio?

14-2 **STOCK SPLIT** Gamma Medical's stock trades at $90 a share. The company is contemplating a 3-for-2 stock split. Assuming that the stock split will have no effect on the market value of its equity, what will be the company's stock price following the stock split?

14-3 **STOCK REPURCHASES** Beta Industries has net income of $2,000,000, and it has 1,000,000 shares of common stock outstanding. The company's stock currently trades at $32 a share. Beta is considering a plan in which it will use available cash to repurchase 20% of its shares in the open market. The repurchase is expected to have no effect on net income or its stock price. What will be Beta's EPS following the stock repurchase?

Intermediate Problems 4–6

14-4 **STOCK SPLIT** After a 5-for-l stock split, Strasburg Company paid a dividend of $0.75 per new share, which represents a 9% increase over last year's pre-split dividend. What was last year's dividend per share?

14-5 **EXTERNAL EQUITY FINANCING** Northern Pacific Heating and Cooling Inc. has a 6-month backlog of orders for its patented solar heating system. To meet this demand, management plans to expand production capacity by 40% with a $10 million investment in plant and machinery. The firm wants to maintain a 40% debt level in its capital structure. It also wants to maintain its past dividend policy of distributing 45% of last year's net income. In 2014, net income was $5 million. How much external equity must Northern Pacific seek at the beginning of 2015 to expand capacity as desired? Assume that the firm uses only debt and common equity in its capital structure.

14-6 **RESIDUAL DIVIDEND MODEL** Welch Company is considering three independent projects, each of which requires a $5 million investment. The estimated internal rate of return (IRR) and cost of capital for these projects are presented here:

Project H (high risk):	Cost of capital = 16%	IRR = 20%
Project M (medium risk):	Cost of capital = 12%	IRR = 10%
Project L (low risk):	Cost of capital = 8%	IRR = 9%

Note that the projects' costs of capital vary because the projects have different levels of risk. The company's optimal capital structure calls for 50% debt and 50% common equity, and it expects to have net income of $7,287,500. If Welch establishes its dividends from the residual dividend model, what will be its payout ratio?

Challenging Problems 7–9

14-7 **DIVIDENDS** Bowles Sporting Inc. is prepared to report the following 2014 income statement (shown in thousands of dollars).

Sales	$15,200
Operating costs including depreciation	11,900
EBIT	$ 3,300
Interest	300
EBT	$ 3,000
Taxes (40%)	1,200
Net income	$ 1,800

Prior to reporting this income statement, the company wants to determine its annual dividend. The company has 500,000 shares of common stock outstanding, and its stock trades at $48 per share.

a. The company had a 40% dividend payout ratio in 2013. If Bowles wants to maintain this payout ratio in 2014, what will be its per-share dividend in 2014?

b. If the company maintains this 40% payout ratio, what will be the current dividend yield on the company's stock?

c. The company reported net income of $1.5 million in 2013. Assume that the number of shares outstanding has remained constant. What was the company's per-share dividend in 2013?

d. As an alternative to maintaining the same dividend payout ratio, Bowles is considering maintaining the same per-share dividend in 2014 that it paid in 2013. If it chooses this policy, what will be the company's dividend payout ratio in 2014?

e. Assume that the company is interested in dramatically expanding its operations and that this expansion will require significant amounts of capital. The company would like to avoid transactions costs involved in issuing new equity. Given this scenario, would it make more sense for the company to maintain a constant dividend payout ratio or to maintain the same per-share dividend? Explain.

14-8 **ALTERNATIVE DIVIDEND POLICIES** Rubenstein Bros. Clothing is expecting to pay an annual dividend per share of $0.75 out of annual earnings per share of $2.25. Currently, Rubenstein Bros.' stock is selling for $12.50 per share. Adhering to the company's target capital structure, the firm has $10 million in total invested capital, of which 40% is funded by debt. Assume that the firm's book value of equity equals its market value. In past years, the firm has earned a return on equity (ROE) of 18%, which is expected to continue this year and into the foreseeable future.

a. Based on this information, what long-run growth rate can the firm be expected to maintain? (Hint: g = Retention rate × ROE.)

b. What is the stock's required return?

c. If the firm changed its dividend policy and paid an annual dividend of $1.50 per share, financial analysts would predict that the change in policy will have no effect on the firm's stock price or ROE. Therefore, what must be the firm's new expected long-run growth rate and required return?

d. Suppose instead that the firm has decided to proceed with its original plan of disbursing $0.75 per share to shareholders, but the firm intends to do so in the form of a stock dividend rather than a cash dividend. The firm will allot new shares based on the current stock price of $12.50. In other words, for every $12.50 in dividends due to shareholders, a share of stock will be issued. How large will the stock dividend be relative to the firm's current market capitalization? (Hint: Remember that market capitalization = P_0 × number of shares outstanding.)

e. If the plan in Part d is implemented, how many new shares of stock will be issued, and by how much will the company's earnings per share be diluted?

14-9 **ALTERNATIVE DIVIDEND POLICIES** In 2013, Keenan Company paid dividends totaling $3,600,000 on net income of $10.8 million. Note that 2013 was a normal year and that for the past 10 years, earnings have grown at a constant rate of 10%. However, in 2014, earnings are expected to jump to $14.4 million and the firm expects to have profitable investment opportunities of $8.4 million. It is predicted that Keenan will not be able to maintain the 2014 level of earnings growth because the high 2014 earnings level is attributable to an exceptionally profitable new product line introduced that year. After 2014, the company will return to its previous 10% growth rate. Keenan's target capital structure is 40% debt and 60% equity.

a. Calculate Keenan's total dividends for 2014 assuming that it follows each of the following policies:

   1. Its 2014 dividend payment is set to force dividends to grow at the long-run growth rate in earnings.

   2. It continues the 2013 dividend payout ratio.

   3. It uses a pure residual dividend policy (40% of the $8.4 million investment is financed with debt and 60% with common equity).

   4. It employs a regular-dividend-plus-extras policy, with the regular dividend being based on the long-run growth rate and the extra dividend being set according to the residual dividend policy.

b. Which of the preceding policies would you recommend? Restrict your choices to the ones listed but justify your answer.

c. Assume that investors expect Keenan to pay total dividends of $9,000,000 in 2014 and to have the dividend grow at 10% after 2014. The stock's total market value is $180 million. What is the company's cost of equity?

d. What is Keenan's long-run average return on equity? [Hint: g = Retention rate × ROE = (1.0 − Payout rate)(ROE).]

e. Does a 2014 dividend of $9,000,000 seem reasonable in view of your answers to Parts c and d? If not, should the dividend be higher or lower? Explain your answer.

COMPREHENSIVE/SPREADSHEET PROBLEM

14-10 **RESIDUAL DIVIDEND MODEL** Buena Terra Corporation is reviewing its capital budget for the upcoming year. It has paid a $3.00 dividend per share (DPS) for the past several years, and its shareholders expect the dividend to remain constant for the next several years. The company's target capital structure is 60% equity and 40% debt, it has 1,000,000 shares of common equity outstanding, and its net income is $8 million. The company forecasts that it will require $10 million to fund all of its profitable (that is, positive NPV) projects for the upcoming year.

a. If Buena Terra follows the residual dividend model, how much retained earnings will it need to fund its capital budget?

b. If Buena Terra follows the residual dividend model, what will be the company's dividend per share and payout ratio for the upcoming year?

c. If Buena Terra maintains its current $3.00 DPS for next year, how much retained earnings will be available for the firm's capital budget?

d. Can the company maintain its current capital structure, the $3.00 DPS, and a $10 million capital budget without having to raise new common stock?

e. Suppose that Buena Terra's management is firmly opposed to cutting the dividend; that is, it wants to maintain the $3.00 dividend for the next year. Also, assume that the company was committed to funding all profitable projects and was willing to issue more debt (along with the available retained earnings) to help finance the company's capital budget. Assume that the resulting change in capital structure has a minimal effect on the company's composite cost of capital so that the capital budget remains at $10 million. What portion of this year's capital budget would have to be financed with debt?

f. Suppose once again that Buena Terra's management wants to maintain the $3.00 DPS. In addition, the company wants to maintain its target capital structure (60% equity and 40% debt) and its $10 million capital budget. What is the minimum dollar amount of new common stock that the company would have to issue to meet each of its objectives?

g. Now consider the case where Buena Terra's management wants to maintain the $3.00 DPS and its target capital structure, but it wants to avoid issuing new common stock. The company is willing to cut its capital budget to meet its other objectives. Assuming that the company's projects are divisible, what will be the company's capital budget for the next year?

h. What actions can a firm that follows the residual dividend model take when its forecasted retained earnings are less than the retained earnings required to fund its capital budget?

INTEGRATED CASE

SOUTHEASTERN STEEL COMPANY

14-11   DIVIDEND POLICY   Southeastern Steel Company (SSC) was formed 5 years ago to exploit a new continuous casting process. SSC's founders, Donald Brown and Margo Valencia, had been employed in the research department of a major integrated-steel company; but when that company decided against using the new process (which Brown and Valencia had developed), they decided to strike out on their own. One advantage of the new process was that it required relatively little capital compared to the typical steel company, so Brown and Valencia have been able to avoid issuing new stock and thus own all of the shares. However, SSC has now reached the stage in which outside equity capital is necessary if the firm is to achieve its growth targets yet still maintain its target capital structure of 60% equity and 40% debt. Therefore, Brown and Valencia have decided to take the company public. Until now, Brown and Valencia have paid themselves reasonable salaries but routinely reinvested all after-tax earnings in the firm; so the firm's dividend policy has not been an issue. However, before talking with potential outside investors, they must decide on a dividend policy.

Assume that you were recently hired by Arthur Adamson & Company (AA), a national consulting firm, which has been asked to help SSC prepare for its public offering. Martha Millon, the senior AA consultant in your group, has asked you to make a presentation to Brown and Valencia in which you review the theory of dividend policy and discuss the following questions:

a. 1. What is meant by the term *dividend policy*?

2. Explain briefly the dividend irrelevance theory that was put forward by Modigliani and Miller. What were the key assumptions underlying their theory?

3. Why do some investors prefer high-dividend-paying stocks, while other investors prefer stocks that pay low or nonexistent dividends?

b. Discuss (1) the information content, or signaling, hypothesis; (2) the clientele effect; (3) catering theory; and (4) their effects on dividend policy.

c. 1. Assume that SSC has an $800,000 capital budget planned for the coming year. You have determined that its present capital structure (60% equity and 40% debt) is optimal, and its net income is forecasted at $600,000. Use the residual dividend model to determine SSC's total dollar dividend and payout ratio. In the process, explain how the residual dividend model works. Then explain what would happen if expected net income was $400,000 or $800,000.

2. In general terms, how would a change in investment opportunities affect the payout ratio under the residual dividend model?

3. What are the advantages and disadvantages of the residual policy? (Hint: Don't neglect signaling and clientele effects.)

d. Describe the series of steps that most firms take in setting dividend policy in practice.

e. What is a dividend reinvestment plan (DRIP), and how does it work?

f. What are stock dividends and stock splits? What are the advantages and disadvantages of stock dividends and stock splits?

g. What are stock repurchases? Discuss the advantages and disadvantages of a firm's repurchasing its own shares.

 THOMSON REUTERS

Use the Thomson ONE—Business School Edition online database to work this chapter's questions.

APPLE'S DIVIDEND POLICY

In this chapter's opening vignette, we discussed Apple's decision to establish a dividend payout policy in 2012. Let's find out what has happened to Apple's (AAPL) dividend policy since the time of this announcement. We can address this issue by relying on data provided in Thomson ONE.

Discussion Questions

1. To get information about Apple's dividend policy, enter its ticker quote (AAPL) and select OVERVIEW > FULL REPORTS > THOMSON FULL REPORTS > FULL COMPANY REPORT. On the next screen, click on STOCK & EARNINGS DATA and scroll down to the "Annual Historical Data" section. What has happened to Apple's dividend per share, dividend yield, and dividend payout over the past 5 years? Provide an explanation for what took place.

2. Compare this information with other firms in the same industry. To see how Apple stacks up against its peers, select COMPARABLES > OVERVIEWS > PER SHARE DATA to get Apple's peers' last annual dividends. Accessing COMPARABLES>OVERVIEWS>ABSOLUTE RANKINGS will give their dividend yields. You can also get this information from the VALUATION COMPARISON in the OVERVIEWS section. Has Apple behaved differently from its peers, or have there been industry-wide shifts?

3. Refer back to the FULL COMPANY REPORT used in Question 1. Manually plot earnings per share, dividends per share, and cash flow per share over time. In the text, we point out that dividends are often more stable than earnings, that cash flows track earnings very closely, and that cash flow per share exceeds dividends per share by a safe margin. Do you see a similar pattern for Apple? Explain.

4. In the "Interim Financial Data" section of the THOMSON FULL COMPANY REPORT, (scroll to the top and click on INTERIM FINANCIAL DATA), identify the dividend declared date, record date, ex-date, and pay date. Explain the significance of those dates. Go back to OVERVIEW and access the "Interactive Price Chart." Can you observe price shifts around these dates? Explain what price shifts you might expect to see.

5. Investors are more concerned with future dividends than historical dividends, so go to ESTIMATES and scroll down to the "Consensus Estimates" on the screen. Click on the "Available Measures" menu to toggle between earnings per share and dividends per share. How do analysts expect Apple's payout policy to behave in the future?

6. Go back to OVERVIEW > FULL REPORTS > THOMSON FULL REPORTS > STOCK SECTION. Scroll down to the "Annual Historical Data" section. Has Apple been repurchasing stock, or has it been issuing new stock? What has happened to its year-end market capitalization over this 5-year period?

Solutions to Self-Test Questions and Problems

Note: Except for Chapter 1, we do not show an answer for ST-1 problems because they are verbal rather than quantitative in nature.

CHAPTER 1

ST-1 Refer to the marginal glossary definitions or relevant chapter sections to check your responses.

CHAPTER 3

ST-2 a.

EBIT	$5,000,000
Interest	1,000,000
EBT	$4,000,000
Taxes (40%)	1,600,000
Net income	$2,400,000

b. Current liabilities = Accounts payable + Accruals + Notes payable
$$= \$3,000,000 + \$1,000,000 + \$2,000,000$$
$$= \$6,000,000$$

NOWC = Current assets − (Current liabilities − Notes payable)
$$= \$14,000,000 - (\$6,000,000 - \$2,000,000)$$
$$= \$10,000,000$$

c. NWC = Current assets − Current liabilities
$$= \$14,000,000 - \$6,000,000$$
$$= \$8,000,000$$

d. FCF = (EBIT(1 − T) + Depreciation) − $\left(\begin{array}{c} \text{Capital} \\ \text{expenditures} \end{array} + \begin{array}{c} \text{Increase in net operating} \\ \text{working capital} \end{array} \right)$
$$= [\$5,000,000(0.6) + \$1,000,000] - [\$4,000,000 + 0]$$
$$= \$4,000,000 - \$4,000,000$$
$$= \$0$$

Note that capital expenditures are equal to the change in net plant and equipment plus the annual depreciation expense.

e. Rattner's end-of-year Statement of Stockholders' Equity is calculated as follows:

Statement of Stockholders' Equity

	Common Stock		Retained Earnings	Total Stockholders' Equity
	Shares	Amount		
Balances, beginning of year	500,000	$5,000,000	$11,200,000	$16,200,000
Net income			2,400,000	
Cash dividends			−1,200,000	
Addition to retained earnings				1,200,000
Balances, end of year	500,000	$5,000,000	$12,400,000	$17,400,000

f. **MVA** $= (P_0 \times$ **Number of shares**$) -$ **Book value of equity**

$= (\$52 \times 500{,}000) - \$17{,}400{,}000$

$= \$8{,}600{,}000$

g. Before we can calculate the firm's EVA, we need to calculate the firm's total invested capital. We know that the firm uses no preferred stock and we know that Assets = Liabilities + Equity. From the information provided in the problem we know:

		Accounts payable	$ 3,000,000
		Accruals	1,000,000
		Notes payable	2,000,000
Current assets	$14,000,000	Current liabilities	$ 6,000,000
		Long-term debt	?
Net fixed assets	15,000,000	Common equity	17,400,000
Total assets	$29,000,000	Total liabilities & equity	$29,000,000

We calculated common equity in Part e, so the only value we don't know on the balance sheet is long-term debt. However, we have enough information to calculate it:

Long-term debt $= \$29{,}000{,}000 - \$17{,}400{,}000 - \$6{,}000{,}000$

Long-term debt $= \$5{,}600{,}000$

Now, we can find the firm's total invested capital:

Total invested capital = **Notes payable** + **Long-term debt** + **Common equity**

Total invested capital $= \$2{,}000{,}000 + \$5{,}600{,}000 + \$17{,}400{,}000$

Total invested capital $= \$25{,}000{,}000$

Now, we can calculate the firm's EVA:

EVA = **EBIT**$(1 - \text{T}) -$ [**Total invested capital** $\times$ **After-tax % cost of capital**]

EVA $= \$5{,}000{,}000(0.6) - [\$25{,}000{,}000 \times 0.09]$

EVA $= \$3{,}000{,}000 - \$2{,}250{,}000 = \$750{,}000$

CHAPTER 4

ST-2   Billingsworth paid $2 in dividends and retained $2 per share. Since total retained earnings rose by $12 million, there must be 6 million shares outstanding. With a book value of $40 per share, total common equity must be $40(6 million) = $240 million. Since Billingsworth has $120 million of total debt, its total debt to total capital ratio must be 33.3%:

$$\frac{\textbf{Total debt}}{\textbf{Total debt} + \textbf{Equity}} = \frac{\$120\ \textbf{million}}{\$120\ \textbf{million} + \$240\ \textbf{million}}$$

$$= 0.333 = 33.3\%$$

ST-3   a. In answering questions such as this, always begin by writing down the relevant definitional equations, and then start filling in numbers. Note that the extra zeros indicating millions have been deleted in the calculations below.

(1) $\text{DSO} = \dfrac{\textbf{Accounts receivable}}{\textbf{Sales}/365}$

$40.55 = \dfrac{\text{A/R}}{\text{Sales}/365}$

$\text{A/R} = 40.55(\$2.7397) = \$111.1\ \textbf{million}$

(2) Current ratio $= \dfrac{\text{Current assets}}{\text{Current liabilities}} = 3.0$

$\phantom{\text{Current ratio}} = \dfrac{\text{Current assets}}{\$105.5} = 3.0$

Current assets $= 3.0(\$105.5) = \$316.50$ million

(3) Total assets $=$ Current assets $+$ Fixed assets

$\phantom{\text{Total assets}} = \$316.5 + \$283.5 = \$600$ million

(4) ROA $=$ Profit margin $\times$ Total assets turnover

$\phantom{\text{ROA}} = \dfrac{\text{Net income}}{\text{Sales}} \times \dfrac{\text{Sales}}{\text{Total assets}}$

$\phantom{\text{ROA}} = \dfrac{\$50}{\$1,000} \times \dfrac{\$1,000}{\$600}$

$\phantom{\text{ROA}} = 0.05 \times 1.667 = 0.083333 = 8.3333\%$

(5) ROE $=$ ROA $\times \dfrac{\text{Assets}}{\text{Equity}}$

$12.0\% = 8.3333\% \times \dfrac{\$600}{\text{Equity}}$

Equity $= \dfrac{(8.3333\%)(\$600)}{12.0\%}$

Equity $= \$416.67$ million

(6) Current assets $=$ Cash and equivalents $+$ Accounts receivable $+$ Inventories

$\$316.5 = \$100.0 + \$111.1 +$ Inventories

Inventories $= \$105.4$ million.

Quick ratio $= \dfrac{\text{Current assets} - \text{Inventories}}{\text{Current liabilities}}$

$\phantom{\text{Quick ratio}} = \dfrac{\$316.5 - \$105.4}{\$105.5} = 2.00$

(7) Total assets $=$ Total claims $= \$600$ million

Current liabilities $+$ Long-term debt $+$ Equity $= \$600$ million

$\$105.5 +$ Long-term debt $+ \$416.67 = \$600$ million

Long-term debt $= \$600 - \$105.5 - \$416.67 = \$77.83$ million

Note: We could have found equity as follows:

$\text{ROE} = \dfrac{\text{Net income}}{\text{Equity}}$

$12.0\% = \dfrac{\$50}{\text{Equity}}$

Equity $= \$50/0.12$

Equity $= \$416.67$ million

Then we could have gone on to find long-term debt.

b. Kaiser's average sales per day were $\$1,000/365 = \$2.74$ million. Its DSO was 40.55, so A/R $= 40.55(\$2.74) = \$111.1$ million. Its new DSO of 30.4 would cause A/R $= 30.4(\$2.74) = \$83.3$ million. The reduction in receivables would be $\$111.1 - \$83.3 = \$27.8$ million, which would equal the amount of cash generated.

(1) New equity $=$ Old equity $-$ Stock bought back

$\phantom{\text{New equity}} = \$416.7 - \$27.8$

$\phantom{\text{New equity}} = \$388.9$ million

Thus,

$$\text{New ROE} = \frac{\text{Net income}}{\text{New equity}}$$

$$= \frac{\$50}{\$388.9}$$

$$= 12.86\% \text{ (versus old ROE of 12.0\%)}$$

(2) $$\text{New ROA} = \frac{\text{Net income}}{\text{Total assets} - \text{Reduction in A/R}}$$

$$= \frac{\$50}{\$600 - \$27.8}$$

$$= 8.74\% \text{ (versus old ROA of 8.33\%)}$$

(3) Total debt before the asset reduction is the same as total debt after the asset reduction. Neither notes payable nor long-term debt was impacted by the asset reduction. However, after the asset reduction equity has declined, so total capital has declined.

$$\text{Total debt} = \text{Notes payable} + \text{Long-term debt}$$

$$\$97.8 = \$20 + \$77.8$$

$$\text{New total assets} = \text{Old total assets} - \text{Reduction in A/R}$$

$$= \$600 - \$27.8$$

$$= \$572.2 \text{ million}$$

Before asset reduction:

$$\text{Total capital} = \text{Total debt} + \text{Old equity}$$

$$= \$97.8 + \$416.7$$

$$= \$514.5 \text{ million}$$

After asset reduction:

$$\text{Total capital} = \text{Total debt} + \text{New equity}$$

$$= \$97.8 + \$388.9$$

$$= \$486.7 \text{ million}$$

Therefore,

$$\frac{\text{Total debt}}{\text{Old total capital}} = \frac{\$97.8}{\$514.5} = 19.0\%$$

while

$$\frac{\text{Total debt}}{\text{New total capital}} = \frac{\$97.8}{\$486.7} = 20.1\%$$

CHAPTER 5

ST-2   a.

$1,000 is being compounded for 3 years, so your balance on January 1, 2017, is $1,259.71:

$$\text{FV}_N = \text{PV}(1 + I)^N = \$1,000(1 + 0.08)^3 = \$1,259.71$$

Alternatively, using a financial calculator, input $N = 3$, $I/YR = 8$, $PV = -1000$, $PMT = 0$, and $FV = ?$ Solve for $FV = \$1,259.71$.

b.

```
   1/1/14        1/1/15      1/1/16      1/1/17
     |  2%  |    |    |    |    |    |    |    |    |    |    |    |
    -1,000                                    FV = ?
```

$$FV_N = PV\left(1 + \frac{I_{NOM}}{M}\right)^{MN} = FV_{12} = \$1,000(1.02)^{12} = \$1,268.24$$

Alternatively, using a financial calculator, input N = 12, I/YR = 2, PV = −1000, PMT = 0, and FV = ? Solve for FV = $1,268.24.

c.

```
   1/1/14        1/1/15      1/1/16      1/1/17
     |      8%      |           |           |
               -333.333    -333.333    -333.333
                                        FV = ?
```

Using a financial calculator, input N = 3, I/YR = 8, PV = 0, PMT = −333.333, and FV = ? Solve for FV = $1,082.13.

d.

```
   1/1/14        1/1/15      1/1/16      1/1/17
     |      8%      |           |           |
   -333.333    -333.333    -333.333    FV = ?
```

Using a financial calculator in begin mode, input N = 3, I/YR = 8, PV = 0, PMT = −333.333, and FV = ? Solve for FV = $1,168.70.

e.

```
   1/1/14        1/1/15      1/1/16      1/1/17
     |      8%      |           |           |
                    ?           ?           ?
                                        FV = 1,259.71
```

Using a financial calculator, input N = 3, I/YR = 8, PV = 0, FV = 1259.71, and PMT = ? Solve for PMT = −$388.03. Therefore, you would have to make 3 payments of $388.03 each beginning on January 1, 2015.

ST-3 a. Set up a time line like the one in the preceding problem:

```
 1/1/14        1/1/15      1/1/16      1/1/17      1/1/18
   |      8%      |           |           |           |
 PV = ?                                          FV = 1,000
```

Note that your deposit will grow for 4 years at 8%. The deposit on January 1, 2014, is the PV, and the FV is $1,000. Using a financial calculator, input N = 4, I/YR = 8, PMT = 0, FV = 1000, and PV = ? Solve for PV = −$735.03.

$$PV = \frac{FV_N}{(1 + I)^N} = \frac{\$1,000}{(1.08)^4} = \$735.03$$

b.

```
 1/1/14        1/1/15      1/1/16      1/1/17      1/1/18
   |      8%      |           |           |           |
                  ?           ?           ?           ?
                                                 FV = 1,000
```

Here we are dealing with a 4-year annuity whose first payment occurs 1 year from today, on 1/1/15, and whose future value must equal $1,000. You should modify the time line to help visualize the situation.

Using a financial calculator, input $N = 4$, $I/YR = 8$, $PV = 0$, $FV = 1000$, and $PMT = ?$ Solve for $PMT = -\$221.92$.

c. This problem can be approached in several ways. Perhaps the simplest is to ask this question: "If I received $750 on 1/1/15 and deposited it to earn 8%, would I have the required $1,000 on 1/1/18?" The answer is no.

$$FV_3 = \$750(1.08)(1.08)(1.08) = \$944.78$$

This indicates that you should let your father make the payments of $221.92 rather than accept the lump sum of $750 on January 1, 2015.

You could also compare the $750 with the PV of the payments as shown below:

```
1/1/14      1/1/15      1/1/16      1/1/17      1/1/18
        8%
├───────────┼───────────┼───────────┼───────────┤
          -221.92     -221.92     -221.92     -221.92
PV = ?
```

Using a financial calculator, input $N = 4$, $I/YR = 8$, $PMT = -221.92$, $FV = 0$, and $PV = ?$ Solve for $PV = \$735.03$.

This is less than the $750 lump sum offer, so your initial reaction might be to accept the lump sum of $750. However, this would be a mistake. The problem is that when you found the $735.03 PV of the annuity, you were finding the value of the annuity *today*, on January 1, 2014. You were comparing $735.03 today with the lump sum of $750 one year from now. This is, of course, not correct. What you should have done was take the $735.03, recognize that this is the PV of an annuity as of January 1, 2014, multiply $735.03 by 1.08 to get $793.83, and compare $793.83 with the lump sum of $750. You would then take your father's offer to make the payments of $221.92 rather than take the lump sum on January 1, 2015.

d.
```
1/1/14      1/1/15      1/1/16      1/1/17      1/1/18
        I = ?
├───────────┼───────────┼───────────┼───────────┤
  -750                                          1,000
```

Using a financial calculator, input $N = 3$, $PV = -750$, $PMT = 0$, $FV = 1000$, and $I/YR = ?$ Solve for $I/YR = 10.0642\%$.

e.
```
1/1/14      1/1/15      1/1/16      1/1/17      1/1/18
        I = ?
├───────────┼───────────┼───────────┼───────────┤
          -200        -200        -200        -200
                                            FV = 1,000
```

Using a financial calculator, input $N = 4$, $PV = 0$, $PMT = -200$, $FV = 1000$, and $I/YR = ?$ Solve for $I/YR = 15.09\%$.

You might be able to find a borrower willing to offer you a 15% interest rate, but there would be some risk involved—he or she might not actually pay you the $1,000!

f.

Find the future value of the original \$400 deposit:

$$FV_6 = PV(1.04)^6 = \$400(1.2653) = \$506.13$$

This means that on January 1, 2018, you need an additional sum of \$493.87:

$$\$1,000.00 - \$506.13 = \$493.87$$

This will be accumulated by making 6 equal payments that earn 8% compounded semiannually, or 4% each 6 months. Using a financial calculator, input $N = 6$, $I/YR = 4$, $PV = 0$, $FV = 493.87$, and $PMT = ?$ Solve for $PMT = -\$74.46$.

Alternatively, input $N = 6$, $I/YR = 4$, $PV = -400$, $FV = 1000$, and $PMT = ?$ Solve for $PMT = -\$74.46$. Note that the sign on the PV amount entered in the calculator was negative because the initial deposit will offset the total amount needed. If the signs on both the FV and PV amounts had been the same, you would have calculated a larger payment than was necessary.

g. $\text{Effective annual rate} = \left(1 + \dfrac{I_{NOM}}{M}\right)^M - 1.0$

$$= \left(1 + \dfrac{0.08}{2}\right)^2 - 1 = (1.04)^2 - 1$$

$$= 1.0816 - 1 = 0.0816 = 8.16\%$$

$\text{APR} = I_{PER} \times M$

$$= 0.04 \times 2 = 0.08 = 8\%$$

ST-4 Bank A's effective annual rate is 8.24%:

$\text{Effective annual rate} = \left(1 + \dfrac{0.08}{4}\right)^4 - 1.0$

$$= (1.02)^4 - 1$$

$$= 1.0824 - 1$$

$$= 0.0824 = 8.24\%$$

Now Bank B must have the same effective annual rate:

$$\left(1 + \dfrac{I_{NOM}}{12}\right)^{12} - 1.0 = 0.0824$$

$$\left(1 + \dfrac{I_{NOM}}{12}\right)^{12} = 1.0824$$

$$1 + \dfrac{I_{NOM}}{12} = (1.0824)^{1/12}$$

$$1 + \dfrac{I_{NOM}}{12} = 1.00662$$

$$\dfrac{I_{NOM}}{12} = 0.00662$$

$$I_{NOM} = 0.07944 = 7.94\%$$

Thus, the two banks have different quoted rates—Bank A's quoted rate is 8%, while Bank B's quoted rate is 7.94%; however, both banks have the same effective annual rate of 8.24%. The difference in their quoted rates is due to the difference in compounding frequency.

CHAPTER 6

ST-2   a. **Average inflation over 4 years $= (2\% + 2\% + 2\% + 4\%)/4 = 2.5\%$**

b. $T_4 = r_{RF} + MRP_4$
$= r^* + IP_4 + MRP_4$
$= 3\% + 2.5\% + (0.1)3\%$
$= 5.8\%$

c. $C_{4,BBB} = r^* + IP_4 + MRP_4 + DRP + LP$
$= 3\% + 2.5\% + 0.3\% + 1.3\% + 0.5\%$
$= 7.6\%$

d. $T_8 = r^* + IP_8 + MRP_8$
$= 3\% + (3 \times 2\% + 5 \times 4\%)/8 + 0.7\%$
$= 3\% + 3.25\% + 0.7\%$
$= 6.95\%$

e. $C_{8,BBB} = r^* + IP_8 + MRP_8 + DRP + LP$
$= 3\% + 3.25\% + 0.7\% + 1.3\% + 0.5\%$
$= 8.75\%$

f. $T_9 = r^* + IP_9 + MRP_9$
$7.3\% = 3\% + IP_9 + 0.8\%$
$IP_9 = 3.5\%$
$3.5\% = (3 \times 2\% + 5 \times 4\% + X)/9$
$31.5\% = 6\% + 20\% + X$
$5.5\% = X$
$X = \text{Inflation in Year 9} = 5.5\%$

ST-3 $T_1 = 6\%; T_2 = 6.2\%; T_3 = 6.3\%; T_4 = 6.5\%; MRP = 0$

a. Yield of 1-year security, 1 year from now is calculated as follows:

$$(1.062)^2 = (1.06)(1 + X)$$
$$\frac{(1.062)^2}{1.06} = 1 + X$$
$$1.064 = 1 + X$$
$$6.4\% = X$$

b. Yield of 1-year security, 2 years from now is calculated as follows:

$$(1.063)^3 = (1.062)^2(1 + X)$$
$$\frac{(1.063)^3}{(1.062)^2} = 1 + X$$
$$1.065 = 1 + X$$
$$6.5\% = X$$

c. Yield of 2-year security, 1 year from now is calculated as follows:

$$(1.063)^3 = (1.06)(1 + X)^2$$
$$\frac{(1.063)^3}{1.06} = (1 + X)^2$$
$$1.13317 = (1 + X)^2$$
$$(1.13317)^{1/2} = 1 + X$$
$$6.45\% = X$$

d. Yield of 3-year security, 1 year from now is calculated as follows:

$$(1.065)^4 = (1.06)(1 + X)^3$$
$$\frac{(1.065)^4}{1.06} = (1 + X)^3$$
$$1.213648 = (1 + X)^3$$
$$(1.213648)^{1/3} = 1 + X$$
$$6.67\% = X$$

CHAPTER 7

ST-2   a. Pennington's bonds were sold at par; therefore, the original YTM equaled the coupon rate of 12%.

b. $$V_B = \sum_{t=1}^{50} \frac{\$120/2}{\left(1 + \dfrac{0.10}{2}\right)^t} + \frac{\$1,000}{\left(1 + \dfrac{0.10}{2}\right)^{50}}$$

With a financial calculator, input the following: N = 50, I/YR = 5, PMT = 60, FV = 1000, and PV = ? Solve for PV = $1,182.56.

c. **Current yield = Annual coupon payment/Price**
$$= \$120/\$1,182.56$$
$$= 0.1015 = 10.15\%$$

Capital gains yield = Total yield – Current yield
$$= 10\% - 10.15\% = -0.15\%$$

Total return = YTM = 10%

d. With a financial calculator, input the following: N = 13, PV = −916.42, PMT = 60, FV = 1000, and $r_d/2 = I/YR = ?$ Calculator solution = $r_d/2 =$ 7.00%; therefore, $r_d = YTM = 14.00\%$.

Current yield = $120/$916.42 = 13.09%
Capital gains yield = 14% – 13.09% = 0.91%
Total return = YTM = 14.00%

e. The following time line illustrates the years to maturity of the bond:

Thus, on March 1, 2013, there were 13 2/3 periods left before the bond matured. Bond traders actually use the following procedure to determine the price of the bond:

(1) Find the price of the bond on the next coupon date, July 1, 2013. Using a financial calculator, input $N = 13$, $I/YR = 7.75$, $PMT = 60$, $FV = 1000$, and $PV = ?$ Solve for $PV = \$859.76$.

(2) Add the coupon, $60, to the bond price to get the total value of the bond on the next interest payment date: $\$859.76 + \$60.00 = \$919.76$.

(3) Discount this total value back to the purchase date (March 1, 2013): Using a financial calculator, input $N = 4/6$, $I/YR = 7.75$, $PMT = 0$, $FV = 919.76$, and $PV = ?$ Solve for $PV = \$875.11$.

(4) Therefore, you would have written a check for $875.11 to complete the transaction. Of this amount, $\$20 = (1/3)(\$60)$ would represent accrued interest and $855.11 would represent the bond's basic value. This breakdown would affect both your taxes and those of the seller.

(5) This problem could be solved *very* easily using a spreadsheet or a financial calculator with a bond valuation function, such as the HP-12C or the HP-17BII. This is explained in the calculator manual under the heading, "Bond Calculations."

ST-3 a. (1) $\$100,000,000/10 = \$10,000,000$ per year, or $5 million each 6 months.

(2) VDC will purchase bonds on the open market if they're selling at less than par. So, the sinking fund payment will be less than $5,000,000 each period.

b. The debt service requirements will decline. As the amount of bonds outstanding declines, so will the interest requirements (amounts given in millions of dollars). If the bonds are called at par, the total bond service payments are calculated as follows:

Semiannual Payment Period (1)	Sinking Fund Payment (2)	Outstanding Bonds on which Interest Is Paid (3)	Interest Payment[a] (4)	Total Bond Service (2) + (4) = (5)
1	$5	$100	$6.0	$11.0
2	5	95	5.7	10.7
3	5	90	5.4	10.4
⋮	⋮	⋮	⋮	⋮
20	5	5	0.3	5.3

[a]Interest is calculated as (0.5)(0.12) (Column 3); for example: Interest in Period 2 = (0.5)(0.12)($95) = $5.7.

The company's total cash bond service requirement will be $21.7 million per year for the first year. For both options, interest will decline by $0.12(\$10,000,000) = \$1,200,000$ per year for the remaining years. The total debt service requirement for the open market purchases cannot be precisely determined, but the amounts would be less than what's shown in Column 5 of the table above.

c. Here we have a 10-year 7% annuity whose compound value is $100 million, and we are seeking the annual payment, PMT. The solution can be obtained with a financial calculator. Input $N = 10$, $I/YR = 7$, $PV = 0$, and $FV = 100000000$, and press the PMT key to obtain $7,237,750. This amount is not known with certainty as interest rates over time will change, so the amount could be higher (if interest rates fall) or lower (if interest rates rise).

d. Annual debt service costs will be $100,000,000(0.12) + $7,237,750 = $19,237,750.

e. If interest rates rose, causing the bond's price to fall, the company would use open market purchases. This would reduce its debt service requirements.

CHAPTER 8

ST-2   a. The average rate of return for each stock is calculated simply by averaging the returns over the 5-year period. The average return for Stock A is:

$$r_{Avg\ A} = (-24.25\% + 18.50\% + 38.67\% + 14.33\% + 39.13\%)/5$$
$$= 17.28\%$$

The average return for Stock B is:

$$r_{Avg\ B} = (5.50\% + 26.73\% + 48.25\% + -4.50\% + 43.86\%)/5$$
$$= 23.97\%$$

The realized rate of return on a portfolio made up of Stock A and Stock B would be calculated by finding the average return in each year as r_A(% of Stock A) + r_B(% of Stock B) and then averaging these annual returns:

Year	Portfolio AB's Return, r_{AB}
2009	(9.38%)
2010	22.62
2011	43.46
2012	4.92
2013	41.50
	r_{Avg} = 20.62%

b. The standard deviation of returns is estimated, using Equation 8.2a, as follows:

$$\text{Estimated } \sigma = \sqrt{\frac{\sum_{t=1}^{N}\left(\bar{r}_t - \bar{r}_{Avg}\right)^2}{N-1}}$$

For Stock A, the estimated σ is 25.84%:

$$\sigma_A = \sqrt{\frac{(-24.25\% - 17.28\%)^2 + (18.50\% - 17.28\%)^2 + (38.67\% - 17.28\%)^2 + (14.33\% - 17.28\%)^2 + (39.13\% - 17.28\%)^2}{5-1}}$$
$$= 25.84\%$$

The standard deviations of returns for Stock B and for the portfolio are similarly determined, and they are as follows:

	Stock A	Stock B	Portfolio AB
Standard deviation	25.84%	23.15%	22.96%

c. Because the risk reduction from diversification is small (σ_{AB} falls only to 22.96%), the most likely value of the correlation coefficient is 0.8. If the correlation coefficient were −0.8, the risk reduction would be much larger. In fact, the correlation coefficient between Stocks A and B is 0.76.

d. If more randomly selected stocks were added to a portfolio, σ_p would decline to somewhere in the vicinity of 20% (see Figure 8.6); σ_p would remain constant only if the correlation coefficient were +1.0, which is most unlikely. σ_p would decline to zero only if the correlation coefficient, ρ, were equal to zero and a large number of stocks were added to the portfolio, or if the proper proportions were held in a two-stock portfolio with $\rho = -1.0$.

ST-3   a. $b = (0.6)(0.70) + (0.25)(0.90) + (0.1)(1.30) + (0.05)(1.50)$
$= 0.42 + 0.225 + 0.13 + 0.075 = 0.85$

b. $r_{RF} = 6\%$; $RP_M = 5\%$; $b = 0.85$ **(calculated in Part a)**

$r_p = 6\% + (5\%)(0.85)$
$= 10.25\%$

c. $b_N = (0.5)(0.70) + (0.25)(0.90) + (0.1)(1.30) + (0.15)(1.50)$
$= 0.35 + 0.225 + 0.13 + 0.225$
$= 0.93$

$r = 6\% + (5\%)(0.93)$
$= 10.65\%$

CHAPTER 9

ST-2   a.   This is not necessarily true. Because G plows back two-thirds of its earnings, its growth rate should exceed that of D, but D pays higher dividends ($3 versus $1). We cannot say which stock should have the higher price.

b.   Again, we just do not know which price would be higher.

c.   This is false. The changes in r_d and r_s would have a greater effect on G; its price would decline more.

d.   The total expected return for D is $\hat{r}_D = D_1/P_0 + g = 12\% + 0\% = 12\%$. The total expected return for G will have D_1/P_0 less than 12% and g greater than 0%, but $\hat{r}_G$ should be neither greater nor smaller than D's total expected return, 12%, because the two stocks are stated to be equally risky.

e.   We have eliminated a, b, c, and d, so e should be correct. On the basis of the available information, D and G should sell at about the same price, $25; thus, $\hat{r}_s = 12\%$ for both D and G. G's current dividend yield is $1/$25 = 4%. Therefore, g = 12% − 4% = 8%.

ST-3   The first step is to solve for g, the unknown variable, in the constant growth equation. Since D_1 is unknown but D_0 is known, substitute $D_0(1 + g)$ for D_1 as follows:

$$\hat{P}_0 = P_0 = \frac{D_1}{r_s - g} = \frac{D_0(1 + g)}{r_s - g}$$

$$\$36 = \frac{\$2.40(1 + g)}{0.12 - g}$$

Solving for g, we find the growth rate to be 5%:

$$\$4.32 - \$36g = \$2.40 + \$2.40g$$
$$\$38.4g = \$1.92$$
$$g = 0.05 = 5\%$$

The next step is to use the growth rate to project the stock price 5 years hence:

$$\hat{P}_5 = \frac{D_0(1+g)^6}{r_s - g}$$
$$= \frac{\$2.40(1.05)^6}{0.12 - 0.05}$$
$$= \$45.95$$

(Alternatively, $\hat{P}_5 = \$36(1.05)^5 = \$45.95$)

Therefore, the firm's expected stock price 5 years from now, $\hat{P}_5$, is \$45.95.

ST-4 a. (1) Calculate the PV of the dividends paid during the supernormal growth period:

$$D_1 = \$1.1500(1.15) = \$1.3225$$
$$D_2 = \$1.3225(1.15) = \$1.5209$$
$$D_3 = \$1.5209(1.13) = \$1.7186$$

$$\text{PV D} = \frac{\$1.3225}{1.12} + \frac{\$1.5209}{(1.12)^2} + \frac{\$1.7186}{(1.12)^3}$$
$$= \$1.1808 + \$1.2125 + \$1.2233$$
$$= \$3.6166 \approx \$3.62$$

(2) Find the PV of the firm's stock price at the end of Year 3:

$$\hat{P}_3 = \frac{D_4}{r_s - g} = \frac{D_3(1+g)}{r_s - g}$$
$$= \frac{\$1.7186(1.06)}{0.12 - 0.06}$$
$$= \$30.36$$

$$\text{PV } \hat{P}_3 = \frac{\$30.36}{(1.12)^3} = \$21.61$$

(3) Sum the two components to find the value of the stock today:

$$\hat{P}_0 = \$3.62 + \$21.61 = \$25.23$$

Alternatively, the cash flows can be placed on a time line as follows:

0		1		2		3		4
12%								
g = 15%		1.3225		1.5209	g = 13%	1.7186	g = 6%	1.8217

$$30.3617 = \frac{\$1.8217}{0.12 - 0.06}$$
$$\underline{32.0803}$$

Enter the cash flows into the cash flow register (remembering that $CF_0 = 0$) and I/YR = 12, and press the NPV key to obtain $P_0 = \$25.23$.

b.
$$\hat{P}_1 = \frac{\$1.5209}{1.12} + \frac{\$1.7186}{(1.12)^2} + \frac{\$30.36}{(1.12)^2}$$
$$= \$1.3579 + \$1.3701 + \$24.2028$$
$$= \$26.9308 \approx \$26.93$$

(Calculator solution: $26.93)

$$\hat{P}_2 = \frac{\$1.7186}{1.12} + \frac{\$30.36}{1.12}$$
$$= \$1.5345 + \$27.1071$$
$$= \$28.6416 \approx \$28.64.$$

(Calculator solution: $28.64)

c.

Year	Dividend Yield	+	Capital Gains Yield	=	Total Return
1	$\frac{\$1.3225}{\$25.23} \approx 5.24\%$		$\frac{\$26.93 - \$25.23}{\$25.23} \approx 6.74\%$		$\approx 12\%$
2	$\frac{\$1.5209}{\$26.93} \approx 5.65\%$		$\frac{\$28.64 - \$26.93}{\$26.93} \approx 6.35\%$		$\approx 12\%$
3	$\frac{\$1.7186}{\$28.64} \approx 6.00\%$		$\frac{\$30.36 - \$28.64}{\$28.64} \approx 6.00\%$		$\approx 12\%$

CHAPTER 10

ST-2 a. Component costs are as follows:

Common: $r_s = \dfrac{D_1}{P_0} + g = \dfrac{D_0(1 + g)}{P_0} + g$
$$= \frac{\$3.60(1.09)}{\$54} + 0.09$$
$$= 0.0727 + 0.09 = 16.27\%$$

Preferred: $r_p = \dfrac{\text{Preferred dividend}}{P_p} = \dfrac{\$11}{\$95} = 11.58\%$

Debt: $r_d(1 - T) = 12\%(0.6) = 7.20\%$

b. WACC calculation:

$$\text{WACC} = w_d r_d(1 - T) + w_p r_p + w_c r_s$$
$$= 0.25(7.2\%) + 0.15(11.58\%) + 0.60(16.27\%) = 13.30\%$$

c. $\dfrac{\text{Retained earnings}}{\text{breakpoint}} = \dfrac{\text{Addition to retained earnings for the year}}{\text{Equity fraction}}$
$$= \frac{0.7(\$34,285.72)}{0.6} = \$40,000$$

At a capital budget greater than $40,000 new common stock would have to be issued, and the firm's WACC would increase above 13.3%. Therefore, only Projects A, B, and C can be accepted for a total capital budget of $40,000.

CHAPTER 11

ST-2 a. *Net present value (NPV):*

$$NPV_X = -\$10,000 + \frac{\$6,500}{(1.12)^1} + \frac{\$3,000}{(1.12)^2} + \frac{\$3,000}{(1.12)^3} + \frac{\$1,000}{(1.12)^4} = \$966.01$$

$$NPV_Y = -\$10,000 + \frac{\$3,500}{(1.12)^1} + \frac{\$3,500}{(1.12)^2} + \frac{\$3,500}{(1.12)^3} + \frac{\$3,500}{(1.12)^4} = \$630.72$$

Alternatively, using a financial calculator, input the cash flows into the cash flow register, enter I/YR = 12, and then press the NPV key to obtain $NPV_X = \$966.01$ and $NPV_Y = \$630.72$.

Internal rate of return (IRR):
To solve for each project's IRR, find the discount rates that equate each NPV to zero:

$$IRR_X = 18.0\%$$
$$IRR_Y = 15.0\%$$

Modified internal rate of return (MIRR):
To obtain each project's MIRR, begin by finding each project's terminal value (TV) of cash inflows:

$$TV_X = \$6,500(1.12)^3 + \$3,000(1.12)^2 + \$3,000(1.12)^1 + \$1,000 = \$17,255.23$$
$$TV_Y = \$3,500(1.12)^3 + \$3,500(1.12)^2 + \$3,500(1.12)^1 + \$3,500 = \$16,727.65$$

Now, each project's MIRR is the discount rate that equates the PV of the TV to each project's cost, $10,000:

$$MIRR_X = 14.61\%$$
$$MIRR_Y = 13.73\%$$

Payback:
To determine the payback, construct the cumulative cash flows for each project:

	Cumulative Cash Flows	
Year	Project X	Project Y
0	($10,000)	($10,000)
1	(3,500)	(6,500)
2	(500)	(3,000)
3	2,500	500
4	3,500	4,000

$$Payback_X = 2 + \frac{\$500}{\$3,000} = 2.17 \text{ years}$$

$$Payback_Y = 2 + \frac{\$3,000}{\$3,500} = 2.86 \text{ years}$$

Discounted payback:
To determine the discounted payback, construct the cumulative discounted cash flows at the firm's WACC of 12% for each project:

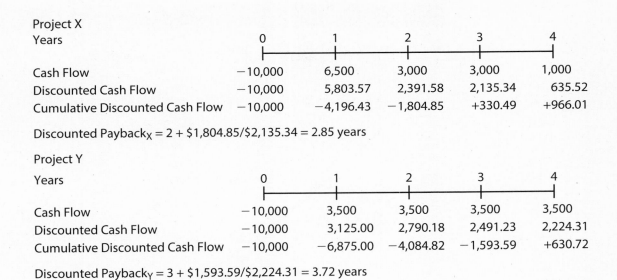

Project X

Years	0	1	2	3	4
Cash Flow	−10,000	6,500	3,000	3,000	1,000
Discounted Cash Flow	−10,000	5,803.57	2,391.58	2,135.34	635.52
Cumulative Discounted Cash Flow	−10,000	−4,196.43	−1,804.85	+330.49	+966.01

Discounted Payback$_X$ = 2 + $1,804.85/$2,135.34 = 2.85 years

Project Y

Years	0	1	2	3	4
Cash Flow	−10,000	3,500	3,500	3,500	3,500
Discounted Cash Flow	−10,000	3,125.00	2,790.18	2,491.23	2,224.31
Cumulative Discounted Cash Flow	−10,000	−6,875.00	−4,084.82	−1,593.59	+630.72

Discounted Payback$_Y$ = 3 + $1,593.59/$2,224.31 = 3.72 years

b. The following table summarizes the project rankings by each method:

	Project that Ranks Higher
NPV	X
IRR	X
MIRR	X
Payback	X
Discounted payback	X

Note that all methods rank Project X over Project Y. In addition, both projects are acceptable under the NPV, IRR, and MIRR criteria. Thus, both projects should be accepted if they are independent.

c. In this case, we would choose the project with the higher NPV at r = 12%, or Project X.

d. To determine the effects of changing the cost of capital, plot the NPV profiles of each project. The crossover rate occurs between 6% and 7% (≈ 6.22%). See the graph on the next page.

   If the firm's cost of capital is less than 6.22%, a conflict exists because NPV$_Y$ > NPV$_X$, but IRR$_X$ > IRR$_Y$. Therefore, if r were 5%, a conflict would exist. Note, however, that when r = 5.0%, MIRR$_X$ = 10.64% and MIRR$_Y$ = 10.83%; hence, the modified IRR ranks the projects correctly, even if r is to the left of the crossover point.

e. The basic cause of the conflict is differing reinvestment rate assumptions between NPV and IRR. NPV assumes that cash flows can be reinvested at the cost of capital, while IRR assumes reinvestment at the (generally) higher IRR. The high reinvestment rate assumption under IRR makes early cash flows especially valuable, and hence short-term projects look better than long-term projects under IRR.

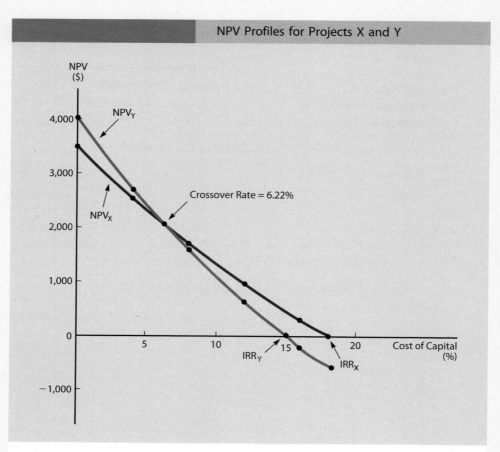

NPV Profiles for Projects X and Y

Cost of Capital	NPV$_X$	NPV$_Y$
0%	$3,500	$4,000
4	2,545	2,705
8	1,707	1,592
12	966	631
16	307	(206)
18	5	(585)

CHAPTER 12

ST-2 a. Estimated investment requirements:

Price	($55,000)
Installation	(10,000)
Change in net operating working capital	(2,000)
Total investment outlay	($67,000)

b. Depreciation schedule:

Equipment cost = $65,000; MACRS 3-year class

	Years		
	1	**2**	**3**
MACRS depreciation rates	33%	45%	15%
Equipment depreciation expense	$21,450	$29,250	$9,750

Note that the remaining book value of the equipment at the end of the project's life is $0.07 \times \$65,000 = \$4,550$.

c.

	Year 0	Year 1	Year 2	Year 3
Investment Outlays:				
Equipment purchase	($65,000)			
Change in NOWC	(2,000)			
Operating Cash Flows over Project's Life:				
Revenues (4,000 × $50)		$200,000	$200,000	$200,000
Variable costs (70%)		140,000	140,000	140,000
Fixed costs		30,000	30,000	30,000
Depreciation		21,450	29,250	9,750
EBIT		$ 8,550	$ 750	$ 20,250
Taxes on operating income (40%)		3,420	300	8,100
AT project operating income		$ 5,130	$ 450	$ 12,150
Add back: Depreciation		21,450	29,250	9,750
EBIT(1 − T) + Depreciation		$ 26,580	$ 29,700	$ 21,900
Terminal Cash Flows:				
Salvage value				10,000
Tax on salvage value				(2,180)
AT salvage value				$ 7,820
Recovery of NOWC				2,000
Project free cash flows	($67,000)	$ 26,580	$ 29,700	$ 31,720

```
 0            1            2            3
 +-----11%----+------------+------------+
-67,000     26,580       29,700       31,720
```

d. From the time line shown in Part c, the project's NPV can be calculated as follows:

$$\text{NPV} = -\$67,000 + \$26,580/(1.11)^1 + \$29,700/(1.11)^2 + \$31,720/(1.11)^3$$

$$= \$4,245$$

Alternatively, using a financial calculator, you would enter the following data: $CF_0 = -67000$; $CF_1 = 26580$; $CF_2 = 29700$; $CF_3 = 31720$; I/YR = 11; and then solve for NPV = $4,245.

Because the NPV is positive, the project should be accepted.

e. Project analysis if unit sales turned out to be 20% below forecast:

Initial projection = 4,000 units; however, if unit sales turn out to be only 80% of forecast then unit sales = 3,200.

	Year 0	Year 1	Year 2	Year 3
Investment Outlays:				
Equipment purchase	($65,000)			
Change in NOWC	(2,000)			
Operating Cash Flows over Project's Life:				
Revenues (3,200 × $50)		$160,000	$160,000	$160,000
Variable costs (70%)		112,000	112,000	112,000
Fixed costs		30,000	30,000	30,000
Depreciation		21,450	29,250	9,750
EBIT		($ 3,450)	($ 11,250)	$ 8,250
Taxes on operating income (40%)		(1,380)	(4,500)	3,300
AT project operating income		($ 2,070)	($ 6,750)	$ 4,950
Add back: Depreciation		21,450	29,250	9,750
EBIT(1 − T) + Depreciation		$ 19,380	$ 22,500	$ 14,700

(Continued)

	Year 0	Year 1	Year 2	Year 3
Terminal Cash Flows:				
Salvage value				10,000
Tax on salvage value				(2,180)
AT salvage value				$ 7,820
Recovery of NOWC				2,000
Project free cash flows	($67,000)	$ 19,380	$ 22,500	$ 24,520

NPV calculation:

0		1	2	3
−67,000		19,380	22,500	24,520

$$\text{NPV} = -\$67{,}000 + \$19{,}380/(1.11)^1 + \$22{,}500/(1.11)^2 + \$24{,}520/(1.11)^3$$
$$= -\$13{,}350$$

Alternatively, using a financial calculator, you would enter the following data: $CF_0 = -67000$; $CF_1 = 19380$; $CF_2 = 22500$; $CF_3 = 24520$; $I/YR = 11$; and then solve for NPV = $-\$13{,}350$.

Because the NPV is negative, the project should not be accepted. If unit sales were 20% below the forecasted level, the project would no longer be accepted.

f. *Best-case scenario:* Unit sales = 4,800; Variable cost % = 65%

	Year 0	Year 1	Year 2	Year 3
Investment Outlays:				
Equipment purchase	($65,000)			
Change in NOWC	(2,000)			
Operating Cash Flows over Project's Life:				
Revenues (4,800 × $50)		$240,000	$240,000	$240,000
Variable costs (65%)		156,000	156,000	156,000
Fixed costs		30,000	30,000	30,000
Depreciation		21,450	29,250	9,750
EBIT		$ 32,550	$ 24,750	$ 44,250
Taxes on operating income (40%)		13,020	9,900	17,700
AT project operating income		$ 19,530	$ 14,850	$ 26,550
Add back: Depreciation		21,450	29,250	9,750
EBIT(1 − T) + Depreciation		$ 40,980	$ 44,100	$ 36,300
Terminal Cash Flows:				
Salvage value				10,000
Tax on salvage value				(2,180)
AT salvage value				$ 7,820
Recovery of NOWC				2,000
Project free cash flows	($67,000)	$ 40,980	$ 44,100	$ 46,120

Project NPV:

0		1	2	3
−67,000		40,980	44,100	46,120

$$\text{NPV} = -\$67{,}000 + \$40{,}980/(1.11)^1 + \$44{,}100/(1.11)^2 + \$46{,}120/(1.11)^3$$
$$= \$39{,}434$$

Alternatively, using a financial calculator, you would enter the following data: $CF_0 = -67000$; $CF_1 = 40980$; $CF_2 = 44100$; $CF_3 = 46120$; $I/YR = 11$; and then solve for NPV = $39,434.

Base-case scenario: The NPV was calculated in Part d as $4,245.

Worst-case scenario: Unit sales = 3,200; Variable cost % = 75%

	Year 0	Year 1	Year 2	Year 3
Investment Outlays:				
Equipment purchase	($65,000)			
Change in NOWC	(2,000)			
Operating Cash Flows over Project's Life:				
Revenues (3,200 × $50)		$160,000	$160,000	$160,000
Variable costs (75%)		120,000	120,000	120,000
Fixed costs		30,000	30,000	30,000
Depreciation		21,450	29,250	9,750
EBIT		($ 11,450)	($ 19,250)	$ 250
Taxes on operating income (40%)		(4,580)	(7,700)	100
AT project operating income		($ 6,870)	($ 11,550)	$ 150
Add back: Depreciation		21,450	29,250	9,750
EBIT(1 − T) + Depreciation		$ 14,580	$ 17,700	$ 9,900
Terminal Cash Flows:				
Salvage value				10,000
Tax on salvage value				(2,180)
AT salvage value				$ 7,820
Recovery of NOWC				2,000
Project free cash flows	($67,000)	$ 14,580	$ 17,700	$ 19,720

Project NPV:

```
0          1          2          3
+----11%----+----------+----------+
-67,000   14,580    17,700     19,720
```

$$\text{NPV} = -\$67,000 + \$14,580/(1.11)^1 + \$17,700/(1.11)^2 + \$19,720/(1.11)^3$$
$$= -\$25,080$$

Alternatively, using a financial calculator, you would enter the following data: $CF_0 = -67000$; $CF_1 = 14580$; $CF_2 = 17700$; $CF_3 = 19720$; $I/YR = 11$; and then solve for NPV = −$25,080.

Scenario	Probability	NPV
Best case	25%	$39,434
Base case	50	4,245
Worst case	25	−25,080
	Expected NPV =	$ 5,711

$$\sigma_{\text{NPV}} = \left[0.25(\$39,434 - \$5,711)^2 + 0.50(\$4,245 - \$5,711)^2 + 0.25(-\$25,080 - \$5,711)^2\right]^{1/2}$$

$$\sigma_{\text{NPV}} = [\$284,310,182 + \$1,074,578 + \$237,021,420]^{1/2}$$

$$\sigma_{\text{NPV}} = \$22,856$$

$$\text{CV}_{\text{NPV}} = \$22,856/\$5,711 = 4.0$$

g. The project's CV = 4.0, which is significantly larger than the firm's typical project CV. So, the WACC for this project should be adjusted upward, 11% + 3% = 14%.

To calculate the expected NPV, standard deviation, and coefficient of variation you would recalculate each scenario's NPV by discounting the project cash flows by 14% rather than 11%.

Best-case scenario:

$$\text{NPV} = -\$67{,}000 + \$40{,}980/(1.14)^1 + \$44{,}100/(1.14)^2 + \$46{,}120/(1.14)^3$$
$$= \$34{,}011$$

Alternatively, using a financial calculator, you would enter the following data: $CF_0 = -67000$; $CF_1 = 40980$; $CF_2 = 44100$; $CF_3 = 46120$; $I/YR = 14$; and then solve for NPV = \$34,011.

Base-case scenario:

$$\text{NPV} = -\$67{,}000 + \$26{,}580/(1.14)^1 + \$29{,}700/(1.14)^2 + \$31{,}720/(1.14)^3$$
$$= \$579$$

Alternatively, using a financial calculator, you would enter the following data: $CF_0 = -67000$; $CF_1 = 26580$; $CF_2 = 29700$; $CF_3 = 31720$; $I/YR = 14$; and then solve for NPV = \$579.

Worst-case scenario:

```
0          1          2          3
|----------|----------|----------|
     14%
-67,000    14,580     17,700     19,720
```

$$\text{NPV} = -\$67{,}000 + \$14{,}580/(1.14)^1 + \$17{,}700/(1.14)^2 + \$19{,}720/(1.14)^3$$
$$= -\$27{,}281$$

Alternatively, using a financial calculator, you would enter the following data: $CF_0 = -67000$; $CF_1 = 14580$; $CF_2 = 17700$; $CF_3 = 19720$; $I/YR = 14$; and then solve for NPV = -\$27,281.

Scenario	Probability	NPV
Best case	25%	\$34,011
Base case	50	579
Worst case	25	−27,281
	Expected NPV =	\$ 1,972

$$\sigma_{\text{NPV}} = \left[0.25(\$34{,}011 - \$1{,}972)^2 + 0.50(\$579 - \$1{,}972)^2 + 0.25(-\$27{,}281 - \$1{,}972)^2\right]^{1/2}$$
$$\sigma_{\text{NPV}} = [\$256{,}624{,}380 + \$970{,}225 + \$213{,}934{,}502]^{1/2}$$
$$\sigma_{\text{NPV}} = \$21{,}715$$
$$\text{CV}_{\text{NPV}} = \$21{,}715/\$1{,}972 = 11.01$$

The expected NPV of the project is still positive, so the project would still be accepted, but it is a risky project.

CHAPTER 13

ST-2 a. The following information is given in the problem:

Q = Units of output(sales) = 5,000
P = Average sales price per unit of output = \$100
F = Fixed operating costs = \$200,000
V = Variable costs per unit = \$50
EBIT = Operating income = \$50,000
Total assets = \$500,000
Common equity = \$500,000

(1) Determine the new EBIT level if the change is made:

New EBIT $= P_2(Q_2) - F_2 - V_2(Q_2)$
New EBIT $= \$95(7,000) - \$250,000 - \$40(7,000)$
         $= \$135,000$

(2) Determine the incremental EBIT:

ΔEBIT $= \$135,000 - \$50,000 = \$85,000$

(3) Estimate the approximate rate of return on the new investment:

$$\Delta ROA = \frac{\Delta EBIT}{Investment} = \frac{\$85,000}{\$400,000} = 21.25\%$$

Because the ROA exceeds Olinde's average cost of capital, this analysis suggests that the firm should go ahead and make the investment.

b. The change would increase the breakeven point. Still, with a lower sales price, it might be easier to achieve the higher new breakeven volume.

$$\text{Old}: Q_{BE} = \frac{F}{P-V} = \frac{\$200,000}{\$100 - \$50} = 4,000 \text{ units}$$

$$\text{New}: Q_{BE} = \frac{F_2}{P_2 - V_2} = \frac{\$250,000}{\$95 - \$40} = 4,545 \text{ units}$$

c. The incremental ROA is:

$$ROA = \frac{\Delta Profit}{\Delta Sales} \times \frac{\Delta Sales}{\Delta Assets}$$

Using debt financing, the incremental profit associated with the investment is equal to the incremental profit found in Part a minus the interest expense incurred as a result of the investment:

ΔProfit = New profit − Old profit − Interest
         $= \$135,000 - \$50,000 - 0.10(\$400,000)$
         $= \$45,000$

The incremental sales is calculated as:

ΔSales $= P_2 Q_2 - P_1 Q_1$
         $= \$95(7,000) - \$100(5,000)$
         $= \$665,000 - \$500,000$
         $= \$165,000$

$$ROA = \frac{\$45,000}{\$165,000} \times \frac{\$165,000}{\$400,000} = 11.25\%$$

The return on the new investment still exceeds the average cost of capital, so the firm should make the investment.

ST-3 a. Total capital = $5,000,000 and remains the same at all levels of debt; Tax rate = 35%; Original shares outstanding = 200,000; EBIT = $500,000 at all levels of debt.

From the data given in the problem, we can develop the following table:

w_d	w_c	r_d	EBIT	Interest[a]	Net Income[b]	Shares Outstanding[c]	EPS[d]
0.00	1.00	5.00%	$500,000	$ 0	$325,000	200,000	$1.63
0.25	0.75	6.00	500,000	75,000	276,250	150,000	1.84
0.50	0.50	8.30	500,000	207,500	190,125	100,000	1.90
0.75	0.25	11.00	500,000	412,500	56,875	50,000	1.14

Notes:

[a]Interest expense is calculated as $w_d \times$ Total capital $\times r_d$.

[b]Net income is calculated as $(\text{EBIT} - \text{Interest})(1 - T)$.

[c]Shares outstanding is calculated as Original shares outstanding at Debt level = 0 $- (w_d \times$ Original shares outstanding at Debt level $= 0)$.

[d]EPS is calculated as Net income divided by Shares outstanding.

b. EPS is maximized at a capital structure consisting of 50% debt and 50% equity. At that capital structure, the firm's EPS is $1.90.

c. Tax rate = 35%; r_{RF} = 3.5%; b_U = 1.25; $r_M - r_{RF}$ = 4.5%.

From data given in the problem, we can develop the following table:

w_d	w_c	D/E	r_d	$r_d(1 - T)$	b_L[a]	r_s[b]	WACC[c]
0.00	1.00	0.0000	5.00%	3.25%	1.25	9.13%	9.13%
0.25	0.75	0.3333	6.00	3.90	1.52	10.34	8.73
0.50	0.50	1.0000	8.30	5.40	2.06	12.78	9.09
0.75	0.25	3.0000	11.00	7.15	3.69	20.09	10.39

Notes:

[a]These beta estimates were calculated using the Hamada equation, $b_L = b_U[1 + (1 - T)(D/E)]$.

[b]These r_s estimates were calculated using the CAPM, $r_s = r_{RF} + (r_M - r_{RF})b$.

[c]These WACC estimates were calculated with the following equation: WACC $= w_d(r_d)(1 - T) + (w_c)(r_s)$.

d. Carlisle's WACC is minimized at a capital structure consisting of 25% debt and 75% equity. At that capital structure, the firm's WACC is 8.73%.

e. The capital structure at which the firm's WACC is minimized is the optimal capital structure, i.e., the capital structure at which the firm's value is maximized. For Carlisle, this capital structure consists of 25% debt and 75% equity. This is not the same capital structure at which EPS is maximized, because the additional risk taken on is not measured in the EPS calculation, but it is measured in the WACC calculation. (That is, the costs of debt and equity increase at additional debt levels, and those component costs are used in the WACC calculation.)

f. As an analyst (on the basis of these data), the recommendation to the firm would be to issue $1,250,000 of debt (calculated as $0.25 \times \$5,000,000$) with a 6% coupon rate (this is r_d at this debt level), and use these funds to repurchase 50,000 shares of common stock.

CHAPTER 14

ST-2 a.

Projected net income	$2,000,000
Less projected capital investments	800,000
Available residual	$1,200,000
Shares outstanding	200,000

DPS = $1,200,000/200,000 shares = $6 = D_1

b. EPS = $2,000,000/200,000 shares = $10

Payout ratio = DPS/EPS = $6/$10 = 60%, or

Total dividends/NI = $1,200,000/$2,000,000 = 60%

c. Currently, $P_0 = \dfrac{D_1}{r_s - g} = \dfrac{\$6}{0.14 - 0.06} = \dfrac{\$6}{0.08} = \$75.00$

Under the former circumstances, D_1 would be based on a 20% payout on an EPS of $10, or $0.2 \times \$10 = \$2$. With $r_s = 14\%$ and $g = 12\%$, we solve for P_0:

$$P_0 = \frac{D_1}{r_s - g} = \frac{\$2}{0.14 - 0.12} = \frac{\$2}{0.02} = \$100$$

Although CMC has suffered a severe setback, its existing assets will continue to provide a good income stream. More of these earnings should now be passed on to the shareholders, as the slowed internal growth has reduced the need for funds. However, the net result is a 25% decrease in the value of the shares.

d. If the payout ratio were continued at 20%, even after internal investment opportunities had declined, the price of the stock would drop to $2/(0.14 - 0.06) = $25 rather than to $75.00. Thus, an increase in the dividend payout is consistent with maximizing shareholder wealth.

Because of the diminishing nature of profitable investment opportunities, the greater the firm's level of investment, the lower the average ROE. Thus, the more money CMC retains and invests, the lower its average ROE will be. We can determine the average ROE under different conditions as follows:

Old situation (with founder active and a 20% payout):

g = (1.0 − Payout ratio)(Average ROE)

12% = (1.0 − 0.2)(Average ROE)

Average ROE = 12%/0.8 = 15% > r_s = 14%

Note that the *average* ROE is 15%, whereas the *marginal* ROE is presumably equal to 14%.

New situation (with founder retired and a 60% payout as explained in Part c):

g = 6% = (1.0 − 0.6)(ROE)

ROE = 6%/0.4 = 15% > r_s = 14%

This suggests that a new payout of 60% is appropriate and that the firm is taking on investments down to the point at which marginal returns are equal to the cost of capital. Note that if the 20% payout was maintained, the *average* ROE would be only 7.5%, which would imply a marginal ROE far below the 14% cost of capital.

CHAPTER 15

ST-2   The Calgary Company: Alternative Balance Sheets

	Restricted (40%)	Moderate (50%)	Relaxed (60%)
Current assets	$1,200,000	$1,500,000	$1,800,000
Fixed assets	600,000	600,000	600,000
Total assets	$1,800,000	$2,100,000	$2,400,000
Debt	$ 900,000	$1,050,000	$1,200,000
Equity	900,000	1,050,000	1,200,000
Total liabilities and equity	$1,800,000	$2,100,000	$2,400,000

The Calgary Company: Alternative Income Statements

	Restricted	Moderate	Relaxed
Sales	$3,000,000	$3,000,000	$3,000,000
EBIT	450,000	450,000	450,000
Interest (10%)	90,000	105,000	120,000
Earnings before taxes	$ 360,000	$ 345,000	$ 330,000
Taxes (40%)	144,000	138,000	132,000
Net income	$ 216,000	$ 207,000	$ 198,000
ROE	24.0%	19.7%	16.5%

ST-3   a and b.

Income Statements for Year Ended December 31, 2014 (Thousands of Dollars)

	Vanderheiden Press		Herrenhouse Publishing	
	a	b	a	b
EBIT	$ 30,000	$ 30,000	$ 30,000	$ 30,000
Interest	12,400	14,400	10,600	18,600
Taxable income	$ 17,600	$ 15,600	$ 19,400	$ 11,400
Taxes (40%)	7,040	6,240	7,760	4,560
Net income	$ 10,560	$ 9,360	$ 11,640	$ 6,840
Equity	$100,000	$100,000	$100,000	$100,000
Return on equity	10.56%	9.36%	11.64%	6.84%

The Vanderheiden Press has a higher ROE when short-term interest rates are high, whereas Herrenhouse Publishing does better when rates are lower.

c. Herrenhouse's position is riskier. First, its profits and return on equity are much more volatile than Vanderheiden's. Second, Herrenhouse must renew its large short-term loan every year, and if the renewal comes up at a time when money is very tight, when its business is depressed, or both, then Herrenhouse could be denied credit, which could put it out of business.

CHAPTER 16

ST-2   To solve this problem, we will define ΔS as the change in sales and g as the growth rate in sales, and then we use the three following equations:

$$\Delta S = S_0 g$$
$$S_1 = S_0(1 + g)$$

$$\text{AFN} = (A_0{}^*/S_0)(\Delta S) - (L_0{}^*/S_0)(\Delta S) - MS_1(1 - \text{Payout})$$

Set AFN = 0, substitute in known values for $A_0{}^*/S_0$, $L_0{}^*/S_0$, M, payout, and S_0, and then solve for g:

$$0 = 1.6(\$100g) - 0.4(\$100g) - 0.10[\$100(1 + g)](1 - 0.45)$$
$$0 = \$160g - \$40g - 0.055(\$100 + \$100g)$$
$$0 = \$160g - \$40g - \$5.5 - \$5.5g$$
$$\$114.5g = \$5.5$$
$$g = \$5.5/\$114.5 = 0.048 = 4.8\%$$
$$g = \text{Maximum growth rate without external financing}$$

ST-3   Assets consist of cash, marketable securities, receivables, inventories, and fixed assets. Therefore, we can break the $A_0{}^*/S_0$ ratio into its components—cash/sales, inventories/sales, and so forth. Then,

$$\frac{A_0{}^*}{S_0} = \frac{A_0{}^* - \text{Inventories}}{S_0} + \frac{\text{Inventories}}{S_0} = 1.6$$

We know that the inventory turnover ratio is Sales/Inventories = 3 times, so Inventories/Sales = $1/3 = 0.3333$. Further, if the inventory turnover ratio can be increased to 4 times, then the Inventory/Sales ratio will fall to $1/4 = 0.25$, a difference of $0.3333 - 0.2500 = 0.0833$. This, in turn, causes the $A_0{}^*/S_0$ ratio to fall from $A_0{}^*/S_0 = 1.6$ to $A_0{}^*/S_0 = 1.6 - 0.0833 = 1.5167$.

This change has two effects: First, it changes the AFN equation, and second, it means that Weatherford currently has excessive inventories. Because it is costly to hold excess inventories, Weatherford will want to reduce its inventory holdings by not replacing inventories until the excess amounts have been used. We can account for this by setting up the revised AFN equation (using the new $A_0{}^*/S_0$ ratio), estimating the funds that will be needed next year if no excess inventories are currently on hand, and then subtracting out the excess inventories that are currently on hand:

Present conditions:

$$\frac{\text{Sales}}{\text{Inventories}} = \frac{\$100}{\text{Inventories}} = 3,$$

so

$$\text{Inventories} = \$100/3 = \$33.3 \text{ million at present}$$

New conditions:

$$\frac{\text{Sales}}{\text{Inventories}} = \frac{\$100}{\text{Inventories}} = 4$$

so

$$\text{New level of inventories} = \$100/4 = \$25 \text{ million}$$

Therefore,

$$\text{Excess inventories} = \$33.3 - \$25 = \$8.3 \text{ million}$$

Forecast of funds needed:

$$\Delta S = 0.2(\$100 \text{ million}) = \$20 \text{ million}$$

$$\text{AFN} = 1.5167(\$20) - 0.4(\$20) - 0.1(1 - 0.45)(\$120) - \$8.3$$
$$= \$30.3 - \$8 - \$6.6 - \$8.3$$
$$= \$7.4 \text{ million}$$

CHAPTER 17

ST-2 $\dfrac{\text{Euros}}{\text{C\$}} = \dfrac{\text{Euros}}{\text{US\$}} \times \dfrac{\text{US\$}}{\text{C\$}}$

$\qquad = \dfrac{\text{€}0.75}{\$1} \times \dfrac{\$1}{\text{C\$}1.02} = \dfrac{\text{€}0.75}{\text{C\$}1.02} = \text{€}0.7353 \text{ per Canadian dollar}$

Ulrike Neumann/Vetta/Getty Image

Answers to Selected End-of-Chapter Problems

Note: This appendix presents some intermediate steps and final answers to selected end-of-chapter problems. Please note that your answer may differ slightly due to rounding differences. Also, some of the problems may have more than one correct solution depending upon the assumptions made in working the problem. Finally, where the selected problems involve a verbal discussion as well as numerical calculations, the verbal answer is not provided.

3-2 $1,000,000
3-4 $20,000,000
3-6 $25,000,000
3-8 Statement a; possibly statement c because of tax refund
3-10 $1,575,000
3-12 $300,000
3-14 $12,681,482
3-16 a. $NOWC_{2013} = \$210,000,000$; $NOWC_{2014} = \$192,000,000$
  b. $FCF_{2014} = \$58,000,000$
  c. Increase in FCF

4-2 44%
4-4 M/B = 4.2667
4-6 ROE = 8%
4-8 NI = $112,500
4-10 $P_0 = \$142.50$
4-12 TIE = 2.25×
4-14 ROE = 23.1%
4-16 ΔROE = +7.2%
4-18 TIE = 6.0×
4-20 Accounts receivable = $405,682
4-22 Sales = $450,000; AR = $45,000; Inv = $90,000; FA = $150,000; CL = $75,000
4-24 a. Current ratio = 3.56×;
    Debt to total capital = 20.05%;
    DSO = 30.3 days; ROA = 6.00%;
    ROIC = 7.54%
  b. Firm: ROE = 3.4% × 1.77 × $450/$315
      = 8.6%
    Industry: ROE = 3.0% × 3 × ROE/ROA
      = 3.0% × 3 × 12.86%/9.00%
      = 12.86%

5-2 PV = $1,292.10
5-4 N = 11.01years
5-6 $FVA_5 = \$1,725.22$; $FVA_{5\ Due} = \$1,845.99$
5-8 PMT = $444.89; EAR = 12.6825%

5-10 a. $895.42
  b. $1,552.92
  c. $279.20
  d. $499.99; $867.13
5-12 a. 7%
  b. 7%
  c. 9%
  d. 15%
5-14 a. $6,374.97
  b. $1,105.13
  c. $2,000.00
  d(l). $7,012.47
  d(2). $1,160.38
  d(3). $2,000.00
5-16 $PV_{7\%} = \$1,428.57$; $PV_{14\%} = \$714.29$
5-18 a. Stream A: $1,251.25; Stream B: $1,300.32
  b. Stream A and Stream B: $1,600
5-20 Contract 2: PV = $10,717,847.14
5-22 a. $802.43
  b. Pymt 1 : Int = $500; Princ = $302.43;
    Pymt 2 : Int = $484.88; Princ = $317.55
  c. $984.88
5-24 a. $279.20
  b. $276.84
  c. $443.72
5-26 $17,290.89; $19,734.26
5-28 $I_{NOM} = 7.8771\%$
5-30 a. E = 63.74 yrs.; K = 41.04 yrs.
  b. $35,825.33
5-32 $496.11
5-34 a. PMT = $10,052.87
  b. Yr.1: Int/Pymt = 24.87%; Princ/Pymt = 75.13%;
    Yr.2: Int/Pymt = 17.36%; Princ/Pymt = 82.64%;
    Yr.3: Int/Pymt = 9.09%; Princ/Pymt = 90.91%
5-36 a. $5,308.12
  b. $4,877.09
5-38 $309,015
5-40 $9,385

6-2 2.25%
6-4 1.5%
6-6 21.8%
6-8 8.5%
6-10 6.0%
6-12 0.35%
6-14 a. r_1 in Year 2 = 6%
  b. $I_1 = 2\%$; $I_2 = 5\%$

6-16   14%
6-18   a. $r_{T1} = 9.20\%$; $r_{T2} = 8.40\%$; $r_{T3} = 7.60\%$;
       $r_{T4} = 7.30\%$; $r_{T5} = 7.20\%$; $r_{T10} = 6.60\%$;
       $r_{T20} = 6.30\%$

7-2   a. 7.22%
       b. $988.46
7-4   YTM = 6.62%; YTC = 6.49%; most likely
       yield = 6.49%
7-6   a. Bond C: $1,012.79; $1,010.02; $1,006.98;
                  $1,003.65; $1,000.00
       Bond Z: $693.04; $759.57; $832.49;
                  $912.41; $1,000.00

7-8   15.03%
7-10 a. YTM = 9.69%
       b. CY = 8.875%; CGY = 0.816%
7-12 a. YTM = 8%; YTC = 6.1%
7-14 a. 5 years
       b. YTC = 6.47%
7-16 $1,067.95
7-18 a. YTM = 8.35%
       b. YTC = 8.13%
       c. YTC = 8.13%
       d. Year 6; YTC = 8.27%

8-2 $b_p = 1.12$
8-4 $r_M = 11\%$; r = 12.2%
8-6   a. $\hat{r}_Y = 14\%$
       b. $\sigma_x = 12.20\%$; $CV_Y = 1.45$
8-8   b = 1.33
8-10 4.2%
8-12 a. $r_i = 15.5\%$
       b(l). $r_M = 15\%$; $r_i = 16.5\%$
       b(2). $r_M = 13\%$; $r_i = 14.5\%$
       c(l). $r_i = 18.1\%$
       c(2). $r_i = 14.2\%$
8-14 $b_N = 1.16$
8-16 $r_p = 11.75\%$
8-18 a. $0.5 million
       d(l). $75,000
       d(2). 15%
8-20 a. $r_A = 11.30\%$; $r_B = 11.30\%$
       b. $r_{p\ Avg} = 11.30\%$
       c. $\sigma_A = 20.8\%$; $\sigma_B = 20.8\%$; $\sigma_p = 20.1\%$
       d. $CV_A = CV_B = 1.84$; $CV_p = 1.78$

9-2 $\hat{P}_0 = \$6.25$
9-4   a. End of Year 2
       b. $37.80
       c. $34.09
9-6 $r_p = 8.33\%$
9-8   a. $125
       b. $83.33
9-10 $23.75
9-12 a(l). $9.50
       a(2). $13.33
       a(3). $21.00

a(4). $44.00
b(l). Undefined
b(2). −$48.00, which is nonsense
9-14 $P_0 = \$19.89$
9-16 6.25%
9-18 a. $P_0 = \$54.11$; $D_1/P_0 = 3.55\%$; CGY = 6.45%
9-20 $35.00
9A-2 a. $P_0 = \$32.14$
       b. $P_0 = \$37.50$
       c. $P_0 = \$50.00$
       d. $P_0 = \$78.28$

10-2 $r_p = 8\%$
10-4 a. $r_s = 15\%$
       b. $r_e = 16.11\%$
10-6 a. $r_s = 16.3\%$
       b. $r_s = 15.4\%$
       c. $r_s = 16\%$
       d. $r_{s\ Avg} = 15.9\%$
10-8 $r_s = 16.51\%$; WACC = 12.79%
10-10 WACC = 11.4%
10-12 a. $r_s = 14.40\%$
       b. WACC = 10.62%
       c. Project A
10-14 11.94%
10-16 a. g = 8%
       b. $D_1 = \$2.81$
       c. $r_s = 15.81\%$
10-18 a. $r_d(1 - T) = 7\%$; $r_p = 10.20\%$; $r_s = 15.72\%$
       b. WACC = 13.86%
       c. Projects 1 and 2 will be accepted
10-20 a. $r_d(1 - T) = 5.4\%$; $r_s = 14.6\%$
       b. WACC = 10.92%

11-2 IRR = 16%
11-4 4.34 years
11-6 a.   5%: $NPV_A = \$3.52$; $NPV_B = \$2.87$
               10%: $NPV_A = \$0.58$; $NPV_B = \$1.04$
               15%: $NPV_A = -\$1.91$; $NPV_B = -\$0.55$
       b. $IRR_A = 11.10\%$; $IRR_B = 13.18\%$
       c. 5%: Choose A; 10%: Choose B; 15%: Do
          not choose either one
11-8 a. Without mitigation: NPV = $12.10 million;
          IRR = 19.86%;
          With mitigation: NPV = $5.70 million;
          IRR = 15.24%
11-10 Project A; $NPV_A = \$30.16$
11-12 $IRR_L = 11.74\%$
11-14 a. HCC; PV = −$805,009.87
       c. LCC; PV = −$686,627.14
11-16 a. $NPV_A = \$14,486,808$; $NPV_B = \$11,156,893$;
          $IRR_A = 15.03\%$; $IRR_B = 22.26\%$
       c. Crossover rate ≈ 11.71%
11-18 a. No; $PV_{old} = -\$89,910.08$;
          $PV_{New} = -\$94,611.45$
       b. $2,470.80
       c. 22.94%

11-20 $10,239.20

11-22 $250.01

12-2 a. $2,600,000

b. $2,000,000

c. $2,700,000; $\Delta = +\$100,000$

12-4 Yes, NPV = $15,301.10

12-6 a. SL: Deprec. = $200,000/yr;
MACRS: $264,000; $360,000; $120,000; $56,000

b. MACRS; $12,781.64

12-8 a. −$178,000

b. $52,440; $60,600; $88,960

c. No, NPV = −$19,549

12-10 Yes, NPV = $921.36

12-12 a. A: $6,750; B: $7,650; $\sigma_A = \$474.34$; $CV_A = 0.0703$

b. Project B

12-14 a. NPV = $37,035.13; IRR = 15.30%; MIRR = 12.81%; Payback = 3.33 yrs.

b. +20%: NPV = $77,975.63; −20%: NPV = −$3,905.37

c. E(NPV) = $34,800.21; $\sigma_{NPV} = \$35,967.84$; CV = 1.03

12-16 a. −$792,750

b. Depr.$_{New}$: $235,000; $376,000; $223,250; $141,000; $129,250
Depr.$_{Old}$: $120,000/yr.
ΔDepr.: $115,000; $256,000; $103,250; $21,000; $9,250

c. $206,000; $255,350; $201,888; $173,100; $168,988 + $118,925 = $287,913

d. Yes; NPV = $11,819.67

12-18 a. A, B, C, D, E; $5,250,000

b. A, B, D, E; $4,000,000

c. B, C, D, E, F, G; $6,000,000

13-2 30% debt and 70% equity

13-4 $b_U = 1.0435$

13-6 a(l). −$60,000

a(2). $40,000

b. $Q_{BE} = 14,000$

c. $Q_{BE} = 8,750$

d. $Q_{BE} = 17,500$

13-8 $r_s = 17\%$

13-10 a. $FC_A = \$80,000$; $V_A = \$4.80$/unit; $P_A = \$8.00$/unit

b. Firm B

c. 50,000 units

13-12 a. $EPS_{old} = \$2.04$; New: $EPS_D = \$4.74$; $EPS_S = \$3.27$

b. 339,750 units

c. $Q_{old} = 316,957$ units; $Q_{New, \, Debt} = 272,250$ units; $Q_{New, \, Stock} = 204,750$ units

14-2 $P_0 = \$60$

14-4 $D_0 = \$3.44$

14-6 Payout = 31.39%

14-8 a. 12%

b. 18%

c. g = 6%; $r_s = 18\%$

d. 6%

e. 28,800 new shares; $0.13 per share

15-2 73 days; 30 days; $1,178,082

15-4 a. 83 days

b. $356,250

c. 6.49×

15-6 a. 32 days

b. $288,000

c. $45,000

d(l). 30

d(2). $378,000

15-8 a. $ROE_T = 11.75\%$; $ROE_M = 10.80\%$; $ROE_R = 9.16\%$

15-10 a. Oct. loan = $22,800

b. $111,300; $297,600; −$155,100; −$22,800; $118,500; $187,800

16-2 AFN = $610,000

16-4 a. $133.50 million

b. 39.06%

16-6 $67 million; 5.01×

16-8 a. $480,000

b. $18,750

16-10 $34.338 million; 34.97 ≈ 35 days

16-12 a. $2,500,000,000

b. 24%

c. $24,000,000

16-14 a. 33%

b. NP = $3,553.2; Bonds = $6,598.8; Stock = $2,514; RE = $28,284

17-2 26.45 yen per shekel

17-4 1 euro = $1.60 or $1 = 0.625 euro

17-8 10.218 kronas per pound

17-10 $r_{NOM-U.S.} = 2\%$

17-12 a. $1.558067

b. Discount

17-14 +$500,000

17-16 $568,092,486

Selected Equations and Tables

CHAPTER 3

Stockholders' equity = Paid-in capital + Retained earnings

Stockholders' equity = Total assets − Total liabilities

Net working capital = Current assets − Current liabilities

Net operating working capital = (Current assets − Excess cash) − (Current liabilities − Notes payable)

Total debt = Short-term debt + Long-term debt

Total liabilities = Total debt + Accounts payable + Accruals

Operating income (or EBIT) = Sales revenues − Operating costs

$$FCF = (EBIT(1 - T) + Depreciation) - \left(\begin{matrix} Capital \\ expenditures \end{matrix} + \begin{matrix} \Delta Net\ operating \\ working\ capital \end{matrix} \right)$$

MVA = (P₀ × Shares outstanding) − Book value of total common equity

$$EVA = EBIT(1 - T) - \left(\begin{matrix} Total \\ invested \\ capital \end{matrix} \times \begin{matrix} After\text{-}tax \\ percentage \\ cost\ of\ capital \end{matrix} \right)$$

2013 Individual Tax Rates: Single Individuals

If Your Taxable Income Is	You Pay This Amount on the Base of the Bracket	Plus This Percentage on the Excess over the Base (Marginal Rate)	Average Tax Rate at Top of Bracket
Up to $8,925	$ 0	10.0%	10.0%
$8,925–$36,250	892.50	15.0	13.8
$36,250–$87,850	4,991.25	25.0	20.4
$87,850–$183,250	17,891.25	28.0	24.3
$183,250–$398,350	44,603.25	33.0	29.0
$398,350–$400,000	115,586.25	35.0	29.0
Over $400,000	116,163.75	39.6	39.6

Married Couples Filing Joint Returns

If Your Taxable Income Is	You Pay This Amount on the Base of the Bracket	Plus This Percentage on the Excess over the Base (Marginal Rate)	Average Tax Rate at Top of Bracket
Up to $17,850	$ 0	10.0%	10.0%
$17,850–$72,500	1,785.00	15.0	13.8
$72,500–$146,400	9,982.50	25.0	19.4
$146,400–$223,050	28,457.50	28.0	22.4
$223,050–$398,350	49,919.50	33.0	27.1
$398,350–$450,000	107,768.50	35.0	28.0
Over $450,000	125,846.00	39.6	39.6

2013 Corporate Tax Rates

If a Corporation's Taxable Income Is	You Pay This Amount on the Base of the Bracket	Plus This Percentage on the Excess over the Base (Marginal Rate)	Average Tax Rate at Top of Bracket
Up to $50,000	$ 0	15%	15.0%
$50,000–$75,000	7,500	25	18.3
$75,000–$100,000	13,750	34	22.3
$100,000–$335,000	22,250	39	34.0
$335,000–$10,000,000	113,900	34	34.0
$10,000,000–$15,000,000	3,400,000	35	34.3
$15,000,000–18,333,333	5,150,000	38	35.0
Over $18,333,333	6,416,667	35	35.0

CHAPTER 4

$$\text{Current ratio} = \frac{\text{Current assets}}{\text{Current liabilities}}$$

$$\text{Quick, or acid test, ratio} = \frac{\text{Current assets} - \text{Inventories}}{\text{Current liabilities}}$$

$$\text{Inventory turnover} = \frac{\text{Sales}}{\text{Inventories}}$$

$$\text{Days sales outstanding (DSO)} = \frac{\text{Receivables}}{\text{Average sales per day}} = \frac{\text{Receivables}}{\text{Annual sales}/365}$$

$$\text{Fixed assets turnover} = \frac{\text{Sales}}{\text{Net fixed assets}}$$

$$\text{Total assets turnover} = \frac{\text{Sales}}{\text{Total assets}}$$

$$\text{Total-debt-to-total-capital ratio} = \frac{\text{Total debt}}{\text{Total capital}} = \frac{\text{Total debt}}{\text{Total debt} + \text{Equity}}$$

$$\text{Total-liabilities-to-assets ratio} = \frac{\text{Total liabilities}}{\text{Total assets}}$$

$$\text{Debt-to-equity ratio} = \frac{\text{Total debt}}{\text{Equity}}$$

$$\text{Times-interest-earned (TIE)} = \frac{\text{EBIT}}{\text{Interest charges}}$$

$$\text{EBITDA coverage} = \frac{\text{EBITDA} + \text{Lease payments}}{\text{Interest} + \text{Principal payments} + \text{Lease payments}}$$

$$\text{Operating margin} = \frac{\text{EBIT}}{\text{Sales}}$$

$$\text{Profit margin} = \frac{\text{Net income}}{\text{Sales}}$$

$$\text{Return on total assets (ROA)} = \frac{\text{Net income}}{\text{Total assets}}$$

$$\text{Return on common equity (ROE)} = \frac{\text{Net income}}{\text{Common equity}}$$

$$\text{Return on invested capital (ROIC)} = \frac{\text{EBIT}(1-\text{T})}{\text{Total invested capital}} = \frac{\text{EBIT}(1-\text{T})}{\text{Debt} + \text{Equity}}$$

$$\text{Basic earning power (BEP)} = \frac{\text{EBIT}}{\text{Total assets}}$$

$$\text{Price/Earnings (P/E)} = \frac{\text{Price per share}}{\text{Earnings per share}}$$

$$\text{Book value per share} = \frac{\text{Common equity}}{\text{Shares outstanding}}$$

$$\text{Market/Book (M/B)} = \frac{\text{Market price per share}}{\text{Book value per share}}$$

$$\begin{aligned}
\text{ROE} &= \text{ROA} \times \text{Equity multiplier} \\
&= \text{Profit margin} \times \text{Total assets turnover} \times \text{Equity multiplier} \\
&= \frac{\text{Net income}}{\text{Sales}} \times \frac{\text{Sales}}{\text{Total assets}} \times \frac{\text{Total assets}}{\text{Total common equity}}
\end{aligned}$$

$$\begin{aligned}
\text{EVA} &= \text{Net income} - [\text{Equity} \times \text{Cost of equity}] \\
&= (\text{Equity})[\text{Net income/Equity} - \text{Cost of equity}] \\
&= (\text{Equity})(\text{ROE} - \text{Cost of equity})
\end{aligned}$$

CHAPTER 5

$$\text{Future value} = \text{FV}_\text{N} = \text{PV}(1+\text{I})^\text{N}$$

$$\text{Present value} = \text{PV} = \frac{\text{FV}_\text{N}}{(1+\text{I})^\text{N}}$$

$$\begin{aligned}
\text{FVA}_\text{N} &= \text{PMT}(1+\text{I})^{\text{N}-1} + \text{PMT}(1+\text{I})^{\text{N}-2} + \text{PMT}(1+\text{I})^{\text{N}-3} + \cdots + \text{PMT}(1+\text{I})^0 \\
&= \text{PMT}\left[\frac{(1+\text{I})^\text{N} - 1}{\text{I}}\right]
\end{aligned}$$

$$\text{FVA}_\text{due} = \text{FVA}_\text{ordinary}(1+\text{I})$$

$$\begin{aligned}
\text{PVA}_\text{N} &= \text{PMT}/(1+\text{I})^1 + \text{PMT}/(1+\text{I})^2 + \cdots + \text{PMT}/(1+\text{I})^\text{N} \\
&= \text{PMT}\left[\frac{1 - \dfrac{1}{(1+\text{I})^\text{N}}}{\text{I}}\right]
\end{aligned}$$

$$\text{PVA}_\text{due} = \text{PVA}_\text{ordinary}(1+\text{I})$$

$$\text{PV of a perpetuity} = \frac{\text{PMT}}{\text{I}}$$

$$\begin{aligned}
\text{PV} &= \frac{\text{CF}_1}{(1+\text{I})^1} + \frac{\text{CF}_2}{(1+\text{I})^2} + \cdots + \frac{\text{CF}_\text{N}}{(1+\text{I})^\text{N}} \\
&= \sum_{t=1}^{\text{N}} \frac{\text{CF}_t}{(1+\text{I})^t}
\end{aligned}$$

$$\text{Periodic rate (I}_\text{PER}) = \frac{\text{Stated annual rate}}{\text{Number of payments per year}} = \text{I/M}$$

$$\text{Number of periods} = (\text{Number of years})(\text{Periods per year}) = \text{NM}$$

$$\text{Effective annual rate (EFF\%)} = \left(1 + \frac{\text{I}_\text{NOM}}{\text{M}}\right)^\text{M} - 1.0$$

CHAPTER 6

Quoted interest rate $(r) = r^* + IP + DRP + LP + MRP$

$$= r_{RF} + DRP + LP + MRP$$

$r_{\text{T-bill}} = r_{RF} = r^* + IP$

$r_{\text{T-bond}} = r^*_t + IP_t + MRP_t$

$r_{\text{C-bond}} = r^*_t + IP_t + MRP_t + DRP_t + LP_t$

r_{RF} with cross-product term $= r^* + IP + (r^* \times IP)$

CHAPTER 7

Bond's value $= V_B = \dfrac{INT}{(1 + r_d)^1} + \dfrac{INT}{(1 + r_d)^2} + \cdots + \dfrac{INT}{(1 + r_d)^N} + \dfrac{M}{(1 + r_d)^N}$

$$= \sum_{t=1}^{N} \frac{INT}{(1 + r_d)^t} + \frac{M}{(1 + r_d)^N}$$

Price of callable bond $= \displaystyle\sum_{t=1}^{N} \dfrac{INT}{(1 + r_d)^t} + \dfrac{\text{Call price}}{(1 + r_d)^N}$

$$V_B = \sum_{t=1}^{2N} \frac{INT/2}{(1 + r_d/2)^t} + \frac{M}{(1 + r_d/2)^{2N}}$$

Accrued interest $=$ Coupon payment $\times \left(\dfrac{\begin{array}{c}\text{Number of days since}\\ \text{last coupon payment}\end{array}}{\begin{array}{c}\text{Number of days}\\ \text{in coupon period}\end{array}} \right)$

Dirty price $=$ Clean price $+$ Accrued interest

Invoice price $=$ Quoted price $+$ Accrued interest

CHAPTER 8

Expected rate of return $= \hat{r} = P_1 r_1 + P_2 r_2 + \cdots + P_N r_N$

$$= \sum_{i=1}^{N} P_i r_i$$

Standard deviation $= \sigma = \sqrt{\displaystyle\sum_{i=1}^{N} (r_i - \hat{r})^2 P_i}$

Estimated $\sigma = \sqrt{\displaystyle\sum_{t=1}^{N} \frac{(\bar{r}_t - \bar{r}_{Avg})^2}{N - 1}}$

Coefficient of variation $= CV = \dfrac{\sigma}{\hat{r}}$

$\hat{r}_p = w_1 \hat{r}_1 + w_2 \hat{r}_2 + \cdots + w_N \hat{r}_N$

$$= \sum_{i=1}^{N} w_i \hat{r}_i$$

$b_p = w_1 b_1 + w_2 b_2 + \cdots + w_N b_N$

$$= \sum_{i=1}^{N} w_i b_i$$

$$RP_M = r_M - r_{RF}$$

$$RP_i = (RP_M)b_i$$

$$r_i = r_{RF} + (r_M - r_{RF})b_i$$

CHAPTER 9

Value of stock $= \hat{P}_0 =$ PV of expected future dividends

$$= \frac{D_1}{(1 + r_s)^1} + \frac{D_2}{(1 + r_s)^2} + \cdots + \frac{D_\infty}{(1 + r_s)^\infty}$$

$$= \sum_{t=1}^{\infty} \frac{D_t}{(1 + r_s)^t}$$

Constant growth stock: $\hat{P}_0 = \dfrac{D_0(1 + g)^1}{(1 + r_s)^1} + \dfrac{D_0(1 + g)^2}{(1 + r_s)^2} + \cdots + \dfrac{D_0(1 + g)^\infty}{(1 + r_s)^\infty}$

$$= \frac{D_0(1 + g)}{r_s - g} = \frac{D_1}{r_s - g}$$

$$\begin{array}{ccc} \text{Expected rate} & = & \text{Expected} \\ \text{of return} & & \text{dividend yield} \end{array} + \begin{array}{c} \text{Expected growth rate, or} \\ \text{capital gains yield} \end{array}$$

$$\hat{r}_s = \frac{D_1}{P_0} + g$$

Growth rate $= (1 - \text{Payout ratio})\text{ROE}$

Zero growth stock: $\hat{P}_0 = \dfrac{D}{r_s}$

Horizon value $= \hat{P}_N = \dfrac{D_{N+1}}{r_s - g}$

Nonconstant growth stock: $\hat{P}_0 = \dfrac{D_1}{(1 + r_s)^1} + \dfrac{D_2}{(1 + r_s)^2} + \cdots + \dfrac{D_N}{(1 + r_s)^N}$

$$+ \frac{D_{N+1}}{(1 + r_s)^{N+1}} + \cdots + \frac{D_\infty}{(1 + r_s)^\infty}$$

$$= \frac{D_1}{(1 + r_s)^1} + \frac{D_2}{(1 + r_s)^2} + \cdots + \frac{D_N}{(1 + r_s)^N} + \frac{\hat{P}_N}{(1 + r_s)^N}$$

$$= \text{PV of nonconstant dividends} + \text{PV of horizon value, } \hat{P}_N$$

PV of horizon value, $\hat{P}_N = \dfrac{D_{N+1}/(r_s - g)}{(1 + r_s)^N}$

$$\begin{array}{c} \text{Market value} \\ \text{of company} \end{array} = V_{Company} = \text{PV of expected future free cash flows}$$

$$= \frac{FCF_1}{(1 + WACC)^1} + \frac{FCF_2}{(1 + WACC)^2} + \cdots + \frac{FCF_\infty}{(1 + WACC)^\infty}$$

Horizon value $= V_{Company \ at \ t=N} = FCF_{N+1}/(WACC - g_{FCF})$

Market value of equity $= \text{Book value} + \text{PV of all future EVAs}$

$$V_p = \frac{D_p}{r_p}$$

$$\hat{r}_p = \frac{D_p}{V_p}$$

CHAPTER 10

$$\text{WACC} = \begin{pmatrix} \% \\ \text{of} \\ \text{debt} \end{pmatrix}\begin{pmatrix} \text{After-tax} \\ \text{cost of} \\ \text{debt} \end{pmatrix} + \begin{pmatrix} \% \text{ of} \\ \text{preferred} \\ \text{stock} \end{pmatrix}\begin{pmatrix} \text{Cost of} \\ \text{preferred} \\ \text{stock} \end{pmatrix} + \begin{pmatrix} \% \text{ of} \\ \text{common} \\ \text{equity} \end{pmatrix}\begin{pmatrix} \text{Cost of} \\ \text{common} \\ \text{equity} \end{pmatrix}$$

$$= w_d r_d(1-T) \quad + \quad w_p r_p \quad + \quad w_c r_s$$

After-tax cost of debt = Interest rate on new debt − Tax savings

$$= r_d - r_d T$$
$$= r_d(1-T)$$

Component cost of preferred stock $= r_p = \dfrac{D_p}{P_p}$

Required rate of return = Expected rate of return

$$r_s = r_{RF} + RP = D_1/P_0 + g = \hat{r}_s$$

$$r_s = r_{RF} + (RP_M)b_i$$
$$= r_{RF} + (r_M - r_{RF})b_i$$

r_s = Bond yield + Risk premium

$$P_0 = \frac{D_1}{(1+r_s)^1} + \frac{D_2}{(1+r_s)^2} + \cdots + \frac{D_\infty}{(1+r_s)^\infty}$$
$$= \sum_{t=1}^{\infty} \frac{D_t}{(1+r_s)^t}$$

$$P_0 = \frac{D_1}{r_s - g}$$

$$r_s = \hat{r}_s = \frac{D_1}{P_0} + \text{Expected g}$$

Cost of equity from new stock $= r_e = \dfrac{D_1}{P_0(1-F)} + g$

$$\frac{\text{Flotation cost}}{\text{adjustment}} = \frac{\text{Adjusted}}{\text{DCF cost}} - \frac{\text{Pure}}{\text{DCF cost}}$$

$$\frac{\text{Cost of}}{\text{external equity}} = r_s + \frac{\text{Flotation cost}}{\text{adjustment}}$$

$$\frac{\text{Retained earnings}}{\text{breakpoint}} = \frac{\text{Addition to retained earnings for the year}}{\text{Equity fraction}}$$

CHAPTER 11

$$NPV = CF_0 + \frac{CF_1}{(1+r)^1} + \frac{CF_2}{(1+r)^2} + \cdots + \frac{CF_N}{(1+r)^N}$$
$$= \sum_{t=0}^{N} \frac{CF_t}{(1+r)^t}$$

$$CF_0 + \frac{CF_1}{(1+IRR)^1} + \frac{CF_2}{(1+IRR)^2} + \cdots + \frac{CF_N}{(1+IRR)^N} = 0$$
$$\sum_{t=0}^{N} \frac{CF_t}{(1+IRR)^t} = 0$$

$$\sum_{t=0}^{N} \frac{COF_t}{(1 + r)^t} = \frac{\sum_{t=0}^{N} CIF_t(1 + r)^{N-t}}{(1 + MIRR)^N}$$

$$PV\ costs = \frac{TV}{(1 + MIRR)^N}$$

$$Payback = Number\ of\ years\ prior\ to\ full\ recovery + \frac{Unrecovered\ cost\ at\ start\ of\ year}{Cash\ flow\ during\ full\ recovery\ year}$$

CHAPTER 12

Taxes paid on salvaged assets = Tax rate × (Salvage value − Book value)

Recovery Allowance Percentage for Personal Property

Ownership Year	Class of Investment			
	3-Year	5-Year	7-Year	10-Year
1	33%	20%	14%	10%
2	45	32	25	18
3	15	19	17	14
4	7	12	13	12
5		11	9	9
6		6	9	7
7			9	7
8			4	7
9				7
10				6
11				3
	100%	100%	100%	100%

CHAPTER 13

$$ROIC = \frac{EBIT(1 - T)}{Total\ invested\ capital}$$

Operating breakeven: $EBIT = PQ - VQ - F = 0$

$$Q_{BE} = \frac{F}{P - V}$$

$$b_L = b_U[1 + (1 - T)(D/E)]$$

$$b_U = b_L/[1 + (1 - T)(D/E)]$$

$$r_s = r_{RF} + \frac{Premium\ for}{business\ risk} + \frac{Premium\ for}{financial\ risk}$$

Net debt = Short-term debt + Long-term debt − Cash and equivalents

CHAPTER 14

$$Dividends = Net\ income - \frac{Retained\ earnings\ required\ to\ help}{finance\ new\ investments}$$
$$= Net\ income - [(Target\ equity\ ratio)(Total\ capital\ budget)]$$

CHAPTER 15

$$\begin{array}{c}\text{Inventory}\\\text{conversion}\\\text{period}\end{array} + \begin{array}{c}\text{Average}\\\text{collection}\\\text{period}\end{array} - \begin{array}{c}\text{Payables}\\\text{deferral}\\\text{period}\end{array} = \begin{array}{c}\text{Cash}\\\text{conversion}\\\text{cycle}\end{array}$$

$$\text{Inventory conversion period} = \frac{\text{Inventory}}{\text{Cost of goods sold}/365}$$

$$\text{Average collection period (ACP or DSO)} = \frac{\text{Receivables}}{\text{Sales}/365}$$

$$\begin{array}{c}\text{Payables}\\\text{deferral period}\end{array} = \frac{\text{Payables}}{\text{Purchases per day}} = \frac{\text{Payables}}{\text{Cost of goods sold}/365}$$

$$\text{Accounts receivable} = \text{Sales per day} \times \text{Length of collection period}$$
$$= (\text{ADS})(\text{DSO})$$

$$\begin{array}{c}\text{Nominal annual}\\\text{cost of}\\\text{trade credit}\end{array} = \frac{\text{Discount \%}}{100 - \text{Discount \%}} \times \frac{365}{\begin{array}{c}\text{Days credit is}\\\text{outstanding}\end{array} - \begin{array}{c}\text{Discount}\\\text{period}\end{array}}$$

$$\text{Simple interest rate per day} = \frac{\text{Nominal rate}}{\text{Days in year}}$$

$$\text{Interest charge for month} = (\text{Rate per day})(\text{Amount of loan})(\text{Days in month})$$

$$\text{Approximate annual rate}_{\text{Add-on}} = \frac{\text{Interest paid}}{(\text{Amount received})/2}$$

CHAPTER 16

$$\text{AFN} = \begin{array}{c}\text{Projected}\\\text{asset}\\\text{increase}\end{array} - \begin{array}{c}\text{Spontaneous}\\\text{liabilities}\\\text{increase}\end{array} - \begin{array}{c}\text{Increase in}\\\text{retained}\\\text{earnings}\end{array}$$

$$= (A_0^*/S_0)\Delta S - (L_0^*/S_0)\Delta S - MS_1(1 - \text{Payout})$$

$$\begin{array}{c}\text{Full}\\\text{capacity}\\\text{sales}\end{array} = \frac{\text{Actual sales}}{\begin{array}{c}\text{Percentage of capacity}\\\text{at which fixed assets}\\\text{were operated}\end{array}}$$

$$\frac{\text{Target fixed assets}}{\text{Sales}} = \frac{\text{Actual fixed assets}}{\text{Full capacity sales}}$$

$$\begin{array}{c}\text{Required level}\\\text{of fixed assets}\end{array} = (\text{Target fixed assets}/\text{Sales})(\text{Projected sales})$$

CHAPTER 17

$$\text{Direct quotation:} \frac{\text{U.S.\$ required}}{1 \text{ unit of foreign currency}}$$

$$\text{Indirect quotation:} \frac{\text{Units of foreign currency}}{1 \text{ U.S.\$}}$$

$$\frac{\text{Forward exchange rate}}{\text{Spot exchange rate}} = \frac{(1 + r_h)}{(1 + r_f)}$$

$$P_h = (P_f)(\text{Spot rate})$$

$$\text{Spot rate} = \frac{P_h}{P_f}$$